The Partisan Press

The Partisan Press

A History of Media Bias in the United States

SI SHEPPARD

McFarland & Company, Inc., Publishers
Jefferson, North Carolina, and London

LIBRARY OF CONGRESS CATALOGUING-IN-PUBLICATION DATA

Sheppard, Si, 1972–
The partisan press : a history of media bias in the United States / Si Sheppard.
p.   cm.
Includes bibliographical references and index.

ISBN-13: 978-0-7864-3282-0
softcover : 50# alkaline paper ∞

1. Journalism — Objectivity — United States — History.
2. Press and politics — United States — History.   I. Title.
PN4888.O25S54 2008   071.3 — dc22   2007038824

British Library cataloguing data are available

On the cover: Richard Canton Woodville, *War News from Mexico*, oil on canvas
27" × 24¾", 1848 (private collection); front cover by TG Design

Manufactured in the United States of America

*McFarland & Company, Inc., Publishers
Box 611, Jefferson, North Carolina 28640
www.mcfarlandpub.com*

To Jack Goldfarb:

לטוב המגיעה ובאהבה, לנשגב היאה בהוקרה.

Contents

Preface

Burke said there were Three Estates in Parliament; but, in the Reporters'
Gallery yonder, there sat a *Fourth Estate* more important far than they all.
It is not a figure of speech, or a witty saying; it is a literal fact.... Literature
is our Parliament too. Printing ... is equivalent to Democracy; invent Writing, Democracy is inevitable.... Whoever can speak, speaking now to the
whole nation, becomes a power, a branch of government, with inalienable
weight in law-making, in all acts of authority. It matters not what rank he
has, what revenues or garnitures: the requisite thing is that he have a tongue
which others will listen to; this and nothing more is requisite.
— Thomas Carlyle, *On Heroes, Hero Worship, and
the Heroic in History*, 1841[1]

    Partisan bias in the media has simmered in the background of political debate through-
out U.S. history.[2] Occasionally it erupts into salience as an issue in itself. The election of 2004
was one such occasion. Popular responses corresponded well to what Richard Hofstadter called
the "paranoid style" in American politics, the process whereby citizens are mobilized by their
commonly held "conspiratorial fantasy" against a perceived fifth-column threat to the republic.[3] This threat, which represents a danger to participatory democracy through its capacity
to manipulate opinion, has manifested itself in the past in such forms as freemasonry, the
Papacy, financial and banking elites, and international communism. To a substantial constituency in contemporary American society, it is the media which now constitutes a key component in an interlinked tripartite domestic axis of evil, incorporating Hollywood and
academia. Having emerged as the modern focal point for populist antagonism, the media is
now in and of itself a participant in contemporary political debate rather than limited to serving its assumed role as the matrix in which that debate takes place.[4] But is this antagonism
justified?
    To begin with, how are we to define the media? At the turn of the millennium the media
in the United States consisted of some 1,600 daily newspapers, over 7,000 weekly newspapers,
over 11,000 magazines and journals, 12,500 radio stations, and 1,500 television stations, not
to mention a plethora of Web sites being operated everywhere from high-tech offices to
parents' basements.[5] Could such a multifarious agglomeration of disparate interests maintain a uniform partisan agenda? Even assuming we could speak of the media as an entity, to
describe it as biased begs the question: compared to what? What is the basis for comparison?

Is the media in the United States biased compared to the media overseas? The answer, bluntly, is no.

So if the U.S. media is not biased on a horizontal continuum (in comparison to its contemporary counterparts in other countries) can it be considered biased on a vertical continuum (in comparison to its past counterparts through American history)? The answer to this question, which I have investigated in researching this book, is, again, no.

This is not to deny that bias influences the style and content of news coverage in its day-to-day depiction of sociopolitical trends and events. But the muted, largely subliminal bias that permeates the contemporary mainstream media today is but a pale shadow of the raw, uncompromisingly partisan bias that was the established business model of the American media from the foundation of the republic until at least the outbreak of the Second World War. The standard of objectivity to which modern news agencies are expected to aspire and against which bias can be measured is in fact a recent and unprecedented phenomenon in American history, one entirely alien to the law of the jungle under which the media operated in the age of Washington, Jackson, Lincoln and Roosevelt.

It has been said the media controls "democracy's most important product: political information."[6] If we are to accept that objectivity in the presentation of political information is an essential aspect of the electorate rendering an informed choice at the ballot box, then intense scrutiny of the extent to which the media is upholding the golden mean of objectivity is a vital social obligation, and contestation over agenda setting in the news is a legitimate focus for political debate. I conclude that this debate is destined to be rendered redundant by cyclical trends in American business and society that are goading the media back into the model of explicit partisanship that characterized the relationship between press and politics at the birth of the republic.

The media has always sought to justify its existence in terms of its fulfilling a social obligation, but this has oscillated throughout history between its duty to tell the *truth* versus its responsibility to describe the *facts*. The subtle differentiation in these terms spawned two rival professional codes of journalistic integrity and two incompatible business models. The contested nature of that differentiation was revealed in 1789, the very year that George Washington, the first president of the United States, was sworn into office, when John Fenno launched the *Gazette of the United States*, his stated intent being "to hold up the people's own government in a favorable point of light and to impress just ideas of its administration by exhibiting FACTS."[7] In reality, however, what Fenno had done was fire the first shot in the struggle between advocates and opponents of Washington for control of public opinion regarding the administration and hence dominance of the political agenda. The terms of this struggle would establish the template for relations between press and president in subsequent administrations until well into the 20th century, when objective news— the facts—finally succeeded subjective opinion — the truth — as the foundation on which to base the reporting of current affairs.

Fenno may have asserted that he was reporting the facts but in reality he was broadcasting the truth as he saw it. This was the assumed role of the editor of his era. Ward's comment on the social obligation of the press in England during the 18th century applies with equal conviction to its counterpart in the United States: "Partisan journalism believed that it served the public sphere not through careful impartiality but by advancing correct political views and causes and by exposing the errors of the other party."[8] It is important to bear in mind, however, that this is a modern interpretation that Fenno and his peers would not have recognized; to them there was no distinction between advancing correct political views and presenting the public with the facts; by definition, one equaled the other.

The rules of the game changed as the nation matured, to the point where the media became big business, with objective detachment in the fulfillment of its duties ostensibly its most hallowed obligation. Now the rules are changing again. The explosive rise of new communications technologies coupled with an ongoing tightening of partisan self-identification along ideological lines represent an irresistible challenge to the monopoly over political information maintained by the contemporary media and the standards of objectivity to which it aspires.[9] The atomized media matrix of tomorrow will be one in which self-selected news sources cater to the predetermined agenda of the individual. Secure in his own made-to-order multimedia environment, the American consumer will at last achieve validation in what has been since Fenno first went to type the universal understanding of agenda setting in the dissemination of the news, namely, that which I agree with is objective; that which I disagree with is biased.

In order to arrive at this conclusion it was necessary to test to their limits the archival material, records, and patience of so many institutions, the key contributors of which were the Library of Congress, the New York Public Library, and the Milton Eisenhower Library at my own Johns Hopkins University. I would also like to thank Professor Matthew Crenson for his encouragement, input and advice. Above all, I owe a debt of gratitude to my beloved wife Christina, who has juggled a fulltime career, newborn twins, and a husband's academic and literary pursuits during the completion of this project. Objectively, she is the greatest, and that is a fact.

Introduction:
Bias — A New Debate?

The media in the United States serves as the milieu in which political debate can take place. The media is no longer free to set its own terms as to how it performs this role. The media has become an issue in that debate itself. "As long as there has been an American press, our elections have been fought in the media," *Time* magazine has observed. "What's notable about Election 2004 is how much of it was fought against the media."[1] It is within this framework that the reelection of George W. Bush in 2004 has been heralded as symbolizing the triumph not merely of a particular candidate or party but of democracy itself over a monolithic, elite-driven and all-pervasive institution dedicated to imposing its own agenda.

That the media represented the most significant hurdle to the reelection of their president was received wisdom on the part of the Republican Party long before — indeed, generations before — the official beginning to the campaign.[2] Speaker after speaker at the Republican national convention in New York made a point of reminding the delegates, the party, and all true Americans who their real enemy was. "For it has been said so truthfully that it is the soldier, not the reporter, who has given us the freedom of the press," Zell Miller noted. "It doesn't matter to him how he is demonized," Rudy Giuliani said of Bush; "it doesn't matter what the media does to ridicule him or misinterpret him or defeat him." "America has done this kind of work before, and there have always been doubters," the president himself declared, citing a *New York Times* critique of the post–World War II occupation of Germany to make a point about Iraq. "Maybe that same person is still around, writing editorials."

As the campaign progressed, conservatives found their worst expectations realized, their assumptions vindicated. The Republican Party was all over the press all year long. The day after the vice-presidential debate in Cleveland, the Republican National Committee (RNC) took issue with Chris Matthews, host of MSNBC's *Hardball*. An RNC news release questioned remarks made by Matthews about the vice president, accusing him of being an advocate for the Kerry-Edwards ticket: "Matthews pinch-hits for Edwards and strikes out the truth." On another occasion, the RNC took exception to a *New York Times* report that Mr. Kerry "essentially voted for one large tax increase" in 1993, not the 98 separate increases asserted by Mr. Bush. "That's a stat only the Kerry campaign would use," the RNC said in a statement. In the waning days of the campaign, after Kerry began touting a report in the *New York Times* that explosives in Iraq may have been stolen because of poor security by American troops, and

The bias game is played even at the apex of the political pyramid; here President George W. Bush displays a none-too-subtle rejoinder to the media coverage of his administration. Previous occupants of the office have felt the same frustration (courtesy of Reuters).

hastily produced a television ad that included the story, the RNC responded with a statement declaring: "Kerry and the *New York Times* ignore facts, stay on attack."[3] During their last debate, Bush himself chided Kerry: "I'm not so sure it's credible to quote leading news organizations"—with a nod toward moderator Bob Schieffer of CBS.

Working above and beyond the official Republican channels, advocates for Bush in print, online, and on the airwaves maintained a round-the-clock vigil to expose the liberal agenda of the media. The ill-starred, Dan Rather—fronted CBS "investigation" into the president's National Guard service during the Vietnam War was easily folded into the overall grand media conspiracy. "Dan Rather is just a small part of a much bigger story," Stephen Hayes concluded. "His careless reporting and, later, dogmatic defense of his errors were but one episode in the media's long offensive against George W. Bush."[4]

To conservatives, therefore, Bush's victory represented a triumph for him, for Jesus, and for America over the forces of secularism, socialism, and treason represented only in a transitory sense by John Kerry. The real enemy, the enduring foe, remains the nation's media. The failure of the latest bid by this entity to cast the elect from their rightful place at the head of the nation's affairs was therefore a cause for exultation, and no small amount of back-patting among the conservative paladins who contributed to the result. "God bless our country," Peggy Noonan exulted in the wake of the election. "Let us savor."

"Who was the biggest loser of the 2004 election?" Noonan asked. "It is easy to say Mr. Kerry: he was a poor candidate with a poor campaign. But I do think the biggest loser was the mainstream media, the famous MSM, the initials that became popular in this election cycle. Every time the big networks and big broadsheet national newspapers tried to pull off a bit of pro-liberal mischief ... the yeomen of the blogosphere and AM radio and the Internet took them down." It was not merely the defeat of King George III's Hessians by American freedom fighters, "It was Agincourt," wrote Noonan. "It was the yeomen of King Harry taking down the French aristocracy with new technology and rough guts. God bless the pajama-clad yeomen of America. Some day, when America is hit again, and lines go down, and media are hard to get, these bloggers and site runners and independent Internetters of all sorts will find a way to file, and get their word out, and it will be part of the saving of our country."

"It will be hard for the mainstream media to continue, in the face of these facts, the mantra that we are a deeply and completely divided country," Noonan concluded, preparing for the next round against the fifth column of American freedom. "But they'll try!"[5]

James Q. Wilson was only one among many conservatives to express relief that on this occasion, at least, "the profound liberal bias among many big-city newspapers and most TV stations did not determine the outcome."[6] "Never before have the establishment media cast aside the diaphanous veils of objectivity with such reckless self-revelation," an outraged John

O'Sullivan declared. And what more overt evidence could be needed to prove the liberal agenda of the media than its tally of editorial endorsements? *Editor & Publisher* counted 213 newspaper endorsements for the challenger and 205 for the incumbent (at least a dozen of whom indicated that their editorial board wanted to endorse Kerry but the publisher or corporate owner insisted they endorse Bush). In terms of the circulation of papers supporting each candidate, Kerry won that race handily, 20,882,889 to 15,743,799. More than sixty newspapers that had backed Bush in 2000 switched to Kerry or declared neutrality.[7] "With such bastions of Republicanism as the *Orlando Sentinel* switching to Kerry, it is hardly surprising that the national media were almost part of his campaign," O'Sullivan concluded.[8]

Such favoritism, of course, was the only factor inhibiting a Republican landslide. "Of all the outrageous aspects of this year's presidential campaign, nothing exceeds the Old Media's overt mission to defeat President Bush. They've always been biased, but this year, they barely tried to hide it," David Limbaugh maintained. "Because of their bias, a large number of people remain in the dark about who John Kerry really is, which is alarming. I dare say that if they had not sheltered Kerry's past and his official record, if they hadn't conspired with Democrats to bring down President Bush, Kerry would be lucky to receive 40 percent of the popular vote."[9]

Fortunately, from their platforms in the new media, Americans like Rush Limbaugh, Michael Savage, Ted Nugent, and G. Gordon Liddy were able to counteract the liberal bias of the old. "Blogs, talk radio, and cable news were not only more influential, but often more intellectually honest than CBS, NPR, and the *New York Times*," Victor Davis Hanson intoned. "The former represented blue-collar America, the latter the sophisticates of the Ivy League and East Coast. Such is our strange society in which democratic populism is now defined by pampered New York metropolitan columnists, billionaire heiresses, financial speculators, and a weird assortment of embittered novelists, bored rock stars, and out-of-touch Hollywood celebs."[10]

"This election has indeed revealed an 'alternative media' of the right," Pat Buchanan chipped in. "But the national press remains what it has been since the 1960s: the most reliably left-wing voting block this side of Bedford Stuyvesant."[11] "Among the legacy media, the mood is what it must have been inside the Kremlin the day after the Berlin Wall fell," Jed Babbin concluded. "Lost power, diminished influence, and the sinking feeling that a lot of people can now ignore you. The term 'legacy media' is a precise one. In the computer biz, 'legacy systems' are old, outdated, and must be replaced if their purpose is to be served. It's happening in the media, and the process is accelerating." The most significant legacy of this trend toward the open identification of the Blue State–dominated media outlets with partisan liberal interests is the creation of a space for alternative media outlets better fitted in terms of ideological slant to service the needs of conservative constituencies:

> The legacy media — CBS, the *New York Times*, and the rest — are rapidly losing their Red State market share to Fox, the *Washington Times*, and the Internet. Advertisers will cling to some of the legacy media because their audiences remain large. But their power to sway opinion has become so small that the migration of audiences to alternate media will soon deprive them of their financial strength. It's hard to keep your market share when you forfeit peoples' trust, when you look down on your audience, and when you hate a large number of your audience and the polls for whom they vote.

From this perspective, the issue of media bias boils down to the single paradigm that defines the way in which conservatives approach the world: If you're not with us, you're against us. "Hate? Can we dare apply such a strong and unqualified term to the media?" Babbin asks. "In short, yes. The legacy media — both here and abroad — hate Mr. Bush and all who support him. Throughout the campaign, they used terms of utter contempt to describe the President, accused him and his advisers of every form of deceit and dishonesty, and gave his opponent immunity from investigation and criticism that is unparalleled in American electoral history." Now that the mask has been stripped from the enemies of George W. Bush in the media, they stand revealed alongside his enemies in Hollywood and academia as the enemies of America itself: "The outrageous bias in the *Post*, the *NYT*, and the others—against Mr. Bush, against conservatives, and conservative principles—forces them to praise America's enemies, and the enemies of our allies."[12]

In this manner, partisan self-identification and pecuniary self-interest serve to reinforce each other in an accelerating spiral that will culminate in the obliteration — by common consent — of any adherence on the part of the media to the concept of objectivity. This business model is increasingly understood as representing the future of the media in America, but not factored into the debate is the reality that it represents a return to the predominant industry standard throughout most of American history.

Conservatives are far from being alone in expressing dissatisfaction with the media. The bookshelves groan under the weight of apolitical tomes critiquing one aspect or another of contemporary journalism.[13] Liberals, too, focus on what they perceive as the shortcomings or biases of the print and electronic news.[14] The left-wing shorthand equivalent to the conservative terms "mainstream," "old," or "legacy" media is "SCLM"—So-Called Liberal Media, so-called because liberals don't consider themselves the beneficiaries of any supposed liberal bias at all. Liberal watchdogs include Fairness and Accuracy in Reporting (fair.org), Media Transparency (mediatransparency.org), and Media Matters for America (mediamatters.org). MoveOn.org maintains an operation, "Fox Watch," in which hundreds of volunteers devote hours of their time to monitor what is in their eyes the wellspring of Republican discourse.[15]

But in the debate over bias in the media, overwhelmingly it is the conservative position that dominates. Conservative publishing imprints release a steady stream of tomes dedicated to exposing the evils of liberalism.[16] Conservative sources within the media itself constantly reference the liberal bias of their rivals.[17] And an entire cottage industry of conservative watchdog organizations exists to monitor and catalogue such atrocities. Prominent examples include the Media Research Center (www.mrc.org), Accuracy in Media (aim.org), Fair Press (fairpress.org), Fight the Bias (fightthebias.com), That Liberal Media (thatliberalmedia.com), the Media Bias Page (akdart.com/media.html), and the Center for Media and Public Affairs (www.cmpa.com).[18]

That the media represents a liberal entity expressly hostile to their interests—to America, to capitalism, and to Christianity — is fundamental to conservative self-identity. To the conservative mind it is only axiomatic that the media would mobilize in force against a Republican administration and Republican legislators. But such overt manifestations of this predetermined agenda represent only the tip of the iceberg. The taint of liberalism pervades every aspect of the media in its interaction with American society at every level.[19] From the cradle to the grave, nothing escapes the purview of liberal bias. "Women's magazines, for example, with their millions of readers, may very well function as liberalism's most prominent mainstream supporters," Evan Gahr points out. "The magazines' news pages also carry frequent paeans to liberal activists.... Let the reader beware: When the subject is politics, a 'womyn' lurks behind every story written by a Cosmo girl."[20] A penitent womyn herself lifted the lid on this process years later, confessing that "when focused on women, the media's liberal bias is more pervasive, more insidious, and more effective."[21] At the same time, "One of the most obvious indicators of liberal bias in the print press is the obituary page," another conservative notes. "This is where we find tributes to those whom left-wing editors regard as 'brilliant,' 'gifted' or 'authoritative' and why. The recent death of Stephen Jay Gould, famed Harvard zoologist and popular science writer, exemplifies how obituaries of public figures serve as a benchmark for liberal standards of distinction."[22]

Conservatives have made the issue of media bias central to contemporary political debate.

Too many attempts to address the issue have become bogged down in the here and now. Debate over the existence, extent and nature of media bias typically focuses exclusively on a very limited range of geographic and historic data. In my opinion the wrong questions are being asked. In response to the assertion that the media in the U.S. is biased, the question should be: compared to what? There are two bases for comparison: the media overseas and the media throughout U.S. history. When measured against both of these control groups the case is extremely weak that a normative bias informs the business model and operational structure of contemporary U.S. media outlets. I will briefly outline the extent of the partisan bias inherent in the media overseas, specifically focusing on the United Kingdom, before commencing my investigation of the patterns of partisan bias throughout the U.S. media since the formation of the republic.

Partisan Norms and the International Media

The issue of media bias, or subjectivity in the media, by definition has to be measured against the golden mean of objectivity, but a precise definition of this term remains elusive. Ward offers a viable characterization in his description of three categories of objectivity: ontological (external objects, facts); epistemological (beliefs and attitudes) and procedural (decisions). "Objectivity" in all three senses contrasts with its opposite, subjectivity. The doctrine of journalistic objectivity, with its stress on facts, procedures, and impartiality, is a hybrid of these three categories: reports are ontologically objective if they are accurate and faithful descriptions of facts or events, epistemically objective if they adhere to good reporting methods and standards, and procedurally objective if they present information in a manner that is fair to sources and rival viewpoints.[23]

Even in a media environment which professes its commitment to these principles as the keystone of its operating standards and business practices, perfect objectivity can never be attained. Every institution seeking to advance its cause through the press aspires to tilt the ensuing coverage in order to obtain, as the Pentagon's 1991 Gulf War media strategy put it, "favorable objectivity."[24] But even if no consensus can be arrived at on the precise terms of media objectivity, its absence is unmistakable. Measuring the extent of media bias is obviously redundant in one-party states, whether de jure, such as Kim Jong-il's North Korea, or de facto, such as Robert Mugabe's Zimbabwe, where all news outlets function as the propaganda extensions of the governing regime. Media objectivity is also effectively compromised to variable degrees in a number of contemporary pseudodemocracies such as Russia, Iran, and Venezuela. Even in functional democracies the state may impinge upon press freedoms, most obviously during time of war.[25] Another concern in liberal states has been that media objectivity may be compromised by non-state actors accumulating too great a news outlet market share and using it to bias the national interest in favor of their personal commercial or political interests. Past examples include Viscount Northcliffe and Baron Beaverbrook, who used their newspaper empires as springboards to service in the U.K. cabinet during World War I and World War II, respectively.[26] More recent examples include Silvio Berlusconi in Italy, who served as prime minister of that country from 1994 to 1995 and from 2001 to 2006, and Rupert Murdoch, dubbed a kingmaker first in Australia and then in the United Kingdom.[27]

These qualifications notwithstanding, liberal democracy remains the environment most conducive to the emergence of a "level playing field" of mass market media competition. Dalton et. al. outline how in coexisting with a partisan political system the media may adopt one of two alternate stances. The first is *external* diversity, in which separate media sources represent particular political viewpoints in their reporting of the news. A clear example of this pattern is the partisan press, with specific newspapers representing the distinct viewpoints of political parties. A contrasting model stresses a pattern of *internal* diversity in which a single medium includes a broad spectrum of the prevailing political viewpoints, for example, a newspaper that balances liberal and conservative columnists on its editorial page.

Under the external diversity model the democratic needs for free expression are represented by the competition between contrasting partisan media. For the individual citizen, the preferred medium provides a clear and reliable cue on how he or she should view and evaluate political phenomena. However, the voter's access to alternative political viewpoints is limited if individuals do not use more than one media source. The media thus largely performs a mobilizing function among already defined political groupings, especially during election campaigns. Ideally, balance within the system is maintained by competition according to free market, level-playing-field principles between media representing rival partisan interests.[28] Media entities committed to the internal diversity model, on the other hand, avoid close ties to political parties in order to maintain their autonomy and commitment to objectivity.

The tabloid press in Britain most closely represent a pattern of external diversity, Dalton and his coauthors conclude in their cross-country comparative analysis. The reader of the typical British tabloid receives a distinctly partisan view of the campaign, which reinforces one political position and consciously under represents another. By contrast, they note the American press most closely represents the pattern of internal diversity.[29] Their analysis focuses exclusively on the contemporary American press. I will argue that this is a divergence from the historic pattern of external diversity in the United States. But first I will expand on the nature of external diversity in the U.K. press, thereby enabling the reader to appreciate the similarity of the U.S. pattern that persisted well into the 20th century.

According to Seymour-Ure, "There have been very obvious historical associations between press and party systems. The growth of competing political parties in nineteenth-century Europe was widely paralleled by the rise of newspapers supporting them."[30] This parallel development emerged in the United Kingdom, which enjoyed a comparative advantage over the rest of Europe in terms of its sociopolitical evolution, by the end of the 17th century. Parliament's decision to allow the Printing Act to lapse in 1695 represented the first easing of legislative restriction of the freedom of the presses, which were swiftly enlisted in the widening partisan divide between the Whigs and the Tories. As early as 1704, Daniel Defoe, in his *An Essay on the Regulation of the Press*, could write that "since this nation is unhappily divided into parties, every side ought to have an equal advantage in the use of the press." The Tory Party certainly took advantage of Defoe, successive ministries employing his talents and those of Jonathan Swift to their advantage. Stevens notes that the last years of the reign of Queen Anne are regarded as the period in which "the periodical essay became an established type in English literature"; forty-five journals were launched from 1712–15, seventeen of which were purely political.[31] By this stage "there was perceived to be a symbiotic relationship between party and print," Knights says. "Partisanship provoked print; and print helped to shape partisanship. In terms of defining partisan identities and allegiances, therefore, the press helped to shape and even to create national party politics."[32]

At the intersection of business and politics, a system was established in which printers willingly attached themselves by the most intimate bonds of patronage to a party or faction or individual within a party. This system survived the transition from Stuart to Hanover, from Tory to Whig, reaching its apogee during the administration of Robert Walpole, the first effectively partisan prime minister.[33] "I believe the people of Great Britain are governed by a power that was never heard of as a supreme authority in any age or country before," Joseph Danvers, MP for Totnes, remarked in 1738; "It is the government of the press."[34] More accurately, it was government through the press. Ministries devoted considerable effort and expense to ensuring that their agenda dominated the national papers, and the opposition fought back with all the resources at their disposal. An editorial in the *London Courant* of August 11, 1781, articulates the extent to which the principle of objectivity was alien to this era:

> The idea of an *impartial* print, and of an *impartial* individual in politics, are equally mean and contemptible. They are both alike avoided and execrated by honest men, because they are both alike destitute of principle. In this hour of ministerial turpitude, it cannot but be competent to every one to discern the ruinous tendency of the measures of the Administration. Every honest man cries out shame upon them, and shuns them as they would a pestilence. Those creatures, and those prints, however, that *affect* an impartiality, observe another kind of conduct. They are base enough to fawn upon Ministry while in power, for what they can get by them, and when justice overtakes them, will be the *first* to cut their throats.[35]

Ironically, the greater the threat represented by an opposition publication, the greater the inducements offered by the government to secure its conversion; to cite just one example, Treasury funds were employed in 1784 to buy into the *Morning Post* and shift its allegiance from Whig to Tory.[36] Of fourteen daily newspapers in existence in 1790, the Treasury provided subsidies to nine, and two more loyal papers were established with the help of government subsidies that year, the *Star* and the *True Briton*.[37] William Cobbett described both papers as "in some sort, the property of the ministers. They were, at any rate, as absolutely at their command as the *Moniteur* is at the command of Bonaparte." Cobbett could have been speaking from experience; his short-lived *Porcupine* was launched in 1800 with £3,000 in support from Treasury funds.[38]

Opposition papers also continued to struggle under the burden of repressive fiscal and political legislation. The 1712 Stamp Act (which was "passed chiefly for political ends" against the Whigs, according to Stevens) created two media worlds — the legitimate elite press and the illicit, unstamped, popular press.[39] Editors who pushed the license of the press too far could find their prints seized and themselves fined or imprisoned, a fate visited even upon members of Parliament such as John Wilkes, whose struggle for freedom of expression in his *North Britain* was the scandal of 1760s London.[40]

Overt state intervention intensified during the crisis of the Napoleonic Wars. In 1798, legislation was passed requiring the recording of the names and addresses of printers and publishers on every copy of a paper, as well as forbidding the export of papers to enemy countries. In 1799, a register of printing presses was introduced. In a pattern that would be paralleled in the United States during its Civil War, official legal harassment was complemented by semi-official intimidation by loyalist mobs.

Unlike the United States in the early 19th century, where the press expanded dramatically, the post-war United Kingdom had a press that remained tightly constrained in circulation, advertising policy, and opinion, thanks to the survival of the stamp tax, advertising duties, and ongoing vigorous enforcement of the Sedition Act.[41] Uninhibited criticism of the government appeared in the illicit, partly underground, unstamped press, among which Cobbett's *Political Register* and Henry Hetherington's *Poor Man's Guardian* were foremost. The government responded in 1819 by passing the Newspaper Stamp Duties Act, which extended the stamp act to pamphlets and other publications.

At the official level, the patronage model survived the war intact and endured into the Victorian era. Drawing a parallel with a pair of notorious, "rotten" parliamentary constituencies that served as sinecures for party loyalists, the *Times* on December 22, 1834, singled out the Gatton and Old Sarum newspapers, saying that "The editorship of one paper was as much a Government appointment as a seat at the India Board or the Admiralty."[42]

Like Parliament, the press was still largely an elite institution that represented the interests of its members in the gentry and mercantile classes. A succession of Reform Acts (1832,

1867, 1872, 1884 and 1885) that broadened the franchise and made Parliament more representative, led in tandem to the emergence of a more open and active national press. This was accomplished through the abolition of the so-called "taxes on knowledge." All restrictions on the size of newspapers were removed in 1825, and the tax on pamphlets was repealed in 1833, the advertisement duty in 1853, the stamp duty in 1855, and the paper duty in 1860. The response was dramatic; in the dozen years between the stamp duty repeal and the Second Reform Act of 1867, the number of daily newspapers doubled, and the circulation of the dailies and the weeklies expanded more than three and a half times.[43] A significant early breakthrough occurred when the *Daily News* debuted on January 21, 1846, with the financial assistance of progressive MPs Sir Joseph Paxton, Sir Joshua Walmsley and Sir William Jackson. "The principles advocated by the *Daily News* will be principles of progress and improvement, of education, civil and religious liberty, and equal legislation." The new publication boasted a prestigious name at its helm: Charles Dickens. The famed author lasted just twenty-six days and seventeen issues as editor, but under better management the *Daily News* flourished and became established as the harbinger of Britain's penny press.[44]

Pervasive political influence, direct or indirect, was maintained even as the media universe expanded. "To get their way, as they usually did, politicians wheedled and cajoled, pleaded and harangued, promised preferential treatment and threatened retribution," Koss relates. "[Prime Minister Lord] Palmerston, incorrigible at the game, set the pace by plying newspapermen with advertising income, sinecures, and invitations to his wife's glittering soirées at Cambridge House.... From all directions and at all levels, politicians joined in the scramble for press support. It was contagious."[45]

The Liberal Palmerston was succeeded as the recognized master of media manipulation by the Conservative Benjamin Disraeli.[46] According to Koss, "Predominantly Liberal when Disraeli took office, the metropolitan press was predominantly Tory when he left it."[47] Disraeli served a long apprenticeship before securing this advantage, however. When Disraeli made "some allusion to the strength of the Conservative party" during an audience with Prince Albert, he got an unexpected, and unwelcome, reply. "What is the use of that," the royal consort said, "the country is governed by newspapers, and you have not got a newspaper."[48] Conservative factional disunity in the mid-19th century left the party's press unable to focus on a coherent message that could serve as a rallying cry against the Liberals. The perils of party propagandists during this period are captured in a letter that Samuel Lucas, editor of the *Press*, wrote to Disraeli, the proprietor of the paper, on July 5, 1853: "In conducting *this organ of a party* I have often to satisfy the requirements of various members of the party who have a stake in the enterprise ... or I have to explain to each respectively the impediments which prevent his views being carried out.... I am to a considerable extent the confidant of individual complaints and representations arising out of the disorganization of our party."[49]

Sensing the lacuna within the ranks of the Conservative press, Disraeli was bombarded with offers from editors desperate to suckle at the patronage teat and willing to offer the services of their publications on mutually advantageous terms. The Conservative mastermind remained aloof, however, much to the frustration of K. H. Cornish, proprietor of the *John Bull*, who wrote to Disraeli in 1859, "I had hoped to have rendered the *John Bull* a nucleus for erecting a Conservative structure ... but as I have been played fast and loose for nearly two years by the Conservative Party, though I refused several handsome offers from their antagonists (one of £1000 a year), I may fairly be excused if I work on my own convictions, regardless of all party men or party measures."[50]

The *John Bull* did not long survive, having been cast adrift from its partisan moorings. Even those papers that successfully maintained their allegiance to the Conservative Party struggled throughout the 1860s, in turn placing a severe drain on Tory resources. "Dependent on the services of the Central Press Agency, established in 1863, these publications tended to resemble one another not only in their contents, but also in their financial distress," Koss observes. "Through the century and beyond, the provinces remained predominantly Liberal terrain."[51]

As a corollary to the greatly expanded and politically aware electorate, the two parties overhauled their campaign mechanisms so as to better coordinate their outreach and appeal. The Conservative Central Office appeared in 1870, the National Liberal Federation in 1877. Coordination of a national media campaign strategy was easier to implement in the United Kingdom than the United States because of the centralization of the major opinion makers in the metropolis of London, which afforded a greater opportunity to shape public opinion. And public opinion was shifting against the Liberals as divisions within the party's ranks over imperialism, free trade and home rule for Ireland threatened its ascendancy.

In groping for an effective populist appeal, both parties seized on the strategy of personalizing the issues of the day in their respective leaders, the Conservative Disraeli and the Liberal William Gladstone. This was particularly relevant for the Liberals as by the time of the passage of the final Reform Act the Conservatives had secured an overwhelming advantage among the metropolitan dailies, while Liberal publications constituted a shrinking minority, even among the provincial dailies.[52] Gladstone seized the way out of this impasse. Through his effective articulation of themes that would resonate in the formal campaign of the following year, during his Midlothian speaking tour of 1879, Gladstone, as Robertson notes, "conveyed his message to a national audience despite a wholesale defection of formerly Liberal journals,"[53] most of which had been won over by the Conservatives between 1855 and 1880. In this instance, "Disraeli was the loser and Gladstone the victor in the 1880 election because Gladstone understood how to campaign *through* the press rather than *with* it."[54] This strategy of proactively imposing an agenda on the media by making yourself the issue and forcing the press to cover you had been intermittently flirted with by U.S. presidential contenders in the past, but into the late 19th century it was still considered beneath the dignity of the presidency for a candidate to actively seek the office. It was William Jennings Bryan who revolutionized the electoral process in the United States with his "whistle stop," coast-to-coast campaign of 1896, specifically in order to offset the wholesale defection of the Democratic papers that year.[55]

The conflict between Liberal and Conservative raged on the editorial pages of their respective newspapers into the first decade of the 20th century. But partisanship in the U.K. press entered a new dimension of intensity after the cataclysm of the First World War, when the Labour Party emerged as a serious contender for power. The Whig versus Tory paradigm represented two sides of the same bourgeois coin. However hard fought their contests, each recognized the other's legitimacy. Even as dedicated a Tory as Lord Northcliffe could write to the Liberal chief whip during the 1911 constitutional crisis, that "If my newspaper can be of any service to whatever government may be in power, I am only too pleased, if without disloyalty to my own party."[56] This era of mutual respect could not survive the 1920s, at the end of which, as one pre-war chronicler notes, after a period of three-party politics, the collapse of the Liberals signified "the simplification of major issues into the two main elements of socialism and anti-socialism."[57] The socialist objectives of the Labour Party made it anathema to the media barons; in their view the Labour versus Conservative paradigm was not a contest between viable alternatives but a struggle for freedom and tradition against an alien and hostile ideology, a worldview that locked in a pattern of institutional hostility towards Labour in the overwhelming majority of the nation's press.

A representative attitude was that of Northcliffe's brother, Lord Rothermere, owner of the *Daily Mail*, who editorialized that a vote for Labour in 1922 represented "a vote for Bolshevism" which would "threaten every man's house and furniture and every woman's clothes and jewelry."[58] After performing strongly in the 1923 general election, despite being subjected to what leader Ramsay MacDonald condemned as a "gross misrepresentation and malignant suppression of facts" by "gutter papers," the first minority Labour government took office in January 1924. It was defeated in the general election in October that year, not least because of the publication of the Zinoviev Letter in Rothermere's *Daily Mail* just four days before the polls opened. Allegedly addressed from Grigori Zinoviev, president of the presidium of the Executive Committee of the Comintern, to the Central Committee of the Communist Party of Great Britain, the letter advocated taking advantage of the diplomatic recognition of the USSR by the Labour government, to intensify communist agitation in Britain, not least in the armed forces. The fact that the letter was a blatant forgery concocted by Secret Intelligence Service operatives based in Riga, who were determined to tip the election to the Conservatives, bothered Rothermere not the least; privately he gloated to Beaverbrook that its publication "altered the situation to the extent of something like a hundred seats."[59]

Even after Labour stormed to power in its own right in 1945, the bitterness lingered. "Why should we ... allow ourselves to be scared by headlines in the capitalist press?" firebrand Minister Anuerin Bevan asked in 1948. "It is the most prostituted press in the world, most of it owned by a gang of millionaires."[60] The frothing bias of the U.K. press from 1945–51 led one American journalist covering the 1950 campaign to express his disgust at the "degradation of the press into unprincipled party organs" characterized by "nothing more than a series of editorial pages," a striking reflection of just how far the U.S. media had strayed from its own partisan roots by this point.

By mid-century, Labour was at last able to command some print firepower of its own in the struggle for the hearts and minds of the populace (see Table 1). Significant contributors to this trend included the launch of a trade union publication, the *Daily Herald*, and the defection of the *Daily Mirror* to Labour in 1945.[61]

TABLE 1. THE DISTRIBUTION IN PERCENTAGES OF PARTISAN EDITORIAL SUPPORT DURING U.K. GENERAL ELECTIONS, 1924–1945[62]

Party	1924	1931	1935	1945
Conservative	72	71	65	52
Labour	5	13	21	35
Liberal	22	16	14	13

According to Thomas, the distribution of editorial fealty in the press paralleled the party system more closely in 1950 than at any time since Labour's emergence as a serious electoral force.[63] The class divide ensured that partisan divisions in the press endured after Labour lost power the following year, but the convergence of the two parties in terms of policy over the ensuing two decades softened the edges of the external diversity that remained the accepted business model.[64] This relative dealignment began to break down in the mid-1970s as the Keynesian consensus disintegrated and class antagonism sharpened. Labour's renewed commitment to socialist objectives and its association with an increasingly militant trade union movement provoked an unusually bitter response from the Conservative press during the snap election of February 1974. Commentators describe the campaign as being distinguished by a "full-blooded campaigning partisanship in the press greater than at any election since the 1950s"[65] and having "ushered in a third phase in press coverage, an era of partisanship rediscovered."[66]

The secular trend away from Labour accelerated during its 1974–79 term in government, as the Conservatives regrouped under the leadership of Margaret Thatcher, and adopted a specifically monetarist policy line, clearly distinguishing them from the Labour alternative for the first time in a quarter century. A key turning point occurred in 1977 when the Rupert Murdoch–owned *Sun* turned against a "tattered, discredited, disastrous [Labour] government" that it accused of being "bogged down by incompetence ... drifting, rudderless" and increasingly dominated by "the Fascist left."[67] In 1979 the *Sun*, the new circulation leader among the daily newspapers, endorsed the Conservatives for the first time.[68]

The general election of 1979 represented the culmination of the transition back to the traditional pattern of a media universe overwhelmingly mobilized against the Labour Party. The government's apparent paralysis as union militancy surged during the "Winter of Discontent" enabled unadulterated support for the Conservative alternative in the nation's press. This was a crucial component in laying the foundation for the emergence of a new monetarist consensus in economic policy. As Thomas notes, while in the short term "the highly exaggerated portrayal of a 'Crisis Britain' allowed for a very effective attack on a discredited, leaderless and union-controlled government unable even to guarantee the most basic needs of its citizens," more fundamentally, "the press played a key role in interpreting the strikes as symbolic of the utter bankruptcy of an ungovernable, union-dominated and over-extended state form."[69] As a direct consequence, "partisanship was more skewed against Labour by the beginning of 1979 than at any other time since before the war. Between 1945–1951 a strongly partisan press had largely cancelled each other out but now, as the Royal Commission [on the Press 1974–77 Inquiry] Minority Report had anticipated, there was 'no balance of political irresponsibility.'"[70]

This imbalance only intensified after the Conservatives assumed power. The new Prime Minister commanded the respect of the broadsheets and absolute fealty from the Tory tabloids, as she conquered the unions at home and the Argentineans in the Falklands. Gilmour notes that the "Thatcher effect" on the popular press "could scarcely have been more fawning if it had been state controlled."[71] Typically there was quid pro quo involved: knighthoods were awarded in 1980 to two editors— Larry Lamb of the *Sun* and John Junor of the *Sunday Express*— for their support during the 1979 campaign, and were later awarded to David English of the *Daily Mail* and Nicholas Lloyd of the *Daily Express* for services rendered while in office.[72] But the overriding justification for the newspaper barons in their total commitment to the Conservative agenda was ideological conformity, a trend that only intensified as Labour spiraled deeper into a reactive socialist mindset. The self-appointed role for the Conservative press as the Thatcherite revolution unfolded was to emphasize its positive aspects while hammering home to readers on a daily basis that there was no viable alternative. "It is difficult to believe that Mrs. Thatcher could have stayed in office for eleven years and introduced Thatcherism to so many areas of British government and life without this dedicated press support," Tunstall concludes. "Throughout the 1980s Mrs. Thatcher's approval rating was six important percentage points better than that of the Conservative Party. Tabloid newspaper Maggiemania certainly played a part in these poll ratings and hence in sustaining Margaret Thatcher in office."[73]

By the time the nation returned to the polls in 1983, the preconditions for what was widely accepted would be a referendum on Thatcherism had already been established. According to Clarke, "The coverage of the general election was an anticlimax, as the terrain of the coverage had been established well before the election campaign began."[74] The *Daily Mirror* was the only national daily newspaper to reject the Conservatives. The rest of the tabloids wholeheartedly shared the agenda of the *Daily Express*, which declared itself "four-square and 100 per cent behind Mrs. Thatcher." A series of *Sun* editorials on the Labour Party during the campaign characterized it as "a desperate, irresponsible, extremist shambles ... which shows the ugly face of rampant extremism and ... has been torn apart and taken over by Marxists ...

with a grotesque parody of a programme ... which is extreme, extravagant and nightmarish ... and which would virtually wipe out freedom."[75] The situation at the *Daily Mail* grew so extreme that a union meeting of at least 60 journalists voted 6–1 in favor of a motion condemning their own paper's election coverage as "too one-sided in favour of the Conservative party." It requested that "the editor give more space and a fair degree of prominence to unbiased factual reports of the positive proposals made by other political parties."[76] Predictably, this grassroots revolt in favor of internal diversity among its own employees was completely ignored by the ownership.

Labour's electoral rout forced it into the long, painful process of adapting to the new political reality. But the party's baby steps in this direction won it few favors from the press, which if anything intensified its pro-Tory bias the more legitimate a threat Labour presented. Much of this animus focused on Neil Kinnock, leader of the party during its transition years until 1992, who was subjected to an orchestrated, unrelenting campaign of personal vilification in the tabloids on a scale unprecedented in the postwar era.[77] As Tony Bevins, a nine-year veteran of the *Sun* and *Daily Mail* before arriving as political editor at the *Independent*, reflected, "The anti-Labour, pro-Tory bias permeates every level of the Tory tabloids; to the point the political reporters see it as their task to generate their own propaganda."[78] This bias extended beyond news reporting and the editorial page to include everything from republishing Tory advertising for free to active collusion in writing articles.[79]

The allegiance of the press to the Conservative Party crystallized during the election campaigns of 1987 and 1992. On the latter occasion, the national dailies split in terms of circulation, 70 percent for the Conservatives to 27 percent for Labour. The raw numbers give no indication of the vehemence with which these preferences were expressed.[80] Once again leading the jihad against Labour was the *Sun*. The election coverage in Murdoch's paper, which for all intents and purposes amounted to an extension of the official Conservative campaign, culminated on April 8 with an issue dedicated to an extensive "Nightmare on Kinnock Street" feature. In the first few pages readers were informed that in the event of a Labour victory, mortgages, taxes, and gas and power prices would go up, the stock market and pound would collapse, and the nation would be subjected to a return of union militancy and an open-door policy on immigration, while homosexuals would rule on planning applications: even loft conversions, home extensions and garages would have to be approved by gay and lesbian groups if Labour took power. On page nine, under the headline "It's Mao or Never for Neil," a psychic asked dead celebrities how they would line up at the polls; it was Winston Churchill, Montgomery of El Alamein, Queen Victoria, and Elvis Presley for Tory leader John Major, Mao, Marx, Stalin, and Trotsky for Kinnock.

On election day, April 9, the front page of the *Sun* featured the Labour leader's head in a light bulb with the headline: "If Kinnock wins today will the last person to leave Britain please turn out the lights." At the foot of the page was a brief editorial: "You know our views on the subject but we don't want to influence you in your final judgment on who will be Prime Minister! But if it's a bald bloke with wispy red hair and two K's in his surname, we'll see you at the airport." Presumably, in the event of a Labour victory, the editors would have decamped to one of the eight "Kinnock Flee Zones" described in the *Sun* on March 13 as part of its "guide to hiding places if Neil gets power." These included Outer Mongolia, the Arctic Circle, and Amish country, U.S.A.

The guiding lights of the *Sun* were spared the perils of exile, as the Conservative Party clung to a narrow majority after the election, precipitating Kinnock's resignation as leader of Her Majesty's Opposition. He placed the blame for his defeat squarely on a campaign of "misinformation and disinformation" on the part of a partisan press which had "enabled the Tory party to win yet again when it could not have secured victory on the basis of its own record, its programme or character."[81] The *Sun* gleefully took full credit for his demise, splashing an infamous headline: "IT'S THE SUN WOT WON IT."

For their own reasons, both sides were happy to conform to the received wisdom that the sustained bias of the Tory press had swung a close election in favor of the Conservatives. A former treasurer of the party, Lord McAlpine, concluded:

> The heroes of this campaign were Sir David English [editor of the *Mail*], Sir Nicolas Lloyd [editor of the *Express*], Kelvin MacKenzie [editor of the *Sun*] and the other editors of the grander Tory press. Never in the past nine elections have they come out so strongly in favour of the Conservatives. Never has the attack on the Labour Party been so comprehensive. They exposed, ridiculed and humiliated that party, doing in their pages each day the job that the politicians failed to do.... This is how the election was won, and if the politicians, elated in their hour of victory, are tempted to believe otherwise, they are in very real trouble next time.

An even more significant endorsement of the powers of electoral mobilization wielded by the tabloids came from the grand dame of the Conservative pantheon, Margaret Thatcher herself, who according to one account told friends that "it was the Tory journalists who won the election and that this should never be forgotten... 'You won it,' she said to Sir Nicholas Lloyd, the editor of the *Express*."[82]

As the Conservative government became bogged down in a mire of scandal in its fourth term, the tabloids flipped en masse to Labour, heralding the ascendancy of Tony Blair in 1997. During the campaign that year, more than twice as many people were reading a newspaper that backed Labour as were reading one that supported the Conservatives; the traditional Tory advantage in the press had been broken for the first time since they had gained ascendancy over the Liberals in the second half of the 19th century.[83] The case that the support of the press barons was a prerequisite for electoral success appeared to have become a self-fulfilling prophecy. But had it? Were the tabloids leading public opinion or following it? Studies of the impact of media on voting patterns in the United Kingdom have yet to provide conclusive evidence that it constitutes a decisive or even formative factor in electoral choice, even during periods of effectively one-party press such as the Conservative heyday of the late 1970s to the early 1990s. Curtice and Semetko report, "Neither the *Sun* nor any of the other pro-Conservative tabloid newspapers were responsible for John Major's unexpected victory in 1992. There is no evidence in our panel that there was any relationship between vote switching during the election campaign and the partisanship of a voter's newspaper."[84] Labour lost power in 1979 because it had lost control of the agenda, not because it had lost control of the media. Voters refused to return Labour to power in three subsequent elections because the party persisted in clinging to a policy agenda that was no longer credible, not because the tabloids told them not to. The electorate finally turned against the Tory government because it had lost moral authority, while Labour under Tony Blair's leadership finally presented a viable alternative, not because the tabloids had jumped ship.

Still the legendary power of the media to make or break a government is widely accepted, not least by the party hierarchies themselves, which are perpetually engaged in a private struggle to woo the media barons. Based on its perception of the fate of its predecessors, both in and out of office, the current Labour administration has adopted as a key component of its governing model a twin-pronged strategy of keeping the press on its side while simultaneously engaging in the manipulation of public relations through direct appeals to the electorate that bypass the gatekeeper role of the media.[85]

As a rule, the mainstream print media in the United Kingdom continues to exhibit qualities of external rather than internal diversity. The opposite scenario currently prevails in the United States where the mainstream print media has evolved to the point where the tenets of objectivity are upheld, or at least aspired to. The U.K. model helps put at least one half of the bias debate in context. "A strongly partisan press, particularly one that favors one party far more than the rest, may not be desirable," Curtice concludes, "but whether it has much influence is another matter. Literary (de)merit should not be confused with political power."[86]

The American Media and the Cycles of Bias

Having provided this brief critique of the media bias issue along a horizontal axis, positioning the U.S. media within the spectrum of contemporary partisan bias in the media internationally, the balance of this text will approach the issue along a vertical axis, measuring the extent to which the contemporary media is biased against the standards of objectivity maintained throughout U.S. history. In other words, having added breadth to this debate, it is my intention to add depth by asking whether modern U.S. media outlets are biased compared to their counterparts in the past. Did Americans enjoy a more balanced perspective on the news 100, 150, and 200 years ago than Americans do today? The answer, categorically, is no.

The extent of the objectivity manifest in the mainstream media of today is not only unusual, it would strike observers from earlier times as morally offensive. Consider the response on August 1, 1832, by the editor of the *Western Argus* in Lyons, New York, to the contents of a newspaper he had received through the mail, which from his description sounds as though it aspired to today's ideal of detachment:

> We have glanced at its editorial columns, and find it what we most of all things abhor and detest, to wit, a neutral paper. It pretends to be all things to all men. Now we wish to be civil to the editor, but we can never consent to an exchange with any such paper, for we verily think they should all, one and all, be thrown out of the pale of the press. If we are asked why, we answer that the editor must be doing violence to his own opinions, or else he had none to abuse; and in either case, he is hardly entitled to the common civilities of his typographical brethren. If he will turn anti [Mason] or democrat, we will exchange with him with pleasure.[87]

The parallels between this editorial and the one published on the far side of the Atlantic in the *London Courant* cited earlier are obvious and speak to the universality of external diversity as the operative business model in a partisan political environment.[88] Having seamlessly made the transition from the mother country to the colonies, external diversity was reflected in every page pouring off the presses in the infant American republic from the first day of its independence. It was only natural that this established relationship between printer and public would flow into the institutionalized divide that emerged between Federalist and Republican parties in the last decade of the 18th century. On September 4, 1798, the *Newark Gazette* decried advocacy of allotting equal time to both sides of the political divide in the pages of the nation's newspapers as a "folly that should not be tolerated." The paper likened such printers to witnesses prepared to lie in testimony to avoid taking a stand for either the accused or the plaintiff: "The times demand decision; there is a right and a wrong, and the printer, who under the specious name of impartiality jumbles both truth and falsehood into the same paper is either doubtful of his own judgment in determining truth from falsehood or is governed by ulterior motives."

On the frontier in Kentucky, the *Washington Mirror* on July 17, 1799, said that treating parties equally was impossible, and that printers who "pretended" neutrality succeeded only in willfully misleading the people. The *Baltimore American*, on May 16, 1797, had already called any claims of objective detachment "all delusion," maintaining that "every party will have its printer, as every sect its preacher." On March 10, 1800, the *New York American Citizen* rejected impartiality as "injurious to the best interests of mankind." No editor was more loyal to the doctrine of external diversity than William Cobbett who in the debut issue of his Philadelphia *Porcupine's Gazette* on March 4, 1797, emphasized to the world:

> PROFESSIONS OF IMPARTIALITY I shall make none. They are always useless, and are besides perfect nonsense, when used by a newsmonger, for ... he that does not exercise his own judgment, either in admitting or rejecting what is sent him, is a poor passive tool, and not an editor. For my part, I feel the strongest partiality for the cause of order and good government ... and against everything that is opposed to it. To profess impartiality here, would be as absurd as to profess it in a war between Virtue and Vice, Good and Evil, Happiness and Misery. There may be editors who look on such a conflict with perfect indifference, and whose only anxiety is to discover which is the strongest side. I am not one of these, nor shall a paper, under my direction, ever be an instrument of destruction to the cause I espouse.[89]

For most of American history there was no news as we understand it, in terms of the reporting of the facts; there was only opinion, and highly partisan opinion at that. To pretend otherwise was to defy common sense. After all, even assuming you could establish a viable publication without the benefit of partisan patronage, if you weren't in the business of words to champion some cause or other, what were you doing there at all? In exercising his rights as a citizen in this milieu of media advocacy, an American would therefore make his choice not between two political camps but between two different worlds, each with its own exclusive and self-contained sources of information. There were papers for Federalists and papers for Republicans; then there were papers for Whigs and papers for Democrats; then there were papers for Democrats and papers for Republicans; and never the twain would meet.

This institutionalized division of the body politic prevailed until the outside world finally intruded on America's self-absorption, first in the fiery cataclysm of World War II, then in the long winter of the Cold War. Under the pressure of meeting these challenges, an enduring bipartisan consensus emerged that for the first time forged a sense of common national purpose. As a by-product it also established the conditions for a national mainstream media market, with all that entailed for enhanced advertising revenue. Driving this process was a new media technology that would take the nationalization of the news to the next level: network television.[90]

This consensus was only patchy, even at its peak, and began to unravel as early as the mid-sixties, but the concept of a national mainstream media survived for the half century after the attack on Pearl Harbor.[91] Its effective disintegration was due to the confluence of five interrelated factors. The first was the fall of the Soviet Union, which liberated America from the all-pervasive communist menace that had acted to mitigate partisan rancor for so long. The second was the 1987 repeal by the Reagan administration of the Fairness Doctrine, which had mandated balance in broadcasting.[92] This decision — a conscious choice to reject the mandate by which the Federal Communications Commission had sought since 1949 to induce *vertical* [i.e. internal] *diversity*, variety within each individual station's programming, in favor of a new doctrine advocating *horizontal* [i.e. external] *diversity*, variety from a broad spectrum of alternatives — allowed for the rise of a new breed of explicitly partisan political commentators on talk radio. The third factor in the break-up of the national media was the emergence of a new wave of communications technologies, particularly cable-access television and the Internet, allowing for the profitable niche marketing of news catering to the ideological needs of particular constituencies. Then there was the election of Bill Clinton, who inspired a backlash of conservative activism on an unprecedented scale, much of which filled out the heretofore empty spaces on talk radio, cable television and the Internet. Finally, there was the rise of a new tabloid/infotainment culture of celebrity, immediacy, and "reality" in which all prior deference to privacy and propriety has evaporated, and in which anyone is fair game.

The idea that there could be a national mass-communications hub from which radiated information of objective value to all Americans arose after World War II, reached its apogee during the reign of Walter Cronkite, and is now in an advanced state of collapse. Less and less able to meet the needs of both extremes of an ever more polarized electorate, the mainstream media is fading away, as network news and newspapers are phased out in favor of cable news and the Internet, outlets that, as Howard Fineman notes, "tend to reinforce the sectarian views of discrete slices of the electorate" rather than present alternatives within a framework that allows for more than one interpretation.[93] Today's American doesn't want cognitive dissonance; today's American wants preexisting assumptions vindicated.[94]

This trend, however, is cyclical, not evolutionary. It represents not a completely new era in media relations, but a return to a previously established model that is deeply rooted in American tradition. The upholders of the mainstream-media concept are uneasy about what this transition represents. "Maybe all the talk about media bias has it backwards," the *Columbia Journalism Review* mused after the election of 2004, "maybe we should start to consider reader and viewer bias instead. Maybe people simply want their own opinions reinforced. Some observers believe we may soon see a partisan news culture driven by economics, as the fragmented media seek audience niches by catering to their politics." But was this a future to aspire to? "We'd rather not live in an America that builds ever-higher and thicker walls between its cultural and intellectual tribes. Such a society won't be stable in the end."[95]

The point is a redundant one, however, for it is no longer possible to obviate this reality, even if the political will existed to do so. The emerging partisan news culture is being driven as much by technology as by economics. "The market for news, entertainment, and information has finally been perfected," Sunstein notes. "We are not so very far from complete personalization of the system of communications."[96] This constitutes a threat to the collective social interest, Sunstein says, because "common experiences, emphatically including the common experiences made possible by the media, provide a form of social glue. A system of communications that radically diminishes the number of such experiences will create a number of problems, not least because of the increase in social fragmentation."[97]

Anderson posits an alternate perspective, that the rise of individualized communications represents "the end of spoon-fed orthodoxy and infallible institutions, and the rise of messy mosaics of information that require — and reward — investigation."[98] Accordingly, society is not so much fragmenting as reconstituting along different dimensions in self-selected communities of interest: "Rather than being loosely connected with people thanks to superficial mass-culture overlaps, we have the ability to be more strongly tied to just as many if not more people with a shared affinity for niche culture."[99]

In the final analysis, stability, like so many other things, exists only in the eye of the beholder. This book is intended to illustrate the extent to which the United States has endured for most of its history as one country harboring two partisan communities that have been as irreconcilable as they have been intellectually self-contained. For a brief half-century, a fragile truce was in effect. It is my contention that, by mutual consent, the cycle of partisan exclusivity is underway again.[100] Americans are choosing sides, not just in how they vote, but where they live and in their sources of information. Those in the media who recognize this new reality, from the most powerful multinational news baron to the humblest blogger, are seizing on this trend to carve out niches for themselves in satisfying the particular needs of one, and only one, ideological constituency. We are witnessing the emergence of a red-state media and a blue-state media, and, once again, never the twain shall meet.[101]

I

The Rise of the Party Press, 1789–1824

The media, in all its evolving forms, has been intimately associated with the decisions and events that have shaped the history of the United States. The part it played in the revolution set the tone for its interpretation in the years to come.[1] As Tebbel and Watts note, "When John Adams declared in 1765, in his *Dissertation on the Canon and Feudal Law*, that he knew of no 'means of information ... more sacred ... than ... [a free] press,' he did not mean it in 20th century terms. Adams and others of his time saw press freedom as the essential weapon required in their power struggle against the Crown."[2] This common understanding of the media's role as partisan instrument, rather than impartial bearer of information, carried over into the debate between federalists and anti-federalists over the ratification of the Constitution, and then into the emerging political divide of the infant republic.[3]

In the America that emerged from the revolution, according to Morton Borden, "The age of blood had passed, replaced by that of ink."[4] But the ink that flowed was too often tinged red with blood. Duels—"affairs of honor"—were a commonplace of life during this period. This was not simply owed to the prevailing social code of the era, but because language— especially the language of politics—was far more confrontational and uncompromising than would be acceptable today.[5] "The public papers will be expeditious messengers of intelligence to the most remote inhabitants of the Union," Alexander Hamilton wrote confidently in *Federalist* 84. But Thomas Jefferson wrote that the newspapers of his day could be divided into four chapters—truths, probabilities, possibilities, and lies—the first chapter being very short and the second not much longer. "Defamation is becoming a necessary of life," Jefferson lamented, "insomuch, that a dish of tea in the morning or evening cannot be digested without this stimulant. Even those who do not believe these abominations still read them with complaisance [and] betray a secret pleasure in the possibility that some may believe them, tho they do not themselves."[6]

As early as the spring of 1790, George Washington, then entering the second year of his (and America's) first presidential administration, wrote, "It is to be lamented that the Editors of different Gazettes in the Union, do not more generally, and more correctly (instead of stuffing their papers with scurrility, and nonsensical declamation, which few would read if they were apprised of the consequences) publish the debates in Congress on all great national questions."[7] In October 1792, Washington wrote Gouverneur Morris: "From the complexion

21

of some of our Newspapers Foreigners would be led to believe that inveterate political dissensions existed among us, and that we are on the very verge of disunion; but the fact is otherwise."[8]

According to Frank Mott, "It must be remembered that in the first quarter of the nineteenth century American newspapers in general reached the lowest ethical ebb of their history. These years comprise a kind of Dark Ages of American journalism. The root of the trouble was in the bigoted partisanship which dominated the press. Loyalty to party was placed above honest reporting, above fair comment."[9] Walt Brown makes the same point; if the period of the early republic did represent the Dark Ages, "then Federalist and Republican editors were the Vandals and Huns whose editorial barbarism brought on the journalistic darkness."[10]

James Lee writes that "those who look over the papers of this era will find that all of the customary courtesies of life were put aside; that the papers of both parties employed the vilest, grossest epithets found in the English language."[11] Editors on both sides of the partisan divide would without hesitation refer to opponents as "insane," "incompetent," "small-minded," "wooden-headed," or some other characteristic involving stupidity. Names of animals, including "jackal," "dog," "skunk," "serpent," "viper," or simply "beast," were favorites, as were words describing an aspect of the opponent's moral nature, "wretch," "coward," "hypocrite," "debaucher," "drunk," "bandit," "carouser," "criminal," and "assassin," being typical. When nouns would not suffice to impart the full extent of an individual's detestability, writers chose adjectives; the opponent might be labeled "worthless," "depraved," "corrupt," "immoral," "malignant," "infamous," "wicked," "vile," or "perverted." On occasion editors would aspire to being a little more imaginative, and would come up with names such as "prating popinjay," "toad-eater," "under-strapper," "addled cat's paw," "guttersnipe," and "double-faced weather-cock."[12] In sum, opposition newspapers, opined the *Gazette of the United States* on July 25, 1801, "must have been written by mad-men for the use of fools."[13]

"The newspapers are venal, servile, base, and stupid," wrote Fisher Ames in 1799.[14] It was an era in which men "with low vitious minds, but some talents and education, become the pimps of faction, English or French," Noah Webster declared, and "abuse the officers of our government, the government itself and the most respectable Americans; foment divisions, inflame parties, spread jealousies, and corrupt the public mind."[15] Many of his contemporaries, even the most partisan, agreed: "A news-paper, generally speaking is the manual of ignorance and rascality," William Cobbett lamented.[16] On March 4, 1799, John Ward Fenno wrote in the *Gazette of the United States*: "The American newspapers are the most base, false, servile and venal publications that ever polluted the fountains of society — their editors the most ignorant, mercenary, and vulgar automatons that ever were moved by the continually rusting wires of sordid mercantile avarice."[17]

"It is impossible to peruse the federal papers of this country; and to observe their utter contempt for truth, their gross scurrility, their repulsive impudence, without feeling an aversion, which ought not to exist, against the very profession which they pursue," Thomas Ritchie complained in his *Richmond Enquirer* on November 7, 1806.[18] Even after the first storm of party politics had passed, the *Washington Monitor*, on August 23, 1808, observed: "It is full time that some effort should be made to purify the presses of the United States, from their froth, their spume, and their coarse vulgarisms. Newspapers of all descriptions teem with bombastic invective, with ridiculous jargon, and empty declamation. The popular taste becomes vitiated, and is prepared to receive the pestilential banquet of every noxious creature that wields a pen or controls a press."[19]

However, for all the opprobrium to which they were subjected, the reality remained that the partisan editor was the key player in the political superstructure of the day. "Modern political oratory is chiefly performed by the Pen and the Press," Benjamin Franklin quipped, and the editors were the gatekeepers of what passed into the public domain.[20] A successful campaign for office was one that conformed to their rules, and there was nothing subtle about the methods involved. As one of the masters of the art, William Duane, reminded Thomas Jefferson in a letter dated January 23, 1809, "Every man of observation knows that fact, that public discussion, argument, and reasoning upon matters of policy, are not addressed to the intelligent and the virtuous part of the community." Emphasizing this point, the editor lectured the president:

> There are in every society large masses of men, who never think or reason; some who have no capacity for thought; many whose judgements are too weak to be constant to any fit ideas; and very many who assume a mask of moderation or liberality only to cover their diabolical selfishness and depravity; very unfortunately this mixture of ignorance, imbecility and hypocrisy is very numerous. It forms perhaps a full third of every society; and it is to the major part of this mass that all public discussions are addressed. They in fact make the majority in all critical times, and are as ready to be thrown into the balance on one side or the other, according to the mode in which they are addressed.[21]

What passes for criticism in the mainstream media nowadays is only a pale, ghostly shadow of what was considered appropriate civic discourse by the wielders of the poison-dipped pens of two hundred years ago. To understand the literary environment in which this nation was forged, a contemporary observer would have to imagine a world where access to the news was entirely in the hands of the "noxious creatures" who broadcast over talk radio and maintain blogs today.

Hamilton and Jefferson

In 1787, Ambassador Thomas Jefferson wrote home to Virginia from Paris that "were it left to me to decide whether we should have a government without newspapers, or newspapers without a government, I should not hesitate a moment to prefer the latter."[22] Eventually he would play a key role in binding the two institutions together, expanding the authority of both.

It is a truism that the manifest desire on the part of the Founding Fathers was that the United States might be governed by an enlightened circle of the best men free of the taint of partisan, party politics. In fact, it was two of the leading lights among those Founding Fathers— Thomas Jefferson, Washington's secretary of state, and Alexander Hamilton, his secretary of the treasury — who were responsible for articulating the first principles of a factional divide that would widen into the country's first party system. Hamilton represented a constituency, centered in New England and based in the major urban trading centers of the Atlantic seaboard, that favored a flexible interpretation of the Constitution, allowing for the assumption of expanded powers by an activist federal government, including public works, a protective tariff, and a standing army, and that leaned toward England in foreign policy. These tendencies were embodied in the Federalist Party. Jefferson represented a constituency, spread across the farms and villages of the South and West, reaching out toward the frontier, that favored strict interpretation of the Constitution and a federal government with limited powers, that stood for free trade, was opposed to public works, considered a standing army a threat to liberty, and tilted towards France in international relations. This constituency evolved into the Republican Party, the ancestor of the modern Democratic Party.

As they were both members of Washington's cabinet, Hamilton and Jefferson were forced to play out their feud by proxy. Each chose to do so through the medium of a hired gun in the press, a hireling sworn to articulate the agenda of his master. These arrangements would define the relationship between politicians and the press for the duration of the antebellum republic. "Lacking partisan structures from which to spread factional points of view, major governmental leaders—whether they supported or opposed the first administration's policies—turned to the press," Richard Rubin notes. "Where they could find willing like-minded editors they utilized them; where they could not, they created and subsidized new journalistic organs to articulate and coordinate the publication of their faction's point of view."[23] This development spawned a whole new generation of editors dedicated to politics as a livelihood. According to Tebbel and Watts, "Where newspapers had been regarded earlier as only one of a printer's products in his efforts to make a living, now they were more often established to represent political parties and advance causes."[24]

Journalism was a profession held in low repute in the 18th century, and relations between politicians and the press in the fledgling republic were edgy, as each defined its role in relation to the other. The day after the House of Representatives approved the First Amendment to the Constitution, protecting the freedom of the press, it debated barring reporters from the House floor. Angry representatives charged reporters with distorting their arguments, mutilating their words, and "throwing over the whole proceedings a thick veil of misrepresentation and error."[25] The debate ended unresolved, but the reporters, who had strategically retreated to the galleries for the duration, found that at its conclusion House doorkeepers barred their return to the floor.[26] When Congress moved from New York to Philadelphia, four seats on window sills were provided for stenographers, and here perched the first congressional reporters, names that would become household words: John Fenno, Philip Freneau, James Thomson Callender, Joseph Gales, Sr., and Samuel Harrison Smith.[27]

The first of these individuals to volunteer for service as the mouthpiece for the Hamiltonian faction was John Fenno, formerly a teacher in Boston and a contributor to Benjamin Russell's *Massachusetts Centinel*, who approached Rufus King in early 1789 about the possibility of establishing a pro-Federalist paper in the nation's capital. The *Gazette of the United States* made its debut in New York on April 15, 1789, promising to attempt "by every exertion, to endear the GENERAL GOVERNMENT to the people."[28] The key to securing this affection was establishing a cult of personality around George Washington. When "the most illustrious PRESIDENT OF THE UNITED STATES" entered New York City on April 25, 1789, Fenno declared with a typical extravagant rhetorical flourish, "many persons who were in the crowd, were heard to say, that they should now die contented—nothing being wanted to complete their happiness, previous to this auspicious period, but the sight of the Savior of his Country."

Such panegyrics notwithstanding, by October publisher and editor Fenno was $400 behind in paying the *Gazette's* expenses and had not even begun to pay back the debts he had incurred in launching the paper. He had to be rescued by Alexander Hamilton. The *Gazette* was given all of the Senate's printing business and most of the Treasury Department's. Hamilton personally loaned Fenno substantial sums, without asking for repayment, on at least two occasions in 1790 and 1791. Editorially, Fenno was assisted by prominent Federalists, including King, Hamilton, and John Adams. Their contributions were made in the form of letters to the editor signed by such pseudonyms as "Publicola," "Davila," "Camillus," "Metellus," "Amicus," "Pacificus," "Catullus," "An American," and "Plain Facts."[29]

The *National Gazette* was in short order denounced by Jefferson as "a paper of pure Toryism, disseminating the doctrines of monarchy, aristocracy, and the exclusion of the influence of the people."[30] On another occasion Jefferson stigmatized "the tory-paper of Fenno" for "rarely admitting any thing which defends the present form of government in opposition to his desire of subverting it to make way for a king, lords and commons." The *National Gazette*, he told his close ally James Madison, was already "under general condemnation for its toryism and its incessant efforts to overturn the government."[31] The master of Montpelier, always on the same wavelength as the master of Monticello, recognized the need to fight fire with fire. As he later explained it: "I entertained hopes that a free paper, meant for general circulation, and edited by a man of genius of republican principles and a friend of the Constitution, would be some antidote to the doctrines and discourses circulated in favor of Monarchy and Aristocracy."[32]

Accordingly, in April 1791, Jefferson and Madison resolved to take active steps "to reclaim [the people] by enlightening them." Jefferson's first choice to serve as the vehicle of this enlightenment was the *Philadelphia General Advertiser*, launched on October 1, 1790 by Benjamin Franklin Bache, the twenty-one-year-old grandson of the great Benjamin Franklin.[33] Jefferson wrote to Bache on April 22, 1791, that his intent to co-opt the editor proceeded "from a desire of seeing a purely republican vehicle of news

The "poet of the revolution," Philip Freneau emerged as the first to take up the pen against the Federalist administration during the early years of the republic. As editor of the *National Gazette* under Thomas Jefferson's patronage, he provided a platform for James Madison and other Republicans to challenge the hegemony of Alexander Hamilton (courtesy of New York Public Library).

established between the seat of government and all its parts."[34] But Bache, who ironically shared a birthday with Fenno, was unwilling at that time to accept the honor of converting his publication into a rival to the *Gazette*. Jefferson and Madison therefore decided to launch their own paper, one that "might go through the states, and furnish a whig-vehicle of intelligence" that would "be generally taken instead of Fenno's." As editor they settled on Philip Freneau, Madison's roommate at the College of New Jersey, who had gone on to captain the privateer *Aurora* during the Revolution and was best known as the author of *The Prison Ship*, a poetic account of his experiences as a prisoner of war.[35] After being initially turned down by Freneau, Jefferson offered him a sinecure to sweeten the deal: "The clerkship for foreign languages in my office is vacant; the salary, indeed, is very low, being two hundred and fifty dollars a year; but it also gives so little to do as not to interfere with any other office one may chuse."[36] The ensuing product, the Philadelphia *National Gazette*, first rolled off the presses in October 1791.[37]

Jefferson and Madison personally assisted in building a list of subscribers for the new paper, as did General Henry Lee in Philadelphia, Daniel Carroll in Maryland, and John Hancock and Samuel Adams in Massachusetts.[38] "I ha[ve given] to Freneau the list of subscribers you sent me," Jefferson wrote his neighbor, Thomas Bell, "I am to pay him for the subscribers, and must get you to settle with them for me." The secretary of state's enthusiasm for the new venture shone through in his appeals: "I am in hopes his paper will give satisfaction," he told Bell, "it is certainly the best I ever saw published in America."[39] That the *National Gazette* was the physical expression of its patron's worldview none could doubt. "I need not write you news, as you receive Freneau's paper," Jefferson wrote to his friend Dr. George Gilmer on May 11, 1792, "in his next after this date will be an interesting report of a committee of Congress on the causes of the failure of the last campaign."[40]

The opening partisan salvo unleashed in the *National Gazette* was the first of a series of eighteen articles penned by Madison. It appeared anonymously in the April 2, 1792, issue under the title "The Union: Who Are Its Real Friends?"

> Not those who promote unnecessary accumulations of the debt.... Not those who study, by arbitrary interpretations and insidious precedents, to pervert the limited government of the Union, into a government of unlimited discretion, contrary to the will and subversive of the authority of the people.... *The real FRIENDS to the Union are those* ... Who are friends to the limited and republican system of government ... Who considering a public debt as injurious to the interests of the people ... are enemies to every contrivance for *unnecessarily* increasing its amount.[41]

Madison pulled no punches in the course of his philippic against the administration. Those endorsing the federalist tendencies of Washington and Hamilton, he implied, were "stupid, suspicious, licentious" creatures, "destitute ... of every quality of a good citizen," possessing "neither the light of faith nor the spirit of obedience."[42]

Freneau continued the literary assault on Hamilton, publishing articles that attacked his *Report on Manufactures* and his excise system, and giving extensive coverage to the most violent anti-Hamilton speeches in Congress, on subjects ranging from frontier defense to the additional assumption of state debts. Hamilton found no respite from an incessant barrage of references to the "numerous evils" of the "baneful" financial system he had constructed, "as unjust in its operation on individuals, as it has been ruinous in its effects on the public."[43]

On June 11 the *National Gazette* posed an increasingly leading series of questions that clearly represented the strict constructionist's perspective on where Hamilton's grand scheme was ultimately leading: "Are not some amongst us avowedly, others notoriously, advocates for monarchy and aristocracy? Are not the principles of all such hostile to the principles of the constitution? Must not such naturally wish to make the constitution by stretching its powers, and aggrandizing a few, the stalking horse to hereditary government?"[44]

Another article contributed anonymously by Madison, "A Candid State of Parties," appeared in the *National Gazette* on September 26, 1792. This essay outlined the emergence of a division within society between an "anti-republican party" which consisted of those who wanted to substitute hereditary for elected representation and believed government could "only be carried on by the pageantry of rank, the influence of money and emoluments, and the terror of military force," and a "Republican party" dedicated to popular government which regarded hereditary institutions as "an insult to the reason and an outrage to the rights of man." The question facing the nation was which of these two parties would "ultimately establish its ascendance." According to Marcus Daniel, Madison's "purpose in writing the essay was not so much to acknowledge the existence of the 'Republican party' as to conjure it into existence."[45]

Hamilton fumed in private about Freneau's "incendiary and pernicious publication" until July 25, when he placed an anonymous little paragraph in the *Gazette of the United States* pointing out that Freneau received a government salary and asking whether this was paid for translations or for publications, "the design of which is to vilify those to whom the voice of the people has committed the administration of our public affairs—to oppose the measures of government, and, by false insinuations, to disturb the public peace?"[46]

"In common life it is thought ungrateful for a man to bite the hand that puts bread in his mouth," Hamilton concluded, "but if the man is hired to do it, the case is altered."[47] Having exposed Freneau, Hamilton turned directly on Jefferson, whom the Treasury Secretary considered "the declared opponent of almost all the important measures which had been devised by the Government" to date. In a letter published anonymously by Fenno's paper on September 15, 1792, Hamilton attacked Jefferson over the impropriety of his relationship with Freneau, who had set up a newspaper that would be "an exact copy of the politics of his employer," and further asserting:

> he is the institutor and patron of a certain Gazette published in this city, the object and tendency of which are to vilify and depreciate the Government of the United States, to misrepresent and traduce the administration of it, except in the single department of which that gentleman is the head ... in support of this paper, thus hostile to the government, in the administration of which he holds so important a trust, he has not scrupled to apply the money of that very government; departing by this conduct from the rules of official propriety and obligation, and from the duty of a discreet and patriotic citizen.[48]

"Can he [Jefferson] reconcile it to his own personal dignity and the principles of probity to hold an office under [the government] and employ the means of official influence in opposition?" Hamilton demanded in print.[49] In private, he took his grievance directly to Washington, asserting "I cannot doubt from the evidence I possess that the *National Gazette* was instituted for political purposes and that one leading object of it has been to render me, and all the measures connected with my department, as odious as possible."[50] On September 9, 1792, Jefferson adamantly denied to the President any guilt on his part in the newspaper war between himself and Hamilton: "I confide that yourself are satisfied that, as to dissension in the newspapers, not a syllable of them has ever proceeded from me."[51] While dissembling to Washington, Jefferson was privately gloating to his associates about the progress his pet publication was making. "Freneau's paper is getting into Massachusetts under the patronage of Hancock and Samuel Adams," an excited Jefferson confided to Thomas Mann Randolph on November 16, 1792. "The people of that state are republican; but hitherto they have heard nothing but the hymns and lauds chanted by Fenno."[52]

Washington, who wasn't buying for a second Jefferson's protestations of innocence, finally felt constrained to intervene on Hamilton's behalf.[53] Jefferson privately recorded that in May 1793 President

> adverted to a piece in Freneau's paper of yesterday; he said he despised all their attacks on him personally, but that there had never been an act of the government ... which that paper had not abused.... He was evidently sore and warm, and I took his intention to be, that I should interpose in some way with Freneau, perhaps withdraw his appointment ... but I will not do it. His paper has saved our constitution which was galloping fast into monarchy, and has been checked by no one means so powerfully as by that paper. It is well and universally known that it has been that paper which has checked the career of the monocrats; and the President, not sensible of the designs of the party, has not with his usual good sense and *sang froid*, looked on the efforts and effects of this free press.[54]

Jefferson dedicated a 4,000-word declaration of innocence to Washington, asserting "in the presence of heaven, that I never did by myself, or any other, or indirectly, say a syllable, nor attempt any kind of influence" over Freneau.[55] In a manifesto that encapsulated both his high-flown ideals and thinly veiled political ambition, the Virginian waxed eloquent on the role of the press: "No government ought to be without censors, and where the press is free, no one ever will. If virtuous, it need not fear the fair operation of attack and defense. Nature has given to man no other means of sifting out the truth either in religion, law, or politics. I think it is honorable for the government neither to know, nor notice, its sycophants or censors, as it would be undignified and criminal to pamper the former and persecute the latter."

Jefferson could not resist concluding that "[Freneau] & Fenno are rivals for the public favor. The one courts them by flattery, the other by censure, & I believe it will be admitted that one has been as servile, as the other severe."[56] Nevertheless, he went on to insist that he never, directly or indirectly, had any influence over Freneau's newspaper. This from the man who allowed Freneau access to his office at night, deliberately leaving confidential reports in plain sight so they might be run the following morning for all the world to see in the pages of the *National Gazette*, sometimes even before Washington had a chance to read them. He also insisted that "I never did by myself or any other, directly or indirectly, write, dictate or procure any one sentence or sentiment to be inserted in his or any other gazette." Jefferson's denials were not credible at the time and, indeed, Freneau, who had the files to prove it, would later charge Jefferson with not only writing much of his publication but with being author of some of its most partisan articles.[57]

Such dissembling was typical of Jefferson, who also channeled money to Charles Holt of the *New London Bee*, Andrew Brown of the Philadelphia *Federal Gazette*, and, most notoriously, rabid anti–Federalist James Callender. In July 1793, barely two months after denying any involvement with partisan politics in his correspondence with the President, Jefferson practically begged Madison to take on Hamilton in print: "Nobody answers him, & his doctrines will therefore be taken for confessed. For god's sake, my dear sir, take up your pen, select the most striking heresies, and cut him to pieces in the face of the public. There is nobody else who can & will enter the lists with him.[58]

As their patrons squabbled, Fenno and Freneau continued their duel of letters. Fenno, the less literary of the two, typically responded to the "malignant effrontery" of the opposition by labeling the administration's critics, among other things, "dismal cacklers," "out of their wits," "propagators of calumny," "villains," "brawlers," "enemies of freedom," and the "worst and basest of men."[59] In one editorial he snapped at the "mad Dogs" and "audacious scribblers" with "disordered imaginations" who "rave about monsters because they are out of their wits."[60]

Freneau was able to make light of Fenno's distress in a manner that always seemed to reflect badly on the aggrieved Federalist. Freneau often chose to return Fenno's salvoes in verse:

> Since the day we attempted the *Nation's Gazette*
> Pomposo's dull printer does nothing but fret;
> Now preaching
> Now screeching
> Then nibbling
> And scribbling
> Remarking
> And barking
> Repining
> And whining
> And still in a pet,
> From morning till night, with the *Nation's Gazette*.[61]

When the federal government moved from New York to Philadelphia, Fenno moved with it, bringing out his first edition in the new capital on November 3, 1790. The 1793 yellow fever epidemic in the city forced the *Gazette* to suspend publication. By the time the contagion had subsided, Fenno was $2,000 in debt. In order to save his business the editor applied to Hamilton for the "assistance long since promised ... with all the pathos I am capable of giving." He asked that Hamilton solicit his supporters for donations to the *Gazette*. "Four Years & and half of my life is gone for nothing; & worse," Fenno pleaded, "if at this crisis the hand of benevolence & *patriotism* is not extended."[62]

Hamilton had previously hesitated to take such direct action, but after enduring two years of assaults from Freneau's *National Gazette* he responded with alacrity to Fenno's plea, raising money by arguing it was critical to the "Federalist cause" that Fenno "be enabled to prosecute a paper." Hamilton enlisted Rufus King to collect $1,000 in New York while he raised a like amount in Philadelphia.[63]

Reconstituted on a more secure basis, the first issue of the *Gazette of the United States & Evening Advertiser* rolled off the presses on December 11, 1793. That left the Federalists in the ascendancy because when Jefferson stepped down from office at the end of 1793 Freneau had to give up his clerkship in the Department of State, resigning on October 11. Bereft of official patronage, his paper could not survive, and the *National Gazette* came to a premature end on October 26.[64] Such an eventuality represented the Achilles' heel of the partisan press in the early years of the republic, when newspapers could not generate on their own the resources they required for institutional independence. It was only by willingly subordinating themselves to rising national and local leaders and their parties that they were able to maintain a free, protected, but dependent voice.[65] If anything upset that relationship, or cut off the flow of funds from political patron to client editor, the publication, irrespective of whatever intrinsic merits it possessed, would be thrown back on its own resources, a contingency few survived. The attrition rate was substantial; of the eighty-one newspapers in operation at the time of Washington's inauguration only twenty-eight were still publishing when Jefferson became president.[66] However, during its brief life the *National Gazette* had more than made its mark. According to Marcus Daniel: "During its short existence, from October 1791 to November 1793, the *National Gazette* had a profound impact on the character of American political discourse. Almost single handedly, Freneau (and his contributors) transformed a hesitant and inchoate sense of opposition to the policies of Alexander Hamilton into a coherent, effective and self-conscious opposition party bursting with political élan and vitality. The emergence of a 'Republican party,' and the success (albeit limited) with which the opposition was able to define the party of government as 'aristocratic' was inextricably bound up with the rhetorical practices of Freneau's newspaper."[67]

After Jefferson's and Madison's efforts to forge a relationship between Freneau and Thomas Greenleaf of the *New York Journal* failed, the gap in Republican ranks was filled by the Philadelphia *General Advertiser* of Benjamin Franklin Bache, who later renamed the paper the *Aurora General Advertiser*. This was to prove a significant choice. According to Jeffrey Pasley, "Bache and the *Aurora* were quite literally constructing the Republican Party during the mid-1790s."[68] Contemporary observers appreciated the development of this phenomenon; the Federalist *Massachusetts Mercury* unhappily admitted that Bache had devised "the most noted engine for spreading filth; and spreads it over the continent, like a blasting mildew, in the pestilential pages of the Aurora."[69] Harrison Gray Otis was another Federalist to lament the manner in which Bache's "poisons are scattered by officious missionaries who prowl through the country, disturbing the silence of the woods and tranquility of the cottage."[70]

For all the ideological satisfaction it provided, the personal cost of publishing and distributing the authoritative voice of Republicanism was ruinous. During the eight years he edited the *Aurora*, Bache lost somewhere between $14,700 and $20,000. At no time was the income from the paper enough to pay his family's living expenses. At the time of his death on September 10, 1798, he was under arrest and bankrupt while his wife Margaret was pregnant with their fourth child.[71] Reflecting its importance, Jefferson and Madison always remained anxious for the financial wellbeing of their media offspring. The *Aurora* and Matthew Carey's *United States Recorder* "totter for want of subscriptions," the vice president wrote Madison. "We should really exert ourselves to procure them, for if these papers fall, Republicanism will be entirely brow-beaten."[72] Their appeals met with some success; yet another Virginian, James Monroe, who called the *Aurora* the "best political paper" in Philadelphia, loaned Bache six hundred dollars after the editor agreed to publish Monroe's "A View of the Conduct of the President," a hostile critique of Washington.

Fenno found out about Jefferson's fundraising and reported that the vice president was "earnestly soliciting his partizans and all their influential men in his part of the country to exert themselves to procure subscriptions to the AURORA, or the paper must fall."[73] The *Aurora* responded by posting the following as a direct challenge to the editor of the *Gazette of the United States*: "To Mr. Fenno: This is to announce you to the world as a scoundrel and a liar; and though you may be generally known as such, I will prove what I say."[74]

Brushing off such inducements to resolve their differences on the field of honor, the Federalists kept up the pressure by opening a new front in the literary war. After a series of meetings with Noah Webster, who gained later fame with his dictionaries, in August 1793 a group of prominent Federalists—including Hamilton, John Jay, Rufus King, James Watson, James Greenleaf, and five others—agreed to subscribe $150 each "for five years without interest towards the creation of a new Federalist newspaper" in New York. Webster moved to the city in order to become editor of the publication, the *American Minerva*, which debuted on December 9, 1793, being rechristened the *Commercial Advertiser* on October 2, 1797. For his pains Webster was hailed by Bache as the "jackall of the British faction" and characterized in the *Aurora* thusly: "If ever a man prostituted the little sense that he had, to serve the purposes of a monarchic and aristocratic junto, Noah Webster, Esq. must be the man."[75]

Partisan divisions had remained in-house during Washington's first term, and the president himself had enjoyed the respect he assumed was the right of office. Even the *National Gazette* did not oppose Washington's reelection in 1792 (though Freneau and a number of other anti-Federalist editors favored New York Governor George Clinton over Adams as vice president).[76] Washington was realistic enough to appreciate that this happy state of affairs could not endure; the President was only too aware that soon "the extravagant (and I may say undue) praises which they are heaping upon me at this moment" would ultimately devolve into "equally extravagant (that I will fondly hope unmerited) censures."

Indeed, the honeymoon was shockingly brief. In short order the President was complaining of the "malignant industry and persevering falsehoods" with which "I am assailed in order to weaken, if not destroy the confidence of the Public."[77] According to Donald Stewart, three events in his second term — the Whiskey Rebellion, the Genêt affair, and the Jay Treaty — "made Washington the object of as concentrated a campaign of vilification as has been known in American political life."[78]

The motivating force behind this vitriolic character assassination was the impingement of the outside world on the relatively tranquil domestic American political scene. While Washington had been content to maintain strict neutrality as the hallmark of his foreign policy during his first four years in office, the widening war in Europe, particularly the entry of Great Britain into the coalition against France, meant it was no longer possible to avoid making zero-sum decisions that would be reflected in the alienation of domestic constituencies. The question of the nature of its relations with France bedeviled the sister American republic during the first quarter-century of its existence. The succession of events in France from the fall of the Bastille to the Declaration of the Rights of Man had won near universal approval on the far side of the Atlantic. But as the reality of the Montagnard coup-d'état, the execution of King Louis XVI (America's benefactor during the struggle for independence), and the

Terror sank in, the earlier burst of enthusiasm on the part of many Americans subsided into doubt and then hostility. While Republicans continued to look to Thomas Paine for guidance on the events in France, Federalists looked to Edmund Burke.[79]

Washington's approval of the Jay Treaty was the final straw as far as Bache was concerned. Having warned that if the treaty were approved "the President will be as sovereign and omnipotent as the Demi-God of a Turkish Seraglio," the August 15, 1795 edition of the *Aurora* used large type to emblazon its incredulity: "We are assured that the President has signed the Treaty, but cannot yet believe it."[80] Once Bache got over his shock he vowed, "I will unmasque the idol we have set up, and shew him to be a man."[81]

In the Republican press, the father of the nation was now labeled "treacherous," "mischievous," "despotic," "a dictator," and "a tyrannical monster," accused of "ingratitude" and "want of merit," characterized as "a spoiled child," and declared guilty of "stately journeying through the American continent in search of personal incense." "The hell-hounds are now in full cry in the newspapers against the President, whom they treat as ill as ever they did me," Adams lamented.[82] For example, "Scipio" writing in the *Aurora* urged Washington to "retire immediately; let no flatterer persuade you to rest one hour longer at the helm of state. You are utterly incapable to steer the political ship into the harbour of safety. If you have any love for your country, leave its affairs to the wisdom of your fellow citizens ... there are thousands amongst them who equal you in capacity, and who excel you in knowledge."[83]

"Will not the world be led to conclude that the mask of political hypocrisy has been alike worn by a CAESAR, a CROMWELL, and a WASHINGTON?" Scipio concluded.[84]

Bache was not afraid to critique Washington's record as commander in chief of the American forces during the Revolution, drawing up a catalogue of failure redeemed only by "the small microscopic exploits of Trenton and Princeton" and accusing the President of having "suffered the war to linger in his hands for seven whole years, notwithstanding he had to contend with some of the most inefficient generals in Europe."[85]

Bache further labeled Washington an "anemic imitation of the English kings," whose qualifications for office could be summed up as those of "a Virginia planter by no means that most eminent, a militia-officer ignorant of war both in theory and useful practice, and a politician certainly not of the first magnitude."[86] "Can it be," Bache wondered, "that one man can have palsied the principles of free born souls ... converted men into eunuchs, and have substituted the distaff for the sword?"[87]

"The publications in Freneau's and [Bache's] papers," the beleaguered President wrote as early as June 1793, "are outrages on common decency."[88] Even literary firebrand Thomas Paine turned on Washington after the president refused to bail him out when he got a little too close to French revolutionary politics and wound up in a Paris prison courtesy of Robespierre. Convinced Washington was "treacherous in private friendship" and "a hypocrite in public life," Paine maintained that "the world will be puzzled to decide whether you are an apostate or an imposter: whether you have abandoned good principles, or whether you ever had any."[89]

Washington wrote Jefferson complaining about those who "publish things that do not, as well as those which do exist; and to mutilate the latter, so as to make them subserve the purposes which they have in view." Washington referred to the abuse by his critics as being couched "in such exaggerated and indecent terms as could scarcely be applied to a Nero; a notorious defaulter; or even to a common pickpocket."[90] The pressure was clearly taking its toll on the father of the nation. In August 1793 Jefferson noted the response of the President to a lampoon that had been published in the *National Gazette*:

> The President was much inflamed; got into one of those passions when he cannot command himself; ran on much on the personal abuse which had been bestowed on him; defied any man

on earth to produce one single act of his since he had been in the Government, which was not done on the purest motives; that he had never repented but once the having slipped the moment of resigning his office, and that was every moment since; that by God he had rather be in his grave than in his present situation; that he had rather be on his farm than to be made Emperor of the world; and yet they were charging him with wanting to be a King. That that rascal Freneau sent him three of his papers every day, as if he thought he would become the distributor of his papers; that he could see in this, nothing but an impudent design to insult him: he ended in this high tone.[91]

At the beginning of July 1796, Washington observed, "That Mr. Bache will continue his attacks on the Government, there can be no doubt, but that they will make no Impression on the public mind is not so certain, for drops of Water will Impress (in time) the hardest Marble." On July 18, Washington wrote his secretary of state, Timothy Pickering, "The continual attacks which have been made and are still making on the administration, in Bache's [paper are as] ... indecent as they are devoid of truth and fairness."[92] Washington finally explained his readiness to leave office as a "disinclination to be longer buffeted in the public prints by a set of infamous scribblers."[93]

Small wonder that in a paragraph omitted from the final draft of his farewell address Washington took a parting shot at the papers, which "have teemed with all the invective that disappointment, ignorance of facts, and malicious falsehood could invent, to misrepresent my politics and affections; to wound my reputation and feelings; and to weaken, if not entirely destroy the confidence you had been pleased to repose in me." Even with that paragraph deleted, Washington was hounded to the end by his adversaries in the press. "Your Address in my mind is fraught with incalculable evils to your country!" William Duane, who was convinced the President's farewell address reflected "the loathings of a sick mind," fumed in the *Aurora*. "Posterity will in vain search for the monuments of wisdom in your administration."[94]

"If ever a nation was debauched, by a man, the American nation has been debauched by Washington," the *Aurora*, determined to get in the last word, declared: "If ever a nation has suffered from the improper influence of a man, the American nation has suffered from the influence of Washington. If ever a nation was deceived by a man, the American nation has been deceived by Washington. Let his conduct, then, be an example to future ages.... Let the history of the Federal Government instruct mankind, that the masque of patriotism may be worn to conceal the foulest designs against the liberties of a people."[95]

The day after Washington left office, the *Aurora* burst forth in joy that "the man who is the source of all the misfortunes of our country is this day reduced to a level with his fellow citizens, and is no longer possessed of powers to multiply evils upon the United States. If ever there was a period for rejoicing, this is the moment — every heart in unison with the freedom and happiness of the people, ought to beat high with exultation that the name of Washington from this day ceases to give a currency to political iniquity, and to legalized corruption."[96]

On this basis Tebbel and Watts observe of Washington that "no president in office was so badly treated by the press except for Lincoln and Franklin Roosevelt."[97] The outgunned Federalist partisans in the press sought desperately to give the president covering fire. "Dead to every normal sentiment that ought to animate the soul — he seems to take a kind of hellish pleasure in defaming the name of WASHINGTON," Fenno declared of Bache.[98] In Fenno's *Gazette*, the author "Americus" expounded on the manifold faults of the editor of the *Aurora*: "He has founded the lowest depths of human depravity, and now exhibits to the world an example of wickedness that no man of his years ever arrived at before. Let none attempt to describe him — language is too weak — no combination of words will come so near to expressing every thing that is monstrous in human nature as BENJAMIN FRANKLIN BACHE. Let him sink into contempt, and let oblivion cover him."[99]

Other citizens were prepared to express their outrage on the president's behalf in more physical terms. In April 1797, while Bache was inspecting the frigate *United States*, he was attacked by Clement Humphreys, son of the vessel's architect, Joshua Humphreys. The younger Humphreys, who pleaded guilty to assault and battery, was shortly thereafter given a diplomatic appointment in Europe by President Adams. "This man [Bache] has celebrity in a certain way," Washington told a correspondent in his retirement, "for His calumnies are to be exceeded only by his Impudence, and both stand unrivaled."[100]

Bache had identified the man from Braintree as Jefferson's chief rival to succeed Washington in 1796, and had drawn the battle lines accordingly, depicting the election as a question of "whether we shall have at the head of our executive a steadfast friend to the Rights of the People, or an advocate for hereditary power and distinctions."[101] However, Adams was the beneficiary of a media honeymoon after his election. The *Aurora* conceded, "It is well known that ADAMS is an Aristocrat only in *theory*, but that WASHINGTON is one in *practice* — that ADAMS has the simplicity of a republican but that WASHINGTON has the ostentations of an eastern bashaw — that ADAMS holds none of his fellow men in slavery, but that WASHINGTON does."[102] In sum, "The republicans are well satisfied with the election of Mr. Adams," with no "apprehension of his putting himself at the head of a party as his predecessor has done."

Adams was wise enough to appreciate that this smooth sailing wouldn't — couldn't — last. As early as the end of April 1797, the president was warning his wife, "I shall soon be acquitted of the crime of *Chronicle*, *Argus* and *Aurora* praise." Which was for the best. As Abigail Adams related, "Their praise for a few weeks mortified him, much more than all of their impudent abuse."[103] The extent to which the President actually preferred being labeled, among other things, "old, bald, blind, querulous, toothless crippled John Adams" by Bache than remaining the beneficiary of his approbation is a matter for conjecture.[104] In any event, the honeymoon ended with a dramatic flourish after Adams's message to a special session of Congress on May 16, 1797, in which the president, in response to the outrages of French privateers against American shipping and the failure of the "XYZ" negotiations with the Directory regime in Paris, advocated increased appropriations for national defense, funding for the construction of three frigates, the arming and convoying of merchant ships, a strengthened militia, additional cavalry and artillery units for the regular army, and the creation of a provisional army in the event of war. Bache took to referring to Adams as "the President by three votes," a "weak old man" in his "dotage," under the direction of Hamilton, by proxy of his adherents in the cabinet.

The yellow-fever epidemic that ravaged Philadelphia in the summer of 1798 momentarily forced a truce between the warring parties (Federalist editors, however, traced the source of the epidemic to a French ship, the *Marseilles*, while Republicans blamed a British vessel, the *Arethusa*). The yellow fever carried off 3,500 souls, including sixty-two who worked for printing establishments throughout the city, eight from the *Aurora* alone. John Fenno's wife Mary died on September 4, Bache on September 10, Fenno himself on September 14.[105]

The twenty-two-year-old John Ward Fenno succeeded his father and swiftly confirmed that partisanship does sometimes run in families. Granted control of the *Gazette* for a few days in 1797, the younger Fenno had seized the opportunity to lash Bache, his father's bête-noire, whom he described as a "poor, silly, emaciated dupe of French villainy," "a base, unnatural, patricidal villain," and "a miserable tool of the most abandoned faction that ever disgraced a free country."[106] After inheriting the family business on a fulltime basis, the younger Fenno confirmed that his purpose was to oppose the "monster Jacobinism ... [and] aspiring demagogues ... and to raise new bulwarks in those quarters where ... the raging madness of Jacobinism may have effected breaches in the barrier round the public weal."[107] This was a task the new editor took personally; having once been described in the pages of the *Aurora* as a "poor little foolish, fluttering thing," the younger Fenno, meeting Bache walking along Fourth Street, attacked the editor with his fists.

Bache, referring to his scuffle with "Fenno's young lady in breeches" on August 8, 1798, maintained: "My cane for a moment became of little use, but soon, grasping it in the middle, made the side of his head or face feel the point of the serril and the top of his skull its weight, having previously taken the impression of his teeth upon the knuckles of my left hand. I completely pinned him in the scuffle against the wall, whilst inflicting the merited chastisement."[108]

Young Fenno, of course, had a different perspective: "I advanced and, seizing him by the collar, struck him at the same instant in the face and repeated my blows as fast as possible. He repeatedly attempted to put his stick in my face; but having closed in with him, his arms were so cramped that his attempts proved very feeble.... I had no weapon but my fist and received no hurt in the transaction."[109]

Whatever the actual outcome of this encounter, Bache's true literary bane was William Cobbett, an Englishman who had served in His Majesty's Armed Forces with the 54th Regiment of Foot in Nova Scotia and New Brunswick from 1784 to 1791. After being mustered out, he left England in March 1792, and after a brief sojourn in revolutionary France set sail for the United States. Upon arrival he addressed a letter to Thomas Jefferson, dated November 2, 1792, listing his current worldly possessions as "youth, a small family, a few useful literary talents, and that is all." Getting to the point, Cobbett placed his literary talents at the disposal of the secretary of state: "Should you have an opportunity of serving me, my onduct shall not show me ungrateful." Jefferson chose not to take up this offer.[110] Given the use to which Cobbett subsequently put his literary talents, Jefferson may have come to regret that decision.[111]

Debuting in March 1797 on the very day Adams was inaugurated, Cobbett's paper, the Philadelphia-based *Porcupine's Gazette*, was intended for those who felt, as he did, "that the insidious influence of revolutionary doctrines was undermining the foundations of all that

The poison pen of William Cobbett (a.k.a. the pugnacious Peter Porcupine) was the most effective weapon in the Federalist literary arsenal during the tumultuous last few years of the 18th century (courtesy of New York Public Library).

was stable, and that this influence must be opposed in every way."[112] Cobbett signaled the start of his counter-offensive by making a veritable declaration of war on the editor of the *Aurora*: "I assert you are a liar and an infamous scoundrel.... You will get nothing by me in a war of words, and ... may as well abandon the contest while you can do it with good grace.... I am getting up in the world and you are going down. [F]or this reason it is that you hate me and I despise you."[113]

Piling it on, Cobbett described Bache as "Printer to the French Director, Distributor General of the principles of Insurrection, Anarchy and Confusion, the greatest of fools, and the most stubborn sans-cullotte in the United States,"[114] and asserted that the editor of the *Aurora*, that "pestilential retailer of sedition," "the white-livered, black-hearted thing Bache, that public pest and bane of decency," was an "ill-looking devil" whose appearance was "just like that of a fellow who has been about a week or ten days in a gibbet," who was considered by "all men of understanding" as "an abandoned liar, as a tool, and a hireling" who should be spurned as one would "a Turk, a Jew, a Jacobin, or a dog."[115]

"No man is bound to pay the least respect to the feelings of Bache," Cobbett concluded in April 1798, in response to some disquiet that he was moving beyond the boundaries of good taste. "He has outraged every principle of decency, of morality, of religion and of nature. I should have no objection to the boys spitting on him, as he goes along the street, if it were not that I think they would confer on him too much honour."[116] Refusing to rise to the bait, Bache contented himself with admitting his "inferiority in the arts of scurrility and defamation." Declining to engage Cobbett, Bache only asked "to have anything but his praise."[117]

Cobbett was even less forgiving, if that is possible, towards other leading Republican editors. The Englishman labeled Scottish rival James Thomson Callender a liar, a drunkard, a "little mangy Scotsman," a "nasty beast," a "little reptile, who, from outward appearances seems to have been born for a chimney sweep," and "an abandoned hireling." Cobbett could scarcely conceal his delight when Callender was hired by the *Aurora*. "[H]aving completely sailed round the world of sedition, [Callender] has hove his shattered and disfigured bark into the harbour of Citizen Benjamin Franklin Bache," *Porcupine's Gazette* declared on April 10, 1798.[118] In an onslaught of character assassination, perhaps unprecedented then and still unrivaled in American print history, Cobbett went on to describe Callender's personal habits: "[He] has a remarkably sly and suspicious countenance; he loves grog; wears a shabby dress, and has no hat on the crown of his head; I am not certain whether he has ears or not.... [He] leans his head towards one side, as if his neck had a stretch, and goes along working his shoulders up and down with evident signs of anger against the fleas and lice."[119]

Porcupine's Gazette claimed a circulation of 2,000 within six weeks of its sensational debut, Cobbett making a point of noting that "these subscribers have been obtained without any of those quack-like mendicant arts that but too often disgrace undertakings of this kind."[120] The paper reached its peak circulation of 2,500 in August 1797, making it the largest of any daily publication, and apparently was one of the most popular papers in the homes of even the most cultured Federalists.[121] However, fellow Federalist editor Benjamin Russell of the *Columbian Centinel* noted on April 10, 1799, that Cobbett "was never encouraged and supported by the Federalists as a solid, judicious writer in their cause; but was kept merely to hunt Jacobinic foxes, skunks, and serpents.... It was ... tho't necessary that the ... party should keep and feed a suitable beast to hunt down these skunks and foxes; and the 'fretful porcupine' was selected for this business."[122]

Cobbett — dubbed "Porcupine Peter, the Democrat Eater" by Freneau — had declared that his feud with Bache would go on "till death snatches one or the other of us from the scene." Bache, aged twenty-nine, was first to die, a victim of the yellow-fever epidemic of 1798. Federalists were quick to grasp the implications. "Bile is the basis of the yellow fever," it was pointed out, "is it surprising that it killed Bache?"[123] *J. Russell's Gazette* greeted the news of the death of the editor of the *Aurora* with the comment, "The Jacobins are all whining at the exit of the vile Benjamin Franklin Bache; so they would do if one of their gang was hung for stealing. The memory of this scoundrel cannot be too highly execrated."[124] John Adams recalled with unbecoming satisfaction that Bache "in his Aurora ... became of course one of the most malicious Libellers of me. But the Yellow Fever arrested him in his detestable Career and sent him to his grandfather from whom he inherited a dirty, envious, jealous, and revengeful Spight [*sic*] against me."[125] The fever itself was represented as divine retribution against the rise of Republicanism. "God has sent out one as a corrective of the other," the *Gazette of the United States* intoned. "Our cities have been punished in proportion to the extent of Jacobinism; and in general at least three out of four of the persons who have perished by pestilence have been over zealous partizans."[126]

Cobbett, whom Matthew Carey labeled "the most tremendous scourge that hell ever vomited forth to curse a people," did not have long to savor his triumph.[127] He was put to flight by a $5,000 libel verdict returned against him for attacking the eminent Dr. Benjamin Rush's treatment of yellow-fever victims. By way of comparison, the cumulative total of the fines imposed in eight convictions under the Alien and Sedition Acts was $2,505. Rather than pay the fine, Cobbett fled back to England, even though he was offered free counsel by Alexander Hamilton (who Cobbett claimed "should think himself honored in defending me"). Otherwise, "because he was unpredictable and uncontrollable," Carol Sue Humphrey notes, "there were few people, Federalist or Republican, who were saddened by his departure."[128]

On January 13, 1800, Cobbett published the farewell issue of *Porcupine's Gazette* from New York, still maintaining that his departure from Philadelphia was the result of his promise to quit Pennsylvania should the Republican candidate for governor in the late election prove victorious. "Knowing, as you now do, that he is elected to that office, there are, I trust, very few of you who will be surprized [sic] to find that I am no longer in that degraded and degrading state."[129]

After returning to Mother England, Cobbett immediately summed up his trans-Atlantic experiences in a pamphlet titled *The American Rush-Light; by the help of which, Wayward and Disaffected Britons may see a Complete Specimen of the Baseness, Dishonesty, Ingratitude, and Perfidy of Republicans, and of the Profligacy, Injustice, and Tyranny of Republican Governments*.[130] But ironically, exposed to the impact of the Industrial Revolution on Britain's rural poor, Cobbett was transformed into a radical reformer. After serving two years in prison for sedition, Cobbett was forced to flee to the United States in 1817. Two years later he departed home to England, this time forever, taking with him a grisly memento—the exhumed bones of Thomas Paine — in his baggage. "I have done myself the honor to disinter his bones," Cobbett reported. "I have removed them from New Rochelle [and] they are now on their way to England."[131] The bones were never seen again, but in the 1830s Cobbett finally achieved his apotheosis—a seat in the House of Commons to round out his career.

Bache was succeeded at the helm of the *Aurora* by William Duane. Born near Lake Champlain, of Irish heritage, he was taken back to Ireland by his mother after his father's death in 1765. Disinherited by his mother for having married a Protestant girl, he left for India in 1787, where he established the Calcutta *Indian World*. His denunciations of scandal in the East India Company and the military, and his "attempting to disseminate the democratic principles of Tom Paine in his paper" led to his arrest without charge and deportation without trial. Washing up in London in 1795, he worked as a parliamentary reporter for the *General Advertiser* and became the editor of the radical London *Telegraph* while seeking restitution for his confiscated Indian property. Ultimately despairing of English justice, he set sail for America, arriving in Philadelphia on the auspicious date of July 4, 1796, where he shortly afterwards found an outlet for his talents at the *Aurora*. After Bache died, his widow Margaret resumed publication of the *Aurora* on November 1, 1798. Duane effectively took control of the paper, though technically it was bequeathed to Margaret, thereby earning the sobriquet "Mother Bache's filthy dish-cloth" from Cobbett. Duane ultimately simplified the issue by marrying his employer and firing back at Cobbett in the *Aurora* on November 5: "All the sluices of *English vulgarity* ... were constantly pouring forth in torrents" from the pen of Porcupine; "our sentiment surpasses pity, for it extends to *contempt*, a contempt excited by the *abject meanness* and *dastardly character* of the calumniator." This missive concluded with an invitation to Cobbett to call at the offices of the *Aurora* to meet the editor or the widow of the former proprietor, who "whether in petticoats or breeches will be ready to give him suitable satisfaction."[132]

A character no less committed to the Republican cause than Bache, or inclined to steer clear of trouble, between 1798 and 1801 Duane was tried in state court for "riot and assault," indicted under the Alien Act, indicted under the Sedition Act, prosecuted and forced into hiding for breaching the legislative privileges of the U.S. Senate, sued several times for libel, and brutally beaten by a gang of Federalist soldiers, among other tribulations. According to an eyewitness, "[T]hey beat him most unmercifully up and down the court — he was covered with blood, his clothes torn off, and so cruelly treated that I thought they would certainly have killed him."[133]

The *Aurora* was not Duane's sole political vocation. He frequented Republican Party meetings and mounted a petition drive against the Alien Law in Philadelphia's Irish community. To counterbalance the Federalist domination of the city's elite militia companies, Duane organized the Republican Greens, a body of men that would be controlled by Republicans. Those serving in the ranks of the Greens were artisans and laborers from working-class and immigrant Philadelphia wards, and their mobilization helped make Philadelphia the backbone of the Republican Party in southeastern Pennsylvania.[134]

Duane and Fenno Jr. picked up where Bache and Fenno Sr. had left off. The *Aurora*, on March 5, 1799, described a John Ward Fenno editorial in the *Gazette of the United States* as a "strange mixture of the incomprehensible and the ridiculous — of vapidity and bombast — egregious vanity & naked hypocrisy — pitiful whining and outrageous rant — which it displays, surpasses any thing perhaps that has ever appeared in a newspaper notorious for all that turpitude which it condemns as well as for the defects which it laments."[135]

The *Gazette of the United States* responded in kind on May 20, 1799: "In the last Aurora is the most singular gallimaufry of falsehood, Democratic, and jailbird impudence, terrified apprehension, and guilty cowardice, signed Wm. Duane.... There can scarcely be a more laughable object than a fellow making pretensions to character, whom every circumstance indicated to have been born in a brothel."[136]

Exchanges continued on this level for the balance of the year. On December 2, the *Gazette of the United States* described Duane as "the gin-drinking pauper who is said to conduct Bache's paper."[137] The *Aurora* replied on December 10, referring to "Fenno, whose enmity to talents is proverbial and ... the natural effect of his stupidity and consequent expulsion at College."[138]

Duane finally emerged victorious; John Ward Fenno sold out in May 1800. Under its new management, Duane cheerfully predicted of the *Gazette*, "We shall hope, among other things, to find less folly and more consistency — more love of country and less hatred of republicanism — because the contrary (with bad company) have ruined and blasted poor Fenno."[139]

However much they resented it, Federalists were forced to recognize the influence of the *Aurora*. According to one Federalist observer, "on every important subject, the sentiments to be included among the democrats, has first been put into the *Aurora*. This was the heart, the seat of life. From thence the blood has flowed to the extremities by a sure and rapid circulation.... It is astonishing to remark, with how much punctuality, and rapidity, *the same opinion* has been circulated and repeated by these people from the highest to the lowest."[140] It was precisely this capacity to maintain the uniformity of opinion that is so critical to party discipline that the Federalists lacked. The fact that there was no Federalist counterpart to the *Aurora* would cost the party dearly.

In condemning the *Aurora* in the House on April 20, 1798, Congressman John Allen of Connecticut argued, "This paper must necessarily, in the nature of things, be supported by a powerful party.... This is the work of a party; this paper is devoted to a party; it is assiduously disseminated through the country by a party; to that party is all the credit due; to that party it owes its existence."[141] But, he continued, more than mere partisan interest was being represented in its pages:

> [T]his business of sowing discord, dissension, and distrust of the Government, [is conducted via] a vile incendiary paper published in this city, which constantly teems with the most atrocious abuse of all measures of Government and its administrators. A flood of calumny is constantly poured forth against those whom the people have chosen as the guardians of the nation. The privilege of franking letters is abused in sending this paper into all parts of the country; and the purest characters are, through this medium, prostrated and laid low in the view of the people ... and this paper is well known always to speak the sentiments of, and be supported by, certain gentlemen in this House. These, sir, are the fruits of the "diplomatic skill of France"— these are the effects of her "means"— these are the effects of "her party in this country."[142]

Thus was the *Aurora*— and, by implication, the Republican Party — identified with the interests of a foreign power. This line of reasoning on the part of the governing party would lead to the first great challenge to the freedom of the press in the history of the republic.

Sedition

Having been cast down as a result of the XYZ affair, the Republicans, said Fisher Ames, "looked around like Milton's devils when first recovering from the stunning force of their fall from Heaven, to see what new ground they could take." Ironically, according to Miller, thanks to the Federalists their fall was cushioned by the Alien and Sedition Acts: "The Republicans landed on their feet, ready to fight on the issue provided them by the administration party."[143]

The campaign in the Republican press against the president was at least as effective in getting under the first lady's skin as it was under his. Writing to her sister in 1797, Abigail Adams fulminated that Bache possessed "the true spirit of Satan, for he not only collects the billingsgate of all the Jacobin papers, but he adds to it the lies, falsehoods, calumny and bitterness of his own."[144] The following year, Abigail lashed out at the "wicked and base" *Aurora*, which was filled with the most "violent and calumniating abuse."[145] She concluded: "the wretched will provoke measures which will silence them e'er long. An abused and insulted publick cannot tollerate them much longer. In short they are so criminal that they ought to be Presented by grand jurors."[146]

The possibility of imposing legal sanctions on partisan critics as an aspect of national policy began percolating through Federalist ranks as the international climate worsened. This was a period when the concept of the "loyal opposition" had yet to be understood. One either supported the President in his course of policy and was loyal, or proffered criticism and therefore branded oneself an enemy of the state. Republican promotion of the Jacobin regime in France was barely tolerable in Washington's day. Now that the prospect of war with the Directory seemed imminent, such philo-Gallicism could only be construed as treason. In other words, as the *Gazette of the United States* put it on June 20, 1798, "He that is not for us, is against us."

The course of events in France offered a particularly stark lesson for Federalist observers about the necessity for civil discourse to be dominated by the established social order. Congressman John Allen recounted that "at the commencement of the Revolution in France, those loud and enthusiastic advocates for liberty and equality took special care to occupy and command all the presses." The Jacobins understood that the press was especially potent in holding sway over "the poor, the ignorant, the passionate, and the vicious." "Over all of these classes," Allen noted, "the freedom of the press shed its baneful effects," and "the virtuous, the pacific, and the rich, were their victims."[147] Just as the French monarchy had been overthrown by calumny and abuse, so, Abigail Adams agreed, "have their emissaries adopted the same weapons in this country and the liberty of the press is become licentious beyond any former period."[148] Underlining the partisan rancor of the era was the conviction on the part of Federalists that a Jacobin fifth column was in place and actively working against U.S. interests. Not until the Red Scare of the 1950s would the nation again actively consider the question of subversion by a foreign power in partisan terms. But during the presidency of John Adams it dominated political discourse. "There is a liberty of the press," declared the Boston *Columbian Centinel* after quoting a "treasonable" statement by the city's Republican *Independent Chronicle*, "which is very little short of the liberty of burning our houses."[149]

A much younger John Adams once wrote in his *Novanglus Essays* that "license of the press is no proof of liberty. When a people are corrupted, the press may be made an engine to complete their ruin."[150] But as president, Adams now complained that the Republican press went to "all lengths of profligacy, falsehood and malignity in defaming our government," and demanded that the "misrepresentations which have misled so many citizens ... must be discountenanced by authority."[151] In 1798, on the pretext of ensuring national security during a period of quasi-war with France, the Federalists moved swiftly to give the president the authority he wanted.

The first of the laws was the Naturalization Act, passed on a strict party-line vote by the Federalist congressional majority on June 18, which required that aliens be residents for fourteen years instead of five years before they became eligible for U.S. citizenship. Congress then passed the Alien Act on June 25, authorizing the president to deport aliens "dangerous to the peace and safety of the United States" during peacetime. The third law, the Alien Enemies Act, enacted by Congress on July 6, allowed the wartime arrest, imprisonment and deportation of any alien subject to an enemy power. "The Libel and Sedition Bill yesterday passed the House, 44 to 41," Bache reported in the *Aurora* on July 11, 1798, "[T]he good citizens of these States had better hold their tongues and make tooth picks of their pens."[152]

Under the terms of the Sedition Act, Congress determined that "if any person shall write, print, utter, or publish ... any false, scandalous and malicious writing ... against the government of the United States, or either house of the Congress ... or the said President ... or to excite against them the hatred of the good people of the United States," that person would be subject to up to two years' imprisonment and a $2,000 fine.[153] The final vote on the measure was highly partisan and highly sectional; only two members from states south of the Potomac cast their votes in favor.[154]

The Boston *Independent Chronicle* commented to the effect that the fear of criticism being exhibited by the administration suggested that it had "insufficient confidence in its own integrity," and went on to denounce the bill as the last gasp of an "expiring Aristocracy."[155] Spurning bile for wit, the *Aurora* greeted Bastille Day with the headline "ADVERTISEMENT EXTRAORDINARY" and these words: "Orator *Mum* takes this *very orderly* method of announcing that a THINKING CLUB will be established in a few days at the sign of the MUZZLE in *Gag* Street. The first subject for cogitation will be: 'Ought a Free People to obey laws which violate the constitution they have sworn to support?' N.B. No member will be permitted to think longer than fifteen minutes."[156]

Other Republican editors were not slow in recognizing the implications of the new legislation. They understood that freedom of the press as a principle was as much a target as they themselves were. James Lloyd of Maryland, who introduced the Sedition Bill into the Senate, "ought to possess that species of immortality by the ruffian who burnt the temple of Ephesian Diana," wrote the New York *Time Piece*. "Let the name of this *Vandal*, this *Goth*, this *Ostrogoth*, this *Hun*, be a bye word through the world; this sacriligist that attempts to burst into the temple of liberty, and defile the altar of American independence." Good republicans, the *Time Piece* continued, "ought to hold him while living to the contempt and execration of mankind, and consign him, when dead, to the abhorrence of posterity."[157]

The passage of the act had an immediate impact, the length and breadth of the country. The editors of the *Savannah Advertiser* in Georgia asserted that "in future no word shall find a place in their paper which has a tendency to vilify the Government of the United States." Charles Holt, editor of the *New London Bee*, who would subsequently be imprisoned as a violator of the act, promised upon its passage to abide by its provisions. "Our correspondents," he wrote, "are desired to observe that the Sedition Bill has passed, and temper their communications accordingly."[158]

Bache remained defiant. On July 19, 1798, the *Aurora* was forced to admit, "Some time ago there were people so wicked as to think America could not have a worse man for President than Gen. Washington; but we learn that they have since, from the most complete conviction, acknowledged the error of their opinion."[159]

The Federalists had already made their intentions toward the editor of the *Aurora* abundantly clear. "Ought not Bache to be regarded as an organ of the *diplomatic skill* of France?" Cobbett wrote in *Porcupine's Gazette* on June 16, 1798. "And ought such a wretch be tolerated at this time?"[160] On June 27, 1798, two weeks before Adams signed the Sedition Bill into law, Bache was arrested on a warrant issued by Supreme Court Associate Justice Richard Peters, who charged him with having libeled the President and the government in a manner tending to excite sedition and opposition to the laws. This indictment was made at common law without benefit of statutory authority. "In Turkey, the voice of the government is the law, and there it is called *despotism*," Bache responded. "Here the voice of the government is likewise the law and here it is called *liberty*."[161]

Washington, on the other hand, even in retirement, continued to deplore the "cowardly, illiberal and assassin-like" efforts on the part of newspapers to "destroy all confidence in those who are entrusted with the Administration."[162] The passage of the Alien and Sedition Acts accordingly secured Olympian approval from the heights of Mt. Vernon: "All secret enemies to the peace and happiness of this Country should be unmasked," Washington said, "for it is better to meet *two* enemies in the *open* field of contest than *one* coward behind the scenes." Better to suppress the Republican press than allow it "to torture, and to disturb the public mind with their unfounded and ill favored forebodings."[163]

The extent to which the Sedition Act was a partisan measure was made explicit by the wholesale assent it received from the Federalist press. Just four days after the passage of the act, the Boston *Columbian Centinel* asked, "Is it not time to ... call to account these monsters of ingratitude, these enemies of order; these friends of darkness—is it not time to silence their tongues, or dash them to the earth[?]"[164] The *Albany Centinel* proclaimed that "it is patriotism to write in favor of our government" and "sedition to write against it." "There is no rigor at all," this paper observed, "in punishing men who, in the teeth of a positive law will publish malicious and willful lies, with design to injure and ruin the government of the people." The *New York Gazette* demanded that Republican editors be "ferreted out of their lurking places" and condemned to punishment. The New York *Commercial Advertiser* declared that anyone who inveighed against the Sedition Act "deserves to be suspected" themselves of sedition.[165] The *Salem Gazette* explained that the "safety of our nation depends" on the Sedition Act, while William Cobbett dutifully compiled a list of seditious newspapers for the benefit of government prosecutors, singling out, among others, the *Baltimore Intelligencer—* "a sink of abuse, scurrility and democracy," edited by "an imp of democracy, as wicked & depraved as his master the Devil."[166]

The administration needed little assistance in picking its targets, and was not shy about exercising its new power. From July 1798 to March 1801, when the Sedition Act expired, the Federalists arrested approximately twenty-five well-known Republicans. Fifteen of these arrests led to indictments. Eleven cases went to trial, ten resulting in convictions.

The first target for the administration was the Republican congressman from Vermont, Matthew Lyon, who had made good in life after running away from his family in Ireland as a teenager and arriving in America as an indentured servant. A budding industrialist and entrepreneur, Lyon had decided to try his hand in politics, and doing so in Federalist New England meant sponsoring a newspaper that would project his agenda to the electorate. As Lyon put it, "I was surrounded by newspapers containing high tone British doctrines flowing in upon us from the hireling presses.... Tory doctrines were flowing freely from the favored presses of Vermont." Accordingly, on April 1, 1793, Lyon launched the weekly *Farmer's Library*, as he told Albert Gallatin, "to break down the undue influence of the Aristo-Tory faction" who were deluging the northeast with an "overpowering flood of anti-Republicanism."[167]

Lyon made his seventeen-year-old son the publisher of the *Farmer's Library* and freely admitted, "I hired a printer, the best Republican essays were selected. My pen was not idle ... by this means the Republican doctrines were scattered through the Northern States." The first issue of the newspaper was introduced by an address of Thomas Paine to the French National Assembly and included an open letter from the French Republic that offered fraternal greetings to the United States: "Single and alone against the coalition of Kings, we have shewn ourselves worthy of being your brothers." But most significant was the slogan on the masthead: "THE FREEDOM OF THE PRESS SHALL REMAIN INVIOLATE."[168]

Already a thorn in the Federalist's side, Lyon made himself a marked man in Congresson January 30, 1798. On the floor of the House, Lyon causally remarked to the Speaker that if he should go into Connecticut, and manage a press there six months, he could turn out the state's entire Congressional delegation. One of the representatives in question, Roger Griswold, happened to be within earshot. He called out from his seat, "If you go into Connecticut, you had better wear your wooden sword!"—a slighting reference to an incident during Lyon's service in the Revolutionary War when the troops under his command mutinied and he was cashiered.[169] When Lyon didn't respond, Griswold approached him, seized his arm, and repeated the remark. Lyon retorted by spitting in Griswold's face.

Federalists exploded in outrage. Lyon was dubbed "Spitting Matt" in *Porcupine's Gazette*, and called the "most pitiful, low-breed blackguard that has ever been heard of in America." Another representative from Connecticut, Samuel Dana, referred to his colleague from Vermont as "a kennel of filth," to be discarded "as citizens removed impurities and filth from their docks and wharves." After a motion to have Lyon expelled from the House failed (52 votes in favor, to 44 against, short of the necessary two-thirds majority), Griswold responded by purchasing a stout hickory walking stick at a store on Chestnut Street and then on February 15 beating Lyon with it on the floor of the House. In desperation Lyon seized the tongs from the House fireplace and fought back until the two men were separated.

Lyon had survived both political and physical assaults from the Federalists so far, but his time was running out. "A sedition bill is talked of in Congress," he warned Vermont on June 20 in his new publication, *The Scourge of Aristocracy and Repository of Important Political Truths*. "Its advocates say it is calculated to suppress the villainous falsehoods which men of

base principles are circulating against the constituted authorities. However ... I do not propose to vote for it, as it will tend to prevent due investigation; nor shall I fear after it is passed,
to expose the truth in my usual way to my constituents."[170]

On that same day Lyon had a letter published in *Spooner's Vermont Journal*, complaining
of an America where, he said, "I see every consideration of the public welfare swallowed up
in a continual grasp for power, in an unbounded thirst for ridiculous pomp, foolish adulation, or selfish avarice."[171] This statement formed the first count of the indictment drawn up
against Lyon under the Sedition Act when as a sitting member of Congress he was sentenced
to four months in prison and fined $1,000, plus court costs of $60.96.

Lyon was transported to a jail in Vergennes where he took up residence in a cell he
described as "the common receptacle for horse-thieves, money makers, runaway negroes, or
any kind of felons." In a corner of this unheated "loathsome dungeon" was a "necessary" that
according to Lyon afforded "a stench about equal to the Philadelphia docks in the month of
August."[172] Despite, or perhaps because of, these legal woes he was triumphantly reelected
while in prison and promptly returned to Congress immediately upon his release. According
to the Federalist *Connecticut Courant*, upon his arrival in Philadelphia he pranced "like a
Monkey ... he was taken as an Ass for his braying, for a Cur by his barking, for a Puppy by
his whining, for a Hog by his eating, for a Cat by his spitting, and for a Lion, by nothing but
his being the greatest of Beasts."[173] He survived another motion for expulsion (49 in favor,
45 opposed, again short of necessary two-thirds majority) and had the last laugh; in the House
ballot to settle the victor of the election of 1800, Vermont was the last state to be called and,
as the state's entire Congressional delegation, Lyon had the pleasure of casting the final and
decisive vote that gave Jefferson the presidency.

Before that could happen, many others who had carried the fight to the Adams administration would feel the sting of Federalist retribution. Dr. Thomas Cooper, editor of the Reading, Pennsylvania, *Weekly Advertiser*, was fined and jailed for six months because he insisted
on calling Adams incompetent.[174] For criticizing the army, Charles Holt, editor of the *New
London Bee*, received a $200 fine and a three-month prison sentence. For reprinting another
paper's criticism of Adams, William Durrell of the *Mount Pleasant Register* in New York also
received a three-month term, but was granted a presidential pardon. Anthony Haswell of
the Bennington *Vermont Gazette* spent two months in jail and was slapped with a $200 fine.
Abijah Adams of the Boston *Independent Chronicle* received a thirty-day jail sentence.[175]

The major pre–1798 Republican papers in New York, the *Time Piece* and the *Journal* were
driven from the political scene by Federalist persecution. John Daly Burk, editor of the *Time
Piece*, settled a libel suit out of court and left New York in 1799, much to the satisfaction of
the New York *Daily Advertiser*, which commented: "May such be the fate of every paper, that
under the hypocritical vizer of false patriotism and hallow-hearted professions of attachment
to the people, aim at the subversion of our fair fabric of law, government, individual security and domestic enjoyment."[176]

By indicting Thomas Greenleaf's widow Ann under the Sedition Act and bringing a state-
level libel action against her foreman, David Frothingham (who was sentenced to four months
in jail and a $100 fine), Secretary of State Thomas Pickering and Alexander Hamilton had the
venerable *Journal* shut down. Additionally, the administration classified the New York *Argus*,
the *Baltimore American*, and the *Richmond Examiner* as leading opposition journals against
which law suits should definitely be brought.

But always Federalists longed to bring the *Aurora* to heel. Duane and three other men
had already been arrested and hustled off to jail on February 11, 1799, when the editor precipitated a riot by attempting to gather signatures for a petition to Congress favoring repeal of
the Alien Act. The brawl took place in the churchyard of St. Mary's Catholic Church in

Philadelphia. Duane and his accomplices were acquitted at the ensuing trial in the statehouse on February 21, 1799.[177]

On July 24, 1799, after Duane accused the British ambassador of dispensing $800,000 in bribes in order to influence the midterm elections and secure an Anglo-U.S. alliance, Federalists had had enough. Washington himself was convinced it was high time to make an example of the obstreperous editor:

> There can be no medium between the reward and punishment of an Editor, who shall publish such things as Duane has been doing for sometime past. On what grounds then does he *pretend* to stand in his exhibition of the charges, or the insinuations which he has handed to the Public. Can hardihood, itself be so great, as to stigmatize characters in the Public Gazettes for the most heinous offences, and when prosecuted, pledge itself to support the allegations unless there was something to build on? I hope and expect the Prosecutors will probe this matter to the bottom. It will have an unhappy effect on the public mind if it not be so.[178]

Secretary of State Timothy Pickering wrote to Adams, claiming that although Duane pretended to have been born in Vermont, he was "really a British subject, and, as an alien, liable to be banished from the United States." With his letter, Pickering enclosed a copy of the *Aurora*, which he claimed contained "an uninterrupted stream of slander on the American government." Pickering added he would forward the offending publication to government attorney William Rawle, "and if he thinks it libelous, desire him to prosecute the editor." On August 1, 1799, Adams replied to Pickering:

> Is there anything evil in the regions of actuality or possibility, that the Aurora has not suggested of me. You may depend upon it, I disdain to attempt a vindication of myself against any of the lies of the Aurora, as much as any man concerned in the administration of the affairs of the United States. If Mr. Rawle does not think this paper libelous, he is not for this office; and if he does not prosecute, he will not do his duty. The matchless effrontery of this Duane merits the execution of the alien law. I am very willing to try its strength upon him.[179]

Duane was duly arrested by a federal marshal on a warrant issued by the ubiquitous Richard Peters.[180] The editor, however, was prepared to offer himself as an even easier target. His opportunity arose when Senator James Ross of Pennsylvania, the defeated Federalist candidate for the governorship of Pennsylvania in 1799, introduced a bill in the U.S. Senate on January 23, 1800, that was clearly intended to wrest the upcoming presidential election from Thomas Jefferson if it became apparent that the Virginian was going to win. The bill would have created a grand committee of six senators and six representatives presided over by the chief justice to rule on electoral returns. The committee's decision, made behind locked doors, was to be final. Although the Federalist majority tried to cloak the measure in secrecy, three copies of the bill were dispatched to the office of the *Aurora*. Describing it as a telling example of a "faction secretly working," Duane printed the proposed measure in full on February 19, 1800, labeling it "a bill to influence and affect the approaching Presidential election, and to frustrate in a particular manner the wishes and interests of the people of Pennsylvania." Because a criminal prosecution under the Sedition Act would be too drawn out and too public to debilitate Duane, the Federalists summoned a new Senate committee to punish the editor for his effrontery. Brushing aside Republican arguments that Congress had no constitutional authority to punish a citizen for challenging its conduct or motives, and that the proposed procedure denied Duane's constitutional right to due process of law, the Federalists, without conducting any hearing, by a straight party vote on March 14, adopted a resolution declaring that Duane's comments were "false, defamatory, scandalous, and malicious," and that publication of the proposed bill was a "daring and high-handed breach of the privileges of this House."

The Senate then invited Duane to appear in person to offer evidence in "mitigation" of his offense, but it refused to permit Duane's lawyers to present evidence or question the constitutionality of its action.[181] The editor therefore told the Senate that he considered himself "bound by the most sacred duties to decline any further voluntary attendance upon that body, and leave them to pursue such measures in this case as in their wisdom they may deem meet." Accordingly, the Senate declared Duane in contempt on March 27, 1800, and issued a warrant to the sergeant-at-arms—signed, in his role as presiding officer of the Senate, by Vice President Thomas Jefferson—calling for the editor's arrest. The Senate spent $300 and employed twenty-two constables in its effort "to ferret out the obstinate democrat," money that was poorly spent, given that Duane openly lived in his own home at No. 106 Market St. and even led a parade of his Republican Greens through the streets of Philadelphia.

Switching tack, on May 14 the Senate resolved to have Duane prosecuted in a court of law rather than in its own august chamber, and the editor was arrested on a charge of seditious libel on July 30. Three days later, Duane was brought before District Court Judge Richard Peters, who bound him over to the October term of court and released him on bail of $4,000. During the October term, Duane obtained a continuance until June 11, 1801, and again was released on $3,000 bail.[182] The action was still pending when Jefferson took office and ordered the suit against Duane dropped on the grounds of the unconstitutionality of the Sedition Act, a decision which roused the *Gazette of the United States* to a paroxysm of italicized outrage:

> If he [Jefferson] has dared to STOP A PUBLIC PROSECUTION, carrying on by the *United States* in one of its *courts of law*, on presentment of a *grand jury*, in any *other* way than by *PARDON* of the offender, I pronounce that he is a *usurper*, that he has *broken the constitution!* [In that event] I shall raise my feeble voice, on the side of a *solemn protest*; I shall appeal to the *representatives of the people* as the *grand inquest* of the nation, and call on them to find a *bill of IMPEACHMENT*, for a HIGH CRIME against the *constitution* and *people* of the United States of America.[183]

Perhaps the most storied saga of persecution under the Sedition Act was the case of James Thomson Callender. A Scottish refugee who once likened His Majesty's government to a "mass of legislative putrefaction" in a tome titled *The Political Progress of Britain*, described by his biographer as "one of the most inflammatory, undeferential, and militant texts to be published in the 1790s," Callender, minus his wife and children, arrived in the United States on 21 May, 1793.[184] He found the social environment to his liking. Soon after settling in Philadelphia, Callender remarked that it was "the happy privilege of an American that he may prattle and print in what way he pleases, and without anyone to make him afraid."[185] He was quickly made aware of the limits of that privilege when, as a congressional reporter, he stirred up trouble, and he was eased out of his job in 1796 at the insistence of William B. Giles of Virginia, Jefferson's champion in the House of Representatives. This loss of employment was the first injustice Callender fancied he suffered at the hands of Jefferson, and he later wrote his supposed benefactor complaining, "A man has no merit in telling the truth but he may claim the privilege of not being the object of persecution from the hero of his encomium."[186] Disappointed and resentful, Callender left Philadelphia for Baltimore, returning the following year, at which time he became acquainted with Republicans Thomas Leiper, a wealthy tobacco merchant, and Alexander Dallas, later Madison's secretary of the treasury. It was through these men that Callender's propagandistic talents were first brought to Jefferson's attention, and in June or July 1797 the vice president met Callender in the downtown printing office of Snowden and McCorkle.

Callender cemented his role as America's leading scandalmonger when he issued his pamphlet *The History of the United States for 1796*, which contained an explosive charge, based on documents received from John Beckley, clerk of the House of Representatives, that Alexander Hamilton had stolen funds from the U.S. Treasury. Desperate to vindicate his reputation for financial integrity, Hamilton chose to respond to the accusation by confessing his affair with Mrs. James Reynolds, admitting to being blackmailed in return for her silence. This, to Callender, was one of the greatest triumphs of his journalistic career. Of Hamilton's confession, he wrote exultantly to Jefferson, "no anticipation can equal the infamy of this piece. It is worth all that fifty of the best pens in America could have said against him."[187] The Federalist response was blistering. Labeling Callender the "foreign tool of domestic faction," Fenno asked, "In the name of justice and honor, how long are we to tolerate this scum of party filth and beggarly corruption, worked into a form somewhat like a man, to go thus with impunity? Do not the times approach when it must and ought to be dangerous for this wretch, and any other, thus to vilify our country and government, thus to treat with indignity and contempt the whole American people, to teach our enemies to despise us and cast forth unremitting calumny and venom on our constitutional authorities."

Callender, Fenno concluded, had published "sufficient general slander on our country to entitle him to the gallows"—hardly an idle threat under the circumstances.[188]

In 1798, equally fearing the Alien and Sedition Acts and yellow fever, Callender relocated to the relative safety of Republican Virginia. His arrival was less than auspicious; he was picked up near a distillery near Leesburgh as a vagrant. When he loudly protested that he was a gentleman, albeit somewhat the worse for liquor, and that he had come to Virginia at the express invitation of Senator Stevens T. Mason, the authorities were understandably dubious. However, Senator Mason put all doubt to rest by hurrying to Leesburgh to secure Callender's release.

From his refuge in Loudoun County (which Callender considered "one of the vilest [counties] in America"), the irritable Scotsman wrote petulant letters to Jefferson hinting that he would find lodging at Monticello more convivial, and complaining, "There is no more safety in Philadelphia than in Constantinople. Besides, I am entirely sick even of the Republicans, for some of them have used me so dishonestly." He had been "so severely cheated, and so often," that he was pondering a return to Great Britain, he said. "I engaged in American controversies not from choice, but necessity; for I dislike to make enemies, and in this country the stile of writing is commonly so gross, that I do not think the majority of such a public worth addressing."[189]

Callender appealed to Jefferson for help in finding a job, and the vice president sent him fifty dollars. Callender only moved as far as Richmond, where by the summer of 1799 he was working for the newly established *Richmond Examiner*, the semiweekly edited by Meriwether Jones that was the forerunner to Thomas Ritchie's *Enquirer*. Callender now launched himself into his most notorious political tract, *The Prospect Before Us*, while continuing to beg for periodic advances from Jefferson in paranoia-laced missives typically warning "I am in danger of being murdered without doors." From time to time he posted batches of proof sheets to Jefferson, who responded by posting another fifty dollars, adding with encouraging approval that "Such papers cannot fail to produce the best effect." In late January or early February 1800, Jefferson received a complete copy of *The Prospect Before Us*. "Such papers," the vice president replied, "inform the thinking part of the nation." He also sent a confidential note to James Monroe asserting that it was "essentially just and necessary" that Callender should be aided.[190] However, some Republicans were concerned at their chief's becoming too closely involved with the fiery editor. John Taylor of Caroline cautioned Jefferson in early 1800 to be circumspect, "because upon any disappointment of his expectations ... there is no doubt in my mind, from the spirit his writings breathe, that he would yield to motives of resentment." Jefferson took such advice to heart. He was careful to note, "You will know from whom this comes without a signature," when corresponding with Callender.[191]

Once described as "a dirty little toper with shaved head and greasy jacket," Callender was often down-at-the-heels and frequently drunk — on one occasion he was physically ejected from the halls of Congress because he was "covered with lice and filth." A popular ditty at Federalist gatherings in the spring and summer of 1798, to the tune of "Yankee Doodle Dandy," went:

> Tom Callender's a nasty beast,
> Ben Bache a dirty fellow;
> They curse our country day and night,
> And to the French would sell her.
> Fire and murder, keep it up,
> Plunder is the dandy;
> When some folks get the upper hand,
> With heads they'll be so handy.[192]

The public response to *The Prospect Before Us* was enthusiastic, and sales were brisk, though the always contrarian Callender fretted, "I had once entertained the romantic hope of being able to overtake the Federal Government in its career of iniquity; but I am now satisfied that they can *act* much faster than I can *write* after them."[193] Just how fast the Federalists could act would soon be made very apparent.

The Prospect Before Us was unprecedented and unsurpassed in its abuse of John Adams, whose "reign ... has been one continued tempest of malignant passion." The president, Callender continued "as never opened his lips, or lifted his pen without threatening or scolding. The grand object of his administration has been to exasperate the rage of contending parties, to calumniate and destroy every man who differs from his opinions.... [He] is not only a repulsive pedant, a gross hypocrite, and an unprecedented oppressor, but ... in private life, one of the most egregious fools upon the continent."[194] Callender accused Adams of contriving "a French war, and American navy, a large standing army, an additional load of taxes, and all the other symptoms and consequences of debt and despotism." Future historians, Callender predicted, "will enquire by what species of madness America submitted to accept, as her president, a person without abilities, and without virtues: a being alike incapable of attracting either tenderness, or esteem." "Take your choice," Callender concluded, "between Adams, war and beggary, and Jefferson, peace and competency."[195] The author himself seemed to be begging to bring the wrath of the administration down upon his head. John B. Walton, a federal job aspirant, sent a copy of *The Prospect Before Us* to Secretary of State Timothy Pickering; Callender had preempted him by audaciously sending a copy to the president himself.

While on his first tour of the southern circuit, Supreme Court Justice Samuel Chase received a copy of *The Prospect Before Us* annotated by fellow Federalist Luther Martin, the attorney general of Maryland and an inveterate bloodhound of sedition. Chase seized on the "atrocious and profligate libel" of *The Prospect Before Us* to bring the full weight of the law down on Callender. Three days after Chase arrived in Richmond on May 21, 1800, a grand jury returned a presentment against the author, citing twenty offensive passages from his latest publication. Callender was arrested on May 27 and brought before the Circuit Court of the United States in Richmond on June 3.

Jefferson arranged for Callender to be represented by Republican lawyers, but there was nothing the defense could do to counteract the naked bias of the presiding judge — Supreme Court Justice Samuel Chase. When Callender's attorneys argued that the Sedition Act should be construed to apply only to false statements of fact and not to statements of political opinion, Chase ruled otherwise, branding Callender's statements "false" without regard to whether they were "opinions." After deliberating two hours, the jury returned a verdict of guilty. Prior to sentencing, Chase sternly lectured Callender on the evils of sowing "dissensions, discontent and discord among the people," and asserted that Callender's attack on Adams was "an attack upon the people themselves," for in order to believe Adams guilty of the "atrocities" charged by Callender necessarily implied that the people who elected him "must be depraved and wicked."[196]

After enduring this harangue, Callender was sentenced to nine months in jail, assessed a $200 fine, and bound over on a $1,200 bond to good behavior for two years. The Republican press was outraged, the *Aurora* being moved to offer an unfinished rhyming couplet which the discerning reader would have little difficulty in concluding: "Cursed of thy father, scum of all that's base, thy sight is odious, and thy name is...." But Callender endorsed the role of martyr with gusto, taking the opportunity while incarcerated to write scathing articles for the *Richmond Enquirer*, the *Richmond Virginia Argus*, and the *Petersburg Republican*, while simultaneously composing a second volume of *The Prospect Before Us* just as abusive as the first, in time for the campaign of 1800, seizing the opportunity to describe the President as "that scourge, that scorn, that outcast of America," a "wretch," "an unprincipled oppressor," "a repulsive hypocrite," and "one of the most egregious fools upon the continent."[197] He also went after Chase, calling him a "detestable and detested rascal." When Chase wrote Callender in reply that he planned to beat the author after his release from prison, Callender vowed, "[I]n case of attack, I'll shoot him."[198] Outright violence was ultimately averted, but in 1804 the House of Representatives voted a bill of impeachment against Chase which found misconduct in his rulings and in his "rude and contemptuous" treatment of the prisoner's counsel during the trial of James Callender, which had been marked by "manifest injustice, partiality and intemperance." Chase only narrowly retained his place on the bench.[199]

The Federalists had overreached in first imposing and then enforcing the Sedition Act, a course of action that turned the tide of popular opinion against them permanently. For all the rancor and venom it was exposed to in the pages of its newspapers, having had a taste of the press being subjected to partisan political oversight, America resolved never to go down that route again. On July 4, 1840, Congress repaid all of the fines paid under the Sedition Act, with interest, to the legal representatives of those who had been convicted. The Congressional committee report on the matter declared that the Sedition Act had been passed under a "mistaken exercise" of power and was "null and void." The unconstitutionality of the act, according to the report, had been "conclusively settled."[200]

The Revolution of 1800

"In the short run," says Pasley, "the Sedition Act was a great 'success' for the Federalists in the sense that many of their principal newspaper targets were either suppressed or severely damaged by the prosecutions. In the long run, however, the Sedition Act failed badly. Not only did it fail to put the partisan Republican press out of business, it seemingly called new men into the field, in greater numbers and with greater intensity than previously."[201] As early as August 16, 1798, the *Gazette of the United States* grumbled, "Since the passage of the Sedition Law, the scum, filth and foam of the *Aurora* Cauldron has flowed more than ever."[202] The *Aurora* itself noted with satisfaction on November 23, 1799, "Alexander Hamilton's partiality for the liberty of the press cannot but be excessively gratified in the encrease of Republican newspapers and the decline of those who have advocated crimes, monarchy, and public extravagance. Within the last sixteen months, more than twenty newspapers have been established upon the avowed basis of democratical republican principles— in the same period those papers which advocate adverse principles have uniformly declined in public consideration and profit."[203]

The pace of newspaper creation continued to accelerate, hitting a new high of seventy-one in 1800, on a wave of more than thirty partisan Republican sheets. In all, eighty-five strongly Republican or Republican-leaning newspapers were published in that election year, two-thirds more than there had been before the Sedition Act was introduced. "If the purpose of the Sedition Act had been to multiply Republican newspapers and to increase vastly their circulation, it could be accounted an unqualified success," Miller concludes.[204]

Contemporaries were well aware of the critical contribution to the Republican clean sweep in the elections of 1800 made by the party's partisans in the press. "The newspapers are an overmatch for any government," Federalist Fisher Ames of Massachusetts conceded. "They will first overawe and then usurp it. This has been done, and the Jacobins owe their triumph to the unceasing use of this engine."[205]

Noah Webster conceded in 1800, "I ... aver that no government can be durable and quiet under the licentiousness of the press that now disgraces our country. Jacobinism will prevail unless more pains are taken to keep public opinion correct."[206] From a Federalist perspective, the problem was, as Miller noted, that "there were not enough prisons in the country to hold the newspaper writers, the politicians, and the plain citizens guilty of violating the Sedition Act in the campaign of 1800."[207]

The influence of the Republican press is all the more remarkable when it is considered that the party had to overcome not only outright persecution in attempting to establish a public voice, but also its status as an institutional minority in the world of the media. By the end of the Washington administration there were scarcely thirty papers that could be classified as Republican, compared to about 120 that were Federalist. This was owed to the fact that the early papers were typically published in the seaports and the commercial towns and they generally supported and represented the Washington-Hamilton policies of sound finance at home and commerce with England abroad. The daily papers, of which there were seventeen when Washington left office, were in most cases devoted to serving the mercantile class; they were filled with the advertisements of importers, and nearly all used the word *Advertiser* in the title or subtitle. As spokesmen for the party that represented urban and commercial interests, Federalist editors had easy access to the advertising revenue that was the life's blood of the newspaper. "The anti-Republican party," Jefferson admitted to a foreign observer in 1795, "live in cities together and can act in a body readily, and at all times; they give chief employment to the newspapers, & therefore have most of them under their command."[208]

In addition to these inherent advantages, the Federalists, as the party that held office, were able to exploit heretofore overlooked loopholes in the system to their considerable advantage. Perhaps the last thing on the great minds of the men responsible for ushering the Constitution into existence was how their newfangled governing construct would promulgate to the people the business it was destined to conduct. Congress was not endowed with a printing agency of its own. Instead, little noticed at the time but destined to have profound implications for the future course of relations between the political system and the press, the Act of September 15, 1789, that created the Department of State assigned to the secretary of state the responsibility of selecting newspapers in which to publish authentic copies of the laws and resolutions passed by Congress. The act authorized the use of "at least three of the public newspapers printed within the United States," but the exact number, the choice of which papers, and the rates of pay were left to the secretary's discretion. On March 2, 1799 the law was amended so that the secretary of state was now required to select at least one newspaper in each state.[209]

Adams's secretary of state, Pickering, carefully scrutinized the credentials of the newspaper editors under consideration; the decisive question was always "the politics to which he is inclined." Republicans complained that as long as Pickering was in power, only those papers which employed "all the arts & retrick Hell can invent to blackguard the Republican printers & all they print" need apply.[210] The *Albany Register*, for example, which upheld the Republican gospel in New York "in defiance of the frowns of power, and in the teeth of the landed aristocracy of this state," claimed that it consistently underbid all other printers on contracts for official printing, yet the jobs were always awarded to Federalist rival the *Albany Centinel.*[211]

The Federalist edge in print was bolstered by another of the perks of incumbency. During the 1790s there were approximately 800 deputy postmasters in the United States, each of whom enjoyed the privilege of franking letters and newspapers and of receiving them postage-free. Since most of these plum patronage posts were held by Federalists, opposition newspapers were, at best, obliged to pay postage while Federalist newspapers invariably traveled for free; otherwise, as sometimes happened, they could be deliberately suppressed in the post office and never see the light of day.

Beyond the *Aurora,* Republican newspapers in 1795 were led by old anti-Federalist publications like Thomas Greenleaf's *New York Journal,* the Philadelphia *Independent Gazetteer,* and the *Independent Chronicle* and *Gazette* of Boston. Other press allies included the Bennington *Vermont Gazette,* the Hartford *American Mercury,* and the Elizabethtown *New Jersey Journal.* According to Pasley, "as late as spring of 1798, the Republican press was relatively inconsequential: unstable, widely scattered, vastly outnumbered, and in many cases, unsure of its mission." Pasley calculates the existence of 51 Republican-leaning newspapers in the country at that point, out of a total newspaper population of 185.[212] The situation was so bad in Connecticut that Charles Holt of the *New London Bee,* when criticized in 1798 for being partisan, replied that since "nine tenths of the newspapers in Connecticut are decidedly partial to one side, and keep the other totally out of sight," it was "the business of THE BEE to print on the other."[213]

Jefferson had from the start recognized the need to spread the Republican gospel. As the 1800 campaign season kicked into high gear, Jefferson wrote Madison, "This summer is the season for systematic energies and sacrifices. The engine is the press. Every man must lay his purse and his pen under contribution."[214]

Republican papers began mushrooming across the United States, emerging in the small towns founded by settlers in western New York and Pennsylvania and the new states of Ohio, Kentucky and Tennessee. Federalist Senator Uriah Tracy toured the backcountry in August 1800 and reported dolefully that the administration's foes were "establishing Democratic presses and newspapers in almost every town and county of the country."[215] And there was a new hard edge to these publications. Where the older newspapers were mostly *Gazettes, Chronicles,* and *Registers,* those founded between the summer of 1798 and the end of 1800 had names that immediately called attention to the highly charged political environment. To the existing *Herald of Liberty* and *Genius of Liberty* were added a *Sun of, Tree of, Guardian of,* and, ultimately, *Triumph of Liberty.* Two papers upheld the *Rights of Man;* one avowed itself a *Friend of the People.* Six new papers included the word *Republican* in the title in an overtly partisan sense. These ranged from the sober *Republican Ledger* of New Hampshire to the masculine *Republican Atlas* of western Virginia.[216]

The new breed of Republican editors made neither secret of, nor apology for their political affiliations. "[The] American people have long enough been imposed upon by the pretended impartiality of printers; it is all delusion; every party will have its *printer,* as well as every sect its *preacher,*" wrote Alexander Martin of the Baltimore *American and Daily Advertiser,* "and it is as incongruous for a publication to be alternately breathing the spirit of *Republicanism* and *Aristocracy* as for a clergyman to preach to his audience *Christianity* in the morning, and *Paganism* in the evening.... Every editor who is capable of soaring above the flattery of villainy, and the adulation of power, has too much at stake, in the contest of liberty against slavery, virtue against vice, and truth against sophistry, to admit of more than a limited *impartiality.*"[217] Duane's battle cry was published in the *Aurora* on March 29, 1800:

"[T]he period approaches when the people will have to chuse between the destruction of their liberties as a nation and the rejection of all those from public stations who have been aiding or abetting in those measures which have brought the nation and constitution into their present jeopardy.... My countrymen! If you have not virtue enough to stem the torrent, determine to be slaves at once.... Let not the persecution of an individual dismay you — better the editor of the Aurora should perish than this tyranny should be established."[218]

John Israel sounded the same theme in the first issue of his Pittsburgh *Tree of Liberty*, founded in August 1800: "When the political ship is tossed by the jarring of contending opinions, we believe with Solon that the individual who does not take part, is unworthy of confidence, and merits exemplary punishment." David Denniston, launching a new paper in New York, the *American Citizen*, promised his readers impartiality in terms of accurately reporting current affairs. "But if by impartiality, it is intended to convey an idea of equal attachment to aristocracy as to republicanism, then this paper necessarily rejects ... an impartiality so ruinous to the best interests of mankind."[219]

The editor of *The Portfolio*, a proposed Philadelphia weekly, declared in his prospectus in 1800 that "he *will not* publish an *impartial* paper," decrying "men of convenient maxims, who cry amen to every creed, and venture on all sides, without being trusted by any. Of such infamous principles the Editor has the deepest abhorrence, and for the silly scheme of Impartiality, he cherishes the most ineffable contempt."[220]

In introducing the *Sun of Liberty* to the public of his native Danbury, Connecticut, Samuel Morse rejected impartiality more explicitly than any editor yet. "A despicable impartiality I disclaim," Morse wrote. "I have a heart and I have a country — to the last I shall ever dedicate the first, nor will I receive, with equal approbation, the production of the friends of slavery and the sons of freedom."[221] Modern observers, drawing the distinction between the southern slave-owning core constituency of the Republicans and the nascent abolitionism of the New England-based Federalists may appreciate the irony of such a statement. However, Morse made the same point to Jefferson in private, confirming that his paper was "dedicated to ... the cause of Republicanism," and promising, "I shall endeavor to promote your election to the next presidency, and [endeavor] if possible that you may get some of the votes from this state."[222]

This partisanship came at a price, of course, and newspaper proprietors were seldom shy about reminding partisan subscribers of their obligations. Under the headline "SOMETHING IMPORTANT," the editor of the Baltimore *American* editorialized in October 1800: "Never did R.G. HARPER want an appointment — Never did Judge CHASE want a fat salary — Never did Mr. AMES want to hold his seat — Nor did Republicans want to turn him out of it, more, than at this crisis, the editor of the AMERICAN wants the payment of monies due to him."[223]

James Lyon, in trying to establish the *Friend of Liberty* in Richmond, Virginia, in 1800, urged "the friends of both [liberty and virtue] — among the Republicans of New Hampshire — of Georgia, and of the intermediate states, to aid in the circulation and support of this paper, which is devoted to their service."[224] Many editors continued to look to a prominent and well-heeled sugar daddy for patronage. Jefferson had adroitly played this game for the better part of a decade. As he told Monroe in 1802, "I as well as most other republicans who were in the way of doing it, contributed what I could afford to the support of the republican papers and printers, paid sums of money for the Bee, the Albany Register, etc. when they were staggering under the sedition law, contributed to the fines of Callender himself, of Holt, Brown and others suffering under the law."[225]

Those intent on a career in print honed their skills in supplications to the powerful, learning to gild naked appeals to partisan interest with the right touch of pathos. John Israel, seeking assistance for his newly established *Herald of Liberty* in Washington, Pennsylvania, wrote Congressman Albert Gallatin in 1798:

Without the support of literary talents a periodical publication must of necessity sink into insignificance and disrepute. Therefore to you, Sir, do I look for that Support, which is in your power to give and which will at the same time be instrumental, and beneficial. The most base and villainous opposition have I borne.... [M]y reputation has been wantonly attacked — all my interests attempted to be ruined — but solus have I been forced to repel these attacks — and stand firm to the post. Now that my friends and the friends of the principles we have professed have returned I look up to them for their friendly aid — not doubting I shall receive it.[226]

Although Republicans were shut out from access to federal printing monopolies, they could and did secure access to patronage at the state level. An early manifestation of this phenomenon occurred in North Carolina, where the *Raleigh Register* was launched under the sponsorship of Nathaniel Macon and several other Tar Heel Republicans who had induced Joseph Gales to transfer from Philadelphia in the fall of 1799. To help Gales finance the project, Republicans, who gained control of the state legislature in 1800, handed him the printing of official state business, taking it away from the Federalist *North Carolina Journal* at Halifax, state printer since 1786.[227]

The Republican press followed three key lines of attack: the Federalist threat to liberty, Federalist subservience to England, and Federalist corruption.[228] By election eve 1800, the Republicans had closed the gap considerably on the Federalist edge in print. Fischer has catalogued 201 newspapers active in October 1800. Of these, 103 were identified as Federalist and 64 Republican, with another 14 impartial and 20 whose partisan leanings were unknown (see Table 2). There were even occasional instances of editorial defection from the Federalist ranks to those of the Republicans (the Newark *Centinel of Freedom* and *Kline's Carlisle Weekly Gazette* being cases in point).

TABLE 2. AMERICAN NEWSPAPERS BY STATE AND
POLITICAL AFFILIATION, OCTOBER 1800[229]

State	Strong Republican	Moderate Republican	Moderate Federalist	Strong Federalist	Other/ Unknown	Total
New Hampshire	1	0	8	1	1	11
Vermont	1	0	3	0	0	5
Massachusetts	4	1	12	5	1	23
Rhode Island	2	0	5	0	0	7
Connecticut	3	0	11	2	0	16
New York	5	0	15	1	9	30
New Jersey	2	1	1	2	0	6
Pennsylvania	12	1	8	5	8	34
Delaware	2	0	0	1	1	4
Maryland	6	1	3	2	2	14
Virginia	8	3	6	0	4	21
North Carolina	1	0	5	0	4	10
South Carolina	0	3	3	0	0	6
Georgia	1	1	2	0	1	5
Kentucky	0	4	0	0	0	4
Tennessee	0	1	0	0	1	2
Northwest Territory	0	0	1	0	1	2
Southwest Territory	0	0	1	0	0	1
TOTAL	48	16	84	19	34	201

A closer look at these statistics reveals that the Republicans were in an even better position than the raw totals would indicate. "Not only were Republican newssheets being established twice as rapidly as Federalist ones, but most of these, as became new members of the faith, were more zealous and partisan than the older organs of the opposite belief," Stewart says. This greater zeal was reflected in the fact that, according to Pasley, at least thirty-three of the Republican editors active from 1797 to 1800 held public office at some point during their lives. The Charleston *City Gazette*, for example, was published by Peter Freneau (brother of Philip), who was secretary of state for South Carolina and Jefferson's political manager in palmetto country. Twelve others served in state legislatures, four became mayors, and two were elected to Congress. By contrast, there were only twenty-two officeholders among the much larger pool of Federalist editors, and thirteen of them never progressed beyond the traditional printer's role of postmaster.[230]

"Many papers commonly regarded as Federalist were either lukewarm in their affiliation or sufficiently liberal to permit considerable criticism of the administration," Stewart continues. "The approximately seventy Democratic gazettes in late 1800 were active in achieving Jefferson's victory; it does not follow that all the others were equally vigorous in Adams' behalf."[231] In fact, John Adams later complained that as president he had received "nothing but insolence and scurrility from the federalists. Look back and read the federal newspapers in Boston, New York and Philadelphia of that period and you will then see how I was treated."[232] In addition to a prevailing distaste towards making partisan appeals on the part of its editors, the uncertain loyalty of the Federalist publications was also a reflection of the feud between Adams and Hamilton for control of the party.

Federalist newspapers that looked to Hamilton for inspiration worked against Adams by extolling the virtues of his running mate Charles Cotesworth Pinckney. The *Gazette of the United States* regularly boosted Pinckney beyond his merits, culminating in the printing of "A Sketch of the Life and Character of Charles Cotesworth Pinckney." Reprinting that column was the best evidence that a paper had fallen under Hamilton's spell; examples included the Boston *Columbian Centinel*, the *Middlesex Gazette*, the *Salem Gazette*, and the *Norwich Packet*.[233] Writing to John Trumbull in September 1800, Adams anticipated his own defeat, and preemptively ascribed the blame for it to Hamilton's malignant influence: "Porcupine's Gazette and Fenno's Gazette, from the moment of the mission to France, aided, countenanced, and encouraged by soi-disant Federalists in Boston, New York, and Philadelphia have done more to shuffle the cards into the hands of the Jacobin leaders, than all the acts of the administration, and all the policy of opposition from the commencement of the government.... If the election of a Federal President is lost by it, those who performed the exploit will be the greatest losers."[234]

As Brown notes, "it is clear that Adams believed that he had been ousted from the presidency by the press."[235] There were partisan Federalist papers loyal to Adams, including the Boston *Columbian Centinel* (probably the largest paper in the country in 1800 with a reported circulation of 4,000), the Hartford *Connecticut Courant*, and the Baltimore *Federal Gazette*. But the incumbent party was slow to mobilize its presence in print. It wasn't until the passage of the Sedition Act and, paradoxically, till the Jeffersonian press war against Adams approached fever pitch, that anything like a concerted Federalist counterattack emerged, and even then tentatively. The Trenton *Federalist* debuted in July 1798, followed by the Richmond *Virginia Federalist* (May 1799), the Charleston *Federal Carolina Gazette* (January 1800), and the *Washington Federalist* (September 1800).[236] But, hampered as they were by an ineffective party organization and the feud between Adams and Hamilton, the Federalists were never able to muster a coordinated mass-media campaign at anywhere near the pitch of intensity maintained by their Republican rivals. Not that this was for lack of initiative on the part of individual Federalist editors. The Hartford *Courant*, for one, shuddered at the prospect of Jefferson as president: "Murder, robbery, rape, adultery and incest will be openly taught and practiced, the air will be rent with the cries of distress, the soil soaked with blood, and the nation black with crimes. Where is the heart that can contemplate such a scene without shivering with horror?"[237]

The ironically-titled Hudson *Balance* undertook in its editorials to prove a brace of propositions: "*First*— That Mr. Jefferson is an infidel. And *Secondly*— That he would be pleased with a subversion of Christianity in this country."[238] Jefferson's deism was a popular target. "You have been, Sir, a Governor, an Ambassador, and a Secretary of State," an op-ed piece in the Philadelphia *Gazette of the United States* addressed Jefferson, "and had to desert each of these posts, from that weakness of nerves, want of fortitude and total imbecility of character, which have marked your whole political career, and most probably will attend you to the grave."[239] The same newspaper employed bold type to warn voters that "the only question to be asked by every American, laying his hand on his heart is 'shall I continue in allegiance to GOD — AND A RELIGIOUS PRESIDENT; or impiously declare for JEFFERSON — AND NO GOD!!!'"[240] Another Federalist publication to use Jefferson's deism as grist for its mill was the *New England Palladium*, which insisted, "Should the infidel Jefferson be elected to the Presidency, the seal of death is that moment set on our holy religion, our churches will be prostrated, and some infamous prostitute, under the title of the Goddess of Reason, will preside in the Sanctuaries now devoted to the worship of the Most High."[241]

The *Connecticut Courant* neatly encapsulated the key points of the Federalist assault when it challenged its readers to consider: "Do you believe in the strangest of all paradoxes, that a spendthrift, a libertine, or an atheist, characters which none of you would trust with the most trifling concern in your own private affairs, is qualified to make your laws and to govern you, and your posterity; to be entrusted with the treasure, the strength, and the destiny of the nation?"[242]

"I have been for some time used as the property of the newspapers, a fair mark for every man's dirt," Jefferson complained as early as February, 1798.[243] Pro-administration papers, Thomas Adams of the *Independent Chronicle* agreed, threw at Jefferson "more corruption and filth than would fill the stables of a modern Augean ... [but] when some bold truth is uttered by a Republican, they send forth most pitiful yellings and yet they do not scruple to traduce and calumniate the purest characters of the Union." Even Callender was moved to grumble that "the newspapers printed under the presidential banner, breathe nothing but irritation, calumny, and every imaginable ingredient of civil discord."[244] Duane put this abuse in perspective when he said that he was proud to be the object of Federalist attacks because "it is a just cause of pride to be an object of fear and hatred to the vilest men in a country."[245]

But the occasional literary broadsides, unforgiving as they were, of which its editors were capable, could not compensate for the sustained, coordinated, and on-message barrage to which the Federalist Party was subjected.[246] Federalists like Fisher Ames might sneer that the Republican press had made "uneducated printers, shop-boys, and raw school-masters ... the chief instructors in politics" during the campaign of 1800, but Jefferson's election without them is unthinkable.[247]

John Adams certainly did not hesitate to ascribe the cause of his defeat to the machinations of the press. On April 16, 1801, the former president wrote to Christopher Gadsen of South Carolina, "'Foreign meddlers,' as you properly denominate them, have a strange and mysterious influence in this country. Is there no pride in American bosoms? Can their hearts endure that Callender, Duane, Cooper and Lyon should be the most influential men in the country, all foreigners and all degraded characters?"[248] He later reflected in the same vein, "If we had been blessed with common sense, we should not have been overthrown by Philip

Freneau, Duane, Callender, Cooper, and Lyon, or their great patron and protector [Jefferson]. A group of foreign liars, encouraged by a few ambitious native gentlemen, have discomfited the education, the talents, the virtues, and the property of the country."[249]

Regarding Jefferson, Adams wrote, "I have no resentment against him, though he has honored and salaried every villain he could find that had been an enemy to me."[250] The outgoing president did not deign to extend these sentiments to his successor in person, however, slipping out of Washington early on the morning that Jefferson was sworn into office.[251]

The Virginia Dynasty

"The Revolution of 1776, is now, and for the first time, arrived at its completion." These were the terms by which Jefferson's ascendancy to the White House was heralded in the pages of the *Aurora*.[252] The *Gazette of the United States*, on the other hand, regarded the transition as "the general ascendancy of the worthless, the dishonest, the rapacious, the vile, the merciless and the ungodly," decrying that "the rabble has broken over all restraint."[253] The perspectives of these two papers, although representing the polar extremes of their respective ideologies, reflected both the abiding partisan division within American society and the burden of expectations that would be placed upon the incoming Republican administration. The struggle to define Jefferson's success or failure in meeting those expectations would rage in print for the duration of his two terms in office. In the final analysis he may be said to have won a pyrrhic victory. The opposition presses consistently failed in their efforts to deflect him from securing his policy objectives but they did succeed in ushering aspects of his personal life and intellectual identity into the public domain where they continue to be debated to this day.

Jefferson's first act as president was to pardon all those indicted under the Sedition Act. "I discharged every person under punishment or prosecution under the sedition law, because I considered ... that law to be a nullity, as absolute and as palpable as if Congress had ordered us to fall down and worship a golden image," he told Abigail Adams. This was the Jefferson of principle that history remembers. But the other side to Jefferson, his opportunism, would also be very evident. Ironically, the man who served as the apostle of free speech while in opposition would establish, in effect, the first official government newspaper upon taking office, setting the standard followed by incoming administrations for the next sixty years. Doubly ironic, the man who rallied the nation against the Alien and Sedition Acts would not prove above resorting to legal means to curtail criticism once he took residence in the White House.

Jefferson appointed as his secretary of state his fellow Virginian James Madison, who promptly set about creating a Republican empire of patronage in the press. Typical of the breed receiving coveted government contracts to publish the laws were the Richmond papers the *Virginia Argus* and the *Examiner*, both edited by members of the Republican Party Central Committee in the state, whose duties included directing and coordinating the efforts of the county committees and communicating "useful information to the people." And the Republicans were just as committed to dispossessing Federalist publications as they were to entrenching the privileges of their own. The Federalists were represented in Richmond by two newspapers, the *Virginia Gazette*, edited by Augustine Davis, and the *Virginia Federalist*, edited by William Rind and Jack Stuart. The Republicans struck first at the state level; Davis lost his position as printer to the Commonwealth, and Smith was dismissed as clerk to the House of Delegates. After Jefferson's elevation to the presidency, Davis was stripped of his federal office as postmaster of Richmond.[254]

In some instances, with the battle now won, Republican papers in safe Republican states could afford to bow out of the lists with honor. In Virginia, for example, a striking number of Jeffersonian papers founded in the late 1790s—the Fredericksburg *Genius of Liberty*, the Winchester *Triumph of Liberty*, and the Staunton *Scourge of Aristocracy*—had disappeared by 1803. A counter-example, with enduring significance for national as well as state politics, was the arrival of Thomas Ritchie on the editorial scene that same year. Ritchie had moved to Richmond where the previous Republican newspaper in the state capital, the *Examiner*, edited by Skelton Jones, had folded because of lack of support. Judge Spencer Roane, under whom Ritchie had read law, wanted another partisan journal established, and Jefferson promised federal backing. The Richmond *Enquirer* first appeared as a bi-weekly on May 9, 1804. As editor, the twenty-five-year-old Ritchie paid little attention to advertising, instead anchoring the paper on political patronage and subscriptions, which increased from 500 to 1,500 during the first eighteen months. "Without patronage," Ritchie's biographer admits, his paper "could not have lived in so strong a Federalist atmosphere as Richmond and in competition with a well established and popular press," the Federalist *Virginia Gazette*.[255] Ritchie's strategy enabled him to edit the *Enquirer* for the next forty-one years, picking up the office of state printer from a grateful Republican legislature in 1814, a role he fulfilled, other than during a brief hiatus in 1834, for the next twenty-five years.

Any diminution of Republican editorial endeavor in its own fiefdoms after Jefferson took office

Monumental Inscription.

" *That life is long which answers Life's great end.*"

YESTERDAY EXPIRED,
Deeply regretted by MILLIONS of grateful Americans,
And by *all* GOOD MEN,

The FEDERAL ADMINISTRATION
Of the
GOVERNMENT of the *United States*:
Animated by
A WASHINGTON, an ADAMS ;—a
HAMILTON, KNOX, PICKERING, WOL-
COTT, M'HENRY, MARSHALL,
STODDERT and DEXTER.
Æt. 12 years.

Its death was occasioned by the
Secret Arts, and Open Violence
Of Foreign and Domestic Demagogues :
Notwithstanding its whole Life
Was devoted to the Performance of every Duty
to promote
The UNION, CREDIT, PEACE, PROSPER-
ITY, HONOR, and
FELICITY OF ITS COUNTRY.

At its birth it found
The Union of the States dissolving like a Rope of snow ;
It hath left it
Stronger than the Threefold cord.

It found the United States
Bankrupts in Estate and Reputation ;
It hath left them
Unbounded in Credit ; and respected throughout
the World.
It found the *Treasuries* of the United States and
Individual States *empty ;*
It hath left them *full and overflowing.*
It found
All the Evidences of Public Debts worthless as rags ;
It hath left them
More valuable than Gold and Silver.

This "Monumental Inscription" in the *Columbian Centinel* mourns the passing of the Federalist Party administration after twelve years in office under Washington and Adams. Note the reference to its demise at the hands of "Foreign and Domestic Demagogues"—a charge the Republican editors in question would have considered the ultimate tribute to their role in the election of Thomas Jefferson (author's collection).

was more than matched by expansion elsewhere. With an eye to institutionalizing their dominance, the Republicans were determined not just to master the swing states but to carry the battle into the Federalist heartland of New England where the Jeffersonian voice was muted, if audible at all; in northern Massachusetts (now Maine), for example, a Republican paper was not established until 1803, after eleven Federalist papers had already appeared. The power to dispense patronage now at Jefferson's disposal in Washington gave his party its chance to break up this monopoly.[256] In July 1801 Attorney General Levi Lincoln wrote the president from Worcester: "If Massachusetts gets right, all will be right. The other eastern states will be with her. A few more Republican newspapers, and the thing is accomplished. Exertions are being made to obtain them. Editors alone are wanting; sufficient encouragement would be given them."[257]

Jefferson himself was intimately involved in the process. In his first year in office he wrote an encouraging reply to a Vermont printer who had complained about that state government's ongoing endorsement of Federalist publications:

> I am sorry to learn ... that the officers in the public employment still use the influence and the business of their offices to encourage presses which disseminate principles contrary to those on which our constitution is built. This evil will be remedied.... Your press having been in the habit of inculcating the genuine principles of our constitution, and your sufferings for those principles, entitle you to any favors in your line which the public servants can give you; and those who do not give them, act against their duty. Should you continue in the business you will have the publications of the laws in your state.[258]

The temptation to indulge the partisan press with public money proved irresistible during the Virginia dynasty's long reign; including the three territories, the total number of authorized papers at the end of 1824 was seventy-six, more than double the number in 1801.

At first blush, the big winner from the election of 1800 appeared to be the Philadelphia *Aurora*. Once Jefferson took power, Duane was given not only the printing of the laws but the larger print jobs authorized by the State Department.[259] However, the *Aurora* was not destined to be the voice of the new administration. On the face of it, this may seem surprising. The logistics of the issue were never in question; as Knudson notes, Duane did establish a stationery store and printing shop in Washington, so he probably would have moved the *Aurora* to the new capital if he had been asked to do so.[260] In part, the decision to endorse another vehicle as its quasi-official mouthpiece reflected a deliberate strategy on the part of the Republican Party to maximize its editorial reach. Knudson adds that Duane was promised the printing of the House journals while still in Philadelphia if he continued marshaling the Republican press from there, in what was still the nation's largest city.[261]

On a more personal level, the issue simply boiled down to the Republican hierarchy being unable to trust Duane in a role that demanded the utmost standards of party loyalty and discipline. This was not owing to any lack of gratitude for the significant contribution at great personal risk that Duane had made to the Republican cause during its sojourn in electoral exile. Shortly after Jefferson stepped down from the presidency, he wrote Duane, telling him, "I cannot conclude without thanking you for ... the many proofs of your friendship and confidence." Jefferson continued to solicit funds for the *Aurora* in retirement, reminding one partisan ally in 1811, "This paper has unquestionably rendered incalculable services to republicanism through all its struggles with the federalists and has been the rallying point for the orthodoxy of the whole union. It was our comfort in the gloomiest days, and is still performing the office of a watchful sentinel."[262]

Nevertheless, however genuine Jefferson's affection, the threshold of his tolerance for Duane's iconoclasm had already long expired. The former President admitted to the same correspondent a few weeks later that while he believed Duane to be "a very honest man and sincerely republican, his passions are stronger than his prudence, and his personal as well as general antipathies render him very intolerant."[263]

The problem was that Duane remained committed to Jeffersonian ideals long after the Republican Party, including Jefferson himself, had adopted a stance of greater ideological flexibility. In the increasingly one-party politics of his home state, Duane led the radical Quid or anti-judiciary faction against Republican Governor Thomas McKean. After the election of 1804, Alexander J. Dallas wrote to Albert Gallatin that Duane was responsible for "a fatal division" in the Pennsylvania Republican Party, adding, "There is reason for Mr. Jefferson himself to apprehend that the spirit of Callender survives."[264] Duane never ceased being in the forefront of national affairs. During the war of 1812 he was named first a lieutenant colonel in the expanded army and then adjutant general for the Keystone State (over the objections of Treasury Secretary Albert Gallatin, who quit the Cabinet in disgust over the appointment). His son, William J. Duane, took over from his father at the helm of the *Aurora* in 1822, married one of Benjamin Bache's younger sisters, entered Pennsylvania politics, and in 1833 became secretary of the treasury under Andrew Jackson. But Duane and his *Aurora* were never destined to serve as the true herald of Jefferson's higher truths.[265] The very talents that made him so effective while in opposition — his willfully defiant anti-authoritarian nature — rendered him too unreliable to serve in government.

With Duane out of the picture, the administration would need to adopt as its paper of record one of the extant publications in Washington, where the announcement that Congress would meet in the new capital on November 17, 1800, had already led to a flurry of activity by the printers. The triweekly *Washington Federalist* was launched in Georgetown on September 25. James Lyon, son of the Vermont representative jailed for violating the Sedition Law, started the *Cabinet of the United States* as a Republican daily around October 1, while the twenty-eight-year-old Samuel Harrison Smith brought out his triweekly *National Intelligencer and Washington Advertiser* on October 31.[266]

Smith and Jefferson had first become acquainted in Philadelphia when Jefferson resided there, through their connections with the Philosophical Society, of which Jefferson was president and Smith secretary. Smith began publishing a Jeffersonian newspaper, the Philadelphia *New World*, in the late summer of 1796, but discontinued it on August 16, 1797. The following month he bought the *Independent Gazetteer* from Joseph Gales, Sr., and on November 16 brought out the first issue of the *Universal Gazette*, which he retained as a weekly edition of the *National Intelligencer* after moving to Washington.[267] The launch of the *National Intelligencer* marked an important precedent in the relationship between the press and the political; according to William Ames, "No newspaper published before the *National Intelligencer* was as intimately identified with a political party and a national administration as was Smith's journal."[268]

According to Culver Smith, the *Intelligencer* enjoyed the significant privilege of printing Jefferson's inaugural address before any other paper, which meant it had been given to Samuel Smith before its delivery. "Subsequent handling of the news confirmed the assumption of other newspapers that the *Intelligencer* was the official paper, expressing the sentiments of the government."[269] Talking of itself in the third person, the *National Intelligencer* proudly confirmed on January 1, 1840, that "it was the medium through which the acts of the executive were authentically announced, and in which its advertisements were published."[270]

Within the first year of the new administration, Smith received printing patronage from the Department of State, including the printing of the laws. This publishing "by authority" meant public recognition and growth in subscriptions. More substantial patronage came from orders for department needs, such as printed forms, passports, circular letters, land patents, "sea letters," and stationery. For the first four years of Jefferson's administration, the State

Department's disbursements to Smith for printing averaged nearly $2,000 per year, comparable to the salaries of State Department staff members at the time.

The *Intelligencer's* political affiliation was no state secret — Callender caught the essence of the relationship when he dubbed the paper "Miss Smith's Silky-Milky National Smoothing Plane."[271] Smith himself never made any secret of the partisan basis of his publication, asserting in 1807 his belief that "the existing administration have uprightly and wisely discharged their duties." He was, therefore, he said, "the friend of the administration, and whatever new dangers may environ them, from the injustice of foreign powers, or from internal machinations."[272] The editor clearly enjoyed the privileges afforded by his insider status. His entry in the *Dictionary of American Biography* describes his household as rivaling Jefferson's as the center of Washingtonian social universe: "His home was the rendezvous of statesmen, authors, musicians, politicians, and editors. He set a lavish table, filled his cellar with rare wines, attended an Episcopal church regularly, enjoyed chess and whist, and drove fine horses."[273] Smith sold his newspaper and retired from journalism in 1810; three years later, President Madison appointed him commissioner of the revenue, an office he held until it was abolished. He subsequently became president of the Bank of Washington and, later still, president of the Washington branch of the Bank of the United States.

Smith had prearranged a smooth, in-house transition at the helm of the *Intelligencer*. As Jefferson's second term drew to a close and Smith first signaled his willingness to sell the administration's vehicle "to a person of sound republican principles," the advertisement attracted a proposal from a former associate, Joseph Gales, who in 1797 had sold Smith his weekly newspaper, the Philadelphia *Independent Gazette*, before moving to North Carolina to publish the *Raleigh Register*. Gales now proposed to acquire the *Intelligencer*, not for himself but for his son, Joseph Jr., who had been dispatched to Philadelphia to find work as an apprentice printer after being expelled from the state university for a breach of discipline and for being "loose in his manners." Gales Sr. persuaded Smith to hire his boy on a trial basis in order to groom him as a prospective editor before ceding him control of the paper. Simultaneously, Smith's wife Margaret labored to "soften & polish his manners." After Smith retired, having deemed the twenty-four-year-old Gales Jr. ready to assume the mantle of editor, young Gales operated the *Intelligencer* single-handedly until 1812, when, in anticipation of converting it from a tri-weekly to a daily he took as a partner his brother-in-law, William W. Seaton, who had cut his teeth at age seventeen working for Thomas Ritchie's *Virginia Patriot*, and later edited the Petersburg *Republican* and *North Carolina Journal* prior to marrying Sarah Gales in 1809 and joining her family's paper in Raleigh. For the next fifty years the duo of Gales and Seaton would faithfully uphold the Republican principles bequeathed them by the *Intelligencer's* founder, exhibiting at all times a "one-ness and identity of all purposes, opinions and interests."[274]

Gales and Seaton's tenure of service to the Virginia dynasty reflected the judicious mix of ideological compatibility and partisan flexibility necessary to survive at the top of the patronage totem pole. Shortly after taking office, Secretary of State James Monroe summoned Gales to his office and brusquely notified him that any reports published on foreign policy would be issued directly by his office, if the *National Intelligencer* were to remain the official organ. In fulfilling its obligations, the paper was rewarded by obtaining the congressional printing in 1819. The paper was so closely identified with the government that its offices were specifically targeted for destruction by the British when they occupied Washington in 1814. According to one eyewitness:

> When he [Admiral George Cockburn] went to burn Mr. Gales's office, whom he called his "dear Josey," Mrs. Brush, Mrs. Stelle & a few citizens remonstrated with him, assuring him that it would occasion the loss of all the buildings in the row. "Well," he said, "good people I do not

wish to injure you, but I am really afraid my friend Josey will be affronted with me, if after burning Jemmy's [James Madison's] palace [the White House] I do not pay him the same compliment — so my lads, take your axes, pull down the house, and burn the papers in the street."

The admiral also reportedly ordered all the "Cs" in the type cases destroyed so that the editors could not vilify his name.[275] Benefiting from the ensuing peace, the *Intelligencer* quickly bounced back and even tightened its grip over the federal patronage as America entered the one-party Era of Good Feelings. After Henry Clay engineered a bill whereby Congress would elect official printers for each session, Gales and Seaton were retained as printers for both Senate and House from 1819 to 1827.

The opposition papers, meanwhile, were trapped in a downward spiral in which each successive Federalist defeat at the polls meant their continued denial of access to the federal largesse that flowed ever more freely into the Republican presses. The reading habits of the Senate, whose members had voted themselves free subscriptions to three papers of their choice, represented an accurate barometer of the shifting partisan balance of power. Of the thirty-two senators in December 1801, twenty-three requested the *Intelligencer*, twenty the *Federalist*, and thirteen took both. By 1803 twenty-seven senators requested the *Intelligencer* while subscriptions to the *Federalist* dropped to eight. Having been made abundantly clear of the way the winds were blowing, the editor of the *Federalist* sold out the following year.[276]

Another Federalist paper at the cusp of extinction was the once mighty *Gazette of the United States*, which John Ward Fenno had sold to Caleb P. Wayne in May 1800. Reeling under the collapse of the Federalist political position, the removal of the capital to Washington, and the seven libel prosecutions he accumulated during his year as editor, Wayne sold the *Gazette* to Enos Bronson on November 2, 1801. By that point the paper's subscription list had dwindled from three thousand to eight hundred. Bronson injected some life into the moribund publication by reviving its duel with Duane, "that prostitute and venal slave" at the *Aurora*, but such shadow boxing could only postpone the inevitable, and the *Gazette* ultimately went the way of its party and its ideology, finally expiring in 1819.[277]

In their isolated redoubts, the Federalists remained capable of lashing out in print throughout their protracted death throes as a national party during the first quarter of the 19th century. As Jefferson's agenda unfolded, the Republican regime was attacked for running down the nation's defenses, truckling to Bonaparte, and threatening the independence of the judiciary.[278] According to Knudson, "No newspaper in the country could match the imposing authority of the Boston *Columbian Centinel* under Major Benjamin Russell, who considered himself the keeper of the Federalist flame of truth and political righteousness" during his forty-two years at the helm.[279] Joseph Dennie's Philadelphia *Port Folio* was described by another authority as "a last permanent sanctuary from Jeffersonian democracy."[280] The Raleigh *Minerva* was the Federalist paper propagating these themes in North Carolina, and the Charleston *Courier* in South Carolina.

Jefferson certainly felt the barbs to which he was subjected by these publications. In fact, early in his first term he had largely written off the threat presented by the Federalist opposition in every sphere save print. "The people are nearly all united," he explained in a letter to General Thaddeus Kosciusko dated April 2, 1802. "Their quantum leaders, infuriated with the sense of their impotence, will soon be seen or heard only in the newspapers, which serve as chimneys to carry off noxious vapors and smoke, and all is now tranquil, firm and well, as it should be.[281]

The "quantum leaders" to which Jefferson referred were the nation's legal, commercial, and industrial elites. The financial reserves available to the Federalist Party from such private sources enabled them to balance somewhat the public funds available to the Republicans. For example, Judge Samuel Chase led a circle of contributors who raised $8,000 to establish the

Baltimore *Anti-Democrat* in 1801. A significant milestone took place in the fall of that year when Alexander Hamilton mobilized the $10,000 in capital necessary to launch his own literary vehicle, the *New York Evening Post*, which debuted on November 16, 1801. Hamilton and his New York friends secretly circulated a founders' list among trusted Federalists, who were each expected to contribute a minimum of $100. As Knudson describes it, the list of the 600 original subscribers to the new paper "read like a roster of the inner councils of the New York Federalist Party."[282] Hamilton himself contributed not less than $1,000. Other prominent backers included businessman Samuel Boyd and merchant Archibald Gracie. The money was not given outright but "loaned," the debt being discharged without payment or protest in 1810.

To take the helm of this new partisan vessel, Hamilton recruited William Coleman, a young Federalist who had just

Dubbed the "Field-Marshal of the Federalist editors" shortly after being installed at the helm of the *New York Evening Post* by Alexander Hamilton, William Coleman would survive his patron by more than twenty years. The editor's literary skill and business savvy enabled his paper to outlast the Federalist Party, making it today the oldest continuously published daily paper in the United States (courtesy of New York Public Library).

recently lost his $3,000 a year sinecure as clerk of the New York Circuit Court in the Republican purge.[283] Less than a year after Coleman started editing the *Evening Post*, James Callender dubbed him "Field-Marshall of the Federalist editors."[284] The *Evening Post* had boasted in its prospectus, "We disapprove of that spirit of dogmatism which lays exclusive claim to infallibility; and willingly believe that honest and virtuous men are to be found in each party." But the paper was a child of its age, and unable to remain above the partisan fray.[285] Just a few months after its first issue rolled off the presses, Duane was complaining:

> The paper of *Alexander Hamilton* at New York has assumed the *full toned* grossness and vulgarity of *Porcupine* and *Callender*—their morals and their principles are congenial; to them nothing is so abhorrent as the Aurora. While we feel a pride in their hatred, and it is a just cause of pride to be an object of *fear* and *hatred* to the vilest men in a community — we shall pursue our course steadily, and laugh at the insolent stupidity which they substitute for argument, and the mendacity which they employ to escape from the exposure of their crimes.[286]

Undeterred, Coleman continued to take aim at his rivals, sometimes in verse:

> Lie on, Duane, lie on for pay,
> And Cheetham, lie thou too,
> More 'gainst truth you cannot say,
> Than truth can say 'gainst you.

Alternatively, Coleman could appeal to the classics, as when he appended Milton's description of Satan, who "Squat[ted] like a toad at the ear of Eve," with the comment, "I beg the devil's pardon for comparing him in any shape with Duane."[287] Surveying this contest, Callender, who could only dream of such influence, remarked, "The people of America derive their political information chiefly from newspapers. Duane upon one side, and Coleman upon the other, dictate at this moment the sentiments of perhaps fifty thousand American citizens."[288]

Notwithstanding these individual initiatives, the Federalists remained incapable of establishing the kind of integrated national network of media outlets that may have given the party a fighting chance against Republican hegemony. "One of [the Republicans'] many plans," John Nicholas wrote to Alexander Hamilton on August 3, 1803, "has ever been to support with all their best energies, both mentally and [financially], their best printers, and with the utmost industry, care and activity, to disseminate their papers and pamphlets. While the Federalists on their part leave their printers to scuffle on the support of their subscribers [which is] I believe a very flimsy and uncertain daily sustenance, and to scribble their own way to conquest!"[289] It was imperative not merely to patronize Federalist publications in isolation but to establish a nationwide network of Federalist papers dedicated to advancing the party cause. The Federalists, it was said, "seldom republish from each other, while on the other hand, their antagonists never get hold of anything however trivial in reality, but they make it ring through all their papers from one end of the continent to the other."[290]

And the Republicans were by no means slackening in their press war against the defeated Federalists just because they now held the reins of power.[291] Postmaster General Gideon Granger issued the following call to arms to members of his party in 1802: "The Federalists have associated in an organized body to destroy the reputation of the present administration by every species of Slander and Calumny which they have ingenuity to invent.... We therefore ardently solicit our friends and all friends of the Republican Principles to be instant in season and out of season in repelling their attack by counter Publications in the Republican News Papers."[292]

British exile James Cheetham, editor of the New York *American Citizen*, the successor to the *Argus*, was the fieriest Republican partisan in the Empire State. A typical broadside was directed at the New York *Gazette and General Advertiser* on March 7, 1801: "Destitute of claim to truth, to integrity, and to honour, it is a fit repository of the filth of the fallen faction, whose means are falsehood and misrepresentation, and whose end, the dissolution of our republican system of government."[293] Cheetham was DeWitt Clinton's leading propagandist during his bitter struggle with Aaron Burr for control of the Republican Party in New York during the early 19th century. Burr responded by launching the *Morning Chronicle*, edited by Washington Irving's brother Peter, on October 1, 1802.

The literary trade was a dangerous business. William Coleman allowed himself to be talked out of challenging Cheetham after the latter accused him of fathering a mulatto child during his youth in Greenfield, Massachusetts, but he did succeed in killing another critic in a duel in 1803 — making him a better (or at least luckier) practitioner of the art than his patron Hamilton. His luck ran out in 1818 after he published a narrative of the misconduct of Democratic judge Henry B. Hagerman while traveling upstate as Judge Advocate. On the evening of April 11, Coleman was overtaken by Hagerman at the corner of Murray and Church Streets and attacked without warning from behind. The judge gave the editor a savage beating with the butt of a rawhide whip. Two years to the day after the attack, Coleman was awarded $4,000 in damages, but he went to the grave in 1829 still paralyzed from the waist down.[294]

The end of the Federalist era had not made those engaged in the business of words any less vulnerable to legal sanction. In addition to their prosecutions under the Sedition Act, the

Federalists had initiated several common-law prosecutions against certain publications for seditious libel. This avenue of retribution remained open even after the expiry of the Sedition Act, and libel suits resulted in the jailing of John S. Lillie of the Boston *Constitutional Telegraph*, Harry Croswell of the Hudson *Wasp*, William Carlton of the *Salem Register*, and Nathaniel Willis of the Portland *Eastern Argus*, during Jefferson's first term. The number of trials was legion; the Hudson *Bee* of June 14, 1803, noted the fact that the latest libel suit against its editor was his thirteenth. William Duane of the *Aurora* had accumulated over sixty libel suits by 1806.[295]

The leading advocate of partisan legal action against partisan papers was none other than the president himself. "Though I have made up my mind not to suffer calumny to disturb my tranquility, yet I retain all my sensibilities for the approbation of the good & just," Jefferson wrote to Congressman Samuel Smith of Maryland on August 22, 1798. "That is, indeed, the chief consolation for the hatred of so many, who, without the least personal knowledge, & on the sacred evidence of Porcupine & Fenno alone, cover me with their implacable hatred. The only return I will ever make of them, will be to do them all the good I can, in spite of their teeth."[296] Jefferson sang a different tune once in office, and the chief source of his recantation was none other than James Callender.

For understandable reasons, no one was happier at Jefferson's victory than Callender, who was under lock and key at the time. "Hurraw!" he crowed. "How shall I triumph over the miscreants! How, as Othello says, shall they be damned beyond all depth!"[297] His joy was to be short lived, however. Jefferson pardoned Callender — as he did all people convicted under the Sedition Act — on March 16, 1801, after Callender had completed eight months of his prison term. Callender's expectations had already long exceeded this obligation, however.

Callender had written to Jefferson from jail on September 13, 1800, "If I live to see a republican president in the chair, I shall have a press of my own in Richmond; and give the aristocrats a cut and thrust volume per annum for some years to come [for] the federal viper will undoubtedly continue to hiss; but I make no doubt of living to trample him in the mire of universal detestation." The following month he wrote again, remarking that "2 or 300 dollars would be quite enough to buy a press &c." and complaining that he had received no reply from Jefferson after sending him several installments of proofs from the second volume of *The Prospect Before Us.*[298]

On February 23, 1801, ten days prior to his release from jail, Callender asked Jefferson for the remission of his $200 fine, on the grounds that he could not leave prison without paying it and that if he did he would have no money left to establish his long-contemplated printing shop in Richmond. On April 12, Callender repeated his plea, explaining that the former state marshal, Edmund Randolph, had refused to remit the fine. Callender listed his endeavors on behalf of the Republican Party, and the costs incurred thereof — "By the cause, I have lost five years of labor; gained five thousand enemies; got my name inserted in five hundred libels," concluding bitterly, "I mention these particulars as this is probably the close of my correspondence with you, that you may not suppose that I, at least, have gained anything by the victories of Republicanism."[299] When this missive failed to elicit a response, Callender wrote further letters to Virginia Governor James Monroe and to Cabinet members Levi Lincoln and James Madison, complaining, of his efforts to solicit Jefferson's help, that "I might as well have addressed a letter to Lot's wife" and asking for appointment as postmaster of Richmond.[300]

Jefferson did ultimately arrange for the court fine to be repaid, but it was too late to assuage Callender's outrage at what he saw as the president's litany of bad faith. When Callender began to hint that he would publicly divulge that he had received money from the then vice president while conducting his campaign against Adams, a flurry of letters passed among Jefferson, Madison and Monroe on the subject of how best to respond to Callender's increasingly strident demands and threats. The president described his relationship with Callender in a July 17, 1802, letter to Monroe: "I as well as most other republicans who were in the way of doing it, contributed what I could afford to the support of the republican papers and printers, paid sums of money for the Bee, the Albany Register &c. when they were staggering under the sedition law, contributed to the fines of Callender ... and others suffering under that law. I discharged, when I came into office, such as were under the persecution of our enemies, without instituting any persecutions in retaliation."[301]

Two days previously Jefferson had written Monroe, "I am really mortified at the base ingratitude of Callender. It presents human nature in a hideous form. It gives me concern, because I perceive that relief, which was afforded him on mere motives of charity, may be viewed under the aspect of employing him as a writer." He went on to assert that "no man wished more to see his pen stopped" and claimed that the financial inducements he offered "were no more than charities, yielded under a strong conviction that he was injuring us by his writings."[302]

For Callender, the final straw was Jefferson's failure to award him the cherished postmastership of Richmond. On July 11, 1801, he and Henry Pace established the Richmond *Recorder*, dedicated to the excoriation of the President. From Philadelphia, Duane led the Republican counterattack against "this *apostate* and new *convert* of federalism." On August 25 he published an article on Callender's dead wife, painting a portrait of her being "overwhelmed by a created [i.e. sexually transmitted] disease, on a loathsome bed, with a number of children, all in a state next to famishing ... while Callender was having his usual pint of brandy at breakfast."[303] It took three days for a copy of the *Aurora* to find its way to Richmond. The following day, September 1, in the pages of the *Recorder*, Callender unleashed his literary weapon of mass destruction against the president: "It is well known that the man, *whom it delighteth the public to honor*, keeps, and for many years past has kept, as his concubine, one of his slaves. Her name is SALLY. The name of her eldest son is TOM. His features are said to bear a striking although sable resemblance to the president himself.... By this wench, Sally, our president has had several children.... THE AFRICAN VENUS is said to officiate, as housekeeper, at Monticello."[304]

"Behold the favorite!" Callender crowed, with biting sarcasm and evident glee. "The first born of republicanism! The pinnacle of all that is good and great! In the open consummation of an act which tends to subvert the policy, the happiness, and even the existence of this country!" In signing off, the author made sure to note that his exposé was the malignant fruit of the President's betrayal. "When Mr. Jefferson has read this article, he will find leisure to estimate how much has been lost or gained by so many unprovoked attacks upon J. T. Callender."[305]

Callender continued to exploit the issue of Jefferson's miscegenation in the pages of the *Recorder* at every available opportunity, both in prose and doggerel. A representative example was published on November 17, 1802:

> Yankee doodle, who's the noodle?
> What wife were half so handy?
> To breed a flock of slaves for stock,
> A blackamoor's the dandy.[306]

The Federalist press could hardly afford to miss this opportunity to republish the allegation that Jefferson was "frolicking with his 'Congo Harem' and adding to the labor force at Monticello by an annual increment of mulattoes."[307] But Callender's revelation of Jefferson's relationship with Sally Hemings made even Federalists, who were happy enough to quote him at length in their publications, uncomfortable at being associated with him. The editor of the

Norristown Herald declared, "The truth is, Callender has no political honesty; no personal merit; and we are sincerely sorry to see such characters on the federal side."[308] Callender was unrepentant. "The original and just cause for introducing the background scenery of Monticello," he asserted, was Jefferson's connivance with the personal attacks by Republican printers. The president "had it in his power, with a single word, to have extinguished the volcanoes of reproach," but "with that frigid indifference which forms the pride of his character, the president stood neuter."[309] As a consequence, "chastisement was promised, and the promise has been kept with the most rigid punctuality. If [Jefferson] had not violated the sanctuary of the grave, Sally and her son Tom would still, perhaps, have slumbered in the tomb of oblivion."[310]

Duane continued to fire salvoes in response, again returning to the issue of Callender's abject failure as a husband and father, writing in the *Aurora*, September 15, 1802, "His unfortunate wife was suffered by him to perish in her own filth until maggots were engendered beneath her ... his children were left to wallow in filth, ignorance and misery, while he was indulging in intoxication on the money bestowed by blind and undiscriminating benevolence!"[311] George Hay, a member of the Virginia governor's executive council and Monroe's son-in-law, adopted a direct approach to the problem. He viciously battered Callender's head with a club and then persuaded a Virginia court to silence the editor on the extremely dubious grounds that English common law entitled the state to require a "common libeler of all the best and greatest men in our country" to post a bond against committing further offenses. Rather than put up the money, Callender went to jail. Released, he drowned in the James River in July 1803.[312]

Whatever relief Jefferson felt when advised of this news swiftly evaporated when Callender's papers were made public, exposing his relationship with the President. Jefferson frantically tried to disassociate himself from *The Prospect Before Us*, but the Federalists were having none of it. Harry Croswell, Federalist editor of the Hudson *Wasp*, concluded;

> It amounts to this then. He [Jefferson] read the book and from that book inferred that Callender was an object of charity. Why! One who presented a face bloated with vices, a heart black as hell — one who could be guilty of such foul falsehoods, such vile aspersions of the best and greatest man the world has yet known — he is an object of charity! No! He is the very man that an aspiring mean and hollow hypocrite would press into the service of crime. He is precisely qualified to become a tool — to spit the venom and scatter the malicious poisonous slanders of his employer. He, in short, is the very man that a dissembling patriot, pretended "man of the people" would employ to plunge the dagger, or administer the arsenic.[313]

On February 5, 1803, Jefferson wrote to a foreign correspondent, warning him not to believe everything he saw in print: "Our newspapers, for the most part, present only the caricatures of disaffected minds. Indeed, the abuses of the freedom of the press here have been carried to a length never before known or borne by any civilized nation."[314] Typically, the President ascribed the source of this cancer within the blossom of liberty entirely to his political adversaries: "The Federalists having failed in destroying the freedom of the press by their gag law, seem to have attacked it in the opposite form, that is by pushing its licentiousness and its lying to such a degree of prostitution as to deprive it of all credit. And the fact is that so abandoned are the Tory presses in this particular that even the least informed of people have learnt that nothing in a newspaper is to be believed."[315]

Jefferson would almost immediately be presented with an opportunity to correct this abuse. Smarting under the lash of the newspapers in his state, Thomas McKean, the Republican governor of Pennsylvania, had petitioned the legislature to do something about the "unparalleled licentiousness" of the press. Finding no redress for his grievances from that quarter, on February 7, 1803, he wrote to the president, soliciting his advice on how to proceed: "The infamous and seditious libels, published almost daily in our newspapers, are become intolerable. If they cannot be altogether prevented, yet they may be greatly checked by a few prosecutions: I have had it for some time in contemplation to make the experiment but as the President, Congress, and several of the principal officers of the U.S. have been frequently implicated, I have declined it until I should obtain your advice and consent. This vice is become a national one, and calls aloud for redress."[316]

In 1798 Jefferson had secretly coauthored, with Madison, the Kentucky and Virginia Resolutions, which nullified the Sedition Act, but this was a manifestation of his commitment to states' rights, not to the universal freedom of expression. Jefferson denied that the federal government under the Constitution had the power to "abridge the freedom of speech, or of the press." But the states, in Jefferson's view, did have this power, and he was a vigorous advocate of their wielding it.[317] As he explained to Abigail Adams, "While we deny that Congress have a right to control the freedom of the press, we have ever asserted the right of the States, and their exclusive right to do so.... In general, the State laws appear to have made the presses responsible for slander as far as it is consistent with its useful freedom."[318]

On February 19, 1803, the President sent McKean, a fellow signatory to the Declaration of Independence, the green light to proceed. Warning him that "on the subject of prosecutions, what I say must be entirely confidential, for you know the passion for torturing every sentiment & word which comes from me," Jefferson continued: "The federalists having failed in destroying the freedom of the press by their gag-law, seem to have attacked it in an opposite form, that is by pushing its licentiousness & its lying to such a degree of prosecution as to deprive it of all credit. And the fact is that so abandoned are the tory presses in this particular that even the least informed of the people have learnt that nothing in a newspaper is to be believed. This is a dangerous state of things, and the press ought to be restored to its credibility if possible."[319]

Jefferson concluded, "I have therefore long thought that a few prosecutions of the most prominent offenders would have a wholesome effect in restoring the integrity of the presses. Not a general prosecution, for that would look like prosecution: but a selected one."[320] Joseph Dennie, editor of the Philadelphia *Port Folio*, was indicted five months later. Jefferson had an abiding distaste for Dennie, who had the effrontery to criticize the grammar and diction of the Declaration of Independence, "that false, and flatulent, and foolish paper."[321] Smoothly integrating Jefferson's scientific pursuits and his alleged trysts with Sally Hemings into an ode that was shades of Horace, Dennie had advised the president on January 22:

> Resume thy shells and butterflies,
> Thy beetles heads, and lizard's thighs,
> The state no more controul:
> Thy tricks, with *sooty* Sal, give o'er;
> Indulge thy body, Tom, no more;
> But try to save thy *soul*.[322]

Dennie was arrested and charged with libel of the government. At the conclusion of his trial, held at the Pennsylvania Supreme Court, Chief Justice Jasper Yates instructed the jury to remember that the more the government is held up to scrutiny, "the more fully will the judgments of honest men be satisfied that it is the most conducive to the safety and happiness of a free people." Dennie was found not guilty.[323]

Harry Croswell was another editor to push the Republicans too far when, on September 9, 1802, the Hudson *Wasp* reaffirmed that "Jefferson paid Callender for calling Washington a traitor, a robber, and a perjurer; for calling Adams a hoary-headed incendiary; and for most grossly slandering the private characters of men whom he well knew were virtuous. These charges, not a democratic editor has yet dared, or ever will dare, to meet in an open and manly discussion." These charge were true, as far as they went. On September 29, 1802, Samuel Smith of the *Intelligencer* declined the opportunity to publish a communication respecting the character and conduct of the now infamous Callender: "The Editor has determined not to disgrace the columns of a Paper that entertains a respect for decency and truth, by republishing the infamous calumnies and vulgarities of a man who has forfeited every pretension to character, or refutations of falsehoods which may recoil on those who propagate them, but cannot impair the well earned esteem in which the first talents and virtues of the nation are held. Without incurring any responsibility for the future, the Editor has prescribed to himself for the present the duty of suffering these base aspersions to perish unnoticed in their own infamy."[324]

However, New York's Republican attorney general, Ambrose Spencer, promptly indicted Croswell on the grounds of his "being a malicious and seditious man, of a depraved mind and wicked and diabolical disposition, and also deceitfully, wickedly, and maliciously devising, contriving and intending, Thomas Jefferson, Esq., President of the United States of America, to detract from, scandalize, traduce, vilify, and to represent him, the said Thomas Jefferson, as unworthy [of] the confidence, respect, and attachment of the people of the said United States."[325] The editor was convicted, but Alexander Hamilton stepped in on appeal in February 1804 to argue before the New York Supreme Court that Croswell deserved a new trial. Political influence ensured that the conviction would stand, but the Republicans were so cowed by Hamilton's eloquence that Croswell was never sentenced.[326]

Further north in New England, at the urging of United States District Judge Pierpont Edwards, who had been named to the bench by Jefferson, a federal grand jury in Connecticut in 1806 returned indictments against six defendants for the common law crime of seditious libel of the president. Those indicted included Thomas Collier, publisher of the *Litchfield Monitor*, and Barzillai Hudson and George Goodwin, editors of the *Connecticut Courant*. This was done, Republicans in the Nutmeg State assured Jefferson, because "Federal Editors have unceasingly issued from their presses, libels as unprecedented in number and grossness, as they were unfounded in truth." The press, these partisans concluded, "we consider as essential to *our* liberties; *its* liberty is inviolable." But it was not fit to charge the administration "with motives subversive of the liberties and happiness of the nation." In 1808 the government dropped the prosecutions of all of the defendants except Hudson and Goodwin, whose case prior to trial was appealed to the Supreme Court for a decision on whether federal courts possessed jurisdiction over the common-law crime of seditious libel. Four years later the Supreme Court ruled against federal common-law jurisdiction.[327]

By this time, the press and the judiciary were the only remaining obstacles to the Republican agenda. "When Jefferson stood for re-election in 1804, he faced a remarkable situation," Mott says. "There was virtually no campaign against him except the sniping of the opposition press. About all that was left of Federalism was a dogged loyalty to its glorious past and a lot of last-ditch newspapers."[328] In his second inaugural Jefferson lashed out at his tormentors:

> During the course of this administration, and in order to disturb it, the artillery of the press has been leveled against us, charged with whatsoever its licentiousness could devise or dare. These abuses of an institution so important to freedom and science, are deeply to be regretted, inasmuch as they tend to lessen its usefulness, and to sap its safety; they might, indeed, have been corrected by the wholesome punishments reserved and provided by the laws of the several States against falsehood and defamation; but public duties more urgent press on the time of public servants, and the offenders have therefore been left to find their punishment in the public indignation.[329]

Given that Jefferson had been reelected in a landslide of such proportions that the Federalist Party had in effect ceased to exist, the president was doing little more than shadowboxing. Thomas Paine, writing in the *American Citizen* on October 20, 1806, asserted that the Federalist papers had lost their influence with the citizens of New York:

> The number of Federalist papers in the city and state of New York are more than five to one to the number of Republican papers, yet the majority of the elections go always against the Federalist papers; which is demonstrative evidence that the licentiousness of those papers is destitute of credit.[330]

Even the Federalist dominance of the press was fading. "Tho' not 1/25 [of the] nation, they command 3/4 of its papers," Jefferson grumbled in 1804. This was an exaggeration; the Republican presence in the nation's newspapers was fast expanding. By 1808 the Republicans had finally gained the upper hand in terms of newspapers by number, though their majority rested upon the support of weeklies rather than dailies. Of 273 pro-party papers, 142 supported the Republicans, while 131 supported the Federalists. Of pro-Republican papers, 114 were weeklies, 11 were semiweeklies, 9 were triweeklies, and 8 were dailies. On the Federalist side, 97 were weeklies, 15 semiweeklies, 5 triweeklies, and 14 dailies. Thus, although more papers backed the Republican Party, the newspapers supporting the Federalists actually printed slightly more total issues per week.[331]

Jefferson's embargo policy of 1807 gave the Federalist Party a new lease on life, reflected in a burst of energy in print. In Massachusetts, Harrison Gray Otis, representing a new, if belated, spirit of professionalism in the party, drew up a survey of Federalist presses in New England, noting how politically active they were, how well they were subsidized by Federalist leaders, and where further financial and other assistance was needed. As a result of this and similar efforts, more than forty new Federalist journals were created during 1808 and 1809 alone, igniting a literary arms race with the Republicans.[332]

The new Federalist papers had a harder edge, reflected in their titles. Harry Croswell's Hudson, New York, *Wasp* featured not only its arthropod namesake on the title page, but the promise "to lash the [Republican] Rascals naked through the world."[333] There was a *Scourge* at various times in Boston, Providence and Baltimore, complementing the *Porcupine* in Baltimore, the *Scorpion* in Worcester, and the *Switch* in Cooperstown. The latter declared in its prospectus its intent:

> To seek, to find, the kennel'd pack
> To lacerate the rascals back
> Detect their crimes, expose their pranks,
> And put to flight their ragged ranks.[334]

The most aggressive Federalist paper was the Baltimore *Federal Republican*, founded by planter and attorney Alexander Contee Hanson, Jr., in 1808. With headlines like "THE RABBLE," Hanson swiftly made his fellow denizens of Charm City familiar with his attitude toward their Republican voting habits. After Hanson spurned Madison's declaration of war on Great Britain in June 1812, asserting "we will never breathe under the dominion, direct or derivative, of Bonaparte," the Republican governor of Maryland, rather than risk bringing Hanson into a civil court on charges of sedition, used his powers as commander in chief of the state militia to have the editor, a lieutenant in the 39th Regiment of the state militia, suspended from his rank for one month, imprisoned, and court martialed. A Baltimore mob took matters into its own hands, attacking and destroying the offices of the *Federal Republican*. Hanson described the episode as "a daring and desperate attempt to intimidate and overawe the minority, to destroy the freedom of speech and of press."[335] This was not a unique fate for a Federalist paper during the flush of patriotic fervor in the first months of the war — mobs drove both the Savannah *American Patriot* and the *Norristown Herald* out of business. In New Jersey, the Federalist editor of the Elizabethtown *Essex Patriot* published a letter he had received: "Your damned tory paper will serve a Baltimore trick if it don't quit printing federal lies about the republicans. If your shop is burned low and your ears cut off 'tis not any more than what you deserve and will get." Five months later the office of the *Essex Patriot* was burned to the ground.[336]

It was Hanson's determination to avoid again being subjected to this fate that culminated in bloodshed. He and his fellow suburbanite Federalists acquired a new office in Baltimore, a fortress-like, three-story brick mansion, stocked it with enough weapons to mount a minor military campaign, and waited for the showdown. The result was tragedy. Federalist shots killed one and wounded several members of the Republican mob that attempted to storm the building. The rioters dispersed but returned in greater numbers, and with a cannon. The commander of the city militia impelled the defenders to surrender. They were led off under guard to the jailhouse where they were incarcerated for their own protection. The mob promptly descended on the undefended newspaper building and leveled it, carting off bricks and lumber.

The next evening, the militia having being dismissed, the mob swarmed over the jailhouse, hauled out those ten of Hanson's men who had been unable to escape, beat most of them senseless (including Hanson and Revolutionary War hero General "Light Horse" Harry Lee), tarred and feathered others, set another man on fire, and killed another Revolutionary War hero, General James M. Lingan.[337] Remarkably, Hanson not only retained control of his paper, continuing to issue the *Federal Republican* throughout the war, but was elected to Congress by grateful Federalists in rural Montgomery and Frederick Counties (in order, it was said, to serve "as a stick jabbed in the eye of Republican Baltimore"), and was later elevated to the Senate.[338]

The Federalists tried hard to fight fire with fire, but their editorial partisans, for all their literary panache and erudition, lacked the common appeal of their Republican rivals.[339] The Federalist ethos was no longer relevant to those citizens who in increasing numbers were reaching out for new homes along the frontier. "Wit and satire should flash like the electrical fire" in the pages of the new Federalist organ, Boston *New England Palladium* founder Fisher Ames asserted. But even while upholding a partisan agenda, he was quick to assure his readers that the Federalist press should remain "fastidiously polite and well-bred. It should whip the Jacobins as a gentleman would a chimney sweeper, at arm's length, and keeping aloof from his soot."[340] The Worcester *Scorpion* made a habit of correcting the grammar of Republican toasts and translation of Latin phrases used in the *National Aegis* while belittling the social status of its editors, "an apothecary, a Cobler and a Stage-Man."[341] Pasley notes the inherent impotence of this failure to cross the class divide:

> Federalist wits filled pamphlets, books, and newspaper back pages with poetry and sketches stuffed with literary allusions and current political references, often so stuffed that they had to be footnoted. While sometimes amusing to the expert reader, these works were like most polite literature in being written for insiders, people who shared the same reference points and would grasp the allusions, puns, and allegories. Young Federalists can be imagined chortling over such material on a slow day at the law office, reaffirming their feelings of superiority, but it is difficult to see how even they could have expected it to change their political fortunes.[342]

In the final analysis, even those opposition editors who inhabited the most rarefied social strata were forced to admit the inescapable reality that America would never again accept Federalist values and hence Federalist rule. "Our fond notions of the superior virtue and information of our countrymen," one correspondent in the *Port Folio* lamented during Jefferson's second term, "we find to be nothing but waking dreams."[343] The situation only worsened as America expanded deeper into the interior of the continent and away from the trade-oriented

Federalist bailiwicks in the major seaports along the coast. Each state that entered the union therefore further diluted Federalist influence, two senators at a time. The new faces on Capitol Hill and in the electoral college — Tennessee, Kentucky, Ohio— represented effectively one party, and hence one-party press states. The immediate frontier beyond the Appalachian mountains opened up to printers, invariably Republican, after 1821, when Samuel Rust patented a less-costly, compact, hand-operated press that could be transported in a horse-drawn wagon and was capable of turning out 250 impressions an hour.[344]

One by one, in despair or resignation, the Federalist presses abandoned the partisan arena in order to concentrate on commerce, science, and the arts, a process Dowling describes as "the Federalist retreat from history." Throughout this long and complex withdrawal Federalism, banished from the civic sphere by a triumphant Jeffersonian ideology, sought an alternative home in what is now dubbed the public sphere, but what the *Port Folio* writers called, in the usual eighteenth-century phrase, the republic of letters.[345]

Fittingly, the last serious challenge to the Virginia Dynasty emerged from within the ranks of the Republican Party when, in 1812, New York City Mayor DeWitt Clinton took on James Madison in America's first wartime presidential election. The Clinton faction introduced a new innovation that would quickly take hold as a standard of future contests: the campaign newspaper. To extend their influence the Clintonians established two new journals outside of New York, the *Pilot* in Boston and the *Whig Chronicle* in Philadelphia. Clinton's chief New York organ, the *Columbian*, helped obtain subscriptions for both of the new papers. The *Pilot* was under the same editorial direction as the *Boston Yankee*, a Republican weekly which in September suddenly switched its support from Madison. Both the *Pilot* and the *Whig Chronicle* disappeared after Clinton's defeat.[346]

By the time Madison made way for Monroe in 1817, the political landscape, and with it the literary environment, had changed dramatically in favor of the Republicans since they first contested a presidential election twenty years earlier. There were only 153 papers in November 1796, 30 to 35 of which were for Jefferson, including eight of the twelve Virginia papers. Four years later, Jefferson's support had increased to 65–70 of the 204 papers then in circulation. By 1808, at the end of the Jefferson's term, his successor, James Madison, could count on the backing of 130–140 out of the 292 papers in circulation. According to *The History of Printing in America*, published by Isaiah Thomas in 1810, it was in that year that the balance of editorial opinion finally shifted in favor of the Republicans, who were endorsed by 159 papers to 157 for the Federalists, with 14 neutral and 29 unidentified. In 1812 a good majority, about 175 out of 330 papers endorsed Madison's reelection. In 1816 barely more than 100 out of 378 papers still stood forlornly by their dying Federalist principles, as Monroe extended the reign of the Republican Virginia Dynasty for another term in office.[347] Even these diehards finally threw in the towel. It was the arch-Federalist Boston *Columbian Centinel* that conceded that President Monroe's well-received swing through New England in 1819 heralded the arrival of an "Era of Good Feelings" free from partisan wrangling.

The newspaper had come of age in America, both encouraging the course of the nation's ever-westward expansion and tagging along in its wake, both feeding off of and contributing to the evolution of partisan government. By the time Monroe settled in to his unopposed second term, the essential qualities that would be the hallmarks of the press during a new era of party politics — the cycle of patronage and partiality — had been well established.

But at what cost? A few months before Jefferson retired from public office he received a letter from 17-year-old John Norvell of Danville, Kentucky, who asked the President how to go about the management of a newspaper in order to best serve the public good. Jefferson's reply reflected just how far the press had fallen in his estimation since the time decades earlier when he had considered a free press more valuable than government itself:

It is a melancholy truth, that a suppression of the press could not more completely deprive the nation of its benefits, than is done by its abandoned prostitution to falsehood. Nothing can now be believed which is seen in a newspaper. Truth itself becomes suspicious by being put into that polluted vehicle....

   I will add, that the man who never looks into a newspaper is better informed than he who reads them; inasmuch as he who knows nothing is nearer to truth then he whose mind is filled with falsehoods and errors. He who reads nothing will still learn the great facts, and the details are all false.[348]

Apparently, young Norvell didn't take this bleak perspective to heart. In fact, his subsequent legacy in print epitomized the career path of the classic partisan newsmonger. In 1817 he acquired the Lexington *Kentucky Gazette*, selling it two years later to buy an interest in the Philadelphia *Franklin Gazette*, where his partner was Richard Bache, son of the Benjamin Franklin Bache of *Aurora* fame. In 1831 Norvell was one of those Democratic editors whom President Jackson was criticized for appointing to postmasterships. Taking up office in Detroit, he remained active in Michigan politics until his death, achieving his apotheosis in representing the state in the U.S. Senate. Norvell's success was a more accurate reflection of the demands of American political culture than Jefferson's gloomy prognostications. The inescapable fact remained that the press was partisan because the electorate preferred it that way.

II

Press, Party and Patronage, 1824–1860

In 1861, just as the nation was undertaking the horrific process of secession and Civil War, William Howard Russell, the famed journalist of the *Times of London* who had practically invented the role of war correspondent during his coverage of the Crimean Campaign, arrived in the United States on assignment to cover the ongoing political crisis. Russell exhibited little respect for the purveyors of the print trade on the western shores of the Atlantic. He wrote of "journals conducted avowedly by men of disgraceful personal character — the be-whipped and be-kicked and unrecognized pariahs of society in New York."[1] He singled out two examples of the breed. The first was the editor of the *New York Herald*: "[James] Gordon Bennett is so palpably a rogue — it comes out so strongly in the air around him, in his eyes & words & smell & voice that one pities the cause which finds in him a protagonist." The second was the editor of the *New York Tribune*: "Horace Greeley is the nastiest form of narrow minded sectarian philanthropy, who would gladly roast all the whites of South Carolina in order that he might satisfy what he supposes is a conscience but which is only an autocratic ambition."[2]

The antebellum American press was considered fair game in the mother country. Charles Dickens, for one, was horrified by the "ribald slander" of the American press, "this monster of depravity."[3] In his *The Life and Adventures of Martin Chuzzlewit* he listed an inventory of the New York newspapers by title: the *Rowdy Journal, Peeper, Family Spy, Keyhole Reporter, Plunderer, Stabber*, and, "the leading journal of the United States," the *Sewer*: "Here's the Sewer's exposure of the Wall Street Gang, and the Sewer's exposure of the Washington Gang, and the Sewer's exclusive account of a flagrant act of dishonesty committed by the Secretary of State when he was eight years old."[4]

But the blackguard editor was something of a stock figure in American novels of the period also. James Fenimore Cooper christened the unscrupulous editor of his 1838 *Homeward Bound* with the significant, if unlikely, name Steadfast Dodge.[5] In John Pendleton Kennedy's 1840 *Quodlibet*, a desperate clique of Quodlibetarian Democrats, having been smote hip and thigh by the Whig *Through Blue Whole Team*, must hire their own journalist for retaliatory purposes. The job applicant is described as "a thin, faded little fellow, whose clothes seemed to be somewhat too large for him. His eye was gray and rather dull, his physiology melancholy, his cheek sunken, his complexion freckled, his coat blue, his buttons dingy, his hair sandy and like untwisted rope. The first glance at the person of this new comer gave every man of the club the assurance that here was an editor indeed." The individual in question assures the committee that failure, rejection, poverty and derision having long since curdled the milk of human kindness in his bosom, he intends to make the Quodlibet *Whole Hog* a monument of partisan rancor.[6] Parodies such as these only ever saw the light of day because they resonated with a public long accustomed, in the words of one contemporary commentator, to an information marketplace in which "too many of our presses are the exclusive property of sects and parties, and their editors but the twilight shadows of bodies without souls."[7]

It is clear that Americans were deeply ambiguous about the role and nature of the press in their political system. However, love or hate the press, none could deny its significance. Whatever Russell's opinion of Greeley, historian James Ford Rhodes says that to read the *Tribune* was to understand the opinions of the nearly two million men who voted for Lincoln in 1860.[8] Congressman (and later Vice President) Schuyler Colfax described the editorial class as "the power that makes Administrations, breaks down & builds up parties, controls or directs public opinion, & in the foreground of the fight, receives all the arrows of the enemy."[9] Colfax was speaking from experience; like many politicians of his day he was able to tout his accomplishments in his own publication, having been a legislative correspondent for the *Indiana State Journal* before purchasing an interest in the *South Bend Free Press*, changing its name in 1845 to the *St. Joseph Valley Register*, the Whig organ of northern Indiana.

The famed French commentator Alexis de Tocqueville remarked in his magisterial study *Democracy in America* that "if there were no newspapers, there would be no common activity."[10] Facilitating the reach of this bustling political milieu to the ever expanding frontiers of the republic was a federal agenda toward information exchange structurally the antithesis of the "taxes on knowledge" model imposed by the governments of Europe.

Postage charged printed material in the antebellum United States was, at most, only 1.5 cents. Letters, by contrast, were charged per page and according to distance; at 25 cents per page, a four-page letter mailed over 450 miles cost one dollar. In effect, cheap newspaper postage was subsidized by letter writers, just as Congress had intended in setting the rates in the Postal Acts of 1792 and 1794. "The generation that drafted the Constitution and the First Amendment," Kielbowicz notes, "adopted below-cost newspaper postage as a means of uniting a fragile nation."[11] As a result, newspapers deluged the mails to the point where the press and the postal service seemed at times indistinguishable (as evidenced to this day by the recurrence of *Post* in newspaper titles). By one estimate, newspapers accounted for no less than 95 percent of the weight of all mail delivered in 1832 while contributing only 15 percent of postal revenue that year.[12]

By 1830, approximately 16 million copies of postage-paying newspapers circulated annually through the mail. For the next fifteen years, until Congress modified rates in 1845, the number of newspapers using the mail grew an average of 2.3 million copies a year. Jacksonville, Illinois, was the largest city in the state in 1831, with perhaps as many as 3,000 residents, but could only support one local newspaper of its own. The citizens compensated by drawing on news sources from other locales; at least 271 residents received 133 different publications—for a total of 486 subscriptions—via the mail.[13]

As cheap as newspaper postage was for individuals, it was cost-free for printers, who enjoyed unlimited exchange privileges. By sending copies of their own publication to other printers, they received a deluge of postage-free papers from all over the U.S. in return. One estimate suggests that printers in the 1840s received an average of approximately 80 exchange newspapers each week, with some printers, particularly in the major cities, receiving many more. Postmaster General Amos Kendall complained to Congress in 1838 of some printers exchanging with up to 600 other newspapers. While these exchanges between printers comprised less than one-fifth of the total number of newspapers handled by the postal system, this network nevertheless formed the backbone of an information system that was truly national in scale. In the age prior to the invention of the telegraph and the emergence of rail travel, even frontier publishers miles away from the nearest navigable water could benefit from the exchange system. In its debut issue in November 1831, the *Sangamon Journal*, for example, featured items culled from the Richmond *Compiler*, *Albany Argus*, *Boston Literary Gazette*, and the *National Intelligencer* in the nation's capital. With this system of exchange in place, events reported in any given locale made their way in short order into an exponentially growing number of newspapers.[14]

"In the days before the telegraph, newspaper exchanges provided the most regular form of political communication nationwide," Baldasty concludes.[15] Using this network it was the editors who built and defined the great parties that emerged out of the Era of Good Feelings, first the Democratic Party of Andrew Jackson, then its Whig and Republican rivals. "The highly political Jacksonian era represents what was probably the high tide of the partisan press," Baldasty says.[16] According to Fish, during the age of Jackson, "newspaper men were the most important single class of party workers."[17] Baldasty agrees that "on the local level, even in small rural counties, editors were among the party's elite, part of the party's core."[18]

The press helped redefine the role and image of the politician as the country made the transition from elite to mass political participation. Robertson makes the point that "where Jacksonian rhetoric differed from Jeffersonian language was in its intimacy and its accessibility. Office seekers acquired nicknames; hack writers scrutinized lives for telling facts (or fictions) about politicians."[19] This process achieved its apotheosis in the "log cabin" mythos of 1840.

A.W. Thayer, editor of the Haverhill, Massachusetts, *Essex Gazette*, maintained that an editor was "a sentinel placed in his country's watch tower."[20] Thayer might have been the very person one contemporary had in mind when he complained of "that rabid arrogance which characterizes all small editors who have learned from the twaddle about 'the Press' to regard themselves as divinely-appointed potentates."[21] But that was how the system worked.

To launch a newspaper was for a party to stake a claim to the town in which it was published. If the enemy already distributed a publication in that town, then battle was joined. In New York State, for example, 65 percent of county seats had rival newspapers by 1830. If a party did not possess a newspaper in that town, then for all intents and purposes it did not exist in that town, if for no other reason than because of the mechanics of the electoral process at the time. An antebellum American did not just saunter up to the polling place on election day and expect to be handed a ballot. He had to bring his own ballot, and the easiest source to secure one of these was in the same place where he got his daily news; at the masthead on the editorial page of his partisan paper.

Although there is no reason to doubt that the partisan attachments of the nation's editors were genuine, the foundation of the entire system rested on cold, hard cash. The editor of the *Army and Navy Chronicle*, published in Washington, noted on July 30, 1840, "Such a thing as absolute independence in the press—an independence of party trammels ... is not and cannot be endured in this country. Every publication must espouse some cause, if the proprietors hope to command success."[22] That same year the best advice Horace Greeley, himself still finding his way in the big leagues of the newspaper game, could give Henry J. Raymond, eleven years before Raymond founded the *New York Times*, was to "attach yourself to some distinct interest in such a manner as to secure its support."[23] Greeley received a sharp lesson in the limits of editorial independence the following year upon the launch of his *New York Tribune*:

My leading idea was the establishment of a journal removed alike from servile partisanship on the one hand and from gagged, mincing neutrality on the other. Party spirit is so fierce and intolerant in this country that the editor of a non-partisan sheet is restrained from saying what he thinks and feels on the most vital, imminent topics; while, on the other hand, a Democratic [or] Whig ... journal is generally expected to praise or blame, like or dislike, eulogize or condemn, in precise accordance with he views and interests of its party. I believed there was a happy medium between these extremes—a position from which a journalist might openly and heartily advocate the principles and commend the measures of that party to which his convictions allied him, yet frankly dissent from its course on a particular question, and even denounce its candidates if they were shown to be deficient in capacity or (far worse) in integrity.

Greeley's assertion of independence notwithstanding, he expected support from the Whigs and sought it less than a month after the paper debuted, writing to party boss Thurlow Weed on May 10: "Thus far I have not had $30 of advertising from Whigs ... though I expected more. I don't want to beg any of it, but I shall have a hard fight to live through the summer without some help."[24]

The cyclical nature of the system was played out in every small town in America, where the newspapers could not survive without party patronage and the parties could not flourish without the support of a local newspaper, a fact recognized by a resolution of the Indiana State Democratic Convention of 1840 that "it is [incumbent upon] our cause to give a generous support to those Democratic papers which ably and honestly defend our principles; and that he who takes such a newspaper and does not pay for it assists to break it down and therefore plays into the hands of our opponents."[25]

Once a publisher had established a reputation, whether on a local or national level, then the tables turned somewhat, and he could become more important to the party, at least in the short term, than the party was to him. Retaining the loyalty of a particularly influential publication could be of inestimable value to the party concerned. When the ailing John Brazier Davis, editor of the *Boston Patriot*, wanted to sell his paper, Massachusetts Republicans feared the publication might fall into the wrong hands. One of Daniel Webster's friends warned the senator: "I have no hesitation in saying that the Boston *Patriot* is the most powerful engine which can be used to direct the politics of Massachusetts, New Hampshire, Maine and Vermont, and it is a most powerful influence in many other states. Hundreds and thousands of Old Republicans, as they are styled, read this as Holy Writ and they read nothing else.... If our friends mean to sustain themselves in New England, and they ought not to suffer the present opportunity to possess this press escape them."[26]

When Tennessee senator Andrew Johnson broke with the editor of the established Democratic organ in Knoxville, he was advised to launch a rival publication as soon as possible: "The present editor must be *killed off*, or else his *constant harping* ... must sooner or later ... poison the public mind against you."[27]

No quarter was asked and none given in the editorial exchanges of the period; the "whole-hog press" of antebellum America was taught, as Hezekiah Niles said, "to wheel and fire at word of command."[28] In a sample broadside from the 1840 campaign, the nominee of the Whig Party, William Henry Harrison, was identified in the pages of one Democratic newspaper as "always a coward, always a foe to the people, always ... rapacious ... and as infamous as [Benedict] Arnold. We know not whether to scorn his imbecility, to hate his principles, or wonder at his impudent effrontery." Conversely, a single paragraph on the Democratic Party's candidate President Martin Van Buren in the Whig press included the words "profligate," "dangerous," "demagogue," "corrupt," "degrade," "pervert," "prostitute," and "debauch."[29] Given that these were the terms with which editors habitually critiqued the ideology, style, and veracity of their peers, it is little wonder that tempers frayed. New York diarist Philip Hone recorded a typical incident in 1831: "While I was shaving this morning I witnessed from the front windows an encounter in the streets between William Cullen Bryant, one of the editors of the Evening Post, and Wm L Stone, editor of the Commercial Advertiser. The former commenced the attack by striking Stone over the head with a cowskin; after a few blows the parties closed and the whip was wrested from Bryant and carried off by Stone."[30]

The laws of external diversity applied to the entire spectrum of the American media milieu, and objectivity under these circumstances was regarded as not merely utopian but positively pernicious. As Jackson loyalist Isaac Hill put it, "In the first place, we view the idea of an impartial paper as preposterous; for there is no man in his sense who does not view one of the great parties ... as being essentially right, and the other wrong; and the man thus convinced of right and wrong would, in our opinion, be equally guilty for treating both parties alike with him who advocated a bad cause knowing it to be such."[31]

The lines of the second party system had firmed up

No newspaper did more to condition the north against slavery than Horace Greeley's *New York Tribune*. Unfortunately, Greeley could never be content with influence, and over the course of more than thirty years made a series of increasingly quixotic tilts at power, the last and grandest of which, a tilt at the presidency itself, cost him control of his beloved newspaper, his sanity, his health, and ultimately his life (courtesy of Library of Congress).

by 1840, and newspapers were the linchpin of the whole system, "the fortresses of party," as Silbey describes them. The mission of those editors who had emerged from the 1830s determined, for whatever reason, that to repudiate the Democratic Party that represented Jackson's legacy was "to harmonize the actions, and promote the efficient organization of the Whig party, as well as to diffuse its principles and arouse its spirit and enthusiasm."

Each editor was aware that his paper's "true office [was] to impersonate its party and give it a language, harmonious, life-like and truthful," to "spread ... the principles and build up the strength of the party." The last issue of one Democratic campaign newspaper, the *Republican Sentinel*, signed off on October 30, 1844, with the remark: "If we have succeeded in turning one repentant Whig from the error of his ways, or in preventing a single Democrat from straying to the camp of Henry Clay, we are content with having labored for the good cause."[32] The Whig partisans in the press, of course, were no less shameless in employing the same propagandistic means to the opposite end.

Two developments in the antebellum era were responsible for the first cracks in the façade of the party-media patron-client relationship. The first was the synergistic elimination of suffrage restrictions and revival of partisan attachment that ensued over the decade following the collapse of the Era of Good Feelings. In 1820, nine of the twenty-four states still chose their electors in the state legislatures. By 1832, only South Carolina still selected its electors in this manner, and of the other twenty-three states, only Rhode Island, Virginia, and Louisiana continued to restrict the suffrage with property or taxation qualifications. As the era of the second party system dawned, the vast majority of the states conducted elections on the basis of effectively universal white male suffrage.[33]

In an environment where newspaper circulation was intimately bound up with partisan mobilization, the inevitable corollary of any broadening of the pool of potential voters would be a corresponding increase in the size of the media market. Many of the new constituencies, such as the Anti-Masons, the trade unions, and the abolitionists, dissatisfied with the lack of receptivity on the part of the established party-press system to their causes, spun out their own social networks and corresponding advocacy literature. An unprecedented window of opportunity had opened for a new breed of publication primed to take advantage of the fragmented market environment.

The first of this new breed appeared on September 3, 1833, when the New York *Sun,* the first of the so-called penny papers, made its debut. Edited by Benjamin Day, its slogan — "It Shines for All" — reflected Day's determination to both undersell and outperform his more insular, niche-oriented rivals. According to Ward, the emergence of the penny press marked the beginning of a paradigm shift within the journalistic profession, during which the previously dominant "ethics of persuasion," which sought to tell people what they ought to believe, gave way before an "ethics of popularity," which used a more accessible style to tell readers what they wanted to know.[34] The gossip, scandal-mongering, and outright frauds with which these proto-tabloids went to press on a daily basis outraged established editorial opinion, but their sales and hence the advertising revenue they generated enabled them to operate independently of either party.[35]

This is not to suggest that a new dawn of objectivity had been heralded by the likes of Day and James Gordon Bennett. Far from it; the penny papers rivaled even the most dedicated of the captive partisan papers in the extent of their commitment to individual causes and candidates. The crucial difference lay in the fact that a penny paper could choose its battles based solely on the idiosyncratic whim of its proprietor. A business model incorporating the independence of action afforded by financial self-reliance, the critical first step towards objectivity, had been established. "Avoiding the dirt of party politics, we shall yet freely and candidly express our opinion on every public question and public man," Bennett declared on August 31, 1835. He explicitly established the link between the profit motive and the *Herald's* eschewing a partisan identity, noting that commercial interests "are beginning to find out that a brief advertisement in our sheet is seen and read by six times as many as it would be in the dull prairies of the Courier & Enquirer."[36]

The socio-political implications of targeting the mass market for the first time, transforming the newspaper industry from an elite medium to a popular one, were noted, in terms that applied equally to either side of the Atlantic, by Edward Bulwer Lytton in *England and the English*, published in 1833 during a similar conjunction of the extension of the franchise, following the passage of the Reform Act in 1832, and the emergence of a popular press: "If the sevenpenny paper were ... to sell for twopence what would be the result? Why ... a new majority must be consulted, the sentiments and desires of poorer men than at present must be addressed; and thus a new influence of opinion would be brought to bear on our social relations and our legislative enactments."[37]

In America, the transition to the new era was signaled on the mastheads of the nation's newspapers, as even those publications committed to representing the interests of financial and industrial elites adapted to the literary tastes and political aspirations of the newly enfranchised mass market. More than half of all newspapers published weekly or more frequently in New York, Boston, Baltimore, Philadelphia, Washington, Charleston, and New Orleans in 1820 had the words "advertiser," "commercial," or "mercantile" in their titles. After 1830, few newspapers were founded with such names; instead they flaunted titles expressing a form of agency, such as "herald" and "tribune."[38]

The second challenge to the essentially provincial scope of the antebellum press was presented by a revolutionary breakthrough in communications technology. Not until the rise of the Internet would a technological innovation have a more profound impact on the newspaper industry than the telegraph. A $30,000 congressional appropriation enabled Samuel Morse to run wires between Washington and Baltimore for a long-distance test of his invention, which paid off in dramatic fashion on May 24, 1844, as Senators and Representatives gathered in the Capitol to witness Morse send the first ceremonial message: "What hath God wrought?" Of more practical interest to the assembled politicians were the reports wired back from Baltimore of the Democratic convention then meeting. When the telegraph announced the nomination of New York's Senator Silas Wright for vice president, Wright declined the honor, also via telegraph, and did so repeatedly until the delegates finally got the message. At a stroke, the viability of the new invention had been demonstrated in the timeliest fashion. The tyranny of distance was overthrown, and newspapermen were among the first to appreciate the practical applications. "There is just one remedy for the ills that journals are heir to," Horace Greeley intoned, "*telegraphic competition. I mean to have it.*"[39] So did James Gordon Bennett, who waxed lyrical in a mid–1844 editorial: "Once this extraordinary invention shall have been fully applied all over the country, the wonderful spectacle will be presented, of a vast continent, as consolidated and united, and possessed as much, nay, in greater degree, of the means of rapid communication as the city of New York. It will tend to bind together with electric forces the whole Republic, and by its single agency do more to guide against disunion, and blend into one homogenous mass, the whole population of the Republic, than all that the most experienced, the most sagacious, and the most patriotic government, could accomplish."[40]

Regular use of the telegraph by the press began on April 11, 1846, when the Philadelphia *Public Ledger* started moving congressional reports by a combination rail and telegraph system, enabling it to publish that part of the previous day's floor activities which had taken place up to 3 o'clock in the afternoon. On June 6, the gap between the telegraphic lines linking Washington to Baltimore, and Philadelphia to New York, was closed, enabling reporters to send mass-market accounts of the congressional agenda to publications in all four cities. Boston was integrated into the network in 1847, Chicago and New Orleans after 1852. For the first time the entire country was being integrated into a single national media market.

An important step in this process took place in early 1849 when Bennett's *New York Herald*, along with the *Sun*, the *Tribune*, the *Courier and Enquirer*, the *Journal of Commerce*, and the *Express*, organized a partnership, the New York Associated Press, to lease a telegraph line for their exclusive use, and to charter a steamer from Halifax, where transatlantic ships stopped before proceeding to Boston and New York. The same news would be delivered to the six member papers at the same time, and they would share the costs evenly. The benefits were manifest. "By means of the electric telegraph the local advantages of the Washington papers are transferred to this metropolis," Bennett gloated in 1849. No longer would his reporters be forced to accept the "wages of corruption from Congress" in the form of patronage, like that "superannuated pensioner of the Whig party, the *Intelligencer*."[41]

This unshackling of political reporting from consolidated elite interpretation would have significant implications for the prevailing norms of governance. Prior to the advent of the telegraph, America was, in the words of Robert Wiebe, a society of isolated, insular "island communities." Slow and sporadic networks of communication severely restricted the interaction among these islands and dispersed the power to form opinion and enact public policy.[42] According to Harold Innis, when the monopoly over knowledge previously maintained at the geopolitical core of the nation was abolished, central authority itself was threatened. By "annihilating time and space," the telegraph crippled the assumed prerogative of a handful of kingpins in the House and Senate to set the political agenda. Accordingly, "power shifted from Washington and issues were no longer settled in Congress." It was for this reason that the rival yet complementary tendencies of abolitionism and secessionism proved impossible to resolve via the established mechanism of legislative compromise.[43]

Speaking for many of his generation, Bennett had anticipated that the revolution in communications technology would serve not merely his own pecuniary interests but as a means to reconcile increasing sectional tensions. In his view, the telegraph would have "a prodigious, cohesive, and conservative influence on the republic. No better bond of union for a great confederacy of states could have been devised.... The whole nation is impressed with the same idea at the same moment. One feeling and one impulse are thus created and maintained from the centre of the land to its utmost extremities.[44]

Ironically, this trend toward standardization of the news contributed to the fragmentation, rather than the consolidation, of national identity. The telegraph significantly accelerated the demise of a quirk essential to the stability of the fragile antebellum two-party system. By as early as the mid–1840s it had become exceedingly difficult to harmonize the interests of both sections in a single party. In order for a party to remain viable both north and south of the Mason-Dixon Line, it was vital that its candidates for elective national office tailor their rhetoric to match the demands of either section according to circumstances. The new era of rapid and intensive national circulation of speeches and statements meant that it was no longer possible for a candidate to say different things to different constituencies. The telegraph therefore imposed *consistency* for the first time on American political debate precisely at the moment that the sections had arrived at a position of mutual *incompatibility* in terms of their interests.

None of Bennett's grand expectations for the telegraph were realized, though no-one tried harder than he did to realize its potential for sectional reconciliation. Southern interests had no more loyal friend in the north than Bennett, and by 1860 his *Herald* was the only New York paper still circulating freely in what would become the Confederacy. But far from being "consolidated and united," the nation was fracturing into ever more independently homogeneous northern and southern sections. In the twilight of his presidency, and on the brink of civil war, James Buchanan would blame the new medium for his woes, and those of America: "I do not know whether the great commercial and social advantages of the telegraph are not counterbalanced by its political evils. The public mind throughout the interior is kept in a constant state of excitement by what are called 'telegrams.' They are short and spicy and can easily be inserted in the country newspapers. In the city journals they can be contradicted the next day; but the case is different throughout the country. Many of them are sheer falsehoods, especially those concerning myself."[45]

Even after stripping aside the evident self-pity in these remarks, the fact remains that new communications technologies that facilitate the flow of information between individuals and social networks do not necessarily result in the homogenization of the cultural milieu in which they operate, least of all in a negotiated geographical construct like the United States. The power to standardize the news inherent in the telegraph ultimately failed to deflect the sociopolitical identity-based mobilization of southern interests that culminated in secession and the Confederacy, and persisted for generations, even after Reconstruction. Network radio and then television would finally succeed in standardizing the news across all sections of the country, only for their hegemony to be broken by talk radio, cable television, and the Internet, heralding the emergence of a new era of balkanized, identity-based news.[46]

Four-Cornered Fight

When the Virginia dynasty finally expired, three members of the cabinet — Secretary of State John Quincy Adams, Secretary of the Treasury William Crawford, and Secretary of War John C. Calhoun — all of them ostensibly good Republicans, entered the lists intent on succeeding Monroe in the election of 1824. All of these would-be Diadochi understood the rules of the political game, and each maintained a loyal mouthpiece in the Washington press as the cornerstone of their campaign.[47] As Adams noted, "in our presidential canvassing an editor has become as essential an appendage to a candidate as in the days of chivalry a 'squire' was to a knight."[48] There was little chivalrous about these new squires of the pen in this modern era, however, where money, not loyalty, represented the bottom line. After Adams pulled State Department patronage from the Washington *National Intelligencer*, that paper formally threw its support to Crawford in June 1824.[49]

Crawford was also backed by the *Washington Gazette*, founded in 1813 by Jonathan Elliot, who had supported him for president in 1816. Since that time Crawford had patronized the *Gazette* with enough Treasury Department printing to enable it to become a daily in 1817. Elliot had also done some printing for Adams, but after losing the State Department's contract for printing the census, Elliot pledged his paper to Crawford's campaign to succeed Monroe, on the grounds that "he could not afford to be [Adams's] friend for nothing."[50] Adams sourly concluded that the masthead on the editorial page of the *Gazette*, "Democracy, Economy, and Reform," meant "Democracy to be used against me, Economy against Calhoun, and Reform against both." As the pressure mounted, he would rail against the publication's "ruffian-like manner," its propagating "scurrility and billingsgate" and being filled with the "foulest abuse" (such as labeling the secretary of state "a mere man of books ... by no means competent to deal with the able, practical and subtle ministers of the European powers").[51] Adams also noted with alarm the literary phalanx lining up behind Crawford outside of the nation's capital as early as September 1822:

> The *National Intelligencer* is secured to him by the belief of the editors that he will be the successful candidate, and by their dependence upon the printing of Congress; the *Richmond Enquirer* because he is a Virginian and slave-holder; the *National Advocate* of New York, through Van Buren [and also through him, the *Albany Argus*], the *Boston Statesman* and *Portland Argus* through William King; the *Democratic Press*, of Philadelphia, because I transferred the printing of the laws from that paper to the *Franklin Gazette*; and several other presses in various parts of the Union upon principles alike selfish and sordid.

When not engaged in disparaging the efforts of Calhoun and Crawford to raise their profiles in the nation's presses, Adams fretted about his prospect of being squeezed between them; "these engines will counteract each other, but I shall be a mark for both sides, and, having no counter-fire upon them, what can happen but that I must fall?"[52]

Adams was the beneficiary of the sudden collapse of one of his rivals. Calhoun had an understanding with the Washington *Republican and Congressional Examiner*, which started publication in August 1823, and whose editor, Thomas L. McKenney, a former Superintendent of Indian Affairs, was a subordinate in Calhoun's War Department. "I think it originated in the War Office and will be Mr. Calhoun's official gazette as long as it lasts," John Quincy Adams noted in his diary.[53]

That was not long. McKenney was under investigation for maladministration in his former office, and when Calhoun decided to drop out of the presidential race in order to focus on the vice presidency, his paper was sold in July 1824 to the Washington *National Journal*, which Adams had backed with printing orders and other favors from the State Department since it had been founded as a semi-weekly by Peter Force, a former member of the Washington City Council, in November 1823. The *National Journal* suddenly found the Adams/Calhoun ticket the most convivial imaginable. With the additional patronage emanating from the War Department, the *National Journal* was able to go to press daily. The editors of the *Intelligencer* were only "sorry to say, to the last moment, [the *Examiner*] had not the least symptom of penance for its Manifold transgressions."[54]

Adams was endorsed outside Washington by the Philadelphia *National Gazette*, Richmond *Constitutional Whig*, and *Niles's Weekly Register* of Baltimore.[55] But the secretary of state also worked quietly to use the powers vested in his office to tilt the playing field in his favor. On October 23, 1824, the editor of the pro–Jackson Trenton *Emporium* publicly raised this as an issue:

> LET IT BE KNOWN—for, peradventure it is not known, by every body, that John Quincy Adams, *has in his pay*, no less than seventy-two *printers of Newspapers*, in these United States. Do you ask how this is possible? It is a matter of fact — and may in a great measure account for the number of papers we find enlisted in his cause in the country. Mr. Adams as Secretary of State, appoints three printers in each state to publish the Laws of the Union, for publishing which they are severally paid out of the National Treasury, generally in a pretty round sum.[56]

The outsiders in the race — Speaker of the House Henry Clay and senator and former general Andrew Jackson — had to rely on local papers to make their case. "This is one advantage at least you enjoy by having no press — you certainly provoke no hostility," Clay backer Senator Josiah Johnston of Louisiana wrote him in August 1824, trying to make the best of a bad situation. But he was very aware of the downside: "It is impossible to present your claims or your chances before the people — or to counteract the united efforts of all parties to withdraw you from the contest." Johnston did what he could to remedy the situation and was able to inform Clay that the Philadelphia *Aurora* had agreed to come out in his favor in September. When Johnston heard that the *Patriot* could "be had in New York for some money," he raced to the city "to accomplish this object — it is in vain to strive against the united influence of the press without one." And he succeeded in his mission. "I have made a running visit to New York," he told Clay. "Secured the *Patriot* & returned this morning. It will at least have the effect to disseminate the truth."[57]

Other Clay backers included the *Argus of Western America* in Kentucky, and the *Liberty Hall* and the *Cincinnati Gazette* in Ohio. Jackson had the strong support of the *Columbian Observer* and *Franklin Gazette* in Pennsylvania and the *Columbian Observer* and *National Republican* in Ohio.

The Philadelphia *Aurora* first raised the possibility of a Jackson presidential bid in January 1822. The venerable newspaper expired soon thereafter, but its niche was quickly filled by the *Columbian Observer*, edited by Stephen Simpson, a former assistant of Duane's, who was joined by a small network of like-minded newspapers around the state. This editorial support swung Pennsylvania's 1823 state convention, called by Duane's political rivals in order to launch the campaign of Calhoun, behind Jackson, making him a national contender and inducing Calhoun to drop out of the race and focus on the vice presidency.[58]

On behalf of its respective heroes, the press was entirely uncompromising towards its rivals. All the candidates were fair game, as were their wives. The *Raleigh Register*, which on October 12, 1824 had summarized Andrew Jackson's career as "a disgusting detail of squabbling and quarreling — of pistolings dirkings & brickbattings and other actions reconcilable neither to regulations nor morals," took after Rachel Jackson seven days before North Carolina voted: "I make a solemn appeal to the reflecting part of the community, and beg of them to think and ponder well before they place their tickets in the box, how they can justify it to themselves and to posterity to place such a woman as Mrs. Jackson at the head of the female society of the U. States."[59]

It was a race like no other. Jackson finished with the most electoral votes (99), followed by Adams (84), Crawford (41) and Clay (37). No candidate having a majority, the election went to Congress for a decision. Under the Constitution, the House was only entitled to choose from among the top three contenders, so Clay was forced to drop out. The Kentucky Colt then threw his support behind Adams, giving him the bare majority of state delegations needed to secure the Presidency. Adams then nominated Clay for the role of Secretary of State.

When Adams was finally confirmed as president, the Philadelphia *Christian Gazette and Youth's Herald* concluded that "the Presidential contest having been closed, it is sincerely to be desired that the disagreements and broils, the vituperations and accusations which it has occasioned may be heard of no more. The notoriety, frequency and apparent malignity of these have been disgraceful to a nation which claims to be civilized and free."[60] It was to be a forlorn hope. Supporters of Jackson immediately cried foul, accusing the Adams-Clay duumvirate of conducting a "corrupt bargain" to steal the White House from its rightful occupant. "Expired at Washington," declaimed one Jacksonian newspaper, "on the ninth of February, of poison administered by the assassin Hands of John Quincy Adams, the usurper, and Henry Clay, the virtue, liberty and independence of the United States."[61] Fired by a burning passion to correct this injustice, the Jacksonians launched a concerted multimedia campaign to undermine the Adams presidency from the moment he took office, in preparation for a rematch in 1828. In an entirely unforeseen corollary, from this personal crusade would emerge the Democratic Party.

Adams was fatally slow in recognizing the danger, and proved dilatory in deploying the primary asset at the disposal of the incumbent, his power to dispense patronage. Edward Everett, a member of Congress representing Massachusetts, warned the president: "If the Administration then discard the principle of bestowing the patronage on their political friends, they turn against themselves not only the expectants but the incumbents.... Our present chief magistrate made the experiment of the higher principle of exclusive regard to merit; and what has been his reward? A most furious opposition, rallied on the charge of corrupt distribution of office, and the open or secret hostility of three-fourths of the officeholders of the union."

"For an Administration then to bestow its patronage without distinction of party is to court its own destruction," Everett concluded.[62] But while his friends fretted that Adams was failing to properly mobilize the press resources at his disposal, his enemies were making an issue of those instances in which the administration was prepared to subsidize its allies in print. On January 24, 1827, nearly a year after North Carolina Senator Nathaniel Macon called for a Senate investigation of executive patronage, the *United States Telegraph* pointed out that the evils of a patronized press continued to flourish: "We, who are in the daily habit of close observation, can see the purposes for which the Democratic Press, the Richmond Whig, the New Hampshire Journal, the Charleston Gazette, and the Frankfort Commentator, have been put under the pay of the State Department. Regularly organized, and knowing the purpose of their master, they originate and circulate the grossest falsehoods and exaggerations which, by the combined operations, is thus thrown into every part of the Union by a simultaneous republication into all the affiliated presses."[63]

In February, in response to the withdrawal of patronage from the *National Intelligencer* and the *Argus of Western America*, a resolution was presented to the House asking Clay to supply not only a list of those papers receiving patronage, but also the reason why printing contracts were withdrawn from papers. Critics charged that the removal of competent printers was "much more effectual and much more dangerous than the Alien and Sedition laws," because patronage operated in such a way that few were cognizant of its significance. Representative James Hamilton of South Carolina accused Clay and Adams of establishing a "Government Press" that was more alarming to liberty than a standing army of 6,000 men. In the Spring of 1828 the House again tried to bridle the administration's dispensation of patronage, accusing Clay of enforcing the "pecuniary censorship of the press," and proposing the abolition of executive privilege altogether, because it was worse than any "Star Chamber code of pains and penalties."[64] No action was taken on any of these measures, leaving the system of patronage firmly in place when it was inherited by the incoming Jacksonians after the election of 1828. With the apparatus in their hands, any scruples they may have retained about the threat it posed to the liberties of the press simply melted away like April snowflakes.

But that was all in the future. Long before the anticipated Adams-Jackson rematch took place, the nation's press would have to adapt to the savage political infighting that characterized the period from 1825 to 1829, a term marked by the most intense partisan competition since the 1797–1801 presidency of John Adams. That meant choosing sides. While some would shy away from or stumble while making that decision, others would emerge whose particular talents were well suited for the new era.

The big loser among the Washington press from the four-cornered presidential dogfight of 1824 was Crawford's paper, the *Gazette*. In March 1825, after failing to curry favor from either Jackson or Adams, Elliot sold the paper to John S. Meehan, who renamed it the *United States Telegraph*. Less than a year later, on February 6, 1826, the paper was again sold, on this occasion to a character from the frontier whose express intent was to use his influence in print as leverage in gaining access to the corridors of power. Duff Green would succeed, briefly, in fulfilling this vision, in the process setting a new precedent for the relationship between administration and court paper. According to Belko, "The *Telegraph* was more than *the* partisan propaganda machine for the Jackson campaign. It was also *the* foremost disseminator of Jacksonian ideology."[65] But from such heights his fall was equally dramatic, definitive proof that in a world centered on patronage, independence of mind, far from being an asset, was a potentially fatal liability.

Kentucky-born-and-bred, Green had shifted to the Missouri territory in 1816 where he rapidly made good, being appointed a brigadier general of the militia, becoming one of the territory's largest landowners, a recognized frontier lawyer, a member of the merchant community in St. Louis, a member of Missouri's Constitutional Committee and later elected to first the lower and then the upper house of the state legislature.

Green's preferred candidate to succeed Monroe in the White House was John C. Calhoun, on purely ideological grounds. Green's brother-in-law, Illinois senator Ninian Edwards, provided the initial contact between Green and Calhoun in the summer of 1823. The meeting went well, Calhoun writing to Edwards that Green was "intelligent and decisive, and must, in time, become important in the West."[66] In December 1823, Green purchased the *St. Louis Enquirer* with a loan of a thousand dollars to use as a campaign vehicle, initially for Calhoun, and then, after the South Carolinian withdrew from the race, for Andrew Jackson.[67]

In Washington on business shortly after the election, Green became "personally acquainted" with Jackson. On his return trip to St. Louis, he traveled in the company of Old Hickory as far as Louisville, Kentucky, where Jackson, Green later recalled, "then urged me to remove to Washington and take charge of a paper opposed to the reelection of Mr. Adams." In September 1825, Calhoun, who was already looking to abandon the Adams-helmed ship of state, wrote to Samuel D. Ingham, endorsing Green as editor for the proposed Jacksonian newspaper. "I think with you as to ... Green's qualifications," Calhoun asserted, "and I have no doubt, that he ought to be encouraged. I will cheerfully do all in my power."[68]

In May 1826, Green succeeded Meehan as editor of the *Telegraph*. He was able to take full financial control of the paper the following month, after Senator John Eaton of

The political eccentricity of Duff Green is hinted at in this formal portrait. He was one of the leading propagandists for Andrew Jackson during the campaign of 1828, but his too fervent support for Vice President John C. Calhoun led to his *Telegraph*'s being toppled from the exalted role of administration mouthpiece by Amos Kendall's *Globe* during Old Hickory's first term (courtesy of Library of Congress).

Tennessee, Jackson's close friend and soon to be his beleaguered Secretary of War, endorsed a loan for Green in the amount of three thousand dollars. In one of Jackson's memorandums, Old Hickory listed nine individuals who had pledged a total of two thousand dollars to cover Eaton. These included South Carolina Congressman James Hamilton, Jr. ($300); Virginia Congressman John S. Barbour ($300); Pennsylvania Congressman Samuel D. Ingham,

Jackson's first secretary of the Treasury ($150); Tennessee Congressman James K. Polk, a future Speaker of the House and President ($100); and Senator John Branch of North Carolina, Jackson's first secretary of the navy, who chipped in another $300.[69]

Green dedicated the *Telegraph* to proving that the Adams administration was one of "bargain, intrigue and corruption." In characterizing the leading lights of the administration he made reference to the "affected airs" of "King John II" and labeled Clay an "arch intriguant" in the Burr conspiracy and as such a "traitor to his country."[70] In the poisonous political atmosphere of the day, Adams was able to confirm the disloyalty of his Vice President when he detected in Green's syntax a "sample of bad English peculiar to Calhoun."[71] Whatever the source of his prose, one of Green's primary avenues of attack against the Adams administration was its patronage of the media. On February 7, 1826, he wrote:

> We refer to that which operates on the press, and which tends to convert this sentinel of freedom into a spy of power ... it is in vain to talk of a free press, when the favor of power is essential to the support of editors, and the money of the people, by passing through the hands of the Executive, is made to operate as a bribe against liberty. It is a most solemn truth, and should be deeply impressed on every mind, that if liberty shall ever expire in our country, it will die of the poisonous draught of corrupt patronage.[72]

This was a typical response during the era of the kept press from those editors on the outside looking in; once Green gained access to those sources of patronage his scruples melted away. When the *National Journal* displaced the *National Intelligencer* as the quasi-official paper of the Adams administration, it secured the printing privileges for the executive branch but not those for Congress. Jackson's supporters chose to make a fight on this issue on behalf of the *Telegraph*, and the struggle was far from being exclusively metaphorical. Green accused Edward Sparhawk, a reporter for the *National Intelligencer*, of willfully and maliciously misinterpreting the *Telegraph's* report of a John Randolph speech on slavery, and warned him not to repeat the offense. When Sparhawk proceeded to do just that, Green attacked him in the rooms of the Senate Committee on Claims on January 25, 1828. Sparhawk charged that Green, "armed with a bludgeon," had pulled his hair and gouged his eyes. Green denied the charge of gouging, but boasted that Sparhawk's "nose was wrung, and his ears, both of them, pulled." Green maintained that he "had no intention to offer to Mr. Sparhawk any other injury"; his sole object being "not to hurt, but to disgrace him."[73]

The *National Intelligencer* retained enough support in the House of Representatives of the outgoing Nineteenth Congress to get reelected by that body as its printer in the spring of 1827 for another two-year term, but when the next Congress convened in December, Green was duly elected printer to the Senate by a vote of 25 to 19.[74] In addition to representing one of the earliest official divisions in the Senate between Jacksonians and pro–Adams National Republicans, the outcome of the struggle represented the first instance of a change of printer resulting from a change of party dominance, and it would be far from the last. "The consideration was not that the new printer was better than the old, but that he had a newspaper operating in the interest of the new majority, deserving the kind of support that would enable his paper to be effective," Smith says. "This was an example of the new trinity of printing, politics and patronage."[75]

Adams was losing critical editorial support to Jackson, both through overt and covert means. Postmaster General John McLean was also quietly subsidizing the *Telegraph* with favors. "I am the servant of the people," he sanctimoniously wrote Jackson, "not of the administration. The patronage placed in my hands is to be used for the public benefit."[76] Adams, later meditating on his defeat, recorded in his memoirs that "some think I have suffered for not turning my enemies out of office, particularly the Postmaster General."[77]

Jackson won an election in 1828 that Hezekiah Niles, editor from 1805 to 1811 of the *Baltimore Evening Post* prior to founding the influential *Niles' Weekly Register,* called "the most rude and ruthless" in the short political history of the young nation up to that time. It was "derogatory to our country, and detrimental to its free institutions and the rights of suffrage, with a more general grossness of assault upon distinguished individuals" than he had witnessed even during the bitter last years of Federalist power.[78] "If the hundredth part of the accusations against public characters is true," Niles observed, "they should all be in jail."[79]

"There can be no question that this election splattered more filth in more different directions and upon more innocent people than any other in American history," Robert Remini agrees. "No one was spared, not the candidates, not their wives, not their friends and supporters."[80] Claude Bowers is another to argue that the election of 1828 unleashed "the most scurrilous campaign of vilification the country had known."[81] In addition to the residue of bitterness generated by the contested outcome to the previous election, the savage partisan intensity witnessed during the campaign of 1828 was at least in part owed to the striking uniformity and regularity of the newspapers arrayed on one side or the other, with a degree of coordination and determination that surpassed even the Republican onslaught against the first President Adams during the campaign of 1800. "Never before had the press been as well organized and as fully used in a presidential election as in the one of 1828," Smith notes. "There were few, if any, independent papers. Printers became partisans and marshaled their type like soldiers to save their country from fancied political danger. Campaign managers begged, bought or otherwise enlisted editors in their cause."[82]

Partisan expectations for the political role of the editor were also evolving. "Until Jackson, political party organization had been so weak that newspapers were a prime element in the ability of a candidate to function," Tebbel and Watts explain.[83] Nearly every candidate had his own newspaper, with its loyal editor, whether he had any organization behind him or not. Although still expected to fulfill this role, editors the length and breadth of the country now began to get personally involved in the emergence of what became the Democratic Party under Jackson.

A key player in this process was New York senator Martin Van Buren, the "Little Magician" at the head of the Albany Regency which dominated New York politics on Jackson's behalf, who fully appreciated the importance of a secure propaganda base for a career in public office. With the political newspapers on side "we can endure a thousand convulsions," Van Buren noted, "without them, we might as well hang our harps on willows." The cycle of patronage, propaganda and reward in New York was epitomized by the career of Azariah Flagg, a member of the Regency who started political life as a Republican editor. Settling in Clinton County in 1811, he rapidly made the *Plattsburg Republican* the party's leading organ in northeastern New York. Unrelenting opposition to DeWitt Clinton brought him Regency approval, seven years as secretary of state, and ten years as comptroller.

The authoritative mouthpiece of the Regency was the *Albany Argus,* founded in 1813. When the editor of the *Argus,* Isaac Q. Leake, refused to endorse the Regency's presidential candidate for 1824, he was hurried into retirement and replaced by Edwin Croswell. The Regency-dominated legislature in New York retained Croswell as state printer from 1823 to 1840, a span of time which led a clutch of other Regency editors, at the helm of such publications as the *Elmira Gazette* and the *Patriot* in Orange County, to start clamoring for "rotation in office."[84] Even while juggling such intramural rivalry, Van Buren continued to tighten his grip over the press in upstate New York. In 1828 the *Buffalo Emporium* sourly noted that the Regency had bought out the *Buffalo Gazaette* and *Black Rock Gazette,* which henceforth would echo "the will of Pope Martin the First."[85]

Regency critics attributed great political power to the *Argus.* James Watson Webb of the *Morning Courier and New York Enquirer* claimed, "There is no office to fill — no executive to nominate — no political plan to organize — and no point to carry by the state, even in the National Councils, that is not first arranged in the office of the Albany *Argus*."[86] The *Argus* even had the effrontery to accuse the Adams administration of persecuting "faithful, well-tried, and patriotic republican printers," while rewarding those that were "subservient." The *New Hampshire Patriot*, the *Eastern Argus*, and the *Frankfort Argus* had been "deprived of government patronage for exposing fearlessly the abuses committed by Mr. Adams."[87]

Jackson was ably supported in Virginia by Thomas Ritchie, editor of the *Richmond Enquirer* and head of the Richmond junto which dominated the politics of the Old Dominion.[88] Ritchie and Van Buren met in the spring of 1823 (ironically, when both were partisans of William Crawford) and became fast friends; fifteen years later Ritchie would write that from "the first moment of my acquaintance with you, I have been your personal and political friend."[89]

The genesis of the modern Democratic Party can be traced to January 1827 when Van Buren wrote to Ritchie pledging his support to Old Hickory. Such a course, the New Yorker put it, would be "the best and probably the only practicable mode of concentrating the entire vote of the opposition & of effecting what is of still greater importance, the substantial reorganization of the old Republican Party," thereby "substituting *party principle* for *personal preference* as one of the leading points in the contest." In order to prosper in office, Jackson would need the "concerted effort of a political party, holding in the main, to certain tenets & opposed to certain prevailing principles."

"Political combinations between the inhabitants of the different states are unavoidable & the most natural & beneficial to the country is that between the planters of the South and the plain Republicans of the North," Van Buren continued. The only alternative was that "geographical divisions founded on local interests or, what is worse prejudices between free and slave holding states will inevitably take their place."[90]

Jackson's supporters in Congress caucused and pledged to establish "a chain of newspaper posts, from the New England States to Louisiana, and branching off through Lexington [a deliberate shot across the bow of Henry Clay] to the Western States." Everywhere the owners and editors of newspapers volunteered to coordinate and promulgate the Jacksonian doctrine in their state. In New Hampshire the go-to man for party building was Isaac Hill of the *New Hampshire Patriot*, a proponent of Crawford in 1824, whose declaration of support for Jackson in March 1827 cost him the state printing. "Hill was the peerless leader of the party during the years of its greatest success," McCormick says. "From his office in Concord, known as the 'Dictator's Palace,' he skillfully guided the actions of the party caucus, which in turn enforced iron discipline on the party in the legislature."[91]

In South Carolina, editors such as Benjamin F. Perry of the *Greenville Mountaineer*, M. D. Richardson of the Sumterville *Southern Whig*, and Richard Yeadon of the *Charleston Courier*, assumed the leadership of Jackson's Democratic Party and led the fight against nullification and disunion. In Massachusetts, the *Boston Statesman* newspaper junto, headed by David Henshaw, Nathaniel Greene and Andrew Dunlap, controlled Democratic Party operations in the 1820s. After this trio accepted patronage appointments from Jackson in 1829, Charles G. Greene assumed editorship of the paper and inherited the tasks of organizing party meetings and drawing up party tickets. Suffolk County Jacksonian meetings were held in Greene's offices, and he served in the state legislature while still editing the *Statesman*.[92] Other prominent Jacksonian editors included J. M. Niles, publisher of the *Hartford Times*; in Ohio, Moses Dawson, editor of the *Cincinnati Advertiser* and Elijah Hayward, editor of the Cincinnati *National Republican and Ohio Political Register*, a member of the Cincinnati Jackson committee who in 1824 had served as chair of the state committee for Jackson; and in Indiana, Elihu Stout, editor of the lone pro–Jackson paper in the state, the Vincennes *Western Star*.

Van Buren wanted to replace Green with Ritchie as the definitive spokesperson for the Jackson movement in the nation's capital, but this proposal was vetoed by Calhoun, who warned, "A paper is already in existence, and it does seem to me that two on the same side must distract and excite jealousy. Each will have its partisans."[93] The Green/Calhoun alliance would extend so far as to be consummated by the marriage of Green's daughter Margaret to Calhoun's son Andrew in May of 1835, but still the South Carolinian foresaw both the genesis of the Democratic Party and the death of his own presidential ambition: "Between the Regency at Albany and the junto at Richmond, there is a vital connection. They give and receive help from each other, and confidently expect to govern this nation."[94]

In 1826, Major Mordecai M. Noah ended a ten-year association with Tammany Hall as editor of the political machine's daily, the *National Advocate*, and launched the *New York Enquirer* to rally the voters of Gotham for Old Hickory. Jackson received another major boost in the Empire State when the *Evening Post*, the voice of Federalism since its foundation by Alexander Hamilton in 1801, declared for him under new editor William Cullen Bryant. Whenever necessary, Jackson's supporters were prepared to be a little more proactive. When Luther Tucker of the *Rochester Daily Advertiser* wanted to support Jackson in 1828, his coeditor balked. The Regency helped Tucker buy his partner out.[95] Other papers to declare for Jackson included the *Aurora and Franklin Gazette* and the *Palladium* in Philadelphia; the *New Hampshire Patriot*; Gideon Welles's *New Haven Journal*; Dabney S. Carr's *Baltimore Republican*; the *Nashville Republican and State Gazette*; the *Charleston Mercury*; and, in the heart of Henry Clay country, Amos Kendall's Frankfort, Kentucky, *Argus of Western America*.

The President was not entirely friendless. In fact, "Adams probably had as many newspapers as Jackson," Smith notes.[96] For a start, Adams had the *National Journal* and *National Intelligencer* at his command in Washington. The editors of the *Intelligencer*, claiming to have discerned "a violence of temper, and a recklessness of consequences" in Jackson, felt they were "induced ... to oppose, with all our slender means, his elevation to an office for which he was never designed by nature, and has not been trained by education."[97]

Outside of the capital, important Adams newspapers included the Richmond *Constitutional Whig*; Charles King's *New York American*; in Philadelphia, the *Democratic* Press (edited by John Binns, publisher of the infamous "Coffin Handbill") and the *National Gazette*; *Niles' Weekly Register* of Baltimore, alongside the *Maryland Republican* and the Baltimore *Marylander*; the *New Jersey Patriot*; the Virginia *Constitutional Whig*; the *Raleigh Register*; the Lexington *Kentucky Reporter*, the voice of Henry Clay in his home town; the *Illinois Gazette*; the *Missouri Republican*; the *Massachusetts Journal*; the *Columbian Centinel* in Boston; and the *Cincinnati Gazette*, source of much of the sensationalist muckraking concerning Jackson and his wife Rachel.

In 1827, the editor of the latter publication, a confidant of Clay's named Charles Hammond, undertook a fact-finding mission throughout the frontier states, accumulating material on Jackson's various escapades, which ranged from the incredible truth to the most salacious gossip, for use in the forthcoming campaign. Clay recommended his mudslinging friend to Daniel Webster, calling Hammond's paper "upon the whole, the most efficient and discreet gazette that espouses our cause," and recommending direct financial support for his efforts.[98] "The course adopted by the Opposition, in the dissemination of Newspapers and publications against the Administration and supporting presses," Clay declared, "leaves to its friends no other alternative than that of following their example, so far at least as to circulate information among the people."[99] Isaac Hill responded in the *New Hampshire Patriot* by maintaining, "Clay is managing Adams's campaign, not like a statesman of the Cabinet, but like a shyster, pettifogging in a bastard suit before a country squire."[100] The *New Hampshire Patriot*, in an article titled "Licentiousness of the Press," complained on September 8, "It will not, we believe, be contradicted, that the Adams presses generally, professing to belong to the old federal party, and of course, to "good society," have in the present contest, lost sight of every decent regard for public reputation and private feelings."[101]

Hill was prepared to fight fire with fire. He published the accusation that Adams, while ambassador to Russia, had once "procured" a virginal American governess to satisfy "the carnal desires of Czar Alexander the First."[102] In fact, the young woman in question had been the maid to Adams's wife and nurse to his son Charles, who had been nothing more than routinely introduced to the czar.

Campaign journals issued solely for the election season, and even more scurrilous than the "legitimate" press, included, for Jackson, *We the People*; the *United States Telegraph Extra*, unleashed by Duff Green; and *The Nose: Or Political Satirist*, published by William Piatt of Jersey Shore, Pennsylvania, which took its name from an inci-

PROVIDENCE.

PEOPLE'S TICKET.

FOR PRESIDENT,

JOHN QUINCY ADAMS.

Whom WASHINGTON, in 1797, considered " the most valuable public character we had abroad ;"

Whom JEFFERSON, in 1785, esteemed so highly that he said to Mr. GERRY—" I congratulate your Country on their prospects in this young man;"

Whom MADISON appointed first to negociate a Treaty for Peace ;

Whom MONROE, with the advice of General Jackson, placed first in his Cabinet ;

Whom THE PEOPLE, in 1824, elevated to the highest station in the world ;

Whose Administration, though assailed from the beginning by an Opposition unexampled for its bitterness and profligacy, has been singularly prosperous;

And who, in less than four years, besides defraying the expenses of government, (great and 'extravagant' as they are said to be by his opponents)—and besides applying upwards of TWELVE MILLIONS to works of public improvement and national defence,—HAS PAID MORE THAN THIRTY-THREE MILLIONS OF THE PUBLIC DEBT.

FOR VICE PRESIDENT,

RICHARD RUSH.

The present able and efficient Secretary of the Treasury—and fearless advocate of the Interests and Honour of his Country

The editorial page of the local party newspaper was where the citizens of antebellum America could find the electoral ticket of their choice. This example, from the Providence *Literary Cadet and Rhode Island Statesman*, dated June 4, 1828, boldly states its allegiance to President John Quincy Adams and his running mate Richard Rush (author's collection).

dent in which the associate editor of the *Telegraph* had tweaked the nose of the president's son in the rotunda of the Capitol.[103] Administration allies in this aspect of the campaign included *The Political Primer, or A Horn-book for the Jacksonites*, a semi-weekly launched in April in Dover, Delaware, costing $6 for the duration of the campaign, and *Truth's Advocate and Monthly Anti-Jackson Expositor*, published by Hammond.[104] The latter paper was just warming up when it introduced Old Hickory to the electorate in the following terms: "You know he is no jurist, no statesman, no politician; that he is destitute of historical, political, or statistical knowledge; that he is unacquainted with the orthography, concord and government of his language. You know that he is a man of no labour, no patience, no investigation, in short, that his whole recommendation is animal fierceness and organic energy. He is wholly unqualified by education, habit and temper, for the station of President."[105]

On March 26, 1827, the *National Journal* published a reprint of an election circular distributed by one Thomas L. Arnold, a candidate for Congress in Tennessee:

> General Jackson spent the prime of his life in gambling, in cock-fighting, in horse-racing, and has all his life been a most bloody duelist; and to cap all his frailties he tore from a husband the wife of his bosom, to whom he had been for some years united in the holy state of matrimony. Robards, the wretched man whose wife was taken from him, did not very long survive the disgraceful transaction; but during the time that he did live, General Jackson lived with his wife in a way that would have subjected any other to an indictment in the County Court for "open and notorious lewdness."
>
> I heard one of the General's prominent friends boasting of it, as an act of gallantry, and said that "the General had driven Robards off like a dog and taken his wife." If General Jackson should be elected President, what effect, think you, fellow-citizens, will it have upon American youth?[106]

Jackson's Nashville Central Committee retorted that Jackson and Rachel had married under the impression that Robards had already granted a divorce, and had remarried in 1793 when the divorce was finally granted, but Hammond, aware that a Kentucky court had found Rachel guilty of desertion and adultery, put to the nation the question: "Ought a convicted adulteress and her paramour husband to be placed in the highest offices of this free and Christian land?"

In June of 1827, Duff Green led the counterattack by raising the specter of impropriety in Adams's relationship with the first lady, at the same time decrying the necessity of doing so, while warning that he would not be so coy in future if the administration continued its assault on Rachel Jackson. "It was not our desire to point the finger of scorn at the *incestuous person*," Green asserted. "It was not our desire to trace the *love* adventures of the Chief Magistrate, nor to disclose the manner, *nor the time*, at which *he*, his brother-in-law, and his father-in-law before him, led their *blushing* brides to the hymenial altar." Only if the administration rekindled their slanders on Jackson's wife, Green warned, would he expose the "leprosy which preyed upon the household" of the president.[107] But Hammond was only warming up. His retort echoes through the ages: "General Jackson's mother was a COMMON PROSTITUTE, brought to this country by the British soldiers! She afterwards married a MULATTO MAN, with whom she had several children, of which number General JACKSON IS ONE!!!"

Hammond also published a list of fourteen "juvenile indiscretions" attributed to Jackson between the ages of twenty-three and sixty, involving public brawls, gunfights, duels, and other acts of mayhem which supposedly documented the general's "intemperate life and character."[108]

The most visually striking product of the Adams propaganda campaign was the brainchild of John Binns, the editor of the Philadelphia *Democratic Press*, who breathlessly recounted how Jackson had approved the execution of six militia deserters after their conviction by a military court, in the wake of his great victory at New Orleans in 1815. Binn's "Coffin Handbill" leaflet, entitled "Some Account of Some of the Bloody Deeds of GENERAL JACKSON," was bordered in black with six black coffins drawn under the names of the six militiamen. In one corner of the handbill Jackson is depicted running his sword cane through the back of a man in the act of picking up a stone to defend himself (an act for which he was later acquitted by a grand jury on the grounds of self-defense). "Gentle reader," the handbill implored, "it is for you to say, whether this man, who carries a sword cane, and is willing to run it through the body of any one who may presume to stand in his way, is a fit person to be our President."[109]

"General Jackson has been assailed," Green lamented, "in the most wanton and inhuman manner — the slanders have been carried into the bosom of his family ... the Billingsgate calendar has been exhausted, and he has been made alternately, a cut throat, adulterer, negro buyer, and cock fighter."[110] In the face of such provocation it is small wonder Jackson spent the entire campaign brooding darkly of revenge: "I am branded with every crime ... and was not my hands tied, and my mouth closed, I would soon put an end to their slanders. This they know not, but suppose when the elections are over all things will die away — not so, I look forward to the first of Dec. next with much anxiety. The day of retribution must come."[111]

Finally, mercifully, it was over. "To the polls!" Green commanded, as election day dawned in the several states. "To the Polls! The faithful sentinel must not sleep — Let no one stay home — Let every man go to the Polls — Let not a vote be lost — Let each Freeman do his duty; and all will triumph in the success of JACKSON, CALHOUN and LIBERTY!"[112] After Pennsylvania and Ohio declared for Jackson, making his election certain, an ebullient Green wrote the general, "It will be a triumph such as never was before achieved in the country.... Excuse my dear Sir the overflowing of a heart that is almost too full to rejoice."[113]

"The presidential campaign of 1828 had been to a large extent a contest among newspapers," Smith notes, and Jackson had won.[114] The *National Journal* reflected the consensus among the pro–Adams press in its depiction of the *Telegraph*, and Green in particular: "Purchased and established to advance the interests of its owners at the expense of truth, and decency, and morality, it has found no slander too vile, no falsehood too gross, no calumny too malicious for its purpose; and the creature employed by its managers — a stranger to decency, destitute of honor ... strikes as he is directed reckless of the consequences, well aware that being a shadow, justice has no terrors for him, and the contempt of mankind cannot reach him."[115]

Given the source, Green would have registered this perspective as approbation, a sentiment shared by the *Charleston Mercury*, which observed that "the opposition papers have long endeavored, by every species of calumny and defamation, to injure the character and destroy the influence of the *United States Telegraph*. Such a course, perhaps, was to have been expected of *them*, seeing that it was principally owing to the exertions of the *Telegraph* that the late Administration was defeated."[116]

Old Hickory

It was in this atmosphere that Jackson was elected, and the air got no more pure once he took office. "No president had a supporting press more vociferously loyal, or more intolerant," than Jackson, Tebbel and Watts claim.[117] Jackson was convinced that the last victim of the campaign that brought him to power was his beloved wife Rachel. She had suffered in silence the slanders of the administration press throughout the year but her health collapsed after the election, and she died just before Christmas. "I shall not go without friends to reward," the president-elect declared at her funeral, "and I pray God that I may not be allowed to have enemies to punish. I can forgive all who have wronged me, but will have fervently to pray that I may have grace to enable me to forget or forgive any enemy who has ever maligned that blessed one who is now safe from all suffering and sorrow, whom they tried to put to shame for my sake!"[118] Those editors who had incurred Jackson's wrath were soon to discover just how implacable his enmity could be.

Once in office, Jackson did not neglect his editorial allies when the sharing of the spoils of victory began. "You may say to all our anxious Adams-ites that THE BARNACLES WILL BE SCRAPED CLEAN OFF THE SHIP OF STATE," Isaac Hill gloated. "Most of them have grown so large and stick so tight that the scraping process will doubtless be fatal to them."[119] In an age defined by partisan attachment, the alternative was so irrational as to defy contemplation: "Shall we ... appoint to office and continue in office the men who have ... libel[ed] the purest patriots in the country?" Hill asked. "Forbid it Heaven!"[120]

Green publicly announced in the *Telegraph* that Jackson would "reward his friends and punish his enemies." In the "distribution of the federal patronage," Green explained to one Jackson supporter shortly before Old Hickory's inauguration, "General Jackson will have much in his power. He can enrich and strengthen his part by a transfer of the lucrative offices into sound hands." With other Jackson men, Green was more forthright. "How is your postmaster?" the editor queried a campaign worker. "Can't I serve you there? Or can't I obtain for you a mail contract? Let me hear from you fully on these points.... I am now in a position where I can serve my friends."[121]

After just ten days of the new regime John Quincy Adams rendered the verdict that "the only principles yet discernible in the conduct of the President" were "to feed the cormorant appetite for place, and to reward the prostituting of canvassing defamers."[122] Jackson's predecessor further complained, "The appointments, almost without exception, are conferred upon the vilest purveyors of slander during the late electioneering campaign, and an excessive disproportion of places is given to editors of the foulest presses. The appointments are exclusively of violent partisans; and every editor of a scurrilous and slanderous newspaper is provided for."[123]

An initial hurdle presented by Postmaster General John McLean was easily overcome. When McLean told Jackson that he would fire pro–Jackson as well as pro–Adams postmasters if he must dismiss men for political activity, the president responded with a direct question: "Mr. McLean, would you accept a seat on the bench of the Supreme Court?" Four days later, the malleable William T. Barry had replaced McLean and the wholesale "reform" began.[124]

All told, Jackson, who personally subscribed to twenty newspapers while president, named nearly sixty journalists to high office (see Table 3).[125] The greatest beneficiaries of the new order were the personnel of the *Boston Statesman*, who won postmaster at Boston, district attorney for Massachusetts, weigher and gauger at Boston, collectorship of the Port of Boston, and navy agent for Massachusetts between them.

TABLE 3. NEWSPAPER APPOINTMENTS TO PUBLIC OFFICE BY THE JACKSON ADMINISTRATION[126]

Editor	Publication	Appointment
Isaac Hill	*New Hampshire Patriot*	Second Controller of the Treasury
Amos Kendall	*Argus of Western America*	Fourth Auditor of the Treasury
Mordecai Noah	*New York Enquirer*	Surveyor of the Port of New York
Dabney Carr	*Baltimore Republican*	Naval Officer at Baltimore
Moses Dawson	*Cincinnati Advertiser*	Receiver of Public Money for the Land Office at Cincinnati
Elijah Hayward	*National Republican and Ohio Political Register*	Commissioner of the General Land Office in Ohio
Andrew Marschalk (Proprietor)	*Natchez Gazette*	Collector of the Port of Natchez
Peter Wagner	*Louisiana Advertiser*	Naval Officer at New Orleans
A.S. Thruston	*Florida Intelligencer*	Collector at Key West

Editor	Publication	Appointment
John Fitzgerald	*Nashville Republican*	Postmaster at Pensacola
Philo White	*Western Carolinian*	Navy Agent
Mary Dickson (Proprietor)	*Lancaster Intelligencer*	Postmaster at Lancaster
John Norvell	*Pennsylvania Inquirer*	Postmaster at Detroit
John M. McCalla	*Kentucky Gazette*	Marshal of Kentucky
David Henshaw	*Boston Statesman*	Collector of the Port of Boston

The *Telegraph* was another big winner. Green advocated the removal of Dr. Tobias Watkins, who had briefly been part-owner of the *National Journal*, as fourth auditor of the Treasury, and George Watterson, who had been a contributor to the *National Journal*, as first Librarian of Congress (that role went instead to *Telegraph's* original editor, John S. Meehan). Two *Telegraph* staff members were appointed to clerkships in Washington, while a third got a temporary job in the State Department. The three editors of the *Hartford Times* were appointed to positions as postmaster at Hartford, customs agent in Boston, and the tax collector in Middletown, Connecticut.

Some Jacksonians professed concern at the excess of the largesse being offered to the party faithful. Thomas Ritchie was one to express alarm at the easy pickings offered to "the Editorial Corps," as he called it. On March 29, 1829, less than three weeks after Jackson took office, Ritchie wrote Van Buren, confessing, "We are sorry to see the personal friends of the President appointed. We lament to see so many of the Editorial Corps favored with the patronage of the Administration."[127]

"A single case," Ritchie continued, "would not have excited so much observation, but it really looks as if there were a systematic effort to reward Editorial Partisans, which will have the effect of bringing the vaunted Liberty of the Press into a sort of contempt."[128] Van Buren passed Ritchie's letter on to Jackson, who in a reply dated March 31, professed to being bemused by the editor's assertions. Claiming he had "only followed the examples of my illustrious predecessors, Washington and Jefferson," which was true in the latter instance, at least, Jackson asserted that while he had not, nor would he ever, "make an appointment but with a view, to the public good ... I cannot suppose mr Ritchie would have me proscribe my friends, merely because they are so." After all, "If my personal friends are qualified and patriotic why should I not be permitted to bestow a *few* offices on them?"[129]

In the Senate, Daniel Webster labored to save the country from what he called "the typographical corps," with some success— of the 319 nominations Jackson sent to the Senate, all but six were eventually confirmed, but of those six, four were identified with the press: Major Henry Lee, Isaac Hill, James Gardner, and Moses Dawson. Amos Kendall and Mordecai M. Noah both squeaked through their confirmations on the deciding vote of Vice President Calhoun, Kendall being confirmed as fourth auditor for the Treasury Department.[130] According to Webster, "Were it not for the fear of the out-of-door popularity of General Jackson, the Senate would have negatived more than half his nominations."[131]

After the Senate rejected Hill for second comptroller of the Treasury by a vote of 33 to 15, he regrouped in New Hampshire, and returned to Washington to represent his state in the Senate. John Milton Niles, Jacksonian editor of the *Hartford Times*, was appointed postmaster of Hartford. In 1835, Niles was appointed to fill the term of a deceased senator. Elected in his own right in 1836, he took a brief hiatus from the Senate at the end of Van Buren's presidency to replace Amos Kendall as Postmaster General, after Kendall resigned to take charge of the *Extra Globe*, editorial voice for the Van Buren reelection campaign.

The first list of publishers of the laws authorized after Jackson took office showed a change of over 70 percent. Of the 78 newspapers having assignments at the end of the Adams administration, only 23 were retained, and a half-dozen more of these were shortly dropped. Of those that were kept, most, if not all, had been either pro–Jackson, like the *Albany Argus*, inoffensive, or practically indispensable because of a lack of alternatives, like the *Arkansas Gazette*.[132]

On the face of it, the millennium had dawned for Duff Green of the *Telegraph*. In addition to his serving as mouthpiece of the incoming administration, with all that promised in terms of the capacity to access patronage, he retained the printing rights in the new Senate and, by 107 votes to 95, was granted the printing rights in the new House.

Green's rivals continued to depict him as occupying the center of the Jacksonian web in Washington. The *Richmond Whig* maintained that he exercised "unbounded influence over the mind of Gen. Jackson," saying, "we understand that no appointment has been made, that Duff was not known to have approved either by signing a recommendation, or by a viva voce expression of approbation."[133] Green's enemies sought to make his influence an issue. "No more successful means could be perused to open the eyes of the people," Henry Clay wrote to a friend, "than to make more and more evident at Washington, the fact, which I believe to exist, that Duff Green is the actual President."[134]

But in reality Green's status rested on shaky foundations. What authority he had was derived directly from Jackson, and that connection was growing more tenuous by the day. The editor had assumed he would be in a position to dictate policy as well as patronage in the new administration, but swiftly became aware that his initiatives were being stymied across the board by other power brokers within the spoils system. Ironically, the power to dispense patronage proved to be a double-edged sword because those who looked to Green for sinecures rounded on him when their applications were denied. During the campaign of 1828, the editors and sponsors of two Boston papers, the *American Statesman* and the *Jackson Republican*, had loaned Green considerable sums of money, $6,000 and $5,000 respectively. When Green failed to acquire patronage for these men, they held him directly responsible. In fact, one of the editors of the *Republican*, Colonel Henry Orne, quickly turned against him, publishing a series of damning articles under the pseudonym "Columbus."[135]

The problem was that Green refused to accept the fact that his role was a subordinate one. He responded by lashing out at those within the new administration he felt were betraying him, sparing no one, not even Jackson. It was the beginning of a rift that would widen between Green and Old Hickory, and that would culminate with his expulsion from the President's inner circle before the end of Jackson's first term.[136]

The man who seized the opportunity afforded by this estrangement owed his livelihood as a budding man of letters to the very man who would become the most consistent and high-profile target of his pen. In 1814, Dartmouth-educated Amos Kendall arrived in Lexington, Kentucky, and got his first break when Henry Clay departed to represent the United States in peace negotiations in Europe. Clay's wife Lucretia offered Kendall $300, plus room and board at the Ashland plantation, to serve as tutor for her five oldest children. The grateful Kendall later beseeched Clay, "[C]ommand my pen or my paper.... If I can assist you now, it will be some compensation to your estimable lady for the kindness she exhibited towards me when I was moneyless, friendless and powerless."

The following year Kendall made his first foray into journalism when he bought a half share in the Georgetown *Minerva*, the print vehicle of Congressman Richard M. Johnson (the famed slayer of Tecumseh who later served as Martin Van Buren's vice president). Along with the editorial role came the offer of the town postmastership.

Ever moving on, in October 1816 Kendall acquired a half share in the Frankfort *Argus of Western America*. In 1817 he lost a fistfight to John N. Farnham of Frankfort-based *The Commentator*, but that couldn't prevent him from taking full control of Farnham's paper later that same year. In 1820, Kendall made an important addition to the *Argus* when he enlisted the editorial assistance of Francis P. Blair, the clerk of the Franklin County Circuit Court.

In the presidential contest of 1824, Kendall was loyal to Clay, whom he described as "the Grecian Pericles, without his propensity to war"—a direct dig at General Andrew Jackson, a man whose "genius is peculiarly martial," Kendall wrote, "his means are always fraught with violence." Even after rejecting as inadequate Clay's offer of a position in the State Department at $1,000 a year, Kendall remained disenchanted with Jackson. In his own words, he "disliked" the general's "violent" and "tyrannical disposition," his lack of "capacity," and his "moral character, particularly the way he obtained his wife."

Kendall's hand was forced in October 1826

The consummate professional, Amos Kendall smoothly made the transition from partisan of Henry Clay to *éminence grise* of Andrew Jackson. The apotheosis of his career, serving as postmaster general under two presidents, demonstrated the blurring of the lines between public service, partisan politics, and pecuniary self-interest typical of the era (courtesy of Library of Congress).

when Jacksonians gave him two-day notice in which to endorse their hero; otherwise they would set up their own paper in Frankfort. "You must determine to aid in putting them [Adams and Clay] down, or go down yourself," Kendall was warned.[137] On November 1, Kendall capitulated. "Let us take up Old Hickory," he announced—on the grounds that the general reflected Jeffersonian beliefs more than the "consolidating principles" of John Quincy Adams. The final break came on December 22, 1826, when Clay transferred the printing contracts for the federal laws in Frankfort from the *Argus* to the *Commentator*. Kendall now declared himself unwilling to "be crushed beneath the wheel's of [Clay's] ambition," and emerged as a leading advocate for Jackson.[138]

Kendall was alert to the potential benefits that could accrue to an editor willing to fly the flag for Jackson in the heart of Clay country. Those who would save the Bluegrass State from Clay, Kendall wrote Blair from Washington, would create "irresistible claims on the administration" and be able to "command anything they may desire." In conclusion, Kendall reported, "we must stay clear and support Jackson and the successor most likely to succeed when the time comes."[139] To that end, Kendall was prepared to bide his time. Rejecting an opportunity to join Duff Green in managing the *Telegraph*, he also turned down offers of senior clerkships from Van Buren and Louis McLane, secretary of the Treasury, before securing a position as fourth auditor of the Treasury on the casting vote of Calhoun — how the vice president must have later regretted that vote! Answerable directly to Jackson, Kendall waited for his opportunity.

That opportunity came in a situation reminiscent of the rivalry between Hamilton and Jefferson during the presidency of Washington. The splits that emerged in the administration during Jackson's first term were reflected in the media mouthpieces of the rival factions. Green was close to Calhoun, but the vice president was drifting away from Jackson on the issue of states' rights, and was locked in a bitter rivalry with Secretary of State Martin Van Buren for the president's affections. Van Buren had the upper hand because of his support for the president during the so-called Petticoat Affair.[140] Calhoun's situation worsened in the spring of 1830 when William Crawford charged that when both men had served in Monroe's cabinet, Calhoun had favored disciplining Jackson for exceeding orders during his invasion of Florida in 1818. Jackson demanded an explanation and found Calhoun's answers unsatisfactory.

Matters reached a crisis point when Jackson attended a birthday dinner hosted by Calhoun on April 13, 1830, an event that was swiftly revealed as a rally for nullification. After enduring twenty-four consecutive toasts extolling nullification principles, the president successfully squelched any misconception that he was prepared to even consider defiance of federal laws with his own toast: "Our Union: It must be preserved." In the aftermath, the angry president blamed Green as the person most responsible for "willfully perverting" the dinner into a political engine. "We must get another organ to announce the policy," he told an aide. This sentiment was echoed in the Jacksonian press. The editor of the *Philadelphia Inquirer* announced in early 1830 that he supported the administration but had never liked Green or the *Telegraph*. Thomas Ritchie of the *Richmond Enquirer* considered Green a "miserable driveller and servile sycophant of Mr. Calhoun." Another administration paper, the *Greensborough Patriot*, noted that Green was "contentious" in dealing with other Jacksonians and did not really serve the party.

"The disposition which Gen. Green has exhibited to identify Gen. Jackson and his friends with the nullifiers of South Carolina," Kendall accurately surmised, "has excited anew their desire for another paper here." Writing from a steamboat at Wheeling, Virginia, Jackson alluded to another grievance: "The truth is, [Green] has professed to me to be heart and soul against the Bank, but his idol [Calhoun] controles him as much as the shewman does his puppits, and we must get another organ to announce the policy, and defend the administration." As long as the official party mouthpiece remained in Green's hands, the president concluded, the administration would be "more injured than by all the opposition."[141] "Green has wholly lost the confidence of the President," Kendall reported to Blair, "and ... there will shortly be a real administration paper here."[142]

"I know the President will enter with zeal into my views," Kendall continued. "Your sentiments in relation to the Bank will make him zealous for you. I think he will be for the paper any hour." By June, Jackson was finally and fully committed to establishing a new voice for the administration. Postmaster General Barry suggested his friend Blair, whose association with Kendall was well known. Kendall immediately fired off a letter to Blair from Washington, asking, "How would you like to be the Editor of a paper here which should have the support of the Executive, and be the *real* Administration paper?"[143] On November 1, 1830, Kendall wrote again to confirm that Jackson "introduced the subject of a newspaper here himself. I told him I had written you to come on. He said, if you come and start a paper you should be supported. So you have, not the word of a King, but of one who is more likely to fulfill it."

Kendall wanted immediate progress: "I shall expect to see you by the middle of November, and your paper ought to appear by the first of December."[144]

Kendall assured Blair that he could expect cooperation from Barry, Secretary of State Van Buren, the War Department, the Treasurer's office, the second comptroller, and the second and fourth auditors. Other department heads, in time, "would throw their patronage into your hands on its being understood, as it will be, that such a step would be acceptable to the President." "The personal exertions of the President and all his particular friends, may be relied on to give the paper circulation," Kendall emphasized.[145]

Blair decamped for Washington posthaste, bringing John C. Rives with him to serve as business manager of the ensuing publication, the *Washington Globe*, which made its debut as a semiweekly on December 7, 1830.[146] Reared in Frankfort, the son of Kentucky's longtime Republican attorney general James Blair, Francis graduated with honors from Transylvania College the same year that Kendall finished at Dartmouth. Blair, like Kendall, had endorsed Clay for president in 1824, only to fall out with the Kentucky Cock during his term as Secretary of State. "I never deserted your banner," he wrote Clay after the fact, "until the questions on which you and I so frequently disagreed in private discussion—(State rights, the Bank, the power of the Judiciary, &c.)—became the criterions to distinguish the parties, and had actually renewed, in their practical effects, the great divisions which marked the era of 1798."[147]

Blair, who stood a scant five feet two inches tall and weighed barely a hundred pounds, failed to make much of an impression on the Washington social scene, but his capacity with pen in hand soon made his reputation. "It is the purpose of the Editor to dedicate this paper to the discussion and maintenance of the principles which brought General Jackson into office, and which he brought with him into office," Blair wrote in his prospectus.[148] These sentiments were reemphasized in the first edition of the *Globe*: "To contribute something to the ends sought to be affected by continuing the administration of the present Chief Magistrate through a second term, is the leading consideration which actuated the Editor in the establishment of this paper."[149] In case anyone missed the point, Jacksonian principles were emblazoned across the masthead of the first issue: "The World is Governed Too Much." The only legitimate object of the government was "to protect men in the pursuit of happiness." Bereft of this protection, "the weak would be the victims of the strong, and the world would be full of violence and crime."[150] Readers of the new paper quickly accustomed themselves to such fulsome panegyrics in praise of the *Globe's* patron as this:

> Andrew Jackson, the "Hero of New Orleans," at the head of the American people, grasping the glorious standard of "*E. Pluribus Unum,*" protecting our rights abroad, fostering our interests at home, and viewing with an eye as unblenching as his country's eagle's, the gathering array of hostile force ... a moral spectacle, sublime without parallel in the history of Republics ... unmoved as the White Mountains of the Granite State ... too deep in the people's affections to be undermined. The storms of faction beat around him unheeded. The cloud rests upon him but a moment and leaves him more bright than before, towering in the sunshine of spotless honor and eternal truth.[151]

Jackson's opponents, of course, had a somewhat different perspective, both on Old Hickory and his propagandists; Clay, for one, blasted the "muckraking scum" of the *Globe* on the floor of the Senate.

In order to ease the *Telegraph* out of the President's inner circle in as non-confrontational a manner as possible, Blair pointed out to its editor the increasing volume of printing business in the capital, of which, in order to help prevent it falling into the hands of interests "whom I consider public enemies," he was prepared to take up some slack so as to relieve the pressure on Green. Therefore, Blair surmised, Green might find it "advantageous" and in "the interests of the great cause" if another press was created under the management of an individual "who could prove rather a coadjustor than a competitor." Blair assured Green the two editors would "not divide" in their efforts "on any great public principle." Blair's letter was immediately followed by one from Kendall. Do not let your enemies establish another press, he urged Green; let Blair do so, for he was "a friend, *personal* and *political.*"[152]

Green wasn't buying it for a moment. "The removal of Blair to this city," he wrote a confidant, "was, no doubt, preparatory to a development, on the part of a portion of the President's friends, in which it was anticipated that I could not cooperate." That "development" was of course the presidential ambition of Martin Van Buren, whose rivalry with Calhoun for the succession had been a hallmark of the administration since the moment Jackson took office. Van Buren "has made a covert war upon me," Green complained, "and nothing but the power of my press and the force of my position has maintained me thus far."[153] Time, however, was running out. Word quickly filtered through the ranks of the Jacksonian press as to the status of the upstart new publication: "We have here a new paper, called the *Globe*, edited by the late editor of the Frankfort *Argus*. He is a man of talent, a gentleman, sagacious, discreet and powerful. He comes here by *invitation* [i.e. of Jackson]. We are his supporters. I wish you to be. Use your influence for him and let your paper notice him."

In order to ensure a secure financial base for its fledgling mouthpiece, the administration applied half-secret (and wholly improper) pressure on federal appointees earning $1,000 or more a year to subscribe or, it was clearly implied, they would find themselves out of a job. Jackson himself told followers. "I expect you all to patronize the *Globe*." Blair claimed 2,000 subscribers in July 1831 and 3,700 by November.[154] Kendall also passed word to department heads that the President wanted to see departmental printing shifted to the new paper, and, to ensure this was done, Jackson issued an executive order requiring all Cabinet members to give him monthly reports on how much money had been spent on printing and who had been given the contracts. Kendall was appointed Postmaster General in 1835 to more effectively coordinate both the enrollment of subscriptions among the personnel of the department and the dissemination of Jacksonian principles through the mail. It was a significant responsibility because Jackson had elevated the office of Postmaster General to the cabinet level specifically in order to tighten control over the patronage at its disposal; with postmasters, clerks, and mail contractors under its purview, the department directly controlled or indirectly influenced approximately 18,000 jobs throughout the U.S.[155]

Immediately upon the paper's debut, the State Department gave the *Globe* the contract to print the United States diplomatic correspondence for the years 1783–89. During the Twenty-Second Congress, Blair received slightly more than half of all printing ordered by the executive departments, worth $47,224.42, and the *Globe* continued to receive this executive patronage throughout the Jackson and Van Buren administrations. Between 1831 and 1837 alone, the *Globe* received $241,000 for printing from all government sources.[156] Reflecting the dog-eat-dog world of partisan journalism, many of these were contracts that had been diverted away from Green's *Telegraph*. Postal contracts provided Blair with another $8,386.50, for printing mail proposals between July 20 and October 11, 1832, amounting to approximately $116 for each day's issue of the *Globe*.[157] The subsidies to Blair were no secret. On September 8, 1832, the Boston *Columbian Centinel* charged that the post office "has been reconverted to a vast machine for electioneering purposes.... The consequence is that our daily mails are made the vehicles of thousands of electioneering papers and tracts, which are scattered through the country at the expense of the people, for the mere purpose of continuing in power the present corrupt rulers."[158]

By the beginning of 1831, then, a triumvirate of publications was now established to herald the dawn of the new order. The *Albany Argus* represented the Jacksonian cause in the North, the *Richmond Enquirer* performed this role in the South, and the *Globe* acted to coordinate the whole from the center of the web in Washington itself. "When the *Globe*, *Argus* and *Enquirer* spoke, there was an echo from every corner of the nation," one commentator wrote of Jackson's early days in office. "They made cabinet officers and custom-house weighers, presidents and tide-waiters, editors and envoys. They regulated state legislatures and dictated state policies. They were the father confessors to the democracy of the country."[159]

The trio of Kentuckians, Kendall, Blair, and Rives, came to be known as Jackson's "Kitchen Cabinet," so called because they semi-covertly entered the White House via the servant's entrance to the scullery.[160] Typically, Kendall would take notes as the president outlined his agenda, often while Jackson lay back on his couch smoking his pipe. He would take these extemporaneous ramblings to Blair at the *Globe*, where they

A less than imposing presence in person — he stood a scant five feet two inches tall and weighed barely a hundred pounds — Francis Preston Blair made up for any physical shortcomings via his astute management of Andrew Jackson's mouthpiece, the *Globe*. His influence earned him a place in Old Hickory's informal "Kitchen Cabinet" (courtesy of New York Public Library).

would write (or rewrite) what was said into publishable form.[161] This prototypical agenda-setting operation would serve as the template for the packaging of news by subsequent presidencies. The range of the multimedia image-management strategies maintained by the Jackson administration has a very contemporary air to it. Jackson was the first president to have a resident portrait painter on call at the White House, Ralph E. W. Earl, widowed husband of Rachel Jackson's niece Jane Caffery.[162] Contemporaries found these initiatives unsettling; the Kitchen Cabinet represented "an influence, at Washington," as one member of the official Cabinet ominously described it, "unknown to the constitution and to the country."[163] The president's multifarious opponents expressed similar views. "The President's press," Nullifier Senator George Poindexter of Mississippi charged, "edited ... by the 'Kitchen Cabinet,' is made the common reservoir of all the petty slanders which find a place in the most degraded prints in the Union."[164]

By his own account, Blair had more influence with Jackson than even the president's trusted political right hand, Martin Van Buren. "Where I am I can do nothing wrong," Blair once wrote to his sister-in-law. "If Van Buren says, 'You are rash in this business, Mr. Blair,' the old hero says, 'You are right, Mr. Blair, I'll stand by you.'"[165]

As attitudes hardened over the nullification issue, Green found himself drawing ever closer to the vice president. Green thought he could still be a Jackson man while representing Calhoun's interests, but in this he was sorely mistaken. Postmaster Barry made this clear during an encounter outside the offices of the *Telegraph*:

GREEN: Am I to understand that support or opposition to Mr. Van Buren was to be considered the test of friendship to the administration?

BARRY: I cannot see how anyone could sustain the administration and assail one of the members of the Cabinet.

GREEN: But your organ, the *Globe*, assails Mr. Calhoun and I learn that friendship or enmity to Mr. Calhoun is to be made the test of friendship or enmity to General Jackson!

BARRY: Mr. Calhoun has assailed Mr. Jackson by the publication of the correspondence and ... if you identify yourself with Mr. Calhoun, then you must abide the consequences.[166]

"The old man," Green surmised, "has the weakness of old age and has become a pliant instrument in the hands of those about him."[167] Calhoun, meanwhile, had prepared a dossier on his record that was intended to prove that he was not hostile to the president. It included all his recent correspondence with Jackson. The vice president first offered Blair what became known as the Calhoun Correspondence, but Blair wouldn't touch it. The *Telegraph* became the first newspaper in which it was published, on February 17, 1831, and even Green was careful not to run it until after he had been reelected as printer over Gales and Seaton to both the incoming House and Senate (by votes of 108–76 and 24–22 respectively). But the political damage was done. Jackson was "thunderstruck" when he read the *Telegraph*, and responded to Green's assertion that the president had approved the publication by snarling that "a more palpable falsehood was never uttered."[168]

The break with Jackson inevitably meant a break with the *Globe*. "When we came to this city," Blair intoned with solemn, wide-eyed, and entirely insincere innocence, "it was our ardent hope that the *Telegraph* and our humbler selves would continue to be friendly laborers in the same field. It is some weeks since that hope has vanished."[169] The *Globe* asserted that Calhoun's publication "was wholly uncalled for. It is a firebrand wantonly thrown into the [Democratic Party]." It was a blunder on an epic scale. "The publication of the controversial matter, designed to ruin Van Buren's prospects, not only had the opposite effect, it drew a line between the *Telegraph* and the *Globe*, definitely proclaiming the former as an instrument of Calhoun, and no longer a voice of the administration," Smith concludes.[170]

After Jackson's cabinet disintegrated in April 1831 over the so-called Petticoat Affair, the *Telegraph* openly blamed Van Buren, and hoped Jackson would "open his eyes to the intrigues which have produced the present unhappy state."[171] In fact, Jackson moved closer to Van Buren, drafting him as his running mate in 1832 in place of Calhoun. "Poor Duff has politically cut his throat & Calhoun is prostrate never to rise again," the president mused after the South Carolinian resigned the vice presidency.[172] "They [Calhoun and Green] have cut their own throats, and destroyed themselves in a shorter space of time then any two men I ever knew."[173] Jackson never forgave his two erstwhile allies for their apostasy. "Duff Green and company will be buried in the oblivion of forgetfulness for the profligate and wicked course they have pursued," he growled to Van Buren on August 8, 1831.[174]

Green moved into outright opposition to Jackson on September 1, 1831, declaring, "General Jackson has disappointed the expectations of his friends, and failed to accomplish the objects for which he was elected, [which] is reasonable cause for refusing his reelection." The problem was, as Green admitted, that "no dereliction on his part can diminish the weight of the objections once so forcibly and so successfully urged against Mr. Clay."[175]

Green initiated a three-pronged strategy to win the presidency for Calhoun. First, he tried to minimize the nullification issue to make the South Carolinian more attractive in the North. Second, he tried to spur the emergence of pro–Calhoun newspapers and grassroots organizations in order to wrest control of the Democratic Party from Jackson. And when that failed, Green traveled from Philadelphia to New York to New Haven, trying to persuade the leaders of the Anti-Masonic Party to nominate Calhoun as their candidate, even making a last-ditch effort to pack the Anti-Mason convention.[176]

Green also brought attention, apparently without a shred of embarrassment, to the administration's patronage of the *Globe*, asserting that this was an example of a "servile Press" that substituted loyalty to Jackson for its duty to the voters.[177] On the sidelines, Gales and Seaton at the *Intelligencer* declared the *Globe/Telegraph* feud a "spicy" affair. To "kill off Duff," Blair later admitted, "was really my interest."[178]

Blair was very nearly spared the effort by Green's remarkable propensity for making enemies. As tempers frayed over the nullification crisis, Green made his inimitable contribution by labeling the members of the Union Party in South Carolina "Tories." Palmetto State representative James Blair warned Green that if he repeated the charge he would have to abide the consequences. Disregarding the threat, Green again used the term in an editorial on December 23, 1832. The following day Blair, a giant in stature, approached Green from behind while walking along Pennsylvania Avenue, and without warning knocked him down with his cane. He then kicked Green into the gutter and jumped on him with all of his three hundred and fifty pounds, breaking the editor's arm, collar bone, several ribs, and dislocating his hip. From his hospital bed the next day Green, not exactly filled with Christmas cheer, dictated an editorial entitled "Brute Force" in which he repeated his former charges, adding that Blair was not only a Tory but a traitor, a coward, and a liar.[179]

Among the other tasks charged to him by the president, Amos Kendall was also responsible for the organization of the Central Hickory Club in Washington, which masterminded Jackson's reelection campaign. This body acted as an unofficial national steering committee, coordinating the distribution of literature and keeping tabs on electioneering activities throughout the nation. Kendall also wrote the "Address of the Central Hickory Club to the Republican Citizens of the United States," which became the de facto party platform.[180] According to Duff Green, Jacksonian officials "take their cue from the party, and few, very few, read any but the party paper, and he who controls the leading papers control[s] the party. What press is the organ of the Jackson party? *The Globe*! Who is the master spirit of the Central Hickory Club? Amos Kendall! Who controls the Globe? *Amos Kendall*!! Thus is all political power resolved into the hands of Amos Kendall!"[181]

Amos Kendall certainly stands out as the man best qualified to be described as the *éminence grise* not merely of Jackson but of the Democratic Party that was his legacy.[182] Congressman Henry A. Wise shrilled in the House in 1838 that the editor was "the President's *thinking* machine, and his *writing* machine — ay, and his *lying* machine!" Kendall, he said was "chief overseer, chief reporter, amanuensis, scribe, accountant general, man of all work — nothing was well done without the aid of his diabolical genius." John Quincy Adams was more succinct but no less inclined to exaggerate two years later when he remarked of Jackson and Van Buren that "both ... have been for twelve years the tool of Amos Kendall, the ruling mind of their dominion."[183]

Many rivals accused Kendall of being the presiding genius behind the throne. In the wake of the bank recharter veto message, the *National Intelligencer* demanded to know, "Are the People ... willing to have AMOS KENDALL rule over them in the name of ANDREW JACKSON?"[184] But in addition to writing for Jackson, the editor performed many other hands-on functions in his role as presidential troubleshooter. It was Kendall who Jackson sent on a tour of the eastern seaboard to ascertain the attitude of the state banks toward removal of funds from the Bank of the United States. Kendall's report that "a considerable number of banks [were] eager to have the deposits" gave the President the green light to proceed.[185] Furthermore, an investigation of the political ties of presidents, cashiers, and directors of the banks chosen to receive the funds prior to 1836 revealed that, of those identifiable, 78.8 percent were Democrats, 21.2 percent Whigs. "Somehow," Pessen writes, "Amos Kendall had been able to ferret out Democratic bankers from among those common folk who alone belonged to the Jacksonian party. 'Pet' banks indeed!"[186] That task fulfilled, Jackson chose to dispose of the incompetent Barry as Postmaster General by appointing him minister to Spain and installing Kendall in his place. In that office Kendall allayed Southern concerns over the circulation of abolitionist material via federal mail by interpreting the Post Office Act of 1836 so as to permit southern justices of the peace to brand a particular piece of received mail as abolitionist, and to fine the local postmaster who did not immediately burn the offending literature.[187]

Though triumphantly reelected in 1832, Jackson would never be free from the carping of the opposition press during his second term, a fact that was brought home when the new Congress of 1833 split on the printing contracts, Green being dumped in favor of Gales and Seaton by the House, but being retained by the Senate. "So you see Congress pays Gales and Seaton for abusing me for the last twelve years, and Duff Green for the last three," Jackson grumbled.[188] This was a reflection of a process by which the partisans of the press, having contributed to the evolution of the Democratic Party from a Jacksonian personality cult to a structured, hierarchical political entity, were drawing the battle lines of a new partisan divide by spurring the emergence of an anti–Jacksonian rival. The origins of what would become the Whig Party can be traced to the summer of 1830 when three editors in Boston, John B. Davis of the *Patriot*, Nathan Hale of the *Advertiser*, and A. H. Everett of the *North American Review*, sent a circular letter throughout the northern and western states urging that old Republicans start political organization for the 1832 election, offering themselves to set up party committees.[189]

Henry Clay undertook to be the standard bearer of the disparate anti–Jacksonians in the campaign of 1832. Once again the newspapers of the nation divided for or against the contenders, each side portraying the contest as a life and death struggle with the survival of the Union, Constitution, etc., at stake. Passions ran high; William Cullen Bryant, editor of the *New York Evening Post*, went so far as to personally cane a Clay supporter he encountered on Broadway. "We are, and have been, and as far as we know, ever shall be, for Mr. Clay, and for no one else!" Gales and Seaton declared in the *Intelligencer*.[190] Isaac Hill's *New Hampshire Patriot*, on the other hand, carried an op-ed piece headlined, "Twenty-one Reasons Why Henry Clay Should Not Be Elected President." Reason number twenty: "Because ... he spends his days at a gaming table and his nights in a brothel."[191]

Blair distributed thirty issues of a campaign supplement, the *Globe Extra*, in the six months leading up to the election, vowing to "throw this paper into every neighborhood of the United States" so that the people "may know and appreciate the measures and principles which guide Gen. Jackson in the administration of the government." Blair used the post office, controlled by the Democrats, to circulate the *Extra*; Democratic congressmen franked the paper; and Democratic editors nationwide, like Thomas Ritchie and Thomas Hart Benton, published the *Extra* prospectus and sold subscriptions to it.

The *Extra* was "sent in bundles by the Administration and its officers, into every town where a Jackson man can be found to distribute them," the *Maine Advocate* reported. That publication was shocked at the organization and innovation exhibited by the new Democratic Party: "Letters are written and *franked* by the different officers at Washington, and sent out in all directions, soliciting 'names and money,' and it is avowed to be their intention to introduce them into every house in the State, if possible.... At what former period have we seen the government officers, and even the President himself ... writing electioneering letters, and circulating papers filled with political trash and vilest falsehoods?"[192]

Blair was fighting Green, who, refusing to endorse Clay and having failed to entice Calhoun to enter the lists, finally settled for endorsing Anti-Masonic candidate William Wirt. Green issued a print run of the *Telegraph Extra* which swelled to 30,000 in the ten weeks before the election and was intended to reach "every hamlet in the country" in order "to counteract the falsehoods" of the Jackson administration.[193]

The defining issue of the campaign of 1832 was the question of the Second Bank of the United States. Renewal of the bank's charter passed both houses of Congress but on July 10, Jackson, who maintained both an abiding distrust of centralized financial institutions and dislike of Nicholas Biddle, the bank's president, issued a veto, declaring his stand "against all new grants of monopolies and exclusive privileges, against any prostitution of our government to the advancement of the few at the expense of the many."

That action electrified the nation's opinion makers, with responses falling predictably along partisan lines. Speaking for the Democrats, the *Washington Globe* labeled the bank "the germ of an American nobility, an instrument to enable the aristocracy of England to ... bring these states into a dependence on the British Isles, not less degrading and more fatal to their interests than their colonial condition." By defying Biddle and the bank, Jackson had done "as our fathers did in 1776," namely assert "the right of our people to freedom, and of our States to independence." The *Globe* found it "difficult to describe in adequate language the sublimity of the moral spectacle now presented to the American people in the person of Andrew Jackson ... in this act the glories of the battlefield are eclipsed — it is the crowning glory of an immortal fame."[194]

The anti–Jacksonians, on the other hand, were appalled. The *Lexington Observer* observed of Jackson's veto message, "It is a mixture of the Demagogue and the Despot, of depravity, desperation and feelings of malice partially smothered. It is the type of the detested hypocrite, who, cornered at all points, still cannot abandon entirely his habitual artifice, but at length, finding himself stripped naked, in a tone of defiance says: 'I am a villain; now do your worst and so will I.'"

This conjunction of Jackson with usurpation and arbitrary power suffused anti-administration editorials. "The Constitution is gone!" wailed the *National Intelligencer*. "It is a dead letter, and the will of a DICTATOR is the Supreme Law!" The *New York Commercial Advertiser* denounced Jackson's assumption of "a DISPENSING POWER" over the law; such a pretension, it said, had "not been exercised with impunity, even in the British monarchy, except in despotic times."[195] Other papers saw Jackson's action as the harbinger not of monarchy but of its antithesis: "The spirit of Jacksonianism," shrieked the *Boston Daily Advertiser and Patriot*, "is JACOBINISM ... its Alpha is ANARCHY and its omega DESPOTISM. It addresses itself to the worst passions of the least informed portion of the People."[196]

An anti-Jackson newspaper in Boston described the president as "the wretched object who impersonates the Chief Magistracy of the country ... broken down in health and intellect ... the slave of the profligate creatures of both sexes by whom he is surrounded."[197] Perforce, the anti–Jacksonians rallied to the election of Clay. "One more opportunity — perhaps the last — is yet afforded us," an Ohio newspaper solemnly declared, "of strangling the monster of despotism before it shall have attained full growth, and checking the full tide of corruption before it shall have become too strong to be resisted. The power still remains in our hands. Let us so use it as men who are to render an account to our God, to our country, to the world — and all will be well." [198] Just as pro–Jackson editors took a leading role in the formation of the Democratic Party, so did their anti–Jackson rivals in mustering the forces of the opposition. All the National Republican editors from Boston — the *Columbian Centinel*, the *Daily Courier*, the *Advertiser*, and the *Independent Courier*— were delegates to the Massachusetts state National Republican convention in 1832.

According to Arthur Schlesinger, two-thirds of the newspapers published in the country supported the Second Bank of the United States during its struggle for survival with Jackson.[199] Not all of this support was disinterested. The bank freely dispensed patronage, buying the allegiance of editors as easily as it did members of Congress. The editors of the *National Intelligencer*, for example, had more than ideological motivations for their staunch defense of the bank. Gales and Seaton owed slightly more than $50,000 to the bank in 1829; they were so heavily indebted that Biddle had refused their requests for additional loans in late 1828 and early 1829, and in 1829 the bank purchased the *National Intelligencer* building under terms of a deed of trust. By January 1832, Gales and Seaton had succeeded in reducing their debt to the bank to slightly less than $12,000, but they were still on shaky financial ground and only too willing to accept Biddle's patronage. They received $1,300 in 1831 and $800 in 1832 for printing speeches and pamphlets favoring the bank.[200]

A striking example of pecuniary needs outweighing partisan loyalty is the volte-face on the bank issue by the *New York Courier and Enquirer*. After serving eight years in the military, the twenty-five-year-old James Watson Webb resigned his commission in 1827 and moved to New York, "a mere boy, to take charge of a political press at the commencement of the political campaign which terminated in the election of Andrew Jackson to the presidency," as he later recalled, buying the *Morning Courier* and merging it in 1829 with the *Enquirer*.[201] Webb, who backed Van Buren to succeed Jackson, became so embroiled in his confrontation with Duff Green, who backed Calhoun, that he finally hurried south to punish "the St. Louis upstart" in the spring of 1830.

Webb arrived in Washington on May 6 with the specific intent of horsewhipping Green before as many members of Congress as could be assembled in one place to witness the event. According to Webb's account in the *Courier and Enquirer* on May 10, he saluted Green as a "poor, contemptible, cowardly puppy," whereupon Green drew a pistol, "about eight inches long." Webb offered to throw away his cane if Green would throw away his handgun. "I will pull your nose and box your ears," he said.

In Green's account, published in the *Telegraph* on May 13, he was approaching the west front of the Capitol when Webb, with cane raised, confronted him, blocking his path to the entrance. Green halted and drew his pistol, whereupon the following exchange took place:

WEBB: Throw away your pistol and I will give you a damned whipping!
GREEN: I do not mean to be whipped by you, nor will I put myself in a position to invite attack from you.
WEBB: Are you not a coward to draw a pistol on an unarmed man?
GREEN: I have no time to waste with you — so you must march out of my path.
WEBB: I will not.
GREEN (cocking and presenting the pistol): You shall!
WEBB: I'll go back.
GREEN: Very well, go backward or forward as you like — but march out of my path.

Webb then retreated up the stairs and into the rotunda of the Capitol, keeping a wary eye over his shoulder the entire time.[202] The two editors kept firing verbal salvoes at each other into 1832, Webb posting handbills declaring, "I publish General Duff Green to the world, as a scoundrel and a coward," Green posting Webb in turn as a "despicable character."[203] Webb, smarting under this insult, sent as his representative Samuel B. Barrell to secure an apology and a retraction of the statement, with the intention of challenging Green to a duel if the apology was not forthcoming. Green responded by administering a cowhide flogging to Barrell, and the matter was allowed to die.

But later that year the *Courier and Enquirer*, which had previously labeled the enemies of Jackson a "trinity of abominations," suddenly switched its support mid-campaign from the president to Clay.[204] Webb's last-minute defection to the anti–Jackson camp caused such a commotion that a Congressional committee looked into the matter and unearthed the fact that loans totaling nearly $53,000 had been made to Webb by the Second Bank of the United States during the preceding year.[205] The *Globe's* Blair nailed Webb as "that two legged, strutting, mouthing, ranting, bullying animal ... who has just 'hopped the twig' and now sits perched on the United States Bank, chanting his cock-a-doodle-doos." Blair, who responded to the decision by Hezekiah Niles to support recharter by noting archly that Niles had "defected to the Bank: *price unknown*,"[206] later admitted being "charmed" with Webb's "honesty and independence in complying with his bargain with the Bank—and the bold, frank and honorable way in which he unsays all that he has said in favor of the President for the price paid for him by Mr. Biddle."[207]

Jackson's opponents were not able to salvage the election for Clay, but in the wake of their defeat they continued to coalesce into a viable political party. Many differing strands of editorial perspective were woven into the support of the majority of the nation's press for the Whig Party from its emergence in the 1830s until its collapse in the 1850s. These included the old Republican papers, the Anti-Masonic press, the anti–Jackson papers in the South, and the Clay papers of the West. The Whig presence was preponderant among the weekly papers of the smaller towns. Whig papers loyal to Clay in his home state, for example, included the Lexington *True American* of Cassius M. Clay and the *Louisville Journal* of George D. Prentice. Even in Tennessee, the heart of Jackson country, the *Knoxville Whig*, edited by "Parson" William G. Brownlow, carried the torch for Clay. But as in the days of the old Federalist press,

The fearsome James Watson Webb was editor of the New York *Morning Courier* and *New York Enquirer*. Even by the standards of a violent age, his aggression, whether in print, on the field of honor, or during a chance encounter on the street, made him a dangerous adversary (courtesy Library Congress).

the Whigs were even more dominant among the dailies of the large cities, where the mercantile classes, who contributed most of the advertising revenue, were generally aligned with the party. As late as 1851, New York City still had only one Democratic paper to half a dozen Whig papers.

It was Webb of the *Courier and Enquirer* who originally popularized the term "Whig" as defining the opposite to Jacksonianism.[208] Webb also stuck the Democrats with the label "Loco Foco" after an incident at a party caucus in 1835 when, after the conservative faction not only staged a walkout but turned off the gas lights in the hall, the remaining delegates continued to conduct business by the light of their Loco-Foco brand matches.[209]

Webb carried his take-no-prisoners attitude into his advocacy for the new party. In 1842, he denounced the temperance champion and Kentucky congressman Thomas Marshall, who demanded satisfaction and seriously wounded Webb in the leg. The editor spent the next two years in Sing Sing Prison for breaking New York's anti-dueling laws.

In addition to taking the field of honour himself, Webb was also responsible for impelling those around him into duels as well. In 1838, Congressman Jonathan Cilley of Maine made some remarks critical of Webb during the course of a debate in the House. Webb demanded satisfaction through his second, Congressman William Graves of Kentucky. Cilley refused Webb's challenge on the grounds that that Webb was not a gentleman, and said that in any case under the Constitution he was not responsible to anyone outside the House for anything he said within it. Graves conceded that Cilley's position was legally proper — but then issued him a challenge of his own, because under the *Code Duello* Cilley's refusal of Webb's challenge constituted an insult to his second. Cilley accepted, chose rifles at eighty yards, and was fatally wounded in the ensuing third exchange of shots. The duel roused such a furor in the country that Congress finally bestirred itself and passed a law which "provided death to all survivors when anyone was killed, and five years' imprisonment for giving or accepting a challenge," which was a step in the right direction, but apparently did little if anything to cool passions.[210] Webb went on to horsewhip people on the street, take his cane to elected representatives on the steps of Congress, and organize the mob that sacked the church of abolitionist preacher Charles Finney.[211]

In 1829, another habitual duelist, William Leggett, who had been court-martialed and forced to resign from the navy in 1826 for that offense, became the associate editor and part owner of Bryant's *Evening Post*. After persuading Bryant to horsewhip a rival editor at the *Commercial Advertiser*, Loco Foco Leggett next took on Webb. He confronted the editor on Wall Street, announced "Colonel Webb, you are a coward and a scoundrel and I spit upon you," proceeded to do so, and then punched Webb in the face. However, he had bitten off more than he could chew on this occasion; Webb retaliated by beating his adversary senseless with his cane.[212] Webb remained at the helm of his paper until it merged with the *World* on July 1, 1861. Having turned Republican during the 1850s, Webb was rewarded by Abraham Lincoln with the mission to Brazil. If rival editors ever reflected on the irony of this least diplomatic of men being awarded a post in the foreign service they held their tongues out of sheer relief at his departing for the safe distance of another hemisphere.

Influential Whig papers in New England included the Massachusetts *Springfield Republican*, founded by Samuel Bowles in 1824 and later edited by his son, and the Boston *Atlas*, coedited by Richard Houghton and Richard Hildreth.[213] But the most prominent Whig newspaperman during the brief life of the party was Edward Thurlow Weed. As a tramp journeyman printer he had held jobs in various localities, from Cooperstown to Albany, before finally becoming proprietor of a little weekly newspaper of his own, the *Republican Agriculturalist*, in the Chenango County town of Norwich. Without financial resources and unable to make the paper pay, he sold out in 1820 and spent another couple of years knocking about as a

journeyman printer be-
fore becoming junior edi-
tor of the anti–Van Buren
Rochester Telegraph, which
he took ownership of
in 1825. Elected to the
state assembly in 1824 on
DeWitt Clinton's People's
Party ticket, when the
anti–Masonic phenome-
non erupted in upstate
New York, Weed dedi-
cated himself to this fresh
crusade. According to
Vaughn, "No man exerted
as great and continuous an
influence on Antimasonry
and did more to make it a
working political instru-
ment than Weed."[214]
Forced to sell his interest
in the *Telegraph* by a boycott of local Masonic subscribers and advertisers,
Weed established the *Anti-
Masonic Enquirer*, which
commenced publication
on February 2, 1828, with
its guns trained on the
Regency. Van Buren's
patronage would turn the
press, which "ought to be
free as air and fearless as
virtue," Weed wrote in
one of the first issues of
his new paper, into "the
muzzled organ of faction
and the tamed beast of
burden of demagogues."[215]

From his power base as editor of the *Albany Evening Journal*, the "Wizard of the Lobby" Thurlow Weed played a formative role in the emergence of the Whig Party. His partnership with William Seward, the
most enduring in the history of American politics, brought his protégé
to the threshold of the White House (courtesy of Library of Congress).

In 1828, Weed also served as campaign manager for John Quincy Adams in western New
York. In 1830, he moved to Albany and emerged as a political boss in his own right, taking
on the Regency with his own machine and his own newspaper, the *Evening Journal*, finally
succeeding Croswell as state printer in 1840.[216] Weed's own experience of elective office
amounted to two terms in the New York State Legislature; the "Wizard of the Lobby" preferred to work his particular brand of magic behind the scenes. One of the first "kingmak-
ers" in American politics, Weed has been described as "another Warwick, making senators,
governors, and state officers," most notably in the election of William Seward as governor of
New York in 1838.[217] "How much I am indebted to you!" Seward gushed in the wake of his
victory. "You are a wonderful being — a mystery — but to me a guardian spirit, where gentle

influences seem to prepare the very atmosphere I breathe with grateful odors." Predictably, Seward greeted his victory with the declaration, as simple as it was no doubt heartfelt, "God bless Thurlow Weed, I owe this result to him."[218]

Seward first encountered Weed by chance in 1825 when, passing through Rochester on an excursion to Niagara Falls, his wagon became bogged down, and the editor came to his assistance. The unlikely partnership between the powerfully-framed, hard-bitten and savvy Weed, and the dapper, diminutive and idealistic Seward would blossom over the ensuing four decades, from serving together in the New York State Legislature as young men, to Seward's elevation from the governor's office to the Senate and the threshold of the White House. The all-pervasive nature of the personal and political bond between the two men, surely the most intimate collaboration of its kind in American history, was overtly manifested when Seward as secretary of state felt constrained to remind his fellow Cabinet members that "Seward is Weed and Weed is Seward. What he says, I endorse. We are one."[219] More prosaically, it was said of the duo that while Seward had the principles, Weed had the votes.[220] The editor's greatest triumph on the national stage was his orchestration of the "Tippecanoe and Tyler too" campaign of 1840 which elevated the first Whig, William Henry Harrison, to the presidency.

Tippecanoe and Tyler Too

During the 1836 campaign, Weed described then vice president Van Buren, running to succeed Jackson, as "a crawling reptile, whose only claim was that he had inveigled the confidence of a credulous, blind, dotard, old man."[221] The Whigs were unable to prevent Van Buren's election, but, as economic conditions deteriorated sharply during his ensuing term of office, Whig editors would follow Weed's lead in describing the rising tide of bankruptcy and unemployment as the inevitable consequence of the nation's being subjected to experiments by a "groveling demagogue" who had "slimed himself into the Presidency."[222] "In fine, a national paralysis, ruined fortunes, gloom, suffering, and a bankrupt treasury, are the prints of General Jackson's footsteps, in which Mr. Van Buren has faithfully followed," the *National Intelligencer* sorrowfully intoned on March 20, 1840.[223]

When a party is forced onto the defensive, it must of necessity attack, so the Democratic papers, rather than coming to the succor of Van Buren, laced into his putative challenger, Henry Clay. In August 1839, the *Globe*, in mock distress, bemoaned the "melancholy spectacle" of Clay, "an aged man ... perhaps for the last time dragging the wreck of fame, of talent, and of existence, through the heat and dust of a political canvass, only to disgrace the close of a career whose commencement, alas, promised so brightly."[224] But the Whigs postponed this apotheosis of Clay by nominating General William Henry Harrison, the victor of the 1811 Battle of Tippecanoe. The initial reaction of the *Globe* in its December 9, 1839, issue was to dismiss the Whig candidate as "nothing but the mummy of defunct Federalism." In a letter to Jackson, Blair professed little concern about the upcoming campaign saying, "We look upon Harrison's nomination as the best the Whigs could make for us."[225]

Unfortunately for the Democrats, their efforts to mark Harrison with the stigma of elitism would backfire spectacularly. In the immediate aftermath of Harrison's nomination, a disappointed Clay partisan fired off to a reporter from a local Democratic paper, the *Baltimore Republican*, an appraisal of the Whig candidate that would appear in print on December 11, 1839: "Give him a barrel of hard cider, and settle a pension of two thousand a year on him, and my word for it, he will sit the remainder of his days in his log cabin, by the side of a sea-coal fire, and study moral philosophy."[226]

Since it had coalesced in the 1830s, the Whig Party had struggled to find some way to connect with the common man of the electorate. Most notably, Whig propagandists had tried, and failed, to inflate the legendary Congressman David Crockett of Tennessee into a rival for Jackson, a tactic that culminated in their erstwhile protégé's political self-immolation and subsequent death at the Alamo.[227] Now the Whigs seized on the sneering reference to hard cider and the log cabin to turn the tables on the Democrats. The remarks circulated through the Whig press like wildfire. "The Log Cabin," said Thurlow Weed, "is a symbol of nothing that Van Buren knows, feels, or can appreciate."[228] On December 20, the *National Intelligencer* reprinted a broadside from the Baltimore *Patriot* that set the tone of the upcoming campaign: "HARD CIDER AND LOG CABIN CANDIDATE.... The Loco-Focos sneer at General HARRISON as a poor man.... It is well known that General HARRISON is, in a pecuniary condition, poor.... THE POOR MAN'S PRESIDENT is the motto on the flag under which we hope to fight."

Illustrating the extent to which the Whig press was taking the initiative in nationalizing the campaign theme, on January 14 the *National Intelligencer* reprinted a similar declaration from the *New York Daily Whig*: "The '*Log Cabin Candidate*' is the term of reproach given to General HARRISON.... These scoffers at Republican simplicity point with exultation to the place of Mr. VAN BUREN, and his servants in livery — his English servants and numerous outriders.... Every "Log Cabin" beyond the mountains and throughout the mighty west will rush to the contest in support of a gallant soldier and veteran statesman, and place him triumphantly in the Presidential chair."[229]

In fact, Harrison, who did not drink hard cider, was earning over $6,000 annually, was not born in a log cabin but in a fine two-story brick home at Berkeley on the James River in

Every motif of the "Log Cabin" mystique that saturated the Whig campaign for William Henry Harrison in 1840 is well represented in this music sheet, "General Harrison's Log Cabin March & Quick Step." Before a log cabin in the wilderness Harrison greets a crippled veteran. The score running through the six bars of music forming the stripes of the flag continues on the wall of the cabin itself. Repeated throughout the notation, marking the treble and bass clefs, are tiny figures of soldiers, bayonets, and cider barrels (courtesy of Library of Congress).

Virginia, and at the time of the campaign owned a palatial Georgian mansion in Vincennes, Indiana.[230] It was true that he also owned a $10,000 estate in North Bend, Ohio, one that he had built for his bride near the turn of the century. It earned him a designation as "the farmer of North Bend," but only the north wing had any logs in it. Nevertheless, the legend was established.[231]

A personal committee headed by Charles S. Todd, editor of the *Cincinnati Republican*, was formed to manage the Harrison campaign, performing every task from preparing his speeches to answering his correspondence.[232] Relishing the opportunity, Harrison's backers competed with each other to extol the plebian virtues of their candidate: "Thrice honored be he whom the splendid palaces, the seduction of official station, the blaze of military and civic renown, could never allure from his attachment to the republican simplicity which he learned between the unhewn rafters of his log cabin," the *Newark Daily Advertiser* intoned on May 16, 1840.

An increasingly frustrated Blair, conversely, found the spectacle of log cabins and hard cider, barouches and white horses, guzzling, boasting and bragging an "insulting display of ... contempt for popular intelligence."[233] Subsequent editions of the *Globe* portrayed Harrison as a "weak, vain old man, in the dotage of expiring ambition," a "gossiping old lady ... who lives on a sinecure clerkship in a city but is pretended to be a FARMER living in a log cabin and drinking hard cider," a "vain, imbecile, garrulous personage who, in his best days, when called into public service by family influence and busy ambition, was always begging certificates from his kindly ... subalterns to cover his disasters and defeats," and a "superannuated imbecile old man in the custody of a committee of keepers," all of which was preparatory to the definitive assessment of the Whig nominee in the pages of the mouthpiece of the Democratic Party: "Is the man insane?"[234] But with momentum on their side, the Whigs responded in mocking verse:

> King Matty he sat in his 'big White House,"
> A curling his whiskers fine,
> And the Globe man, Blair, sat by his side,
> A drinking his champaigne wine, wine, wine,
> A drinking his champaigne wine.[235]

Some Whigs were more direct. "A sure method to kill fleas," Cleveland-based *The Axe* snapped, "is to spread *The Globe* over them."[236]

Major boosters of the "Hard Cider" candidate included Weed's *Albany Evening Journal*, the *New York Express*, the *Louisville Journal*, the *Advertiser* and the *Atlas* of Boston, and, in Harrison's Buckeye home state, the *Cincinnati Gazette* and Columbus-based *Ohio State Journal*.[237] Duff Green made his return to public affairs when he established the Baltimore *Pilot & Transcript*, an organ dedicated to the election of William Henry Harrison, on April 2, 1840. Green also published *The Tippecanoe Text Book*, *The Log Cabin Cabinet*, and *The Tippecanoe Song Book*.

As one measure of the increased interest in the election of 1840, there were 58 Democratic temporary campaign papers (up from 10 in 1836), and 101 for the Whigs (up from 14).[238] A new player on the national stage of partisan journalism made his debut during campaign of 1840 in this capacity. Having begun his print career as a fifteen-year-old apprentice to the East Poultney, Vermont, *Northern Spectator* five years earlier, Horace Greeley arrived in New York City in August 1831 seeking his fortune with "twenty-five dollars in his pocket and his red-handkerchief bundle on his shoulder." In 1834, Greeley and a partner launched a new literary weekly, the *New Yorker*. When the partnership dissolved in 1836, Greeley took sole ownership of the publication as his share. Shortly afterwards Greeley, then twenty-eight, was co-opted by Weed to manage the Whig campaign journal, the *Jeffersonian*, during the 1838 midterm elections. "In casting about for an editor," Weed would later recall, "it occurred to me that there was some person connected with the *New Yorker*, a literary journal published in that city, possessing the qualities needed for our new enterprise." These traits included his being "a strong tariff man, and probably an equally strong Whig."[239] Having satisfied his patron's expectations in the midterm elections, Greeley was assigned responsibility for a new publication with a similar function, the *Log Cabin*, two years later. Greeley, now an ardent Whig who had attended the party's first national convention in Harrisburg as a delegate from New York, introduced this vehicle on July 11, 1840, and made its agenda abundantly clear in his prospectus:

> THE EXTRA LOG CABIN is now published, and for sale at this office. It contains a fine PORTRAIT OF GEN. HARRISON; A FULL REFUTATION OF THE WHITE SLAVERY SLANDER, also of the falsehood that Congress refused a vote of thanks to Gen. Harrison for his bravery and Conduct in the War, with Engravings of the GOLD MEDALS which were voted for him by Congress; engravings of OLD FORT DEFIANCE and FORT MEIGS; the Battle-Guards of WAYNE'S VICTORY, TIPPECANOE and THE THAMES, with full authentic accounts of the several Battles and other Military Operations in which Gen. Harrison has been engaged, Gen. Harrison's LETTERS TO BOLIVAR, SHERROD WILLIAMS, JAMES LYONS, &c.&c.—the whole forming a compendious and eloquent record of the CHARACTER, SERVICES, PRINCIPLES AND OPINIONS of General Harrison, and a conclusive refutation of the malignant slanders which have been uttered against him.[240]

In the cockpit of the New York partisan press, where the *Courier and Enquirer*, *American*, *Express*, and *Commercial Advertiser* were the established Whig papers and the *Evening Post*, *Journal of Commerce*, *Sun*, and *Herald* leaned Democratic, Greeley immediately made his mark by launching into what would become recognized over the next thirty years as his trademark pseudo–Manichean style of outraged moral hectoring. "Wherever you find a bitter, blasphemous Atheist and enemy of Marriage, Morality, and Social Order," the *Log Cabin* maintained, "there you may be certain of one vote for Van Buren."[241]

The Illinois equivalent to Greeley's publication was the *Old Soldier*. "Every Whig in the state must take it," the young Abraham Lincoln brusquely informed county committeemen, "[and] you must raise a fund ... for extra copies ... for distribution ... among our opponents." In Ohio there sprang up at least seventeen variations on this theme. In addition to the regular Whig press, the Chillico *Log Cabin Herald*, the Cleveland *Hard Cider for Log Cabins*, the Steubenville *Log Cabin Farmer*, and the Elyria *Old Tip's Broom* were made available to the discerning voter of the Buckeye State. Similarly, the *Snag Boat* of Raymond, Mississippi, the *Flail* in Brattleboro, Vermont, the *Sucker* in Alton, Illinois, the *Settler* in Fredonia, New York, the *Harrisonian* of Athens, Georgia, and the *Tippecanoe* in Greencastle, Indiana, ensured that every community, North or South, no matter how isolated, was able to fully appreciate the glory that was William Henry Harrison. Epitomizing the common theme of such publications, the Chicago *Hard Cider Press* admitted straight up it "went for Harrison without a why or wherefore."[242]

And these campaign vehicles were even able to turn a profit—the circulation of Greeley's paper, for example, shot up to eighty thousand from forty-eight thousand, increasing at a rate of nearly five thousand per week.[243] The proceeds were such that in the aftermath of the campaign, and shortly after his thirtieth birthday, Greeley was able to launch a daily, the *New York Tribune*, on April 10, 1841.[244]

The flip side for the Whigs, in the campaign to portray their candidate as the new Cincinattus, was the equally well orchestrated litany of defamation to which Van Buren was subjected. The president was relentlessly associated in the pages of the Whig press with that characteristic most fatal to the political prospects of any presidential aspirant: effeminacy. After enduring a scurrilous three-day tirade in the House from Congressman Charles Ogle, labeled "The Regal Splendor of the Presidential Palace," in which he was depicted as dining off plates of gold and admiring himself in golden-framed mirrors nine feet high and four and half feet wide, Van Buren was described by the *Louisville Journal* as being in such a rage "that he actually burst his corset."[245] There was no room for honesty in such a charged political climate. After conscience-stricken fellow Whig congressman Levi Lincoln decried the "unwarranted and undignified attack" on the president the day after the Ogle omnibus concluded, Greeley brushed him off by attacking those "Artful Dodgers" who forged "a pretended speech of Mr. Lincoln."[246] If Van Buren was credited with any masculine qualities at all it was only for James Gordon Bennett of the *New York Herald* to wonder out loud whether there might not be Kinderhook children "with light hair and small, cunning eyes" who had no knowledge of "their father."[247]

Van Buren's forebears had pioneered framing the terms of an election by pitting the solid republican values of the South and West against the effeminacy of the Northeast during their campaign against John Adams in 1800. They had used the same terms to good effect against his son a generation later. Some Democrats were able to appreciate the irony of having the tactic turned against their candidate in 1840. "We have taught them to conquer us!" the *Democratic Review* wryly conceded.[248]

Some Democrats gave as good as they got. Wilbur F. Storey, the nineteen-year-old editor of the Indiana *La Porte Herald* attacked a Whig editor as unworthy of mention, and then labeled him "a degraded being, an abandoned reprobate, entirely reckless of truth, deceitful and treacherous, a filthy and loathsome blackguard, an object of pity and contempt rather than of ridicule." The following year, Storey moved to South Bend where he reported on the front page that the Whig candidate in a congressional race had died, forcing the voters to choose the Democrat.[249]

Amos Kendall had resigned as postmaster general on May 9 to take control of the president's reelection campaign, but in arguing the Democratic case he made the fullest possible use of the government payroll. One of his gambits was to "request" of all postmasters that they secure subscribers for the *Extra Globe*: "Every farmer, mechanic, and workingman should have one; and if they cannot well spare a dollar each, two or more should unite to-gether to take one." The former postmaster general hoped that this little chore would be "compatible" with the "inclination and sense of duty" of his erstwhile employees. The ploy was apparently a success: "A few Whig postmasters," the *Globe* reported blandly, "have returned rude and insulting replies" to the circular; but most "disposed of the prospectus as requested" like "true gentlemen."[250] The compliant postmasters collected subscriptions and remitted them postage-free. Post office headquarters recorded the subscriptions—sometimes 400 a day—before turning them over to the *Globe*.[251]

At Van Buren's suggestion, a campaign paper, the *Rough-Hewer*, published in conjunction with the *Argus*, was established in Albany to counteract Greeley's *Log Cabin*. Illinois Democrats brought out a similar paper, the *Old Hickory*. In Pennsylvania there was the *Magician*, in Ohio the *Democratic Rasp*, *Hickory Club* and *Kinderhook Dutchman*. Perennial Democratic stalwarts included the *Bay State Democrat*, the *Ohio Statesman*, the *Baltimore Republican*, the *Kentucky Gazette*, the *Nashville Union*, and the *Richmond Enquirer*.[252]

Viewed through the prism of the intervening decades, it is impossible to determine from the partisan press of the era where the truth lies in any assessment of anything relating to the campaign. Is it a fact that, as according to a Whig interpretation, a speaker's lips "glowed with a Promethean fire" during an address? Or is the Democratic depiction of the same individual as a "gorged itinerant raver" more accurate?[253] When Whig papers speak of an address as incorporating a "most vigorous and beautiful appeal to the intellect and heart," how can such an account be reconciled with the Democratic assessment of the same speech as "pompous, florid declamation"?[254]

One thing was certain, as the victorious Harrison was first to point out: "Ask the subsidized press what governs its operations, and it will open its iron jaws and answer you in a voice loud enough to shake the pyramids—MONEY! MONEY! I speak not at random—facts bear me testimony."[255]

A GLOBE TO LIVE ON!

Blair and Kendall are here portrayed as conjoined twins after Kendall resigned his cabinet post as postmaster general on May 16, 1840, to undertake editing of the *Extra Globe* during the presidential campaign that year. Blair exclaims, "Amos: you are an Atlas! and can support the Globe!" to which Kendall replies, "Yes! Frank, and <u>can</u> make the Globe support me," a reference to the widespread rumor that Kendall had a large stake in the campaign paper's profits. Kendall holds in his left hand a paper with the words "List of Subscribers 100,000 Office Holders," a commentary on Kendall's employing thousands of federal postmasters to distribute the *Extra Globe*, and on the practice of requiring public employees to contribute a portion of their salaries to support electoral politics (courtesy of Library of Congress).

Manifest Destiny

"The sun of Reform and Liberty has at length risen in our long oppressed and misgoverned country," Greeley's *Log Cabin* crowed on March 6, 1841. "The administration of Martin Van Buren terminated on Wednesday of this week." In his stead Harrison was inaugurated "amidst an unprecedented concourse of rejoicing, sympathizing Freemen."[256] But fate would not allow the Whigs to savor their triumph for long.

For the incoming Whigs the first task was to sweep anyone tainted by association with the Democratic Party from access to federal patronage. They went to work with a vengeance. The first Democratic appointments as postmaster general—Barry, Kendall, and Senator John M. Niles—had between them removed 1,892 postmasters over the three terms of Jackson and Van Buren. After the election of Harrison, the incoming Whig appointee, Francis Granger, removed 1,085 postmasters during his mere four-and-a-half months in office.[257]

Inevitably, Blair and Rives were stripped of their printing privileges by the new Whig majority in the Senate. Henry Clay was determined to dismiss them "on the ground of infamy of character of the print and the Printer.... [The Senate] owed it to the purity of the national character to disconnect themselves at once and forever from those men."[258] The *Globe's* contracts were revoked on a straight party vote of 26–18.

Over the course of his thirty-day presidency, Harrison had enough strength to appoint Duff Green as governor of the Florida Territory and name Green's son Todd as minister to Russia. But any further Whig expectations were dashed when their hero, having over-exerted himself at his inaugural, contracted pneumonia, and died one month after being sworn in to office. On April 10, 1841, "a day of most unseasonable chill and sleet and snow," Greeley lamented, "our city held her great funeral parade and pageant in honor of our lost President, who had died six days before." Greeley chose "that leaden, funeral morning, the most inhospitable of the year," to issue the first edition of his new publication, the *New York Tribune*. He wasn't shy about admitting the partisan motivation or finances behind the new venture: "I had been incited to this enterprise by several Whig friends, who deemed a cheap daily, addressed more specifically to the laboring class, eminently needed in our city, where the only two cheap journals then and still existing — the Sun and the Herald — were in decided, though unavowed, and therefore more effective, sympathy and affiliation with the Democratic Party. Two or three had promised pecuniary aid if it should be needed."[259]

Harrison's death had elevated his running mate, John Tyler, to the Presidency. Now the Whigs faced an essential problem; Tyler wasn't a Whig, and he proceeded to veto Whig measures. On the last day of the 1841 session, Tyler was repudiated by the Congressional Whig caucus. In September of that year his entire Cabinet, bar Webster, resigned en masse. Speaking for orthodox Whigs everywhere, the *Lexington Intelligencer* snarled, "If a God-Directed thunderbolt were to strike and annihilate the traitor, all say that Heaven is just."[260]

The breakup of the Whig Cabinet forced Gales and Seaton to make the difficult decision to retain their allegiance to Clay and oppose the president. In September 1841, Tyler made Thomas Allen's *Madisonian* the official newspaper of his administration. "I can no longer tolerate the *Intelligencer* as the official paper," the President remarked. "Besides assaulting me perpetually, directly, it represses all defensive articles.... There is a point beyond which one's patience cannot endure."[261]

Duff Green, ever amenable to states' rights interests, was appointed to London in 1841 as an executive agent to President Tyler, with a roving commission to obtain inside information for a new commercial treaty with England. His unstinting advocacy of human bondage earned him the sobriquet "American ambassador of slavery" from John Quincy Adams. Green later secured the consulship at Galveston and then landed in Mexico City as the president's unofficial emissary, sounding out the prospects for the sale of California.[262]

Henry Clay, the Whig nominee for the election of 1844, expected to face off that year against ex-president Van Buren. But the Democratic convention instead nominated its first "dark horse" presidential candidate, James Knox Polk of Tennessee. Whigs professed to be delighted; the *New York Tribune* labeled Polk a "third-rate partisan" and "a buffoon," while his running mate, George M. Dallas, was denounced as "a very Jacobinic, loose-principled, Texas Locofoco."[263] To the *National Intelligencer*, Polk's nomination "may be considered as the dying gasp, the last breath of life, of the 'Democratic' party."[264] But in fact the Democrats had serendipitously stumbled onto the formula for a successful presidential candidacy. Polk's very anonymity was his chief asset because that made it easier for the electorate to project its aspirations onto him. Clay, on the other hand, had that most crippling of political liabilities, an extensive record of achievement in government. Every vote he ever cast, every quip he ever made, could be used in evidence against him. To the *Globe*, Clay's life had been "a continued series of brawls and violence, and disregard of laws the most sacred in the eyes of God and Man," and Democratic papers the length and breadth of the nation dedicated themselves during the campaign to reminding voters, in intimate detail, of every one of these incidents.[265]

During the presidential contest of 1844, at least sixty-three special campaign newspapers were published for Clay, forty-three for Polk, and four for Liberty Party candidate James

Birney.[266] The most interesting of this breed made its debut in June 1844 when young lawyer and rising Empire State Democrat Samuel J. Tilden and his good friend John L. O'Sullivan, co-founders of the influential *United States Magazine and Democratic Review* in 1837, collaborated to launch a newspaper in New York dedicated to the election of Polk. The first issue of the *New York Morning News* appeared on August 21, 1844, supplemented by a weekly campaign sheet, aptly enough labeled *The Campaign*, "designed to place every Democrat in possession of all the material arguments and evidence in support of his noble cause, in a condensed form, and to enable them to lay before his neighbors of opposite or unsettled politics."[267] O'Sullivan ran himself so ragged during the campaign that his mother was moved to comment to a friend in mid–October, "My John looks worn and fatigued — he can find no rest until after this Presidential contest." Her son's imprecations were far from subtle; likening the Whigs to street walkers—"A fair and showy exterior — all smile and blandishment without, but all deceit and death within"— he urged subscribers to "do your duty to your principles, your country and humanity" by voting in the defense of "the sacred cause of the very manhood, the very humanity that is in us."[268] But when it was all over, in the judgment of the *Richmond Enquirer*, "there was no single individual to whom the Union was more indebted than John Louis O'Sullivan for the vote of New York," and hence the election of Polk.[269] During Polk's term, O'Sullivan would rise to become, according to Frederick Merk, "the high priest of the doctrine of Manifest Destiny," a phrase O'Sullivan coined to define an era and an ethos.[270]

The *Morning News* greeted the outcome of the election with the simple salutation "OUR COUNTRY IS SAVED." Clay's partisans in the press, on the other hand, carried the shock of his final defeat to their graves. Gales and Seaton never registered greater personal anguish in their more than thirty years as editors of the *National Intelligencer*: "The disappointment and pain with which this result of the late animated canvass has filled our breasts it would be mere affectation for us to deny, or to attempt to conceal from our readers. Wholly unexpected, the event took us completely by surprise. Not for even a moment apprehended, the blow came upon us with a staggering force."[271]

Greeley, who "profoundly loved Henry Clay," issued a *Clay Tribune* campaign supplement to his *New York Tribune*, and freely admitted it was no secret that "from the day of his nomination in May to that of his defeat in November I gave every hour, every effort, every thought to his election.... I gave heart and soul to the canvass." He sent his wife Molly to find refuge on a farm in rural Massachusetts while he camped out in his office, living without sleep and giving up to six speeches a day on Clay's behalf: "I traveled and spoke much ... and I gave the residue of the hours I could save from sleep to watching the canvass and doing whatever I could to render our side of it more effective."[272] Marking the first manifestation of what would become a regular feature in American politics, Greeley blamed Clay's loss on the presence of a third party. "On your guilty heads shall rest the curses of unborn generations," he chastised Liberty Party voters, whom the Whigs maintained had taken enough votes in New York to throw the state to Polk: "It is hard that an ultra Slavery candidate should be elected by the abolitionists."[273]

Ironically, while the end of Tyler's term in the White House effectively spelt the death knell for his mouthpiece, the *Madisonian*, Clay's narrow defeat did not augur well for the Democratic Party's paper of record, the *Globe*. Blair had retained patronage during Van Buren's term of office but found himself on the outside with the incoming Polk administration. For one thing, Blair was too close to such Democratic leaders as Thomas Hart Benton and Martin Van Buren, who had opposed Polk's nomination. Blair was also personally opposed to the annexation of Texas, an issue dear to Polk's heart, and was suspected of holding antislavery views. Polk also suspected that Blair would devote the duration of his term to controlling the Democratic nomination for 1848.

Polk ally Major John P. Heiss, former publisher of the *Nashville Union*, reportedly raised $35,000 from Simon Cameron and other well-heeled politicians to buy out Blair and Rives.[274] Polk was good enough to offer Blair the embassy to Spain (the offer was refused) but the last issue of the *Globe* rolled out on April 30, 1845. The following day the paper came out under new management and with a new masthead, the *Union*.[275] Heiss took over from Rives as business manager, and Polk succeeded in cajoling Thomas Ritchie, veteran editor of the *Richmond Enquirer*, to take the reins from Blair. This action startled Andrew Jackson, who called the removal of Blair "the most unexpected thing I ever met with," and warned his protégé that it could "result in injury to the perfect unity of the democracy."[276] But Young Hickory was adamant that his choice was the correct one: "I must be the head of my own administration," Polk responded, "and will not be controlled by any newspaper."[277] During his term in office the president used the *Union* to present his views to the public and keep recalcitrant Democrats in line. Of necessity, party leaders had to subscribe to the paper to remain abreast of the administration's agenda, as well as the latest capital gossip.[278]

Ritchie's pedigree as a partisan editor of the Jefferson and Jackson school was impeccable. His launch of the *Richmond Enquirer* on May 9, 1804, had been greeted by his being labeled a "double-faced villain ... a bug hardly worth the effort of crushing" by maverick Virginia Republican John Randolph.[279] But long before Ritchie moved to Washington to take over at the helm of the *Union*, "he held the politics of the Old Commonwealth in the hollow of his hand," the *New York Times* wrote. In 1824, Gales and Seaton urged Ritchie to publicize a certain candidate "because, there being no national central committee, you come the nearest to the character of such a committee." Four years later, William C. Rives, the

Thomas Ritchie, long-serving editor of the *Richmond Enquirer*, survived the dog-eat-dog game of Virginia journalism for decades before making the fatal mistake of stepping up to the national arena. The lure of serving President James K. Polk as editor of his administration's mouthpiece, *The Daily Union*, proved irresistible but the timing was inopportune, as the second party system was beginning to fracture along sectional lines. Unable to satisfy any of the factions of the rapidly fragmenting Democratic Party, Ritchie lost the confidence of all, including his patron Polk (courtesy of Library of Congress).

leading Jacksonian congressman in Virginia, had written of the *Enquirer* that "there is not a political aspirant in the nation who does not anxiously court the countenance of such a paper, and at this moment, Van Buren, I know, and most probably Calhoun, and all the rest of the candidates for the presidential purple, are in close correspondence with Ritchie, and suing for his support."[280]

Ritchie was a loyal Jacksonian but he had never quite exhibited the pure, undiluted hero worship characteristic of Blair. At the time of the bank veto, recalled Martin Van Buren, Ritchie "scarcely ever went to bed ... without apprehension that he would wake up to hear of some coup d'etat by the General which he would be called upon to explain or defend."[281] Though never fully trusted by Jackson, Ritchie became, alongside Blair and Edwin Croswell of the *Albany Argus*, one of the most influential press spokesmen of the Democratic Party. No less an observer than Van Buren ascribed to the *Enquirer* "an influence greater than any other press in the Union." Ritchie's career achieved its apogee in 1844 when he became the unofficial field marshal of the Polk campaign; in that role Ritchie "probably contributed more than any other man in the union towards elevating Mr. Polk toward the presidency," concluded *Niles' Weekly Register*.[282]

Ritchie had a decades-long rivalry with John Hampden Pleasants of the *Richmond Whig*, whose father was Governor of Virginia from 1822 to 1825, and who described the Democrat as, among other things, "the old mesmerized driveller of the *Enquirer*." Ritchie retorted in kind, referring to Pleasants as "an indecent and factious slang-whanger." The back-and-forth nearly resulted in a duel in 1843 when Ritchie's oldest son, William, requested an appointment with Pleasants on the field of honor. The crisis was averted on that occasion, but when the elder Ritchie moved to the capital his sons took over at the *Enquirer* and they were spoiling for a fight.

Pleasants was very familiar with the risks involved for a southern editor trying to ply his trade within the boundaries set by the region's peculiar code of honor. When he wrote that the Democrats had changed their old policy of electing idiots and elected a lunatic as governor instead, O. Jennings Wise, the governor's son, had to go to the *Whig* office and beat the editor severely with a rattan cane.[283] But after Thomas Ritchie, Jr., accused Pleasants of planning to start an abolitionist journal, a base falsehood if ever there was one, and then labeled him a coward in print in response to his denials, Pleasants was forced to call Ritchie out.

At dawn on the appointed day, the editor of the *Whig* showed up with a revolver in his coat pocket, a pistol in each hand, a bowie knife in his vest, and a sword cane under his left arm. The editor of the *Enquirer* arrived armed with two pistols and a cutlass in his belt, a revolver in his pocket, and a pistol in each hand. The two men started out two hundred yards apart. Pleasants walked towards Ritchie, who opened fire at thirty yards. Pleasants was hit repeatedly but kept staggering toward Ritchie until he finally collapsed. He was carried from the field and died two days later.[284]

Such incidents were part of the fabric of life across the South.[285] "It is understood," the globetrotting Harriet Martineau observed, "that in New Orleans there were fought, in 1834, more duels than there are days in the year, fifteen on one Sunday morning."[286] Tempers showed no sign of cooling more than twenty years later; in 1858, the drama critic of the New Orleans *Daily Delta*, Emile Hirairt, offended several gentleman admirers of a singer with his caustic comments concerning her voice. Faced with a veritable plethora of challenges, he accepted two, killing the second protagonist in an exchange of shotgun fire.

But the heartland of the *Code Duello* was the state of Mississippi, where a citizen could not append the sobriquet "gentleman" unless he was prepared to uphold his rights upon the field of honor. Mississippi governor Henry Foote fought at least three duels in his native state, and, for good measure, one in Alabama. At least eleven antebellum Mississippi editors participated in duels, and three of them were killed. By comparison, six Virginia and six South Carolina editors fought duels during the same period, two from each state never returning to their respective presses.

One need only consider the storied record of the Vicksburg *Sentinel*—from its founding in 1837 until, mercifully, it expired during the Civil War—to appreciate the risk to life and limb inherent in plying the newspaper trade in the antebellum South. During the paper's early years, its editors were involved in a series of duels and brawls over their position on a widespread cotton-speculation controversy. In 1842, *Sentinel* writer James Fall was wounded in a duel with the president of the Railroad Bank, occasioned by an uncomplimentary story. Editor James Hagan survived a duel with the editor of the rival *Vicksburg Whig* before being gunned down in 1843 by the son of a judge about whom he had written some unkind remarks. In 1846, editor T. E. Robins was shot at ten paces by a J. M. Downes; a few days later, Robins's replacement as editor, Walter Hickey, was challenged by Downes's second. Hickey killed the challenger in the ensuing duel but was himself wounded in a later confrontation. He recovered and moved on to Texas, only to be killed in a fight there. Another editor, James Ryan, was killed by the publisher of the competing *Whig*; his replacement, John Lavins, was jailed for writing threatening editorials. A man named Jenkins, who succeeded Lavins, was murdered, and his successor, F. C. Jones, committed suicide.[287]

Dr. George Bagby, a Virginia editor himself, wrote in the 1850s: "The Virginia editor is a young, unmarried, intemperate, pugnacious gambling gentleman. Between drink and dueling-pistols he is generally escorted to a premature grave. If he so far withstands the ravages of brandy and gunpowder as to reach the period of gray hairs and cautiousness, he is deposed to make room for a youth who hates his life with an utter hatred and who can't keep drunk for more than a week at a time."[288]

The two brothers who edited the *Richmond Examiner* in the early 19th century both died in duels. Edgar Allan Poe challenged one of the paper's later editors, John Daniel, but showed up too drunk to shoot. Daniel, wounded in the right arm on another occasion, had to fire with his left in subsequent duels. But he continued to abuse northerners and southerners impartially, labeling the treasurer of the Confederacy a reckless gambler unfit for office. The treasurer duly called him out and put a bullet in his thigh.[289] In Kentucky, proslavery Charles Wickliffe killed the editor of the *Lexington Gazette* over an anonymous antislavery article. He was tried and acquitted, but the next editor disagreed with the verdict in print. Wickliffe challenged him too and this time was killed at eight feet.[290]

These pugnacious attitudes spilled over with expansion into the West; things got so bad that at one point the *Kansas City Times* suggested that someone should stuff and preserve a specimen Kansas editor before the race became altogether extinct.[291] Joseph Charless, who founded the St. Louis *Missouri Gazette* in 1808, was assaulted, spat on, shot at, and had his office burned down; the editor of the rival *Inquirer* then waylaid him on the street and beat him severely with a cudgel. One editor in San Francisco, pressed for time, posted a notice on his door: "Subscriptions received from 9 to 4, challenges from 11 to 12 only."[292] A dispute over whether or not to send aid to the snowbound Donner party moved General James Denver, secretary of state of California, to kill Edward Gilbert, editor of the *Alta California*. Apparently this was a popular move; Denver went on to serve as a congressman and territorial governor, and had a city in Colorado named after him.[293]

In Washington, Ritchie Sr., like Blair and Green before him, found it impossible to satisfy all of the factions within a Democratic Party that was increasingly divided along sectional lines into a series of personal fiefdoms, each claiming to represent mainstream party values and demanding that its position be recognized as such in the party's court paper. Carrying out this delicate balancing act on a daily basis taxed even the most sensitive of partisan editors who were only too aware that one misstep could have perilous repercussions.

The Whigs were immediately able to capitalize on the divisions opened by the demise of Blair. Although they were unable to prevent the Democratic majority from electing Ritchie as House printer when Congress convened in December 1845, they did succeed in having the rates cut to 20 percent below what had been paid since 1819. In the summer of the following year, the opposition was able to further embarrass the administration when, supported by a handful of dissident Democrats, they forced through both houses a bill providing that the clerk of the House and the secretary of the Senate let the printing each session to the lowest bidder. Ritchie submitted the lowest bid and continued to serve both houses, but the *Union's* revenues had been cut to the point where it now operated at a loss.[294]

In February 1847, a final humiliation was visited upon Ritchie after he accused those senators who had opposed the administration's military bill of handing a victory to Mexico. Since the editorial appeared only hours after John C. Calhoun had critiqued Polk's handling of Mexican affairs, the attack appeared directed against him personally. Calhoun's allies mobilized to bar Ritchie from the Senate floor and, their having secured the support of enough mischievous Whigs, by a vote of twenty-seven to twenty-one the Senate barred its doors to its own printer, the august body not deigning to readmit him until June of the following year.[295] Ritchie ultimately found himself being marginalized by Polk even before the end of his term in office; the President swiftly tired of his hand-picked editorial advocate, complaining of his "constitutional infirmity," his inability to keep a secret. "All he knows, though given him in confidence, he is almost certain to put it in his newspaper," Polk grumbled.[296]

According to William E. Ames, during the period that Congress underwrote the political organs of the nation's capital, up to 1846, nearly two and a half million dollars was directed into the pockets of the Washington publishers. No publication had received more generous treatment than the *National Intelligencer*, whose receipts showed a gain of just over $1 million from the regular congressional contracts, with an additional $650,000 from the publication of archival material — the *Annals* and *American State Papers*. Blair and Rives received half a million dollars in congressional contract money during their fifteen years in Washington. Duff Green was paid nearly $400,000 before he was forced from the scene in the 1830s, and he received an additional $54,000 for publishing documents relative to public lands. The other major beneficiary was Thomas Allen, editor of the *Madisonian*, who lapped up the federal largesse dispensed by his patron, "His Accidency" John Tyler, to the tune of $258,000.[297]

The Polk administration further widened the scope for patronage when at the end of its term it created a new cabinet office, the Interior Department, responsible for the General Land Office, which made the widest possible use of newspapers, placing advertising of land sales in newspapers every quarter. According to Smith, "The policy seems to have been to shift the advertising each quarter so that more papers could have a share ... it served as a means of giving favors to papers that the State Department did not have on its list."[298]

In a bid to revive the magic of 1840, as the campaign season of 1848 dawned, there was strong support for the nomination of Mexican War hero General Zachary Taylor among the Whig press, including Weed's Albany *Evening Journal*, the Philadelphia *North American*, the *Herald* and *Courier and Enquirer* in New York, and Alexander Bullitt's *New Orleans Picayune* in Taylor's native Louisiana. Although the *National Intelligencer* was cool towards Taylor, the only major dissenter — on the grounds that since Taylor had no known party affiliation and had never even voted, he was not qualified to serve as the presidential nominee of the party — was Horace Greeley's *Tribune*. Whig papers zeroed in on Democratic nominee Lewis Cass, "a base intriguer, and unprincipled demagogue," according to the Springfield (Massachusetts) *Republican*, June 1, 1848, which added, "None have played the sycophant, none have bended in abject submission to the South, more basely than he."[299] Democrats sought to make an issue of the Whig bias in the press. Party broadsheet *The Campaign* warned members, "We must count upon a host of presses ... upon streams of money, contributed by the rich merchants and the greedy manufacturing capitalists, being poured out against us."[300] But the party was hamstrung by division into a popular sovereignty faction, loyal to Cass, and a free-soil faction that broke away and put forth its own nominee, former President Martin Van Buren, guaranteeing the election of Taylor.[301]

Taylor, a career military man, was not a believer in the spoils system. However, as Smith notes, "His principal appointed officials did not have the handicap of reservations about the spoils of victory, and they succeeded in giving Taylor's short presidency a record for proscription that outdid that of any previous president."[302] In his selection of newspapers to print the laws in the states and territories for the Thirty-first Congress, Secretary of State John Clayton managed to find substitutes for *every single one* of the selections made by his predecessor, James Buchanan. Upon taking office, Taylor had revived the failed *Republic* as his mouthpiece, and retained Bullitt and John G. Sargent of the *New York Courier and Enquirer* as editors.[303] After Taylor's demise in July 1850, the *National Intelligencer* was revived as the official party organ, replacing the *Republic*, which had sided against incoming President Millard Fillmore.

The fact that it was Daniel Webster who took over as secretary of state for Fillmore should have signified a break with the cycle of federal patronage for the partisan press. After all, it was Webster who at the National Republican convention in 1832 likened the "purchased or pensioned" press to the fettered press of other countries, explaining that the press cannot be trusted in such circumstances "because it is under a power that may prove greater

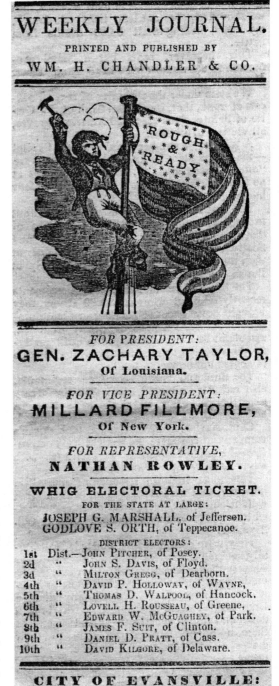

A Whig ticket for Zachary Taylor, published in the Evansville, Indiana, *Weekly Journal* during the campaign of 1848, features a military motif appropriate for the hero of Buena Vista, symbolically nailing its colors to the mast for "Old Rough and Ready." (author's collection).

than the love for truth." It was Webster who called Jackson's mass appointment of editors to public office "reprehensible" on the grounds that it "It degrades both the government and the press ... turns the palladium of liberty into an engine of party ... so completely perverts the true object of government [and] so entirely revolutionizes our whole system, that the chief business of those in power is directed rather to the propagation of opinions favorable to themselves rather than to the execution of the laws."[304]

And it was Webster who, at the Whig convention in 1840, had suggested the establishment of an independent printer of government laws and business, because no man should be compelled to give his money "to pay another man to persuade him not to change the government." However, once again, the cycle repeated itself as the temptation to secure partisan ends in office overcame whatever principles might have been espoused when isolated from power. Webster set about making a clean sweep of his predecessor's appointments; in only two sessions he effected a turnover of 60 percent of Clayton's choices, and the deciding factor, as always, was pure politics. For example, Webster could not renew the contract with the *Albany Evening Journal* because that was Weed's paper, and Weed was anathema to the Fillmore wing of the Whig Party in New York State. In fact, the *Evening Journal* was so obnoxious that Fillmore even proposed to buy it from Weed, and was prepared to offer a generous premium to do so. When Weed refused to sell out, the president's friends created the *New York State Register* at Albany, which became the organ of the Fillmore Whigs and, naturally, got the printing contract from Webster.[305]

The changing of the guard represented by the incoming Democratic administration of Franklin Pierce was marked in traditional style; Pierce's secretary of state, William L. Marcy, made almost a clean sweep of the publishers of the laws, changing all but six

The Lynn News.

LYNN, ESSEX COUNTY, MASS.

Lynn, Friday Morning, Aug. 27, 1852.

Whig National Nominations.

ELECTION, TUESDAY, NOVEMBER 2.

SCOTT & GRAHAM.

FOR PRESIDENT,
WINFIELD SCOTT,
OF NEW JERSEY.

FOR VICE PRESIDENT,
WM. A. GRAHAM,
OF NORTH CAROLINA.

General Winfield Scott's nickname, "Old Fuss and Feathers," lent itself less readily to electoral propaganda, and, with the Mexican War rapidly receding into memory, military themes were less appropriate for the campaign of 1852. This Whig ticket published in the *Lynn News* (Lynn, Massachusetts) is more subdued than the efforts of past years, perhaps a reflection of the entropy that was shortly to overwhelm the party (author's collection).

(four of which were in the territories) on the list of the outgoing Whig administration. When fellow Democrat Buchanan succeeded Pierce in the White House, there was another shuffle of the publishing rights, with at least twenty-nine changes being made.

By now the entire mechanism of government printing was coming into question. The cost had skyrocketed during the Pierce administration. For printing, paper, and related processing, the bill for the two Congresses during his term (Thirty-third and Thirty-fourth) was $3,899,000 — more than the cost for all previous years since 1819 combined.[306] An investigation conducted by the aroused Thirty-fifth Congress found that more money had been spent than appropriated, and culminated in the prosecution and conviction of the superintendent of public printing.

The management of the *Union* was implicated in the scandal. The mouthpiece of the Democratic Party had fallen on troubled times. Thomas Ritchie had surrendered control of the *Union* to A. J. Donelson on April 15, 1851.[307] Donelson lasted less than a year before handing off to General Robert Armstrong, who had served on Jackson's staff at the Battle of New Orleans during the War of 1812. When Armstrong, who was described by one acquaintance as "wholly destitute of literary culture — incapable of writing a sentence," died (a corollary, perhaps, of his alleged capacity to consume fifty-six bottles of wine in a twenty-four hour period), A. O. P. Nicholson, the former editor of the *Nashville Union* and an old friend of President Pierce, took over, bringing with him a fellow Tennessean, former congressman Harvey Watterson. Nicholson stepped down after Buchanan was inaugurated. The new president installed his friend John Appleton as editor, but then moved him up to assistant secretary of state, leaving William A. Harris to take his place. Once Harris took control of the *Union*, he announced that he would spare no expense or effort to "make it the great central organ of the Democratic Party."[308] Buchanan finally appointed General George W. Bowman as superintendent of public printing and prevailed upon him to buy out the *Union*. Bowman's publication came out on April 13, 1859, still proclaiming itself to be "a thoroughly Democratic Paper," but with the name *Constitution* substituted for *Union*, the latter a loaded term during a period of worsening sectional tension.

In 1860, a select committee of the Senate investigating the state of public printing reported that it was "the unanimous opinion of the committee that the present system of public printing is the worst that could have been adopted, and from its very nature inviting not only a profuse expenditure, but corrupting in its tendencies."[309] Even those once deeply implicated in the network of patronage agreed that the system was out of control. The "scenes ... in regard to the public printing ... were sickening to every patriotic mind," former president Martin Van Buren wrote to Francis Preston Blair on May 6, 1860.[310]

Change was in the air. An act establishing the Government Printing Office was introduced as a resolution in the House on March 26, 1860. The measure passed the House by a vote of 120–56 and the Senate by a 31–14 margin. The act creating the Government Printing Office became law on June 23, 1860, and although it did not officially open until March 4, 1861, with the inauguration of Abraham Lincoln, printing operations began almost immediately.

By this time Bowman had already bailed out of the *Constitution*, leaving his associate editor, William Browne, in charge. Browne promptly got offside with Buchanan by showing too much sympathy for the secessionist South. After the *Constitution* rejected the administration's stance on secession set forth in the President's fourth annual address to Congress in December 1860, an irked Buchanan wrote to the paper's editor on Christmas Day notifying him that the administration was pulling the plug on any further patronage:

> I have read with deep mortification your editorial this morning in which you take open ground against my message on the right of secession. I have defended you as long as I can against numerous complaints. You have a perfect right to be in favor of secession, and for this I have

no just right to complain. The difficulty is that the "Constitution" is considered my organ, and its articles subject me to the charge of insincerity and double dealing. I am deeply sorry to say that I must in some authentic form declare that the "Constitution" is not the organ of the administration.[311]

"I advocated secession," an unrepentant Browne proudly declared in his final issue, adding that any attempt to enforce the laws in a seceded state would provoke "a war the most calamitous, the most unholy, the most infamous that was ever declared since the world began." By the end of January 1861, the *Constitution*, deprived of its small executive subsidy, had passed out of existence, and with it passed the official presidential organ as an American institution.[312] There was a postscript to this dénouement, characteristic of the age. Browne, having announced that he was suspending publication of his paper until he could arrange "its reissue elsewhere under better and more favorable auspices," removed to the more genial environment of Richmond, soon thereafter emerging as assistant secretary of state of the Confederate States of America.[313]

The only vestige of the old order still standing was the State Department's right to select the vehicles for the printing of the laws. Here it was still business as usual and the debut Republican secretary of state, William Seward, a former U.S. senator and governor of New York, was as adept at the art of patronage as any of his Democratic predecessors. He immediately made an almost complete change in assignments of publishers, dropping all but three of the Buchanan administration's choices, two of these in the far west.

This remnant of the newspaper patronage system did not long survive the Civil War.[314] It was caught in the crossfire of the struggle between Congress and the executive branch over the direction of Reconstruction. Hidden in the appropriation bill approved in March 1867 was a provision that stripped the secretary of state of the right to appoint newspapers in the former Confederate States, giving this power instead to the clerk of the House of Representatives. This authority was extended to all states a few weeks later. The system of publishing the laws itself expired in 1875.

A House Divided

The second party system collapsed long before the traditional system of printing patronage expired. The cause, simply put, was sectionalism, as the nation split into irreconcilable halves along the issue of slavery. Cutting across partisan lines, the ongoing presence of slavery within the nation provoked the emergence of an abolitionist press that against all odds defiantly expanded its reach as the decades wore on.[315] The first abolitionist newspaper, Benjamin Lundy's *Genius of Universal Emancipation*, was founded in 1821. Adding their voices to the swelling chorus were the *Freedom's Journal*, first published in 1827 by the Rev. Samuel Cornish and the first black college graduate in the United States, John B. Russworm, Bowdoin, Class of 1826; William Lloyd Garrison's the *Liberator*, which appeared on New Year's Day in 1831; and the *North Star*, under the guidance of Frederick Douglass, in Rochester beginning in 1847.

Douglass was only one of many abolitionists whose crusade in print was countered by mob violence; in his case this meant his house being burned down. Other abolitionist presses that were sacked included John Greenleaf Whittier's Philadelphia *Pennsylvania Freeman* and the Utica *Standard and Democrat*. The greatest sacrifice in the abolitionist cause was made by Elijah Parish Lovejoy, whose Alton, Pennsylvania *Observer* was wrecked no fewer than three times. On the final occasion, on the night of November 7, 1837, Lovejoy himself was killed.[316]

The abolitionists most vulnerable to mob violence were those prepared to preach the gospel on the borders of the cotton kingdom itself (penetrating to its core, as its denizens would be the first to point out, being ill advised). In Kentucky, the plant of the Newport *Free South* was destroyed. Another resident of the Bluegrass State to suffer the same fate was James G. Birney, the presidential nominee of the Liberty Party in 1840 and 1844, who had been driven into exile in 1836 after he began publishing the abolitionist weekly *The Philanthropist.* When he tried to start again in Cincinnati, his printing shop was wrecked.

Determined to avoid the same fate, Kentucky firebrand Cassius M. Clay procured a three-story red-brick building in Lexington at 6 North Mill Street, as the headquarters for his emancipationist *True American,* which debuted on June 3, 1845, under the motto "GOD AND LIBERTY!" He and his friends lined the doors and window shutters with sheet iron to prevent the building being fired. He purchased two small brass cannons in Cincinnati, loaded them to the muzzle with bullets, slugs and nails, and placed them breast high on a table facing the entrance, directly across from double doors that opened in the middle and were fastened with a chain "so that only one person at a time could make his way in to certain death." An ample supply of pikes and muskets lined the walls. In the event that these defenses failed, Clay had arranged an escape route for his employees via trapdoors leading to the roof and thence across neighboring buildings. For himself, he reserved a keg of powder with which to blow the establishment and everybody in it to the hereafter when resistance no longer became possible. "This," Clay stated, "I should most certainly have done, in case of the last extremity," for "I knew that if the office was once taken, after the bloody defense I intended to make, my life was forfeited, and I was determined to fire my magazine and send as many of them into eternity in my company as possible."[317] These elaborate fortifications were rendered impotent on August 18, 1845, when the good citizens of Lexington, taking advantage of the opportunity presented by Clay's being utterly debilitated with fever, took possession of his office, removed all the presses, and deposited them at the rail

The hardening sectional lines of the 1850s ultimately made it too dangerous even for so fearless an iconoclast as Cassius Clay to overtly criticize slavery south of the Mason-Dixon Line. Working the combustible intersection between journalism and politics in Kentucky nearly cost him his life on more than one occasion. His reward was to be posted by Lincoln as minister to Russia, an appointment celebrated with this Brady portrait (courtesy of Library of Congress).

station, destination anywhere north of the "peculiar institution," as slavery was sometimes called. The *True American* was back in business by October, still datelined Lexington, but printed in Cincinnati. After many vicissitudes in the cause of emancipation, Clay ultimately received his reward in the form of being appointed minister to Russia by Lincoln during the Civil War.

The increasing salience of the abolitionist cause in the North inevitably provoked a reaction in the South, which felt that the established political system and its affiliated broadcast mediums were failing to effectively defend Southern honor and Southern interests. Thomas Ritchie's last significant contribution to the republic, his pursuit of compromise during the secession crisis of 1850 (Osthaus says that "the victory of political moderation owed as much to Thomas Ritchie as to any other single person") created a sectional backlash when sixty-four Southern congressmen of both parties called for the establishment of a Southern newspaper. The signatories to "The Southern Address" sneered that Washington papers like the *Union* and the *Intelligencer* made "the maintenance of political parties their supreme and controlling object, but [there are] none which consider the persecution of sixteen hundred millions of property, the equality and liberty of fourteen or fifteen States, the protection of white man against African equality, as paramount over or even equal to the maintenance of some political organization which is to secure a President."[318] The *Southern Press* answered the call, making its debut on June 17, 1850, but the new paper barely lasted two years, a reflection of temporarily abating sectional tensions, but also of the underlying nature of Southern culture.

The expansion in the number of newspapers published in the U.S. had more than kept pace with the expansion in the nation's size and population (see Table 4). American literature was coming of age. The antebellum era was energized by the pens of such luminaries as Edgar Allen Poe, Walt Whitman, Nathaniel Hawthorne, Henry Wadsworth Longfellow, Henry David Thoreau, Ralph Waldo Emerson, and Herman Melville. A new breed of publications (such as *Harper's*, founded in 1850; *Frank Leslie's Illustrated*, founded in 1855; and *The Atlantic*, founded in 1857) was called into being to serve as a forum for these and other authors.

But as the nation matured it became evident that the emergence of its great writers, great newspapers, and great editors was increasingly a Northern phenomenon. In part this was a corollary of social realities—the 1850 census concluded that over twenty percent of the adult white population of the South could not read, compared with three percent in the middle states and less than one-half of one percent in New England. Accordingly, while Alabama was the most literate Southern state, with 60 newspapers and periodicals in circulation, by comparison New York had 428, Pennsylvania 310, Ohio 261, and even Illinois sustained a market for over a hundred different publications.

TABLE 4. EXPANSION OF U.S. NEWSPAPERS IN CIRCULATION, 1760–1860[319]

Year	Total Newspapers	Free Population (In Millions)	Free Population Per Newspaper
1760	18	1.270	70,555
1775	37	2.100	56,756
1790	96	3.232	33,667
1800	234	4.403	18,816
1810	366	6.048	16,524
1828	861	10.845	12,596
1840	1,404	14.575	10,381
1850	2,302	19.988	8,683
1860	3,343	27.489	8,223

The absence of an active readership also reflected the weak nature of party identity in the rural, insular, patriarchal South. Even during the 1840s, the peak decade of antebellum two-party competition, the South had remained largely resistant to the siren call of the party press. Accordingly, there was no correlation between newspaper competition and voter turnout; for all the fire and brimstone in print, come election time Southern voters remained mobilized along traditional patrimonial lines. Whatever partisan attachments had emerged became less prevalent and collapsed entirely as sectional passions reached their peak at the end of the decade. "The closed society of the South from the 1850s through the 1870s reflected a closed press reinforcing and reiterating community views," Osthaus notes.[320] Each twist in the spiraling sectional confrontation during the 1850s—the collapse of the Missouri Compromise, the Dred Scott decision, "Bleeding" Kansas, John Brown's raid on Harper's Ferry, the breakup of the Democratic Party and the election of Lincoln in 1860—was marked by a more vigorous defense of explicitly Southern interests by the Southern press.[321] As a consensus emerged in the South in favor of overt secessionist nationalism, the expression of alternate opinions became not merely unprofitable but outright dangerous. In such an atmosphere the existence of a vigorous publishing market became a superfluous luxury—after all, how many newspapers does a town, state or society need when they all express the same point of view?[322]

But even as party distinctions blurred in the South, they sharpened in the North. According to Mark W. Summers, "The 1850s were the halcyon days of the hireling press."[323] "Neutrality in this country and this age," one prominent paper admitted, "is an anomaly."[324] Census data from 1850 reported that there were 1,620 partisan newspapers in 1850 with a combined daily circulation of over two million (nearly one copy for every voter); by contrast there were only 83 independent newspapers with a total circulation of only three hundred thousand, concentrated in Boston, Philadelphia, and New York.[325] "Indeed, political sponsorship in one form or another constituted the dominant economic and ideological base of American newspapers through much of the nineteenth century," says Ponder.[326]

Everything, it seemed, was politically relevant. John W. Forney of the Philadelphia *Press*, advising an associate on how to extol the virtues of a local fire company, said he would call upon his readers to observe "the fine, self-denying heroism of these firemen's devoted lives; of their protection of our homes; and I would adjure them to remember Douglas and follow Walker, and never cease to war upon the infamies of Lecompton."[327]

Despite entering the decade ensconced in the White House, the one player not destined to be a factor in the grand political drama of the 1850s was the Whig Party, whose ramshackle coalition was dealt a death blow in the landslide defeat of 1852. Horace Greeley, for one, recognized that the writing was on the wall. "The Whig party had been often beaten before," he reflected, but this rout proved the party "practically defunct, and in an advanced stage of decomposition."[328]

Northern Whigs, watching their southern counterparts being subsumed into what they perceived as an all-embracing united front on behalf of the budding Confederacy's "Slave Power," pondered their options. Alliance with the hereditary Democratic foe, the party which spawned the likes of Pierce and Buchanan, traitors to the North, was not an option. "The political, numerical, intellectual, moral, and physical power and strength of the country resides north of the 'Mason and Dixon's line,'" wrote Thurlow Weed, "but our 'dough-faces' have frittered it away."[329] The only alternative was to sponsor the development of a political entity that truly reflected a northern perspective on slavery and the tariff. Many Whigs flirted with the nativist Know Nothing movement, which made its explosive political debut mid-decade.[330] But by the end of the 1850s, Northern interests had effectively coalesced around another new party, bringing it to the threshold of the White House.[331]

When members of this fledgling movement, a still largely inchoate mishmash of former

Whigs, veterans of the Free Soil campaign, abolitionists, and Democrats outraged at their party's sponsorship of the Kansas-Nebraska Act, approached Horace Greeley for assistance in promulgating their agenda, he promised to do what he could, but reminded them that the true measure of their success would lie in the righteousness of their cause. "We [editors] will try and do what we can," he wrote. "But remember that editors can only follow where the people's heart is already prepared to go with them. They can direct and animate a healthy public indignation, but cannot create a soul beneath the ribs of death."[332] Greeley did have one enduring suggestion to make, when Asahel N. Cole, editor of the Friendship, New York, *Genesee Valley Free Press*, contacted him to suggest a name for the new party. "Call it Republican," Greeley replied, "no prefix, no suffix, just Republican." In May 1854, Cole's newspaper became the first to display the party name in its masthead.[333]

In their debut performance in the midterm elections of 1854, the Republicans proved that they did indeed have soul, exhibiting real strength in many northern states. But building an effective operating structure for the movement as a whole, one capable of challenging for the presidency, would take time and organization. At this point the great editors were prepared to step in and help facilitate the process of converting disparate clumps of anti–Democratic voters into fully-fledged Republicans. The time had indeed come "to bury our beloved [Whig] party; it is dead," Greeley wrote Joseph Medill, editor of the *Chicago Tribune*. "But we have many fool friends who insist it is only in a comatose state and will recover.... I dare not yet in New York announce the demise of the party and call for the reorganization of a new one. But do you go ahead on the Western reserve and commence the work. I like the name for it. If you can get the name Republican started in the West it will grow in the East. I fully agree to the new name and the new christening."[334]

Greeley's enthusiasm for the new crusade quickly butted up against the limitations of his own political ambition. Greeley had his heart set on the Republican gubernatorial nomination in 1854, and according to Thurlow Weed, he had, "as both he and his friends thought, every reason to expect this."[335] He was therefore sublimely disappointed to be passed over, and his mortification only increased when the convention selected his former employee Henry J. Raymond, editor of the *New York Times*, for lieutenant governor. "No other name could have been so bitterly humbling to me," he complained to Weed in terms that could have only confirmed in Weed's mind the wisdom of not finding a place for Greeley on the ticket. "I should have hated to serve as Lieutenant Governor, but I should have gloried in running for the post." Greeley swallowed his pride and backed the Republican ticket in the fall campaign, but the moment the results were all in he turned his wrath on his erstwhile colleagues. "The election is over, and its results sufficiently ascertained," Greeley wrote to Weed on November 11, 1854. "It seems to me a fitting time to announce to you the dissolution of the political firm of Seward, Weed, and Greeley, by the withdrawal of the junior partner."[336] This manifesto was brushed off by the two senior partners at the time; the long-term implications only became apparent at the Republican national convention nearly six years later, and by then it was too late.

James Gordon Bennett

Even as the verbal and literary jousts of peacetime were being superseded by the first shots of the Civil War, the faint glimmerings of a new press, one wedded to the individual passions of its editor as opposed to the dictates of a party, were beginning to emerge. It wasn't much — in fact for a considerable period the entire burden was carried by one idiosyncratically solitary individual — but it was a start.

Amidst all the ebbs and flows of partisan and sectional sentiment there was one man determined to shrug off the constraints of party loyalty and publish the news in the national interest as he saw it. And he set an example to be followed. According to Tebbel and Watts, beginning in 1835 with the arrival of James Gordon Bennett and his *New York Herald*, a new era of journalism began in which editors might be partisan, and might even be involved in politics themselves, but at the same time were independent entrepreneurs who could afford to be independent because they were the proprietors of money-making newspapers that did not need the support of politicians or parties to survive. It was a major turning point in the relationship between the press and the parties.[337] The new era was marked by "the beginning of an *attempt* to be objective in the news columns, which Bennett and the others succeeded finally in separating from editorial comment appearing on an editorial page," Tebbels and Watts write. "In the two decades before the Civil War, candidates and presidents alike had for the first time to deal with a press that, by and large, they could not buy with direct or indirect patronage."[338]

"I have endeavored to secure a high position in parties, and to settle myself in life," Bennett ruminated miserably in his diary in 1831. "I have always failed — why so?"[339] The answer lay simply in the fact that during an era which prized party loyalty above all else, Bennett insisted on steering his own erratic course through the rocky shoals of antebellum politics. A journeyman printer and campaign worker for Tammany Hall who rose to be a member of a Democratic Ward Committee in New York City in 1831, Bennett became an associate editor of Mordecai M. Noah's *New York Enquirer* in late 1827. After James Watson Webb merged his *Morning Courier* with the *Enquirer* in 1829, Bennett rose to the position of associate editor of the new paper, but quit when it flipped to support Clay and the Second Bank of the United States in 1832.

Bennett launched the *New York Globe* at the end of October 1832, as a campaign vehicle for Jackson. When it folded after Jackson was returned to office, Bennett importuned Vice President Van Buren for the U.S. consulship in Bremen. This came to nothing, as did his efforts to secure an editorial position on the *Washington Globe*. In January of the following year he began working for the Jacksonian Philadelphia *Pennsylvanian*, becoming editor in May. But in November, after publicly differing with the administration over banking policy, he was forced out. According to Bennett, "Amos Kendall and the irresponsible cabal at Washington [were] the prime movers" in his dismissal. Bennett had learned his lesson; never again would he be a party editor.[340]

In fact, Bennett had an unlikely trump card. Even while attacking the Second Bank in print, Bennett was privately sending Nicholas Biddle reports on the plans and attitudes of the Van Buren leaders in New York. In return he was later to beg Biddle for a loan of $4,000 in order to establish his own paper. On May 6, 1835, Bennett launched his *New York Herald*, a new penny paper of four four-column pages. His capital totaled $500, his office was a Wall Street cellar furnished with a few packing cases covered with planks, and Bennett himself comprised the entire staff, yet in less than a year the paper was selling almost 15,000 copies daily.

Bennett's technical innovations made the *Herald* a landmark in the history of American journalism. The paper was unabashedly targeted at the mass market. It included news from hitherto-disdained fields of life, including the police courts, sporting fields, theaters, and finance. In 1838, Bennett pioneered the concept of establishing a corps of European correspondents. He was the first editor to use the telegraph extensively in reporting stories, and his was the first newspaper to accompany news articles with illustrations. But most of all, Bennett defiantly and jealously guarded his right to pursue an independent course in his editorial policy. Almost uniquely, Bennett was free from the dictates of political patrons. In the first edition of his paper the editor asserted: "In *débuts* of this kind many talk of principle — political principle, party principle — as a sort of steel-trap to catch the public. We mean to be perfectly understood on this point, and therefore *open disclaim all steel-traps — all principle, as it is called, all party, all politics....* We shall support no party, be the organ of no faction or coterie, and care nothing for any election or any candidate, from President down to constable."[341]

This policy of total non-alignment would not last long, but to the end, if Bennett was to offer an endorsement it was in response to the merits of the candidate in question, not loyalty to any party. His could be the most partisan paper in New York, but it was also the most fickle. Bennett was a loyal Democrat until offering his support to Harrison in 1840; switched back to the Democrats and Polk in 1844; then flipped again to endorse Taylor in

The scandal-mongering style of James Gordon Bennett shattered established journalistic conventions and made him a pariah among his peers. But the success of his business model enabled him to break free of the party patronage that guided the editorial policy of every other publication of the day (courtesy of Library of Congress).

1848; then back again to Pierce in 1852; then skipped lightly over his Democratic values (and own immigrant past) to flirt with the nativist Know Nothing movement in 1854-55. He shrugged off his own virulent racist and anti-abolitionist principles to back Fremont in 1856; he became President Buchanan's most loyal press ally before turning on him at the end of his term; he urged the nation to reject Lincoln in 1860 but endorsed him in 1864; and he backed Grant after the Democrats failed to nominate Chief Justice Salmon Chase in 1868.

The combination of this independent line in editorial policy with the unprecedented sensationalism of the *Herald's* news coverage unsettled and offended Bennett's fellow editors.[342] Even Benjamin H. Day, who had founded New York's first penny press newspaper, the *Sun*, in 1833 as a twenty-three-year-old, fulminated in print against "the notorious vagabond Bennett; the veriest reptile that ever defiled the paths of decency," whose "only chance of dying an upright man will be that of hanging perpendicularly upon a rope."[343] That sentiment was echoed by The *Cleveland Morning Leader*, which considered Bennett "the arch enemy of all good," while the *Utica Morning Herald* depicted him as "an architect of ruin" and "a social and intellectual pariah, whom society has cast from its bosom with loathing; a creature from whom honest men instinctively recoil."

Henry J. Raymond, founding editor of the *New York Times*, christened Bennett with his enduring moniker "Old Satanic." Bennett, who had a habit of referring to himself as the "Napoleon of the news," had a correspondingly low opinion of Raymond, who in the pages of the *Herald* was "likened to a monkey, prying into everything, continually chattering over small discoveries, and always very busy about very insignificant trifles. In fact, he is the monkey editor, chattering and skipping about, and playing the very mischief among the crockery."[344]

"Write him down, make respectable people withdraw their support from the vile sheet," one observer urged the discerning public, "so that it shall be considered disgraceful to read it, and the serpent will be rendered harmless."[345] But in fact Bennett always enjoyed playing his role as social upstart to the hilt. "Newspaper abuse made Mr. Van Buren chief magistrate of this republic, and newspaper abuse will make me the chief editor of this country," he boasted.[346] And Bennett could give as good as he got. Bennett, who lived on "defamation, slander, obloquy, beastliness," and "lies," was horsewhipped seven times in the public streets, Horace Greeley of the *New York Tribune* would write, not including the "sundry kickings out of hotels" or "the crushing ceremony of a company leaving the table when he ventured to sit down among them." And this was relatively benign treatment; "Of course, such conduct could not go unscourged even in New York. If he had lived further South, he would have been simply beaten to death or shot."[347] Bennett was only too happy to reply in kind. "Horace Greeley, BA and ASS," went a typical *Herald* jibe, "is probably the most unmitigated blockhead concerned with the newspaper press. Galvanize a large New England squash and it would make as capable an editor as Horace."[348]

But Bennett's greatest foe — and chief physical threat — was his old employer James Watson Webb. The editor of the *Courier and Enquirer* considered Bennett a moral "pestilence," a "worthless vagabond," and a "disgusting obscenity," who should be ousted from Manhattan because his paper was afflicted with "moral leprosy." Prostitutes, Webb continued, regard the *Herald* as "their special organ." Indeed, a gentleman would as soon choose a wife in a brothel as marry a woman who read the *Herald*. The solution was to fight the *Herald* as though it was a pestilence: "The creed of *all* should be —*purchase* not, *read* not, *touch* not."[349]

Deliberately courting trouble, on January 19, 1836, Bennett published extremely embarrassing revelations about Webb's misfortunes in the stock market, shedding crocodile tears as he did so. It was only "with heartfelt grief that we are compelled to publish the following awful disclosure of the defalcations of our former associate, Col. Webb," Bennett wrote. It was only with "pain, regret, and almost with tears in our eyes," Bennett insisted, that he published the exposé. The real pain began the following day when Webb chased down his former employee, punched him in the face, and then started beating him with his cane.[350]

Bennett tried to pass the incident off with a laugh: "The fellow, no doubt, wanted to let out the never-failing supply of good humor and wit, which has created such a reputation for the Herald, and appropriate the contents to supply the emptiness of his own thick skull."[351] But, apparently not yet satisfied, Webb caught up with Bennett again on Wall Street in May after the *Herald* had accused the *Courier and Enquirer's* editor ("a man up to the eyes in whiskers and infamy") of stock-jobbing, claims which resulted in a grand jury being called.[352] As Bennett described the incident, Webb "pushed me down the stone steps, leading to one of the broker's offices, and commenced fighting with a species of brutal and demoniac desperation characteristic of a fury."[353] Bennett also dubiously asserted that he landed a punch of his own on the formidable Webb, "which may have knocked down his throat some of his infernal teeth, for anything I know."[354]

A third brawl, with the same results, took place in July. Bennett also received public beatings from William Leggett, editor of the *New York Evening Post*, and Peter Townsend, editor of the *New York Evening Star*. The *New York Sun* then took to calling Bennett "common flogging property."[355] But even bruises make good publicity; Bennett had been "horse-whipped, kicked, trodden under foot, spat upon, and degraded in every possible way," one observer remarked, "but all this he courts because it brings him in money."[356]

There were two issues on which Bennett was consistent throughout his career. The first was Manifest Destiny. In the summer of 1843 the *Herald* proclaimed, "The Anglo Saxon race is intended by an overruling Providence to carry the principles of liberty, the refinements of civilization, and the advantages of the mechanic arts through every land, even those now barbarous. The prostrate savage and the benighted heathen, shall yet be imbued with Anglo Saxon intelligence and culture, and be blessed with the institutions, both civil and religious, which are now our inheritance. Mexico, too, must submit to the o'erpowering influence of the Anglo Saxon."[357]

The second issue dear to Bennett's heart was race. He incessantly played on New York's hatred and fear of African Americans—as Bennett referred to them, "the eternal," "the everlasting," "the infernal," or just "the Almighty Nigger." Bennett remained the best friend of the South among the major newspapers throughout the accelerating sectional crisis of the 1850s. He lashed out at any of his rivals if they so much as hinted at concerns over the future course of slavery. The *Sun*, Bennett said in 1838, was "entirely in the abolition interest" and declining so rapidly as a result of competition from the *Herald* that it resembled a real newspaper only so much "as a respectable nigger generally gets to an Anglo Saxon."[358]

Bennett leaped to the defense of the Kansas-Nebraska Act, adding belligerently that his was "about the only Northern newspaper that had the moral courage to come out boldly in its support," and wrote, "We have been true to our principles on slavery from the first: we have opposed, at no small cost to ourselves every anti-slavery movement that has originated in the North during the last thirty years, and intend to die in that belief and that course."[359] Even as sectional lines hardened, Bennett continued to boast that for two score years, "through good and evil report, the *New York Herald* has been the only Northern journal that has unfailingly vindicated the constitutional rights of the South," and he continued to take editorial potshots at what he called "Black Republicans" and their allies in the press, such as the "nigger-worshipper" Horace Greeley.[360]

The endorsement of the *New York Herald* was as welcome as it was transient; every president sought it, none could maintain it. "It is quite unnecessary for me to say that I have not been invisible to the vast influence of the *Herald* throughout the late canvass," Franklin Pierce acknowledged after his election in 1852. He swiftly found out that influence was double-edged. After Pierce rejected Bennett's claim to the consulate in Paris, the editor turned all his guns on the beleaguered president, representing him in the pages of the nation's top-selling daily publication as "imbecile," "blundering," "treacherous," "weak," "cowardly," "wicked," "corrupt," "reprobate," "degraded," and ultimately "too mean to hate, too pitiable even to despise."[361]

In 1856, Bennett shocked everyone by filing away his pet phrase for the newborn Republican Party—"nigger worshippers"—and endorsing its debut candidate for president, John C. Fremont. Democratic candidate James Buchanan found himself represented in the *Herald* as "cold," "timid," an "old fogy," and a "superannuated dotard" with an "utter want of human sympathy."

Bennett's overriding concern was his contempt for Philadelphia editor John Forney, who was leading the Buchanan campaign and would become his editorial spokesman if he were elected. But once Buchanan *was* elected, Bennett trimmed his sails to the wind yet again, and during his term in office the president had no more loyal ally in the press. Buchanan, who had fallen out with Bennett years before, scrambled to patch up their relationship upon taking office. "I rejoice that our former friendly relations are to be restored," the president wrote "I am truly sorry they were ever interrupted; and this not only for my own sake, but that of the country. The New York *Herald*, exercising the influence which signal ability and past triumphs always commands, can contribute much to frustrate the sectional party which now so seriously endangers the Union, and to restore the ancient friendly relations between the North and the South."[362]

Buchanan gave the *Herald* access to reports well in advance of other papers, allowed its Washington correspondents to get advance tips on changes in policy or personnel, and, on at least one occasion, the president sent Bennett an advance copy of his State of the Union Address. "Buchanan owes more to Mr. Bennett than all his [other] partisan journalists and fulsome flatterers put together," Horace Greeley sourly observed. But when Buchanan failed to appoint Bennett to the consulate in Turin at the end of his term, he rapidly found himself the chief object of Bennett's wrath over the secession crisis. "The *Herald* ... from a spirit of malignity ... takes every occasion to blame me for my supineness," the outgoing President complained.[363]

Railsplitter

In the space of less than eight years, Whig partisans in the press such as Thurlow Weed and Horace Greeley had presided over the disestablishment of their old party and its reconstitution in a new, exclusively northern, Republican form, which elected its first president, Abraham Lincoln, in 1860.[364] This background is important to bear in mind when considering the trajectory of Lincoln's career because, say Tebbel and Watts, "of all the presidents, Lincoln was most involved with the press, owed the most to it, and suffered the most from it."[365]

Lincoln was a corporation lawyer and former one-term Whig congressman who had joined the Republican Party in response to the passage of the Kansas-Nebraska Act in 1854, tilting unsuccessfully for the party's vice presidential nomination in 1856. He knew how the newspaper game was played. As the silent partner and financial supporter of the Springfield, Illinois, German-language newspaper, the *Illinois State Anzeiger*, Lincoln signed a contract with publisher Theodore Canisium stating that if the paper should "in political sentiment" depart from the Republican platforms and if it should ever print "anything opposed to, or designed to injure the Republican Party, said Lincoln may, at his option, at once take possession of said press, types, &c. and deal with them as his own."[366] In fact, the *Anzeiger* never defected and after his election as president, Lincoln withdrew and Canisius became full owner. The paper was discontinued shortly afterward, as Lincoln had another reward for his friend: appointment as U.S. consul to Samoa.[367]

Therefore, when Lincoln sought the nomination of the Republican Party to take on Democratic senator Stephen A. Douglas in the election of 1858 he knew he needed heavyweight backing from the newspaper bosses first. He was supported by Charles L. Wilson, editor of the *Chicago Journal* and a dominant figure in the powerful Cook County delegation, but was opposed by "Long John" Wentworth, mayor of Chicago and editor of the *Chicago Daily Democrat*, who had his own eye on the nomination.

Lincoln ultimately owed his place on the ballot to a conclave held in the Illinois State Library on April 21 of that year, nearly two months prior to the Republican state convention at which he formally received the nomination. The principles in attendance—Dr. Charles A. Ray, who, along with Joseph Medill, was co-owner of the *Chicago Tribune*; William Bross, editor of the *Chicago Democratic Press*; and George T. Brown, editor of the *Alton Courier*—in addition to Norman B. Judd, chairman of the Republican state committee, reached a consensus that Lincoln was "the first and only choice of the Republicans of Illinois for the United States Senate."[368]

But Lincoln's campaign fell afoul of the grand strategy masterminded by Horace Greeley of the *New York Tribune*. Greeley had been an early and eager advocate for the Republican cause; his proselytizing for what would become the Grand Old Party earned him a beating from Democratic congressman Albert Rust of Arkansas in 1856.[369] However, the editor was prepared to make short term sacrifices whenever necessary in order to secure his ultimate goals. For that reason, Greeley consistently exhibited the utmost respect for Lincoln's opponent — the "Little Giant," Stephen Douglas, the author of the Kansas-Nebraska Act — quite deliberately in order to worsen the split between North and South within the Democratic Party. "Don't you smell that they all believe already that he and I are in cahoots, as they say — secretly leagued to humble and ruin 'the South?'" Greeley wrote Schuyler Colfax in 1860. "Everything I have done to favor him since '57 inclusive is treasured up and used to diffuse and deepen the impression that he is a disguised Abolitionist, and virtually of the Black Republicans."[370]

The subtleties of Greeley's strategy escaped many Republicans, especially in Illinois. "I like Greeley," Lincoln wrote to his law partner and confidant William Herndon, "think he intends right, but I think he errs in his hoisting up of Douglas, while he gives me a downward shove." In Lincoln's opinion, someone should "put a flea in Greeley's ear" and set him straight, sentiments he reiterated in a letter to Senator Lyman Trumball: "What does The *Tribune* mean by its constant eulogizing and admiring and magnifying of Douglas? Does it, in this, speak the sentiments of Republicans at Washington? Have they concluded that the Republican cause, generally, can best be promoted by sacrificing us here in Illinois?"[371] During the course of a mission east to find out the answer to that question, Herndon was granted a twenty-minute interview by Greeley which was enough to convince him that the *New York Tribune* "evidently wants Douglas sustained and sent back to the Senate." In Boston, Herndon told abolitionist minister Theodore Parker that Greeley, who he labeled "capricious, crotchety, full of whims, and as wrong-headed as a pig," was going to "lower the Republican flag" in Illinois for the sake of Douglas.[372]

Greeley reassured Herndon that he was not trying to influence Illinois politics, urging the Republicans there to "paddle your own dug-out." When Lincoln was formally endorsed as the party's nominee for the Senate, Greeley reprinted his "House Divided" speech in full, calling it "concise and admirable." But the tone of his editorials did not alter; he continued to maintain that a Lincoln victory would drive Illinois Democrats into a position of "virtual subservience to the Slave Power." Herndon retorted that Greeley was in fact "daily playing into the hands of the pro-slavery camp" and that his "hearty Douglas position" rendered him a "natural fool." Even after Lincoln, who won the popular vote, was denied election by a 54–46 Democratic majority in the Illinois State Legislature, Greeley remained unrepentant: "Your course may prove wiser in the long run," he told Herndon, "but ours vindicates itself at the outset."[373]

The narrow margin of Lincoln's defeat, and his widely-reported success in more than holding his own against the Little Giant in their famed series of debates, stamped him as presidential material. Lincoln's arrival on the national political stage was heralded by the favorable notice he received in Republican papers and the hostility of the Democratic press. The *Cincinnati Enquirer*, for example, responding to a Lincoln speech in 1859, wrote "It is, in a single expressive word, trash — trash from beginning to end; trash without one solitary oasis to relieve the dreary waste that begins with its nearest and ends with its furthest boundary."[374]

Lincoln began his tilt for the Republican nomination in 1860 with the hometown backing of the *Chicago Democrat*, the *Press*, and the old Whig papers, the *Journal* and the *American*.[375] But according to Pollard, "Lincoln's ultimate triumph might have been impossible but for the influence of two leading newspapers and the men behind them." These were the two *Tribunes*, Joseph Medill's in Chicago, and, ironically, Horace Greeley's in New York.[376]

Medill was co-owner with Dr. Charles H. Ray of the *Chicago Tribune*, an early and firm supporter of Lincoln that referred to Douglas and the Democrats as the "anti–American party."[377] During the Civil War, Lincoln would tell Medill, "You and your *Tribune* have had more influence than any other paper in the North-west in making this war."[378] Medill played a key role in Lincoln's nomination at the 1860 Republican convention in hometown Chicago when, at the conclusion of the second ballot, the editor was able to get the message through to David Cartter, chairman of the Ohio delegation, that Governor Salmon Chase, the Buckeye State's favorite son, could have "anything he wants" if the Ohio delegation went over to Lincoln. Cartter rose at the next roll call to announce the shift of four votes from Chase to Lincoln. And the deed was done. Lincoln was nominated and Chase went on to become secretary of the treasury in his administration.[379]

Greeley made his contribution to Lincoln's nomination by undermining the candidacy of "Honest Abe's" chief rival, Senator William Seward of New York. Greeley dedicated his time in Chicago to badmouthing Seward and boosting Edward Bates of Missouri. On the critical third ballot, Greeley flipped the 48 votes committed to Bates onboard the Lincoln bandwagon.[380] Lincoln was thus the beneficiary of the split within the nascent Republican Party in

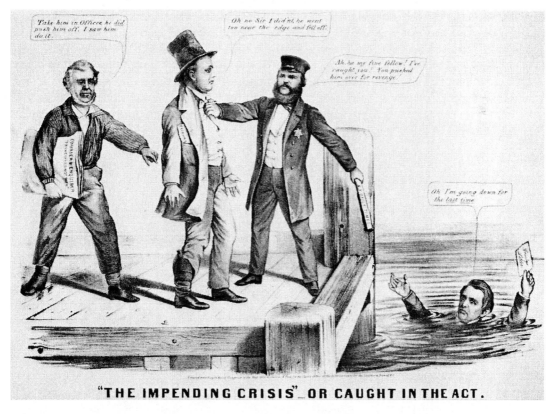

"THE IMPENDING CRISIS"_ OR CAUGHT IN THE ACT.

The repercussions of the 1860 Republican convention, nominating the dark horse Abraham Lincoln and not the favorite, William Seward, are depicted in this Currier & Ives cartoon. Horace Greeley, who was widely regarded as having machinated Seward's defeat out of spite towards the senator's patron Thurlow Weed, is confronted by fellow editors James Watson Webb and Henry J. Raymond. The title of the print is derived from Hinton Helper's influential 1857 antislavery pamphlet *The Impending Crisis* (courtesy of Library of Congress).

the Empire State between the Seward faction, comprised largely of old Whigs and represented by the *Albany Evening Journal*, the paper of Seward's political mastermind Thurlow Weed, and Henry J. Raymond's *New York Times*, and the anti–Seward faction, dominated by former Free Soil Democrats, and represented by Greeley's *New York Tribune* and William Cullen Bryant's *New York Evening Post*.[381]

Predictably, the Seward organs were mortified by the defeat of their champion at the hands of the upstart Lincoln. "Misrepresentation has achieved its work," began a mournful editorial in the *Albany Evening Journal*. "The timid and credulous have succumbed to threats and perversions ... the recognized standard bearer of the Republican Party has been sacrificed upon the altar of fancied unavailability. The sacrifice was cruel and unnecessary."

Webb also opened fire on Greeley in the *Courier and Enquirer*. Responding to the latter's denials of having engineered Seward's defeat, Webb, who described Greeley as "a viper" and "a coarse man" with "none of the instincts of a gentleman," declared that "a more deliberate and wicked falsehood than this never found publicity, even through the columns of the *Tribune*.... It was under the garb of friendship that the viper struck the blow; it was as the long-tried and well known friend of Seward, shedding crocodile tears over his unavailability, that he poisoned the minds of the leading men in the Convention and created doubts in regard to Mr. Seward's strength."[382]

The election of 1860 was the first four-cornered fight since 1824. Lincoln as the Republican nominee enjoyed the luxury of a divided opposition; the Democratic Party had split into an anti-administration, Northern faction, represented by Stephen Douglas, and a pro-administration, Southern faction, represented by Vice President John C. Breckinridge. In addition, a hybrid of Whig holdouts and the dying Know Nothings, called the Constitutional Union Party, had nominated John Bell. Each contender could count on the fulsome support of a segment of the press. Sometimes too fulsome; the Easton, Pennsylvania, *Times* wryly commented that a good way to illuminate the towns and villages of the nation with gas during the campaign of 1860 would have been to ignite the editors of their local newspapers.[383]

If such a policy had been adopted, even the smallest of American communities would have been the beneficiaries of the subsequent illumination. Joseph C. G. Kennedy, head of the Census Bureau, pointed out that the 1860 census "strikingly illustrates the fact that the people of the United States are peculiarly 'a newspaper-reading nation,' and serves to show how large a portion of their reading is political. Of 4,051 papers and periodicals published in the United States ... three thousand two hundred and forty-two, or 80.02 percent, were political in their character." However, while the total number of newspapers had doubled since 1850, far exceeding the increase in population during the decade, this expansion was a reflection of politicization, not urbanization; only 126 communities in the United Sates in 1860 could boast a population exceeding 3,200 people. The 3,242 partisan newspapers must therefore have blanketed the myriad small towns and villages across the land. The census of 1860 identified 259 partisan newspapers in Illinois, for example, which contained only 133 towns with populations exceeding 1,500.[384] It was these communities that would serve as the battleground for the last campaign of the antebellum era.

The stakes had never been so high in an election, and the partisan advocates of the press were correspondingly apocalyptic in their rhetoric. "Keep before the people," Republican campaign broadsheet *The Railsplitter* urged the party faithful on August 15, 1860, "that the Democratic Party is composed of Knaves, plunderers and political mountebanks, that sell themselves to the highest bidder for power, place or self ... that it has become the rendezvous of thieves, the home of parasites and blood-suckers, the enemy of God and man, the stereotyped fraud, the sham, the hypocrite, the merciless marauder, and the outlawed renegade and malefactor."[385]

Boston had five Republican organs—the *Advertiser*, the *Atlas and Bee*, the *Journal*, the

Traveller, and the *Saturday Evening Gazette*. Other papers for Lincoln in New England included the *Portland Daily Advertiser*, the *Providence Daily Journal*, the *Springfield Daily Republican*, the *Courant* and the *Evening Press* of Hartford, and the *Journal and Courier* and the *Palladium* of New Haven.

In New York City the *Tribune* ("Douglas has brains," Greeley sneered, "so had Judas"), the *Times*, the *Evening Post*, the *World*, the *Courier and Enquirer*, and the *Commercial Advertiser* were Lincoln papers, as were the nearby *Brooklyn City News*, the *Advertiser* and the *Mercury* of Newark, and the Jersey City *Daily Courier and Advertiser*. In upstate New York the Republican banner was flown by the *Albany Evening Journal*, the *Commercial Advertiser* and the *Express* of Buffalo, the *Rochester Evening Express*, and the *Syracuse Journal*. In Pennsylvania there were three major Republican papers in Philadelphia — the *Daily News*, the *Evening Bulletin*, and the venerable *North American and United States Gazette*— in addition to the *Harrisburg Telegraph* and the *Daily Pittsburgh Gazette*.

Major Republican papers in the Midwest included the *Gazette* and the *Commercial* in Cincinnati; the *Intelligencer* in Wheeling; the *Leader* and the *Herald* in Cleveland; the *State Journal* in Columbus; the *Journal* in Indianapolis; the *Advertiser* and the *Tribune* in Detroit; the *Sentinel* and the *Wisconsin* in Milwaukee; the *Tribune*, the *Journal*, and the *Democrat* in Chicago; and the *State Journal* in Lincoln's own Springfield.

The prominent Douglas papers in the North were the *Boston Herald*, the Providence

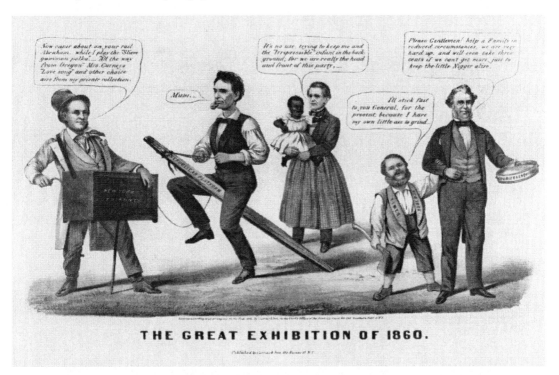

THE GREAT EXHIBITION OF 1860.

In this anti-Lincoln cartoon from 1860, the Republican candidate, riding on a wooden rail, is tethered with a cord to Horace Greeley's index finger, and is dancing to the abolitionist tune the editor grinds out from his *New York Tribune* organ. Lincoln's lips are padlocked shut, a reference to his refusal to campaign in person, so the artist has embodied the Republican platform in the persona of Seward holding an African-American infant and complaining, "It's no use trying to keep me and the 'Irrepressible' infant in the background; for we are really the head and front of this party." Two more New York editors, Henry J. Raymond and James Watson Webb, offer their support at right (courtesy of Library of Congress).

Post, the Albany *Atlas and Argus*, the *Courier* and the *Republic* of Buffalo, the *Brooklyn Evening Standard*, the Philadelphia *Press*, the Washington, D. C. *States and Union*, the *Pittsburgh Post*, the *Cincinnati Daily Enquirer*, the *Cleveland Plain Dealer*, the *Indianapolis Sentinel*, the *Detroit Free Press*, the *Milwaukee Press and News*, the *Daily Chicago Times*, and the *Springfield Register*.

While Douglas had not one significant press ally in New York City, Breckinridge enjoyed the support of the *Herald*, the *Journal of Commerce*, and the *Daily News*, in addition to the Brooklyn *Eagle*. All of these papers equally vociferously backed the fusion ticket ultimately forged between the three anti–Lincoln candidates in the Empire State. Other Breckinridge organs in the North included the *Boston Post*, the *Newark Evening Journal*, the *Philadelphia Pennsylvanian*, the Washington *Constitution*, the *Bangor Daily Union*, the *Concord Democratic Standard*, the *Hartford Daily Times*, the *Syracuse Daily Courier and Union*, the *Harrisburg Patriot and Union*, the *Columbus Capital City Fact*, and the *Cleveland National Democrat*. The only significant Breckinridge paper west of Ohio was the *Madison Argus and Democrat*.

Appropriately, most of Breckinridge's Northern support went the way of the Confederacy. The *Pennsylvanian* and the *Constitution* died even before Fort Sumter was fired upon. The *Daily Union, Democratic Standard*, and *National Democrat* collapsed before the close of 1861. The *Argus and Democrat* disappeared in 1862 and the *Capital City Fact* ceased publication in 1864. Thus, only five of the twelve leading Northern papers for Breckinridge in 1860 survived the Civil War.

Bell was represented in the free states by the Washington *National Intelligencer*, the *Boston Daily Courier*, the *Philadelphia Evening Journal*, the *Cincinnati Daily Times*, and the Jersey City *American Standard*.[386]

Although accused of being a sectional candidate, Lincoln's claim to the presidency was not received with universal approbation even in the North. As the *New York Herald* commented after the convention in Chicago, "The conduct of the Republican Party in this nomination is a remarkable indication of small intellect, growing smaller."[387] Bennett considered Lincoln merely "a third-rate Western lawyer," although an improvement over Seward, "the shrewdest demagogue and traitor whom the country has ever produced."[388]

Vanity Fair, which dubbed Lincoln "a characterless candidate, supported by an aimless party," looked forward to utilizing the most prominent physical traits of the Republican nominee to its advantage during the campaign, alluding to "certain characteristics which, if there is any power in newspaper fun, will go far towards defeating him."[389] Less delicately, the Albany *Atlas and Argus* called Lincoln the ugliest man in the Union, ungainly as a scarecrow, and with the complexion of an octoroon. The New Albany, Indiana, *Daily Ledger* conjectured that his education had been held back because he was too ugly to be accepted by a respectable school. In Wisconsin, the *Prairie du Chien Courier* concluded that Lincoln resembled "a monkey taking medicine." The *New York Leader* made no effort to conceal its disgust: "A horrid looking wretch he is! Sooty and scoundrelly in aspect — a cross between the nutmeg dealer, the horse-swapper, and the nightman.... He is a lank-sided, slab-sided Yankee of the uncomliest visage and dirtiest complexion."[390]

Even in the erstwhile friendly territory of Massachusetts, the *Springfield Republican* described Lincoln as "the leanest, lankest, most ungainly mass of legs, arms, and hatchet-face ever strung upon a single frame. He has most unwarrantably abused the privilege which all politicians have of being ugly." Apparently on aesthetic grounds alone the paper concluded, "We would regard his election as a national calamity."[391]

But the real fire emanated from south of the Mason-Dixon Line, where Lincoln had almost universally been excluded from the ballot and had a correspondingly total absence of editorial support. "Since even the most conservative journals charged the Republicans with plotting to subvert the white race in the South, it is difficult to see how Southern readers could have maintained anything resembling an objective, balanced view of Lincoln and his party," Reynolds notes. "In the absence of contradictory Northern arguments, most Southerners apparently had little trouble believing the allegations of Southern secessionist papers."[392]

There was a tightly woven nexus between politics and the press in the South.[393] John Marshall of the Austin *State Gazette* was state chairman of the Democratic Party in Texas from 1858 to 1861. A. B. Norton, editor of the Austin *South Intelligencer* and *Fort Worth Chief*, placed Governor Sam Houston's name in nomination at the Constitutional Union Party's convention.[394] Leading "Fire Eaters" maintained their own secessionist organs, like Ethelbert E. Barksdale's Jackson *Mississippian* and Robert Barnwell Rhett's *Charleston Mercury* which, although frequently quoted in Southern papers and regarded in the North as a barometer of secessionist sentiment, boasted a circulation of only 500.

Breckinridge dominated the Southern political press during the campaign of 1860. He enjoyed the support of a clear majority of the papers in Florida, Alabama, Texas, Arkansas, South Carolina, and Georgia; pluralities in Virginia, Louisiana, North Carolina, and Mississippi; and nearly matched the tally of endorsements for favorite son Bell in Tennessee. Key supporters in the Deep South included the *Montgomery Advertiser and State Gazette*, the Atlanta *Daily Intelligencer and Examiner*, the New Orleans *Daily Delta*, and the *Jackson Mississippian*. In the upper South, Breckinridge was endorsed by the *Enquirer* and the *Examiner* in Richmond, the Raleigh *Press*, and the *Louisville Daily Courier*.

Bell was endorsed by over a third of the Southern papers, being most enthusiastically received in Tennessee and Louisiana. Key allies in the press included the Nashville *Republican Banner*, the Memphis *Enquirer*, and the *Louisville Daily Journal* in the upper South, and the *Richmond Whig*, the *Raleigh Register and North Carolina Gazette*, the *New-Orleans Bee* and the New Orleans *Weekly Picayune* in the Deep South.

Douglas placed a weak third among the Southern papers. "The living and the dead are separated at Charleston," the New Orleans *Daily Delta* crowed. "The real, breathing, true and unconquerable Democracy, with seventeen sovereign States at their back, will meet the niggerites of the North on their own ground."[395]

Advocates for the Little Giant included the *Daily Louisville Democrat*, the *Memphis Daily Appeal*, the Augusta *Daily Constitutionalist*, the *Mobile Daily Register*, and the New Orleans *Daily True Delta*. But an ally of Douglas wrote from Grenada, Mississippi, explaining that the press of his state was "generally in the hands of young and inexperienced men controlled by the ruling dynasty. When a scheme is put on foot the [Jackson] Mississippian roars and all the little country papers yelp, the cross road and bar room politicians take it up and so it goes, and if anyone opposes them they raise the cry of abolitionist and traitor, two words of awful import in this country."[396] On July 3 the Newbern *Daily Progress* admitted it was the only paper in North Carolina "that had said a good word for Douglas," and the situation was equally dire for the Little Giant in many other states of the Deep South.[397]

The Spartanburg, South Carolina, *Spartan* called Douglas "a traitor to his party, traitor to his principles," and reasoned "he must prove traitor to the South." The Fayetteville *North Carolinian* declared, "We are opposed to Mr. Douglas, to his view, to his theory and his sentiments—in fact to the man." The Opelika, Alabama, *Southern Era* argued that Douglas "deserves to perish upon the gibbet of Democratic condemnation, and his carcass to be cast at the gates of the Federal City, in order that demagogues and renegade partisans might view with horror the dreadful retribution which stern justice will, sooner or later, visit upon them."[398]

Bell did not escape his share of excoriation. The *Dallas Herald* labeled him "a fossilized relic of a remote period.... These antiquarian gropers [the Constitutional Union delegates] have impiously disentombed this honored mummy from the tomb of the Pharaohs and have set him up in public places again to be gazed at with more wonder than he ever inspired during his palmiest days."[399]

Heightened tensions among fellow Southerners often spilled over into outright violence long before Dixie turned its guns on the North. One such incident transformed Lynchburg, Virginia, into the Tombstone of the fabled West. When George and William Hardwick of the pro–Breckinridge *Lynchburg Daily Republican* confronted Joseph and Robert Button of the pro–Bell *Lynchburg Daily Virginian*, according to one eyewitness, all four started shooting "as if by common consent." When the smoke cleared, both Button brothers lay mortally wounded.[400]

Not every publication south of the Mason-Dixon Line considered the election a referendum on the division of the Union. Some border South papers, such as the Nashville *Union and American*, the Lexington *Kentucky Statesman* (which considered "the disunionist howl" as "nothing but absurdity, mendacious malignity, and despicable hypocrisy"), and the Raleigh *North Carolina Standard*, were opposed to secession. The Nashville *Republican Banner* denounced the secessionists for concocting "the vilest, most damnable, deep laid and treacherous conspiracy" to "chloroform" Southerners with sectional prejudice, while the *Memphis Enquirer* urged its subscribers, "Let every man put his foot down on disunion; it is no remedy for Southern wrongs; or it is only the mad man's remedy." Most obdurate on this question was *Brownlow's Knoxville Whig*, edited by the fiery Parson Brownlow since 1838, which boasted the largest circulation in Tennessee, with 12,000 subscribers. Although an ardent advocate of slavery in the territories, Brownlow vigorously denounced the "wicked" and "treacherous" secessionists and vowed to resist "the fire-eating, union-dissolving, political charlatanism of the Southern extremists."[401] With the writing on the wall in September, he drew his own particular line in the sand: "I propose when the Secessionists go to Washington to dethrone Lincoln, to seize a bayonet and form an army to resist such an attack and they shall walk over my dead body on the way."[402]

However, in the papers of the Deep South, the universal theme was uncompromising rejection of the Republican Party and its nominee. In one example the Corsicana, Texas, *Navarro Express* articulated Lone Star State expectations of the future under the Republican heel: "As soon as Lincoln is installed into office ... he will wave his black plume Southward. With the army and navy ... he will invade us. He will issue his ukase, enfranchising the negroes, and arming them; he will confiscate property, and commend us to the mercy of torch and steel. Of this we are not left to doubt."[403]

With the prospect of Lincoln's election making their blood run cold, Southern editors were almost frantic in their protracted, region-wide campaign of denunciation. Typically, the *Clarksville Chronicle* in Tennessee wrote Lincoln off as a "soulless and brainless demagogue."[404] Through an act of projection of almost mind-numbing proportions, the *Charleston Mercury* labeled Lincoln a "bigot and extremist,"[405] concluding, "Faugh! After him what decent white man would be President?"[406]

The Southern press hinted that there was black blood in the Republican ticket itself, and some retailed the allegation that Lincoln's running mate, Hannibal Hamlin, was a mulatto. One Alabama paper snarled, "A free nigger to preside in the United States Senate: how would Southern Senators like that? The humiliation and disgrace of the thing would certainly be something, but the smell would be awful."[407] "Think of it," the Newberry, South Carolina, *Rising Sun* agreed, "a nigger in principle, elected President, and a mulatto, for Hamlin is said to be one, sitting as Vice President and presiding in the Senate. What Southern man could submit to sit under the shadow of such a creature."[408]

Lincoln's sole advocate in the Southern press was Archibald Campbell, editor of the

Wheeling Intelligencer, which at the time was in Virginia. Campbell attended the 1860 Republican national convention and served as secretary of the Republican executive committee in Virginia. The almost total absence of Southern support notwithstanding, Lincoln was elected the sixteenth President of the United States—which promptly commenced disuniting even before he took office, beginning with the secession of South Carolina on December 20. Lincoln's partisans chafed at the dithering impotence of the outgoing James Buchanan. "The imbecile old creature has completely shown the white feather," the *Chicago Tribune* snapped, as the Southern states slipped out of the Union one by one. "But the country has only to endure six weeks more of this miserable cowardice, incompetency and disloyalty."

As the crisis over Fort Sumter continued, the *Tribune's* loathing of the lame duck President reached boiling point: "His Excellency, James Buchanan ... is tottering through the sumptuous solitude of the White House, a chattering imbecile, a hopeless, helpless prisoner of vicious counselors, pandering to bad passions in others which age has extinguished in himself, alternately telling his beads and writing weak supplications for newspapers—an object of mingled compassion and contempt."[409]

The stage was set for the Civil War, and the press would play a critical part in it.

III

From Civil War to Gilded Age, 1860–1896

The Civil War was the crucible of the American nation and the nation's press was there not merely to report the facts but to weave itself into the story it was telling — always needling, cajoling, damning, or praising, with one eye on the needs of its particular audience, and the other on the verdict of history. By 1860 there was little room for dissent in the papers of the South, and none at all after the fall of Fort Sumter. But the Northern papers accurately reflected the entire spectrum of Northern opinion, including the substantial constituency that questioned the conduct of, or justification for the war. The power of the media barons, who possessed the priceless capacity to shape the news, was a constant presence that decision makers in both civilian and military spheres at the highest levels had to take into account for the duration of the conflict. Finding the correct balance in responding to this unprecedented challenge was not the least of the problems faced by the Lincoln administration in its war to preserve the Union.[1] Conversely, sometimes the newsmakers got a little too close to the action for their own comfort. The presses of Greeley's *Tribune* were stormed during the New York draft riots of July 1863 but Raymond, who had somehow obtained two Gatling guns which he mounted in the first-floor publication office of his building, kept the mob at bay from the headquarters of the *Times*.

The accelerated tempo of the news during the war left telegraph offices inundated with stories being wired in from multiple fronts, and editorial offices struggling to assimilate the raw material. There were occasions when the demand for information ran ahead of the technology available to provide it; a breaking news story would not uncommonly be headlined, "Important if True." However, this unprecedented pressure did have longer-term implications. Because the newspapers were constantly fighting the clock to get to press, they increasingly resorted to running with wire service bulletins that avoided the typically discursive narrative format of the day in favor of relatively detached reports in the "inverted pyramid" style. As Dicken-Garcia notes, it was during the Civil War that "news came to be treated as a product," as opposed to an exercise in subjective literary interpretation.[2]

Mechanization, a component of the industrial revolution then consummating its worldwide socioeconomic hegemony, helped institutionalize this commodification of the news. One observer was struck by the newfound urgency of the news process during a tour of Greeley's *Tribune* offices where he witnessed "the great engine of the 19th century, steam engines in every part of the huge building, four editors at humble tables, with pen & scissors in hand, preparing for 100,000 readers & more, with telegraphic dispatches every hour, from every part of the Union."[3]

Mechanization helped the number of papers in print keep pace with America's burgeoning population. Only 65 dailies were published in 1830; by 1870 this figure had grown to 574; it was 971 by 1880, 1,610 by 1890, and over 2,200 newspapers were printed every day at the dawn of the 20th century.[4] Innovations in production and distribution also ensured that more papers were more readily available to more people than ever before. The average circulation of daily papers climbed from 2,200 a day in 1840 to 8,007 in 1904 and 16,684 in 1925. In 1870, only two papers had a circulation of over 100,000; by 1890 there were eight. That decade, the leading papers of New York City sold over 300,000 copies a day. As a corollary, newspaper revenue from advertising doubled from 1870 to 1880, nearly doubled again over the next decade, and then continued to steadily expand in the 20th century.[5] Put another way, in 1879, U.S. publications' total revenues amounted to approximately $89 million, of which 56 percent came from sales and subscriptions, while 44 percent came from advertising. By 1914, revenues had climbed to almost $419 million, with advertising contributing 61 percent, and sales and subscriptions dropping to 39 percent.[6] This evolution in the newspaper business model brought down prices, and, by weakening the link between the papers and patronage, would have significant long-term implications for the relationship between press and party. Joseph Pulitzer, the influential publisher of the *St. Louis Post-Dispatch* and later the *New York World*, praised advertising revenue for liberating newspapers from the stranglehold of party controls.[7] "As they expanded their circulation and their revenues, and as their investments multiplied, journals increasingly shifted from a political enterprise to a big business," Kaplan says. "The constraints of the market and the incentives of profit-making weighed ever more heavily on the conduct of journalism."[8] In that sense, "The interests of corporate America in reaching all potential consumers fortuitously coalesced with democracy's ideal of including all citizens in the nation's cultural and political dialogues."[9]

The combination of technology and good business sense also militated against partisan bias. By definition, it was in the interests of wire services such as the Associated Press to sell their reports to as many different papers as possible. In his study of the Wisconsin press, Donald L. Shaw found a strong relationship between increased use of wire service stories and a sharp drop in biased reporting. Comparing wire and non-wire stories over the period 1852–1916, Shaw judged non-wire stories to exhibit bias approximately fifteen times as frequently as wire stories.[10]

Certainly, a growing handful of the major papers had the will and the capacity to transcend their traditionally subservient role and emerge not just as conduits of party ideology but as true bearers of the news. By the 1870s, newspapers were "made to sell," the elderly James Watson Webb lamented in a letter to James G. Blaine in 1876. "When you and I were editors we did not follow, but made, public sentiment; and we also made presidents. But things have changed now."[11]

In January 1871, Henry Watterson, editor of the *Louisville Courier-Journal*, wrote that "the time has passed" when editors of the partisan press were "men of second-rate abilities, [who] served mainly as squires to their liege lords, the politicians."[12] The following year, William Cullen Bryant in the New York *Evening Post* claimed that the "jackal days of journalism are gone, happily never to return.... The journalist is no longer the camp-follower of this or that party, shouting the battle cries of his leaders, and picking up such booty in the way of office as his generals may choose to throw to him. He is himself a leader, a centre of political power, directing the course of parties, and only losing his power when he becomes partisan."[13] Charles Dana declared that his New York *Sun* would wear "the livery of no party, and [discuss] public questions and acts of public men on their merits alone."[14]

However, there remained definite limits as to how far down the path of objectivity editors schooled in an atmosphere of pure partisanship were prepared to travel. George William Curtis, the editor of *Harper's Weekly* from 1853 to 1892, was careful to draw the distinction between independence and objectivity. For him, membership in one or other of the two major parties was not just natural but necessary: "The man who thinks that both are equally bad, and who does not care which prevails, is a man without opinions, or without principle, or without perception, and in either case is wholly unfit to be an editor." Curtis considered editorial independence a service, not a threat, to the party system: "The more deeply an independent journal sympathizes with the principle and purpose of a party, the more strenuously will it censure its candidates and leaders, for the purpose of keeping the principle pure, and of making the success of the party a real blessing."[15] Curtis was not afraid to practice the partisan politics he preached. Defeated in a run for Congress in 1864, he lost in his bid to become senator in 1866 and lost again in what he thought was a lock on the nomination for governor at the Republican state convention in New York in 1870. After being appointed to head President Grant's Civil Service Commission in 1871, he subsequently became a key figure in both the Liberal Republican campaign of 1872 against Grant and the Mugwump defection to Grover Cleveland in 1884.[16]

This blurring of the lines between journalistic responsibilities and political ambition was endemic throughout the period. Editors of major papers in New York City alone who took seats in Congress included Henry Raymond of the *Times* (1864), Joseph Pulitzer of the *World* (1884), Amos Cummings of the *Sun* (1886) and William Randolph Hearst of the *Journal* (1902). The career path of James G. Blaine offers a classic example of employing journalistic talents as a springboard for political ambition.[17] Two months after taking over as editor of the *Kennebec Journal*, the incoming Whig majority in the Maine legislature designated his publication the state paper, with a contract to print all official notices. Blaine traded up to become editor of the *Portland Daily Advertiser*, Maine's most influential paper, in 1857. He won election to the state legislature in 1858; became chairman of the Republican State Committee; and by 1860 was Speaker of Maine's House of Representatives. In 1862 he won election to the U.S. House of Representatives, where he joined fellow print veterans House Speaker Schuyler Colfax, proprietor of the South Bend, Indiana, *Register* and Minority Leader James Brooks, formerly editor of the *New York Daily Express*. The election of 1864 brought ten more newspapermen into the House.

In the Civil War Senate sat Republican Henry Anthony, owner of the *Providence Daily Journal*, and Democrat B. Gratz Brown, editor of the *Missouri Democrat*.[18] During his twenty-five years in the Senate, from 1859 until his death in 1884, Rhode Island's Henry Anthony never relinquished editorial control of the *Daily Journal*, which served as the mouthpiece for the state's Republican Party and textile industry. Joseph Hawley was another to mix the newspaper business with politics over the span of several decades. The chairman of the Free Soil Party's State Committee and editor of the party's newspaper, the *Charter Oak*, in 1856 he took a leading part in organizing the Republican Party in Connecticut, and in 1857 became editor of the *Hartford Evening Press*. After serving with distinction in the Federal army throughout the Civil War, Hawley served as governor of Connecticut from April 1866 to April 1867. A few months after stepping down from that office he bought the *Hartford Courant*, which he merged with the *Press*, making it the most influential newspaper in his state and one of the leading Republican papers in the country. From this foundation Hawley would go on to a distinguished career in national politics that included two stretches in the House and one in the Senate.

The bottom line remained that even if the pace and scale of the newspaper business was evolving, its underlying operating principles would not have appeared at all alien to previous generations of newspaper readers. "Every newspaper writer and every printer had been educated for half a century in the belief that no journal of any respectability could be established without the consent of politicians and the pecuniary aid of party," a contemporary wrote; the press therefore remained "the slave of the two political oligarchies."[19] To give just one example, when new owners took control of the Hunterdon, New Jersey, *County Democrat* in 1867, they established their credentials by announcing that the Democratic county committee had "approved and sanctioned" the sale on the expectation that the incoming management would uphold the traditional business practices of the paper. These included accepting cords of hickory during election years, in lieu of the two-dollar annual subscription; placing notices of Democratic meetings in news columns; enlivening the pages with sketches of the Democratic symbol, the rooster; and encouraging advertisers to employ political themes in their commercials, an example being the Albaugh Dry Goods Company with its 1866 slogan, "The Veto Sustained: Popular Prices for Clothing."[20]

Passing judgment on his peers in the August 12, 1880, issue of *The Nation*, Edwin L. Godkin remarked that "traditions of party fealty and advocacy ... too strong to be overthrown" still dominated the press.[21] "Nineteenth-century newspapers imported the rigidities and exclusions of the parties' strategic agenda into the public sphere, and continually shored up the party's dominion over public discourse," Kaplan confirms. "The daily partisan paper spoke in emphatic, argumentative, and often personal tones. It addressed its audience as committed political participants and in some sense as one engaged citizen speaking to another."[22] What had happened to the promised dawn of an objective media? On the surface, progress away from dogmatic allegiance to the patron party appeared to be the emerging, even dominant trend among the nation's papers. In New York State in 1869, according to *Rowell's American Newspaper Directory*, there were 108 Democratic and 159 Republican newspapers, making 267 partisan papers in all. Ten years later, the number of partisan newspapers had increased to 290, but they were now in a minority compared to the 325 independent and nonaffiliated newspapers. In some states there was an absolute decline in the number of partisan newspapers in print over the same period. There were 70 Democratic and 149 Republican newspapers in Illinois in 1869; ten years later only 67 Democratic and 106 Republican newspapers survived (see Table 5 and Table 6.)[23]

TABLE 5. PARTISAN VS. INDEPENDENT PRESS, 1869[24]

Newspapers	New York	California	Ohio	Illinois
Partisan	52%	54%	76%	75%
Independent	33%	24%	15%	16%

TABLE 6. PARTISAN VS. INDEPENDENT PRESS, 1879[25]

Newspapers	New York	California	Ohio	Illinois
Partisan	37%	31%	44%	41%
Independent	42%	54%	47%	48%

The number of partisan papers in Detroit also declined over the course of the late 19th century, from 40 to 60 percent partisan in the 1860s and 1870s, to 18–34 percent in the 1880s and 1890s.[26] By 1890, 25 percent of the more than 9,000 Northern weeklies (rising to one-third of weeklies published in the Northeast) were self-proclaimed independents, and 24 percent of the region's 1,300 dailies asserted independence as well. Of the 144 Northern urban papers whose sales reached at least 10,000 copies a day, a total of 56, or 39 percent, had declared their independence. So too had 19 of the 28 metropolitan journals with circulations of 50,000 or more, a striking 68 percent.[27]

But these figures belie two important countervailing trends. The first is that the siren call of easy party money proved irresistible to many editors who still couldn't make ends meet without it. This was particularly true of the smaller rural publications that lacked the necessary population and hence advertising revenue base to go their own way. Despite the increasing salience of advertising revenue, subscriptions and party and official funds remained vital to the survival of most publications well into the 20th century. Even in Detroit, the *Post* made its position — you get what you pay for — abundantly clear to the Republican Party on the eve of campaign season 1872:

> For Grant and Wilson
>   To meet the demands of the Republicans of Michigan and to advance their cause, the WEEKLY POST will be sent to subscribers until after the election at the rates given below.
>   The Post has no sympathy with the sickly inanity that the Republican Party has accomplished its mission. No party has ceased to be useful while it retained the vitality which initiates all the practical reforms of its age and it is the crowning glory of the organization which has done so much for the country....
>   With these convictions ... the POST proposes to utter no uncertain sound during the canvas just now opening ... and it depends upon those who are Republicans ... to aid in extending its circulation.[28]

Secondly, even the biggest of the metropolitan papers might be entirely independent of patronage financing and yet entirely biased in favor of one party or the other simply because that was the inclination of management, typically the owner and/or the editor. James Gordon Bennett had proved decades earlier that independence of party ties need not in any sense mean objectivity in his approach to the issues of the day.[29]

Even if not being directly subsidized by one or the other party, many newsmakers were the beneficiaries of softer forms of patronage. According to Summers, most editors could be co-opted by the offer of a $1,200 postmastership, which let them send their newspapers free under the official frank and let them harass rival presses by confiscating circulars, finding out their subscribers' names and convincing them to cancel, or fostering newspaper-supporting clubs.[30] More ambitious media insiders acquired government jobs, took favors, hired themselves out as lobbyists, and acted as advisers, errand runners, and campaign organizers for politicians they liked, and attended political conventions to pull the wires against those they didn't. In this environment, says Summers, "Newspapers were more than echoes of party organizers, much less objective reporters of political affairs. They proclaimed themselves as a power in their own right."[31]

Whitelaw Reid represents a classic study in this new, if not obviously improved, mode of relationship between journalist and politician. Shortly before taking over as managing editor of the *New York Tribune* he had exclaimed, "Independent journalism! That is the watchword of the future in the profession. An end of concealment because it would hurt the party; an end of one-sided expositions."[32] But these fine sentiments did not deter him from steadfastly heaping calumny upon the Democratic Party (which the *Tribune* on one occasion referred to as "a myth, a reminiscence, a voice from the tomb, an ancient, fishlike smell") over several decades, nor from accepting the appointment by the Harrison administration as Minister to France, nor from securing the Republican Party's vice presidential nomination at its 1892 national convention. Another to follow this path was Charles Emory Smith. A journalist with the *Albany Morning Express* and *New York Evening Journal*, he graduated to editor and part-owner of the *Philadelphia Press*. He was subsequently appointed minister to Russia and, later still, postmaster general of the United States.[33]

Even the vaunted capacity of the wire services to standardize the news while stripping it of subjectivity could be compromised when the wire services themselves were being deliberately biased. It had dawned on some of the more forward-thinking politicians of the age that courting the masters of this new medium would obviate the need to inveigle their way into the hearts of any number of the editors of provincial and small-town newspapers. One of the quickest off the mark in this regard was perennial Republican presidential hopeful James G. Blaine. His connections paid off in 1876 when, shortly before the GOP national convention, at which Blaine was widely considered the frontrunner to secure his party's presidential nomination, a Democratic House investigating committee charged him with using his influence as Speaker to secure a land grant for a railroad in Arkansas and with selling the railroad's bonds at a liberal commission. Blaine privately secured possession of the notorious "Mulligan letters," which had been named as proof, before they could be placed on record, and he never surrendered them. In a dramatic bid to uphold his honor, he did condescend to read portions of the letters, out of chronological order, to the House, a performance that culminated in his theatrically-timed physical collapse. Summers notes that "it was perhaps no coincidence that the Washington bureau of the Associated Press, friendly as ever to Blaine, failed to send along the letters in question to its readers on the day that it reported Blaine's theatrical triumph. Indeed, it tried to suppress them all, until the special correspondents banded together to force their transmission along the wires."[34]

Blaine ultimately came up just short at the convention, but the eventual nominee, Rutherford Hayes, was another beneficiary of wire-service largesse. The manifest bias of the Associated Press was so blatant, both throughout the campaign of 1876 and during its bitterly contested aftermath, that Democrats dubbed it the "Hayesociated Press."[35] When Tilden's backers called mass meetings to protest the election being stolen, William Henry Smith, a loyal Republican and confidant of Hayes before taking over the Western Associated Press in Chicago, wrote to one of his reporters in Ohio, "I suggest that we can best subserve the interests of the country and the press by making no reference to them in our reports."[36]

According to Summers, for decades after Appomattox, "most journals remained the partisan shills, long on rant and short on news (especially local) that they had been since Andrew Jackson's day."[37] The official position as commissioned by the U.S. government in 1881, was that in the wake of the Civil War, "the great mass of the newspapers of the United States continued to be conducted in the interests of one or other of the existing parties, and still continue to be so conducted, and they will so continue for an indefinite time to come." Furthermore, "It is neither unnatural nor improper that this relationship should exist."[38] It just made life easier. Democrats and Republicans both appreciated the fact that when looking for their party's perspective on current events they didn't have to waste much time flipping through the Gilded-Age equivalent of the magazine rack. "A single glance at the masthead often told the whole story," Summers says. "One did not have to ask the politics of the Hudson *True Republican* or the Linn *Unterrified Democrat*."[39] In most major cities there was a relative stasis throughout the Gilded Age. In Cleveland, the Democratic *Plain Dealer* battled the Republican *Herald* and *Leader*. In St. Louis the *Globe Democrat*, Republican, struggled for the hearts and minds of Midwesterners with the *Republican*, Democrat. Even in the territories, the battle went on; the *Press-Gazette* pleaded the Democratic case for the residents of Oklahoma City in the morning, while the *Times-Journal* published the Republican perspective in the afternoon.[40]

"We publish a Republican paper because we are Republicans, and have faith in Republican principles," the Chicago *Daily Inter Ocean* notified its readers the week it commenced publication; "Republican in everything, independent in nothing," was its boast. The LaCrosse, Wisconsin, *Democrat* on the other hand remained proudly "Democratic at all times and under all circumstances."[41] Mark "Brick" Pomeroy, the editor of the *Democrat* during the Civil War, went so far as to express a fervent hope that should Lincoln succeed in his bid for reelection, "some bold hand will pierce his heart with dagger point for the public good."[42] When he relocated to Manhattan to launch the *New York Democrat*, he made his intentions immediately clear by referring to Republican congressman and perennial presidential hopeful "Beast Brute Blundering Butchering Blear-eyed Blackguarding Bag Faced Ben Butler" in his headlines, and standing a small statue of the former Civil War general outside his office door complete with the inscription "Thief Robber and Woman Insulter."[43]

Vicious polemics were a standard trope of editorial dialogue throughout the era. Mark Twain, campaigning for James Garfield in 1880, made a wry observation on the prevailing tendency in the nation's press to counter policy with personal abuse when he told an audience at the Hartford, Connecticut, opera house "I have never made but one political speech before this. That was years ago. I made a logical, closely reasoned, compact powerful argument against a discriminating opposition. I may say I made a most thoughtful, symmetrical, and admirable argument, but a Michigan newspaper editor answered it, refuted it, utterly demolished it, by saying I was in the constant habit of horse whipping my great grandmother."[44]

This institutionalized bias also made it difficult to discern reality from wishful thinking in the news of the day. Reporting on the Connecticut Republican state convention of 1876, for example, the Democratic *New Haven Evening Register* found the convention floor "half full, while the galleries were almost empty." The keynote address "fell flat on delegates and audience alike. Even the mention of the name of the Republican candidate for the presidency created no enthusiasm." A second speaker was "long and rambling," a third "long and tiresome." In contrast, the reporter for the Republican *Morning Journal and Courier* related that "every available seat in the body of the hall was filled, while a large number of citizens occupied seats in the galleries." The keynote speaker "was loudly applauded," the second speaker spoke "impassioned words exciting tumultuous applause," and the third delivered "an able and telling speech which excited renewed enthusiasm."[45]

The persistence of partiality in the nation's media led one contemporary critic to claim that the "astonishing" credit that the New York *Sun* received for actually reporting that Grover Cleveland had won the presidential election of 1884 in fact represented only the most backhanded approbation. "The compliments ... showed how rare and wonderful a thing this was in American political journalism," Smythe points out. "Yet ... to compliment a paper upon printing the news with exactness and impartiality ought to be almost as offensive as to compliment a man upon his honesty or a woman upon her chastity."[46]

Look Away

No one could say that the nation hadn't been warned. The newspapers of the cotton kingdom, headed by such leading Southern nationalists as John Daniel of the *Richmond Examiner*, Roger Pryor of the *Richmond Enquirer*, and John Forsyth of the *Mobile Advertiser and Register*, had clearly signaled that the election of Abraham Lincoln in 1860 meant secession. "The South," opined the Augusta *Southern Confederacy*, "will never permit Abraham Lincoln to be inaugurated President of the United States; this is a settled and sealed fact. It is the determination of all parties in the South. Let the consequences be what they may, whether the Potomac is crimsoned in human gore, and Pennsylvania Avenue is paved ten fathoms deep with mangled bodies, or whether the last vestige of liberty is swept from the face of the American continent, the constitutional South will never submit to such humiliation and degradation as the inauguration of Abraham."[47]

According to the *Charleston Daily Courier*, in the heartland of secession country, Lincoln's triumph at the polls "determined the failure of the great American experiment of self-government."[48] If the Union had failed then the genesis of a new Southern nation dedicated to the preservation of slavery was the only recourse, and the newspapers of the budding confederacy were to be, as always, at the vanguard of the struggle. In Fredericksburg, Virginia, shortly to be the site of one of the bloodiest battles of the Civil War, the *Herald* identified its own kind as the source of the sectional divide, and, with the cynicism born of despair, offered the mass euthanasia of the entire journalistic profession as a solution to the crisis: "Newspaper and Telegraphs have ruined the country. Suppress both and the country could be saved now."[49]

Sensing its participation on the threshold of history, the secessionist press everywhere across the South was caught up in an exaltation of messianic righteousness, fueled by a heady cocktail of resentment, defiance, and exhilaration.[50] The Harrisonburg, Virginia, *Rockingham Register and Advertiser* had no second thoughts about remaining in the Union with Northern folk: "Infidels, free-lovers, amalgamationists, they are, and as such can make the Devil himself grow pale over their acts of wickedness."[51] The *Richmond Examiner* called for the South to march on Washington and deliver it from "Lincoln the beast ... the Illinois Ape."[52]

The *Atlanta Daily Intelligencer* expressed its opinion that should an abolitionist come South "at this excited time ... we would not give a dime for his life. He would be strung up to the nearest live oak — and permitted to dance upon nothing."[53] The Charlotte, North Carolina, *Bulletin* went further, demanding total obeisance to the doctrine of secession among its fellow Southerners: "We spit upon every plan to compromise, come from what source it may. A Southern man who would now offer to compromise with the Northern States is a traitor to the South, and ought to be branded, if possible, with a more prominent mark than was placed upon the murderer CAIN. May he be accursed forever."[54]

Across the South this consensus was imposed, where necessary by force. Less than a month after the surrender of Fort Sumter, Confederate rangers enforced total conformity in the Lone Star State by sacking and torching the offices of the *San Antonio Alamo Express*. "The morning light displayed the charred ruins of the *Alamo Express*, the last Union paper in Texas," editor James P. Newcomb later recalled.[55]

One by one, the Union men were dispossessed, Union voices silenced. The last to go down, literally with the flag still flying, was *Brownlow's Knoxville Whig*, which spat defiance at the secessionists, reminding them that while cotton was "King," "Kentucky and Missouri hemp, as a necklace for traitors, is an article of still greater value for home consumption."[56] Parson Brownlow held out for the Union, even after Tennessee finally seceded on June 8, determined to "battle on beneath the folds of the Star Spangled Banner as the only sacred shield of a common nationality."

The heat was on, but Brownlow continued to excoriate the Davis administration in Richmond, asserting, "I shall continue to say just what I please until my office is closed or destroyed by brute force.... I will starve, or beg my bread ... before I will surrender to this vile heresy of Secession." Brownlow was finally arrested by Confederate commissioners and charged with treason to the newborn republic in December. "Now this hoary-headed and persistent traitor ... deserves death and we vote to kill him," opined the Columbus, Georgia, *Times*. Brownlow could consider himself lucky that his ultimate sentence was expulsion to the North. The last laugh would be his. After the Union retook Knoxville, Brownlow returned home and resumed publication, but with the name changed to *Brownlow's Knoxville Whig and Rebel Ventilator*. He was elected Governor of Tennessee in 1865 and served two terms before resigning and selling his newspaper in 1869 in order to accept a seat in the U.S. Senate, where he served until 1875. Upon his return to private life he bought back the *Whig* and continued to edit it until his death in 1877.[57] He never forgot nor forgave those who had risen against the Union. "Let them be punished — let them be impoverished — let them be slain," he fulminated, "and after slain, let them be damned!"[58]

Attitudes were hardening in the North, too. The *Philadelphia Morning Pennsylvanian*, the voice of the Buchanan administration in the City of Brotherly Love, continued to pump out anti-abolition screeds over the secession winter, but was clearly being kept alive solely by virtue of patronage from Washington. When that dried up the moment Buchanan left office, the *Morning Pennsylvanian* had just enough energy left to sing the praises of the emerging Confederacy before expiring. Its obituary was left to the *Philadelphia Sunday Dispatch*: "Ill done, bad and faithless servant."[59]

Honest Abe

Shortly after Lincoln took office, the *New York Herald*, commenting on the administration's patronage appointments to date, remarked, "It is evident that Mr. Lincoln has determined upon an evacuation of the *New York Tribune* office, if he has not decided about Fort Sumter."[60] Less propitious circumstances for building a viable administration cannot be imagined, but even in a time of crisis Lincoln recognized the rules of the political game still applied. The relations between politicians and press remained as symbiotic as ever. For evidence of this Lincoln had to look no further than his own immediate circle where his vice president, Hannibal Hamlin, and four members of his Cabinet had been editors at one time or another.

In navigating the state of flux generated by the transition to a new administration led by a political unknown at the head of a neophyte party during a period of crisis, the president-elect had to be careful in deciding exactly who his friends in the print trade really were. James Harvey, Washington correspondent for the *North American*, wrote Lincoln's private secretary, John G. Nicolay, on November 25, 1860, warning him that "one Hanscom, a newsgatherer of the N.Y. Herald" was in Springfield and intended to establish a new paper in Washington. Hanscom, Harvey continued, "is known here as one of the most unscrupulous & notorious of all the corrupt gang who infest this Capital." Indeed, Harvey considered his employment by the *Herald* proof of his low character: "That paper has just such agents & no other." The real object of the new publication, Harvey continued, "is a speculation on the Government, and a lobby machine to operate upon the Republicans in Congress." He urged Nicolay to warn Lincoln against Hanscom, adding: "The attempt will be made to impress upon the public that it is his [Lincoln's] organ, & to impress the pockets of his friends, for the support of adventurers." Hanscom in fact brought out the first issue of the *National Republican* the day after Harvey penned his missive sounding the alarm against the project which, bereft of administration support, failed.[61] Harvey would be rewarded for services rendered by being appointed minister to Portugal.

Lincoln made substantial use of government patronage to reward loyal editors and sway the allegiance of others (see Table 7). It was simple quid pro quo. One observer recalls the president remarking in 1864 that "no man, whether he be private citizen or President of the United States, can successfully carry on a controversy with a great newspaper, and escape destruction, unless he owns a newspaper equally great, with a circulation in the same neighborhood."[62] Every editor had his price; and patronage was the instrument through which a president could shape the editorial environment to his advantage.

TABLE 7. NEWSPAPER APPOINTMENTS TO PUBLIC OFFICE
BY THE LINCOLN ADMINISTRATION[63]

Individual	Newspaper	Appointment
George W. Fogg	*Concord Independent Democrat*	Minister to Switzerland
James F. Babcock	*New Haven Daily Palladium*	Collector of Customs at the Port of New Haven
George Dawson	*Albany Evening Journal*	Postmaster at Albany
Charles A. Dana	*New York Tribune*	Assistant Secretary of War
James S. Pike	*New York Tribune*	Minister to Holland
Bayard Taylor	*New York Tribune*	First Secretary of the Legation in St. Petersburg
William H. Fry	*New York Tribune*	First Secretary, Turin Legation
John Bigelow	*New York Evening Post*	Consul General at Paris
Horace N. Congar	*Newark Daily Mercury*	Consul at Hong Kong
Jacob R. Freese	*Trenton State Gazette*	Commissioner of the Board of Enrollment, 2nd District, NJ
George Bergner	*Harrisburg Telegraph*	Postmaster in Harrisburg
Russell Errett	*Pittsburgh Gazette*	Paymaster in the Army
John S. Prettyman	*Milford Peninsular News & Advertiser*	Consul at Glasgow
John F. McJilton	*Baltimore Patriot*	Surveyor of the Port of Baltimore
James C. Welling	*Washington National Intelligencer*	Assistant Clerk in the United States Court of Claims
Archibald W. Campbell	*Wheeling Intelligencer*	Postmaster in Wheeling
Frederick Hassaurek	*Cincinnati Daily Commercial*	Special Treasury Agent and Collector of Customs at Puget Sound
James H. Barrett	*Cincinnati Daily Gazette*	Commissioner of Pensions
William Dean Howells	*Columbus Ohio State Journal*	Consul in Venice
Edwin Cowles	*Cleveland Leader*	Postmaster in Cleveland
John D. Defrees	*Indianapolis Journal*	Superintendent of Public Printing
John W. Dawson	*Fort Wayne Times*	Governor of Utah Territory
John L. Scripps	*Chicago Press & Tribune*	Postmaster in Chicago
Charles L. Wilson	*Chicago Daily Journal*	First Secretary, London Legation
George Schneider	*Chicago States-Zeitung*	Consul at Elsinore, Denmark
David L. Phillips	*Springfield Illinois State Journal*	U.S. Marshal for the Southern District, Illinois
Theodore Canisius	*Springfield Illinois Staats-Anzeiger*	Consul at Vienna
Rufus King	*Milwaukee Sentinel*	Minister to the Papal States

Individual	Newspaper	Appointment
Carl Roeser	*Manitowoc Wisconsin Democrat*	Clerk in the Treasury Department
Peter L. Foy	*St. Louis Missouri Democrat*	Postmaster in St. Louis
Henry Boernstein	*St. Louis Anzeiger des Westen*	Consul at Bremen
Charles L. Bernays	*St. Louis Anzeiger des Westen*	Consul at Zurich
William F. Switzler	*Columbia Missouri Statesman*	Military Secretary of State for the Conquered State of Arkansas
John Teesdale	*Des Moines Iowa State Register*	Postmaster in Des Moines
Daniel W. Wilder	*Leavenworth Weekly Conservative*	U.S. Surveyor General for Kansas and Nebraska
Thomas J. Dryer	*Portland Oregonian*	Commissioner to Hawaii
James Harvey	*Philadelphia North American*	Minister to Portugal

The manner in which Lincoln finessed the political conversion of John W. Forney affords a representative example of this process. During the Pierce administration, the Philadelphian Forney, then a Democrat, had been a partner in the administration organ, the *Washington Daily Union*, and in 1856 had backed his friend James Buchanan for president. After Buchanan failed to get Forney appointed the editorship of the *Union*, elected Senator from Pennsylvania, or appointed to his Cabinet, Forney turned on the administration. He founded the *Philadelphia Press* in 1857 and used it to back Senator Stephen Douglas in his struggle with the president over Kansas and other issues. Early in 1860, the Republican majority shrewdly capitalized on the Buchanan-Forney split, and elected Forney as Clerk of the House of Representatives. Forney returned the favor by continuing to blast Buchanan and exacerbating the split within the Democratic Party in Pennsylvania by openly supporting Douglas for president over Buchanan's vice president, John Breckinridge.

Lincoln appreciated Forney's aid, and following his election wrote to the editor and tendered him his friendship. In March 1861, when Forney's bid for reelection as Clerk of the House was defeated, Lincoln was instrumental in having Forney chosen as Secretary of the Senate, making him the beneficiary of the administration's awarding of substantial advertising contracts. In the same month, prior to the outbreak of war, Lincoln tendered Forney's son a commission as lieutenant in the Marine Corps.

Now solidly behind the Republican president, Forney launched the weekly *Washington Sunday Morning Chronicle* on March 31, 1861, upgrading it to a daily, the *Daily Morning Chronicle*, on November 3, 1862. In addition to securing the lion's share of the public notice advertising from the executive departments, ten thousand copies of the *Chronicle* went daily on government order to the Army of the Potomac. In turn, Lincoln appointed one of the paper's editorial writers, Daniel R. Goodloe, as one of the commissioners of emancipation in the District of Columbia. He also appointed one of Forney's brothers-in-law and associates in the business management of the *Chronicle*, William Reitzel, as a route agent for the post office, and one of Forney's cousins, who was also connected with the paper, was given a sinecure in the Interior Department.[64]

Two more pro–Lincoln Philadelphia editors patronized by the administration were Morton McMichael, proprietor of the *North American*, and James S. Chambers, publisher of the *Evening Bulletin*. McMichael's paper received a generous amount of advertising, principally in the form of proposals for the coal, pork, beef, and other supplies necessary to carry on the war, plus the right of publication of the laws passed by Congress. In addition, four of McMichael's sons enjoyed favors in the form of military promotions or civil appointments.[65]

Over and above enjoying the grant of advertising contracts from the administration, Chambers secured the position of navy agent, while his seventy-three year old father was made superintendent of warehouses in the customs service at Philadelphia, earning $1,200 per year. Casper Souder, Jr., a reporter for and shareholder in the *Evening Bulletin*, received appointment as inspector of customs at Philadelphia, with an official salary of $1,905 per year.[66]

Patronage could also help bind the various factions of the Republican Party more closely to the administration, for example helping assuage the lingering bitterness of the Weed/Seward faction over Lincoln's nomination. Among the federal plums accruing to *Albany Journal*, two of Weed's subordinates received lucrative postmasterships in the state capital, another was appointed assistant secretary of state to Seward, while a fourth was appointed a clerk to Secretary of the Senate Forney. "Editors seem to be in very great favor with the party in power," the *Baltimore Evening Patriot* observed at the end of March 1861, "a larger number of the fraternity having received appointments at its hands than probably under any previous Administration."[67]

Copperheads

Of course, many small-town editors, out of love for the Union or fealty to the Republican Party, were prepared to stand by the president without expectation of reward. In 1847, Jane Grey Swisshelm established the *Pittsburgh Saturday Visiter*, an abolition and women's rights paper, which in 1856 was merged with the weekly edition of the *Pittsburgh Journal*. In 1857 she moved to St. Cloud, Minnesota, where she launched the *St. Cloud Visiter*. Her bold editorial stance provoked a mob into destroying her office and its contents and throwing her printing press into the river. Undeterred, she shortly afterwards began to publish the *St. Cloud Democrat*. When Abraham Lincoln was nominated for the presidency, she spoke and wrote on his behalf and for the principles of which he was the representative. When the Civil War began and nurses were wanted at the front, she was one of the first to respond. After the Battle of the Wilderness, she had charge of 182 badly wounded men at Fredericksburg for five days, without surgeon or assistant, and saved them all.

But there were just as many editors who, for reasons ranging from partisan stubbornness to genuine horror at the bloodshed engulfing the nation, were prepared to defy the Administration and determined to bring down the president. On the day Fort Sumter was taken, the Jersey City, New Jersey, *American Standard* left its readers with absolutely no doubts as to who was responsible for the fratricidal conflict now erupting, when it labeled Lincoln "the American Cain."[68] There were no fewer than eight pro-states'-rights papers in Baltimore, fueling that city's antipathy to the Union cause. The editors of the *South* (as succinct a title as ever there was) proclaimed secession "a righteous and holy cause," and said, "We are ready to stand by it to the last. If it is rebellion we are content to be rebels—if treason, traitors."[69] Such publications were defined by Union men as the "Copperhead" press, after the venomous snake.

Copperhead publications typically took the high road, criticizing the war effort on the grounds of defending constitutional rights, while taking the low road of savage race-baiting. Emancipation represented "another step in the nigger business, and another advance in the Robespierrian highway of tyranny and anarchy," the editor of the Canton, Ohio, *Stark County*

Democrat snarled.[70] "If this is a war ... of Abolition," the Democratic editor of the Oshkosh, Wisconsin, *Courier* stated in an editorial, "then the sooner the Union goes to the devil the better." Nelson Abbott, the editor of the Macomb, Illinois, *Eagle*, defined the Republican agenda in the following terms: "It is nigger in the Senate and nigger in the House. It is nigger in the forenoon and nigger in the afternoon. It is nigger in motions and nigger in speeches. It was nigger the first day and it has been nigger everyday. Nigger is in every man's eye, and nigger in every man's mouth. It's nigger in the lobby and the proceedings are black with nigger.... The nigger vapor is a moral pestilence that blunts the sense of duty to the constitution and destroys the instinct of obedience to the law."[71]

Lincoln was never popular in staunchly anti-abolition, Irish, and Democratic New York City, and failed to carry it in either of his presidential campaigns. Logically, it was the heartland of Copperhead sentiment. Only five of New York City's seventeen papers supported Lincoln in any degree — the *Times, Evening Post, Sun, Tribune,* and *Commercial Advertiser.* Nine of the others were frankly pro-slavery, and of these, five were firmly in the Copperhead camp.[72]

As much ink was spilled as blood in the cause of blue and gray during the Civil War, and nowhere was the literary assault on Abraham Lincoln more fervid than the offices of the *La Crosse Democrat,* where the arch–Copperhead Mark "Brick" Pomeroy labeled the President "The Widow-Maker of the 19th Century" and openly wished "some bold hand will pierce his heart with dagger point for the public good" (courtesy of Library of Congress).

Outside of New York, leading Copperhead papers included the *Detroit Free Press,* the *Cincinnati Daily Enquirer,* the *Dayton Daily Empire,* the *Indiana State Sentinel,* and, most notoriously, the *Chicago Times,* edited by Wilbur F. Storey; the *La Crosse Democrat,* edited by Marcus Mills "Brick" Pomeroy; and the *Columbus Crisis,* edited by Samuel Medary.

Storey's motto was "To print the news and raise Hell!" As editor of the *Detroit Free Press,* Storey had been the spokesman for the Democratic Party in Michigan, and perhaps the entire Northwest, for a decade prior to the outbreak of the Civil War. According to one account, Storey "had a wider fame and fewer friends than any other newspaperman in Michigan."[73]

Storey's acerbic pen had a habit of making him enemies. In 1870 he would be horsewhipped by five members of the Lydia Thompson Burlesque Troupe (whom he had described as "A large limbed, beefy specimen of a heavy class of British barmaids") on Wabash Avenue. But it was during the Civil War that Storey made his name as Abraham

Lincoln's most trenchant journalistic critic north of the Mason-Dixon Line, cancelled subscriptions be damned. "I don't wish to perpetuate my newspaper," Storey snarled. "*I am the paper!* I wish it to die with me so that the world may know I was the *Times!*"[74]

The *Times* was prepared to offer qualified support to the war effort until Lincoln issued the Emancipation Proclamation, which Storey, an inveterate racist even by the standards of the day (a typical discussion of African-American life would begin with "Negro Civilization: Its Bestiality and Degradation"), called "a monstrous usurpation, a criminal wrong, and an act of national suicide"[75] which would be remembered "in all history as the most wicked, atrocious and revolting deed in the annals of civilization."[76]

From that moment on, in the pages of the *Times*, "Czar Abraham" was depicted as "a creature of pity and contempt; an irresolute, vacillating imbecile,"[77] who was "mean, wily, illiterate, brutal, unprincipled, and utterly vulgar";[78] "a blunderer, a charlatan ... a crude, illiterate bar-room witling,"[79] who was the possessor of "whatsoever in human nature is false, treacherous, weak and cowardly."[80]

Even the Gettysburg Address received a negative review in the *Times*, being labeled "an offensive exhibition of boorishness and vulgarity." And Storey was just warming up: "We did not conceive it possible that even Mr. Lincoln would produce a paper so slipshod, so loose-jointed, so puerile, not alone in its literary construction, but in its ideas, its sentiments, its grasp. He has outdone himself. He has literally come out of the little end of his own horn. By the side of it, mediocrity is superb."[81] "The cheek of every American must tingle with shame as he reads the silly, false and dishwatery utterances of the man who has been pointed out to intelligent foreigners as the President of the United States," Storey concluded.[82]

By January 1864, Storey had concluded that the only logical course of action available to the nation was "the extermination of the residents of New England, the hanging of [Horace] Greeley ... and the expatriation of the whole tribe of Washington officials, from Old Abe down to his doorkeeper."[83] Little wonder the *Chicago Tribune* called upon "the government, citizens and people of Illinois" to "suppress the *Times*, hang its editor, burn its equipment and annihilate all white men connected with it."[84] In his report to the War Department, Captain William James, Provost Marshall of the First District of Illinois, in discussing the role of "the wicked, reckless and debauched newspaper press of the State," singled out the *Times* as "chief among these instigators of insurrection and treason, the foul and damnable reservoir which supplied the lesser sewers with political filth, falsehood and treason. The pestilent influence of that paper in this State has been simply incalculable."[85]

The editor of the *Horicon Argus* and then the *Milwaukee Daily News* during the 1850s, "Brick" Pomeroy was rewarded for his loyal propagandizing on behalf of his Democratic Party by being appointed a deputy U.S. marshal. In 1860, he purchased a one-third stake in the *La Crosse Daily Union and Democrat*. But he was a loyal Douglas man, taking time off to attend the convention in Baltimore at which the Little Giant finally secured the nomination of the northern wing of the Democrat Party.

In November, Pomeroy launched his own *La Crosse Democrat*. His initial response to secession was hostile. "We contend," he declared, "that no state has the right to secede — has no right to declare herself free from the laws which govern the Union; and every sane man must insist upon this principle." Pomeroy sounded almost downright Republican in his contempt for the lame duck President: "What a weak and imbecile old fool Jim Buchanan is," he editorialized. "Buchanan is a traitor to his Country — a traitor to his party — a traitor to his word." He asked his readers to add an extra line to their prayers: "Save our Country, but damn our President."[86]

Pomeroy was quick to rally to the colors in the wake of Fort Sumter. But the specter of abolition cooled his Unionist ardor. "We are willing to fight till death for the common good of a common people, but will not be forced into a fight to free the slaves," he reasoned. "The real traitors in the north are the Abolitionists."[87]

A three-week tour of the St. Louis sector and a two-month term in Arkansas at the head-quarters of the Army of the Southwest, during which he was exposed to the full horrors of war, completed Pomeroy's conversion from dissident to full-blown Copperhead.

Pomeroy subsequently shocked even the more jaded of his contemporaries by placing the caption "THE WIDOW-MAKER OF THE 19TH CENTURY" over a front-page picture of the president. "Lincoln," the embittered editor expanded, "is but the fungus from the corrupt womb of bigotry and fanaticism." Other terms commonly associated with the president in the pages of the *Democrat* were "fool," "blockhead," "moron," "flatboat-tyrant," "despised despot," "imbecile," and "orphan-maker." Pomeroy characterized the war as "insane" and labeled it "a murderous crusade for cotton and niggers."[88]

Seeking divine intervention for a Democratic victory in the election of 1864, Pomeroy prayed, "May God Almighty forbid that we are to have two terms of the rottenest, most stink-ing, ruin-working smallpox ever conceived by fiends or mortals, in the shape of two terms of Abe Lincoln's administration."[89] Pomeroy employed an endless series of literary gambits in his bid to serve as the vehicle through which the omnipotent presence could work its magic over the electorate. This included catchy verse. To the tune of "When Johnny Comes March-ing Home," the *Democrat* suggested:

> The widow-maker soon must cave,
> Hurrah! Hurrah!
> We'll plant him in some nigger's grave,
> Hurrah! Hurrah!
> Torn from your farm, your shop, your raft,
> Conscript how do you like the draft?
> And we'll stop that too,
> When Little Mac takes the Helm.[90]

As election day approached, Pomeroy's appeals grew more shrill, and acquired a menac-ing undertone of implied violence. "He who pretending to war for wars against the constitu-tion of our country is a traitor and Lincoln is one of these men," Pomeroy insisted, "and if he is elected to misgovern for another four years, we trust some bold hand will pierce his heart with dagger point for the public good."

Lincoln's reelection did little to soften Pomeroy's mood. "If Old Abe ever comes into our office to tell one of his stories, or crosses our path, we'll go for him," the editor promised. "Dare not assassinate Lincoln! We'd shoot him as quick as any man."[91] He even went so far as to recommend an appropriate epitaph:

> Beneath the turf the widow-maker lies,
> Little in everything except in size.

So Pomeroy did not retreat a single step when word of Lincoln's assassination reached LaCrosse. Dipping his pen in gall, the editor rejoiced that "God generously permitted an agent to make a martyr of the president.... [W]e feel to thank God for calling Lincoln home, wher-ever that may be."[92]

Pomeroy decamped for New York after the war, leaving a trail of outraged Union men in his wake. "He out-jeffed Jeff Davis in treasonable utterances and out-deviled the Devil in deviltry," one rival concluded.[93]

Samuel Medary, a former state senator and editor of the *Columbus Ohio Statesman*, played a key role in the outcome at the Democratic national convention of 1844. Andrew Jackson gave a letter of recommendation to Medary, the chair of the Ohio delegation, with instructions to present the name of James Knox Polk to the convention in the event of a deadlock. When the proper time came Medary produced the letter. Polk was nominated by acclamation.

Medary served as temporary chair of the Democratic national convention that nominated James Buchanan for president in 1856. Buchanan subsequently appointed him governor of the territory of Minnesota where he served from 1857 to 1858 before taking over the same office in "bleeding" Kansas.

Returning to Columbus in late 1860, Medary launched the *Crisis* on January 31, 1861. His publication swiftly became a clearinghouse for all anti-administration propaganda. One of its chief activities was the publication of every speech uttered in public by the leading Copperhead officeholder, Ohio congressman Clement L. Vallandigham, himself the one-time editor of the *Dayton Western Empire.*

Describing the President as a "half-witted usurper," Medary wrote, "Lincoln is running our country to perdition.... [E]verybody not crazy with 'negro on the brain' knows it." After Lincoln's first year in office, Medary charged that he "ought to be impeached, either for violating the Constitution or for incompetence and idiocy."[94]

Things kept going from bad to worse until the issuance of the Emancipation Proclamation, which Medary greeted with the assertion, "We have at last hit upon the lower round of our national existence."[95] Medary, who in March 1863 had his plant smashed by a mob largely made up of Union veterans of the 2nd Ohio Cavalry, stuck to his guns.[96]

Finally, on May 20, Medary was indicted on conspiracy charges by a federal grand jury in Cincinnati. His trial date was set for October, but his health collapsed and he died before he could get his day in court, unlamented by his Republican rivals. Describing him as "one of the vilest scoundrels that ever lived," who "ruined more young men through his wiles and false doctrines than any other man of his age," the *Nevada Gazette* concluded that "when Sam Medary died one of the devil's own children went home to his father's house."[97]

Suppression

No one took the disloyalty of the Union press more personally than the Union generals fighting the war. Not only were they forced to endure a constant stream of criticism, second guessing, and unsolicited advice from the editorial pages, they also suffered constant headaches from the presence of reporters around camp and on campaign.

The swarms of reporters passing in and out of the front lines presented an unprecedented problem for the military brass. Correspondents had accompanied the army to war for the first time in Mexico from 1846 to 1848, but their stories presented no threat to national security, as the distance to their editors was so great and communications so poor that their stories didn't appear in the papers until long after the events they depicted took place. In 1861, with battles raging almost literally on the doorsteps of the major publications, it was a very different story.

Reynolds notes that throughout the war "there is no question that northern journalists were responsible for the transmission through their papers of key information to the Confederates." Braxton Bragg, for example, learned of Union general Rosecran's risky plan to divide his army east of Chattanooga from the *Chicago Times;* other Confederate generals found General William Sherman's plans for his Georgia campaign detailed in the *New York Times.* Robert E. Lee was an avid reader of the Union press. He learned of McClellan's impending departure from Harrison's landing in August 1862 from the *Philadelphia Inquirer,* enabling him to launch his highly successful attack against General John Pope at Second Manassas, and was apprised of Grant's planned movements, expected reinforcements, and even of his "secret" meeting with other generals during the Wilderness Campaign of 1864 by the *New York Daily News*.[98]

The authorities in Washington tried to stem the tide of information flowing across Confederate lines by making examples of some of the perpetrators. Malcolm Ives, a reporter assigned to set up a Washington bureau for the *New York Herald*, was arrested in February 1862 on the order of Secretary of War Edwin Stanton because he persisted in eavesdropping in the War Department after being repeatedly told to leave. Imprisoned in Fort McHenry, he was not released until the following June. Secretary of the Navy Gideon Welles had B. S. Osborn, a reporter for the *New York Daily News*, arrested in 1865 on the grounds that he had divulged the target and date of the amphibious assault on Wilmington, North Carolina, the previous December.[99]

But the real burden fell on the front-line officers, whose frustration mounted as this additional burden was thrust upon them. Many responded with increasingly severe reprisals. Ambrose Burnside, having returned to active duty as a corps commander during the Wilderness Campaign in 1864, not only had *New York Times* correspondent William Swinton arrested, but ordered him shot the same day. Swinton was ultimately spared by Grant, who had his sentence commuted to expulsion from the army's lines.[100]

Another correspondent to fall foul of a Union commander during the Wilderness Campaign was Edward Crapsey of the *Philadelphia Inquirer*, who made himself very unpopular with the Union army during the Wilderness Campaign when he (along with two correspondents for the *New York Herald*) was captured by Confederate raiders. Although the three newspapermen managed to escape during a run-in between their captors and Union cavalry, their letters and papers remained in Confederate hands, and all the reports of the fighting they had compiled, including the long casualty lists of the Army of the Potomac, were published two days later in a Richmond newspaper.

A month later, Crapsey filed a report that noted: "Grant's presence saved the Army, and the nation, too; not that General Meade was on the point to commit a blunder unwittingly, but his devotion to his country made him loath to risk her last army on what he deemed a chance. Grant assumed the responsibility and we are still ON TO RICHMOND." Meade took immediate offense and had the reporter arrested. The following day, large cardboard placards bearing the words "LIBELLER OF THE PRESS" were tied across Crapsey's chest and back. Then he was paraded past Meade's old division, drawn up in long lines, while a regimental band played the "Rogue's March." After that he was taken to the edge of camp by a corporal's guard and expelled. This spectacle, Meade wrote his wife, took place "much to the delight of the whole army, for the race of the newspaper correspondents is universally despised by the soldiers."[101]

There was a postscript to this incident. After returning to Philadelphia, Crapsey convened a conclave of correspondents all of whom swore that Meade's name would not be mentioned again during the campaign except in connection with defeats; all future credit for victories would go to Grant. As a result, Meade's name barely appeared in print at all for the next six months, putting a serious crimp in the general's political prospects, and possibly his place in history.[102]

The potential for such retaliation left the Union officer corps in a no-win situation. Whatever the partisan motivation of the various publications determined to cover the war, they could all agree on one thing — the paramount, inviolable virtue of freedom of the press, which to the beleaguered military authorities they seemed to value more than the Union itself. After General Henry W. Halleck expelled all correspondents from the Union lines in the East, the *New York Times* responded on behalf of its newsmongering brethren: "More harm would be done to the Union by the expulsion of correspondents than those correspondents now do by occasional exposures of military blunders, imbecilities, peccadilloes, corruption, drunkenness, and knavery, or by their occasional failure to puff every functionary as much as he thinks he deserves."[103]

No one in uniform was a more dedicated foe of the press than General William T. Sherman, whose enmity dated from the publication of a December 1861 headline in the *Cincinnati Daily Commercial* which proclaimed, "GENERAL WILLIAM T. SHERMAN INSANE." The article went on to state that Sherman, while commanding in Kentucky, had gone "stark mad" and had been relieved when commanders became aware of his mental collapse, concluding that it thanked God the army had not been crippled "through the loss of the mind of a general."[104]

Sherman, who vowed "to get even with the miserable class of corrupt editors yet," was supposed to have once greeted the report that three journalists had been killed during an engagement with the enemy by remarking, "Good! Now we shall have news from Hell before breakfast."[105] He did in fact label reporters the "most contemptible race of men that ever existed," with "the impudence of Satan." He warned that if any members of this breed entered his camp they would be arrested, charged with spying, "tried by court martial and if possible shot or hung."[106]

"Jeff Davis owes more to you newspapermen than to his army," Sherman once snapped at a startled reporter. In August 1862, Grant ordered Sherman to arrest Warren P. Isham, correspondent for the *Chicago Times* and brother-in-law of the paper's editor Wilbur Storey. Isham spent ninety days in incarceration. Sherman wired Grant that he was happy to perform this duty since he "regarded all these newspaper harpies as spies, and they should be punished as such."[107] Nor was the general's opprobrium reserved exclusively for Democrats. "If I could have caught Mr. Greeley during the war," he once said, "I would have hung him."

During the Vicksburg campaign, Sherman, who growled about the presence within his camp of "some half-dozen little whipper-snappers who represent the press, but are in fact spies, too lazy, idle, and cowardly to be soldiers,"[108] issued an order letting the fourth estate know exactly where it stood: "Any person whatever ... found making reports for publication which might reach the enemy, giving them information, aid and comfort, will be treated as spies." To show that he meant business, after a setback during the Vicksburg campaign, Sherman ordered the arrest of *New York Herald* correspondent Thomas W. Knox, who had accused the general of mismanagement and called for him to be replaced. "I am going to have the correspondent ... tried by court martial as a spy," the general wrote to Admiral David Porter, "not that I want the fellow shot, but because I want to establish the principle that such people cannot attend our armies, in violation of orders, and defy us, publishing their garbled statements and defaming officers who are doing their best." The court duly found Knox guilty and ordered him evicted from army lines.[109]

After being petitioned by the press, including Bennett's arch rivals, the *New York Times* and the *Tribune*, the president had the verdict countermanded. "I am now determined to test the question," Sherman raged to Grant. "Do they [reporters] rule or the commanding general? If they rule I quit.... I will never again command an army in America if we must carry along paid spies."[110] Grant was able to smooth enough of his subordinate's ruffled feathers to incline him out of his threatened resignation. But Sherman remained far from satisfied with the outcome. He warned that "if the press be allowed to run riot, and write up and write down at their pleasure, there is an end to constitutional government in America, and anarchy must result."[111] But in the final analysis, he was prepared to wash his hands of the decision: "Mr. Lincoln, of course, fears to incur the enmity of the *Herald*, but he must rule the *Herald* or the *Herald* will rule him; he can take his choice."[112]

Sherman was correct that Lincoln was determined to be more circumspect in his dealings with the press. But then, a general is immune from the political repercussions of his actions where a politician is not. The freedom of the press came under greater threat during the Civil War than at any time since the expiry of the Sedition Act. Lincoln was forced to walk a fine line between restraining his generals from taking excessive disciplinary action against the newspapers, and authorizing such action himself, authority formally granted by Congress on July 11, 1862, when it passed what became known as the "Treason Act," targeted at individuals who gave aid and comfort to the enemy "through the expression of disloyal statements."

Without seeking legislative approval, the administration had already taken unilateral action against several publications. The locus for federal retaliation was New York, where on June 27, 1861, a meeting of the Association of the Democratic Editors of the State of New York presided over by U.S. representative Benjamin Wood, the brother of New York Mayor Fernando Wood, who had recently acquired the *New York Daily News*, convened to accuse the Republican Party of "enmity to liberty" and resolve that "the attempt to muzzle the Democratic Press by mobs and terrorism, to prevent citizens from expressing their honest opinions, calls for and deserves the earnest condemnation of every true friend of law, order and liberty." Accordingly, "in view of the many manifest violations of the fundamental principles of the Constitution, it becomes the duty of the Democratic Press and of all friends of free institutions, to unite in resisting these alarming strides towards a despotic and consolidated system of government."[113]

The response from Union loyalists was to assert the primacy of the national interest over the First Amendment. On August 19, Edward Everett, most recently vice presidential running mate to John Bell, published an article in the *New York Ledger* on the topic of "Northern Secession Journals" in which he decried the "absurdity" of allowing "the systematic and licentious abuse of a government which is tasked to utmost in defending the country from general disintegration and political chaos" by "pernicious journals," because of some "all but superstitious devotion of the people to the liberty of the press." Raymond of the *New York Times* chimed in with his observation that Everett's position "is clearly just.... Speech should only be free when it is loyal.... Whenever the press becomes dangerous to the existence of the government, it must be checked by the law."[114] Even Horace Greeley endorsed this position; while freedom of the press was "clearly recognized and solemnly guaranteed" in law, "all who would exercise it are authoritatively notified that abuses of it will subject the offenders to punishment." Legitimate criticism of government policy must not justify "an attack upon a Government's existence."[115]

Happily, from the perspective of the loyalists, the federal government had already set in motion the process by which it would rein in the license of the press. On August 15 a grand jury for the circuit court of the United States for the Southern District of New York was convened under foreman Charles Gould to determine the legality of indicting Northern newspapers that openly opposed the war. According to the grand jury, "There are certain newspapers within this district which are in the frequent practice of encouraging the rebels now in arms against the federal government by expressing sympathy and agreement with them, the duty of acceding to their demands, and dissatisfaction with the employment of force to overcome them. Singled out were the *New York Daily News*, *Journal of Commerce*, *Day Book*, and *Freeman's Journal*, and the *Brooklyn Eagle*. The grand jury noted that it was "aware that free governments allow liberty of speech and of the press to their utmost limit, but there is, nevertheless, a limit." Then it arrived at the point: "The conduct of these disloyal presses is, of course, condemned and abhorred by all loyal men; but the grand jury will be glad to learn from the Court that it is also subject to indictment and condign punishment."

Under this pretext, one week later, the newspapers named by the grand jury were suspended from the mail, per order of the postmaster of New York. The legal justification was the War Department's General Order No. 67, which ordered that all correspondence and communications, verbal or written, that put the "public safety" at risk, should be confiscated. The penalty for undertaking such correspondence or communications, according to the order, was death.[116]

The U.S. marshal for the Eastern District seized three thousand copies of the *Daily News* that had been sent to Philadelphia, and shortly after the paper was suspended, not to reappear for eighteen months. The *Day Book* collapsed entirely, later being revived with the title *The Caucasian* to more explicitly assert its principles. James A. McMaster, editor of the *Freeman's Journal*, was arrested by order of Secretary of State Seward, charged with treason, and imprisoned in Fort Lafayette, where he was held eleven weeks before being released without ever having been brought to trial. The price for survival paid by the *Brooklyn Eagle* was the resignation of its editor, which according to his successor, was ordered by Postmaster General Montgomery Blair "as a 'sine qua non' of having the paper's standing restored." It was further understood that his successor "should be a 'union' man who would be acceptable to the leading Union men of Brooklyn."[117]

In the final edition of the *Day Book*, its editor N.R. Stimson wrote: "An attempt is now being made to suppress all the organs of opinion in the North that differ with the will of the party temporarily in possession of the Federal Government."[118] As the year progressed, the evidence mounted that this policy was actually in effect.

Early in the morning of August 19, 1861, the offices of the Westchester, Pennsylvania, *Jeffersonian* were broken into and all the equipment was destroyed, a fate that elicited little sympathy from the *Philadelphia Inquirer*, which condoned the mob action on the grounds that "the traitorous expressions of the sheet have long been annoying to the residents of this place."[119] Five days the paper was shut down by federal marshals "upon the authority of the President." When a court handed the paper back to editor John Hodgson, Postmaster Blair barred it from the mails.[120]

On the morning of August 22, 1861, Amasa Converse, editor of the *Philadelphia Christian Observer*, a Presbyterian newspaper, published a letter that described federal troops killing Southern women and pillaging homes. That afternoon he was arrested and his newspaper confiscated. In order to escape prosecution, Converse fled to Richmond, where he resumed publication on September 19.

The administration also attempted to bring the "secessionist" press to heel in Maryland. A total of nine newspapers in Baltimore were suppressed during the war, either temporarily or permanently, and two more were forced to suspend publication after the arrest of their editors. In September 1861, Blair barred from the mail the *Daily Exchange*, (which described the war as "a wicked and desperate crusade"), the *South* (which announced it had been established "to further the Confederate cause"), and the ironically titled *Daily Republican* (which labeled the administration "The Despotism of Lincoln and Co."). When the editors of these three papers continued to attack the administration, Secretary of War Stanton ordered their arrests. When they continued to prove obstreperous after serving prison time, the military authorities in Maryland finally stepped in to suppress these and other "treasonable" newspapers.[121] Other newspapers suppressed included the *Louisville Courier*, the *Boone County Standard*, and the *New Orleans Daily Crescent*. Even in faraway California, Democrats were subject to the restraining influence of federal interference with the mails. In February 1862 eight newspapers—the *Placerville Mountain Democrat*, the *Los Angeles Star*, the *Weekly Stockton Argus*, the *Stockton Democrat*, the Visalia *Equal Rights Expositor*, the *Visalia Post*, the *Tulare Post*, and the *San Jose Tribune*—all lost their postal rights.

Federal authorities began targeting Copperhead editors for arrest almost as soon as the first shots were exchanged between North and South. The Flanders brothers, co-editors of the Malone, New York, *Franklin County Gazette*, were arrested on October 21, 1861, and carted off to Fort Lafayette. More than a dozen Democratic editors were seized by federal marshals in 1862; the list included Archibald McGregor of the Canton, Ohio, *Stark County Democrat*; Dr. Edson B. Olds of the Lancaster, Ohio, *Eagle* and Daniel Sheward of the Fairfield, Iowa, *Constitution and Union*. Daniel Flanagan, editor of the Mason, Ohio, *Democrat* was arrested the day after reprinting an anti-draft article, tried before a military commission in Cincinnati, and sentenced to six months imprisonment in Fort Delaware.[122]

Dennis A. Mahony of the *Dubuque Herald* was a committed foe of Lincoln, who he stigmatized as "the exponent of Personal Liberty Bills, Nigger Suffrage and Equality, Beecherism, Stoweism, Niggerism, and a dozen isms and Tom fooleries upon which the entire North under the lead of Abolitionized Massachusetts has gone mad." Around 3:30 A.M. on August 14, 1862, a federal marshal and two aides called at Mahony's residence, arrested the protesting editor, and carted him off to a waiting steamboat to begin the first leg of a long journey that took him to Old Capitol Prison in Washington. No formal charges were ever filed against him. After nearly four months of confinement he was released on November 11 alongside several others (including David Sheward, editor of the Fairfield, Iowa, *Constitution and Union*, and two judges) after expressing a commitment they "would not prosecute Federal or State officers who had been concerned in our arrest."[123]

Mahony responded by traveling to New York City with a manuscript drafted during his time behind bars that would be published as *The Prisoner of State*. He dedicated the book to Secretary of War Stanton in a missive that began: "Sir — Having considered for some time to whom it was most appropriate to dedicate a work describing the kidnapping of American freemen by arbitrary power, and their incarceration without trial or the judgment of any court in Military Prisons, no one has so well earned the unenviable distinction as yourself of having your name connected so imperishably with the infamy of the acts of outrage, tyranny, and despotism which the book, I hereby, dedicate to you, will publish to the American people." Mahoney concluded two pages later, "I am, sir, one of the many hundred victims of the despotism of the arbitrary power of which you have become the willing, servile, and pensioned tyrant."[124]

In the meantime, Mahony went right back to unleashing venom against the Administration. Lincoln's Emancipation Proclamation of January 1, 1863, was the last straw. The editor flirted with treason when he stated that the proclamation excused Democrats from further support of the war. "Abolition," an editorial stated, "created the Administration, has shaped its policy ... and must be left to furnish the material requisites of men and money." For good measure, the editorial added that "Lincoln, his Cabinet, Congress, and all, should be hurled into the Potomac."[125] More pointedly, Mahony asked those of his readers who were under arms, "Are you, as soldiers, bound by patriotism, duty or loyalty to fight in such a cause?"[126]

Albert D. Boileau, editor of the *Philadelphia Evening Journal*, a Copperhead mouthpiece, was arrested on January 23, 1863, after printing an article that compared Lincoln's "intellectual capacities" with those of Jefferson Davis. The rumor was that Lincoln personally ordered the arrest because he came out second-best in the comparison. And the arrests continued. John Kees, the editor of the *Circleville Watchman* in Ohio, was arrested in June 1863. Archibald McGregor, editor of the *Stark County Democrat*, was arrested in October. The *Watchman* was shut down, but McGregor's paper remained in circulation under the guidance of his wife who, two weeks after her husband's arrest, remarked in an editorial, "The administration is drunk with power, addicted to tyranny, [and] characterized by imbecility."[127] The *Philadelphia Evening Journal*, was suspended in 1863. Boileau was sent as a prisoner to Fort McHenry, from which he was released a few days later, after a written apology and a promise to behave in future.

Many officers with military commands acted on their own initiative against publications they considered deleterious to the war effort, without waiting for specific instructions from Washington. Major General John C. Fremont, appointed commander of the Department of the West in July 1861, ruled over his fiefdom with an iron fist, banning the five blacklisted New York papers and the *Louisville Courier*, and suppressing the *St. Louis Morning Herald*, the *War Bulletin*, and the *Missourian*. After being criticized for failing to display similar zeal in actual combat, he arrested Francis P. Blair, Jr., founder of the *St. Louis Democrat* and a brigadier general under Fremont's own command, and Charles G. Ramsey, editor of the *St. Louis News*.

In the spring of 1863, Major General Samuel Prentiss, headquartered in Helena, Arkansas, and commanding the Department of the Southwest, prohibited under "General Order No. 19" the circulation of the *Chicago Times*, the *Milwaukee News*, and the *La Crosse Democrat* within his jurisdiction. "Brick" Pomeroy, on assignment for the *Democrat* and correspondent for the other two papers, was summoned to Prentiss's office where he was read the riot act, ordered out of the area, and threatened with being arrested and hanged as a spy if he returned.[128]

In April 1863, the administration named General William Rosecrans the Union military commander of Missouri. He immediately gave orders to halt the circulation of opposition newspapers in that state, and the postmaster in St. Louis duly halted distribution of Columbus-based *The Crisis* and the *Chicago Times*. In June the postmaster in Wheeling, West Virginia, who also happened to be publisher of the *Wheeling Intelligencer*, banned the *Crisis* from the mail in his state on the grounds of "disloyalty to the government of the United States."

Ohio served as the front line during the struggle to define the limits of free speech during wartime. Ambrose Burnside, reassigned to command the Department of the Ohio as penance for his ineptitude at the Battle of Fredericksburg, was determined to impose a hard line. He issued General Order No. 38 in April 1863, announcing, "The habit of declaring sympathy for the enemy will no longer be tolerated.... Persons committing such offenses will be subject to military procedures." Burnside did not wait long before demonstrating that he meant business. After Clement Vallandigham delivered a speech on May 1 in which he asserted, among other things, that the "wicked a cruel war" was being waged deliberately in order "to erect a Republican despotism on the ruins of slavery," Burnside dispatched troops to the ex–Congressman's home to haul him off in the middle of the night and take him into custody. When William Logan, Vallandigham's successor at the *Western Empire*, denounced the action in a scathing editorial, he too was arrested and soon joined his hero in a Cincinnati jail.[129]

On June 2, Burnside, overruling a temporary restraining order issued by a federal judge on the grounds of the paper's "repeated expression of disloyal and incendiary statements," sent a squad of soldiers to seize the presses of the *Chicago Times*. That step nearly sparked a civil war within the Civil War, for Chicago was a Democratic city with a Democratic mayor and city council. A crowd gathering in Court House Square quickly swelled to 20,000 strong, and violence was only narrowly averted. The Illinois legislature promptly deplored Burnside's act as "so revolutionary and despotic" that it was "equivalent to the overthrow of our government."[130] Even Republican papers joined in the protest; the *New York Times* warned that "for a military officer to march a company of soldiers into a man's house or office and suppress him of his business, because he deems him guilty of a violation of law, is simply a piece of madness." Lincoln finally countermanded the order, forbidding the general to use General Order No. 38 against newspapers in future without presidential approval. Silencing Storey was counterproductive, Lincoln explained, because "the irritation produced by such acts is ... likely to do more harm than the publication would do." The *Times* reopened after three days, while

Burnside, humiliated, submitted his resignation to the president, who rejected it.[131] Storey got in some parting shots of his own, describing Burnside as "the butcher of Fredericksburg" and the "assassin of ... liberty," but noting the general "was not the head butcher and assassin; he was only the creature, the mean instrument, the puppet, the jumping-jack of the principal butchers and assassins."[132]

Half a dozen Democratic papers were suppressed in the Hoosier State after General Milo S. Hascall was named commander of the Military District of Indiana, a subdivision of General Burnside's Department of the Ohio. Hascall issued "Order No. 9" as a supplement to Burnside's General Order No. 38. Hascall's edict said that all newspapers (and speeches) that advised resistance to measures intending "to bring the war policy of the Government into disrepute" would be considered a violation of General Orders No. 38. Hascall's edict added, "The country will have to be saved or lost during the time this Administration remains in power, and therefore he who is factiously and actively opposed to the war policy of the Administration is as much opposed to his Government." When the editor of the South Bend-based *St. Joseph County Forum* announced that he intended to defy Hascall's authority, his paper was shut down. In 1863, when the editor of the Plymouth, Indiana, *Democrat* labeled Hascall "a donkey" for threatening the freedom of the press, he was promptly arrested — giving him the satisfaction of at least being proven right.[133]

When Brigadier General John M. Schofield arrested William McKee, editor of the St. Louis, Missouri, *Democrat*, Lincoln wrote, "I regret to learn of the arrest of the Democratic editor. I fear this loses you the middle position I desire you to occupy." Later, Lincoln felt compelled to write to Schofield again in a communication that came closest to articulating a specific administration policy on the question of freedom of the press: "You will only arrest individuals and suppress assemblies and newspapers when they may be working palpable injury to the military in your charge, and in no other case will you interfere with the expression of opinion in any other form or allow it to be interfered with violently by others. In this you have a discretion to exercise with great caution, calmness, and forbearance."[134]

Most Unionists, both those in the press game and in the public at large, expressed little sympathy for the victims of federal suppression. John W. Forney's *Philadelphia Press* spoke for many when he wrote: "Let us unite the North by any means.... Silence every tongue that does not speak with respect of the cause and the flag."[135] Even during wartime, however, there were some prepared to make a stand on civil libertarian grounds. Concerned at the extent of the arbitrary power being wielded by the administration, on June 8, 1863, newspaper publishers of the New York metropolitan area called a meeting to protest infringements on freedom of the press by the federal government. Horace Greeley was one of the moving spirits and presided as chair. Four declarations were approved, the first stating, "While we ... emphatically disclaim and deny any right as adhering in journalists or others to incite, advocate, abet, uphold, or justify treason or rebellion, we respectfully but firmly assert and maintain the right of the press to criticize firmly and fearlessly the acts of those charged with the administration of the government." The editors also denied "the right of any military officer to suppress the issues or forbid the general circulation of journals printed hundreds of miles from the seat of war."[136]

But still the arrests kept coming. On July 8, 1864, Lewis Baker, the editor of the *Wheeling Daily Register*, was taken into custody by federal troops. Lincoln overturned the arrest, but Baker remained ungrateful, asserting that he would remain free only "until some petty fool of Abraham Africanus sees fit to again attempt to wreak the black malice of a rotten heart upon my personal liberty."[137] Also in 1864, military authorities moved against the *Newark Daily Journal* after it responded to Lincoln's call for more troops by suggesting, "Those who desire to be butchered will please step forward at once.... We hope that the people of New Jersey will ... swear to die at their own doors rather than march one step to fulfill the dictates of that mad revolutionary fanaticism which has destroyed the best government the world ever saw.... Let the people rise as one man and demand that this wholesale murder shall cease." The paper's editor, E. N. Fuller, was charged with inciting insurrection and discouraging enlistments. He was tried in a criminal (rather than a military) proceeding and fined, then immediately returned to his paper where he editorialized that Lincoln "has betrayed his country and caused the butchery of hundreds of thousands of the people ... in order to ... put in force a fanatical, impracticable idea."[138]

Even more ominously, where the authorities were slow to take action against particularly obnoxious Copperhead publications, pro–Union mobs, sometimes from a local community, sometimes comprised of soldiers, would take the law into their own hands. The *Philadelphia Palmetto Flag*, whose editor had written in defense of the assault on Fort Sumter, was the first Northern paper to suffer the effects of mob violence. In the aftermath, the paper ceased publication and its editor headed south. A few days later, on June 18, 1861, the *Boonville Weekly Observer*, a Democratic paper in Missouri, was wrecked by a mob. The weekly *Democratic Standard*, published in Concord, New Hampshire, was wrecked by soldiers on August 8, 1861. The editor, John B. Palmer, was financially ruined, reduced to publishing an open letter in Democratic newspapers appealing for money to buy food for his family, but the editor of the rival *Patriot* exhibited no sympathy, publishing an extra on the mob violence in which he declared "it ought to have been done long ago."[139] In many cases, to assess the partisan nature of the mob violence that took place against the press during the war one need look no further than the name of the publication in question. For example, on August 12, 1861, an angry mob invaded the offices of the Bangor, Maine, *Democrat*, carried the furniture and type cases into the street, and celebrated the Union cause around a bonfire while the paper's editor was placed in jail for his own safety. The offices of the Starke County, Ohio, *Democrat* were wrecked; and the editor of the Essex County, Massachusetts, *Democrat*, was tarred and feathered and ridden out of town on a rail. The Bridgeport, Connecticut, *Advertiser and Farmer* was sacked on August 22, 1861, by Union troops, in full view of more than five thousand onlookers.

"Indiana, Ohio, Illinois, and Pennsylvania were the political battlegrounds in 1863 and witnessed the destruction of more Democratic newspapers than the other Northern states," Klement observes. In Indiana alone, under the tolerant auspices of Governor Oliver P. Morton, mobs caught up sooner or later with the *Terre Haute Journal*, the *Lafayette Weekly Argus*, the *Rockport Democrat*, the *Richmond Jeffersonian*, the *La Porte Democrat*, the *Franklin Democrat*, the *Vincennes Western Sun*, the *Princeton Union Democrat*, and the *Columbia City News*.[140]

"Nowhere in the North was the purpose of the people to kill off that segment of the press injurious to the Union cause more prominently displayed than in Ohio," says Harper. More than a score of antiwar newspapers were put out of business temporarily or permanently by either the federal government or mob violence.[141] On March 5, 1863, during a blinding snowstorm, about a hundred soldiers armed with sabers and revolvers did a thorough job of wrecking the offices of the *Columbus Crisis* before returning to nearby Camp Chase. Neither the governor of Ohio nor the camp commander offered an apology for the incident. In the span of one month alone, March 1864, Unionist mobs ransacked the offices of the *Greenville Democrat*, the *Fremont Ohio Messenger*, and, always eager to express the true depths of their feelings for Samuel Medary, the *Columbus Crisis* on two separate occasions.

The Triumvirate

A major domestic concern for the administration throughout the war was the attitude of the triumvirate of New York newspapers—the *Times*, the *Tribune*, and the *Herald*—whose national influence was so great that it had the capacity to significantly bolster or seriously undercut the administration's own efforts to shape public opinion. This grew more critical as the clock ticked down to Lincoln's reelection.

The editor most loyal to Lincoln was Raymond of the *Times* who had cut his teeth in the print trade at the *New Yorker* while still at college, having been recruited at age eighteen by Greeley, who considered him "a valued contributor to the literary side." He rose swiftly to become Greeley's chief assistant in 1841, the year the *Tribune* was founded.[142] Two years later he joined Webb's *Courier and Enquirer*. Raymond was an active Whig, editing a weekly campaign newsletter, the *Grapeshot*, for Zachary Taylor in 1848. The following year, not yet thirty years old, Raymond was elected to the New York State Assembly. Reelected to a second term in 1850, he was promptly chosen Speaker. The same year he became managing editor of a new literary journal, *Harper's*. In 1851, Raymond quit the *Courier and Enquirer* to found his own paper, the *New York Times*. The following year, Raymond traveled to Baltimore to report the proceedings of the Whig national convention, and was given a seat as a delegate. In 1854, through the machinations of Thurlow Weed, he was elected lieutenant governor of New York. Greeley, who felt that honor was due him, never forgave Weed, or his protégé Seward.[143]

In 1861, this time as a Republican, Raymond was again elected to the State Assembly, where he again was chosen Speaker. Although his bid for the U.S. Senate seat from New York was thwarted in 1863, Raymond was voted chair of the platform committee at the 1864 Republican National Convention and then chair of the National Union executive committee of Lincoln's reelection campaign in 1864. "Raymond," said Lincoln, "is my lieutenant general in politics."[144] He even found time that year to eke out a victory by 464 votes in his own race for a House seat in Congress.

The editor of the *Tribune* proved to be one of Lincoln's biggest disappointments in office. "When 1860 dawned, history set a stage for Horace Greeley on which he might have played the greatest part ever offered to an editor," Harper says. "He failed, utterly and miserably."[145] One of Lincoln's constant headaches during the war was trying to find some way to make use of "Uncle Horace" Greeley, who had swung from urging the "errant sisters" of the secessionist South be allowed to depart in peace before the assault on Fort Sumter to demanding "Forward to Richmond!" in its wake.

By the beginning of 1862, Lincoln and Greeley appeared to have come to a secret agreement regarding official information and freedom of the press. The go-between was Robert Walker, former U.S. senator from Mississippi, secretary of the treasury under Polk and governor of Kansas. In 1861 he had joined forces with James Gilmore, a retired New York cotton broker and occasional contributor to *Tribune*, to publish the *Continental Monthly*, an antislavery journal pressing Lincoln toward emancipation. Greeley promised to help fund the *Continental Monthly* if Gilmore and Walker could feed him information from the White House and cabinet meetings. Walker notified Lincoln that he favored cultivating a "good relationship" with Greeley — in other words, providing "information that will be of value to him" — because that way "we can keep him from going off on tangents."

On November 21, 1861, Lincoln wrote to Walker affirming that the arrangement "meets my unqualified approval, and I shall further it to the extent of my ability, by opening to you — as I do now — fully the policy of the government — its present and future intentions when formed — giving you permission to communicate them to Gilmore for Greeley." Lincoln went on to say that he had the "utmost confidence in Mr. Greeley," who was a "great power" in the land. "Having him firmly behind me," the President added, "will be as helpful to me as an army of one hundred thousand men." Under the terms of this de facto relationship, Greeley would refrain from attacking the administration for as long as Lincoln continued to feed him inside information. The president felt that from this point Greeley would be "my mouthpiece," provided the arrangement remain secret: "I must not be known to be the speaker."[146]

These expectations were to be swiftly frustrated on both sides. Greeley was too independent-minded to serve any administration in any official capacity. His constant needling of Lincoln to force the pace of emancipation left the two men constantly at odds throughout the war, to the point where Greeley conspired to have Lincoln replaced on the Republican ballot for president in 1864 by a more ardent abolitionist, while conducting ad hoc peace negotiations with Confederate representatives that same year.[147] But Lincoln had the skills to take the wind out of Greeley's sails. After the editor insisted that the president undertake peace negotiations with Confederate agents congregating on the Canadian side of Niagara Falls, Lincoln surprised the editor by agreeing — then empowering him to conduct the negotiations. Much against his will Greeley set off bearing Lincoln's terms for peace. The affair was a fiasco; Greeley botched the negotiations and in any event the Confederate agents had no authority to discuss terms.[148]

Henry J. Raymond lived in the shadow of James Gordon Bennett and Horace Greeley after launching the *New York Times* in 1851, but the paper he founded would ultimately surpass their publications and emerge as the leading newspaper in the city. Raymond, a loyal soldier for the Republican Party, held a variety of public offices throughout his editorial career (courtesy of Library of Congress).

After enduring the predictable and entirely characteristic failure of all his schemes, Greeley finally came out foursquare for the president: "Henceforth we fly the banner of ABRAHAM LINCOLN," he declared. "We must re-elect him, and God helping us, we will."[149]

Lincoln himself made the laconic observation, "It is important to humor the *Herald*," but how he was to maintain himself in the good graces of its editor was a never-ending conundrum.[150] Bennett's disenchantment with the fragmenting Democratic Party in 1860 seemed to offer hope of a Republican rapprochement with the *Herald*. "We have no regrets to express," Bennett assured his readers, "over the broken down democracy. We congratulate the American people that this corrupt and demoralized party of juggling and swindling spoilsmen, with political vagabonds and vagrants as its managers, has at last broken to pieces from their quarrels."[151] But Bennett then emerged as one of the leading lights of the fusion campaign in New York that sought to unite the squabbling anti–Republican candidacies into one ticket in order to deny Lincoln a majority in the electoral college and thereby throw the decision into Congress.

When that gambit failed, Bennett took it in stride, blithely advising President-Elect Lincoln to step aside in favor of some other individual more acceptable to both North and South. Doing so would "render him the peer of Washington in patriotism." Should Lincoln fail to follow this sage advice and persist "in his present position in the teeth of results as his election must produce, he will totter into a dishonored grave, driven there perhaps by the hands of an assassin, leaving behind him a memory more execrable than that of Arnold — more despised than that of the traitor Cataline!"[152]

As the Southern states fell away from the Union one by one, Bennett upheld their right to secession and was a trenchant critic of the administration which he accused of dragging the nation into an unnecessary war. "The masses of the population reprobate the blood-thirsty imbecility of the Washington government," Bennett snapped less than a month after Lincoln was sworn in as president. "In the annals of history there would be found no parallel of a people, from such a height of prosperity as the United States have attained, so recklessly plunged its future destiny into an abyss of ruin, if the present mismanagement of affairs is allowed to continue."

The next morning, April 10, New Yorkers enjoying the *Herald* with their breakfast read Bennett's pledge of support for vigilante action to remove Lincoln from office: "Our only hope now," he wrote, "against a civil war of an indefinite duration seems to lie in the overthrow of the demoralizing, disorganizing and destructive [Republican] sectional party, of which 'Honest Abe Lincoln' is the pliable instrument."[153] Later that day the telegraph wires began chattering with the news of the assault on Fort Sumter.

Northern outrage forced Bennett to let some of the Southern air out of his sails; when demonstrating crowds demanded that he show his true colors Bennett hastened to have the *Herald* building bedecked in the Stars and Stripes.[154] But it still left him vulnerable. On April 15, the morning Lincoln issued a proclamation calling for the states to raise a militia 75,000 strong for the defense of the republic, the *Times* attacked the *Herald* in a stinging editorial titled "A QUESTION A GOOD MANY PEOPLE ARE ASKING": "Is there to be no limit to the *Herald's* open advocacy of treason and rebellion? That print has done everything in its power to encourage and stimulate the secession movement. It has vilified the Government, belied the people of the Northern States, scattered broadcast throughout the South the most infamous falsehoods concerning the public sentiment in this City, and done everything in its power to incite the South to the open war into which they have at last plunged the country."[155]

Lincoln commissioned Thurlow Weed to seek out what terms Bennett demanded for his commitment to the war effort. Lincoln gave the task to Weed, he said, because of Weed's "considerable experience in belling cats." But it seemed a strange choice — Weed had not been on speaking terms with his fellow editor for over thirty years, not since Bennett had accused Weed of distributing funds to swing Anti-Masonic votes to John Quincy Adams in 1828. The current crisis superseded old grudges, however, and the two agreed to meet, whereupon Weed told Bennett, "Mr. Lincoln deemed it more important to secure the *Herald's* support than to obtain a victory in the field."[156] Bennett then sent his own emissary to Lincoln, pledging his paper's unconditional support "for the radical suppression of the Rebellion by force of arms." As a sign of good faith, Bennett offered the president his son's sailing yacht as a contribution to the revenue service — securing "in consideration thereof for its owner the appointment of lieutenant in the same service."

The yacht *Henrietta*, named after the younger Bennett's mother, was duly inducted into the service, and Bennett Jr. received his commission as third lieutenant in the Revenue Cutter Service. The *Henrietta* cruised off the Long Island Coast during 1861 and saw service at Port Royal, South Carolina, the following year, before being withdrawn from service in April 1862. Lieutenant Bennett tendered his resignation the following month, which was approved.[157] These nautical concessions apparently failed to incline Bennett's favor toward Secretary of the Navy Gideon Welles, who received many a broadside from the *Herald* during the war. Bennett considered him "the Connecticut fossil," who urgently needed replacement by "a living man." In return, Welles considered Bennett "a vagabond editor without principle or reputation."[158]

In December 1863 the *Herald* declared, "We abandon 'Honest Old Abe' as a hopeless case." The *Herald* continued:

> President Lincoln is a joke incarnate. His [first] election was a very sorry joke. The idea that such a man as he should be president of such a country as this is a very ridiculous joke. His debut in Washington society was a joke.... His inaugural address was a joke.... His cabinet is and always has been a standing joke. All his state papers are jokes. His letters to our generals, beginning with those to General McClellan, are very cruel jokes.... His emancipation proclamation was a solemn joke.... His title of 'Honest' is a satirical joke.... His intrigues to secure renomination and the hopes he appears to entertain of a re-election are, however, the most laughable jokes of all.[159]

Bennett subsequently launched a crusade to draft military hero General Ulysses Grant for the presidency: "Certainly it could be the last evidence that we were a besotted and blinded people if, with a man like General Grant within our reach, we should coldly pass him by to re-elect the imbecile joker who has dragged the country into the slough of slaughter and corruption."[160]

Greeley was convinced of Lincoln's impending political demise as late as August 1864, writing, "Mr. Lincoln is already beaten. He cannot be elected. And we must have another ticket to save us from utter overthrow."[161] The constant buzz of speculation about who would emerge from the Republican convention as the party's nominee left the New York *World* chortling, "It would be difficult to determine which are more damaging to the prospects of Mr. Lincoln in his candidacy for reelection — the heavy blows in front which his manly opponents are dealing, or the stabs in the back inflicted by his professed friends."[162]

Benjamin Wood's paper was predictably unimpressed with the outcome of the Republican convention, where Unionist Democrat Andrew Johnson of Tennessee was selected as Lincoln's running mate. the ticket consisted of "two ignorant, boorish, third-rate backwoods lawyers," according to the *Daily News*.[163] Even in Lincoln's home state, the Springfield *Illinois Staats-Anzeiger*, a paper once secretly owned by him, deserted the cause in the most emphatic way, declaring henceforth that it would "protest against his reelection under all circumstances and at any price. No reasons of expediency can influence us to ever accept Lincoln as our President again."[164]

The dynamics of the campaign changed when the Copperhead-dominated Democratic convention nominated General George McClellan as its candidate but declared the war a failure and demanded its immediate cessation. The opening sentence of *Harper's* on September 10, 1864, declared: "The platform of the Chicago Convention will satisfy every foreign and domestic enemy of American Union and Liberty."[165] Joseph Medill of the *Chicago Tribune* was even less enthralled by the Democratic nominee, a man it characterized as a "stick in the mud," a "do nothing," a "copperhead," and "hostile to the best interests of humanity," who was nominated at a convention notable for the "most unblushing and shameless utterances of treason" by a party comprised of "bloated aristocrats" and the "great unwashed of the Celtic persuasion."[166]

Even Bennett, who considered Lincoln "a failure, militarily, socially, and as a statesman," was outraged by the peace plank the Democratic Party crafted for McClellan to run on. "The greatest and most disgraceful of all the political failures resulting from the war is the Chicago platform," he fumed, concluding that if Lincoln were reelected, "he will owe his success in a great degree to that Copperhead platform outrage upon the people of the loyal states."[167] Raymond was more succinct; every man at the Democratic convention was labeled a "black hearted traitor" in the pages of the *New York Times*.

With public opinion turning in his favor after the electrifying news of Atlanta's surrender to Sherman, Lincoln was able to whip the recalcitrant Republican press into line and enjoy the solid backing of his party.[168] The Republicans were able to go on the offensive, weaning papers away from the Democrats. Zornow records how Edward Sturznickel, editor of the Erie *German Spectator*, owed money to local Democrats, who attempted to foreclose on his property. Sturznickel appealed to the Republicans for aid. Two additional Pennsylvanian papers, the York County *True Democrat* and Lehigh County *Patriot*, were in similar straits and appealed to the Union Central Committee for aid.[169]

The race-baiting thrust of the Democratic campaign was spearheaded by the party's allies in the press. Just prior to election year, a pamphlet titled *Miscegenation: The Theory of the Blending of the Races, Applied to the American White Man and Negro* materialized in New York City endorsing "race mixing" as a means to invigorate the country and strengthen society. "All that is needed to make us the finest race on earth is to engraft on our stock the Negro element." The pamphlet upheld miscegenation as the apotheosis of abolitionism and the Republican Party, and contained a long section urging the Irish of New York to overcome their hostility to African Americans and "intermarry with them as Lincoln wished." The pamphlet generated a minor sensation that continued to bubble during the campaign. Only after the election was it revealed as a fraud perpetrated by two New York *World* journalists—managing editor David Croly and one of his reporters, George Wakeman—who were deliberately trying to stir up a racist backlash against the administration.[170]

Such shenanigans notwithstanding, Lincoln ultimately coasted to a landslide victory, setting the stage for the final act of the Civil War. The last shot of that war—the one that murdered Lincoln—temporarily forced a ceasefire to the partisan sniping of the press. Even Bennett felt moved to exclaim, "We must all mourn with sad and sickened hearts the success of the great crime which has removed our beloved and trusted President ... one of the most solid, brilliant and stainless reputations of which in the world's annals any record can be found."[171] But it also sparked one last spontaneous spasm of violence throughout the North and—reflecting their mixed record during the conflict, and the low regard in which most Americans held the press establishment—newspapers that had opposed the Union cause were often the targets of this inchoate rage. When word of Lincoln's assassination arrived in far-off San Francisco, a mob surged up Montgomery Street, bent on revenge against newspapers that had blasphemed the president and were known to have secessionist sympathies. The *Democratic Press* was the first victim, followed in order by the *News Letter*, the *Monitor*, the *Occidental*, and *L'Union Franco Américaine*. While the mob wrecked the offices and broke the presses, an immense crowd gathered in the street, cheering and applauding.[172]

Reconstruction

The Southern press, like the other institutions of the region, was devastated at the end of the Civil War. According to one estimate, only twenty-two daily newspapers were still being published throughout the entire Confederacy when Lee surrendered at Appomattox, compared to sixty-six prior to the war. The number of weeklies had dropped to 182 from 633.[173]

All the South had left was its allegiance to the Democratic Party. Republicans were not welcome in Dixie, nor were their newspapers. In 1868, only 200 people in Virginia subscribed to Greeley's *New York Tribune*; another 117 subscribed in North Carolina, 96 in Tennessee, and 50 in Texas. The other seven ex–Confederate states had fewer than 20 subscribers each.[174]

In the South, the platform of each party was its race. Southern Democrats, of course, were only too happy to point out that they were far from being alone in playing the race card. On one occasion, the Cleveland *World* remarked that "10,000 bobtail gorillas trained to put folded paper in a slot would exercise as much judgment and understanding as 10,000 Republicans in Louisiana and Georgia."[175] But race was only one of a number of issues in the North. In the South it was *the* issue.[176] Even Parson Brownlow of *Brownlow's Knoxville Whig*, erstwhile martyr to the Union cause, identified fully with the instincts and motivations of his subscribers on "the nigger question." In an editorial on February 6, 1864, Brownlow drew out the nightmare vision of African American equality the South had incurred upon itself through the folly of secession: "Nigger here, nigger there, nigger yonder, and nigger everywhere — nigger in the church, nigger in the social circle, nigger in the woodpile ... nigger at the polls, nigger at the dining table, black nigger, greasy nigger, odorous nigger, and nothing but grinning, wooly-headed nigger."[177] In January 1865, Brownlow proclaimed, "[the] nigger is the rebellion and the rebellion is the nigger, and to put down the one we have got to get rid of the other." His alternatives ranged from segregation to forced colonization of African Americans, either to "a suitable country" or to a separate "territory ... within such degree of latitude as are adopted to their nature."[178]

In the South, racial and political solidarity were indistinguishable. The Democratic Party served as the rallying point for white supremacy, while Democratic newspapers provided a forum through which whites expressed their resistance to federal Reconstruction and their rejection of civil rights. These were the twin evils intimately and indelibly associated in Southern hearts and minds with the Republican Party. In 1874, the Jackson, Tennessee, *Whig and Tribune* remarked on Reconstruction that "the evils, the seeds of race bitterness and antagonism, its agitation has sowed, will rankle in the hearts of the insulted whites of the South, and the deluded Negroes, for years. However, it has doubtless accomplished one good, it has damned the Republican Party for all times to come."[179]

The terms for political debate across the South were headlined by the *Mobile Daily Register* on July 9, 1870, and echoed by editors throughout the region:

> A WHITE MAN'S GOVERNMENT.
> A WHITE MAN'S PARTY.
> A WHITE MAN'S PAPER.
> WE FIGHT ON THAT LINE.
> THE WHITE REPUBLIC OF WASHINGTON.
> ALWAYS WHITE!
> ALWAYS DEMOCRATIC!
> ALWAYS CONSTITUTIONAL!
> REGISTER FOR THE GREAT CAMPAIGN OF 1870![180]

Democratic editors universally derided those Republican publications that emerged in the South during Reconstruction as "nigger papers." In Richmond, the *New Nation* was labeled the "New Nigger Nation" and referred to as "this stinking nuisance" by its rivals. In Alabama, the editor of the Democratic *Tuscaloosa Independent Monitor* referred to the *Demopolis Southern Republican* as the "Demopolis Negro Newsrag," while his counterpart at the helm of a Mississippi paper characterized the *Vicksburg Weekly Republican* as a "filthy, slimy, stinking, negro equality, negro-loving, white man-hating, hate-engendering organ of perjured scoundrels." The *Mobile News* labeled the *New Orleans Tribune* a "filthy, black republican, negrophilist journal." In Georgia, hostile editors referred to John Emory Bryant of the *Augusta Loyal Georgian* as "the mulatto Republican" and a "hybrid bastard." Stretching the English language beyond breaking point in the inexpressible passion of his outrage, the editor of the *Arkansas Gazette* asserted that his rival at the helm of the city's Republican newssheet suffered from "black vomit," the inevitable result of "the effects of trying to swallow the moral tergiversations and nigrescent politics of that stramentous journal."[181]

White Republicans in the South were tarred with the brush of race treachery and suffered accordingly in the Democratic press. The editor of the *Houston Telegraph* referred to Republican papers in his state as "the mongrel press of Texas." Another Houston editor vilified his Republican counterparts in Austin as "nigger speculators," while the editor of the *Seguin Journal* called the editor of San Antonio's Republican paper a "contemptible, penniless, characterless, stealing carpetbagger."

Since they dominated what remained of commerce and industry in the South, Democrats could cripple any publication that breached the color line by withholding crucial advertising. In Georgia, the editor of the *Quitman Banner* hinted broadly that he was "ashamed for every one who is so lost to the proud feelings of a white Southerner" as to advertise in the Republican *Bainbridge Weekly Sun*.[182] Where social ostracism and economic boycott failed, violence would be resorted to without scruple to uphold white supremacy. Violence remained a staple of Southern political culture, a trait satirized in Mark Twain's *Journalism in Tennessee*. An old editor, fresh from a shooting, advises his young assistant who will be taking charge of the office: "Jones will be here at three — cowhide him. Gillespie will call earlier, perhaps — throw him out of the window. Ferguson will be along about four — kill him.... The cowhides are under the table, weapons in the drawer, ammunition there in the corner, lint and bandages up there in the pigeonholes. In case of accident, go to Lancet, the surgeon downstairs. He advertises; we take it out in trade."[183]

Some Southern papers, the story went, had a man on their staff to attend exclusively to the fighting part of the business. "If the writing editor branded you a liar," David Macrae wrote, "and you went in Southern fashion to demand satisfaction, he handed you over to the fighting editor." Macrae was startled, in visiting the offices of the *Mobile Tribune* in Alabama, to see a sign on the door which read: "Positively no admittance until after two o'clock. Except to whip the editors."[184]

The racial politics of Reconstruction aggravated this code of personal honor to the point where publishing a Republican newspaper in the South was to court danger on a daily basis. The editor of the *Holly Springs Sun* in Mississippi was attacked twice on his first day of publication. The owner of the *Augusta National Republican* was whipped, as was the editor of the *New Orleans National Republican*. In Mississippi, after the Republican editor of the *Columbus Press* had labeled his Democratic counterpart at the *Columbus Index* a liar, the latter publicly beat him with a cane. James Sener of the *Fredericksburg Ledger* survived a beating with a bruised face and a broken arm. Pierce Burton, editor of the Demopolis, Alabama, *Southern Republican*, was brutally pistol-whipped. In Wilmington, North Carolina, the assistant editor of the *Post* was waylaid and beaten, and in Louisiana a judge infuriated by remarks about him in the *Opelousas St. Landry Progress* severely caned one of its editors. In Georgia John Bryant of the *Loyal Georgian* was beaten and Joel Griffin of the *Southwest Georgian* shot at. D. A. Webber of the St. Francisville, Louisiana, *Feliciana Republican* was murdered, as was Lewis Middleton, editor of the *West Point Times*. Mobs sacked a number of Republican presses, including the *True Southerner* in Virginia, the *Rutherford Star* in North Carolina, the *Houston Union* in Texas, the *Maryville Republican* in Tennessee, the *Sun* in Talladega, Alabama, and at least four papers in Louisiana — *Blackburn's Homer Iliad*, the *St. Landry Progress* in Opelousas, the *Attakapas Register*, and the *Rapides Tribune*.[185] Ultimately, even the suggestion that he might be disloyal to his race was enough to justify a Southern man taking the law into his own hands. In 1890, P. B. Hamer of the Marion, South Carolina, *Pee Dee Index* was beaten and thrown down a flight of stairs by J. H. Evans and W. J. McKerall of the *Marion Star* after he suggested that the editors were "politically a mite pro-negro."[186]

Because of their inability to find advertisers and subscribers, Republican papers throughout the South were dangerously reliant on the patronage afforded them by Republican state governments. The Democratic "redemption" of the Southern states cut off access to this largesse, and the Republican press—which peaked in the South at 163 papers in 1871, roughly 29 percent of the total in circulation—wilted immediately thereafter.

By 1877, the year the Hayes administration pulled the last federal troops out of the South, and the last Republican state administrations lost office, the number of Republican papers had shrunk to seventy-six. Four years later, the Republican total had fallen to forty-three, twelve of which were in Tennessee (and eleven of these were based in the Unionist east of the state). By 1880 there were only six Republican papers left in North Carolina, another six in Louisiana, five in Texas, four in Arkansas, three in Alabama (all of them in the belt of northernmost counties), two each in Florida, Georgia, and Virginia, one in Mississippi, and none in South Carolina.[187]

With the African-American community now stripped of federal protection, "Redeemer" white state governments grew bolder in imposing Jim Crow restrictions on civil rights. Segregation on public transportation, such as trams and trains, was a critical first step. Southern papers played their role in shaping the public mood. Typically, the Forest, Mississippi, *Register* waxed indignant at the spectacle of African-American state senator Robert Gleed attempting to rise above his station one day on the Mississippi Central Railroad: "Old Bob Gleed, the flat-nosed, thick-lipped, long-heeled, goat-scented, state senator from Lowndes ... packed his stinking carcass into the ladies car." The editor was happy to report that Gleed was promptly knocked unconscious for his effrontery.[188]

By the end of the 19th century, the way had been smoothed for the final solution of the "Negro problem" in the South: disenfranchisement. Southern editors were at the forefront of the drive, spanning the entire old Confederacy, to strip African Americans of the right to vote. Unless this measure was undertaken, argued the Selma, Alabama, *Southern Argus*, "the 90,000 Negro voters in the State will devitalize the numbers of all parties; and from the poisonous fountain, corruption and death will penetrate to every extremity of the administration."[189]

Typical of the rejoicing over the final victory of white supremacy was the editorial tirade in 1901 of the Enterprise, Alabama, *Weekly Enterprise*, which gloated, "The day of the long-legged, lantern-jawed, slab-sided, pigeon-toed, jangle-kneed, box-ankled, turkey-trodden, unforgotten political polawog has gone, the day of white supremacy dawneth and the black clouds of Ethiopia are receding from the American horizon." No longer would elections be decided by the intrigue of counting "dead niggers and dogs." From now on, man and dog would "bow to the behest of Caucasian rule."[190] Looking back on the era, a well-known Mississippi editor recalled with pride (if less than perfect grammar) the role that he and his editorial cohorts had played in redeeming the South: "At the conclusion of the war a bold and untrammeled press, with great writers weilding [sic] the editorial pen, fired the heart of the people of Mississippi, and stirred them to action, which finally culminated in the overthrow of the negro horde and the retirement of his allies, the scalawag and the carpetbagger. The press led the fight which resulted in a glorious victory for justice, right and decency, the restoration of demrocracy [sic] and the returning of government to its rightful owners."[191]

The emergence of a one-party state in the South institutionalized the political divisions of the Civil War. For decades after Appomattox, citizens on both sides of the Mason-Dixon Line were urged to vote as they had shot. To the *Philadelphia Inquirer*, published on October

30, 1876, the overriding issue of the campaign that year was "whether the Rebel Democracy are to be victorious over the loyal Republicans at the polls, after they were beaten by loyal Republicans in the field." A typical Republican rallying cry was this Gilded-Era, election-day appeal issued by the *Poughkeepsie Daily Eagle*: "Let us clinch to-day by the ballot the bloody victory of the bullet. The South will to-day vote as Lee and Jackson fought. Let us to-day vote as Grant and Sherman fought. Vote for humanity! Vote for continued prosperity! Vote for plenty of work and good wages! *Vote for a tariff!* Come out! Come out!"[192]

The Southern press would continue to serve as the watchdog of the white social order during the long night of Jim Crow. Southern papers would be directly involved in the hurly-burly of politics in the old Confederacy — editors rising from the county paper office to the governor's chair, for example, included W. D. Jelks of Alabama, James K. Vardaman of Mississippi, James Stephen Hogg of Texas, Robert Taylor of Tennessee, and Keen Johnson of Kentucky. But wrapped up in its one-party, one-issue milieu, the Southern press would contribute little to the national political debate.

Perhaps the sole significant exception was Henry Watterson, who got his start as a young

Few editorial voices in the one-party South carried much weight nationally; the exception was "Marse Henry" Watterson of the *Louisville Courier-Journal*. His long career in print, that began as editor of the Confederate version of *Stars and Stripes* as a young man during the Civil War, culminated in his winning the Pulitzer Prize for his editorials endorsing U.S. entry into World War I (courtesy of Library of Congress).

man during the Civil War, not fighting for the South but writing for it. His *Rebel* was the *Stars and Stripes* of the Confederacy. When the war ended, he settled in a Cincinnati suburb and became editor of the *Evening Times*. After moving to Nashville, he was approached by the rival proprietors of the *Louisville Courier* and the *Journal*. Taking over as editor of one, he quickly subsumed the other. When the first edition of the *Courier-Journal* hit the streets of Louisville, Watterson, only twenty-eight-years-old, had a long and influential career ahead of him.[193]

The Gilded Age

The twenty years after Reconstruction was abandoned are commonly referred to as the Gilded Age. During this era, the last of the frontier was tamed and America emerged as an industrial power. It was a period when great fortunes were made and lost, reformers struggled to scour cronyism from the political system, and the partisan balance of power between the two parties frequently teetered on a knife-edge. The press played a key role in all of these phenomena.

It was a period of great opportunity, but also great risk for those committed to the business of print. In the teeth of a serious economic recession during the middle third of the decade, "the 1870s saw the most dramatic rise in the number of total newspapers in the history of the United States," says Jeffrey B. Rutenbeck. The total number of newspapers in incorporated places rose from 5,091 in 1870 to 9,810 in 1880 — a 93 percent increase, compared to a 37 percent increase in the previous decade and a 29 percent increase in the decade to 1890. New York's total newspaper circulation increased by 51 percent during the 1870s, California's by 65 percent, that of Illinois by 45 percent, and that of Ohio by 95 percent.[194] But like everything else during this era of unbridled capitalism, the newspapers attempting to make sense of it all suffered a startlingly high attrition rate. Of the 5,871 journals reported in the 1870 U.S. census, 1,904 disappeared within the next ten years. In 1880, a total of 85 dailies and 1,042 weeklies were established, but in the same year proprietors suspended publication of 56 dailies and 777 weeklies.[195]

By and large, the unwritten rule of partisan journalism remained that if you paid the piper, you called the tune. Editors of the proprietary press understood the risks involved whenever they contemplated any deviation from the party line. Manton Marble nearly bankrupted his *New York World* in 1862 when he adopted an increasingly critical tone towards the Lincoln Administration's policies and handling of the Civil War. Cut off by the Republican Party, Marble secured an emergency $2,000 loan from prominent Democratic lawyer Samuel Barlow in August. The shift in the *World's* editorial perspective was marked; as McJimsey notes, "while Marble was excoriating the administration, Barlow was setting about to secure support for the *World* within the Democratic Party."[196]

In September, Marble sold out three quarters of his 25 percent interest in the *World* to a consortium of buyers led by Barlow and including August Belmont, Samuel J. Tilden, and Fernando Wood, Copperhead mayor of New York and boss of Democratic fiefdom Mozart Hall. In Marble's words, "The hour struck, the opportunity came. I seized it.... [I]nterest seemed to me for once to coincide with duty."[197] By the end of 1863, after a financial merger with the *Albany Argus*, Marble had made the *World* an organ of the Democratic Party.

"Much of the capital invested in the nineteenth-century newspaper," Kaplan says, "came from politicians in hot pursuit of elected office. Ownership of a party organ — possession of a journalistic mouthpiece — crucially enhanced a politician's prestige and power."[198] A favored party tactic involved bailing out failing independent papers as a cost-effective means of establishing a partisan presence. The *Indianapolis Sentinel*, for example, owed its rescue from foreclosure and the auction block to a joint stock company organized with Democratic Party committee funding. Heading the stockholders' list were the secretary of state, the state auditor, the treasurer, and one of the state's most prominent Democratic congressmen.[199]

The prospect of enough money changing hands to change editorial opinion, and therefore change votes, was always being raised. On the face of it, the presidential campaign of 1868 was marked by the usual affirmation of one candidate and denigration of the other by the respective party presses. The *New York Post*, for example, labeled Democratic contender Horatio Seymour "childless, scheming, not studious, selfish, stealthy, earnest of power, feeble, insincere, timid, closefisted, inept, too weak to be enterprising." The *Hartford Post* called him "almost as much of a corpse" as ex–President Buchanan, who had just died, and continued: "Seymour is a little creature; his face is an outlined wriggle. Its expression is a dodge. He has a smooth tongue, feeble health, a constant fear of aberration. His art is to wheedle the vain, promise the ambitious, and charm the religious."[200]

But behind the scenes, party activists were working to tilt the papers in their favor. R. W. Latham wrote Democratic kingpin Samuel Tilden on July 13 that Washington correspondents were "in an organized state" and could be controlled for Seymour if $3,000 to $3,500 per month was made available. The Republicans, Latham said, had declined to pay them in cash, "but offer largely in case of success. This doesn't suit." Latham advised that the money should be distributed through F. P. Stanton, who had been a worker for Supreme Court Chief

Justice Salmon Chase. If Stanton has charge of it, "you must succeed," Latham said. Montgomery Blair wrote Tilden that the *New York Herald*'s editor James Gordon Bennett, a booster of Chase prior to the Democratic convention, who endorsed Republican candidate Ulysses S. Grant afterwards, might be won over by the offer of a diplomatic post: "Bennett looks to position, and there is no getting him without assurance of it.... Chase got his support, I am sure, by promising him this mission if he was elected.... If Seymour could support Chase for the Presidency for his doings about impeachment I cannot see why he could not appoint Bennett for helping save the country. Seymour ought not, under any circumstances, to be approached on this matter. But I think we might legitimately hold out hopes to Bennett and keep our promise of support in good faith."[201]

In fact, it was the Democrats who suffered from the fickle loyalty of those press barons ostensibly arrayed in their ranks. In mid–October, Manton Marble's *World* published an editorial calling for the Democratic Party to "remove or neutralize" those factors having an adverse impact upon the campaign. "We still have nearly three weeks for action," it declared, "and where so slight a counterpoise would suffice to turn the scale, prompt action ... will accomplish wonders."[202] This advice was widely interpreted as proposing that Seymour and Blair step down from the Democratic ticket. Shortly afterwards, in Washington, the *National Intelligencer* endorsed the *World*, asserting that the Democrats should rally behind embattled incumbent Andrew Johnson as its presidential standard bearer.

Democratic leaders were mystified. One wrote to Tilden: "We were completely puzzled with Marble's course. How could he have come out with such an article without consideration?"[203] But whatever the incentive for the *World*'s apostasy, the defection of the *Intelligencer* was inspired by the decision of Grant's campaign manager W. E. Chandler, after consultation with A. T. Stewart, Morgan, Greeley, Pierrepont, and General Sickles, to "invest" in the paper. On October 19, Chandler wrote Washburne that he was about to carry out his plan. "I shall act with caution," he promised, "and get what I bargain for before I pay for it. They are a mercenary, unprincipled set, but the effect produced through the country by such acts as that in the *World* today, which I've telegraphed to Grant, and similar acts in the *Intelligencer* is tremendous, and now is the time to smash the Democratic party in pieces." Chandler piously concluded, "I may be mistaken in dealing with such scoundrels—pitch defiles—but I am conscious of the purity of my own motives and I do not want to lose this opportunity of demoralizing the Democracy. I hope you approve, and Grant too, if he finds out."[204]

Marble's inconsistency in the fulfillment of his partisan obligations constantly embroiled him in personal and financial trouble. After the *World* attacked the notorious Tweed Ring, Marble was rapped over the knuckles by prominent New York Democrat William Cassidy, who warned him in a letter on May 13, 1869, "Perhaps it is the highest office of journalism to stand aloof and above and independent of, parties and sects and events—and to turn opinion into wholesome channels. But this tone is incompatible with party devotion, or with association with other journals."[205] Advertising, both political and commercial, fell to the lowest levels in the paper's history that year. "Marble's flirtations with independence were beginning to cause problems for his business," Rutenbeck notes.[206]

Corporate bigwigs as well as politicians—and the line could be easily blurred—also maintained discreet but still more or less direct control over media conduits to public opinion. And woe betide the editor who turned on his patron. In 1884, Henry G. Davis, coal magnate and Democratic heavyweight in West Virginia, pulled the plug on Lewis Baker, editor of the party's foremost paper in the state. Having previously endowed Baker not just with state printing contracts and political confidences but substantial loans, Davis foreclosed, forcing him to sell out and leave the state.[207]

The greatest conundrum facing the partisan paper was how to respond to division within the patron party. In the mid–1860s, the leading Republican journal in Michigan, the *Advertiser and Tribune*, was caught up in an intra-party feud and refused to endorse the slate of Republican candidates belonging to the faction led by Senator Zachariah Chandler. In response, a "joint stock company" led by Chandler and including senatorial candidate William Howard, Governor Henry Crapo, and future senator Thomas Ferry, founded a rival Republican paper, the *Detroit Daily Post*, in 1866. They appointed Carl Schurz as editor with the explicit intent, according to one observer, to "offset the lukewarm if not hostile influence of the Tribune and at the same time properly chastise it."[208] The *Advertiser and Tribune* and *Post* continued their very public brawl until 1877 when, two years after Chandler was defeated in his bid for reelection to the Senate, the two papers merged.

The combined publication remained resolutely and absolutely loyal to the Republican Party. The *Post and Tribune* edition of October 15, 1888, for example, contained within its four pages one news report deriding a Democratic rally; three commentaries and analyses predicting a likely Republican election victory; a story of a Detroit Democratic family converting *en masse* to the Republican Party; an editorial jibe over factional squabbles in the Democratic Party, including two accounts of internal Democratic conflicts; and lastly, news of local election bets where no Democrats were willing to place money on the party's chances of winning.[209]

The Republican Party, of course, had a considerable stake in ensuring that this loyalty was retained. When the *Post and Tribune* was acquired by James Scripps in 1891, the sale was contingent upon Scripps and his managing editor, Michael Dee, maintaining the paper as an advocate of Republican policies and candidates. Dee was quick to reassure the head of the state Republican Party that even though Scripps also controlled the Democratic *Detroit Evening News*, he would never be "fool enough to sacrifice my business to my opinions.... I intend to make [the *Post and Tribune* a] first class Republican paper and have abundant means to do it."[210]

The partisan picture was most dramatically scrambled by the fission of the Republican Party into Liberal and Stalwart factions in 1872. Behind the Liberal movement were four of the most noted newspaper editors in the country: Horace White of the *Chicago Tribune*, Samuel Bowles of the *Springfield Republican*, Murat Halstead of the *Cincinnati Commercial*, and Henry Watterson of the *Louisville Courier-Journal*. These men came to be known collectively as the Quadrilateral, a reference to the four fortified towns in northern Italy that maintained the Austrian occupation. They held regular meetings, formulated policies, and used their papers in an effort to organize public opinion in support of their goals.[211] Other influential Liberal Republican publications included such daily papers as the *New York Tribune*, still owned by Horace Greeley but now edited by Whitelaw Reid, and the *New York Evening Post* of William Cullen Bryant, along with weeklies like Edwin L. Godkin's *Nation* and George William Curtis's *Harper's*.[212]

Not all Liberal Republican opposition to the Grant administration was disinterested. Patronage was a double-edged sword for a President — while its judicious application could create allies in the world of the press, the withholding of its benediction could make the most bitter of enemies. Such was the case with Charles A. Dana. The managing editor at the *New York Tribune* until forced out by Greeley in 1862, Dana joined the staff of the War Department, rising to assistant secretary of war in 1864. Dana took control of the New York *Sun* in 1868. Having loyally supported Grant's ascendancy to the White House, Dana expected — and thought he had received — a commitment from Grant to a lucrative position as customs collector for the Port of New York. When these expectations were dashed, Dana turned overnight into one of Grant's harshest critics.[213]

The Liberal Republicans ultimately resolved to split the party and run their own candidate against Grant, holding their convention in Cincinnati to select a nominee. The career of Carl Schurz, who presided over the convention, reflects the porous boundaries between the worlds of politics and the press. One of the "Forty-Eighters," the German refugees fleeing the backlash to the revolutions of 1848, he settled in the Midwest and immediately became involved in Republican politics, seeking office and attending the 1860 national convention. Appointed minister to Spain by Lincoln, he returned to the United States to enlist, rising to the rank of major general during the Civil War.

After returning to civilian life, Schurz worked as Washington correspondent for the *New York Tribune*, then as editor-in-chief of the *Detroit Post* and, after 1867, as co-editor and part owner of the German-language *Westliche Post* in St. Louis. Elected senator from Missouri in 1868, he established the Liberal Republican movement in the Show Me State, which elected his protégé, B. Gratz Brown, governor in 1870. Schurz served as secretary of the interior for President Hayes, and then moved to New York where he became editor-in-chief and one of the proprietors of the *Evening Post* in 1881 and took over as editor of *Harper's Weekly* in 1892.

The Quadrilateral tried to engineer the nomination of Charles Francis Adams at the Liberal Republican convention in Cincinnati. According to Smart, they were outmaneuvered by Reid, who secured the nomination for his chief at the *New York Tribune*, Greeley.[214] Other accounts ascribe Greeley's success to the mischievous Dana. Since, in his estimation, Grant could not be defeated, why not bring forward the "philosopher of the *Tribune* as a sacrificial lamb?"[215] Irving Stone considered Greeley unique among the defeated presidential contenders that he chronicled, in being "the only one ... who was in effect nominated by the opposition."[216] But this may be giving Dana too much credit. His managing editor, Amos J. Cummings, maintained afterwards that "Mr. Dana started Greeley's

A "Forty-Eighter"— a member of the German refugee exodus fleeing the backlash to the revolutions of 1848 by emigrating to the United States — Carl Schurz served his adopted country as a diplomat and on the battlefield during the Civil War. Moving seamlessly from journalism to politics, he was elected to the U.S. Senate, chaired the Liberal Republican convention in 1872, and served as Secretary of the Interior for President Hayes, before rounding out his career with spells as editor of the New York *Evening Post* and *Harper's* (courtesy of Library of Congress).

candidacy for the Presidency merely as a joke. I warned him that his efforts would be taken seriously, but up to the very morning of the day the Cincinnati Convention met, he insisted that Greeley had no chance of getting the nomination."[217]

As Greeley's running mate, the convention selected Governor B. Gratz Brown of Missouri, who got his start in politics as editor of the *St. Louis Democrat*. With such a ticket, "One might have thought that Greeley's fellow editors would have rallied to his support," Tebbel and Watts note, "since he was the first of their number ever to be nominated for the presidency, but they deserted him *en masse*."[218]

The *Nation* greeted Greeley's nomination by remarking that a greater degree of incredulity and disappointment had not been felt since the news of the first battle of Bull Run. And the *Nation* was only one of the Liberal Republican publications to return to the fold and perforce endorse Grant. Years later, W. A. Linn, managing editor of the *New York Evening Post*, recalled the proprietor's reaction to the first reports of the outcome of the Cincinnati convention: "Well," Bryant mused, "there are some good points in Grant's administration, after all." Bryant proceeded to draft the *Post's* editorial response — "Why Mr. Greeley Should Not Be Supported for the Presidency" — himself. The salient points included Greeley's lack of moral courage; the fact that his one consistent policy, advocacy of the high tariff, rendered him "a thorough-going, bigoted protectionist, a champion of one of the most arbitrary and grinding systems of monopoly ever known in any country"; and ultimately for "the grossness of his manners."[219] Still shaking his head in despair at the feckless flippancy of the convention's choice, Bryant concluded, "I should at any time beforehand have said that the thing was utterly impossible — that it could not be done by men in their senses, but bodies of men as individuals will sometimes lose their wits." In private, writing to his friend Hamilton Fish, Thurlow Weed was even more blunt: "Six weeks ago I did not suppose that any considerable number of men, outside of a Lunatic Asylum, would nominate Greeley for President."[220]

The *New York Times* headlined the conclusion of the Liberal Republican convention as "THE END OF A FARCE!" and described its nomination of Greeley as "the biggest joke of the nineteenth century."[221] "If anyone could send a great nation to the dogs," the *Times* editorialized, "the man is Greeley."[222]

Greeley's qualifications for the nation's highest office were not exactly stellar. His entire career in public office amounted to filling out a ninety-day unexpired term in Congress from December 5, 1848, to March 4, 1849.[223] The editor had unsuccessfully sought election to the House in 1850, 1868 and 1870, and to the Senate in 1861 and 1863.

Furthermore, Greeley had a public record, going back decades, of taking positions on controversial issues, leaving him the unlovely option of either upholding his previous stances, and thereby appearing extreme, or repudiating them, and thereby appearing insincere. Greeley himself had once observed, "A man says so many things in the course of thirty years that may be quoted against him." He was to discover how right he was during his bid for the presidency. As Van Deusen notes, "If ever a man had to eat his own words, it was Horace Greeley in the campaign of 1872."[224]

Stalwart Republicans in the press lined up against their Liberal rivals and went to work for Grant's reelection with alacrity. But the Democratic organs that year faced a peculiar conundrum — could they honorably endorse Greeley, as the national party had done? After all, Greeley had been aiming broadsides at them for over three decades. A typical effort ran: "Point wherever you please to an election district which you will pronounce morally rotten, given up in great part to debauchery and vice, whose voters subsist mainly by keeping policy offices, gambling-houses, grog-shops, and darker dens of infamy, and that district will be found at nearly or quite every election giving a majority for that which styles itself the 'Democratic' Party.... Every one who chooses to live by pugilism, or gambling, or harlotry, with

The Bath Daily Times.

Friday Evening, September 20, 1872.

I would sum up the policy of the Administration to be a thorough enforcement of every law; a faithful collection of every tax provided for; economy in the disbursement of the same; a prompt payment of every debt of the nation; a reduction of taxes as rapidly as the requirements of the country will admit; reduction of taxation and tariff to be arranged so as to afford the greatest relief to the greatest number; honest and fair dealings with all other peoples, to the end that war, with all its blighting consequences, may be avoided, but without surrendering any right or obligation due to us; a reform in the treatment of Indians, and, finally, in securing a pure, untrammeled ballot, where every man entitled to cast a vote may do so just once, at each election, without fear of molestation, or proscription on account of his political faith, nativity, or color,

U. S. GRANT.

REPUBLICAN NOMINATIONS.

FOR PRESIDENT,

ULYSSES S. GRANT,

Of Illinois.

FOR VICE PRESIDENT,

HENRY WILSON,

Of Massachusetts.

"General Grant never has been beaten, and he never will be.—*Horace Greeley.*

For Electors of President and Vice President,

At Large { SAMUEL E. SPRING,
{ ALEXANDER CAMPBELL.
First District JAMES H. McMULLAN.
Second District JOHN H. KIMBALL.
Third District JAMES ERSKINE.
Fourth District MORDECAI MITCHELL.
Fifth District WILLIAM McGILVERY.

nearly every keeper of a tippling-house, is politically a Democrat."[225]

The issue rent the leading Democratic paper in Michigan, the *Detroit Free Press.* Two of the owners steadfastly refused to bow to the inevitable and accept Greeley. The third owner, editor William Quinby, according to one of his reporters, "believed the Free Press would lose prestige among the steadfast loyal and intelligent followers and leaders of the Democratic Party should it prove disloyal to the party's official actions.... In his opinion, the party could better afford to support the absurd nomination of Mr. Greeley than go to pieces over such an issue."[226] The *Detroit Advertiser and Tribune* foresaw the outcome of the confrontation: "Like an ancient hen struggling with a piece of garbage whose dimensions were not accurately estimated beforehand, the [Free Press] will be seen choking away at the subject for a while.... But it will worry Greeley down and ... advocate the ticket."[227]

The prediction proved accurate as Quinby was able to raise the requisite capital to buy out his partners' interests, and the *Free Press* was finally able to swallow the "garbage" of Greeley's nomination. The *Detroit Post* was quick to accuse the *Free Press* of betraying its subscribers by switching from opposing to supporting Greeley: "The Free Press' advocacy [of an anti–Greeley position] was designed to be a pledge and an inducement to all anti–Greeley Democrats to subscribe for that paper and rely upon it as a faithful organ to represent their sentiments during the campaign. Many of them did subscribe ... in full faith that it would continue to be their organ and advocate their faith and policy. But the Free Press has hoisted the [pro–Greeley] ticket and deceived and betrayed all those who trusted in its pledge."[228]

Nevertheless, from 1872 until the upheaval of 1896, with Quinby at the helm, the *Free Press* remained the leading Democratic voice in Michigan. Greeley's presidential bid, however, was beyond resuscitation. In quick succession he lost financial control of the *Tribune* to his managing editor ("You son of a bitch, you stole my newspaper!" Greeley shouted at Reid), his wife

This 1872 Ulysses S. Grant ticket from the *Bath Daily Times* features the President's personal manifesto at the top, and at the bottom a testimonial to his invincibility, contributed by his opponent — just one of the myriad of aphorisms scattered throughout more than thirty years of journalism by Horace Greeley that his opponents were only too delighted to use as ammunition against him (author's collection).

passed away, he suffered the worst defeat in a presidential election of the post–Civil War era, his mental and physical health collapsed, and he died even before the electoral college could meet.[229] There was a shakeout among the Liberal press barons in the wake of Greeley's demise. Dana, for one, remained unrepentant. His *Sun* greeted Grant's reelection with:

> GREELEY DEFEATED
> FOUR MORE YEARS OF FRAUD
> AND CORRUPTION[230]

However, Reid and Halstead both returned to the Republican fold, while White was forced out by his partners on the *Chicago Tribune*.[231] Reid was quickly rehabilitated, but Halstead was never truly forgiven for his apostasy; the Senate approved Reid's nomination by President Benjamin Harrison as minister to France in 1889, but rejected Halstead's as ambassador to Germany.[232]

Another big loser from the fluctuating state of politics during the Grant administration was Manton Marble, who incurred further Democratic opprobrium for his wholesale support of the Liberal Republican faction and his endorsement of Charles Francis Adams for President. When the Liberal Republican convention nominated Greeley, the *World* was aghast saying; "Mr. Greeley is not our choice, and we regret his nomination." Marble further antagonized Democrats by refusing to swallow the party line and endorse Greeley. In a July 2 article, Marble fired back at critics in the Democratic press, declaring that "the World scorns the petty, servile critics who have arraigned its course and impugned its motives since the preposterous action of the Cincinnati convention." In his view such "small critics, at once insolent and servile, seem to have no conception of the great change which has come over the spirit of American journalism within the last twenty years." The "old" idea of political journals, Marble explained, was that they were "mere lackeys who wore the livery of party chiefs, dependent on their patrons and bound to obey orders on penalty of dismissal." However, according to Marble, in the modern world, "vigorous, healthy journals of both parties despise and loathe this degrading standard of their duties."[233]

"Bad as we think the Cincinnati movement in its results," Marble elaborated, "we nevertheless rejoice in it for the striking demonstration it has given of the superiority of the great journals of the country to party dictation.... The fact that their views cross those of the herd of office-seekers and party wire-pullers, is of the slightest possible consequence to these established journals, which laugh at the feeble organs that are not yet emancipated from the old dictation of the temporary party chiefs, whom independent journals can make and unmake."[234]

These were fine principles, but Marble then almost immediately began backsliding. On the eve of the Democratic pseudo-convention called to endorse Greeley's candidacy, he reminded readers of his obdurate resistance to his erstwhile rival's nomination, but meliorated this with a declaration that he was doing so with the long-term interests of the Democratic Party at heart: "Such a feat of degulition will be performed at Baltimore tomorrow or next day, when the Democratic party will gulp down Mr. Greeley; and as this amazing meal has been decided on, we can only wish the Democratic party a happy digestion. The World will contribute no slime to give the animal a slippery passage down the throat of the devourer; but when the thing is done, it will do whatever may be in its power to aid the digestion, and prevent the Democratic party from going into torpid and prolonged stupor by reason of the heavy load upon its stomach."[235]

Marble then completely collapsed and swallowed the party line — and Greeley with it — whole: "The World is, of course, bound by its reiterated pledges and promises, and by its sense of fidelity to the Democratic party, to acquiesce in what was done yesterday at Baltimore."[236] In a post-election editorial, Marble attempted to retrospectively justify his position:

We loyally surrendered our own judgement to the decision of the Democratic National Convention, and tried to carry with us the protesting members of the party whose views we had shared previous to the nomination. We have always thought it more important to preserve the unity and uphold the discipline of the Democratic party than to secure its support for any candidate of our preference. We have always felt that the best part of our work as a public journal, and an organ of Democratic opinion, consisted in enlightening and educating the public sentiment of the party during the intervals between our great quadrennial contests for the control of the Federal Government.[237]

Marble was fiercely loyal to 1876 Democratic presidential nominee Samuel J. Tilden, drafting the party's platform on the candidate's behalf and serving as Tilden's self-appointed representative in Florida during the crisis over that state's electoral vote.[238] However, he had already paid the ultimate price for cultivating a maverick editorial reputation; his deteriorating financial situation had forced him to sell out of his stake in the *World*.[239] A month later, in an editorial on May 22, the new management conceded that the discerning reader may have noted a change in the paper's political stance: "To the public a change has for some time been suggested in the altered political tone of the paper. The exclusive devotion to the nomination of Governor Tilden at St. Louis, which was an unvarying characteristic under Mr. Marble's management, has disappeared, and while no unkindness or injustice is now shown towards the Governor, the possibilities of other candidates are more favorably considered. Moreover, the advocacy of Free Trade, which Mr. Marble never intermitted for a day, assumes ... a less conspicuous and less pertinacious quality."[240]

Tilden or Blood

In the immediate aftermath of the centennial election of 1876, a special correspondent for the *Chicago Tribune* wrote an extensive commentary accounting for the victory of the Democratic candidate, millionaire corporation lawyer and governor of New York Samuel J. Tilden — in New York and, apparently, the nation. He made a point of assessing the role of the Empire State media during the campaign, and his conclusion, that "never before have the great political parties in a Presidential struggle received so little valuable support from the respective newspapers supposed to be in sympathy with them," speaks volumes about the expectations placed upon the media of the Gilded Age by contemporaries.

The correspondent details the manner in which Bennett's paper "of course, followed its usual course, patting both sides on the back alternately," making it "of no use to either party." Shockingly, "The *Herald* printed simply what it regarded as news, and favored neither party in its reports of meetings, conferences, etc." Even after having squeezed out Manton Marble as editor, the new proprietors of the *World* were nevertheless "forced to countenance him in the paper to maintain its standing in the party." This manifest lack of enthusiasm crept into print: "It has blown hot and blown cold, according to fancy, clearly showing it had no stomach for the job it had in hand." By the same token the *Tribune*, which had soured on the Grant administration, "was worse than useless to the Republicans, for, while it claimed to be working in the Republican interest, it did so in a half-hearted manner which acted more like a wet blanket on the party than a stimulant. It was so bitter in its opposition to men that it lost sight of principles."

Tilden's chief ally was the *Sun*, which "has been, in this campaign, the sharpest, ablest, and most influential" paper in New York. Dana took on his Republican rivals of all stripes and "he has knocked their pins from under them every time." But while conceding his skill, the Chicago man excoriated the editor's apostasy: "What an instance of moral prostitution does Mr. Dana present!" In his evolution from being Greeley's managing editor to endorsing the election of "an arrant secessionist ... [h]e has done more than any one man, besides Mr. Tilden, to secure this result."[241]

The assumption that the election was secure, however, proved premature. Tilden's rival, the Civil War major general and governor of Ohio Rutherford B. Hayes, had an ally among the ranks of the New York Republican press who would prove willing to go above and far beyond any previously established boundaries of partisan politicking. The press had played an influential role in setting the stage for previous presidential contests but never before had an election been stolen (or saved, depending on your point of view) by a single publication.

The GOP had singled out Tilden as the Democratic nominee even prior to his election as governor of New York when he was instrumental in breaking the stranglehold of "Boss" Tweed's Tammany Hall over Manhattan. As a candidate for the presidency, Tilden was subjected to an incessant barrage of savage personal attacks by a well-prepared Republican press. Hayes's own biographer admits of Tilden, "There was hardly a crime save murder of which he was not charged by the regular Republican newspapers of the country."[242] Added to this were the ad hominem personal attacks. The *Chicago Tribune* labeled Tilden "as cold as 32 degrees below zero," and assessed his character by saying, "He's weazened, and shrimpled, and meanly cute. There is nothing about the man that is large, big, generous, solid, inspiring, powerful, or awakening. He's a small, lazy, odorous, ungainly, trickling stream, winding along and among the weeds that have grown up in the track of the great river, long since dried up."[243]

The *Albany Evening Times* was no less caustic: "Supreme selfishness, and a cold, unscrupulous, cunning nature are his marked characteristics. The intensity of his selfishness has never been relaxed even by the softening influence of married life, and he seems to be as destitute of magnetism or emotion as a mummy."

Zeroing in on Tilden's failure to embrace "the softening influence of married life," Thomas Nast encapsulated the implied Republican campaign theme of gossip and stereotype pictorially in the pages of *Harper's* week after week by depicting Tilden wearing a dress. But Tilden had one very special enemy. In 1871 he had committed to print his assessment of the bias exhibited by "the immense preponderance of the Republicans in journalism," singling out the *New York Times* as "this local cancer, directly under the focus of that journalism."[244] Ironically, the *Times* had been a staunch supporter of Tilden during his struggle against "Boss" Tweed. In 1871 the paper had informed the voters of the 18th Assembly District in Manhattan that they "ought to esteem it an honor and a privilege to elect SAMUEL J. TILDEN to the Legislature. He has shown himself a gallant, conscientious, efficient foe to corruption. We appeal to every Republican to vote and work for him."[245] But as Tilden had predicted, the *Times* was to emerge as his bête noire five years later, both indirectly and directly costing him the presidency. Eckenrode says, "The final outcome of the election was determined, in great part, by a [single] newspaper, the New York *Times*. This journal had distinguished itself in the campaign above a thousand other partisan sheets by its persecution of the Democratic candidate, whom it libeled in every possible way."[246] Tilden's biographer agrees: "Had it not been for the stubborn resistance of that journal, Tilden's election might have been quietly acknowledged."[247]

The *Times* vilified Tilden from the beginning of the campaign to its end and beyond. The paper published a major three-page exposé on August 23 titled: "AN INFAMOUS RECORD. TILDEN AS SECESSIONIST ... A SYMPATHISER WITH REBELLION ... HIS PRETENSIONS AS A REFORMER EXPOSED...."[248] Further character assassination, which was widely disseminated through the Republican press nationally, followed on a regular basis.[249] The Tilden campaign sought to neutralize the impact of the Republican press by maintaining a centralized

campaign structure dedicated to promulgating the Democratic message via direct dissemination of literature to the voters and by cultivating relationships with those publications still
susceptible to the lure of the big-city sales pitch. The *Times* related the manner in which
Tilden's "Bureau of Correspondence" contacted the unaffiliated papers of the nation offering
to furnish them with "correspondence, original matter, and extracts, suitable for publication,
free of cost," thereby affording "the advantages of organization during the campaign, giving
it the benefit of the political information which the committee has facilities for obtaining
from all parts of the country." The Bureau noted that "great care will be taken that the same
[material] is not sent to any two papers in the same county, or likely to be seen by the same
readers."[250]

Nevertheless, the *Times* on Monday, November 6, the day before the election, radiated
confidence: "THE CLOSE OF THE CANVASS: REPUBLICAN SUCCESS CERTAIN. THE ELECTION
OF HAYES AND WHEELER BEYOND DOUBT ... THE DEMOCRATS UTTERLY DESPERATE AND
DEMORALIZED.[251] The reality was very different. All Tuesday night the reports pouring in
from around the country showed Tilden slashing into the Republican majorities from four
years earlier and picking up state after state, including the big prize, New York.

The next morning Charles Dana's *Sun* declared flatly, "TILDEN IS ELECTED," and
remarked, "The blow dealt at the party in power by an indignant people is as stunning to the
Republicans as it is gratifying to every honest and patriotic man in the Union." The *World*
was equally satisfied: "Peace on earth to men of good will. The magnificent victory has been
won by a party for the salvation of the people." The *New York Evening Post* (which may have
had a vested interest — majority shareholder and co-editor John Bigelow was Tilden's campaign manager and looked to be secretary of state if his candidate won) listed 209 Electoral
votes for Tilden to 160 for Hayes. The *New York Herald* went to press with the headline "THE
RESULT — WHAT IS IT?" but conceded that "returns seem to indicate that Governor Tilden has
been elected."[252] The *New York Tribune*, which on the eve of the election had warned against
a president being imposed by "rifles at the South and repeaters at the North," went to press
on Wednesday with the headline "TILDEN ELECTED." Although the paper labeled the impending flood of Democratic civil service aspirants "as incapable, dishonest and vile an army of
cormorants as ever robed by authority or stole under a license," it conceded, "With last night's
counting of the votes, Gov. Tilden ceased to be the candidate of a party — today he is elected
President of the whole country."[253]

The editorial response throughout the rest of the country devolved along strict and
entirely predictable partisan lines. The *Boston Daily Advertiser* conceded Tilden's election,
describing it as "the triumph of the solid South and the slums of New York. The men who
were the enemies of the Government and waged war against it, and the men who are enemies
of all Government, have turned the scale. Their purposes are not good, but evil."

"Tilden is elected," the *Indianapolis Journal* despaired. "The announcement will carry
pain to every loyal heart in the nation, but the inevitable truth may as well be stated." Nowhere
was that pain felt more keenly than at the *Chicago Tribune*: "Lost. The Country Given Over
to Democratic Greed and Plunder," it lamented; "Tilden, Tammany and the Solid South Are
to Rule the Nation." On the other hand, words failed the *Newark Morning Register*: "How can
we speak the fullness of our hearts over this great triumph of National Democracy?" The
Shreveport Times hailed the "Grand Jubilee of Honest Men Throughout This Grand Universe,"
saying that "the carnival of thieves, state and national, is at an end."[254]

In Bangor, Maine, the *Commercial* greeted Tilden's apparent election with the rapturous
headlines "HALLELUJAH! THE REPUBLIC SAVED! VOX POPULI! VOX DEI!" By way of illustration the front page was decorated with woodcuts of an eagle, two large crowing roosters,
two smaller roosters, the Goddess of Liberty, two more eagles, the names of the states casting

electoral votes for Tilden arranged in the "Democratic Pyramid," the names of the states for Hayes in a "Republican Pyramid," a wet, downcast rooster representing the Republican standard bearer ("After the Shower!") and a few more giddy salutations: "The Millions Have Spoken and Liberty Is Proclaimed Throughout the Land," "The Golden Age Begins," and "The Republic Given a New Lease on Life." The editor liked the display so much he ran it on the front page for two more days.[255]

In Ohio, Hayes went to bed after hearing that Tilden had carried New York. "From that time," he noted in his diary, "I never supposed there was a chance for Republican success."[256] The next morning he wrote a letter to his son conceding, "I bow cheerfully to the result," and told reporters, "I am of the opinion that the Democrats have carried the country and elected Tilden." The governor of New York himself issued a brief statement to the New York *World*, saying, "My election was due to the issues."

Amidst all the Democratic rejoicing there was at

THE DAY THEY CELEBRATE.

ANNUAL POULTRY ERUPTION OF THE AVERAGE COUNTRY PAPER ON THE VILLAGE ELECTION.

The Gilded Age played midwife to a new breed of partisan weekly magazines, such as the Democratic *Puck* (which made its English-language debut in March 1877) and its Republican counterpart *The Judge* (first appearing in October 1881), which added a splash of color to the political debate of the day. Actual post-election headlines in the ultra-partisan papers of the day were only slightly less giddy than the one parodied in this *Puck* cartoon (author's collection).

least one man who had had a premonition of what was about to happen next. "Nothing but a revolution can now defeat us," warned J. J. Faran, editor of the *Cincinnati Enquirer* a week before the election. "I have no doubt the Republicans will get up one or threaten one."[257] How right he was.

In summing up the majesty of the American electoral process, the *New York Tribune* noted, "We can offer to foreigners no more significant hint of the greatness of the Republic, its sound foundation of prosperity, and the belief of the people in that prosperity, than the calm good humor with which one great party will receive its defeat at the hands of another."[258]

Calm good humor was noticeably absent in the newsroom of the *New York Times* on election night, where editor in chief John Foord, political editors George Shepard and Edward

Cary, and managing editor John C. Reid, pored over the returns as they chattered in over the telegraph. A fellow journalist described Reid, who held his post at the helm of the paper from 1872 to 1889, as "not a pleasant or popular person," whose "red, bloated features warned of his hot temper, his angry little eyes of a disposition to tyrannize."[259] Nothing made Reid angrier than Democrats. A Union veteran of the Civil War who had been taken prisoner during the Atlanta campaign in 1864 and incarcerated in the Confederacy's Richmond Libby Prison, Reid harbored an abiding hatred for the party. When the Democratic National Chairman, an overconfident Abram S. Hewitt, sent a messenger to the *Times* building inquiring what majority it conceded to Tilden, Reid defiantly snapped, "None!" The Republicans were in fact still fighting hard for every vote; communiqués from Republican chairmen in Louisiana and Florida had conceded those states to Tilden but Republican National Chairman Zachariah Chandler had suppressed the telegrams and they did not reach press or public.

About 3:45 A.M. the four members of the editorial council were discussing how to put the best spin on the results when the drama took an unexpected new twist — ironically, in the form of a dispatch from Democratic headquarters. Dan A. Magone, chairman of the Democratic Committee for New York, cabled, asking, "Please give your estimate of the electoral votes secured for Tilden. Answer at once." An accompanying telegram from Senator William Barnum of Connecticut, a member of the Democratic National Committee, asked for specific results from Florida, Louisiana, and South Carolina — the three Southern states still under Republican-dominated Reconstruction governments, with Republican-dominated canvassing boards.

Cary immediately saw the opportunity. He persuaded the others that if the Democrats were still not sure they possessed an electoral majority the door was not yet closed on a Republican victory. While Reid set out to inform Zachariah Chandler of this possibility, Cary prepared an editorial headlined "A DOUBTFUL ELECTION." It read that although "in some of the States where the shot-gun and rifle clubs were relied upon to secure a Democratic victory there is only too much reason to fear that it has been successful," nevertheless, "At the hour of going to press the result of the Presidential election is still in doubt." It included a table assigning 181 Electoral votes to Hayes (including South Carolina and Louisiana) versus 184 to Tilden, with the four from Florida still uncertain.

Around 6:30 A.M., just as the *Times* hit the streets, Reid arrived at Republican headquarters, the 5th-Avenue Hotel. The building appeared deserted — despondent Republicans had all retired for the night. Reid, on his way to the reception desk to find the room number for Zachariah Chandler, collided with William Chandler, a general assistant to the Republican National Committee (though no relation to its chairman). Attired in a military coat, an immense pair of goggles, and a hat pulled low over his ears, William had just arrived by train from New Hampshire. "Damn the men who brought this disaster upon the Republican Party!" he exclaimed, clutching a copy of the *New York Tribune*. Reid retorted, "There is no question of the election of President Hayes. He has been fairly and honestly elected."

The two men went to William's room and counted electoral votes. William had to admit that if all the disputed states went Hayes's way, he would be elected with 185 electoral votes to Tilden's 184. Reid wanted to immediately telegraph leading Republicans in the still-doubtful states of South Carolina, Florida, Louisiana, California, and Oregon, but William insisted they first contact Zach Chandler.

After twice knocking on the doors of the wrong persons, William admitted to Reid that he did not know the number of Zach Chandler's room. He returned to the lobby to find the right number, got it, and began kicking and pounding at the door. Reid joined in, remarking, "We'll wake up the whole house and have the police down on us if we don't look out." Finally, Zach Chandler, dazed, sleepy, discouraged, and still in his nightgown, answered. It took some time before he could comprehend the scenario articulated by Reid. Ultimately the chairman told William and Reid, "Very well, go ahead and do what you think necessary," and returned to bed.

Reid and William Chandler rushed to the hotel's telegraph office, only to find it closed — it was 6:55 A.M. and the office would not reopen until 8:00 A.M. Reid ordered a carriage brought to the hotel entrance on Twenty-third Street. While they waited, he dictated messages to William, who wrote them down in shorthand:

> To Governor Chamberlain of South Carolina:
> Hayes is elected if we have carried South Carolina, Florida and Louisiana. Can you hold your State? Answer immediately.

William Chandler signed his own name to the dispatches to Oregon and California, forging Zachariah Chandler's name to the dispatches to South Carolina, Florida and Louisiana.

From the moment the two Republicans' transport arrived, in Reid's account, "probably the quickest time ever made by a carriage from the Fifth-Avenue Hotel to the Western Union was made that morning." Reid rushed into the telegram office and handed the shorthand drafts to the clerk, ordering him, "Get these dispatches off as quickly as possible and charge the Republican National Committee." The clerk, who recognized Reid, replied, "The National Committee has no account here and we can't do it. Why not charge them to the *New York Times* account?" Reid agreed and countersigned the telegrams.[260]

Later that morning, setting the tone for the party line in unmistakable terms, Zachariah Chandler declared, "Hayes has 185 votes and is elected." *The New York Times* was now unequivocal in its Thursday morning edition: "THE BATTLE WON. A REPUBLICAN VICTORY." The other Republican papers were getting the scent. "HAYES POSSIBLY ELECTED," the *New York Tribune* headlined. "HOPE!" read the banner of the *Chicago Tribune*. "WHILE THERE'S LIFE THERE'S HOPE."

The election would be bitterly contested in both Houses of Congress and the Supreme Court all the way through to the week of the inaugural. There was widespread fear of a second civil war. "The democratic house of representatives can be depended on to protect the rights of the people, who have fairly elected Samuel J. Tilden," the *St. Louis Times* counseled, adding however, "If it is necessary to employ force to maintain their action, there are a half million of men who will volunteer to go to Washington at twelve hours notice." Henry Watterson, editor of the *Louisville Courier-Journal* and completing a vacated congressional term at the time, reported from Washington that the election was being stolen and urged a radical response: "On the law the Democratic Party plants itself and means to stand until it is driven off at the point of the bayonet. It is for our people to determine ... whether this shall be done. If they will rise in their might ... and will send a hundred thousand petitioners to Washington ... there will be no usurpation and no civil war. The conspirators will be thwarted."[261]

As matters progressed, out of the control of the Democratic Party, its newspaper organs grew still more shrill. The Terre Haute, Indiana, *Journal* snarled, "The Tilden men of the north and south will not be cheated or counted out. We appeal to our brethren, to democratic governors and democrats everywhere to stand fast in the faith; to come up to the grand work which the hour may yet call for. We say it that these United States by a quarter of a million majority have called Samuel J. Tilden to the chair of state. The majority rules. The majority will fight if there are no other means to save this country."

But the Republicans never wavered one iota from the certainty established by the *New York Times* in the early hours of the morning of Wednesday, November 8, 1876, that Hayes was elected, and they had the partisan advantage to impose it on the electoral commission deciding the issue. The last vestige of Democratic resistance crumbled after Hayes pledged to Southerners the end of Reconstruction in return for his taking office.[262]

On Saturday, March 3, the day after the electoral commission ultimately ruled in favor of Hayes and the day before the new president took office, the *Washington Union*, a newspaper founded by Tilden as the national organ of his campaign, went out of business. "Fraud has triumphed, and triumphed through the treachery of Democrats," the paper cried in its final edition. "Honest men of irresolute nature and dull perception have assisted, but corruption led the way."[263]

Charles Dana printed a picture of Rutherford Hayes on the front page of the *New York Sun* with the word "FRAUD" stamped across his forehead after the electoral commission confirmed his election. The *Sun* advised its readers to stay away from the inauguration and to snub the new president socially, even going so far as to decline invitations to his dinners. "He should be made to feel it daily and hourly that he is only tolerated, and is nothing more than a fraudulent President."[264] Dana continued to refer to the chief executive as "His Fraudulency, Mr. Hayes," for the balance of his term. Grudges died hard. When Hayes died in 1893, Lem Seawright of the Choctaw, Mississippi, *Plaindealer* wrote, "R. B. Hayes, the only man that ever stole the presidency, is dead. Let us hope he has gone where stealing is not a legitimate business."[265]

Little changed in the interval before the next presidential contest. Whatever one's opinion about the outcome in 1876, there were no demands for reform. The actions of the *New York Times* were not considered to have broken any journalistic standards of objectivity, or violated any moral code, because there were no such boundaries. The *Times* was recognized as a legitimate extension of the Republican campaign and was simply behaving as such. That was the way most people, especially most politicians, liked it. In an address to the Ohio Editorial Association in 1878, Congressman James Garfield of Ohio, who would emerge as the Republican presidential nominee in 1880, made clear the limits of "objectivity" as he understood them:

> I have no sympathy with the Utopian idea of "independent journalism." ... Let the journalist defend the doctrines of the party which he approves; let him criticize and condemn the party which he does not approve, reserving always his right to applaud his opponents or censure his friends, as the truth will require, and he will be independent enough for a free country.[266]

Garfield was close to the press, especially his good friend Whitelaw Reid, editor of the *New York Tribune*. Other editorial allies included George A. Benedict of the Cleveland *Herald and Gazette*; W. C. Howells of the *Ashtabula Sentinel*; and Lyman Hall of the Ravenna, Ohio, *Democratic Press*. "It was these editors, and their papers, who were among Garfield's earliest supporters and who, joined by a large part of the Ohio press, began to generate the public enthusiasm that led to his nomination for the presidency," Tebbel and Watts note.[267]

Ma, Ma, Where's My Pa?

On July 21, 1884, the *Buffalo Evening Telegraph*, in three bold front page columns, revealed to its readers:

A TERRIBLE TALE

A DARK CHAPTER IN A PUBLIC MAN'S HISTORY

THE PITIFUL STORY OF MARIA HALPIN AND GOVERNOR CLEVELAND'S SON

The story, endorsed the following day when the *Boston Journal* published its own investigative report, was out. Now the sordid tale of Grover Cleveland, the governor of New York and Democratic candidate for President, the widow Maria Halpin, and their "illegitimate" boy, Oscar, was revealed to the world. The *Evening Telegraph* was far from finished. Five days after the publication of the "Terrible Tale," it splashed more revelations, editorializing, "The libertine is a foe of the home, and is therefore, in a certain sense, a traitor to the Republic."[268]

The two papers, carefully chronicling every lascivious detail imparted to them, no matter how dubious the source, added ever more coarse strokes to their portrait of Cleveland as moral monster, a drunkard and whoremonger who on one occasion became involved in a brawl over a prostitute in a saloon that continued until the protagonists "were both nearly naked and covered in blood."[269] Further "revelations" emerged: how Cleveland had made his apartment in downtown Buffalo "a harem" and, his lust unslaked, had foraged for victims "in the city and surrounding villages."

The division between Cleveland and Blaine, wrote the Reverend George Ball of the Hudson Street Baptist Church in Buffalo, was that "between the brothel and the family, between indecency and decency, between lust and law ... between the depra-

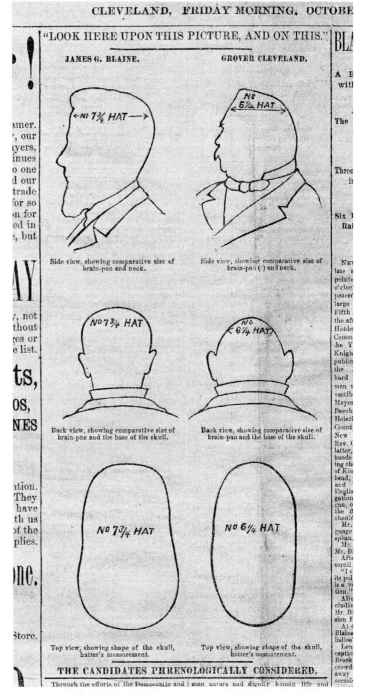

For the benefit of the undecided voter in 1884, the *Cleveland Leader* offered this handy election-eve comparison of the brainpans of the respective candidates. In the event, the superior phrenological qualities of James G. Blaine did not outweigh his ethical agnosticism in the minds of most voters, and he narrowly lost to the cranially limited, but honest, Grover Cleveland (author's collection).

dation of women and due honor, protection, and love of our mothers, sisters and daughters."[270]

"We do not believe the American people would elevate to the Presidency of the United States a betrayer of women, a man of shameless and profligate life," the *Boston Journal* concluded.[271] Some Democrats professed to be unconcerned. "What of it?" shrugged Senator George G. Vest of Missouri. "We did not enter our man in this race as a gelding." But these were only the opening salvoes in what would go down in history alongside the contest of 1828 as one of the slimiest presidential campaigns on record. Under the headline "Infamous Campaign Methods," the *Washington Post*, which held Cleveland's opponent, Republican senator James G. Blaine of Maine, responsible for the mud bath, asserted, "The history of political parties, not only in the United States but in all other countries where elections are held, would be searched in vain for any parallel to the baseness of the treatment accorded Grover Cleveland by the Blaine party in this campaign." "All the proprieties that have hitherto obtained even in the most exciting political contests have been set at naught," it continued. "The floodgates of slander have been kept wide open. Hired liars by the hundred have been kept busy in the manufacture and dissemination of dastardly calumnies. The Blaine press, with few exceptions, has reeked with filth, and men 'clothed with the livery of Heaven to serve the devil in' have wallowed through the slums to gather patches and shreds of calumny to sell to the Blaine managers."[272]

Ironically, Cleveland's chief selling point in winning the nomination had been his integrity, which Democratic strategists portrayed in stark relief to the charismatic but fundamentally dishonest character of Blaine.[273] The Republican candidate was so scandal-tarred that his nomination provoked a slew of defections from the ranks of the Republican press. "Some strange novelties appear," Thomas Bayard wrote fellow Democratic senator Henry C. Davis, "and to find *Harper's Weekly*, the New York *Times*, the *Evening Post*, the New York *Herald*, etc., all aiding the Democratic nominee is enough to make a man stare."[274]

Republicans deserting Blaine for Cleveland were labeled "Mugwumps," and there is a fairly direct lineage between this faction and the Liberal Republicans who contested with Grant during his presidency. Leading Mugwumps, in addition to the papers listed by Bayard, included the *Springfield Republican*, the *Transcript* and the *Herald* in Boston, and the *Philadelphia Record*, plus the weekly *Nation*. In the editorial opinion of the *New York Times*, which displayed the Mulligan letters on its front page, Blaine was exposed as "a prostitutor of public trusts, a scheming jobber, and a reckless falsifier."[275]

Whitelaw Reid this time remained loyal to the GOP. In Duncan's account, Reid "worked closely with Blaine during the campaign as confidant, adviser, and shield against demands from importunate ward and district leaders."[276] Reid kept up the fight to the end. The November 1, 1884, election-eve editorial in the *Tribune* urged its readers "to weight the consequences of supporting an immoral candidate and a corrupt party, united to-day in a conspiracy for plunder and spoils." But Reid's publication and the *Commercial Advertiser* were the only partisan Blaine papers in New York. In fact, the ranks of the Republican press in the major cities was so depleted that the party's national committee had to resort to the antebellum device of establishing a temporary paper in New York for the duration of the campaign. Erstwhile apostate Liberal Republican editor Murat Halstead received the dubious honor of running the paper.[277]

Blaine received greater support in the traditionally Republican Midwest, where the Springfield *Illinois State Journal* introduced news of Cleveland's speeches with a standing headline: "WHAT THE FAT BOY SAYS."[278] "Great Britain hates Blaine; it hated George Washington," the *Auburn Daily Advertiser* solemnly intoned. "It loves Cleveland; it loved Benedict Arnold. Voters don't forget it. The campaign is Great Britain against the United States; Cleveland against Blaine."[279]

On October 31, as the campaign wound to its climax, the *Cleveland Leader* threw its last rhetorical bomb at its namesake. While breathlessly reporting on a Blaine rally in Brooklyn in one article and still harping on the Halpin scandal in another dedicated to the "Utter Heartlessness and Depravity of the Vile Democratic Candidate," the rest of the front page was devoted to a phrenological study of the rival candidates. The skull shapes and measurements of Blaine and Cleveland were illustrated from various angles so as to better inform the undecided voter on their respective merits. "No one who admires those superior intellectual qualities which are known to have their seat in the lower and back part of the head" would hesitate before voting for Cleveland, the *Leader* remarked. Those more impressed by the "qualities of intellect and character indicated by a head which is larger at the crown than at the base, which rests upon a neck instead of commingling with it," would naturally incline towards Blaine.[280]

Made aware of information calling Blaine's marital record into question, Cleveland famously refused to act on it, remarking, "The other side can have a monopoly of all the dirt in this campaign." His fellow Democrats, already hammering at Blaine's shady reputation for influence peddling and abuse of office, were less scrupulous. The *Indianapolis Sentinel* broke the story that Blaine and his wife had had their first child just three months after their marriage. The paper concluded "There is hardly an intelligent man in the country who has not heard that James G. Blaine betrayed the girl who he married, and then only married her at the muzzle of a shotgun.... If, after despoiling her, he was too craven to refuse her legal redress, giving legitimacy to her child, until a loaded shotgun stimulated his conscience — then there is a blot on his character more foul, if possible, than any of the countless stains on his political record."[281]

By the time the campaign drew to a close, both contenders had been saturated in filth. "The Democratic candidate and myself have been maligned, libeled and outrageously attacked in many of the newspapers of the country," Blaine complained; "The truth is that in no campaign in a generation has there been such vilification and so much scandal news printed."[282]

The dénouement of the Blaine campaign took place in New York where he was subjected to two body blows from the press — one the direct result of a positive action from a Democratic newspaper, the other an incident exacerbated by years of negative spin from the Republican papers.[283]

Cleveland was the inadvertent beneficiary of a shuffle in the ranks of the Democratic Party press. One of the big losers to emerge from the campaign of 1884 was Charles Dana, who was continuing to steer his *New York Sun* on an erratic course through the rocky political shoals of the Gilded Era. After backing the ill-fated Samuel Tilden in 1876, Dana endorsed Republican candidate James Garfield four years later, his only concession to the Democratic candidate being "General Hancock is a good man, weighing two hundred and fifty pounds."[284]

In 1884, Dana chose to swim against the tide of the Mugwump defections to Cleveland. He had previously split with the state's governor after Cleveland had refused to appoint one of his friends to his military staff.[285] Dana was to pay a fearsome price for his petulance; by abandoning the party's candidate in favor of independent candidate General Benjamin Butler, the *Sun* forfeited its place as spokesman for the Democrats.

Primed to take advantage of this void in party attachment was loyal Democrat Joseph Pulitzer who, in May 1883, fresh from his devoutly partisan editorial control of the *St. Louis Post-Dispatch*, arrived in New York to rescue the nearly bankrupt *World* and make it the flagship for a new genre of "yellow" journalism — popular, accessible, and cheap.

"The *Post and Dispatch* will serve no party but the people," Pulitzer had announced upon launching that paper at the end of 1878, but his concept of "the people" was a highly partisan one: it "will be no organ of Republicanism, but the organ of truth." His opening declaration of principle at the *New York World*, set forth in the editorial on May 11, 1883, struck the same tone: "There is room in this great and growing city for a journal that is not only cheap but bright, not only bright but large; not only large but truly Democratic — dedicated to the cause of the people rather than that of the purse potentates."[286]

In fact, "The *World's* coverage of the campaign of 1884 was partisan journalism at its worst," Smythe says.[287] In 1884, Pulitzer backed Grover Cleveland for president while in the process of being elected to Congress himself from New York's Seventh District on the Tammany Democratic ticket. (Fealty to his editorial obligations forced him to quit only four months into his term.) "Every column of our paper tells the story of our devotion to the principles of the Democratic party," the *World* boasted. While the *Sun's* circulation fell to 85,000 from 137,000 during the campaign, circulation of the *World*, only 15,000 when Pulitzer took over, soared past 100,000, boosting it toward the milestone of being the first American newspaper to top one million.[288] "We ... believe the success of THE WORLD is largely due to the sound principles of the paper rather than

The name Joseph Pulitzer is indelibly linked with the award for journalistic excellence that celebrates his contribution to the profession. But he himself was a product of the rough-and-tumble reporting of the Gilded Age, and his career is distinguished by its fiery, partisan advocacy and tabloid sensationalism, the very term "yellow journalism" being derived from Richard Outcault's "Yellow Kid" comic strip which Pulitzer's *New York World* introduced in 1895 (courtesy of Library of Congress).

to its news features or its price," he wrote. The paper's circulation, he added, "should cheer the supporters of CLEVELAND and the friends of honest government generally." For Pulitzer, journalism, business and partisanship were intimately bound together.[289] Pulitzer gave voters four reasons for voting for Cleveland: "He is an honest man. He is an honest man. He is an honest man. He is an honest man."[290]

Dana's *Sun* shrilled that if Cleveland won, "the course debauchee might bring his harlots to Washington and hire lodgings for them close to the White House." Defending the Democratic nominees' youthful indiscretions ("How many unmarried men are there in the world who are in a position to safely and conscientiously cast the first stone at the offender?"), Pulitzer retorted, "If Grover Cleveland had whole family of illegitimate children, as he has not, he would be more worthy of the Presidential office than Blaine, the beggar at the feet of railroad jobbers, the prostitute in the Speaker's chair, the representative and agent of corruptionists, monopolists and enemies of the Republic."[291]

When Blaine attended a fundraising dinner at the fashionable Delmonico's restaurant on the evening of October 29, Pulitzer already had his response locked and loaded. The following morning the *World* spread a Walt McDougall cartoon headed "THE ROYAL FEAST OF BELSHAZZAR BLAINE AND THE MONEY KINGS" across all seven columns, showing Blaine at the banquet with such titans of industry as Jay Gould, Andrew Carnegie, John Jacob Astor, William H. Vanderbilt (wearing a crown), and Chauncey Depew, their diamond breastpins glittering as they guzzled Gould Pie, Lobby Pudding and Monopoly Soup, while ignoring a starving couple and their child begging for a share.

The accompanying news report, headed "MAMMON'S HOMAGE," read: "From Rum, Romanism, and Rebellion, Mr. Blaine proceeded to a merry banquet of millionaires.... The rock-ribbed Republican clergymen who waited on Mr. Blaine yesterday ... adopted a series of resolutions in which, emulating the malicious lying and slandering of scurvy politicians, they assailed the character of the Democratic candidate, Grover Cleveland, an honest, upright, truthful man, and beslavered with unctuous praise the notorious self-convicted corruptionist and 'continental' liar James G. Blaine.... Are they in sympathy with the workingman? What humbug! Are they in sympathy with labor? Fraud! Are they not mostly railroad kings, Wall Street millionaires, greedy monopolists, lobbyists, speculators?"[292] The cartoon hit a nerve; within an hour the *World* had sold every copy and had to run off thousands of extras. The Democrats made much of it in the run-up to election day, printing enlarged versions to plaster on walls and carry in parades. Recalling the 1884 campaign, Cleveland himself acknowledged his debt to Pulitzer: "How brilliantly and sturdily the *World* then fought for the Democracy. It was here, there, and everywhere in the field, showering deadly blows upon the enemy and it was won against such odds and by so slight a margin as to reasonably lead to the belief that no contributing aid could have been safely spared. The contest was so close that if it had lacked the forceful and potent advocacy of Democratic principles at that time by the New York *World* the result might have been reversed."[293]

But the real damage had come earlier in the day on October 29, during a mammoth rally of ministers convened by the Republican Party at the Fifth-Avenue Hotel. The intent of the meeting was to effect the consummation of the religious vote with Republican Party through a final crescendo of denunciations of the Halpin scandal. But the event would be remembered only for one remark let slip by master of ceremonies the Reverend Dr. Samuel D. Burchard, a comment that would have been shorn of context and entirely inconsequential in terms of its political impact had it not jibed so neatly with an underlying streak of bigotry that ran through the Republican Party, one that bubbled up through its newspapers into the public domain.

The warning signs should have been apparent in the actual makeup of what was supposed to be a multi-denominational rally. In fact it was almost entirely composed of characteristically Republican Methodists and Presbyterians. There were no Episcopalians, only one Rabbi, and just two Catholics in attendance. The significance of that last point became only too obvious when the Reverend Burchard made his introductory address. "We are Republicans," he told Blaine, "and don't propose to leave our party and identify ourselves with the party whose antecedents have been *rum, Romanism and rebellion*. We are loyal to our flag. We are loyal to you."

If race baiting was a staple of Democratic editorial opinion after the Civil War, the Republican equivalent was xenophobia. One of the original constituencies of the Republican Party during the 1850s was its erstwhile rival, the nativist Know Nothing movement, and the social networks of this old pseudo-fraternal organization persisted within the Republican Party decades after their formal merger. President Grant and both of his vice presidents, Henry Wilson and Schuyler Colfax, had been Know Nothings at one time. It should come as no surprise that the enduring irritant for the Republican Party during this period was Irish Catholicism. No community in the North was more consistently or virulently anti-abolition, less inclined to support the Republican Party, or more skeptical about the Civil War, traits which culminated in the New York Draft Riots of July 1863. Organs of Republican opinion responded in kind. The *Chicago Tribune* characterized the Irish as "blear-eyed sots" and "the voting tool of corrupt Democratic leaders." The *Freeport Journal* spoke scornfully of the "Irish 'cattle' who disgrace our soil." The *Cincinnati Commercial* called the Irish "stuffed apes." The *Detroit Advertiser and Tribune* labeled Irish Americans "locusts." And the *Chicago Western Railroad Gazette* described the Irish as "knaves," "voting cattle," and "filthy, stinking, God-forsaken wretches" after Democrats swept the spring elections of 1863.[294]

These divisions remained in place after the Civil War. While Catholicism represented tradition, WASP Protestantism advocated progress. Catholics favored parochial schools, Protestants public education. Catholics opposed Sabbath laws, Protestants promoted them. Catholics rejected prohibition, Protestants endorsed it. Accordingly, Olson notes, "While the Republican Party seemed bent on crusading to change American socially, the immigrant Catholics turned to the Democratic Party because it opposed such crusades and respected the prerogatives of local communities and groups."[295]

During the 1868 campaign, Republicans intensified their attacks on the Democrats' association with what they labeled "that abomination against common sense called the Catholic religion." Four years later, *Harper's Weekly* asserted that the Catholic Church was "loud in its denunciation of American civilization," that it furnished "three-fourths of the criminals and paupers who prey upon the Protestant community," that it never ceased its "attacks upon the principles of freedom," and that "its great mass of ignorant voters have been the chief source of our political ills." It charged the Jesuits had forged an alliance with Tammany Hall and the Ku Klux Klan, and called upon "every sincere Protestant to labor ceaselessly to defeat the schemes of the Jesuits, and drive their candidate back to a merited obscurity."[296] *Harper's* harped on the same theme in 1876, asserting, "The Roman Catholic priesthood holds in abject discipline the whole body of our Democratic voters.... There is no room for dissent in this remarkable political organization. From the pulpit, the confessional, the church door, the lecture room, Roman Catholics are directed to obey the suggestions of their oracle at the Vatican.... The Vatican directs the policy of the ruling section of the Democratic Party."[297]

The alliterative remark of the Reverend Burchard therefore has long been considered so decisive to the outcome of the presidential race in 1884 because it resonated with Irish voters accustomed to Republican papers like the *Indianapolis Journal* openly speaking of "the imported cattle, mostly Irish" that comprised the Democratic Party and of elections being stolen by "unterrified hordes of bog-trotting repeaters."[298] Despite Republican efforts at outreach, the *New York Tribune* still hadn't got with the program when it noted with approval the high tone of a parade for Blaine in Manhattan: "There were no newly-arrived immigrants in line, as was the case in the Cleveland parade."[299] Blaine belatedly sought to make amends, telling an audience in New Haven, "I should esteem myself of all men the most degraded if ... I could ... make a disrespectful allusion to that ancient faith in which my revered mother lived and died." But that single comment crystallized years of Catholic distrust of the Republican Party and held enough Irish Democrats in line for Cleveland to eke out a 1,047-vote margin in New York State and hence the Presidency.[300]

There would be still more drama to come before the end. The Associated Press and the Western Union Telegraph Company, which had been acquired by Wall Street financier Jay Gould, had maintained an overt bias in favor of Blaine throughout 1884. "I want you to win,"

William Henry Smith, joint general manager of the Associated Press in New York and Chicago, told his dear friend Whitelaw Reid at the outset of the campaign, "and to win a tremendous victory." Democrats, still smarting from out the outcome eight years earlier, were hypersensitive to the possibility of letting another election slip through their fingers because of Republican chicanery. As the days ticked by without any concession from Blaine, the *New York Times* reported that Gould was personally supervising the filing of AP news reports "and keeping back returns favorable to Cleveland." Returns were being sent out in lumps of unidentified election districts which were reported "in amounts and at times to suit the schemes" of the Blaine camp. Meanwhile, Western Union messages containing reports from Democrats were being bungled, and the figures revised by the operators. The *New York Herald* snapped that "during the last two days Gould, by false reports through his telegraphic agencies, has been ... preparing Republican partisans for a fraudulent claim that the vote of New York has been cast for Blaine.... It is the official returns of the ballots of the people of New York honestly counted, and not Jay Gould and his Western Union Telegraph Company that are to determine the electoral vote of this state."[301] It wasn't until Friday, with mobs roaming Manhattan chanting "We'll hang, we'll hang, we'll hang Jay Gould! Blood, blood, Jay Gould's blood!" that the financier, from the safety of his 150-foot yacht in the Hudson River, signaled his concession by personally sending Cleveland a congratulatory telegram. "CLEVELAND HAS WON — JAY GOULD GIVES UP NEW YORK STATE," the *Chicago Herald* headlined.[302]

The diehard Republican press would take some convincing. The *Los Angeles Times* declared Blaine elected on the morning of November 5, 1884, and clung to that view until November 16.[303] Only the *Chicago Tribune*, the other paper to finally concede Cleveland's election that day, could match such overtly partisan behavior when it finally conceded, "A conjunction of the anti-draft Copperheads of New York harbor, aided by a handful of Prohibitionists, and the anti–Union Rebel Democrats of the South has triumphed."[304] The paper's editor exhibited even greater despair in private. "The defeat of our grand and patriotic party ... by the confederates of the South and their slum allies around New York City filled me with bitterness and mortification," moaned Joseph Medill. "I have looked upon it as the most shameful episode of American political history."[305]

Many others held similar views about the election of 1884, less because of the result than the nature of the campaign. "Then and later contemporaries recalled the campaign with a sort of disgusted wonder as a spectacle they had never seen before and hoped never to see again," Summers records. It would be wrong to consider the tactics employed by either side as unorthodox; what happened that year simply represented the logical culmination, indeed the apogee, of the approach taken by the media in previous elections. Only now, finally, had the electorate reached the limit of its endurance towards ad hominem character assassination of its candidates for the nation's highest office. In the future, while no one seeking the presidency could expect to be spared an onslaught of criticism regarding their ideology, motivations, or qualifications, a kind of gentleman's truce would prevail that did spare intrusion into their personal lives by the mainstream media. Of course, this de-escalation of the journalistic arms race may have been as much owed to the desire to channel resources where they could be most effective as it was to any moral crisis among the practitioners of the trade. After all, "There was another reason that 1884 was an end as well as a beginning to 'terrible tales,' and it may have been the strongest," Summers notes, "the low road simply did not work."[306] But whatever the motivation, personal issues that previously would have been splashed across multiple columns in partisan newssheets — Franklin Roosevelt's paralysis, Joe McCarthy's alcoholism, John F. Kennedy's womanizing, and Richard Nixon's psychiatric counseling — were deemed beneath notice. This state of affairs survived long into the next century, until the rise of a "new" media ethic led to the tearing down of every barrier.[307] The contemporary presidential campaign is once again saturated with every detail of a candidate's personal history that can be laid bare under the relentless spotlight of investigative "journalism."

When Cleveland conceded the White House to Benjamin Harrison in 1888, the wheel of patronage turned full circle again. Less than a month after Benjamin Harrison took office in 1889, the *Nation* was already able to list seven Republican partisans in the media who had been granted offices or ambassadorial postings by the new administration (see Table 8).

TABLE 8. NEWSPAPER APPOINTMENTS TO PUBLIC OFFICE
BY THE HARRISON ADMINISTRATION

Individual	Newspaper	Appointment
Whitelaw Reid	*New York Tribune*	Mission to France
Allen T. Rice	*North American Review*	Mission to Russia
John A. Enander	*Chicago Hemlandet*	Mission to Denmark
Murat Halstead	*Cincinnati Commercial Gazette*	Mission to Germany
J.S. Clarkson	*Iowa State Register*	First Assistant Postmaster General
Ellis H. Roberts	*Utica Herald*	Assistant U.S. Treasurer, New York
John New	*Indianapolis Journal*	Consul General in London

Reflecting the importance of New York in Harrison's electoral college strategy, the *Nation* listed three more Empire State editors hoping for a share of the spoils—Charles E. Fitch of the *Rochester Democrat & Chronicle*, who wanted an appointment as internal revenue collector; Col. W. J. Morgan of the *Buffalo Commercial Advertiser*, who wanted to be collector of the Port of Buffalo; and John M. Francis of the *Troy Times*, who was described as "so eager to get into almost any kind of office" that he had been to Washington in person to see about it."[308] Other press appointments included William Henry Smith, who controlled the Western Associated Press, to

The steadfast, orthodox loyalty of Whitelaw Reid to the Republican Party after he wrested control of the *New York Tribune* from the failing Horace Greeley was rewarded by a succession of plum patronage positions, including the coveted posts of minister to France and minister to the Court of St. James's. In 1892 he was even prepared to accept his party's call to serve as running mate to President Benjamin Harrison and thereby risk election to the social oblivion that was the vice presidency (courtesy of Library of Congress).

collector of the Port of Chicago, and James Comly, editor of the *Ohio State Journal*, to the diplomatic post in Hawaii.[309]

At its 1892 convention, the Republican Party passed over incumbent Levi Morton to name Whitelaw Reid, then serving as U.S. ambassador to France, as President Harrison's running mate for the rematch with Grover Cleveland that year. Of course, there was nothing that might incline the delegates to rally around the incumbent vice president to be found in the pages of the *New York Tribune*. "If readers of the *Tribune* had not known who Harrison's vice president was, they would not have learned it from the editorial pages of Reid's paper from the time of his last weeks in France, early in 1892, to the opening of the national convention in Minneapolis in June," Duncan says.[310] Although the Harrison-Reid ticket went down in flames that November, the erstwhile editor was still able to salvage something from the wreckage of his Republican affiliations; he was appointed by the next Republican president, William McKinley, to the American delegation in Paris that concluded the war with Spain, while another Republican president, Teddy Roosevelt, appointed him minister to the Court of St. James's in 1908. In the meantime, Reid and his fellow partisans in the press would be accorded an unprecedented opportunity in which to express the full extent of their loyalty. The last campaign of the 19th century would be marked by a totality of media bias unprecedented in American history.

IV

The Newspaper Barons, 1896–1960

By the dawn of the 20th century, most Americans got their news from what Theodore H. White described as the "proprietary press ... something owned by businessmen for making money."[1] This did not mean the triumph of infotainment over civic obligation; far from it. In 1952, the three leading newspapers in San Francisco printed half as much political information as the same papers did in 1896, even though the number of pages per issue had increased fourfold.[2]

What was distinctive about this new era, according to the standard accounts of media history, was the triumph of objectivity as the prevailing business model in the industry. Until the late 19th century, these accounts maintain, journalism had been defined by partiality and subjectivity. Newspapers were partisan vehicles of persuasion, and a journalist's literary talents were in large part measured by the subjective values of wit, eloquence, ability to attract readers, and talent in stirring popular agitation. The shift toward objectivity introduced a new catalogue of values: rhetorical restraint, fairness to other views, fidelity to facts, use of authoritative sources, and independence from partisan loyalty.

The transition to norms of objectivity within journalism was consummated with the adoption of the news model, what Hackett and Zhao call "the most profound influence on journalism ethics since the arrival of periodic news publishing in the seventeenth century." The nature of news called for a different set of values. News was descriptive, empirical, novel, observational, and factual. Opinion, by contrast, was discursive, analytical, and argumentative. The newspaper as an organ of opinion lacked incentive to make objectivity its primary ethical norm. But once news became the main editorial purpose, the norms of factuality and independence moved to the heart of journalism ethics, in theory and in practice. The public came to expect news as a distinct product, and the industry adjusted its business model accordingly.[3] Another force impelling this evolution was the increasing salience of advertising revenue, which rose from 44 percent of total newspaper income in 1880 to 55 percent by 1900. Schudson notes that "this did not diminish the reliance of newspapers on circulation but, on the contrary, made circulation more firmly the measure of a newspaper's competitive standing.... Circulation became less a private matter of pride and income, more a public and audited indicator of the newspaper's worth as an advertising medium." It was more important than ever for newspapers to maximize their subscriber base. The trendsetter was the *New York*

World which succeeded in broadening its appeal through vivid use of color and illustrations, through targeting news to specific constituencies (with separate sections focusing on sports, show business, women's interests, etc.), and through adopting a professional detachment toward its coverage of partisan politics.[4]

The titles of late 19th century publications that addressed the role of the journalist in society, such as *Guide to Authorship*, *How to Write for the Press*, and *The Blue Pencil and How to Avoid It*, suggest the arrival at a consensus on an industry standard of objectivity. *Hints to Young Editors* explicitly defined objectivity in bipartisan terms: "There is no reason why the news of a Republican paper should not be read by a Democrat with as much confidence as a paper of his own party, and vice versa. It is only by presenting clear, unbiased records of fact that any benefit can be derived from the accompanying comments." Edwin Shuman, the literary editor of the *Chicago Tribune*, published the first comprehensive journalism textbook, *Steps into Journalism*, in 1894, asserting, "It is the mission of the reporter to reproduce facts and the opinions of others, not to express his own." He quoted approvingly from an Associated Press directive to its employees:

> All expressions of opinion on any matter, all comment, all political, religious or social bias, and especially all personal feeling on any subject, must be avoided. This editorializing is the besetting sin of the country correspondent and a weariness to the flesh to the copy-reader who has to expunge the copy's colourings and invidious remarks about individuals. Opinions are the peculiar province of the editorial writer. The spirit of modern journalism demands that the news and editorials be kept distinctly separate. The one deals with facts, the other with theoretical interpretations, and it is as harmful to mix the two in journalism as it is to combine church and state in government.[5]

Another index of the desire for an industry benchmark of objectivity was the formation in 1908 of the first school of journalism at the University of Missouri. By 1917, eighty-four U.S. colleges were offering courses in the field; by 1987 this total had risen to 812. The journalistic value system advanced in academia helped standardize practices across the industry. As objectivity became technically defined as a method rather than a universalizing discourse, it gradually came to be defined as straight, factual reporting, ultimately being reduced to the reporting of factual descriptions and statements produced by accredited sources.[6] As technological advances revolutionized news, this ethos was imprinted on the business model of the fledgling film, radio, and television industries, ultimately becoming embedded in court rulings and FCC regulations. Under the terms of the latter's 1949 Fairness Doctrine, each broadcaster was required to maintain standards of fairness and balance by affording "reasonable opportunity for discussion of conflicting views on issues of public importance." It was an attempt to mandate internal diversity.[7]

According to Graham Knight, the cultivation of objectivity and professionalism in journalism was closely linked to the emergence of a new middle class of salaried intellectuals employed in bureaucratic institutions. By contrast with the old middle class of self-employed commodity producers, the work orientation and career commitment of this new middle class was based on the ideals of objectivity and ethical neutrality.[8] Walter Lippmann had illustrated this point in the 1930-31 *Yale Review* when he noted that reporting could not be considered a profession until "modern objective journalism was successfully created, and with it, the need of men who would consider themselves devoted, as all the professions ideally are, to the service of truth alone." Journalists now aspired to the idealized professional objectivity (and status) of lawyers, doctors, and scientists.[9]

In sum, Hackett and Zhao conclude, under the terms of this new, professional, market-oriented business model, "the political values expressed in the commercial media tended increasingly to be implicit and hegemonic (dominant and consensual), rather than explicit, abrasive, and partisan." To this end, the commercial press no longer assumed that readers were the followers of a particular party or faction, or even that they were active participants in political life. Instead, it increasingly addressed or positioned readers as citizens of the whole nation, as spectators of politics, and perhaps above all as consumers.[10]

The problem with this interpretation is that while it may reflect the stated policy of the industry, and does contain an element of truth in that the template of objectivity was widely adopted as an industry standard, the better to maximize sales, in reality editors manipulated the shell of objectivity to serve as a Trojan Horse, the ideal mechanism with which to wage ideological warfare—for what argument is more persuasive than one developed in a detached style by credible sources in an authoritative forum? Behind the façade — the professional journalistic standards, the foreign correspondents, the impersonal and anonymous wire stories, the carefully segregated news and op-ed pages— objectivity stretched no further than disinterestedly reporting precisely those issues about which management had no previously determined opinion. Coverage of everything management deemed important was slanted to fit its agenda, the only question being the degree to which this partiality crept in. Bias remained rampant in reporting on international relations, with key publications actively proselytizing for or against American intervention prior to the outbreak of war in 1898, 1917 and 1941; on key social trends, for example race, female suffrage, and prohibition; and, as always, on partisan politics. These enduring cleavages were woven deep into the social fabric. According to Michael Barone:

> The high tide of partisan media may have been in New York in the 1920s, when the city had more than a dozen daily newspapers, each targeted at a different ethnic and partisan niche. The new tabloids— Captain Joseph Patterson's *Daily News*, and Hearst's *Daily Mirror*, with their screaming headlines and big pictures— were aimed at the masses of Irish, Italian, and Jewish immigrants. The *Herald Tribune* was for Anglo-Saxon Republicans. The *Times*, with its seeming independence from both political parties, was the favorite of upscale German Jews, who were diffident toward both waspy Republicans and Tammany Democrats. Pulitzer's *World* was aimed at Protestant Democrats, Hearst's *Journal* and *American* at Catholic Democrats. Yet to come were the tabloid *Post*, targeting Democratic Eastern European Jews, and *PM*, directed to Jewish left-wingers. No one read all of these newspapers; who would have time? People picked up the one whose coverage seemed to make the most sense of the world for them. Everyone expected their paper to be partisan.[11]

The big-city newspapers at least had the option of crossing party lines when they felt it was in the national interest. True independence came at a price, and only the press in the major metropolitan centers, with access to a deep enough pool of subscription and advertising revenue, could afford to pay it. It is notable that what expansion there was in the number of independent newspapers kept pace with America's urbanization. The level of independent publications rose only from 5 percent to 9 percent during the entire period from 1810 to 1850. By the middle 1870s it was 25 percent, increasing to 28 percent in 1880, 36 percent in 1892, 40 percent in 1900, and 48 percent in 1940.[12]

But America's demographics still tilted rural at the dawn of the 20th century, and the big fish who had the resources and a point to prove could monopolize the political dialogue in the small towns with a personal newspaper. Years before the shoot-out at the OK Corral, politics in the Arizona Territory was personal and unforgiving, and so were the newspapers. One candidate for office breathlessly labeled his rival "servile, self-asserting, and stupid," and went on to add "As the gaily painted moth, clothed from the slime and filth of earth, which flits around the lighted candle and finally expires in the flame, so this worthless upstart, but yesterday dragged from the gutters of political and social corruption, and clothed, for an hour, from the spoils of official prostitution, awaits his doom in the flame of honest, popular indignation which will soon accomplish the extirpation of the infamous rabble of which he is an acknowledged member."[13]

When there were two such big fish, a "this-town's-not-big-enough-for-the-two-of-us" scenario could arise. For example, in the frontier country of Montana, rival copper kings in Butte owned the *Daily Miner* and the *Anaconda Standard*. On November 9, 1898, the two rivals had perspectives on the outcome of that week's election for mayor between the Democrat Daly and the Republican Clark that were as diametrically opposed as they were mutually irreconcilable. According to the *Daily Miner*:

> By coercion, intimidation and bribery the returns show that the Dalycratic ticket has managed to force itself upon Silver Bow County. A more disgraceful election was never witnessed in Montana. The freedom of the ballot and honesty in elections has become a farce in the light of the methods used by the Dalycratic heelers.
>
> That the Dalycrats bought all the purchasable element no one in the city doubts. Election day, every irresponsible loafer and bum in the city was shouting for Marcus Daly and jingling in their pockets the price of their votes. The better element, the representative elements of Butte, does not appear to be in the majority in Silver Bow County. The returns show that good government by and for the people was beaten.

According to the *Anaconda Standard*, on the other hand, "In spite of a wholesale buying of votes, repeating and fraudulent balloting as indulged in by an unscrupulous opposition, the forces of honesty and decency in Silver Bow County were rewarded yesterday when the entire Democratic ticket won by a handsome majority. That the lying and thieving tactics of the Clark forces availed them little is proven by the results of yesterday's balloting."[14]

The smaller rural papers still depended on the patronage of county printing contracts and on direct subsidies from the parties. "Ever since I have been in the newspaper business it has been considered that a political campaign was a legitimate source of extra revenue to a party newspaper, and I do not think the custom has staled," wrote the owner of the *Daily Yellowstone Journal*, a Republican paper in Montana, in 1908. "There has never been a campaign in which the paper has not been paid something.... For 1902 we received $400; for 1904, $600; for 1906, $500, and I recall that in 1906 I was thanked by the committee for being so reasonable."[15]

"The newspapers of the great cities seldom acknowledge allegiance to any political party," another Republican editor, John Kautz, of the Kokomo, Indiana, *Tribune*, observed after the election of 1900. "They make of themselves chiefly commercial enterprises, buying and selling news, with money-getting their only purpose. The mercenary spirit is in everything they do." Kautz was firmly above such irresolution, and so was his paper: "It is only in the country newspapers that are willing always to make their party's cause their own, to fight under its standard, to stand with it in the fiercest contests. Such a Republican paper is Kokomo *Tribune* and such it has been for more than fifty years."[16]

Kautz was far from alone. As late as 1931, some 34 percent of the 1,500 dailies and 42 percent of the 8,300 weeklies in the North declared their fealty to either the Republicans or the Democrats.[17] Another 18 percent of the dailies and 9 percent of the weeklies maintained informal party ties as "Independent Republican" or "Independent Democratic" papers.[18] A publication fitting this bracket was one that did not accept direct subsidization from a particular party but simply chose to endorse it as a matter of course. An example of the breed, destined to be more influential than most, made its debut on June 3, 1895, in Emporia, Kansas. "The new editor of the GAZETTE desires to make a clean, honest local paper," the proprietor, William Allen White, declared by way of introduction. "He is a Republican and will support Republican nominees first, last, and all the time. There will be no bolting, no sulking, no 'holier than thou' business about his politics."[19] Many Democratic editors had boldly issued similar proclamations when bringing their publications to market, and had confidently expected to uphold such a commitment for the duration. But a political tornado then gathering in the Midwest was shortly to break on the national scene, one that would leave in its wake established partisan and editorial alignments more dazed and disoriented than at any time since the Civil War.

Sixteen to One

"The People have triumphed over the Plutocracy," the *New York World* rejoiced as Grover Cleveland reclaimed the White House from Republican Benjamin Harrison in 1892, "Men are stronger than money."[20] Such joy would be short-lived, however. A financial panic struck almost simultaneously with Cleveland's return to office and the nation plunged into the pit of a depression. In the midterm elections of 1894, the voters visited their wrath upon the Democratic Party, annihilating its majorities in both houses. "In one day the people have wiped out a National party as a schoolboy would sponge his slate," the *New York Tribune* noted with satisfaction. "Two years ago they had a freak of foolishness and were deceived. It has cost them in two years more than the four years of civil war."[21]

By the middle of the decade, economic conditions and social cohesion had deteriorated to the point where the two-party system itself was under threat. Across the South and West, a new agrarian protest movement was rising, the Populist Party, to

William Allen White purchased the *Emporia Gazette* in 1895 and established a national reputation the following year with his editorial "What's the Matter with Kansas?" This stinging critique of the radical environment that had incubated William Jennings Bryan accurately expressed the orthodox values of a host of other small-town Republican editors. The "Sage of Emporia" would later flirt with the wild side himself, aligning with progressive Republicans like Roosevelt and La Follette (courtesy of Library of Congress).

challenge the fiscal orthodoxy upheld by both Republicans and Democrats. The Populists demanded reform such as a graduated income tax, direct election of senators, an eight-hour working day, and, most of all, an inflationary monetary policy through the coinage of silver at a weight ratio of 16 ounces to 1 ounce of gold.

Papers such as the *Advocate*, the *Farmer's Alliance*, and the *Representative*, and the magazine *National Economist*, articulated Populist issues and grievances, proposed political and economic reforms, and mobilized mass support for candidates in elections scattered throughout the South and West. The organizational vehicle that synthesized and organized the channels of communications for the Populists was an umbrella unit, the National Reform Press Association, which came into existence after 1890 when various Southern and Western *Farmer's Alliance* editors coalesced into a propaganda organ of the People's Party. "Considering the geographic distances encompassed by the Populist movement, without the National Reform Press Association the People's Party would have lacked any organizational centrality and ideological coherence," Rubin says.[22]

The Populists had contested the presidential election in 1892, carrying four western states. By 1896 they had a strong, mobilized, and growing presence in Congress and in many state legislatures. The Democratic Party faced the prospect of not only losing the White House to the Republicans but being supplanted by the Populists, and going the way of its ancestral Federalist and Whig enemies.

At the local level, the Democrats were able to forestall the Populist political ascendancy in their political fiefdom of the "Solid South" through the tested formula of fraud, intimidation and violence. "It is the religious duty of Democrats to rob Populists and Republicans of their votes whenever and wherever the opportunity presents itself and any failure to do so will be a violation of true Louisiana Democratic teaching," the foremost party paper in northern Louisiana asserted. "The Populists and Republicans are our legitimate political prey. Rob them! You bet! What [else] are we here for?"[23]

But at the national level, the man who defused the Populist threat and in the process transformed the Democratic Party was a two-term House member from Nebraska named William Jennings Bryan. Control of the Democratic convention in 1896 had already passed from President Cleveland to the more radical wing of the party, led by such men as Illinois governor John Peter Altgeld and the one-eyed South Carolina senator "Pitchfork" Ben Tillman (who won his nickname after threatening to impale Cleveland on that farm implement). Then Bryan rose to speak. No one was prepared for what happened next. At one stroke, Bryan repudiated the administration, co-opted the Populist agenda, and laid claim to the nomination with perhaps the single greatest oration in American history. "You shall not press down upon the brow of labor this crown of thorns," Bryan thundered at the awestruck delegates. "You shall not crucify mankind upon a cross of gold."

Bryan's nomination opened new fault lines in American politics that took generations to heal. The Populists, checkmated, had no choice but to endorse Bryan and slowly fold themselves into the Democratic Party. Urban and eastern Democrats, on the other hand, deserted the party in droves. With one exception, Cleveland and every member of his Cabinet disowned the nominee of their party and endorsed splinter Gold Democrat John M. Palmer for president. The lone holdout was Hoke Smith, the secretary of the interior and owner of the *Atlanta Journal*. Cleveland asked for, and got, his resignation.[24]

Bryan was in the business of print himself, as a feature writer and editor at the *Omaha World-Herald* (on behalf of which he covered the 1896 Republican convention, where he witnessed the nomination of his rival, William McKinley). Later, he founded his own publication, *The Commoner*, as a vehicle for his views. But being acquainted with the rules of the newspaper game won him no favors whatsoever from the other players. The report on the Democratic convention made by the *Philadelphia Press* on July 10 set the tone for the ensuing campaign:

> The Jacobins are in full control at Chicago. No large political movement in America has ever before spawned such hideous and repulsive vipers.... The Altgelds and Tillmans who have thrust aside the old leaders of the Democracy and have seized the reins of control incarnate a spirit of Communism and Anarchy which is new to America on any large scale.
>
> This riotous platform is the concrete creed of the mob. It is rank Populism intensified with hate and venom. It rests upon ... chartered Communism, and enthroned Anarchy. Such a noxious and nefarious profession of faith has never before been made in this country even by an escaped band of lunatics. It begins with falsehood, advances through war upon the social fabric and ends with the unleashing of the mob.
>
> The platform in every vital part appeals to everything that is low and debased and vicious in human nature. In its moral quality and in its public policy it bespeaks the most lawless, irresponsible, incendiary group of besotted leaders who have ever been thrown to the surface even in the worst paroxysms of American demagoguism.

Hardly less caustic was the *Richmond Times*: "In a spasm of hysteria, the convention ran off and nominated a mere youth, who was scarcely known of, because he rattled off before it

a studied piece of sophomorical rhodomontade that did not contain a single sound proposition and abounded in nonsense and anarchy in equal proportions from beginning to end."
The *New York World* agreed, "The expected happened in the Chicago platform. The unexpected
happened in the nomination for President. Lunacy having dictated the platform, it was perhaps natural that hysteria should evolve the candidate."[25]

In the Chicago press, the Democratic convention was labeled "an aggregation of populism, socialism and idiocy," precipitating a crisis "greater than the Civil War." Even the
Democrats' longstanding editorial enemies shed crocodile tears at the spectacle. "The ass of
ignorance, reaction, cupidity, and communism has pulled over himself the lion's skin of a great
political party with a long and in many respects distinguished history," The *New York Journal of Commerce* solemnly lamented.

"Probably no man in civil life has inspired as much terror without taking life as Bryan,"
the *Nation* wryly observed. Print organs across the country ranging from the *Nation* to the
Commercial & Financial Chronicle, presented a solid wall of opposition to the Democratic nominee, who was labeled an anarchist, a socialist, a communist, a revolutionary, a cheap orator,
a mountebank, and an opportunist. "He is a despicable demagogue, without a spark of patriotism," growled the *Chicago Tribune*.[26] Others repudiated the company he kept: *Harper's
Weekly* endorsed McKinley in October, ostensibly out of fear that Bryan would be a puppet
of Altgeld, "the ambitious and unscrupulous Illinois communist."

"Down with the fanatics!" cried the *Springfield Republican*. "National dishonor, private robbery, the exaltation of anarchy ... the damnation of the Constitution," were the patent objects
of the silver movement to the *Philadelphia Inquirer*. In the *New York Mail & Express*, the Bryan
campaign was labeled "the hysterical declaration of a reckless and lawless crusade of sectional
animosity and class antagonism." "No wild-eyed and rattle-brained horde of the red flag ever
proclaimed a fiercer defiance of law, precedent, order and government," it continued.[27]

The *New York Times* (which had backed Democrat Cleveland in 1884, 1888 and 1892),
advised its readers to "Repudiate the Repudiators," the "intoxicated rabble" who had seized

control of the Democratic
convention. Adolph Ochs,
publisher of the *Times*,
admitted to his wife that
he "doubted very much
whether there were many
men in the United States
whose future was so heavily
dependent upon [McKin-
ley's victory] as mine."[28] He
personally led a *Times* contingent that carried silk ban-
ners with the *Times* logo
emblazoned on them down
Broadway during a march of
businessmen for McKinley.[29]

In this *Puck* cartoon, the Populist serpent Bryan devours the Democratic donkey. The reality was that
by appropriating the key planks of the Populist platform in his bid for the presidency, Bryan effectively
forced the third party to subsume itself within the Democratic organization. But in this instance the
medium is the message — the demonic depiction of Bryan is typical of how he was represented in the
overwhelming majority of the nation's presses during his first battle for the White House (courtesy of
Library of Congress).

The vituperative attacks on Bryan were only to be expected from the Republican press. Of more concern was the almost total isolation of Bryan by the Democratic papers. "Never had the shift in newspaper sentiment been so widespread," Paul W. Glad notes.[30] In New York the *Sun*, the *Herald*, the *World*, and the *Evening Post* (which referred to Bryan as "the chief of blatherskites") bolted the Democratic ticket, along with the *Brooklyn Eagle*, leaving William Randolph Hearst's *Morning Journal* as the city's only major newspaper for Bryan (not that Hearst's characterization of Bryan would have won him many votes: "He follows the truth as he sees it, though it lead him to political destruction. His spirit is rather that of a prophet").[31] The defection of Democratic newspapers in New England — including the *Herald*, the *Globe* and the *Post* of Boston, the *Springfield Republican*, the *Hartford Times*, the *New Haven Evening Register*, the *Bridgeport Evening Farmer*, and the *Providence Daily Journal* — was made complete when the *Boston Evening Despatch*, the only paper of any significance left in the region to support Bryan, collapsed two weeks before the election after local businesses pulled their advertising.[32] No such fiscal inducements were necessary in New Hampshire for the hitherto Democratic *Manchester Union* to declare: "For the first time in its history the Union refuses to place at the head of its editorial column the name of the candidate selected by a National Convention of its party. That candidate has been placed upon a platform which no true Democrat can intelligently and sincerely support."[33]

Elsewhere in the Northeast the *Buffalo Enquirer* and *Buffalo Courier*, the *Philadelphia Record* and *Times*, the *Trenton Evening Times* and the *Lowell Morning Times* bolted Bryan. Apostates in the Midwest included the *St. Paul Globe*, the *Cincinnati Post*, and the Chicago-based *Chronicle*, whose defection deprived the Democrats of a single major paper in the Windy City. In Baltimore, the *Sun* and the *News* rejected Bryan, as did the *Record* (which noted that it was precisely because it "has been a firm supporter of Democratic principles [that it now] repudiates, condemns and spits upon this communistic, populistic deliverance").

Only in the South could Bryan expect to count on the balance of media support for his campaign. Josephus Daniels of the *Raleigh News & Observer*, for example, described the nomination of Bryan as a "virile" one, and depicted the Democratic campaign as "a conflict of men against money."[34] The *Fayetteville Observer* was so committed to Bryan's cause that it published the full text of the platform of the North Carolina Democratic Party *every day* on its editorial page throughout the campaign.[35] The *Atlanta Constitution* described Bryan, "the brilliant young Nebraskan," as "a born leader of the people ... the very embodiment of the principles for which the people are contending in the present crisis."[36]

However, even south of the Mason-Dixon Line there was resistance to Bryan and free silver. Although Bryan posed no threat to the color line, the binding force of the one-party Solid South, for the first time since the Civil War, editorial voices were raised against the nominee of the Democratic Party. Some of those who did so paid a fearsome price. In the election controversy of 1876, Democratic kingpin Henry Watterson of the *Louisville Courier-Journal* had blustered in print from his seat in the U.S. House of Representatives (where he had agreed to serve as a placeholder for an uncompleted term) that Tilden had been fairly elected and would "be driven from that position only by bayonets." Now he turned his back on Bryan, whom he scorned as "a boy orator ... a dishonest dodger ... a political fakir ... not of the material of which the people of the United States have ever made a President, nor is he even of the material of which any party has ever before made a candidate."[37] As a result, the *Courier-Journal* lost half its circulation in just twelve months. It took years to rehabilitate the paper, and it was in no position to endure the same ordeal the next time Bryan took on McKinley. "He is four years older," Watterson said in endorsing the Democratic standard bearer, "he must have learned something." Watterson certainly had.[38]

Other southern papers that declined to support the Democratic ticket in 1896 included

The Wausau Herald.

R. E. POWERS.   J. J. LOHMAR.
POWERS & LOHMAR,
Proprietors.

TERMS: $1.50 per Year, in Advance.

Advertising Rates Furnished on Application.

R. E. POWERS.   -   -   Editor.

WAUSAU, WIS., OCT. 9, 1896.

NATIONAL

Democratic Ticket

FOR PRESIDENT—
WILLIAM J. BRYAN,
OF NEBRASKA.
FOR VICE PRESIDENT—
ARTHUR SEWALL,
OF MAINE.

Democratic State Ticket.

For Governor—
W. C. SILVERTHORN.
Lieut. Governor—
H. H. HOARD.
Sec. of State—
C. M. BUTT.
Treasurer—
W. F. PIERSTORFF.
Attorney General—
H. I. WEED.
R. R. Commissioner—
C. F. KALK.
Ins. Commissioner—
F. W. THAL.
Superintendent—
F. L. CLEARY.
For Member of Congress, Ninth District
W. W. O'KEEFE.
For Member of Assembly—1st district,
DR. E. C. FISH.
For Member of Assembly—2d district,
E. J. ANDERSON.

Democratic County Ticket.

Eor Sheriff,
CARL KRONENWETTER.
For County Treasurer,
C. F. PAFF

the *Mobile Daily Register*, the *Atlanta Journal*, and the *Chattanooga Daily Times*. "After death comes the Judgment," warned the *Charleston News and Courier*. "Northern and Eastern States which have been faithful to the Democratic Party in all times of distress and tribulation will not be with the South in its wild career toward financial ruin." Elsewhere it was a mixed bag. In New Orleans, the *Times-Democrat* endorsed Bryan, while the *Picayune* could not swallow free silver. In Texas, the *Galveston Daily News* and *Austin Daily Statesman* opposed the ticket, while the *Houston Daily Post* enthusiastically backed it. In Nashville, the *Banner* bolted the ticket, the *American* remained loyal.[39]

Bryan's press support was strongest, not surprisingly, in the populist Western states where the sentiment for silver was at its peak. In Denver, the *Republican*, the *Times*, and the *News* all backed Bryan, as did the *Tribune*, the *Herald*, and the *News* of Salt Lake City. Pro-Bryan papers in the Midwest included the *St. Louis Republic*, the *Detroit Evening News*, the *Indianapolis Sentinel*, the *Cincinnati Enquirer*, the *Cleveland Plain Dealer*, and the *Columbia Register*. Rare Bryan-boosters in the "Enemy's Country" of the Northeast included smaller papers such as the *Daily News* and the *Mercury* of New York, the Philadelphia *Item*, the Pittsburgh *Post*, and the Springfield *News*.

In Detroit, while the Democratic *Free Press* defected to McKinley and gold, James Scripps led the Republican *Post and Tribune* into the embrace of Bryan and free silver. Ex-governor Russell Alger wrote to Scripps, pleading with him to keep the faith: "The *Tribune* has long been the leading Republican organ of the state and while you own its title and are paying its bills, still in a sense it is the property of the organization that has made the country great. It seems to me, it is your duty to permit it to heartily support both the ticket and platform. Can you not assure the Republicans of the state that, no matter what your views may be, the *Tribune* shall support the party heartily?"

The answer was no.[40] But such stubbornness was exceptional, even among those Silver Republicans who sympathized with the Democratic nominee and his

This ticket from the Wausau *Herald* in 1896 is unusual for two reasons; it is one of the last of a dying breed, the editorial page straight ticket, which by the end of the 19th century was being phased out in favor of the contemporary polling booth; and it propagates the cause of William Jennings Bryan, identifying it with a defiant minority among its peers (author's collection).

platform. The countervailing forces of partisan loyalty, pressure from subscribers and advertisers, and the threat of social ostracism usually held sway. In any event, those rare exceptions where there was a swing in editorial opinion in favor of Bryan could do little to offset the stampede in the opposite direction. "The newspapers which do not repudiate the Chicago platform are the ones to be pitied," the *Los Angeles Times* noted. "They go along, vainly trying to stem the tide of public opinion, and, like a schoolboy walking through a graveyard after nightfall, they endeavor, by whistling, to keep up their courage and drive away the spooks."[41]

On July 11, 1896, the *New York World* wrote off Bryan's chances and expressed concern for the Democratic Party's long-term prospects: "As the party is doomed to defeat by its platform, the ticket is of minor consequence, except as it bears upon the future of the party. A political organization can survive being made odious. There is peril in making it ridiculous." Pulitzer maintained that his apostasy was a temporary phenomenon, necessary for the rehabilitation of the party, and signaled his intention to return to the Democratic fold in four years time when, presumably, the virus of Bryanism had been expunged: "*The World* remembers that the Democratic Party has blundered frightfully in the past, and has survived and recovered from the effects of its unwisdom. We desire to see the old and splendid historic organization left after defeat in such a condition that the fragments can be made to cohere again in 1900."[42] The *New York Sun* followed a similar line, urging Democrats to "go to the polls and clear the way for the new Democracy by firing directly at Bryan a ballot for William McKinley!"[43]

Those editors still on the fence could be nudged in the right direction by being reminded of their pecuniary interests. Advertisers opposed to free silver warned publishers that they would pull their ads if Bryan were elected: "In making the choice of which cause to espouse in the present campaign, it behooves every newspaper in the country to consider the question of its own individual commercial interest."[44]

In his response to the media monolith ranged against him, Bryan sought to make light of the situation, and in doing so to draw a distinction between editorial and popular support: "We do not have all the newspapers with us in this fight, but an editor only votes once and I have known some editors who have had so little influence that they could not even control the one vote which the law gives them. We would be glad to have the newspapers with us, but ... we would rather have the people with us at the polls."

The *New York Times* noted in an editorial reply that Bryan had spoken "with a curious mingling of alarm and resentment of the newspapers.... Two ideas seem to be in his mind. One is that the newspapers are all against him. The other is that they do not represent popular opinion." The *Times* went on:

> The first impression is substantially correct. The newspapers are practically all against him, and against the revolutionary and dangerous ideas which he is trying to spread. ... The fact is easily explained. As a class, the newspaper writers are, necessarily, well-informed, clear-headed, quick-witted men, familiar with the interests of their readers and the principles that govern them. Their views in regard to the broad issues involved in this canvass are not shallow or fleeting, but are based on knowledge and study and observation and on discussion with practical men of affairs. For this reason they readily see through the sophistries, delusions, and fallacies that captivate Mr. Bryan and his followers.[45]

The *Times* was asserting here that the disinterested *rationality* characteristic of the newspapers distinguishes them from the partisan *irrationality* exhibited by the Democratic Party and its nominee for President. Bryan and his value system were accordingly excluded from the mainstream of political debate. The electoral contest, therefore, was not one between viable alternatives, but rather between legitimacy (McKinley) and illegitimacy (Bryan). The

Times arrived at this conclusion not on the basis of *subjective* interpretation of the *truth*, but after *objective* study of the *facts*.

To cite a specific instance whereby the *Times* cloaked the promulgation of a highly partisan agenda in the guise of the prevailing industry standard of objectivity, on September 27 the paper published a letter signed "Alienist" from "an eminent expert on nervous diseases" that cited "incidents of Mr. Bryan's errabund tendencies" and argued that "his utterances prove him to be of unsound mind; it classes him as a political 'mattoid.'" According to "Alienist," the symptoms of mattoidism exhibited by Bryan include "a bad hereditary history, a life of restlessness and mental vagabondage; an intense, overmastering and growing egotism; grandiloquent ideas that are almost, if not quite, delusional; a morbid querulousness and sensitiveness to criticism; fixed ideas about gold and silver, classes and masses, &c., that are not reasonable or reasonably defended, but are passionately affirmed and reiterated; a confused and illogical mental state, and an oratorical monomania."[46]

In an editorial in the same issue and on the same page, the *Times* was forced to agree that it, too, found in Bryan's speeches evidence of his mental deterioration: "What, however, most of all entitles us to say that Mr. Bryan is of unsound mind, whether we call this condition unsoundness in English or insanity in Latin, is that his procedures are not adaptation of intelligent means to intelligible ends."

For several succeeding days the *Times* published a number of letters and interviews in which other "alienists" attested to Bryan's "unsoundness." On September 29, for example, under the headline, "IS MR. BRYAN A MATTOID — LEADING ALIENISTS ANALYZE THE DEMOCRATIC CANDIDATE," the paper published a roundtable discussion of Bryan's mental and emotional stability by the leading mental health professionals of the day. One such expert found himself in agreement with the author of the mattoid thesis, concluding, "It can readily be seen that Mr. Bryan, if elected, would accomplish great harm to the country. His degenerate theories, if he were to put them into execution, would probably prove beyond doubt to the world at large his evident mental deterioration."

"Dr. Hammond," the reporter continued, "suppose for a moment that you are on the witness stand on a criminal trial, sworn to tell the truth to the best of your knowledge, and answer this hypothetical question for me. If a man comes to you and said: 'A friend of mine has adopted a theory about which he is continually talking; he is eaten up, as it were, with vanity, and refuses to listen to anyone who controverts his theory; he continually rails against existing institutions and declares that he alone is competent to rectify the ills. Do you think his mind is failing?' What would your answer be?"

"I should tell the man," answered Dr. Hammond, "that his friend was undoubtedly insane."

Other expert opinion rendered Bryan unworthy of serious psychoanalysis. "'I do not think,' said Dr. Spitzka, 'that Mr. Bryan was ever of a large enough calibre to think clearly and consecutively. His mental territory is not sufficiently extensive to enable him to form a comprehensive judgement on a topic of such wide importance as the one he is so dangerously muddling up.'"[47]

Shortly afterward, the "Alienist" wrote again to the paper expressing satisfaction "that some of our political organizations and civic communities have been made conscious by my letter that they were ruled by mattoids. In many instances it seemed that they knew they had been crudely conscious of having been, as it were, 'queered,' but mental science supplied the missing word in the charade."

The "Alienist" went on to note with some alarm that "a careful perusal of all the speeches of Mr. Bryan in the last three weeks shows most strikingly that the condition I feared is making headway.... The steady and intense dwelling upon one idea, combined with the unremitting and arduous articulation of it leads necessarily to a second stage of mattoidism." Tragically, "Bryan has become, in a certain alienistic sense, self-hypnotized by the imagined luminousness of his own Ego."[48]

"The campaign is simply disgusting," Edwin L. Godkin, editor of the *Nation*, remarked to a friend. "We shall win, but what a victory!"[49] Many papers resolved to exercise their privilege not merely to demonize Bryan but to refuse any right of reply. This was justified as being, objectively, in the public interest. As the *Hartford Courant* noted, "We have had a letter from a local disciple of Mr. Bryan.... We have two reasons for not printing this communication. One is that we can put the space it would occupy to much better use, and the other is that The Courant is not published for the purposes of diffusing Populistic campaign literature. We keep our readers sufficiently well informed as to Mr. Bryan's sayings and doings; that's news. We draw the line at expository commentaries on the Bryan prophecies by Hartford disciples."

In a similar vein, the *New York Evening Post* justified its policy of publishing material entirely and exclusively of a nature inimical to the electoral prospects of Bryan on the grounds that "we print this paper for the purpose of disseminating our own views and, as a rule, not of disseminating the views of people who differ from us." In expanding upon its position the paper explained:

> [I]t is the duty of every editor or publisher not to print what he conscientiously believes will do harm.... [I]t is the business of an editor to keep a strict watch on his columns, and let nothing in which he thinks will work mischief, either social or political. This is his first and great duty. The duty of promoting 'free speech and free thought' is quite secondary to it. Free speech and free thought have on various occasions in the history of the world done great harm. Therefore both speech and thought have to be more than 'free' to entitle them to promotion or circulation at the hands of a decent citizen. They have to be rational, moral, and well-expressed, and in his eyes more likely to promote the general good than the general injury.

"To sum up, the reason why we are not willing freely to admit Bryanites to our columns is that we believe their platform to be from top to bottom irrational, immoral, and anarchistic," the *Evening Post* concluded. "We hold that it would be morally wrong of us to allow either cunning or silly people to spread this story among the ignorant and the thoughtless through our columns."[50] The newspapers, by acting as the gatekeepers of what was, objectively, rational, moral, and legal, thereby served an intensely partisan role throughout the campaign.

The snobbery and chauvinism of the Northeastern media during its war against Bryan raised hackles throughout the South and West. "The New York papers give a great deal of reading matter and very brilliant colored supplements, but they fail in one important essential of newspapers—they don't give the news," the *New Orleans Times-Democrat* groused. Throughout the campaign, "they have twisted and distorted the news in a most remarkable manner, and have fed their readers on the most absurd stories until it seemed impossible for them to know the truth when they saw it."[51] Although the partisan affiliations have reversed, the same constituencies maintain identical perspectives today.

Rejected by business, the clergy, and the incumbent president of his own party, as well as the media, Bryan went down to defeat fighting. Cut off from the people by the intervening firewall of the hostile press, Bryan did something unprecedented for a presidential contender; he hit the road, intending to personally introduce himself and his message to as many voters as possible. The spectacle of a candidate for the nation's highest office soliciting votes on his own behalf gave the elite media just one more reason to heap opprobrium upon the Nebraskan. "God save the country from such stupidity, from such everlasting shame, from such an insufferable spectacle," as Bryan in the White House, snapped the *Cleveland Leader*. "But Bryan with all of his cheap demagoguery, his intolerable gabble, his utter lack of common sense, and his general incapacity in every direction, is a typical Democrat of the new

No 2

Three-time presidential aspirant William Jennings Bryan is here depicted in a characteristic campaign pose. Prior to his nomination, the expectation was that a contender for the presidency remained above the fray and campaigned through surrogates. Bryan was confronted by such a barrage of concentrated media opposition in 1896 that he had no other option but to disregard over a century of tradition and actively seek the office on his own behalf. His bid to bypass the media and personally appeal directly to the voters failed, but it set the pattern for ensuing campaigns dominated by radio, television, and the Internet (courtesy of Library of Congress).

school. His weapon is wind. His stock in trade is his mouth."[52] It was true that Bryan's chief asset was his powerful oratory. But if he was to have any chance at getting his message across, he had no choice but to break with tradition. It was all very well for the Republican candidate to run an old-school campaign, meeting with delegations on the front porch at his home in Canton, Ohio. Bryan had to force the newsmen to follow his campaign and quote his words. He had to make news. In this way the inveterate bias on the part of the media spurred the development of the modern presidential campaign. "It used to be the newspapers educated the people," Bryan told a crowd in Des Moines; "but now the people educate the newspapers."[53]

It wasn't to be. In 1896 the received wisdom was that the press retained the power to make presidents, and "never was that power more forcibly illustrated," the *Washington Star* observed in the aftermath of Bryan's defeat. "In Boston, New York, Brooklyn, Philadelphia, Baltimore, Chicago, and Louisville, where the Democratic newspapers repudiated the Chicago ticket and platform and allied themselves with their Republican and independent contemporaries for sound money, Democratic majorities were wiped out, and all of those cities were gathered into the sound-money fold. It is the brightest chapter in the history of the American press, and it will never be surpassed."[54]

The McKinley press struggled to find the appropriately profound terms in which to express the profundity of its relief and satisfaction at the result. "The country has spoken. It has given answer to those who discredited its patriotism and honor. It has swept into an abyss that is bottomless and whence nothing can emerge the weird, grotesque and menacing elements that threatened it," the *Alameda Daily Argus* concluded, "all the dark forms that threatened the land from behind the mask of free silver have been dispersed and dispelled."[55] "The people have stood by the commandment 'Thou shalt not steal,' which a desperate coalition of cranks and crooks has been endeavoring to repeal," the *Chicago Tribune* rhymed with evident pleasure.[56]

The post-election wrap-up of the *New York Tribune* represents, in my opinion, the defining example of the extreme partiality, the absolute absence of objectivity, and, in a word, the all-consuming partisan bias, endemic not merely in this one campaign but in the great preponderance of the history of American journalism. The editorial, titled simply "GOOD RIDDANCE," reads in full:

There are some movements so base, some causes so depraved, that neither victory can justify them nor defeat entitle them to commiseration. Such a cause was that which was vanquished yesterday, by the favor of God and the ballots of the American people.

  While it was active and menacing, it was unsparingly denounced and revealed as what it was, in all its monstrous deformity. Now that it is crushed out of the very semblance of being, there is no reason why such judgment of it should be revised. The thing was conceived in iniquity and born in sin. It had its origin in a malicious conspiracy against the honor and integrity of the nation. It gained such monstrous growth as it enjoyed from an assiduous culture of the basest passions of the least worthy members of the community. It has been defeated and destroyed because right is right and God is God.

  Its nominal head was worthy of the cause. Nominal, because the wretched, rattle-pated boy, posing in vapid vanity and mouthing resounding rottenness was not the real leader of that league of hell. He was only a puppet of the blood-imbrued hands of Altgeld, the anarchist, and Debs, the revolutionist, and other desperadoes of that stripe. But he was a willing puppet, Bryan was, willing and eager. Not one of his masters was more apt than he at lies and forgeries and blasphemies, and all the nameless iniquities of that campaign against the Ten Commandments. He goes down with the cause and must abide with it in the history of infamy. He had less provocation than Benedict Arnold, less intellectual force than Aaron Burr, less manliness and courage than Jefferson Davis. He was the rival of them all in deliberate wickedness and treason to the Republic. His name belongs with theirs, neither the most brilliant nor the least hateful on the list.

Good riddance to it all, to conspiracy and conspirators, and to the foul menace of repudiation and anarchy against the honor and life of the Republic. The people have dismissed it with no uncertain tones. Hereafter let there be whatever controversies men may please about the tariff, about the currency, about the Monroe Doctrine, and all the rest. But let there never again be a proposition to repeal the moral law, to garble the Constitution, and to replace the Stars and Stripes with the red rag of anarchy. On those and other topics honest men may honestly differ, in full loyalty to the Republic. On these latter there is no room for two opinions, save in the minds of traitors, knaves, and fools.[57]

The conjunction of pecuniary self-interest, partisan attachment, and the prevailing interpretation of the framework of objectivity had mobilized a formidable array of media opposition against Bryan. Having passed through such a maelstrom he could do little but be philosophical. "With all the newspapers of the country against us, our 6,500,000 votes is a vindication of which we have a right to be proud," he remarked after the fight was over.

Citizen Hearst

The campaign of 1896 marked the national debut of perhaps the greatest in the pantheon of press barons. In 1880, mining magnate George Hearst, a member of the lower house of the California legislature, took control of the *San Francisco Daily Examiner* as payment of a gambling debt, in order to foster his political career. Although he ultimately lost a quarter of a million dollars on the paper, it served its primary purpose, for George Hearst rose to the U.S. Senate in 1887. The *Examiner* also fulfilled another role that same year — enabling twenty-three-year-old William Randolph Hearst to cut his teeth in the journalistic trade when his father bequeathed control of the paper to him.

Ever the non-conformist, Hearst, a Democrat at staunchly Republican Harvard, raised such an all-night ruckus when Grover Cleveland was elected that he was suspended from the school.[58] His business model boiled down to one basic rule: spend money to make money. He made a clear signal of his intentions when he personally committed $80,000 in a bid to bring the 1888 Democratic convention to San Francisco.[59] That effort established what would be a recurring pattern throughout the ensuing six decades for Hearst where politics was concerned: ambition, extravagance, and failure.

In 1895, Hearst acquired the New York *Morning Journal.* Immediately after Bryan made his "Cross of Gold" speech, Hearst emissary Willis J. Abbot seized the attention of "the Commoner" (as Bryan was known) and the two men held an impromptu conference in a bathroom adjacent to the convention hall. Abbot confessed that while Hearst had up to this point opposed free silver, he was intent on boosting the *Journal* and saw the opportunity presented by being the only Democratic paper in the nation's largest city as too good to pass up. Bryan immediately signed on to the idea and, over the din outside, helped Abbot draft a comprehensive telegram to Hearst.[60] During the campaign the *Journal* proceeded to depict McKinley as "bound hand, foot and tongue to the most corrupt combination that ever exhibited itself openly in an American presidential campaign." Bryan so appreciated Hearst's efforts on his behalf that the day before the election he wrote the *Journal* a telegram that read, "The *Journal* deserves great credit for its splendid fight in behalf of bimetallism and popular government. Its influence has been felt in the West as well as in the East."[61]

Hearst's next project was to engineer a war against Spain in order to liberate Cuba. In the process, the brash young upstart challenged Joseph Pulitzer for the dominant share of

America's biggest media market, New York. He did so by taking sensationalist journalism to its logical, tabloid conclusion. The result was an ever more hysterical rivalry between the *Journal* and the *World* in their coverage of the Cuban insurrection against Spain. It was an age of Yellow Journalism, named after the *Journal's* cartoon character the Yellow Kid. In 1898, in large part due to the public opinion he had done so much to shape, Hearst got what he wanted. "How do you like the *Journal's* War?" Hearst's mouthpiece crowed on its masthead.[62] Hearst and Pulitzer immediately grappled to assert their ownership of this great crusade, in battles fought daily with screaming headlines and pulsating panegyrics dedicated to the crusade's heroes. "Each claimed the conflict as his own personal property," George Creel wrote, and "rivalry reached the stage of utter madness."[63] According to Joseph E. Wisan, "The Spanish-American War would not have occurred had not the appearance of Hearst in New York journalism precipitated a bitter battle for newspaper circulation."[64]

"The newspapers of your country seem to be more powerful than the government," Spanish Prime Minister Canovas del Castillo ruefully remarked. The demonstrated ability of the Lord of San Simeon to not merely report on but to shape current affairs worried many com-

William Randolph Hearst parlayed his father's money into a career in journalism after being evicted from Harvard, acquiring his first newspaper in 1887. By the time he died in 1951 he had established the template for the multi-market, multimedia news baron who manipulated his infotainment empire in a bid to shape the national debate. His business savvy was not matched by his political acumen, and in his twilight years the Lord of San Simeon was left brooding over a long sequence of misfires and near misses in his quest for public office (courtesy of Library of Congress).

mentators. "A blackguard boy with several millions of dollars at his disposal," lamented *Nation* editor Edwin L. Godkin, "has more influence on the use a great nation may make of its credit, of its army and navy, of its name and traditions, than all the statesmen and philosophers in the country."[65] Hearst felt the same way about it, without any of the reservations. In an editorial published after the Spanish capitulation he wrote:

> The newspaper is the greatest force in civilization.
> Under republican government, newspapers form and express public opinion.
> They suggest and control legislation.
> They declare wars....
> The newspapers control the nation.

In the spring of 1900, Hearst engineered his own election as president of the National Association of Democratic Clubs, which under his leadership grew to more than three million members. He won the position after agreeing to open a newspaper in Chicago at the request of Democratic chairman James K. Jones. On July 4, the first edition of *Hearst's Chicago American* was published to greet the opening of the Democratic National Convention in Kansas City, after William Jennings Bryan himself wired the publisher, "Start the presses."

"The fact that your newspaper was established not merely to make money, but because of your desire to aid the Democratic leaders that you should duplicate in Chicago the splendid work done by the *Journal* and the *Examiner* in '96 ought to commend the paper to the friends of democracy," Bryan told Hearst. "And I am confident that a large circulation awaits the Chicago *American*."[66] Old guard Democrats on the party's national committee were so concerned about Hearst's influence that they rejected New York and Chicago as convention sites in 1904, out of fear that his newspapers in those cities could sway delegates. When St. Louis landed the convention the national, committee reserved the right to change the site if Hearst should launch a newspaper there.

At this time, Hearst's guns were still trained squarely on the Republican Party, which responded in kind. Theodore Roosevelt once publicly rebuked Hearst for "reckless utterances" which "appeal to the dark and evil spirits of malice and greed, envy and sullen hatred."[67] In print, Roosevelt was even more acerbic: "He preaches the gospel of envy, hatred, and unrest. His actions so far go to show that he is entirely willing to sanction any mob violence if he thinks that for the moment votes are to be gained by doing so." In sum, Hearst "is the most potent single influence for evil we have in our life."[68]

Hearst's own electoral history was a string of embarrassments, near-misses and disasters. His success in 1902 at being elected to the first of two terms in Congress from a safe Democratic seat in New York marked the highpoint of his political career. After finishing runner-up for the presidential nomination at the Democratic National Convention of 1904, he threw himself into a third-party bid for the New York mayoralty the following year, losing by an almost certainly illegally padded margin of 3,471 votes to the Democratic candidate. In 1906, this time running for governor, Hearst was the only member of the Democratic state ticket to lose. Hearst lost another third-party tilt for the mayoralty in 1909 and was subsequently rejected by the Democratic Party in his bids for a Senate nomination in 1914, the mayoral nomination in 1917, the governor's mansion in 1918, and a gubernatorial or Senate nomination in 1922. The sting of repudiation would add bitterness to Hearst's increasingly conservative political outlook. By the time another Roosevelt began to consider a presidential bid, Hearst was far from the friend to the Democratic Party that he had been thirty years earlier.

The assassination of McKinley in early 1901 elevated Theodore Roosevelt, that "damn cowboy," to the presidency. More than a changing of the guard was in play here. Roosevelt combined a larger-then-life personality with a new approach to public relations that made him the first media president. "One of the keys to the Roosevelt years was that for the first time in American history reporters became part of the White House operation," George Juergens says.[69] The quickening pace of the relationship between the press corps and the White House was not lost on the president's political opponents. "I say to you in all seriousness," Ben Tillman declared in the Senate on January 17, 1906, "that Theodore Roosevelt owes more of his success as a public man to the newspaper men of this country than any other one instrumentality.... The news is colored and sifted to suit his idea of what ought to be to maintain the great popularity which he has won, to preserve in the public imagination of the people the hold he has on them."[70]

Bryan, running on silver and anti-imperialism, had lost again in his 1900 rematch with McKinley, both in the electoral college and, by a much wider margin, in the nation's press.

"Janus-faced trickster," "quack nostrum doctor," "fake prophet," "safe-breaker," "blatant demagogue," and "apostle of sedition and class hatred" were just some of the choice epithets used to label Bryan in the Republican newspapers, which in many locales were the only newspapers. In Philadelphia, out of forty-two daily and weekly publications, not one endorsed the Democratic ticket.[71] In 1904 the Democrats turned to a conservative, sound-money candidate, Judge Alton B. Parker. The party was much more competitive in the media stakes—in metropolitan New York alone the *Times*, *Herald*, *World*, *Evening Post*, and *Brooklyn Eagle*, all backers of McKinley four years previously, switched to Parker.[72] But this support could not mitigate Parker's landslide defeat to Roosevelt, and its transitory nature would be painfully evident four years later. Even in Bryan's last campaign in 1908, "Democratic papers were as scarce as pearls on an Eastern seashore," Louis W. Koenig writes, and Republican papers were still unforgiving. "For Mr. Bryan, this is annihilation," the *New York Times* summed up after the Commoner's third consecutive loss, "and in his case the crushing defeat of ambition evokes not one spark of pity."[73]

The exception to the rule was the *New York World*, which had been responsible for the only drama of the 1904 campaign with its October surprise allegations that leading industrial trusts were buying immunity from persecution during a second Roosevelt term, with major contributions to his campaign fund. Four years later the *World* again sought to land a last-minute bombshell, this time with a serialized investigative report on bribery and blackmail in the shadowy struggle for control of the Panama Canal. The *World* was not afraid to name names, including Roosevelt's brother-in-law and the brother of the president's anointed successor, GOP candidate William Howard Taft.

Among the anti–Roosevelt papers running the allegations was the *Indianapolis News*, which was secretly owned by Vice President Charles W. Fairbanks, who bitterly resented being passed over for his party's nomination and was doing everything in his power to sabotage Taft's campaign.[74] The Republican candidate barely held Indiana, by less than 11,000 votes, while the party lost the governorship, a senate seat, and twelve out of fifteen congressional races, a string of misfortunes it laid at the door of the *News*. Roosevelt agreed, publicly lashing out on December 7 at what he called "the potent forces for evil in the community." The *World* replied in a sixteen-hundred word editorial the following day, taking full responsibility for the Panama Canal allegations and raising the stakes by directly accusing the president of lying about the particulars of the matter, and calling for a Congressional investigation.

Roosevelt responded by sending a message to the U.S. attorney for New York saying, "I do not know anything about the law of criminal libel, but I should dearly like to have it invoked against Pulitzer of the World.... Pulitzer is one of those creatures of the gutter of such unspeakable degradation that to him even eminence on a dunghill seems enviable.... If he can be reached by a proceeding on the part of the Government for criminal libel in connection with his assertions about the Panama Canal, I should like to do it."

Not waiting for a reply, Roosevelt sent a special message to Congress on December 15, contending, shades of the Federalist Sedition Act, that unjust criticism of government leaders demeaned the nation in the eyes of the world and therefore represented a crime against the state: "In point of encouragement of iniquity, in point of infamy, of wrongdoing, there is nothing to choose between a public servant who betrays his trust ... and a man guilty as Mr. Joseph Pulitzer has been in this instance.... It is therefore a high National duty to bring to justice this vilifier of the American people, this man who wantonly and wickedly ... seeks to ... convict the Government of his own country in the eyes of the civilized world of wrongdoing of the basest and foulest kind."

Pulitzer accepted the challenge, and immediately dictated his reply:

Mr. Roosevelt's attack on the World can be explained only on the theory that he believes he can muzzle the paper, and our recent impeachment of his veracity seems to be the straw that broke his autocratic back.... [W]e do not intend to be intimidated by Mr. Roosevelt's threats, or by Mr. Roosevelt's denunciations, or by Mr. Roosevelt's power....

So far as the World is concerned its proprietor may go to jail ... but even in jail The World will not cease to be a fearless champion of free speech, a free press and a free people.

It cannot be muzzled.[75]

In choosing to make its stand, the *World* was forced to endure immense pressure from the federal government, both overt and underhanded. While the paper fought a series of legal holding actions in the courts, according to Don Seitz, Pulitzer's business manager, "the Administration placed an extraordinary number of secret agents upon the *World's* trail. Its mail was opened in the post office; the portfolios of its messengers between New York and Washington were examined and the Pulitzer Building itself filled with spies."[76]

The conflict dragged on through the lower courts until finally, on January 3, 1911, nearly two years after Roosevelt had left office, the Supreme Court unanimously upheld the New York decision that if Roosevelt or any other plaintiffs wanted to sue for libel they would have to do so the same way as everyone else, as private citizens through the state courts. According to Juergens, "Pulitzer had won a famous victory, one which for all his other achievements belongs among his greatest contributions to American journalism."[77] Pulitzer's partisan motives were never forgiven by the Republican establishment, perhaps to their political disadvantage. A conversation between President William Howard Taft and his wife one morning in 1911 provides an instructive glimpse into the president's political limitations. Taft refused to accept a copy of the *World* from the first lady. "I have stopped reading it. It only makes me angry," the President explained. "But you used to like it very much," Mrs. Taft replied. "That was when it agreed with me, but it abuses me now and I don't want it," the President snapped. "You will never know what the other side is doing if you only read the *Sun* and the *Tribune*," Mrs. Taft insisted. "I don't care what the other side is thinking," The President declared, bringing the conversation to an end.[78]

The more typical editorial line of the day was maintained by the *Los Angeles Times*, launched by the archreactionary Harrison Gray Otis and kept on the same conservative keel by his son-in-law and successor Harry Chandler. "The *Times* was not an organ of the Republican Party of Southern California," says David Halberstam, "it *was* the Republican Party.... [I]f anything the Republican Party was an organ of the *Times*."[79] "To win the endorsement of Harrison Gray Otis, a political candidate needed to have two qualifications," Gottlieb and Wolt note: "he had to be against organized labor, and he had to be a Republican."[80] In time, the candidate had to prove he was the right kind of Republican. The GOP in California during the early years of the 20th century was split into progressive and conservative wings and the *Los Angeles Times* was irrevocably wedded to the latter faction. "Through the use of the Times and the initiation of powerful 'employer unions,' Otis led the businessmen of the city, and his newspaper became their ideological spokesman," Gottlieb and Wolt conclude.[81]

Understandably, this contributed to what could charitably be described as friction between Otis and the progressive Republicans. Running for Governor in 1910, San Francisco Assistant District Attorney and self-styled "Lincoln-Roosevelt" Republican Hiram Johnson was speaking in Los Angeles when someone in the audience shouted out, "What about Otis?" Johnson, warming up, replied, "In the city of San Francisco we have drunk to the very dregs of infamy; we have had vile officials, we have had rotten newspapers." Then he got to the point: "But we have nothing so vile, nothing so low, nothing so debased, nothing so infamous in San Francisco as Harrison Gray Otis. He sits there in senile dementia with gangrene heart and rotting brain, grimacing at every reform, chattering impotently at all things that are decent, frothing, fuming, violently gibbering, going down to his grave in snarling infamy. He is the one thing that all Californians look at when, in looking at Southern California, they see anything that is disgraceful, depraved, corrupt, crooked, and putrescent — that is Harrison Gray Otis."[82]

Otis responded by headlining that Johnson was as "QUALIFIED AS [A] CIRCUS CLOWN" for office.[83] Reliably in lockstep with the GOP presidential nominee every four years, the editor faced his greatest crisis in 1912. Otis was devoted to incumbent Republican president William Howard Taft, on a personal as well as political level. The two exchanged gifts, and Otis had been appointed by Taft in 1910 to a three-man commission representing the U.S. at the Mexican independence centennial celebration. But Taft was under siege by his predecessor and former patron Theodore Roosevelt, who wanted his old job back and was prepared to challenge his former protégé to get it. Otis laced into Roosevelt, labeling him "Teddy the terrible" and a "subordinate devil in the lower regions, a cleaner of cuspidors in Tophet," but couldn't stop him sweeping the California GOP primary.

After Roosevelt was defeated at the Republican convention, his supporters bolted the party and launched the "Bull Moose" Progressive alternative, selecting none other than California governor Hiram Johnson as Roosevelt's running mate. The *Times*, livid at their defection, described them as "coiling and hissing and seething with the virus of anarchy."

"The movement that you head," an editorial addressed to the Bull Moose leaders declaimed, "is overripe, it is overrotten. The garbage barrel is the proper place for it." Every day, the *Times* printed the same words, entitled "Attitude of this Journal," on its editorial page:

> FOR THE COUNTRY AND THE FLAG
> FOR THE CONSTITUTION AND THE COURTS
> FOR UPHOLDING THE HONOUR OF THE ARMY AND NAVY
> FOR ORDERLY LIBERTY UNDER LAW
> FOR AN OCEAN-TO-OCEAN HIGHWAY;
> FOR TRUE FREEDOM IN THE INDUSTRIES
> FOR UNSHACKLED LABOR, NATION WIDE
> FOR PRESIDENT TAFT
>
> AND AGAINST HIS ALLIED ANTAGONISTS
> AGAINST POLITICAL FADS, FREAKS AND FRENZY
> AGAINST THE BIG NOISE AND THE BIG STICK
> AGAINST THE NEW FANGLED JUDICIAL RECALL
> AGAINST FREE TRADE AND FREE SOUP
> AGAINST UNION CONSPIRACY AND MISRULE
> AGAINST THE UN-AMERICAN CLOSED SHOP

Holding the Progressives responsible for Taft's defeat, Otis never forgave them, particularly Roosevelt's running mate Hiram Johnson. When the GOP undertook the delicate task of reaching accommodation between the loyalists and insurgents in order to fight the 1916 campaign on a common platform, the *Times* sniffed, "Whenever a crook ... or any member of the Johnson plunderbund shall make an appearance at a Republican Club banquet, let us receive him courteously, welcome him warmly, and tell the steward to keep an eye on the silverware."[84]

Predictably, Otis blamed Johnson for the narrow loss in California by the Republican candidate that year, Charles Evan Hughes, thereby enabling the reelection of Woodrow Wilson by the narrowest of margins. According to the *Times*, "there was undoubtedly a treasonable combine in northern California between Johnson and Wilson supporters.... [T]he words Benedict Arnold are today being coupled with Governor Johnson's name."[85]

Ivy League

Media politics in the Democratic Party were equally fragmented. Navigating the danger-ous waters of editorial opinion represented not the least of the challenges faced by presiden-tial aspirants, as the primary system increasingly dominated the selection of delegates and hence the floor of the convention. One of the first contenders to emerge victorious from this process, Woodrow Wilson, was in a crucial respect a media candidate. He had a powerful friend, George Harvey, the president of Harper and Brothers, publishers of Wilson's books (such as *A History of the American People*), owner and editor of the *North American Review*, and editor of *Harper's*. Harvey had had his eye on Wilson ever since attending his inaugura-tion as president of Princeton University in 1902. It was Harvey who proposed Wilson for president of the United States at a dinner meeting of the Lotos Club in Manhattan on the eve-ning of February 3, 1906, who featured the Princetonian on the cover of his magazine later that year, and who pushed for Wilson to be chosen by the New Jersey legislature for the U.S. Senate. Wilson turned down the honor but Harvey was undeterred.[86] In the wake of Bryan's third defeat, on May 15, 1909, the lead editorial in *Harper's* stated, "We now expect to see Woodrow Wilson elected Governor of the State of New Jersey in 1910 and nominated for Pres-ident in 1912 upon a platform demanding tariff revision downward."[87] Within the faction-riddled Democratic Party, this overt support from the conservative wing came at a price. On July 7, 1909, Hearst's *New York American* ran a front page article headlined "WALL ST. TO PUT UP WILSON FOR PRESIDENT."[88]

After cutting his journalistic teeth at the *Springfield Republican*, Harvey had joined the *New York World* in 1885 as Pulitzer's man in the Garden State, where he joined the governor's staff and by 1890 had been appointed insurance commissioner. So he knew New Jersey poli-tics, and he knew who the power brokers were. In January 1910, over lunch at Delmonico's restaurant in New York with the boss of the party in the state, former Senator James Smith Jr., who had sent three sons to Princeton, Harvey broached the idea of running Wilson as the Democratic candidate for governor of New Jersey. After some consideration, Smith warmed to the idea. Wilson would make a good figurehead at the top of the ticket. He could facili-tate a Democratic takeover of the state legislature, smoothing Smith's return to the Senate and enabling him to take his kingmaker skills to the national level at the 1912 national convention.

Harvey took the proposal to Wilson and told him: "If I can handle the matter so that the nomination for Governor can be tendered to you on a silver platter without you turning a hand to obtain it, and without any requirement or suggestion of any pledge whatsoever, what do you think would be your attitude?" Wilson paced the carpet in his study, deep in thought. Then he replied: "If the nomination for Governor should come to me in that way, I should regard it as my duty to give the matter very serious consideration."[89]

Wilson gave his final go-ahead after meeting with Harvey, Smith and Henry Watterson of the *Louisville Courier-Journal* at Harvey's fine summer home on the Jersey shore one Sun-day evening late in June 1910. In the great swing toward progressive reform and the Democ-ratic Party that year, Wilson was elected governor in the fall and carried a Democratic majority into the legislature. Ironically, Wilson in office proved to be no mere mouthpiece for the machines. He turned on Smith, denying him the Senate nomination he so desired, and pushed through a number of progressive measures that won him a reputation for reform.

Wilson's electoral success immediately elevated him to presidential caliber. "I congratu-late you and your state and our republic upon your splendid victory," Joseph Pulitzer wrote in the wake of Wilson's victory, "and I must thank you warmly for the intellectual delight your great speeches have given me."[90] Pulitzer took Wilson's presidential ambitions under his wing, taking steps to "present Dr. Wilson's Presidential possibilities to the press and to the country." "As to the Presidency," he told his editors, "build up Wilson on every suitable occasion showing the greatest possible sympathy for and appreciation of his remarkable talents and character."[91]

Unsolicited offers of support from around the country began pouring in to Trenton. "We don't even know that you would like to be president," George D. Armistead of the *San Antonio Daily Express* wrote to Wilson. "We are going to elect you anyway. All we ask is you keep the course that you seem to have marked out."[92] Other early editorial converts in the South included the *Raleigh News and Observer*, owned and edited since 1894 by Josephus Daniels (who would serve as Wilson's secretary of the navy after he took office), and in Atlanta, the *Journal* and the *Georgian*.

However, the reform course Wilson had set meant breaking with his original boosters. Harvey had blazoned "For President: Woodrow Wilson" at the masthead of the editorial page of *Harper's* on November 11, 1911. But after Wilson repudiated his backing, anxious to disabuse any notion on the part of western progressive Democrats that he was the candidate of the eastern conservative wing, Harvey turned on him.[93] So did Henry Watterson who never forgot nor forgave Wilson's apostasy. "Beneath the veneering of scholarly polish," the editor warned, "lay the coiled serpent of unscrupulous ambition."[94]

At the same time, Wilson made a powerful enemy by spurning the overtures of William Randolph Hearst, and doing so in no uncertain terms: "Tell Mr. Hearst to go to hell," the Governor remarked. "God knows I want the Democratic nomination, and I am going to do everything legitimately to get it, but if I am to grovel at Hearst's feet, I will never have it."[95] Hearst's subsequent campaign against Wilson, according to Startt, represented "a brutal, prolonged, and personalized assault. It was, in fact, a comprehensive, nationwide press offensive that lasted through the spring and one that played an important role in dethroning Wilson as the frontrunner for the nomination."[96] To block Wilson, Hearst settled on the governor's chief rival for the nomination, House Speaker Champ Clark. Hearst began his Clark boost late in 1911 when he had Alfred Henry Lewis write a laudatory article about the "Honorable Champ" in *Cosmopolitan Magazine*.

Matters worsened when Oscar Underwood announced his candidacy for the nomination in February 1912. Wilson's position in the South was severely weakened, as such papers as the *Birmingham Age-Herald*, the *Birmingham News*, the *Mobile Register* and the *Montgomery Times* all switched from Wilson to their favorite son. Other papers to forsake Wilson for Underwood throughout Dixie included the *Atlanta Constitution*, the *Florida Times-Union*, and the *Memphis Commercial Appeal*.[97]

In addition, Hearst stole the *Atlanta Georgian* from Wilson's corner by purchasing it and sending lieutenant John Temple Graves south to edit it. He then bought out the *World To-Day*, renaming it *Hearst's Magazine*, and put one of his premier writers, Alfred Henry Lewis, in charge. Lewis delivered a ten-page diatribe at Wilson's expense in the May issue. On March 14, 1912, Hearst released a long statement explaining why he opposed "Professor" Wilson's nomination. After describing the governor as a Federalist, a Tory, and a modern Judas, Hearst concluded, "He is a perfect jackrabbit of politics, perched upon his little hillock of expediency, with ears erect and nostrils distended, keenly alert to every scent or sound and ready to run and double in any direction on the slightest intimation of danger."[98]

Wilson attempted to fight back by making Hearst himself a campaign issue. "William Randolph Hearst has 'decided' I am not to be nominated," Wilson declared at one whistle stop. "What an exhibition of audacity. What a contempt he must feel for the judgment and integrity of the American people."[99] But it was apparently all to no avail. Wilson's campaign foundered on the rock of the Hearst-Clark alliance in the Illinois primary on April 9, 1912. "I am profoundly grateful to all who aided in carrying Illinois for me," Clark telegraphed the *New York American*. "Among them was the powerful influence of the Hearst newspapers, which have stood by me loyally, manfully, and unselfishly from the beginning from Massachusetts to California."[100]

An important Wilson ally was Edward W. Scripps, whose media empire ("the concern," as he called it) in 1912 consisted of thirty-two newspapers in sixteen states, mainly small city publications in the West and South; the Newspaper Enterprise Association, a national newspaper feature service; and the United Press Association. H. N. Rickey, editor in chief of the Scripps papers in Ohio, was committed to "do everything possible to encourage the candidacy of Woodrow Wilson."[101] W. P. Porterfield, editor in chief of the Scripps papers in California, told his boss, "We are going up and down the line for Woodrow Wilson," but he had to admit, "My chief reason for desiring the success of the Wilson ticket, is to defeat Hearst's professed attempt to deliver the California delegation to Clark."[102]

Also on Wilson's side heading into the convention in Baltimore were such magazines as the *World's Work*, *Outlook* (which would back Roosevelt in the general election), the *Independent*, the *Nation*, *Collier's*, and the *Review of Reviews*, and such newspapers as the New York *World*, *Times*, and *Evening Post*; the *Philadelphia Record*, the *Chicago Daily News*, the *Cleveland Plain Dealer*, the *Kansas City Star*, the *Raleigh News and Observer*, and the local *Baltimore Sun*.[103] Wilson's managers made a point of noting "the splendid support which his candidacy is receiving on the eve of the convention from the independent press of the country, without which no Democratic nominee can win."[104]

It was the local paper which was to prove most influential, possibly even decisive in Wilson's nomination. When the *Baltimore Sun* issued a firm editorial endorsement of Wilson, headlined "Name the Strongest Candidate!" on July 1, Wilson was moved to write Charles Grasty, president of Sunpapers, "I need not tell you how deeply I am gratified by the editorial. It is as extraordinary as it is reassuring to receive such support as I am receiving from newspapers of the country and newspaper editors in whose integrity we all believe."[105]

According to Startt, Wilson had more cause to be grateful to Grasty than he knew. Grasty had visited Bryan at his hotel early in the convention to let him know that the *Sun* would soon make its sup-

The career of Woodrow Wilson can be interpreted as one instance after another of failing upwards, from Princeton to Trenton to the White House. Playing the media game was a vital component in taking that last step (courtesy of Library of Congress).

port of Wilson "more pronounced." Grasty urged Bryan to do the same. A few days later, on Sunday, June 30, while the exhausted delegates were in recess, Bryan telephoned Grasty. Would he care to drive Mr. and Mrs. Bryan out into the Maryland countryside? Soon the three were enjoying a ride through Green Spring Valley north of the city. Returning via Falls Road, Grasty invited the Bryans for supper at his home, an offer that was readily accepted. Following the meal, the men fell into a lengthy conversation about the convention, and about Wilson's candidacy in particular. Bryan still expressed doubts about the New Jersey governor, but Grasty reassured him that "on the question of Wall Street taint Wilson was letter perfect." Grasty also helped swing the allegiance of Senator Clarence W. Watson of West Virginia, originally an opponent of Wilson, whose influence extended to the Virginia and Kentucky delegations. Given the fluid nature of convention politics, Grasty's efforts may have been enough to tip the balance towards Wilson on the 46th ballot and secure him the majority he needed for the nomination.[106]

Once Wilson had emerged from the Democratic convention as the party's presidential nominee, additional major papers lining up behind his candidacy included the *Springfield Republican*; the *Globe* and the *Herald* in Boston; the *Newark Evening News*; the *Philadelphia Public Ledger*; the *Pittsburgh Post*; the *Cincinnati Enquirer*; the *Milwaukee Journal*; the *Madison State Journal*; the *Globe-Democrat*, *Post-Dispatch*, and the *Republic* in St. Louis; the *Detroit Free Press*; the *Oklahoma City Daily Oklahoman*; the *Denver Rocky Mountain News*; the *Sacramento Union*; and all the leading southern newspapers.[107]

There were some major shakeouts to come, however, as a three-cornered fight emerged during the campaign. The biggest defection from the Democratic ticket was the Scripps chain. After the Bull Moose convention nominated Roosevelt, Scripps began writing his editors, urging them to support the entire Progressive ticket. While Scripps had not changed his view that Wilson stood for a great deal "of what we stand for," the problem was his party "was even more detestable than ... Taft's party."[108] After being informed of Roosevelt's conduct after surviving an assassination attempt, Scripps telephoned his son James with instructions as to how "the concern" should proceed. James then telegraphed all the Scripps editors: "ON HEARING OF ROOSEVELTS ATTEMPTED ASSASSINATION E.W. SCRIPPS STATED THAT ROOSEVELT'S SPEECH AFTER HE WAS SHOT PROVES NOT ONLY HIS COURAGE AND SINCERITY BUT HIS TRUSTWORTHINESS. THAT A MAN CANNOT LIE FACING DEATH.... SINCE OUR LAST DOUBT HAS BEEN REMOVED A MUCH MORE FRIENDLY ATTITUDE TOWARDS ROOSEVELT IS ADVISED."[109]

One of the Roosevelt's most loyal and influential allies during his Bull Moose campaign was Frank Munsey, publisher of *Munsey's Magazine* and a chain of newspapers in Boston, Philadelphia, Baltimore and Washington, D.C. Whatever interest Munsey may have taken in the Democratic nominee evaporated after Robert Davis, his confidant and the longtime editor of his magazines, described Wilson as "the human anti-climax" in a letter to the publisher.[110] Not only was Munsey's *Boston Journal* the only Roosevelt paper in Boston, in September the publisher bought out the *New York Press* for a reported $1 million to provide Roosevelt with a voice in that city.[111]

In addition to *Munsey's*, other magazines for Roosevelt included the *Outlook* (which had supported Wilson for the Democratic nomination), the *Saturday Evening Post*, and the *American Review of Reviews*, which was edited by Albert Shaw, an old friend of Wilson's. The Bull Moose candidate picked up another major editorial ally in the middle of October when Robert Collier forced his pro–Wilson editor Norman Hapgood to resign, and personally took over management of *Collier's* magazine, converting it into a pro–Roosevelt publication — a move Wilson decried as "nothing less than a national calamity."[112]

Roosevelt's apostasy precipitated a crisis for Republican editors across the nation. Those remaining loyal to Taft included the *Boston Evening Transcript*, the *New York Tribune*, the *St. Louis Globe-Democrat*, the *San Francisco Chronicle*, and of course the *Los Angeles Times*, in addition to national magazines the *Forum*, *Leslie's Weekly*, and the *Independent*.

In a striking blow for party regularity, Roosevelt was described as "insufferable ... intolerant ... an unheeding dictator" in the pages of the Marion, Ohio, *Star*: "His prototype in history was Aaron Burr, the same towering ambitions; the same ruthlessness in disregarding the ties of friendship, gratitude and reverence; the same tendency to bully and browbeat ... the same type of egotism and greed for power."[113] Warren G. Harding, editor of the *Star* since 1884, who placed Taft's name in nomination at the tempestuous Republican convention of 1912, would go on to be elected to the Senate from Ohio in 1914, deliver the keynote address at the GOP convention in 1916, and be elected president in 1920.

As the campaign wound to its climax, traditionally Democratic papers initially resistant to Wilson began returning to the fold. Even Watterson's *Louisville Courier-Journal* finally, reluctantly, editorialized that "being a daily newspaper and unable to take to the woods, [it] would perforce be obligated to support his satanic majesty."[114] Watterson's hatred of Roosevelt may have helped him rationalize this decision; he had called the Rough Rider "a self-confident, supercilious iconoclast" who had been "brutal and reckless" in office and whose intervention in detaching Panama from Colombia represented "villainy from start to finish." Watterson was even less forgiving to the former president on the comeback trail in 1912. On April 27 he wrote, "If that one of the Caesars who goes by the name Nero was insane, Theodore Roosevelt, aspiring to be an imitation Caesar, is insane. He carries all the marks typical of the perverted understanding; the devilish streak of wickedness, the ignoble malignancy, the logical intensity and inaccuracy of the lunatic."[115]

Hearst remained problematic. On September 13 he published a front page editorial in his own name, deriding Wilson's credentials on the tariff issue, declaring that "Mr. Wilson's dogmatic ... declarations have all the positiveness of the pedagogues who has theories on everything and experience in nothing."[116] Hearst himself declined to endorse Wilson, and he allowed his papers to offer only grudging backing. The *New York American* was content to speak of him as "the hand and voice of the Great Average."[117]

But in the final analysis, Wilson believed the small papers were as important to his cause as the larger ones. In a speech to the Democratic Press Association of Missouri he stated, "I feel that ... particularly the country newspapers ... are responsible for the exact slant which opinion is to take with regard to public matters."[118] Startt notes that Wilson was correct to acknowledge their importance, for as the editor of one of those small Democratic newspapers put it, they had "at all times sounded the note of Democracy without wavering or flinching."[119]

Upon taking office, according to Richard L. Rubin, it was Woodrow Wilson who imbedded the presidency's relationship with the press into the structure of the American political process. Shortly after his inauguration in 1913, Wilson made the presidential press conference into a formal and regularly scheduled part of the president's responsibilities, making it "an institutionalized channel of political information for both the press and the mass public."[120]

The specter of executive intervention in the press during time of war returned to haunt the media after Wilson led America into the First World War. Congress passed the Espionage Act of 1917, a law that included provisions for punishing anyone intentionally making false reports that interfered with military operations, willfully obstructing the draft, or willfully causing, or attempting to cause, "insubordination, disloyalty, mutiny, or refusal of duty, in the military or naval forces of the United States." The act carried with it a maximum penalty of twenty years in prison and a $10,000 fine. An amendment, the Sedition Act, passed the following year, broadened the powers of the Espionage Act to include "any disloyal, profane, scurrilous, or abusive language" about the form of government of the United States, the Constitution, the flag, or the military, as well as "any language intended to incite, provoke, or encourage resistance to the United States, or to promote the cause of its enemies." These laws were used to convict more than one thousand individuals out of the nearly twenty-two hundred prosecuted.[121] The jailing of four-time Socialist presidential candidate Eugene V. Debs for sedition is well known (he wasn't released until by order of President Harding in 1921), but Victor Berger, a Socialist member of Congress, was also convicted of treason and expelled from the House of Representatives; his paper, the *Milwaukee Leader*, was banned. Another Socialist daily, the *New York Call*, was denied mailing privileges. Also excluded from the mails by Postmaster General Albert Burleson were the *Masses*, the *International Socialist Review*, the *Gaelic American*, and the *Irish World* (the President overrode orders of exclusion on behalf of the *Nation* and Norman Thomas's *World Tomorrow*).[122]

Eight tumultuous years under Wilson left the American people aching for a return to "normalcy" in the presidential election of 1920.[123] They found this term personified (indeed, coined) by the Republican nominee, Ohio senator Warren G. Harding, the former editor of the *Marion Daily Star*. The liberal press was mortified that cabalistic negotiations in the infamous "smoke-filled room" at the Republican convention had culminated in the nomination of what they perceived as a non-entity. The *New York Times* professed "astonishment and dismay" at the news that a "senatorial cabal," characterized by "imbecility" and consisting of "white livered and incompetent politicians," had nominated a "respectable Ohio politician of the second class." The *New York Post* considered his nomination "an affront to the intelligence and the conscience of the American people." The *New Republic* characterized him as a "party hack" bereft of "moral and intellectual qualities," while the *Nation* labeled him "an animated automaton."[124]

Most of the press disagreed, however. Shortly before the election, the reporters who had been covering Harding's campaign hosted a dinner in his honor: "There isn't a man here who is not impressed with your character. If you don't make a fine President, our judgment is no good and we are in the wrong trade."[125] An overwhelming majority of the voters felt the same way. They elected Harding in a landslide over Democratic nominee, Ohio governor and former editor of the *Dayton Daily News* James M. Cox.[126]

Democrats were quick to finger the culprit for their defeat. "Discontent with the Democratic Administration of affairs, assiduously cultivated by the controlled newspapers and periodicals, has taken form in a vote adverse to the Democratic candidates," explained the *Raleigh News and Observer*. "The Republican Party is the party of special privilege, and privilege can afford to make liberal investment in propaganda."[127] It would be closer to the truth to say that the press was in tune with the national mood and both had firmly tilted towards the Republican Party as the Jazz Age began. Nothing succeeds like success, as the saying goes, and good times typically mean good relations between White House and press. "The business of America is business," Harding's successor Calvin Coolidge declared, and who was prepared to argue? Indeed, *New York World* correspondent Charles Merz, writing in the *New Republic*, went so far as to complain in 1926 that "no ruler in history ever had such a magnificent propaganda machine as Mr. Coolidge; and certainly it would be impossible for anybody to use it more assiduously. The unanimity with which the press supports him is one of the major phenomena of our time."[128]

Happy Days are Here Again

When Coolidge declined to seek another term in 1928, Herbert Hoover stepped up as the Republican standard bearer and easily shrugged off the challenge of Democratic contender Al

Smith. The Republican campaign had been innovative in presenting Hoover as a media candidate and he took office on good terms with the press.[129]

These amicable relations were not destined to long survive the dénouement of the Roaring Twenties. The Wall Street crash in October 1929 heralded the onset of a crippling global economic depression. As the situation worsened, Hoover's standing with the press rapidly deteriorated. Paul Anderson wrote in the *Nation* on October 14, 1931, that relations had reached a state of mutual antagonism "without parallel during the present century. They are characterized by mutual dislike, unconcealed suspicion, and downright bitterness."[130]

Sensing an opportunity, Democratic Campaign Committee chair John J. Raskob brought two newcomers to run the National Committee in Washington shortly after Hoover was inaugurated — Jouett Shouse as executive director and Charles Michelson as publicity director. Raising millions in loans from Smith backers, including Herbert H. Lehman, Bernard Baruch, Pierre du Pont, and Vincent Astor, in addition to Raskob himself, Shouse was able to fund Michelson's ambitious media offensive. "The campaign that Michelson orchestrated was a masterpiece of its kind, even by today's standards, when such propaganda machinery has been raised to a fine art," Tebbel and Watts maintain.[131]

Attacks on the president reached critical mass, not just in liberal weeklies such as the *Nation* and *New Republic* but also in *Scribner's*, the *Atlantic*, *Current History*, *Harper's*, *Survey Graphic*, and the *North American Review*, among others. Tebbel and Watts also note, however, that Michelson had succeeded in giving the Democrats some parity in the media, not dominance over it: "The combined circulation of all these journals did not begin to equal the mass coverage of those magazines which continued to beat the drums for Hoover and defend him throughout his administration; they would not, in fact, have begun to approach the circulation of even one of them, the *Saturday Evening Post*.[132]

One of the few bright lights for the Democrats in 1928 had been the election of Franklin D. Roosevelt as governor of New York. Roosevelt's power base in the nation's largest state automatically made him a presidential contender; his pedigree, personality, and activist program made him the frontrunner. However, Roosevelt's path to the nomination was far from smooth. His first hurdle was neutralizing Hearst, who had (somewhat reluctantly) backed Hoover in 1928, largely because of his personal grudge against Democratic candidate Al Smith, who had snatched the New York Democratic gubernatorial nomination away from him in 1918 and again in 1922, on the latter occasion vetoing his bid for the Senate too. In the process Smith had urged the voters of "this city, this state, and this country ... to get rid of this pestilence that walks in the darkness."[133] Hearst's support for the embattled Hoover stretched until June 1931, when, after Hoover issued a public statement that proposed a one-year moratorium on the payments of World War I reparations and war debts, Hearst announced that he could no longer tolerate the president's internationalism.

Intrigued by the policies unfolding in the Empire State, Hearst sought further details about the freshly reelected governor in January 1931 from E. D. Coblentz, editor of the *New York American*, and told Coblentz, "As Roosevelt is a probable Presidential nominee and the one whom we are most likely to support we should keep him and his policies before the nation. There has been no adequate promotion of him in our papers. We should begin now to see that there is. Please see him, and tell him of our desire to publicize him nationally."

After duly meeting with the governor, Hearst's underling reported a positive impression. Satisfied, Hearst wired back, "Of course we will handle all of Roosevelt's important utterances in a conspicuous way not only in New York but throughout the country."[134]

Less than a year later, however, after reflecting on the Groton-educated Roosevelt's internationalist tendencies, including his ultimate heresy, commitment during the 1920 campaign to U.S. entry into the League of Nations, Hearst's ardor had cooled considerably.

Roosevelt dispatched intermediaries to Hearst in a bid to privately reach an accommodation on the League issue. Hearst was having none of it. "He made his numerous declarations publicly when he said he WAS an internationalist," Hearst editorialized. "He should make the declaration publicly that he has changed his mind and is NOW in favor of keeping the national independence which our forefathers won for us; that he is NOW in favor of not joining the League or the League Court."

"I must say, frankly," Hearst continued, "that if Mr. Roosevelt is not willing to make public declaration of his change of heart, and wants only to make his statement to me privately, I would not believe him."

Just two days later, at a meeting of the New York State Grange on February 2, 1932, Roosevelt gave Hearst what he wanted. "The League of Nations today is not the League conceived by Woodrow Wilson," the Democratic vice presidential candidate of 1920 asserted, but was rather "a mere meeting place for the political discussion of strictly European political national difficulties. In these, the United States should have no part."[135]

The response among informed commentators was scorn. "It will be generally regretted, we think," the *New York Times* editorialized, "that Governor Roosevelt should have been so plainly swayed by political motives in this public recantation." One Roosevelt ally reported from Washington that "Hearst's cohorts here are having the time of their lives raucously laughing at the manner in which their chief brought the Governor of New York to his knees. They boast that from now on Roosevelt is at Hearst's mercy."[136] But as Freidel notes, while "Roosevelt had come in sackcloth and ashes and prostrated himself before Hearst ... the humiliation was an essential step toward the ultimate triumph."[137]

In the wake of Roosevelt's abject submission, the hostility of the Hearst empire diminished very suddenly. But Roosevelt still did not qualify as Hearst's first choice for the Democratic nomination. Scorning to endorse the leading anti–Roosevelt contender, Al Smith, the Lord of San Simeon instead swung behind the least–Wilsonian of the Democratic aspirants, House Speaker John Nance "Cactus Jack" Garner, the representative from Uvalde, Texas, with whom he had served in the 58th and 59th Congresses, and in whose district he controlled a newspaper, the *San Antonio Light*. Speaking in an NBC radio address on January 2, 1932, Hearst asserted, "It is about time that the Democratic Party got back upon the high road of Americanism." The man best qualified to lead the party on this path was Garner, "a loyal American citizen, a plain man of the plain people, a sound and sincere Democrat; in fact another Champ Clark." According to Hearst, the other Democratic candidates "are all good men in their way, but all internationalists— all, like Mr. Hoover, disciples of Woodrow Wilson, inheriting and fatuously following his visionary policies of intermeddling in European conflicts and complications."[138] The Hearst endorsement caught no by surprise more than Garner himself. "I never did know why Mr. Hearst supported me," he said years later. "It stopped me from breathing for a while." When the Speaker got his breath back, he repaid Hearst's generosity by reversing his opposition to a federal sales tax in accordance with the publisher's editorial point of view.[139]

Hearst's endorsement counted for more than good publicity. California was Hearst's heartland, where he controlled 47.6 percent of daily circulation, 56 percent on Sundays. In order to prevent Roosevelt sweeping California's primary, Hearst entered an independent Garner slate headed by none other than William Gibbs McAdoo, Woodrow Wilson's secretary of the treasury and son-in-law who had fought Al Smith for 103 ballots at the Democratic convention of 1924. According to the account of McAdoo's close friend Thomas Storke, editor of the *Santa Barbara News-Press*, "Hearst had asked him personally to head a delegation for Garner. Hearst had promised all-out support and had also promised McAdoo the same support if he should run for the U.S. Senate."[140]

"I could get nothing but evasion from the Democratic Party leaders, and was finally compelled to run a separate Garner ticket," Hearst complained. "In doing this I had to make my combinations with Mr. McAdoo." The Hearst/McAdoo/Garner slate easily outpolled Roosevelt in California, securing 211,913 votes to the New Yorker's 167,117.[141] True to his word, Hearst backed McAdoo's successful Senate race in November.

By the time the Democratic convention opened in Chicago on June 27, 1932, it was clear that Roosevelt had a majority of the delegates but not the two-thirds majority required for the nomination.[142] The press was distinctly cool on him. "The times call for courage and action," the Scripps-Howard newspapers declared in a front page editorial. "We have those qualities in [Alfred E.] Smith. There are other men who possess them. Judged by his performance Roosevelt does not." Only one of a half dozen New York City daily newspapers supported the governor of the state, and of the five Chicago daily newspapers that would be read by delegates during convention week, he enjoyed the support of none. Popular and influential columnists Walter Lippmann, H. L. Mencken, and Will Rogers also favored an alternative to Roosevelt.[143]

As the Democrats convened, Hearst had key men positioned to influence the outcome to his satisfaction.[144] His secretary, Joseph Willicombe, was sent to Chicago with the California delegation with instructions to keep in constant touch with San Simeon by phone and wire. Another trusted employee, George Rothwell Brown, was assigned to maintain a close liaison with Speaker Garner in Washington. According to Oliver Carlson and Ernest Sutherland Bates, John Francis Neylan, Hearst's chief legal counsel and financial advisor, had already concluded that Garner had no real shot at the nomination, and had privately come to an arrangement with Roosevelt's manager, James Farley, to back the New Yorker in exchange for the Texan's being offered the vice presidency.

After three ballots, Roosevelt had failed to secure the necessary two-thirds majority required for the nomination. At 9:15 A.M. on Friday, July 1, the weary delegates voted to adjourn until 8:30 P.M. The leaders of the anti–Roosevelt coalition were confident that the New Yorker had peaked, and that his support would begin to melt away once the convention reconvened. Farley phoned Neylan in San Francisco, urging him to arrange for Garner's support to be thrown to Roosevelt. Neylan contacted Hearst in Los Angeles with a blunt message: "Roosevelt must have California and Texas now."[145] Simultaneously Hearst was being importuned that morning by a man whose well-honed people skills were evident by the mere fact that he was on intimate terms with both Hearst and Roosevelt: Joseph P. Kennedy.

Kennedy got straight to the point. If the Roosevelt candidacy collapsed, the delegates would stampede towards Hearst's least-favorite choice: Woodrow Wilson's secretary of war, Newton D. Baker, an internationalist's internationalist. "Do you want that man Baker running our country," Kennedy asked, "that great defender of the League of Nations, that ardent internationalist whose policies you despise? No, of course you don't. But that's just who you're going to get if you keep holding out your delegates from Roosevelt, for if the convention cracks open, it'll surely be Baker. And then where will you be?"

"If you don't want Baker, you'd better take Roosevelt," Kennedy concluded, "because if you don't take Roosevelt, you're going to have Baker."

"All right. Is that my choice?" asked Hearst. "Could I get [Maryland Governor Albert] Ritchie?"

"No, I don't think so," Kennedy replied. "I think if Roosevelt cracks on the next ballot, it'll be Baker."

"All right," Hearst concluded. "I'll turn to him."[146]

Shortly afterwards, Brown was contacted by Willicombe, who told him, "Mr. Hearst has a request to make of you. He wants you to go to Speaker Garner and say to him that he is very fearful that on the next or some subsequent ballot delegations will desert Roosevelt, and that the nomination will then go to some candidate who will repeat the disasters to the party and the country of 1924 and 1928."

"I knew it was perfectly true that Roosevelt was through if Garner did not save him," Brown recalled. "There was no other way.... I said, 'tell Mr. Hearst I shall do exactly as he requests.'"[147]

Brown walked into Garner's office in the Capitol at approximately 11:00 A.M. that morning. "'Mr. Speaker,' I said, 'I have a message for you from Mr. Hearst.'"

"He looked at me inquiringly from under his shaggy white eyebrows, and led the way into the embrasure of the south window. I think he knew what was coming. We stood in silence for a while, looking out on the beautiful green park."

"Mr. Hearst is fearful that the nomination will go either to Baker or to Smith, unless you throw your strength to Roosevelt," Brown said. "He regards Baker as an internationalist and a reactionary. If Smith should be nominated, we will have the fight of 1928 all over again, with the party torn asunder, and all hope of electing a Democrat gone."

"'Say to Mr. Hearst that I fully agree with him,'" Garner replied. "'He is right. Tell him I will carry out his suggestion and release my delegates to Roosevelt.'"

"I knew it was settled, and that William R. Hearst had made the next President of the United States, Franklin D. Roosevelt," Brown concluded.[148]

Hearst continued to regard Roosevelt as strictly the lesser of two evils. He endorsed the Democratic candidate, but coolly, more in terms of emphasizing the faults of the incumbent president rather than extolling the virtues of his challenger. However, Hearst was wily enough to send an effusive note of goodwill to Hyde Park on the eve of the election: "Well, sir, you made a marvelous campaign, one that has stirred the mind and heart of the nation. I believe you will be triumphantly elected, but in any case I shall retain an enduring admiration for yourself and your great work, and an abiding enthusiasm for your inspiring utterances. I think the country greatly needs you and the practical expression of your truly democratic ideas in the government, and I hope to learn Tuesday that the country has realized its need and made you our President."[149]

Hearst would send no such communication four years later. By then he had already made abundantly clear where he stood.

New Deal

If there was one quality Franklin Roosevelt brought to the presidency it was his skill at manipulating the press. He did it superbly, far better than any of his predecessors, even the other Roosevelt, and he would not be equaled until Ronald Reagan, whose approach was entirely different. Few reporters could be said to "love" Reagan, but Roosevelt commanded the genuine love, affection, and admiration of most the correspondents who crowded into the Oval Office, or gathered around his car, or besieged him wherever he appeared. His jauntiness, cockiness and self-confidence inspired the same kind of frustrated rage among Republicans that Reagan's similar attributes provoked later in Democratic ranks.[150]

Rubin notes of Roosevelt that "to pierce what he considered was the screen of a 'Tory' press required both a strong will and skills to manipulate mass popularity to achieve his own programmatic objectives."[151] When he took office, the prevailing economic crisis paradoxically gave him a honeymoon period in which the press was reluctant, in the national interest, to second guess his agenda. Even a pro–Hoover columnist like Mark Sullivan reasoned that it would be "almost unpatriotic" to make life difficult for Roosevelt as he tried to lift the nation out of the Depression. The real challenge would be retaining at least a fair share of media opinion once the bloom was off the rose. Roosevelt's inherent charm was his chief asset in this respect; deploying it to best effect meant offering unprecedented access to reporters. With only rare exceptions, Roosevelt stuck faithfully to his promise to hold two press conferences every week, meeting publicly with the press 337 times during his first administration, 374 times in the second, 279 in the third, and 8 times in the three months of his fourth term.[152]

Beyond this formal commitment was an ongoing campaign of informal cajolery and sweet talk. The Roosevelt White House opened a larger pressroom off the main entrance of the West Wing, providing correspondents with desks, typewriters, telephones, and, importantly, a poker table. The President and first lady tickled egos by inviting journalists to social functions as guests rather than reporters. Franklin and Eleanor also hosted annual receptions for White House correspondents, had groups of them in for Sunday night scrambled-egg suppers, and threw picnics for them at Hyde Park.[153]

Arthur Krock of the *New York Times* maintained that the Roosevelt administration employed "more ruthlessness, intelligence, and subtlety in trying to suppress legitimate, unfavorable comment" than any other he had ever known. In addition, in a throwback to a previous era, Roosevelt had so generously spread patronage among journalists that the Baltimore *Sun's* Frank Kent commented that there were "almost as many newspaper men in the New

The presidency of Franklin Roosevelt is a perfect instance of the man meeting the moment. Had he been born a generation earlier his unique people skills would have been rendered irrelevant by the absence of a technology capable of projecting his voice to the nation. Had he been born a generation later the merciless glare of television would have spotlighted his physical disabilities and rendered him ineligible for the office in the first place. But coming to power during the brief window when radio was the national medium of communication enabled FDR to establish himself through his weekly "fireside chats" as a fixture in the homes and lives of the American people. For the first time a president was able to use the media to appeal directly to the voters (courtesy of Library of Congress).

Deal as there are in the press gallery." Taking public relations posts in the new federal agencies, the former correspondents helped those of their brethren remaining in the press corps keep up with the dizzying pace of New Deal reform. In another innovation, in order to come to terms with complex economic terms and policy issues on deadline, reporters increasingly came to rely on government press releases.[154]

These efforts yielded mixed results. "On the president's side were an overwhelming majority of the Washington Press corps," Tebbel and Watts note. In 1936, according to Seldes, "The Washington correspondents voted nineteen to one for Roosevelt. In the Chicago *Tribune*, New York *Tribune*, and other towers of Landonism, the vote among the working reporters was about the same ratio."[155]

However, survey research conducted by Rostow indicated substantial majorities of Washington correspondents supported their paper's political point of view and slanted their stories accordingly.[156] Other reporters were induced to submit politically correct material by the established norms of the editorial environments where they worked. Nowhere were these expectations more vividly enforced than at the Hearst press. Rostow quotes one Hearst reporter: "Hearst decided he wanted the McLeod Bill to go through. We were instructed that we were in favor of the bill and were to go out and make everyone else in favor of it. We were instructed to get one hundred telegrams from various people sent to Congress saying they favored the bill. I don't think I found a single person who knew what the bill was or cared, but we got the telegrams because of the obligations [we] felt to the paper."

According to another Hearst reporter, "We do just what the Old Man orders. One week he orders a campaign against rats. The next week he orders a campaign against dope peddlers. Pretty soon he is going to campaign against college professors. It's all the bunk, but orders are orders."[157]

Roosevelt highlighted this issue when, speaking before the American Society of Newspaper Editors, he sought to divide reporters, whom he asserted played by the rules of objectivity, from their employers, whom he accused of agenda-setting: "In the newspaper game those boys down here in Washington have as high a standard of ethics and morals and fair play as any profession in the United States. I take my hat off to them. But a lot of them labor under a very big handicap. It does not trace back, of necessity, to their editors. It traces back to the owner of the paper essentially."[158]

On a lighter note, after being greeted with a giant banner reading "UNDOMINATED CHICAGO TRIBUNE, THE WORLD'S GREATEST NEWSPAPER" while on a visit to Chicago to dedicate a bridge near the Tribune Building, Roosevelt, in his next press conference back at the White House, made a point of singling out the *Tribune's* Washington correspondent: "Come up here, Walter Trohan, I want to see an undominated reporter." Everyone in attendance, well aware of just how dominating the *Tribune's* Colonel McCormick could be, roared with laughter.[159]

Roosevelt's key advantage was a technological innovation that enabled a president for the first time to go over the heads of the press and directly to the voters. The commercialization of the radio forever broke the monopoly of the written word over mass communication. Radio made its debut on the political scene in 1924. Four years later both campaigns spent approximately a half million dollars apiece broadcasting their messages to the approximately nine million radio sets then in use. By 1932, the number of radio sets in use had doubled to eighteen million, and by 1935 had jumped again to twenty-six million.[160] Roosevelt seized this opportunity to project himself and his message, unedited, into the homes of the American people. His legendary "Fireside Chats" built up a loyal constituency among the dispossessed who looked to him as much for the sense of strength and purpose inherent to his messages as their actual content.[161]

The mainstream media, aware it was being disintermediated, reacted with alarm at the prospect of losing its accustomed place in the national political debate. Thomas Woodlock wrote an article for *Barron's* in which he labeled the radio an instrument that invoked "mass emotion," making it possible for a leader to create a "direct democracy" and thereby "thwart the intentions of the founding fathers to restrain the influence of mass emotion and distil from it the more carefully considered will of the people."[162]

Roosevelt was aware of this discomfort and relished rubbing it in. Speaking in a 1937 Fireside Chat, the president pointedly omitted mentioning the print press as a source of political education in America. "Five years of fierce discussion and debate—five years of information through the radio and moving pictures," he observed, "have taken the whole nation to school in the nation's business."[163]

The president would need all the good humor he could muster for the trials that lay ahead. Perhaps the first shot across his bow took place on July 17, 1933, when S. W. Adams, editor of the Gladewater, Texas, *Journal*, announced he had had enough. In a letter addressed to "Mr. Franklin D. Roosevelt, Dictator of the United States," Adams challenged the new president, who had been in office all of four months, to either stop dictating to small businessmen or "boldly declare that democracy is dead" and shout "Long live fascism!"

"There is," Adams continued, "no title inferior to that of dictator who ... usurps dictatorial powers, and becomes a tool of greed.... I denounce you," he continued, "as the greatest scourge a free people ever suffered." Somewhat incongruously, he closed the letter, "yours truly."[164] This tirade might be easily dismissed for the Lilliputian manifesto it was if it did not so quintessentially encapsulate the sentiments of such a broad spectrum of the nation's opinion shapers. From the mightiest press baron to the lowliest county seat editor, the lineup of literary opposition to Roosevelt's reelection was unprecedented in its scope and ferocity. And it was striking how fast that opposition was concentrated. Only eight months into Roosevelt's term of office the *Literary Digest* headlined its summary of press opinion: "Open Warfare on the New Deal."[165]

The New Deal era of the 1930s was marked by dislocation and distress, by innovation and experiment. As if Roosevelt's reforms in economic, labor, and welfare policy were not threatening enough, millions of people desperate to find some way out of the Depression were swept up by the appeal of demagogues such as radio preacher Charles Coughlin or Huey Long, the "Kingfish" of Louisiana, or by schemes such as Dr. Francis E. Townsend's Old Age Pension Plan. These challenges to the established order took place against a global backdrop of revolution, civil war, and totalitarian aggrandizement, both communist and fascist. The pace of change and the dangerous directions it threatened to go left many people convinced that the traditional American commitment to the virtues of the free market, if not capitalism itself, was under siege. Columnist Arthur Krock articulated the unease of this constituency when he noted that after just 49 1/2 days in office, Roosevelt "possesses, is seeking and has been offered more absolute power than the sum of the arbitrary authority exercised at various times in history by Generals Washington, Lee, Grant and Sherman, Presidents Jackson, Lincoln and Wilson, and all the emperors of the Ming dynasty."[166] No one was more sensitive to the extent of this crisis than the editors of the great newspapers. They were in a position to lead a counterattack, and they did so with all the firepower at their command.

The press undertook a trial run for its contest with Roosevelt by concentrating its firepower on Upton Sinclair's nominally Democratic "End Poverty In California" (EPIC) gubernatorial campaign during the 1934 midterm elections.[167] Sinclair, the original "muckraking" journalist and author of *The Jungle*, among multiple other titles, was an unabashed socialist running on a platform of punitive taxation, public works, and worker cooperatives. Naturally, the press was united against him to a degree unprecedented since the days of William

Jennings Bryan. The *Oakland Tribune* took the precaution of consulting with its attorneys about how much it could lie about EPIC and get away with; not all of its compatriots were so scrupulous.[168] Not one newspaper in the entire state of California was prepared to endorse Sinclair for governor.

The *Los Angeles Times* made no secret of its bias against Sinclair, whom it labeled a "life-long socialist, associate and collaborator of radicals, admirer, defender, and self-proclaimed instructor of Communist Russia" and warned that were he elected "the state would be thrown into chaos, at the mercy of riotous, Red-incited mobs."[169] Every day the paper carried, on its front page, a box of "Sinclairisms." Sinclair on the sanctity of marriage: "I have had such a belief.... I have it no longer." On religion: "a mighty fortress of graft." On bankers: "legalized counterfeiters." On the American Legion: the "riot department of the plutocracy" and conductors of "drunken orgies." Nearly all of the quotes were out of context; some of the most inflammatory were actually dialogue from characters in Sinclair's novels.

While Chester Rowell, editor of the *San Francisco Chronicle*, drafted the platform that Republican governor Frank Merriam ran on, Kyle Palmer, the political editor of the *Los Angeles Times*, raised funds and wrote speeches for the governor while at same time directing his paper's coverage of the campaign.

Late in the campaign, the *New York Times* sent Turner Catledge out to report on the political scene in California. Scanning the *Los Angeles Times*, he saw stories on Governor Merriam's every appearance, but no mention of EPIC rallies or speaking engagements by Sinclair. When he queried Palmer about it, the paper's political editor snapped, "Turner, forget it. We don't go in for that kind of crap that you have back in New York—of being obliged to print both sides. We're going to beat this son-of-a-bitch Sinclair any way we can. We're going to kill him."

Palmer had already been "loaned" to Hollywood to work under Motion Picture Industry Association head Will Hays. Palmer, under the official title "public relations director of the Motion Picture Producers Association" helped organize a "tithe" of studio workers earning over $100 a week, who were assessed one day's wages to contribute to a fund earmarked for the election. This fund was used to finance the production of several movie "newsreels" which the studio heads sent to all the theaters in the state. These "newsreels" depicted mobs of the "unemployed" (actually crowd scenes from other movies) waiting at the border for word of Sinclair's election, and featured "interviews" with shaggy, Bolshevik-looking people who explained that they were looking forward to a Sinclair victory because "his system vorked vell in Russia, vy can't it vork here?"[170] Sinclair's "system" never got the chance because he went down in flames in the election.

With Sinclair disposed of, the press could concentrate on the real enemy. Leading the charge was William Randolph Hearst, now more powerful than ever. Hearst was a major beneficiary of the wave of newspaper consolidation that had taken place during the first quarter of the 20th century. In 1900, eight chains controlled twenty-seven papers and perhaps 10 percent of national daily circulation; by 1920 approximately sixty chains owned three hundred dailies and accounted for over one-third of the daily circulation in America, equivalent to over twelve million papers a day.[171] By 1930 only 20 percent of 1,400 cities had any daily newspaper competition. During the Depression period from 1931 to 1936, several hundred additional newspapers suspended publication, so that by 1935 not only were there less papers in circulation than in 1915, but sixty-three companies controlled 328 newspapers with 41 percent of all daily circulation and 52 percent of all Sunday sales.[172] Both in the number of papers and the proportion of buyers reading Hearst papers, the peak years of his empire, 1932–1935, corresponded almost perfectly with the opening years of the New Deal (see Table 9 and Table 10 on page 230).

TABLE 9. HEARST CIRCULATION AS PERCENTAGE
OF TOTAL CIRCULATION IN NINE MAJOR CITIES, 1932[173]

City	Daily	Sunday
San Francisco	61.8	71.8
Los Angeles	59.3	62.7
Boston	44.0	35.7
Washington	42.4	41.7
Chicago	38.3	46.6
Detroit	35.1	35.1
New York	33.3	35.9
Baltimore	29.8	52.1
Pittsburgh	28.8	57.5

TABLE 10. HEARST CIRCULATION
AS PERCENTAGE OF NATIONAL CIRCULATION[174]

Year	Daily	Sunday
1932	13.9	22.5
1933	14.0	23.7
1934	13.5	23.4
1935	13.8	24.5
1936	10.6	22.9

Hearst warmly approved of Roosevelt's first month in office, referring to the president's "bold and sustained action" which "has banished lethargy from our government."[175] Hearst approved of the reflationary National Industrial Recovery Act (NIRA) and, in foreign policy, Roosevelt's decision to reject both discussion of debt reduction with any nation in default of its payments and plans for international currency stabilization. "This administration has realized so many of the ideals of us American-minded folk that I would hate to see it lose power or prestige," Hearst wrote in September 1933.[176]

But Hearst, along with most publishers, balked when Hugh Johnson attempted to bring the printing industry under the umbrella of the NIRA by imposing a code requiring minimum wages, maximum working hours, restrictions against the employment of children, and allowing workers the right of collective bargaining (which provided the impetus for the formation of the American Newspaper Guild). Hearst exploded that the code was "in direct violation of the Bill of Rights ... an abridgement of freedom of the press," and he was prepared to fight it "with every means at my command ... even if it costs me every nickel I possess."[177]

A strike in San Francisco in mid–July 1934 is considered the turning point in Hearst's relationship with Roosevelt. In print, Hearst held provisions of the NIRA that required all employers to negotiate with workers' representatives responsible for the increase in labor unrest. In private, he raged against NIRA-inspired "State Socialism, Communism, extortion, confiscation, demagogic military regimentation, continued business disturbance and industrial discouragement."[178]

By August 1934, Hearst was alarmed enough to cable Coblentz, "Recovery is being retarded by visionary schemes of unsound radicals. Even American institutions are endangered."[179] Early in April 1935, Hearst finally drew a line in the sand, instructing his editors that it was time to "settle down to a consistent policy of opposition to this administration."

A Hearst executive passed word down the chain: "The Chief instructs that the phrase Soak the Successful be used in all references to the Administration's tax program instead of the phrase Soak the Thrifty hitherto used, also he wants the words Raw Deal used instead of New Deal."[180]

The criticism was as unrelenting as it was omnipresent. "By false representation the present Administration was elected, the American system was scrapped, and a political socialistic system under dictatorial direction installed in its place," Hearst fulminated in one editorial.[181] "President Roosevelt has repudiated his office. He has repudiated the Constitution. He has repudiated the fundamental Democratic doctrine of state rights," he accused in another. The last point was undeniable. The first two, if taken seriously, were grounds for impeachment.[182] On June 19, in addressing Roosevelt's progressive taxation proposals, Hearst truly unburdened himself:

> [The] President's taxation program is essentially Communism.
>
> It is, to be sure, a bastard product of Communism and demagogic democracy, a mongrel creation which might accurately be called demo-communism, evolved by a composite personality which might be labeled Stalin Delano Roosevelt.
>
> It contains the mistakes of both individuals, the evils of both systems, and is Russian in manner and utterly un–American in method and principle.
>
> It is a violation of the basic spirit of American institutions, a betrayal of the American ideals of equality and justice.
>
> It is primarily vindictive in purpose.
>
> It divides a harmonious and homogenous nation into classes, and stimulates class distinction, class discrimination, class division, class resentment, and class antagonism.[183]

In October Hearst declared in an interview that Roosevelt would be rejected at the polls because he had too many "foreign, fascistic ideas of personal dictation." Hearst conceded that he was at last burning his bridges with the Democratic Party: "I guess we will have to depend on the Republican Party to rescue the country from experimental socialism and restore it to sound and stable Americanism."[184] Keeping up the pressure, an article entitled "AWAKE, AMERICAN PATRIOTS!" published in the *Los Angeles Examiner* on November 24, 1935, by Robert H. Hemphill, "financial authority" of the Hearst press, declared: "I do not know what catastrophe will be required to shock this nation into a realization of the enormous consequences which are planned and ARE BEING EXECUTED by the Federal Administration and its little band of fanatic adventurers.... This little band of revolutionary radicals PROPOSE TO OVERTHROW THIS GOVERNMENT. AND THEY ARE DOING IT!"[185]

In public, Roosevelt never lost his sense of humor. "What's old W. R. doing now to stir up the animals," he once shouted gleefully at a Hearst reporter. "Give him my regards."[186] But the antipathy was mutual. In November, Roosevelt told Joseph Kennedy, a mutual friend of both men who was attempting to effect a reconciliation, that "there was no man in the United States who was as vicious" an influence as Hearst. Kennedy dropped his proposed mediation.[187]

Opposing Roosevelt could be a family affair. Colonel Rutherford R. McCormick, undisputed overlord of the *Chicago Tribune* since 1911, was joined in his campaign against the New Deal by the *New York Daily News*, whose publisher was captain Joseph Patterson, McCormick's cousin and a former classmate of Roosevelt in Groton days, and the *Washington Herald*, a Hearst paper edited by Eleanor Medill ("Cissy") Patterson, Joseph's sister. Under McCormick, the *Tribune* was no less Republican than it had been in the days it was owned by his grandfather, Joseph Medill, but McCormick combined his inimitable brand of partisan conservatism with a flair for the dramatic. In 1935, the Democratic Party, in a coup dubbed the "Bloodless Revolution," had ended eighty years of Republican rule in Rhode Island by repealing the state's rotten borough electoral system and ousting the existing Supreme Court justices. McCormick responded by having the star that represented Rhode Island cut out of the flag hanging in the lobby of the Tribune Building to signify that the state had forfeited its right to be considered part of the Union. He only restored Old Glory after being advised that such an act constituted flag desecration.

The *Tribune* had never exhibited the least susceptibility to Roosevelt's famous charm, despite McCormick and Roosevelt being old schoolyard chums at Groton. In 1920 the paper had labeled FDR — at the time the running mate of Democratic candidate James M. Cox — "the one half of one percent Roosevelt."[188] It didn't take long before McCormick was ready to signal that his patience with the New Deal was at an end. In an editorial on October 7, 1933, he wrote, "Many ardent supporters of the New Deal feel that the Constitution, both as a framework of government and as a declaration of rights, is obsolete, but the real issue is whether we shall continue to maintain our free society or exchange it for one based on the principle of authority." He followed this up with the accusation that Roosevelt was intent on "creating a half-way house for some stronger man to move to some other location, either Fascist or Communist."[189]

Colonel Robert McCormick began his tenure at the helm of the *Chicago Tribune* in 1911 as a bona-fide, small-government, isolationist conservative, values faithfully reflected in the pages of the newspaper founded by his grandfather, Joseph Medill. McCormick's seething frustration with the New Deal made him so eager to see a Republican returned to the White House that he jumped the gun on election night in 1948 and emblazoned a wrong call in block capitals on his front page, a wrong call so egregious it has passed into legend (courtesy of Library of Congress).

The president again tried to laugh off the accusation that he was intent on overthrowing the republic, suggesting to a *Tribune* reporter that he "tell Bertie he's seeing things under the bed."[190] But the criticism only became more personal. "Business cannot prosper when the President of the United States embarks upon a plan to destroy the constitution," McCormick snapped in June 1935. "Is not Roosevelt's partiality for the unemployed, his coldness to the soldiers, and his hostility to the industrious," the Colonel mused out loud in October that year, "accounted for by his having been unemployed when out of office, never having fought for his country, and having never earned his living?"[191] In its January 1, 1936, edition, the *Tribune* made its declaration of war:

> Get rid of the men who have broken faith, been false to their word, untrue with their promises, and dishonest with the American people. Turn out the wasters who have hoisted the national debt to the 30 billion dollar mark. Turn out the men who have abused their diplomatic immunity, traded secret information for profit, treated desperate situations vaingloriously and in high spirits dealt lightly with the miseries of their fellow countrymen.

Turn out the men responsible for the reduction of the country's food supply, for the boosting of its costs, for the weeds that grow on fertile acres, for the impairment of honorable obligations, for the silly schemes for robbing those who have and giving it to those who envy.

Turn out the men who buy elections. Turn the rascals out. Clean house.

Stop the speculation and destruction. Call a halt while there is yet something to be saved and in time to save it. Restore the national honor. Return the national sanity. Give the people back their faith in government. Time still remains the opportunity is at hand. It cannot be the destiny of the United States to run like the Gadarene swine violently down a steep place and perish in the sea.[192]

These words ran under the phrase "Turn the Rascals Out," which appeared on the editorial page masthead as the *Tribune*'s "Platform for 1936" and continued daily thereafter. Subsequently, the slogan "Only [x number of] days remain to save your country. What are you doing to save it?" was inserted daily at the bottom of the masthead. Still not satisfied, McCormick ordered his switchboard operators to answer every telephone call with the same query.

A frequent target for critics was the president's "Brain Trust," his informal circle of advisers, a lineal descendant of Jackson's Kitchen Cabinet. "We are having," the *Saturday Evening Post* editorialized, "government by amateurs ... who, having drunk deep, perhaps, of the Pierian Spring, have recently taken some hearty swigs of Russian vodka." Not to be outdone in either vituperation or dependence upon classical allusions, H. L. Mencken spoke of the Brain Trust as a "Camorra of quarrelling crackpots" issuing "slimy false pretenses and idiotic contradictions." The *Washington Herald* singled out Rexford Tugwell for special attention, noting his "Communistic" and "subversive" characteristics and concluding, "Treason to American principles is revolution, and Mr. Tugwell's call to revolution is treason."[193]

Mencken, the founder of *The American Mercury*, despised everyone he considered his intellectual inferior (which was pretty much everyone — in 1931 the Arkansas state legislature passed a motion to pray for his soul after the "Sage of Baltimore" raised the entire state to the "apex of moronia"). But he had a special loathing for Roosevelt. The President was "a blood-brother of Lenin," he said. "The smile of the sonofabitch in the White House and the smile of Holy Joe in Moscow," he wrote, "have a great deal in common." Mencken traced the problem back to Roosevelt's alma mater. That "god-damn university, Harvard," Mencken observed during the 1936 campaign, "will have a lot to answer for to history for the Roosevelts." Theodore, said Mencken, had "the manners of a saloon bouncer and the soul of a stuck pig." But Franklin was "the synthesis of all the liars, scoundrels and cheapskates of mankind."[194]

According to Best, both the agenda and the frustration of the press were evident as election year dawned. In his view there is no doubt that by the beginning of 1936 a majority of the press — and virtually all major columnists — harbored serious misgivings about Roosevelt's policies, and others had now begun to seriously question Roosevelt's fitness for his office. "While Walter Lippmann had lagged behind most other columnists in grasping, or at least acknowledging, the dangers of the New Deal, he was one of the earliest to focus on Roosevelt's megalomania and its implications," Best writes. "Yet most newsmen were aware that the failures and dangers of the New Deal were not understood by the mass of Americans despite their efforts to point them out."[195]

The press response to Roosevelt's State of the Union Address set the tone for the ensuing campaign coverage. The *New York Herald-Tribune* labeled the President's message "simply a political harangue, extraordinary chiefly for its heat and frankly demagogic appeal." Roosevelt had, "for the first time made the fomenting of hatred among Americans his OPEN goal." The *Washington Post* concluded that Roosevelt had used Congress "as Hitler uses the Reichstag, as a sounding board from which he can exalt himself and denounce all opposition."[196]

The only thing missing was a champion who could rally all true Americans against, as

McCormick put it, "all the lazy, all the worthless, all the larcenously inclined, all the muddle-heads, all who hope to profit from disorder including the gangsters, and all whose vote can be bought by the four billion dollar corruption fund," who were in the corner of "the play-boy of the White House."[197]

The press scoured America high and low, looking for such a man. They found their shining knight, somewhat incongruously, in the person of Alf Landon, the mild-mannered, politically moderate governor of Kansas. The boost–Landon movement was led by a number of progressive Republican newspapermen from Kansas, including William Allen White of the *Emporia Gazette* (a particular disappointment to Roosevelt, who had on occasion invited him to the White House so he could get "a few helpful thoughts from the philosopher of Emporia"), Roy Roberts and Lacy Haynes of the *Kansas City Star*, and approximately ten other editors from the Sunflower State. After meeting with Landon in Topeka in December 1935, Hearst dispatched word throughout his empire to promote the governor. The entire gamut, from Merryl Rukeseyer, Hearst's financial columnist, turning out two columns on Landon's economic policies, to Damon Runyon writing an article for *Cosmopolitan*, was spanned.[198]

The Landon campaign was in many ways media-driven. William Allen White was largely responsible for drafting the Republican Party platform. Roy Roberts acted as Landon's campaign manager. Alfred H. Kirchhofer, managing editor of the *Buffalo Evening News*, was director of publicity for the GOP in 1936. Appropriately, Landon's running mate was plucked straight from the publisher's office. Frank Knox, a former "Rough Rider" with Teddy Roosevelt, took up journalism as a trade and by 1927 had become general manager of all twenty-seven of Hearst's dailies. Founder of the legendary (or notorious) *Manchester Union Leader* in New Hampshire, Knox bought out the *Chicago Daily News* in 1931 and used it to label Roosevelt's New Deal "alien and un–American" and "a complete flop."

Predictably, Hearst wasn't impressed with the Democratic convention that renominated Roosevelt: "What a travesty of American ideals, what a burlesque of Jeffersonian Democracy, what a political farce, what a Christmas pantomime with administration clowns and pantaloons, all joking and laughing and playing Bolshevik pranks on the public. What a chance for Harlequin himself, attired in red and yellow patchwork of alien policies, to tell his bedtime stories."[199]

Neither was McCormick pleased. While the Democratic convention attracted the headline "THE SOVIETS GATHER AT PHILADELPHIA," its Republican counterpart was hailed "OPEN CAMPAIGN TO SAVE U.S." The same unique brand of evenhandedness was applied to the *Tribune's* coverage of the campaign. Readers were alerted, "RECORDS SHOW ROOSEVELT AIM A REVOLUTION," while a Landon rally would typically be headlined "GOV. ALF M. LANDON TONIGHT BROUGHT HIS GREAT CRUSADE FOR THE PRESERVATION OF THE AMERICAN FORM OF GOVERNMENT INTO LOS ANGELES."

Putting his money where his mouth was, McCormick was the single biggest individual financial contributor to the Landon campaign.[200] "His greatest sacrifice, however, was not money but journalistic integrity," Smith says. "As the campaign intensified, the *Tribune* abandoned even the pretense of impartiality."[201] On one day in October, *Tribune* readers could find no mention of the president of the United States in their morning newspaper. On the following day there was a short piece on page 13, reporting that the president had cancelled his regular White House press conference, "presumably to avoid embarrassing questions about recent campaign developments."[202]

After a Roosevelt parade through Chicago that attracted half a million people, a *Tribune* photographer paid a city street cleaner all of twenty-five cents to strew Roosevelt buttons on the pavement and then be photographed sweeping them up. The intention was to demonstrate popular indifference to the president, but it backfired when the rival *Chicago Times* gleefully exposed the hoax, complete with an affidavit signed by the suborned municipal worker.[203] Undeterred, the *Tribune* a fortnight later printed a photograph of a dog tag embossed with a social security number. According to the accompanying article, workers being enrolled into the social security program would be required to wear them. The *Tribune* ignored the denials, refused to issue a retraction, and actually reprinted the photograph on election day.[204] Hearst employed a similar tactic, issuing a front-page, eleventh-hour claim on the eve of the election that contributing wage earners would never get their money back, headlined "DO YOU WANT A TAG AND A NUMBER IN THE NAME OF FALSE SECURITY?"[205]

More than a decade before Joseph McCarthy initiated the first of his witch hunts, the tactic already loomed large in the nation's press. Hearst, who had earlier accused Roosevelt of "fascist ideas of personal dictation," swung to the other extreme during the 1936 campaign, asserting, "The real candidate — the unofficial candidate of the Comintern — is Franklin D. Roosevelt."[206] Near the end of September, ten Sunday newspapers of the Hearst chain splashed across their front pages "proof" that "through its Comintern in Moscow and its puppet organization in the United States, Soviet Russia is taking an aggressive part in the Presidential campaign in America — ON THE SIDE OF THE NEW DEAL." This "proof" consisted of a translation from Russian of a speech made months earlier by Earl Browder in which the Communist Party candidate issued the new Marxist doctrine authorizing the tactical formation of a proletarian "united front" with other "progressive" forces if necessary to advance the class struggle. In case anyone missed the point, this functionally meaningless missive was helpfully condensed by Hearst to read "Communists can join ... in ... supporting Roosevelt."[207]

When Roosevelt repudiated various accounts of Communist support, the *Tribune* replied: "The question is not whether Mr. Roosevelt repudiates or accepts communism. It is whether he has done and proposes to do things which Communists recognize as their own."[208] McCormick was constantly offering unsolicited advice on this subject to Landon during the campaign. A typical missive was this telegram of September 21: "THE COMMUNIST ALLIANCE IS PRETTY WELL PROVED ALSO CORRUPTION IN THE ALPHABETICAL AGENCIES. IN THE CURRENT EXCHANGE OF THE HOSTILITIES IS THERE NOT ROOM FOR A NOTE OF IDEALISM. LOVE OF COUNTRY AND ITS PEOPLE. I LEAVE THE SUGGESTION WITH YOU."[209]

Landon's running mate chimed in, too: "In plain English," Knox's *Chicago Daily News* editorialized, "the Communist International at Moscow has authorized American Communists to vote for Roosevelt, in order to play up to other American radical groups and to defeat Landon and Knox."[210]

Columnists great and small volunteered to play their part in the great crusade against Bolshevism. The *New York Herald-Tribune* published the daily jeremiads of Preston Davie, whose columns typically appealed to voters "save our country, our homes, and our children from Communism," and always concluded:

> Will you join us?
> Call, write or telephone,
> Forty-one East Forty-Second Street,
> Twelfth floor, Vanderbilt 3-5600[211]

In the *New York American*, Hearst continued to address the president and his associates as "you and your fellow Communists." On October 8, 1936, the *American* printed a poem, under an inflammatory cartoon, of which the first stanza read:

> A Red New Deal with a Soviet seal
> Endorsed by a Moscow hand,
> The strange result of an alien cult
> In a liberty-loving land.[212]

Clarifying his position while vacationing in Europe, Hearst cabled from Amsterdam defending himself from allegations of slander leveled by Roosevelt's "conglomerate party of Socialists, Communists and renegade Democrats," by explaining:

> "I have not stated at any time whether the President willingly or unwillingly received the support of the Karl Marx Socialists, the Frankfurter radicals, Communists and anarchists, the Tugwell Bolsheviks and the Richberg revolutionists which constitute the bulk of his following. I have simply said that he does receive the support of these enemies of the American system of government and that he has done his best to deserve the support of all such disturbing and destructive elements."[213]

The following day, Hearst's *New York American* had the following headlines on pages one and two:

ROOSEVELT HAS [COMMUNIST CANDIDATE EARL] BROWDER'S AID

SOCIALIST-LABORITE SAYS COMMUNISTS BACK ROOSEVELT

NEW DEAL STILL AIMS AT SOCIALIST STATE[214]

Hearst continued his red-baiting into the last days of the campaign. A front-page story in the *San Francisco Examiner* attacking the Works Progress Administration (WPA) asserted, "Taxpayers Feed 20,000 Reds on New York Relief Rolls."[215] On election eve he took out full-page ads in papers across the country, including one in the *Buffalo Evening News* that pointed out, "Mr. Roosevelt recognized Stalin. And later, Stalin recognized Roosevelt. The documents have been printed. Moscow has told all the Communists in America to vote for Roosevelt, the Friend of Russia, the *camarade* of Communism. Are you surprised at that?"[216]

McCormick continued to exhibit pleasure at the progress of his protégé during the campaign. In response to a Landon rally in New York, McCormick wired, "YOUR MADISON SQUARE SPEECH WILL GO DOWN AS ONE OF THE GREATEST IN POLITICAL HISTORY."[217] When NBC asked McCormick about Landon's chances of carrying Chicago, the editor radiated confidence. "Landon will carry Chicago. Chicago is as honest as Maine and ... [t]he revelations that the Russian communists are backing Roosevelt ... have profoundly shocked hundreds of thousands of traditional Democrats who will put the salvation of their country above partisan habit."[218]

On October 31, Roosevelt addressed a rally at Madison Square Garden in New York, telling the assembled masses, "I should like to have it said of my first Administration that in it the forces of selfishness and of lust for power met their match. I should like to have it said of my second Administration that in it these forces met their master." The *New York Herald Tribune* responded to the speech by asserting that it confirmed the accuracy of a comment by Swiss psychologist Carl Jung, who had described Roosevelt as possessed of "the most amazing power complex, the Mussolini substance, the stuff of a dictator absolutely."[219] Colonel McCormick saw in it the prospect of his imminent triumph. "Mr. Roosevelt's speech in Madison Square Garden last night was the speech of a man who was beaten and knew he was beaten," the *Tribune* announced, in total defiance of both conventional wisdom and objective reality. "Mr. Roosevelt was on the defensive from start to finish. The speech was the speech of a defeatist.... Mr. Roosevelt is at the end of his road. And he knows it."[220]

Despite the circulation of his paper slumping by nearly 100,000 in the run-up to the election, McCormick stuck to his guns. Flailing about for any straw of comfort, the *Tribune* reported a swing to Landon among, of all people, businessmen arriving at the airport: "An informal poll taken among the arrivals showed a 9 to 1 sentiment for the Republican candidate."[221] On the front page of the *Tribune's* election-eve issue, the headline blared "NEW DEAL GIRDS FOR 4 YEARS OF SWEET REVENGE — MAPS TERROR DRIVE AGAINST ALL FOES." The article predicted that a "horde of investigators, spies, sleuths, and undercover men of the administration will be turned loose on those who opposed Roosevelt."[222] The front page editorial, titled "PAUL REVERE MUST RIDE AGAIN," declared:

> You as an American have a double duty tomorrow. One is to vote for Landon, the Republican Party, and the republican form of government. The other is to see that others do....
>
> You should realize that Nov. 3 is the most fateful day in the history of the American people. Do not consider that statement an exaggeration. If Landon is not elected you may have seen the last of free government as you have known it....
>
> [I]f you cherish your rights and privileges as an American, if you would avoid autocracy and dictatorship.... If you love your country and want to preserve it, see that Mr. Roosevelt is defeated.[223]

There were islands of support for the administration in the sea of ink spilled against it. The Scripps-Howard papers, which had supported La Follette in 1924 and Hoover in 1928, backed Roosevelt in both 1932 and 1936; Roy Wilson Howard personally assured Roosevelt as the 1936 campaign heated up, "We are going to give you — or honestly attempt to give you — a full 100% of our support."[224] Another important ally of the New Deal was J. David Stern, owner and publisher of the Camden, New Jersey *Courier*, the *Philadelphia Record*, and, from 1933 to 1939, the *New York Post*. The allegiance of the *Post* (the most partisan Democratic paper in the country, one prepared to fight fire with fire by trumpeting headlines like "PRO-HITLER STAFF AT HEADQUARTERS OF REPUBLICANS") helped make New York the most friendly territory in the nation for the Democrats, where they could stack four papers (including the *Times*) up against five for the GOP.[225] But the Democrats were outnumbered four to one in Chicago; the *Times* was the only paper carrying the banner of the New Deal against McCormick's *Tribune* and Hearst's *Herald & Examiner* in the morning, and Knox's *Daily News* and Hearst's *American* in the afternoon.

Elsewhere it was a familiar story. The smaller chains — Block, with seven dailies, and Gannett, with 18 — were almost exclusively Republican with varying degrees of enthusiasm. The *Philadelphia Inquirer*, *Detroit Free Press*, *Denver Post*, and, predictably, Chandler's *Los Angeles Times* were all vociferously anti–New Deal. The *San Francisco Chronicle*, *Seattle Times*, *Portland Oregonian*, and *Kansas City Star* swung in behind Landon. Of more concern to the White House, the *Baltimore Sun*, *St. Louis Post Dispatch*, and *Omaha World-Herald*— which all endorsed Roosevelt in 1932 — refused to do so four years later. In justifying its decision the *World-Herald* explained:

> Mr. Roosevelt, as earnestly and passionately as Hitler once did, assails our own capitalist system.... From this 'economic tyranny,' from the 'palace of privilege,' he purposes to rescue us by a bold declaration of war upon the existing economic order, just as did leaders in other lands.
>
> By his sweeping onslaught Mr. Roosevelt has precipitated uncompromising war between the government he heads and private enterprise.... This newspaper believes the American system, both economic and political, is not so desperately sick, so hopelessly beyond cure, that it is necessary to kill and replace it with an order alien to our traditions, repugnant to all our aspirations.[226]

Joseph Pulitzer II, publisher of the *Post-Dispatch*, justified his rejection of Roosevelt through his opposition to the president's "collectivism," saying, "Collectivism is the deadly enemy of liberalism, although paradoxically in this country collectivist measures have been fostered in the name of liberalism. Collectivism is incompatible with human freedom, with individual liberty and with equality of opportunity. If democracy embraces collectivist measures it will end by destroying democracy."[227]

Even in the one-party South, papers such as the *Dallas News*, the *Houston Post*, and the *Jacksonville Florida Times-Union* supported Landon in every way save by explicit endorsement.[228]

Just how pronounced was the bias against the President? During the 1936 campaign, Roosevelt commissioned a survey from the Democratic National Committee which examined 204 newspapers in cities of 100,000 people or more, not including those in the southern states where, according to the compiler, Carl Byoir, "there is no contest." The results were as follows (see Table 11).

TABLE 11. NEWSPAPER PREFERENCE DURING 1936 CAMPAIGN

Position	No. of Newspapers	Total Circulation
Pro-Roosevelt	50	6,462,814
Anti-Roosevelt	123	15,527,461
Independent	31	1,672,246
TOTAL	204	23,662,521

Of the Pro-Roosevelt papers, a significant number, with a circulation of two and a half million, were in New York alone, which meant that outside of the Empire State there was a circulation in large Northern and Western cities of approximately 4 million for the president and 13 million against.[229] Providing confirmation, another survey published in the *New Masses* at the end of October, which analyzed the "admitted or effective editorial attitude" of every U.S. newspaper with a circulation of at least 50,000, found that those for Landon had a combined circulation of 14,347,000, to 6,996,000 for Roosevelt, with 1,651,000 neutral.[230] One final study concludes that of the fifty dailies with a circulation of 135,000 or more, 75 percent were pro–Landon, 20 percent were for Roosevelt. The eighty papers that endorsed Landon represented 67 percent of the circulation.[231]

In addition, "the anti-press case could be made much worse by testing the specific gravity of the papers officially listed as pro–Roosevelt," George Seldes says. Just as Thomas Jefferson's hired editorial guns had consistently outperformed their Federalist rivals, so "the pro–Landon press was strong in its support and extremely active in propagandizing the electorate.... [T]he same cannot be said for the pro–Roosevelt press."[232] In his recollection of the campaign, postmaster general and FDR confidant James Farley remarked, "In some sections of the country the entire press was hostile to the Roosevelt administration. We received constant complaints from individuals in those areas who said it was impossible to get our side of the story."[233]

The seal on the impending Republican triumph was set by the *Literary Digest*, which had employed mail-in polls that had accurately predicted the victor in the past three presidential elections. In its authoritative final forecast, the *Literary Digest* concluded that Landon would receive 54.89 percent of the popular vote and carry 32 states with 370 electoral votes. Roosevelt was given 40.70 percent of the vote and sixteen states (the solid South plus Kentucky, Maryland, New Mexico, Oklahoma, and Utah).[234]

It was not to be. While his party rolled up majorities of 75–16 in the Senate and 331–88 in the House, Roosevelt won 60.8 percent of the popular vote and all but two states, Maine and Vermont. Not that the two Yankee bastions in question were ever of two minds about their decision: "VERMONT STANDS FIRM WHILE REST OF NATION FOLLOWS STRANGE GODS," ran the headline in a Burlington newspaper. But it did provide ammunition for Democratic quips. Two of Hearst's sons, John and William, strolled into a New York nightclub on election night, hoping to put the events of the evening behind them. "Ah," sang out the quick-witted master of ceremonies, "here come Maine and Vermont!"[235]

Hearst himself took the defeat in good grace. When he called Hyde Park on election night to congratulate the president, John Boettiger, Roosevelt's son-in-law, took the call. "We have been run over by a steam roller, but there are no hard feelings at this end," Hearst said, sentiments reflected in his empire's editorials over the next few days.[236] The *Chicago Tribune* was less conciliatory: "Millions who voted for Mr. Roosevelt are due for a sharp awakening and it should not be long delayed."[237] Down but not out, McCormick ascribed Roosevelt's victory to a coalition comprised of a gamut, from "the Communists in New York to the would-be slave drivers in the South; from the beneficiaries of inside tips on the stock market to the penniless creatures supported by the dole."[238]

There is some evidence that the rarified atmosphere in which they operated helped convince the Roosevelt-haters that their boy actually had a chance in 1936. Certainly, the overwhelming extent of Landon's defeat took many by surprise. "Perhaps this is the 'revolution' of which we have been hearing," the *Grand Rapids Herald* ruefully remarked.[239]

What had happened to the truism that the press made presidents? "Election Day, 1936, was judgment day for America's Daily Press," the *Christian Century* intoned in the aftermath of Landon's defeat.[240] A study of fifteen major cities by the *New Republic* showed that, omitting the few neutral dailies, 71 percent of the total circulation belonged to Landon papers, but they delivered only 31 percent of the votes. Only two papers in all Massachusetts endorsed Roosevelt for a second term but he carried the state easily. In Los Angeles, pro–Roosevelt newspapers had a combined circulation of just 74,252 — but Roosevelt polled ten times as many votes in the city. No Detroit daily backed Roosevelt but he buried Landon in the Motor City by a 2–1 margin. In Chicago, home of the New Deal-hating *Tribune* and *Daily News*, Roosevelt carried forty-eight out of fifty wards.[241]

Had the pro–Landon agenda of the great press barons worked against their candidate? Had Hearst gone too far? Even a Republican paper like the *Hartford Courant* felt impelled to remark during the campaign, "It seems entirely in keeping to say that the gratuitous and intemperate support that Mr. Hearst is now giving to Governor Landon is no more welcomed by that gentleman than the support of violent radicals is welcomed by President Roosevelt."[242]

In 1936, *Fortune* magazine conducted a poll which asked, "Do you think the influence of the Hearst papers upon national politics is good or bad?" In areas with no Hearst press, the response was 10.7 percent good, 27.6 percent bad, and 61.7 percent don't know. In areas with one or more Hearst paper circulating, the response was 10.5 percent good, 43.3 percent bad, and 46.2 percent don't know — perhaps an instance of familiarity breeding contempt?[243] "The election of 1936 marked the climax of Hearst's reputation for influence in national politics," Carlisle says. "During the primaries and the election campaign itself, Hearst's influence became a political issue in itself." While Landon struggled to free himself from Hearst's embrace, "Democratic Party leaders found Hearst's association with Landon useful, and they helped to enforce the notion that Landon was under Hearst's control."[244] "I sometimes think," Roosevelt once reflected, "Hearst has done more harm to the cause of democracy and civilization in America than any three other contemporaries put together."[245] Whatever Hearst's actual relationship to democracy and civilization, he may have been responsible for a commensurate level of damage on Landon.[246]

"While the influence of the print press seems to have detracted from the margins of Roosevelt's victories in certain localities," Rubin concludes, "Roosevelt's active utilization of a variety of communications strategies neutralized much, if not all, of the press's negative efforts."[247] Other presidents had secured reelection by either co-opting or defying the press. Roosevelt was the first to successfully go around them. In many ways, this was the most significant outcome of the election. "To my view, the outstanding thing about the campaign was the lack of influence of the newspapers," Secretary of the Interior Harold Ickes reflected afterwards. "Never have the newspapers, in my recollection, conducted a more mendacious and venomous campaign against a candidate for President, and never have they been of so little influence."

At the December Gridiron dinner, Roosevelt could not resist a satirical barb about the newspapers' campaign coverage: "This character Roosevelt was a villain. He combined the worst features of Ivan the Terrible, Machiavelli, Judas Iscariot, Henry VIII, Charlotte Corday and Jesse James.... I began to believe it myself. Didn't I read it in the columns of our great papers?"[248] In a more serious vein, the president concluded, "There is a growing tendency on the part of the public not to believe what they read in a certain type of newspaper. I think it is not the editorial end, because, as you know, very few people read the editorials.... Lack of confidence in the press today is not because of the editorials but because of the colored news stories and the failure on the part of some papers to print the news."[249]

A quantifiable gap had emerged between the owners of the papers and the people who bought them. And if those who shaped the news couldn't even predict the shifting allegiances of the people, how could they presume to direct them?

"Dewey Defeats Truman"

If Roosevelt ever expected more balanced coverage from the media during his second term he was swiftly disappointed. According to Winfield, "From 1936 through 1940 Franklin D. Roosevelt had to contend with the increasing animosity of American newspapers.... The president's major adversaries were not the opposition party and Congress but rather their mouthpieces in the media."[250] "As you know, all the fat-cat newspapers— 85% of the whole — have been utterly opposed to everything the Administration is seeking, and the best way to describe the situation is that the campaign of the spring, summer and autumn of 1936 is continuing actively through the year 1937," Roosevelt complained to his ambassador in Spain, Claude G. Bowers. "However, the voters are with us today, as they were last fall."[251]

In the nation's capital, Cissy Patterson, who had bought out and merged the Washington *Times* and *Herald* from Hearst, declared, "This administration has been marked by the transparent encouragement of left-wing agitators and plotters against our government."[252] Nor was there any love lost for the president in Chicago after his reelection; venomous as always, the *Tribune* continued to characterize the unfolding New Deal as the "importation of European methods employed by dictatorships both communist and fascist."[253] Back from a trip through the dictatorships of Europe, Frank Knox wrote Amos Pinchot that the experience had "driven home upon me with renewed force that, consciously or unconsciously, Roosevelt has been leading the country straight toward the fascist philosophy."[254]

According to White, "Owners, to Franklin Roosevelt, were the repository of press sins and shortcomings, to whom all responsibility could ultimately be attributed." Editors, no less than reporters, were required to dance to their tune. "It's not the editors," the president explained at a press conference in August 1938. "Hell, most of the editors have got families. They cannot lose their jobs. They have to write what the owner tells them to."[255]

Speaking in a similar vein at a press conference in early 1939, the president charged, "Quite a number of newspaper owners are deliberately putting before the American people deliberate misrepresentations of fact.... I have in front of me, oh, about eight or ten different newspapers. There isn't one story or one headline in all of those papers that does not give, to put it politely, an erroneous impression — not one." Roosevelt maintained that the American people were beginning to realize that the opinions of the "agitators ... of the newspaper owner variety" were "bunk — b-u-n-k, bunk; that these agitators are appealing to the ignorance, the prejudice and the fears of Americans and are acting in an un–American way."[256] Privately, Roosevelt wrote of his enemies, McCormick and Cissy and Joe Patterson, that they "deserve neither hate nor praise — only pity for their unbalanced mentalities."[257]

Because much of the press was isolationist in outlook, as the war clouds gathered toward the end of the decade, editors could add the charge of "warmonger" to their already extensive panoply of anti–Roosevelt criticisms. After the president bypassed Congress to conduct the Lend-Lease deal with beleaguered Britain in 1940, the *St. Louis Post-Dispatch* declared that not only had "Mr. Roosevelt today committed an act of war," but also he had become "America's first dictator."[258]

Pressure for governmental oversight of the media once again intensified. In 1940, Congress passed the Alien Registration Act (with only four dissenters), making it unlawful to publish "any written or printed matter advocating, advising, or teaching the duty, necessity, desirability, or propriety of overthrowing or destroying any government in the United States by force or violence." This legislation was much less significant in the war effort against the Axis Powers than it was for the ongoing campaign to weed out left-wing subversives, something that only intensified after the war.

Even as they continued to flail away at Roosevelt, it was clear to the more perceptive of his critics that they could not take on the New Deal directly.[259] The failure with Landon had brought home the fact that an era had passed, and that to be competitive the Republican Party had to turn to a fresh face, one free from association with the old guard of the Hoover era. The result was one of the most memorable campaigns in history, in which Roosevelt, running for an unprecedented third term, was matched against the darkest of the dark horses ever nominated for president, a candidate who owed his political existence entirely to the media, and to one man in particular.

The father of the new Republican order was Henry R. Luce, who founded *Time* magazine in 1923, later bringing out *Fortune* (1930) and *Life* (1936). The son of a missionary, Luce called journalism a "calling," and often remarked, "Show me a man who thinks he's objective, and I'll show you a man who's deceiving himself." He openly asserted that newspapers should put "intelligent criticism, representation and evaluation of the men who hold offices of public trust" on the front page.[260] This criticism and evaluation was refracted through a partisan lens. "Luce's Republicanism was something almost organic to him, as much a part of him as his Presbyterianism," David Halberstam notes. "Believing in the things he did from his religion and his God, it was impossible to be anything other than a Republican."[261]

Luce's flagship publication reflected his brand of conservative internationalism, an agenda that put him offside with the White House. "Roosevelt hated him [Luce]," explained *Time* editor T. S. Matthews. "He thought he had an unfavorable, unfair press from Luce. He was right, too, because Luce's theoretical idea was to have *Time* fifty-one percent against the government — no matter who they were. With Roosevelt, instead of fifty-one percent, it was about eighty-nine percent."[262] Roosevelt professed disinterest, once remarking of *Time* magazine that "beginning with the first number ... I discovered that one secret of their financial success is a deliberate policy of either exaggeration or distortion. Pay no attention to them — I don't."[263]

In return, Luce manifested a curious love-hate relationship with Roosevelt throughout his presidency, an equivocation quite unlike the attitude of his wife, Clare Booth Luce, who was elected to Congress from Connecticut's Fourth District in 1942, and who unreservedly loathed the president and his entire circle of "ramsquaddled, do-gooding New Deal bureau-

Through his trinity of popular titles — *Time, Life,* and *Fortune*— Henry Luce, seen here with wife Clare, sought to modernize both the publishing industry and the Republican Party, by making them both more colorful and more accessible. The presidential nomination of Wendell Willkie, the least likely candidate of the 20th century, was largely created by Luce, because it was an ideal fit for his agenda — selling more magazines and putting a Republican in the White House. He finally secured both objectives with the election of Dwight Eisenhower (courtesy of Library of Congress).

crats." Although he voted for Hoover, Luce was starstruck after his first meeting with Roosevelt. "My God!" he exclaimed afterward. "What a man! What a man!"[264]

When asked why so many of his reporters were fans of the New Deal, Luce ("il Luce" to irreverent wits at *Time*) would invariably reply, "Damned Republicans can't write."[265] *Time* writer Tom Griffith noted that "it bugged Luce" that FDR photographed so well and "made a terrific *Life* cover" while most Republican candidates "looked like accountants." "God how he hates Roosevelt, as I do too," *Life* editor John Shaw Billings once wrote. Yet when Billings wanted to run a picture in the magazine of the president in a wheelchair, Luce flatly refused.[266]

Luce found his champion in the most unlikely persona imaginable — the Hoosier Democrat Wendell Lewis Willkie. As president and CEO of Commonwealth & Southern Corporation, the nation's largest electric-utility holding company, Willkie made headlines during the late 1930s by leading the fight against the Tennessee Valley Authority. It was a fight Willkie ultimately lost, but it provided him with a platform to continue arguing the case for private utilities specifically and free markets in general, in various public statements for the *Atlantic* and in pieces for the *Saturday Evening Post* ("Idle Men, Idle Money") and the *Reader's Digest* ("The Faith that is America"). His efforts earned him a cover story in the July 31, 1939 issue of *Time* magazine. They also encouraged him to switch parties.

The prime mover behind the Willkie phenomenon was the young and energetic Russell Davenport, managing editor of Luce's business magazine *Fortune*. Davenport, who first met Willkie in August 1939 at a roundtable sponsored by his publication, came away saying, "I have just met the man who ought to be President of the United States." He introduced the Indianan to media barons like the Cowles brothers and to Luce, who noted in a memo, "I think of Willkie as a force of Nature. I think of Davenport as a force of Spirit. When the two met — the chemical reaction produced an event of political history."[267] The influence of the press attained unprecedented scope in 1940; while the Hearst empire had *discovered* Landon four years earlier, the Luce empire effectively *manufactured* Willkie's candidacy from scratch.

According to Robert E. Burke, it was in 1940 that the Willkie campaign really broke into the open with the publication of a piece entitled "We the People" in the April issue of *Fortune*. This article appeared under Willkie's name, although it was largely the work of Davenport, who also contributed an editorial underlying its importance.[268] Davenport ultimately resigned as editor to become Willkie's full-time campaign manager, as "Willkie for President" clubs began mushrooming across the nation.

Luce was the driving force behind this phenomenon. Willkie's biographers agree on his importance to Willkie's unlikely political ascendancy. "Willkie became Luce's hero," Charles Peters says. "The puffery from Luce's publications was shameless and endless."[269] Luce emphasized this agenda in a communiqué to his employees: "*Time* will not allow the stuffed dummy of impartiality to stand in the way of telling the truth as it sees it."[270] Steve Neal remarks that in the lead-up to the Republican convention, "Luce's publications, which had already been friendly to Willkie, abandoned any pretense of objective coverage of the Republican contest and portrayed 'Davenport's man' as the defender of American democracy."[271] *Life* published an unprecedented eleven pages of Willkie puffery in its May 13 issue. "In the opinion of most of the nation's political pundits," it began, "Wendell Lewis Willkie is by far the ablest man the Republicans could nominate for President at Philadelphia next month."

"By June 1940, *Time* and *Life* virtually demanded that Willkie be nominated," Herzstein writes.[272] The Luce publications deliberately ran down Willkie's rivals for the Republican nomination, Ohio senator Robert Taft Jr. and New York attorney general Tom Dewey, inflicting permanent damage on the political careers of both men by fixing the "can't win" label on the former and the "cold fish" label on the latter. A representative campaign report in the June 10 issue of *Time*, for example, declaimed, "While Tom Dewey, with bravado, was fumbling with the topic of foreign affairs, while Taft appeared to be running toward the wrong goal posts, Willkie seized the ball."

In addition to Luce's empire, Willkie also had in his corner the Cowles newspapers in Minneapolis and Des Moines (as well as the Cowles magazine *Look*), *U.S. News & World Report*, and the Scripps-Howard chain (ardent supporters of Roosevelt in 1932 and 1936), which endorsed Willkie on June 19, declaring, "With all due respect to the other Republicans who seem to have a chance, Willkie stands out among them like an oak in a thicket." [273] The *Saturday Evening Post* gave Willkie most of its June 22 issue, including an article by General High Johnson, which said he would be a great President, an article by Willkie himself titled "Five Minutes to Midnight," and an editorial which said the world crisis required bold new leadership. *U.S. News* published a cover photograph of Willkie in his World War I uniform accompanied by a strong endorsement.

Time's June 24 issue convention preview featured "The Story of Wendell Willkie," a three-page feature which stated, "Win or lose, the spectacular campaign of Wendell Willkie belonged with the great U.S. political stories." The magazine advised Republicans that a vote for Willkie was a vote for "the best man the party had to lead the country in a crisis." In all, Willkie's face was splashed across a half dozen of America's most popular magazines during convention week. "Reprints of pro–Willkie editorials, news stories and magazine articles, all appearing as though by magic within the last few days, are being scattered around the Republican National Convention Hotels," the *Cleveland News* reported on June 21. "Early arrivals among the delegates are talking of little else." [274]

According to Neal, writing in the days before the advent of cable television and the Internet, when the big three networks held a virtual monopoly over the nightly news, "In an era when national magazines shaped public opinion, Willkie became an instant celebrity, a star. Having the support of *Life*, *Look*, and the *Saturday Evening Post* were roughly equivalent of CBS, NBC, and ABC getting together on a candidate in the age of television." [275] And still the pressure mounted. On June 27, the day balloting for the Republican presidential nomination began, the *New York Herald-Tribune* ran an unprecedented three-column, front-page editorial hailing Willkie's bid for the presidency, announcing that the Hoosier candidate "seems to us to be heaven's gift to the nation in time of crisis. Such timing of the man and the hour does not come often in history." [276]

Willkie had been a Democrat until the previous year, had never held public office, had not contested any primaries, and arrived at the convention with the fewest number of delegates. Some diehards on the convention floor never warned to him. Colonel McCormick of the *Chicago Tribune*, selected as a delegate at large by the Illinois GOP, committed to Tom Dewey after issuing the heartfelt declaration that "as a soldier who served in a division which lost 23,000 men killed and wounded in the last war, which sacrifice was all in vain, I will vote against any platform pronouncement calculated to involve the United States in the present tragic struggle." [277] But with the galleries packed with his supporters keeping up the rhythmic chant "We want Willkie," the Hoosier made ground until he finally emerged victorious on the sixth ballot. [278]

It had been staged to look spontaneous, "Mr. Smith goes to Washington" incarnate, with Willkie, as *Life* put it, being "swept into the front rank of Republican contenders by a mass wave of spontaneous, volunteer, amateur enthusiasm." But Taft, for one, privately complained of losing the nomination to a propaganda campaign "engineered from Wall Street." [279]

"To Luce," Herzstein says, when the Republican nominee took the fight to Roosevelt in the fall, "Willkie's campaign was a crusade, not a news story." [280] The Luces contributed $14,700 to the Willkie campaign, the maximum allowed under the Hatch Act. Luce himself would telephone his secretary in the middle of the night with some masterstroke of political strategy or defining oratory, and she would dash to the office to dispatch it to the Willkie campaign train on Luce's private wire. Whenever he was in town Willkie would stride into Luce's office unannounced (not even Luce's father could do that) and put his feet up on the desk for long strategy sessions.[281] Dissatisfied with an election-eve editorial in *Life*, Luce rewrote it himself, concluding his missive by arguing, "This is the most important election since 1860 ... because this *may* be the last time in this century that free men will determine what men and what principles govern them.... May God help us to be wise and brave in order that we and our children may be forever free."[282]

The Democrats again sought to turn the media bias against them to their advantage. At a speech in Philadelphia on October 23, Roosevelt refuted Willkie's charge that the New Deal had failed to bring about economic recovery, by comparing the *New York Times* financial section with the editorial page, which supported the Republican candidate. "Wouldn't it be nice, if the editorial writers of the New York *Times* could get acquainted with their own business experts?" the president remarked.[283] Privately, Roosevelt sniped that the press barons could not distinguish between "an objective news story and a free reader for a furniture store."[284]

While the Republican old guard in the press accepted Willkie as the lesser of two evils, some of the venom was missing from the previous contest. Hearst hadn't lost any of his distaste for Roosevelt; on one occasion he characterized the president's new running mate, Secretary of Agriculture Henry Wallace, as "a young gentleman who would not make a very creditable soda fountain clerk." But while he dutifully supported the Republican nominee, he did so without great enthusiasm or much hope: "Every time Mr. Willkie speaks he says something — but it is generally something which Mr. Roosevelt has said before and said better."[285]

But overall Roosevelt's support in the press declined even further from the previous election. In 1932, Roosevelt had enjoyed the editorial support of about 41 percent of the daily newspapers which took sides, and a little larger proportion of the weeklies. In 1936 he was endorsed by 37 percent of the dailies and probably over 40 percent of the weeklies. By 1940 he retained the backing of little more than 25 percent of the dailies and somewhat more than a third of the weeklies.[286] The day after the American people returned Roosevelt to office for an unprecedented third term, Harold Ickes handed out a statement at a press conference noting, "We elected a President who was supported by less than 23 percent of our daily press." Ickes continued: "This reveals an unprecedented and progressively perilous situation requiring public consideration. Although we are fortunate in having free communication over the air, I am convinced that our democracy needs, more than ever before, a truly free press that represents no class or economic group and that will re-win the confidence of our citizens because it is worthy of re-winning that confidence."[287]

Willkie's homespun appeal could not survive the new alignment of the political chessboard that emerged from the tangled wreckage of Pearl Harbor. Luce's agenda was results-driven and his benediction could prove as transient as it was effusive. By the 1944 election season he was writing memos to his subordinates warning them not to get stuck in a "Willkie-or-else" position; when his erstwhile protégé emerged from the Wisconsin primary — after forty speeches in thirteen days — with zero delegates, Luce felt "a certain sense of relief from a long and painful situation," sentiments reflected in a *Time* post mortem that Wisconsin had voted "against a crusade which had never been clearly defined." Willkie blew up at his one-time patron over their last dinner together: "Harry, you may be the world's best editor, but you are certainly the world's worst politician."[288]

Luce had already settled for Tom Dewey as the Republican nominee, but again came up short in the fall.[289] He and everyone else associated with the press would shortly come to miss the old master. If Roosevelt had continually frustrated them, he had won their respect; for his successor they held nothing but undiluted contempt. So passionate was their loathing that it clouded their judgment and led to the most embarrassing agglomeration of wrong calls on one election night in the history of the press.

Roosevelt, when peevish, would consign reporters he considered liars to his "Ananias Club," who would be felled as was Ananias when Peter rebuked them. But whatever issues of the moment Roosevelt had with individual reporters, his real enemy was their publishers, whom he considered the real threat to press freedom. "I have little fear," he wrote, "that freedom of the press will be abridged from external assault in this country. The danger is from internal corruption."[290]

Harry Truman, who took over as president after Roosevelt died on the cusp of victory in the Second World War, possessed little of his predecessor's capacity to absorb criticism and none of his tact in responding to it.[291] He actually told one reporter in 1951, "I think a publisher, or any newspaperman, who doesn't have a sense of responsibility and prints a lot of lies and goes around slandering without any basis in fact — I think that sort of fellow can actually be called a traitor."[292]

Truman lumped *Time, Life* and *Fortune* together as the "Loose" publications, placing them in the same category with *Look, Newsweek, Collier's*, the *Saturday Evening Post*, and most metropolitan newspapers, as part of a vast conspiracy to "misrepresent and belittle the President." The "Loose" magazines were "just too damn big anyway," he believed, and they had "too much power over people and what they think." The big publishers, he added, "have always been against me," and he had always been against them, with an exception made for his son-in-law, Clifton Daniel of the *New York Times*, "just the nicest boy he can be."[293]

As far as the rest of the media went, "I'm saving up four or five good, hard punches on the nose, and when I'm out of this job, I'm going to run around and deliver them personally,"[294] Truman once growled. It remains a matter of conjecture as to who the recipients of this rage would have been, but it's fairly safe money to bet that number one on the ex-president's hit list would have been Henry Luce. Truman once told the editor to his face, "Mr. Luce, a man like you must have trouble sleeping at night. Because your job is to inform people, but what you do is misinform them." Luce said of Truman, "If he and I just had the time to talk things over, we'd find we agreed on most things." Truman said, "I told him I doubted that very much, and I did, and I still do."[295]

Not that Luce was the only subject of Truman's ire. "The old SOB who owned and edited the *St. Louis Post-Dispatch* and *New York World* [Joseph Pulitzer] was in my opinion the meanest character assassin in the whole history of liars who have controlled the newspapers — that includes old man Hearst and Bertie McCormick," Truman once declared. "I'll make a bet, however, that hell has become almost untenable for the devil since Old Pulitzer, Horace Greeley, Charles Dana and the old Copperhead, Bill Nelson [founder of the *Kansas City Star*] and William Allen White arrived."[296] Advances in communications technology provided no succor. "I had thought that pictures [newsreels] and the radio would cure the news liars but they (the liars) have taken over both."[297]

The man from Independence, Missouri, burned through whatever reserves of media good will he inherited with remarkable alacrity. Patience on both sides rapidly ran thin. On June 9, 1948, during a campaign swing through the Midwest, Truman told a reporter for the Spokane *Spokesman-Review* that his publication and the *Chicago Tribune* were the worst two newspapers in America. In a front-page editorial the following day, the *Tribune* lashed back: "Mr. Truman has added his name to the long list of political crooks and incompetents who have regarded THE TRIBUNE as first among their foes.... Thanks in no small measure to THE TRIBUNE, the people of this nation know Mr. Truman for the nincompoop he is and for the vote-stealing, graft-protecting, gangster-paroling, Prendergast man that he is."[298]

The editors of the nation consoled themselves in the knowledge that Truman, the accidental president, could never survive in the White House on his own merits. By 1948, the Democratic Party was in chaos; the left-wing had broken away under the Progressive banner led by former vice president Henry Wallace; the South bolted in the name of segregation and rallied behind the Dixiecrat South Carolina governor Strom Thurmond. Truman's fortunes were at such a low ebb that the *Washington Post* recommended that his party at their convention in Philadelphia "surrender to the inevitable," deny Truman the nomination and nominate a "custodian" in his stead. The *New York Post* went one better, informing the Democrats that by handing the nominating to Truman, "The party might as well immediately concede the election to Dewey and save the wear and tear of campaigning."[299]

Most of the papers that joined the rally around Roosevelt during World War II reverted to their natural partisan stances with a vengeance once the war was over. Dewey, again the Republican nominee, didn't lose a single endorsement from 1944 and picked up scores of others. In the president's home state of Missouri, fourteen dailies with a circulation of 1,326,397 supported Dewey, while Truman had the backing of thirteen with an aggregate circulation of just 44,569.[300] The *St. Louis Post-Dispatch* justified its decision on the grounds that the president lacked "the stature, the vision, the social and economic grasp, the sense of history required to lead the Nation in a time of crisis."[301] The Scripps-Howard chain of nineteen newspapers was almost pitying in its rejection of Truman, saying of this "good man, a good American" that "it was his misfortune, not his fault, that experience and training had not prepared him for the crushing responsibilities that fell upon him."[302]

It was all over bar the counting, and everyone knew it. Elmo Roper, pollster for the *New York Herald-Tribune*, ceased conducting polls in September on the grounds that monitoring the precise margin of Truman's impending defeat was no longer worth the time or effort. Richard L. Strout wrote in the *Christian Science Monitor* on October 14, "It is now as certain as anything can be in the course of American politics that Gov. Dewey is elected and the nation knows it, and yawns over the final three weeks of the campaign, whose outcome was certain before it began."[303]

It seemed the only man left in America still prepared to ignore expert opinion was Harry Truman. Barnstorming the nation, he savaged his opponents—Dewey, Congress, big business, and, not least, the media. Always it came down to a single issue: who can you, the people, trust—the biased reality the press presents to you, or the truth as your president sees it? "I came out here so you might see and understand the things for which I stand, and so that you might get the truth and the facts, which you haven't been getting through the press," he explained on one campaign swing.[304] In New York on October 28, the president stated that he had visited nearly all the great cities of the nation "to tell the people what the issues are. They couldn't find out otherwise because 90% of the press is against us—90% of the radio commentators are against us; and the only way you can find out the truth is for me to come out and tell you what the truth is."[305] Uncharacteristically, Truman was only slightly exaggerating—the papers backing Dewey represented 78.55 percent of the total national circulation, to only 10.03 percent prepared to endorse the President.[306] "Give 'em Hell, Harry!" people would shout "We just tell the truth, and they think it's Hell," Truman would reply.

The following day, wrapping up his campaign in St. Louis on the way back to Independence, Truman returned to this theme, accusing the press of undertaking a "smear campaign on your President ... in all its vile and untruthfully slanted headlines, columns and editorials," led by "Hearst's character assassins" and the "McCormick-Patterson saboteurs," ever since he had unveiled his liberal program in September 1945.[307]

But the press wasn't buying it. Confidence in Dewey's victory was so universal that major publications prior to the election began to publish special reports, magazine articles, columns, editorials, and front-page news stories on the nature of the incoming Dewey administration.

Harry Truman enjoys the last laugh the day after the shocking electoral upset in 1948 that guaranteed him four more years in the White House. The result was a vindication of the President's belief that the American people, when presented with the facts, could see through the lies propagated by the media, an institution Truman brooded about in private and lashed out at in public (courtesy of Library of Congress).

Life captioned a full-page picture of Dewey in its November 1 issue, "The next President travels by ferry boat over the broad waters of San Francisco Bay." *Time* published an advertisement for the November issue of the *Kiplinger Washington Letter* that asked, "What will Dewey do as President?" The October 30 issue of *Kiplinger Magazine* "elected" Dewey not just in 1948 but in 1952 as well, with its feature story that asserted "Dewey will be in for eight years." Nationally syndicated columnists Joseph and Stewart Alsop told readers, "The first post election question is how the Government can get through the next ten weeks.... Events will not wait patiently until Thomas E. Dewey officially replaces Harry S. Truman." The *Detroit Free Press* solved this particular conundrum by suggesting that Truman — "a game little fellow who never sought the presidency and was lost in it, but who went down fighting with all he had" — should appoint Dewey's foreign-policy advisor John Foster Dulles as secretary of state so that international relations would not be disrupted during the interregnum between election day and Dewey's inauguration.[308] Perhaps most embarrassed of all in retrospect was John O'Donnell, writing for the *New York Daily News* and *Washington Times-Herald*, who established his own little niche in history by asking, "So what will Harry do after January 20? We don't care much."

This miasma of wishful thinking persisted into election day itself. The *Washington Post* editorial that morning summed up the campaign as "duller and less significant than any similar contest in recent years," and remarked that frankly it would be a miracle if the Democrats, "wedded to a candidate of something less than towering stature," managed to pull off a victory in their factionalized condition.[309] Fred Othman wrote in the *Washington Daily News*, "The ballots haven't been counted at this writing, but there seems to be no further need for holding up an affectionate farewell to Harry Truman, who will go down in history as the President that nobody hated." [310]

But the most legendary *faux pas* in the history of American journalism would belong to Arthur Sears Henning, the seventy-one-year-old Washington bureau chief of the *Chicago Tribune*. At 9:00 A.M. on election day, before most votes had been cast, let alone counted, Henning confidently wrote the next day's lead announcing Dewey's victory. That evening, when the first returns showed ominous strength for Truman, Henning obstinately ignored them. "Oh, that's just nonsense; that's nonsense," he assured nervous colleagues. "Forget it, the AP is all wrong." Henning headed to WGN's radio studios to report on the Republican sweep, and in his absence the *Tribune's* editors revised his story and recalled the first edition. They tracked down most copies that had already hit the streets, but forgot about the newsstand in the *Tribune's* own lobby. It was there that the rival *Chicago Herald Examiner* gleefully acquired a stack of first editions, making sure to pass a copy on to the President. On the same day that Truman triumphantly held aloft the *Tribune's* infamous three-word banner headline, "DEWEY DEFEATS TRUMAN," Henning's thirty-four-year tenure as Washington bureau chief was abruptly terminated.[311]

No doubt, this misreading of the political situation was partially owed to laziness and over-reliance on conventional wisdom — after all, all of the reputable polling agencies were wide of the mark in their election forecasts, too. But it is also true that the major media houses were guilty of interpreting and reporting the news in terms of what they wanted to hear. Joe Thorndike, managing editor of *Life*, wrote Luce after the election, admitting, "I do think that we ... were misled by our bias."[312] When asked for his own perspective at a press conference on December 2, Truman remarked, "As soon as the people got the facts, they voted right. They couldn't get the facts from your columns and things, so I had to go out and tell them."[313]

Not even a personal triumph on the scale of his reelection, which was complemented by restored Democratic majorities in both houses of Congress, could assuage Truman's animus towards the press. The President was simply not inclined to let bygones be bygones, and hostility towards the "fact murderers" who controlled the media would be a recurring theme of his second term. He made his intentions clear in a tart letter to Elmo Roper in which he asserted, "People in general have lost faith in the modern press and its policies. That is a good thing too. No one segment should be able to control public opinion.... The publishers' press is a very small part of our population. They have debauched the responsibility they owe to the country and the people have shown them just how they like it.[314]

In his State of the Union message to the incoming 81st Congress in January 1949, the president asserted, somewhat disingenuously, "I have no bitterness in my heart against anyone — not even the bitter opposition press and its henchmen, the paid columnists and managing editors, and the bought and paid-for radio commentators." He warned the assembled legislators to remember, "You have learned that the people do not believe in the kept press and the paid radio." In his original conclusion, excised at the last minute, Truman was to have added "We have the greatest republic in the world if we remember that the people elect us to do what we think is right and not what some pollster or misguided editorial writer tells us to do."[315] Truman's disdain toward the press was even more evident in a piece he kept filed in his desk drawer:

> The men who write columns for the classified press sell their writing ability just as ... [loose] ladies sell their bodies to the madam of a bawdy house....
>
> In many cases the publisher only wants talent to present his distorted view point. Hearst, Pulitzer, Scripps-Howard, Gannett, Bertie McCormick and the Patterson chain are shining examples. Many a great and talented scribbler has sold his soul to these purveyors of "Character Assassination." The old Moslem [assassins] of Mesopotamia have a much better chance of a considered judgement in the end than have these paid mental whores of the [controllers] of our so called "free press."
>
> This so called "free press" is about as free as Stalin's press. The only difference is that Stalin frankly controlled his and the publishers and owners of our press are always yapping about the Constitution and suppressing a free press."

The president wrapped up this extraordinary diatribe by concluding, "The Hearst, Knight, Pulitzer, McCormick-Patterson, *L. A. Times*, *Dallas News*, and the *New Orleans Times-Picayune* are the worst news editors in the business—but I'm happy to say their thinking readers are aware of their mishandling of the facts and their political influence is not what they'd like to have it."[316] At the Jefferson-Jackson Day dinner later that year, Truman summed up his victory, telling his fellow Democrats, "This one-sided barrage of propaganda seems overwhelming at first. There are no full-page ads on our side. In fact, all we have on our side is the people. Thank God for that!"[317]

At least Harry never entirely lost his sense of perspective. "It seems that every man in the White House was tortured and bedeviled by the so-called free press," Truman lamented. "They were lied about, misrepresented and actually libeled, and they have to take it."[318] However, he was man enough to admit that "when I read what the lousy press of the days of Washington, Jefferson, Jackson, Lincoln, Grover Cleveland, and Woodrow Wilson had to say about those men, I'm comforted, for I've had it easy by comparison."[319]

I Like Ike

The press recovered from its shocking loss to Truman fairly rapidly. Mao's victory in China was the spur for many to start giving Harry hell. After the fall of Chiang Kai-Shek, for example, Halberstam says, "*Time* was now committed and politicized, an almost totally partisan instrument."[320] As the conflict in Korea ebbed and flowed with no end in sight, criticism of Truman mounted, while his standing in the polls tumbled. After the midterm elections of 1950 went badly for the president, he couldn't help grumbling, "One of the main difficulties with which we are faced now is the campaign of the 'big lie.' There are certain chain newspapers in this country that are using a Soviet propaganda program.... A free press is a free press because it is supposed to freely publish the facts on both sides of every question. That is not done in the Hearst, McCormick, and Roy Howard press." "However," Truman concluded, somewhat disingenuously, "I am not particularly worried about their influence because I don't think they have any."[321]

As Truman's authority deteriorated, however, his emboldened enemies in the press, sensing blood, began to press the assault with renewed vigor. The patience of the *Chicago Tribune* was first to snap. On February 13, 1951, the paper demanded that he immediately be stripped of the presidency: "When the time comes for the impeachment of Truman, the articles of the bill will fall into two classes, each backed by overwhelming evidence. One is Truman's violations of the Constitution, which he is sworn to uphold and defend; the other is his ... institution of Prendergast spoils politics in the White House [which] has brought the presidency to its lowest position in history." The editorial concluded by asserting, "Truman is crooked as well as incompetent. That is sufficient ground for the impeachment of any official." Eleven days later an indignant Truman wrote to Attorney General J. Howard McGrath, fuming that the allegations of corruption represented "libel, and criminal libel at that." Truman authorized McGrath to "go after these people with hammer and tongs," encouraging him to "proceed with whatever action is necessary to get the right result."[322] However, no further action on this matter was undertaken. Presumably, McGrath advised Truman that the administration had no case and the president, no doubt still fuming, let the matter drop.

By the beginning of 1952, even Harry Truman could no longer go on denying that the writing was the wall. Bogged down in Korea, buffeted by mini-scandals, plagued by McCarthy's anti-red witch hunts, and facing a challenge within his own party for the presidential nomination, Truman finally recognized that it was time to throw in the towel. Typically, he resolved to keep to himself his decision not to seek another term, until he was ready to announce it. "In that way," he noted, "I can nail the lies of the sabotage press and the lying air commentators and the columnists whose business it is to prostitute the minds of the voters."[323]

The problem for the opinion makers in the Republican Party was that their frontrunner for the nomination in 1952, Senator Taft, would not make a strong candidate, and his isolationism would not sit well with internationalist Republicans like Luce, even if he was elected. But who could challenge "Mr. Republican" for the hearts and minds of the Republican delegates?

The answer lay in Europe where Dwight D. Eisenhower, the supreme commander of NATO, maintained his headquarters. "Harry fell in love with Eisenhower as people fall in love with beautiful girls," one confidant of Luce's noted. "Harry really fell for him. He idolized Eisenhower as he did almost no one else."[324] Luce flew to Paris to personally petition Eisenhower to return home and run for the presidency.

Luce and his media empire played a key role in Eisenhower's nomination.[325] On the eve of the Republican convention, Eisenhower's managers distributed copies of *Time*, out a day early on Luce's orders, with a highly prejudiced account of the Taft managers "stealing" delegates.[326] "Eisenhower was right for the country for a large number of reasons, therefore it was *Time's* duty to explain why the country needed Ike," Luce explained in the aftermath of the campaign. "Any other form of objectivity would have been unfair and uninvolved."[327] As they had more than a half-century earlier when concentrating their firepower on William Jennings Bryan, key figures in the media were once more explicitly conflating subjective bias in favor of one candidate with what was objectively in the best interests of the nation.[328]

Eisenhower was the overwhelming choice of editorial opinion in the fall, over Democratic candidate Adlai Stevenson. Stevenson's only relatively secure base of editorial support was in the traditionally solid South, including the *St. Louis Post-Dispatch*, the *Louisville Courier-Journal*, and the *New Orleans Item*. Many newspapers— the *New York Times* among them — had committed to Eisenhower even before Stevenson was nominated. The best Stevenson's own family newspaper, the Bloomington *Daily Pantagraph*, could offer was to remain neutral.[329] In the final analysis, a total of 933 daily newspapers with over 40 million readers supported Eisenhower, compared to only 202 dailies with less than five and a half million readers that endorsed Stevenson. In at least nine states— Delaware, Maine, New Hampshire, South Dakota, North Dakota, Rhode Island, Utah, Vermont and Kansas— the Democratic nominee received not a single endorsement (see Table 12 on pages 252–253).

TABLE 12. NEWSPAPER EDITORIAL ENDORSEMENTS BY STATE/TERRITORY, 1952[330]

State/Territory	Eisenhower		Stevenson		Neutral	
	No.	Circulation	No.	Circulation	No.	Circulation
Alabama	8	383,134	7	80,277	2	94,582
Alaska	4	12,002				
Arizona	6	160,870	4	14,291		
Arkansas	10	74,651	9	196,655	6	48,052
California	78	3,191,339	13	558,979	8	41,270
Colorado	12	450,910	4	20,209	3	27,162
Connecticut	20	664,666			3	24,649
Delaware	2	84,356				
District of Columbia	3	600,620			1	226,573
Florida	13	421,868	5	167,030	6	185,084
Georgia	8	207,498	12	534,831	5	33,884
Hawaii	2	125,687			1	10,808
Idaho	7	90,800	2	17,338	1	5,665
Illinois	52	3,488,969	4	35,420	15	121,541
Indiana	38	1,064,526	13	150,533	12	145,005
Iowa	32	758,777	2	20,084	4	37,724
Kansas	41	441,619	2	3,444	2	8,400
Kentucky	6	90,344	11	464,327	7	50,417
Louisiana	9	192,498	1	99,260	8	359,778
Maine	6	178,496			3	55,201
Maryland	7	638,246	2	38,700	3	20,536
Massachusetts	22	1,494,921	2	115,325	11	577,563
Michigan	35	2,005,534	1	3,381	5	131,591
Minnesota	21	902,508	1	7,670	2	9,152
Mississippi	7	39,851	4	94,974	3	36,618
Missouri	26	1,269,176	13	441,708	5	16,562
Montana	8	33,736	1	29,788	2	29,217
Nebraska	15	404,873	2	30,460	2	13,664
Nevada	5	22,159	1	10,914		
New Hampshire	3	31,432			3	52,246
New Jersey	13	765,400	1	44,038	5	181,026
New Mexico	10	68,860	1	11,985	3	14,235
New York	71	7,542,539	7	418,387	9	458,510
North Carolina	6	249,813	13	297,070	16	236,755
North Dakota	10	136,765			1	5,456
Ohio	49	2,553,119	5	175,097	16	154,259
Oklahoma	18	497,665	11	70,224	14	61,778
Oregon	13	342,190	2	204,449	1	7,373
Pennsylvania	83	3,316,391	5	99,637	14	195,385
Rhode Island	4	222,221			1	7,309
South Carolina	7	275,956	5	88,280	3	22,889
South Dakota	10	121,410			1	16,162

State/Territory	Eisenhower		Stevenson		Neutral	
	No.	Circulation	No.	Circulation	No.	Circulation
Tennessee	15	700,662	3	126,893	5	33,573
Texas	38	1,563,190	13	139,650	16	356,663
Utah	1	92,365			2	130,158
Vermont	8	78,438			1	3,529
Virginia	16	534,378	5	62,794	9	117,902
Washington	19	823,866	1	18,749	2	15,838
West Virginia	16	279,216	8	167,124	1	11,421
Wisconsin	17	413,253	4	398,483	5	34,323
Wyoming	3	25,474	2	8,323	3	8,257
TOTAL	933	40,129,237	202	5,466,781	250	4,417,402
PERCENTAGES	67.34	80.24	14.52	10.88	18.14	8.88

The margin of Eisenhower's advantage in the press widens even further when subjective judgments on the extent of the overt bias in favor of a particular candidate are factored into the balance. According to one study, Eisenhower was the beneficiary of such market leaders as the *Chicago Tribune*, the *Indianapolis Star* and the *Los Angeles Times* actively proselytizing on his behalf, while enthusiasm for Stevenson's cause did not extend far beyond the Charleston, West Virginia, *Gazette* and the Great Falls, Montana, *Tribune*.[331]

In addition to his being on the back foot in the city and state papers, not a single mass-circulation magazine with a national distribution was in Stevenson corner.[332] *Life* asserted that Stevenson had aligned himself with the "Acheson faction" within the administration and "its softness on Communism" that had watched the advance of communist power "with feelings ranging from complacency to connivance ... treason was afoot during this calamity."

Stevenson seized his opportunity to highlight the issue of partisan slant in the media when, at a September 8 lunch in Oregon hosted by the state's newspaper editors, publishers and radio broadcasters, he remarked on the phenomenon that "the overwhelming majority of the press is just against Democrats ... automatically, as dogs are against cats." Nearly all of the papers "rushed to commit themselves" to Eisenhower in the spring of 1952, Stevenson said, "long before they knew what [he] stood for, or what his party platform would be, or who his opponent was, or what would be the issues of the campaign."

"I am, frankly, considerably concerned when I see the extent to which we are developing a one-party press in a two-party country," Stevenson concluded.[333] The response from the intended target of this rebuke, the press, was muted. "There is some substance to Governor Stevenson's good-natured criticism that a one-party press has developed in the United States," the *Washington Post* admitted. However, they added, "We suspect that the proportion of papers indorsing the Republican nominee reflects less automatism than the conviction that change is overdue and that it is necessary to counteract the subtle bribery of a party long in power."[334]

Predictably, while the press shrugged off Stevenson's critique, he did receive the Olympian approbation of Harry Truman, who noted privately, "You gave them exactly what they needed.... You stuck the rapier into the spot where it was tenderest and where it needed to be stuck."[335] At a press conference on September 11, three days after Stevenson's Oregon address, Truman warmed to a theme already dear to his heart, the challenge to a viable democracy presented by a one-party press. As the president explained, "Newspapers—especially daily newspapers—have become big business, and big business traditionally has always been Republican. I suggest every American bear this in mind, and add a dash of salt to every Republican helping of news, especially in those many papers and magazines which do not give a fair balance of news between the two major parties. If democracy is to work properly, the people must be able to read and hear not only the Republican story but the Democratic as well."[336]

The personal and editorial agendas of the nation's most prestigious newsmakers during the balance of the campaign prove that they were capable of tuning out or rising above the disapprobation of a lame duck president for whom they had no respect. After Nixon's "Checkers speech," Philip Graham, editor of the *Washington Post*, personally wrote the paper's response, saying that the Republican vice-presidential nominee had "eloquently and movingly" answered the charges against him. He even censored the Herblock cartoons that so enraged Nixon in the two weeks leading up to election day.[337] "As for Ike," Halberstam notes, "Graham's commitment was total." Among other responsibilities, he served as master of ceremonies for the key Eisenhower-Nixon fundraiser in Washington on the eve of the election.[338]

The biggest media "scoop" of the campaign, the charges that Nixon was able to indulge in a lifestyle far above his station only thanks a secret campaign slush fund established by his corporate benefactors, first appeared in the *New York Post*, which, according to Nixon, "was and still is the most partisan Democratic paper in the country. It had done an unusually neat smear job, but I did not expect anything to come of it."[339] In fact, the revelations almost cost Nixon his place on the Republican ticket; at the eleventh hour he was able to salvage his political career by going directly to the American people in a televised address. Nixon's presentation, dubbed the "Checkers" address, in reference to his gratuitously sentimental exploitation of the love his children bore for the family pet, set the template for future appeals.

Having played his part in securing Eisenhower's nomination, Henry Luce personally contributed thirteen thousand dollars to the Republican cause, but more importantly he loaned the services of *Fortune* publisher C. D. Jackson and *Life* editor Emmet John Hughes to the Eisenhower campaign. It was Hughes who conceived and wrote Ike's decisive "I shall go to Korea" speech on October 24.[340]

Harry Truman continued to rail against this elite collaboration against his candidate, his party, and his administration, into the twilight of the campaign. Stumping for Stevenson in St. Louis on November 1, in his last campaign speech as president and his last speech outside of Washington, D.C., Truman again singled out the press, snapping that "the two-party system is all right for the common people, but not, apparently, for the publishers of newspapers. They don't see any threat to our political system in having almost all the newspapers on one side."[341] But it was to no avail. Even if the American electorate was receptive to this message, it had turned its back on the messenger. Twenty years of Democratic dominance in Washington was brought to a crashing end in a Republican landslide. Picking through the rubble, there was one irony in the results for Truman to reflect on; for all the calumny he directed toward the one-party press, the only region to remain loyal to Stevenson was the one-party South. Such subtleties probably did little to alter the president's perspective, or his mood. On December 6 he took his parting shot at the press in the pages of his diary: "To hell with them. When history is written they will be the sons-of-bitches—not I."[342]

In the aftermath of the Republican triumph, Luce could not conceal his glee around the office. "Look at him," a *Time* researcher commented sourly, "only gravity is holding him down."[343] Eisenhower, who always answered every letter and honored every request for a meeting from Luce, subsequently appointed his wife Clare as ambassador to Italy, where she served for four years.[344] "During the Eisenhower presidency," Boughman remarks, "*Time* assumed the role of house organ."[345] Luce didn't think this should surprise anyone. "I am a Protestant, a Republican and a free enterpriser," he declared. "I am biased in favor of God, Eisenhower and the stockholders of Time Inc.—and if anybody who objects doesn't know this by now, why the hell are they still spending 35 cents for the magazine?"[346]

Things didn't get any easier for Stevenson in his rematch against Eisenhower four years later. The papers that endorsed Eisenhower accounted for 60 percent of the total circulation, Stevenson papers a mere 10 percent."[347] Eisenhower even enjoyed the backing of many of the major African-American newspapers, including the *Amsterdam News* in New York, the *Pittsburgh Courier, Louisville Defender* and the *Afro-American* in Baltimore.

The true value of Eisenhower's hidden-hand style of government was only properly appreciated in retrospect.[348] At the time, the president, indeed the entire political establishment, was overshadowed by the series of events that ensued when the junior senator from Wisconsin made a Lincoln Day speech on February 9, 1950, to the Republican Women's Club of Wheeling, West Virginia. "I have in my hand a list of 205 cases of individuals who appear to be either card-carrying members or certainly loyal to the Communist Party," was how the speech, and the phenomenon, began. The press was intimately associated with the explosive saga that was McCarthyism. Never before or since has one individual so comprehensively captured the media spotlight, or maintained so intense a love-hate relationship with its practitioners, as Joe McCarthy.

True, McCarthy could be cruel. He would target critics in the press, accusing them of writing stories that "might well have emanated from Moscow itself," articles that were "almost 100 percent in line with the official instructions issued to all Communists and fellow travelers." His preferred, almost reflexive, response was to simply compare hostile newspapers with the *Daily Worker*. By 1951 this category included publications as diverse as the *New York Times* and the *Post*, the *Madison Capital-Times*, the *St. Louis Post-Dispatch*, the *Denver Post*, the *Christian Science Monitor*, the *Nation*, the *New Republic*, *Time*, *Life*, and *Newsweek*. Whenever he deemed it necessary, McCarthy wouldn't hesitate in resorting to more concrete retaliation. After his most consistent hometown critic, the *Milwaukee Journal*, remarked during the 1950 campaign, "We wonder if the senator's friends shouldn't persuade him to see a psychiatrist," McCarthy called for a boycott of the newspaper. "Keep in mind," he lectured state business groups, "that when you send checks over to the *Journal* ... you are contributing to bringing the Communist Party line into the homes of Wisconsin."[349]

On occasion he could even be violent. On December 15, 1950, McCarthy attacked nationally syndicated columnist Drew Pearson on the Senate floor, labeling him a "Moscow-directed character assassin" and an "unprincipled liar and fake" with a "twisted, perverted mentality." But such a verbal tongue-lashing was relatively mild compared to his behavior three nights earlier in the men's cloakroom of Washington's Sulgrave Club, when McCarthy had physically attacked Pearson, striking him in the face and kneeing him twice in the groin. He had to be hauled off by California Senator Richard Nixon. "If I hadn't pulled McCarthy away, he might have killed Pearson," the future president told a friend. Nixon escorted McCarthy outside and spent the next half-hour trying to locate his colleague's automobile, the junior senator from Wisconsin being too drunk to remember where he had parked it.[350]

But at the same time McCarthy's roguish charm, hard-drinking habits, and readiness to impart an exclusive at all hours of the day, endeared him to many reporters on the beat, even those who despised him personally or opposed him on ideological grounds. If nothing else he was always news, and news is what makes or breaks the business. Therein lay the great irony at the heart of McCarthyism. Certainly, McCarthy had some powerful allies in the press; according to Willard Edwards of the *Chicago Tribune*, McCarthy "just fitted into what we had been saying long before." Accordingly, "we gave him complete support. We never criticized him in any way. We just went all the way with him editorially."[351] The senator also enjoyed the support of the Hearst and Scripps-Howard chains.[352] But his supposed enemies in the media ultimately did at least as much to promulgate his agenda as his friends. By accident or design, McCarthy had stumbled onto a foolproof method by which to make himself the

Renowned Red-baiter Joe McCarthy actually knew nothing about unmasking communists but did know a great deal about how to manipulate the media: always provide good copy, always be accessible, never stand still — be prepared to move on to a fresh target the moment public interest in an old case wanes — and never apologize for anything. This strategy kept him in the headlines for four tempestuous years until he finally bit off more than he could chew when he took on the U.S. army and flamed out on public television (courtesy Library of Congress).

absolute center of the national media whirlwind. If you keep making statements outrageous enough to demand attention, all the while moving from one target to the next too fast for those covering you to ascertain the veracity of your charges, they have to keep taking you at face value and their coverage must reflect that. The *New York Times* and the *Washington Post* might flail at you on their editorial pages, but on the front page, where it counts, all they can do is report what you say, day after day after day.[353]

Secretary of State Dean Acheson, one of McCarthy's primary targets, recognized the implications of this process. Addressing the American Society of Newspaper Editors in 1950 he told them, "Now I don't ask for your sympathy. I don't ask you for help. You are in a worse situation than I am. I and my associates are only the intended victims of this mad and vicious operation. But you, unhappily, you by reason of your calling, are participants. You are unwilling participants, disgusted participants, but nevertheless, participants, and your position is far more serious than mine."[354]

The great press organs themselves agonized over this reality; they fully understood what was happening but were impotent to counteract it. "It is difficult, if not impossible, to ignore charges by Senator McCarthy just because they are usually proved exaggerated or false," the *New York Times* lamented. "The remedy lies with the reader."[355]

"The press was baffled by McCarthy," Oshinsky notes, "And utterly fascinated. Like everyone else, it recognized the paradox of giving serious attention to someone so manipulative and devoid of truth. But it saw no alternative. Unable to ignore McCarthy, the press became his captive, offering its services until the political process finally rose up to silence him."[356]

In the end, the media did not precipitate, but merely presided over, the downfall of Joseph McCarthy. He destroyed himself, a victim of his own success. The rout of the Democratic Party in 1952, something he had done so much to bring about, restored both ends of Pennsylvania Avenue to the Republican grasp. In order to remain in the public spotlight, McCarthy would now have to spin his own party into the web of the Communist conspiracy and in doing so he would unleash forces over which even he had no control. Bayley points out that most of the nation's newspapers, and even most of those on McCarthy's "fellow travelers" list, supported the Republican Party in the fifties, and most of them also supported McCarthy during the first four years of his red-baiting crusade. As long as the people McCarthy was accusing of treason were Democrats, they were happy to play along. It was only when it became obvious, in the early months of 1954, that those being accused of tolerating Communists in government were part of the Republican administration of President Eisenhower that Republican publishers began to see McCarthy in a new light.[357] "The primary function of a newspaper is to tell the people what is happening," Bayley concludes. "In the case of McCarthy, the press did not properly fulfill this function. Nor does the press deserve credit for its final wolf-pack descent on McCarthy when it became apparent that he intended on going right on attacking the Republican Eisenhower administration with the same vigor and venom he had expended on Truman's Democrats. Criticism of McCarthy at this point was easy and unimportant."[358]

McCarthy was never more than shadowboxing in his accusations that the media represented a Soviet fifth column. From the beginning, the press was a willing participant in the Cold War united front against Communism.[359] The *New York Times* not only endorsed Eisenhower for president in both 1952 and 1956, it suppressed the story of U.S. involvement in the 1954 coup that brought down President Jacobo Arbenz of Guatemala,[360] and after Kennedy was elected, at the behest of the White House, it sat on leads about the Bay of Pigs invasion[361] and the Cuban Missile Crisis.[362] But one of the enduring legacies of the McCarthy era was that a new division emerged in the press, one that superseded any confrontation along strictly party lines. "Real" conservatives, still smarting from the internationalist wing of the party having stolen the GOP nomination from their beloved Taft, resolved that from then on, in order to represent the real America, it wasn't good enough any more for a publication simply to be Republican. If it didn't fully endorse McCarthy's vision of the Red Peril, then it was cast into the heretical circle of the elite media — what the *Chicago Tribune* dubbed the "pantywaist press." This categorization, which in conservative eyes managed to be both amorphous in its makeup but homogenous in its propagation of un–American ideas and candidates, has been a pillar of the rightist worldview ever since, even (or perhaps especially) in the eyes of individuals and institutions which themselves could not be more establishmentarian.

The *Tribune* was one of the first to draw this line. In a July 1950 editorial headed "IS IT FEMINISM?" McCormick's paper asked whether the *New York Herald-Tribune* and the *New York Post* followed similar editorial policies because they were both owned by women "who seem to prefer the overbearing arrogance of Englishmen to the deferential courtesy of Americans." The *Washington Post*, the *Tribune* maintained, belongs to Eugene Meyer but was dominated by Mrs. Meyer and "on the Red side of purple." *Time* magazine, the *Tribune* added, has the same approach because "Henry Luce has borrowed Dorothy Thompson's panties and is unable to fill them out completely." This approach was representative of an ongoing process on the part of the conservative press to differentiate itself, the voice of the people, from the "prestige media," the voice of the elite. Responding to a report that Truman read four newspapers each day — the *New York Times* and the *Herald-Tribune*, the Baltimore *Sun*, and the *Washington Post*—a *Chicago Tribune* editorial in April 1951 remarked, "The selection gives a good indication of why he is so frequently out of touch with what the people of the United States are saying and thinking. There is little wonder that the little chump doesn't realize he's a chump."[363]

Things returned to a new equilibrium in the latter half of the decade. The media calmly acquiesced in playing its part in the united front against the invidious Red Menace to all facets of society. The political balance of the nation's newspapers and weekly magazines remained firmly right of center. The major columnists— James Reston, Walter Lippmann, Arthur Krock, the Alsop Brothers, Marquis Childs, and Doris Fleeson — hovered around the center. In the days before talk radio most radio commentators— Alastair Cooke, Erwin E. Canham, Eric Sevareid, and Edward R. Murrow — reflected a kind of centrism in their five weekly 15-minute commentaries. There were Paul Harvey, Fulton Lewis, and, during the McCarthy era, Walter

Winchell on the right, and Edward Morgan on the left, but they were the exceptions. Television news was devoid of editorializing, and while the opinion programs on radio and television such as "American Forum of the Air" and "Author Meets the Critics" could be disputatious, they were at least marked by a degree of civility.[364] In retrospect it is apparent that the Eisenhower years, defined by a universally respected president and an omnipresent external threat, would mark the closest the American media would ever come to attaining the golden mean of objectivity — or, perhaps more accurately, to attaining an industry-wide consensus on the parameters of subjectivity.

But even in this all–American era of coonskin caps, Hula Hoops, and segregated drinking fountains, did conservatives feel they were experiencing a golden age of media influence? Were they happy with the status quo, with the warm indulgence on the part of editors and reporters towards Ike, with the united front against communism,[365] with the upright moral tone that reflexively proselytized against everything from rock and roll to the ambiguous relationship between Batman and Robin? Hardly. That was not the way they saw the world, heard it, read it, felt it. "Radio and television commentators as well as a great proportion of the working press are on the other side," Nixon complained in December 1954. "They stick the needle into us every night and every day, and frankly I simply don't know how we're going to be able to counter-act it until we've developed a corps of people ourselves who will at least give us an even break in reporting the news."[366]

Even in an era when the Republican Party could take for granted the overwhelming support of the nation's press, when the media was fully committed to the Cold War, when issues like feminism, abortion and homosexuality were not mentioned in polite company, and even civil rights was only just emerging as the locus for serious national debate, conservatives were convinced that they were an oppressed majority held at knifepoint by a hostile, alien, elite-driven clique that monopolized the media. Looking back at the fifties, "Put together all the influential media and you get a score of something like liberals 95, conservatives 5," Viguerie and Franke lament. "Or perhaps it was more like 97/3. That's the sort of monopoly enjoyed by Pravda in its Soviet heyday."[367] If that was how conservatives felt at the end of an era when they had enjoyed almost total dominance over the entire spectrum of the media, their outrage when cracks started to emerge in that dominance during the following decade can begin to be appreciated.

V

The Liberal Media?
1960–Today

According to the received wisdom regarding the 1960s, just as the electoral dominance of the Democratic Party began to crumble, the media suddenly flipped from being the voice of the conservative establishment to being a propaganda vehicle for the liberal agenda.

There is some truth to this assertion. There is no doubt that the center of gravity in the nation's elite media shifted from being center right to center left during the course of the decade. Crucially, this was most obvious in the manifest favoritism shown by the leading publications and, more importantly, by the three television networks, toward the civil rights movement and, to a lesser extent, in their criticism of the Vietnam War. Race, therefore, was the wedge that split the elite media from the Republican Party it had considered its own for more than a hundred years.

The slavery question, which was a race question, had been responsible for bringing the Republican Party into being in the first place. The core of the opposition to slavery was centered in the Northeast. As the political expression of this region, the Republicans inherited from their distant Federalist and Whig forebears the mantle of the party which represented the interests of the establishment. The South, from time immemorial, has chosen to define itself through opposition to the Northeast, an essential hostility that reached its apogee in secession and Civil War. The Democratic Party, the physical manifestation of the South, by definition therefore became the voice of the anti-establishment. Even when the Democrats almost totally monopolized power during the two decades from 1933 to 1953, for most of that time under the leadership of the Groton- and Harvard-educated Franklin Roosevelt, because of their Southern roots they remained — to establishment eyes — the opposition. Under all circumstances, the establishment remained loyal to its Republican Party, the government in exile, and the press coverage of the era reflected this reality.[1]

This entire paradigm was stood on its head in the early 1960s, and it wasn't because the media had been swept off its collective feet by the dash and charm of Camelot. It was because the civil rights issue had again forced its way onto the political agenda. This time the Republican Party, which in a paternal, patronizing manner had always at least paid lip service to the welfare of African Americans in the past, was now determined, in the words of Barry Goldwater, to "go hunting where the ducks are," among white southerners energized by the backlash against elite-driven, federally mandated desegregation.[2] As the Democrats under Kennedy and Johnson moved towards civil rights, the Republicans, in one of the great realignments of American political history, emerged as the champions of states' rights.

The ascendancy of the Sunbelt Republicans represented a deliberate challenge to the Northeastern establishment that had assumed its lease over the party extended in perpetuity. The great press organs of the establishment reacted in dismay to the Goldwater campaign for the GOP presidential nomination, but his candidacy did not make them any less Republican; their response was to head off the conservative insurgency in-house by boosting establishment hopeful New York governor Nelson Rockefeller in the primaries and then, when that failed, by endorsing Pennsylvania governor William Scranton at the convention.

It was this blatant meddling in internal GOP factional politics, not some mass defection to the Democratic enemy, which fatally poisoned the relationship between the conservative movement and the elite press. If one moment symbolizes the gulf that had suddenly opened between the Republican Party and the nation's media, it occurred at the GOP convention at the Cow Palace in San Francisco in 1964 when, for the first time in the history of the republic, the Republican Party singled out the press as its enemy and turned on it with savage fury. When Dwight Eisenhower urged the delegates to "scorn the divisive efforts of those outside our family, including sensation-seeking columnists and commentators who couldn't care less about the good of our party," the convention exploded, as Teddy White wrote, "in applause, shouts, boos, catcalls, horns, klaxons, and glory." The delegates, and then the gallery, turned almost in unison and directed their rancor towards the press tables and television booths above the convention floor. As another observer recalled, "The delegates stood on their chairs, shouting, raving, shaking their fists and cursing the reporters in the press section."[3]

In the wake of Goldwater's nomination, a vast percentage of the press did break with generations of tradition to endorse the Democratic incumbent, Lyndon Johnson. But by and large this represented little more than a "Mugwump"-style tactical switch in order to chastise the conservatives for their capture of the Republican Party. On the whole, the nation's mainstream newspapers remained establishment Republican. When the GOP nominated the establishment-worthy Richard Nixon in 1968, they drifted back into their traditional political moorings almost en masse.[4] That wasn't enough to placate conservatives, who observed, with mounting frustration, the nation's elite press being infiltrated by a new generation of reporters infused with the same Baby Boomer ethics as those activists then engaged in capturing the Democratic Party.[5]

The reality was that, aside from a few idiosyncratic exceptions, by the end of the 1960s, the blatant, partisan electioneering style that had characterized the newspapers of a previous generation was fading into the past. Objectivity was the new standard; in order to retain their credibility under this criterion, everyone in the mainstream media was careful to at least pay lip service to separating news reporting from editorial opinion.

A driving force in this trend was the consolidation of the newspaper business under the umbrella of a handful of corporate conglomerates whose agenda was strictly business. The inevitable corollary was a decline in the diversity of perspectives on the news. Prior to the First World War, a majority of cities had commercially competing daily newspapers; by the end of the 1960s, less than 3 percent of cities did. By the 1970s, twenty corporations controlled more than half of the sixty-one daily newspapers sold each day.[6] The big losers were the old school owner/editors who had had driven the business for decades by carving out their own empires of opinion. Liebovich confirms, "These brash media figures, who dictated policy and ideology, gave way to conglomerates—corporations whose leaders sought to entertain as much as inform and who saw presidential politics not as ideological struggles in which they must enmesh themselves but marketable commodities that demanded election-year packaging."[7]

Some professed to miss the traditional model of cutthroat newspaper rivalry, if not for the color then at least for the clarity it brought to election season. "When editorial policy, often of a partisan tone, permeated the entire content of the press, the loyal reader had cues of considerable clarity," V. O. Key wrote. "The partisan press put a degree of order into the confusing world of politics. The modern press tends to convey all its disorders."[8]

All the Way with JFK

The infinitesimal margin between victory and defeat in the presidential election of 1960 gave Richard Nixon plenty of scope to find other people to blame for his failure. The media was high on his list. Nixon first became aware of a media conspiracy actively working against him when as a young congressman he led the House Un-American Activities Committee investigation in the Alger Hiss case. In Nixon's mind, the media establishment rallied around Hiss, one of its own, and against him. On one level this antipathy was simply a response to his agenda as a resolutely anti-red conservative Republican. But on a deeper level Nixon was convinced he was being victimized because he came from the wrong side of the tracks, the wrong side of the country, and hadn't had the benefit of going to the right schools. This persecution complex, a manifestation of his abiding insecurity, became embedded in Nixon's psyche; a brooding antipathy towards the media was a trademark of his subsequent political career.

Nixon, for example, couldn't help but remark on the way "so many reporters in 1960 became caught up in the excitement of Kennedy's campaign and infected with his personal sense of mission." As evidence, Nixon seized on a passage from Teddy White's *The Making of the President 1960*: "By the last week of the campaign, those forty or fifty national correspondents who had followed Kennedy since the beginning of his electoral exertions into the November days had become more than a press corps—they had become his friends and, some of them, his most devoted admirers. When the bus or the plane rolled or flew through the night, they sang songs of their own composition about Mr. Nixon and the Republicans in chorus with the Kennedy staff and felt that they, too, were marching like soldiers of the Lord to the New Frontier."

To provide further verification, Nixon lamented in his memoirs, "Writing to me after the election, Willard Edwards, the *Chicago Tribune's* veteran political analyst, put it more bluntly. He referred to the 'staggering extent of ... slanted reporting' [as] one of the most, if not the most, shameful chapters of the American press in history."[9] In his final assessment on the role of the media in the campaign of 1960, Nixon concluded, "During the campaign they quite naturally—and as often as not, perhaps quite unconsciously—favored the candidate of the party of their choice."[10]

But was Kennedy popular with reporters simply because he was a Democrat? Or was it because he was approachable and responsive, and his campaign pioneered such innovations as providing transcripts of the candidate's speeches, issuing daily quotes for reporters, and seeing to their travel needs? Was Nixon unpopular with reporters for no reason other than he was a Republican? Or did his ill-concealed contempt for the entire profession have something to do with it?[11]

Was the vice president the victim of a concerted media campaign against him? There is some evidence of coolness towards Nixon among the Republican loyalists in the press. "I don't know, I don't know," Henry Luce told a group of his editors prior to the 1960 election. "I just don't like Nixon. I guess we have to support him, but I don't like him.... You know, I never liked Nixon. But I *like* Kennedy. I don't agree with Kennedy on most things, but I *like* him."[12] "This is a heck of a year for *Time* to turn objective!" one leading Republican groused.[13]

But a glance at the figures shows virtually no movement at all in terms of endorsements from the previous election. Kennedy was backed by 16.42 percent of the newspapers in 1960, only a marginal improvement from Adlai Stevenson's 15.76 percent in 1956. In other words, for all the nascent glamour of the emerging Camelot, it was strictly business as usual come election time for most editors.

In fact, circumstances conspired to give conservatism a powerful voice at the opening bell of election season. As the significance of the first-in-the-nation New Hampshire primary increased, so did the prominence of the state's leading newspaper, the *Manchester Union Leader*, which, under editor William Loeb, advanced its hard-earned reputation as the most conservative publication in the country every campaign.[14] With the candidates effectively trapped in New Hampshire for months on end and at his mercy, Loeb had a unique capacity for getting under liberal skins. John F. Kennedy subjected himself to a second helping of punishment by deciding to wind up his 1960 campaign in Manchester where he was greeted by a Loeb editorial asserting that "no one in his right mind" could vote for the Massachusetts senator that year. Kennedy lost his famous cool, growling that he could not think of an American newspaper "more irresponsible" than the *Union Leader* or a publisher "who has less regard for the truth" than Loeb — who responded by labeling Kennedy a "spoiled brat."[15]

And it wasn't as though Nixon was bereft of allies in the media during the fall campaign. Although Kennedy was feebly endorsed by the *Times*, elsewhere in New York, Nixon could rely on the *Herald-Tribune* (whose chief editorial writer, Raymond K. Price, became his chief speech writer) and the *Daily News* (which labeled Kennedy the "British-tailored nominee of the America Stinks Party.")

In addition to the *Tribune*, Nixon was endorsed by the *Daily News* and *Sun-Times* in Chicago; the *Chronicle* in San Francisco, as well as the *Times* in Los Angeles; the *Herald* in Boston, Kennedy's back yard, as well as the *Chronicle* in Houston, Lyndon Johnson country; the *Washington Star*, and the *St. Louis Globe-Democrat*, one of whose editorial writers, Patrick Buchanan, became another of his speech writers; and the Hearst chain (13 papers) as well as the Scripps-Howard chain (19 papers). Individual allies in the press included C. L. Sulzberger of the *New York Times*; Richard L. Wilson of the Cowles publications; and syndicated columnist Joseph Alsop. But the weight of this support was never enough, in Nixon's mind, to balance what he considered the active, calculated animosity of the "elite" media, as manifested in such publications as the *New York Times*, the *Washington Post*, the *Boston Globe*, and the *St. Louis Post-Dispatch*. No matter how high he rose or low he fell, hatred of this elite remained Nixon's lodestar during the ensuing peaks and troughs of his career.[16]

The outcome of the California gubernatorial campaign of 1962 only confirmed the reality that he had constructed in his own mind of a media united against him. Nixon had grown accustomed to slavish loyalty from the press in his native state; his career had been nurtured, defended and promoted in particular by the *Los Angeles Times*.[17] Rarick goes so far as to say, "In his early career, he was for all practical purposes the creation of the *Los Angeles Times*."[18] On the eve of Nixon's famous "Checkers" speech, the *Times* had splashed a "We Stand By Nixon" editorial across its front page: "The personal tragedy of an upright man sacrificed unjustly to satisfy the clamor stirred up by the cunning objectives of his political enemies would by no means be as deplorable as would be the loss to the public of a career genuinely dedicated to the public interest." Nixon continued to bask in the glow of such adulation during his two terms as vice president, while the *Times* continued to micromanage Republican politics in California for the duration of the 1950s, juggling candidates for high office to suit the needs of the day.[19]

But Nixon returned to a different California. Kyle Palmer had died, the man who had discovered Nixon and effectively dominated the Republican Party in the state for decades (he was referred to as "the Little Governor"), and after Norman Chandler's son Otis took over the paper, the *Times* became more evenhanded. Although it reported the campaign fairly, the *Times* was unstinting in its praise of Nixon, who it described as "an outstanding Congressman," who "served California with distinction" in the Senate and was "the most effective Vice President in the long history of that office." The paper ultimately endorsed the entire Republican ticket, including its gubernatorial candidate: "As never before, we must have for governor a man of strong and unwavering leadership, of dynamic leadership. That is why the *Times* believes that Richard M. Nixon should be elected governor."[20]

But it was not enough, either to swing the electorate, which voted to reelect Pat Brown by a clear majority, or to mollify Nixon after he lost. The performance by the tired and emotional former vice president the following morning was a case study in neuroses gone wild.

Stepping up to the microphone, brushing aside his press spokesperson, Herb Klein, who had been fielding reporters' questions, Nixon announced, "Now that Mr. Klein has made a statement, now that all the members of the press are so delighted that I lost, I would just like to make a statement of my own." Nixon then launched into a rambling discourse that was ostensibly a political critique but in fact represented the eruption of more than a decade's worth of suppressed rage against the press. His conclusion has entered political legend:

> And as I leave the press, all I can say is this: For 16 years, ever since the Hiss Case, you've had a lot of fun — a lot of fun — that you've had an opportunity to attack me and I think I've given as good as I've taken.
>
> I leave you gentlemen now and you will now write it. You will interpret it. That's your right. But as I leave you I want you to know, just think how much you're going to be missing. You won't have Nixon to kick around any more, because, gentlemen, this is my last press conference....
>
> I believe in reading what my opponents say and I hope that what I have said today will at least make television, radio, the press first recognize the great responsibility they have to report all the news and, second, recognize that they have a right and a responsibility, if they're against a candidate, give him the shaft, put one lonely reporter on the campaign who will report what the candidate says now and then. Thank you, gentlemen, and good day.

As Nixon stalked away he told Klein, "I know you don't agree. I gave it to them right in the ass. It had to be said, goddamit. It had to be said."[21] The press subsequently fell all over itself denying Nixon's accusation of premeditated bias against his campaign. Otis Chandler published a front page announcement the next day, reminding Nixon that the *Times* had endorsed him in every one of his campaigns (twice for the House, for the Senate, twice for vice president, for president, and for governor): "The *Times* published three editorials and seven editorial cartoons supporting Mr. Nixon's candidacy. We continue today to believe that he was the best qualified candidate for governor, as we said in our endorsement editorial."[22] That still wasn't enough for Nixon, who canceled his subscription a few days later.[23]

In fact, "Nixon's critique of the campaign was plainly inaccurate," Rarick says. "Nixon was annoyed, not because the *Times* and other newspapers had covered the campaign of 1962 unfairly, but because he yearned for the pro–Nixon bias of a bygone day."[24] Halberstam draws the same conclusion, "The truth was the reporting on [Nixon]'s and Pat Brown's race was fair and balanced.... [H]e had never encountered equal treatment before in California and he found it devastating."[25]

Liberals assumed that Nixon had written his own political epitaph, but conservatives saw it differently. Far from ostracizing Nixon they rallied around him. Nixon received thousands of letters of support. Former President Eisenhower spoke for the Republican Party when he commented, "Dick did have a point about bias in reporting and the arrogant sort of journalistic sharp-shooting that occurs daily in all too many publications."[26] As Ambrose puts it, "Nixon began at his last press conference the start of his next campaign.... Campaigning meant bashing the Democrats and their allies, the reporters. Nixon was the best there was at that, and the one who enjoyed it the most."[27]

AuH$_2$O

Nixon hungered to get back into the political game, but for the moment the spotlight had shifted to a newcomer. Those conservatives looking for the definitive moment when they were deserted by their long-term paramour, the media, cite 1964, the year the Republican Party nominated Barry Goldwater. The GOP slogan that year was "A choice, not an echo." To conservatives, the media made its choice in 1964 to oppose Goldwater and, by definition, has upheld that choice every year since.

True-believer conservatives in the press flocked to the Goldwater banner. William Loeb threw the support of his *Manchester Union Leader* behind the Arizona senator, and did his utmost to damage the prospects of New York governor Nelson Rockefeller, showing no compunction about hitting the presumptive favorite for the GOP nomination where he was most vulnerable. "We have never had a wife-swapper in the White House," the *Union Leader* declaimed, in reference to Rockefeller's divorce and remarriage. "We believe that, even though we are inhabiting an age of loose morals, the people will not accept a wife-swapper as President."[28]

But such fervor was hugely outweighed by the rising tide of editorial opposition to Goldwater as the year progressed. During the campaign, *Time* noted that "in a press establishment that normally swings, preponderantly, behind the Republican presidential candidate," publishers "are taking sides with unprecedented speed and in a pattern for which history provides no precedent."[29] Larry O'Brien, an aide to the president, told him bluntly, "It is obvious the press generally is engaged in a total drive to stop Goldwater."

"The editorial support of the nation's press and national magazines is, generally, as solid a Republican resource as the labor unions are a Democratic resource," Teddy White remarked. "But, one by one, starting in August, the regional newspapers and then the national magazines—which, in Republican terms, have always been more Catholic than the Pope—cut their traditional candidate adrift or scorched him with editorial gunfire. Papers that had never before gone Democratic now lined up behind the Democratic candidate."[30]

According to White, the desertion on September 18 of the Hearst papers, Republican since 1932, was the hardest blow for the Goldwater campaign to take. The Cowles and Scripps-Howard chains also came out for Johnson. "By the end of September the best papers in the Republican heartland had checked in—sometimes at the rate of seven or eight a day—with their switches to the Democrats," White observed. These included many publications that had turned their backs on the Democratic Party during the New Deal, such as the *Plain-Dealer* and the *Press* in Cleveland, the *Denver Rocky Mountain News*, and the *Indianapolis Times*, all endorsing a Democrat for the first time since 1936, and the *San Francisco News*, which had last endorsed a Democrat when FDR first ran in 1932.

In order to advocate the election of Lyndon Baines Johnson, therefore, many papers had to shake off an antipathy toward his party, the party of Roosevelt, Wilson and Bryan, that had been the keystone of their existence for decades, and in some instances the very reason for their inception. On July 13, for example, Joe Lastelic, a reporter at the *Kansas City Star*, had notified the White House of an eyebrow-raising impending announcement that his paper was committed to Johnson's reelection. "That will be the first time that a Democrat has won our endorsement in this century," Lastelic explained. "The last man to have it was Grover Cleveland [in 1892]. Please tell the President. It's going to be sensational. [Publisher] Roy A. Roberts, known throughout the country as a good Republican and kingmaker, is going to write it."[31] This reversal in time-honored partisan association was complemented by three more defections from the Republican column: the *Herald Weekly* of Camden, Maine, for the first time since its 1869 founding; the *Syracuse Post Standard*, for the first time in its sixty-five year history; and the upstate New York *Binghamton Sun-Bulletin*, which had refused to endorse a Democrat for President in every election since it first rolled off the presses in 1822.

In October, the defections continued: the *Detroit Free Press*, the *Philadelphia Bulletin*, the *Baltimore Sun* (Republican since 1932), and the grand old lady of Republican journalism, the *New York Herald-Tribune*, which on October 4 published an editorial declaring:

> For the Presidency: Lyndon Johnson.
>
> Travail and torment go into those simple words, breaching as they do the political traditions of a long newspaper lifetime. But we find ourselves, as Americans, even as Republicans, with no other acceptable course.
>
> Senator Goldwater says he is offering the nation a choice. So far as the two candidates are concerned, our inescapable choice — as a newspaper that was Republican before there was a Republican party, has been Republican ever since and will remain Republican — is Lyndon B. Johnson.[32]

The piece went on to excoriate the Republican nominee for thirty more column inches. *Life* magazine also announced its support of Johnson in October, the first time any Time Inc. publication had endorsed a Democrat. The *Atlantic Monthly*, which had not endorsed any candidate in over 100 years, formally opposed Goldwater.[33] "For the good of the Republican Party, which his candidacy disgraces, we hope that Goldwater is crushingly defeated," the *Saturday Evening Post* editorialized. "Goldwater is a grotesque burlesque of the conservative he pretends to be. He is a wild man, a stray, an unprincipled and ruthless jujitsu artist like Joe McCarthy."[34]

Goldwater's position was worst among the major papers with a daily circulation of more than 100,000 subscribers. Nixon had the support of 87 of the approximately 125 publications in this class, to 22 for Kennedy in 1960. In 1964, Johnson won the endorsement of 82 of the major papers to Goldwater's 12.[35] Goldwater found himself almost completely shut out in the major dailies that dominated the media markets in urban centers ranging from Cleveland to Miami to San Francisco. But Johnson was not content to bask in the accolades of newspapers serving the constituencies he had already locked up. He assiduously courted opinion makers in the marginal states where votes were still up for grabs. Devereux notes the success of this strategy: "In the border states, the White House's connections to the media brought on board the Democratic coalition most of the influential voices in the press."[36]

The low-hanging editorial fruit could be plucked easily enough after exposure to the legendary Johnson Treatment. To solidify the *Washington Post's* support for LBJ, publisher Katherine Graham arranged a luncheon at the White House between her editorial board and the president on April 15, 1964. As Graham related in a letter, Johnson's performance won him rave reviews from the *Post* personnel: "I cannot tell you how much yesterday's lunch meant to all of us here at the Post. It made a very deep impression on many of the men and especially on those who had not known you personally before. Fritz Beebe, the Chairman of our Board who is also head of Newsweek, had to return to Washington today and said to me, 'I'm still in a daze from yesterday's wonderful experience....' They were all full of admiration, as was I."[37]

A key mountain-state ally for LBJ was Palmer Hoyt, publisher and editor of the *Denver Post*. White House aide Walter Jenkins, in a memo dated September 13, reported to the president his satisfaction at the extent of the commitment to the Democratic cause: "I talked to Palmer Hoyt last night as you suggested. He is editorializing for you today. Tomorrow he is comparing Miller and Humphrey and coming out for Humphrey. Tuesday he is coming out for you and Humphrey as a team so he is actually having a three day series of editorial support. He is distributing copies to all columnists and commentators and particularly asking the columnists who write for his paper to make appropriate comment."[38]

Further evidence of the explicitly partisan agenda at the *Denver Post* is contained in an October Democratic National Committee (DNC) report which noted that Hoyt was "concerned about the distribution of the smear literature by GOP precinct workers, who, he says, outnumber Democrats by a 2 to 1 margin in Colorado. He would like ... anything else we [the DNC] have to counter and discredit this smear literature. A feature writer on the *Denver Post*, Lev Chapin, has done an analysis of the [pro–Goldwater] book, *A Choice Not an Echo*. Hoyt will send it to us and we can reprint it if we like."[39]

Returning the Field newspaper chain to its traditional Democratic allegiance was a priority for the Johnson campaign. With a heavy investment in a sector that favored high consumer demand and low tariffs, the Field family had joined other major retailers (most notably Edward Filene in Boston) in endorsing FDR and the New Deal, only to back Nixon over Kennedy in 1960. Early in January 1964, *Chicago Sun–Times* editor Emmett Dedmon and other top journalists at the Field newspapers spent several days at the Johnson ranch in Texas. Positive feedback from this excursion drew Field himself into LBJ's orbit. He received an invitation to the White House and, on February 2, a personal call from the president. Both the *Sun-Times* and the *Daily News* endorsed Johnson, who sent several letters to Field thanking him for his support, noting in one that "the support of your papers may well be the difference which will ensure an Illinois vote for the continuation of [our] program."[40]

John Cowles, a Luce Republican and publisher of a chain of newspapers including the *Minneapolis Tribune* and *Des Moines Register*, had endorsed Nixon in 1960 but switched to Johnson in 1964, the White House cementing the relationship by appointing Cowles to a presidential advisory panel on international affairs in September of that year. Johnson was quite consistently shameless in exploiting the office of the presidency if it gave him the opportunity to establish a rapport with a potentially useful ally in the media. Having hosted a lengthy luncheon at the White House for the top editors at Scripps-Howard in mid–March of 1964, after meeting with publisher Sam Newhouse that same month, Johnson agreed to give an address at the dedication of the Newhouse School at Syracuse University and ordered federal government mediation to help end the five-year strike at Newhouse's *Portland Oregonian* newspaper. As a consequence, only two Newhouse chain papers declared for Goldwater, compared to thirteen for Johnson, with the *Oregonian* and *Globe-Democrat* officially neutral.[41] Both Newhouse papers in Syracuse, the *Herald-American* and *Post-Standard*, endorsed Johnson, the publisher of the former writing to the president that "our support will not be limited to the announcement but rather we intend to promote the ticket with vigor and enthusiasm throughout the campaign."[42]

Scripps-Howard papers in the South that backed Johnson in 1964 included the *Birmingham Post-Herald* (which helped to balance the pro–Goldwater *Birmingham News*, a Newhouse publication that refused to toe the company line) and the *Memphis Commercial Appeal*, which broke its post-1936 policy of endorsing Republicans for the presidency. A Newhouse paper that did come through for Johnson in the South was the *New Orleans Times-Picayune*. A DNC survey of the state reported that "[publisher John] Timms says that as a result of the endorsement of Johnson by his two New Orleans papers he believes Johnson will carry South Louisiana by a large enough margin to offset Goldwater's strength in Northern Louisiana."[43] Another significant coup for the president in Dixie was the backing of John S. Knight, who had never previously endorsed a Democrat for the presidency. Winning over the Knight chain secured LBJ the critical, albeit reluctant, support of the *Miami Herald* and *Charlotte Observer*. In his native Texas, Johnson enjoyed the backing of the *Houston Post* (which was owned by the family of Oveta Culp Hobby, who served as secretary of health, education, and welfare in the Eisenhower administration), the *Corpus Christi Caller-Times*, the *Dallas Times Herald*, the *San Antonio Express*, and the *San Antonio Evening News*.

The only solace for the Republican nominee, and a harbinger for the future, were the unprecedented inroads Goldwater made in editorial opinion south of the Mason-Dixon Line, outside of the Lone Star State. "It's been a long time since Southerners have had a presidential candidate they could support with pride and enthusiasm," the *Charleston News and Courier* declared.[44] In Mississippi, the *Natchez Democrat* endorsed Goldwater, the first time it had endorsed a Republican for anything since 1865: "We have reached a point where we can no longer close our eyes to the fact that the national Democratic Party and its nominees ... support and advocate everything that is repulsive and obnoxious to our belief."[45]

Goldwater won fewer than half as many endorsements as Nixon had in 1960, and they were from newspapers with a total circulation of only one-quarter of those backing the Republican candidate four years earlier. In the final analysis, Johnson won endorsements from 440 newspapers (42.47 percent of all papers), with a combined daily circulation of 27.6 million readers (61.5 percent of all readers). Goldwater was endorsed by 359 dailies with 9.7 million readers.

In the entire nation, only three major newspapers stood by their traditional allegiance to the candidate of the party of Lincoln: the *Los Angeles Times*, the *Chicago Tribune*, and the *Cincinnati Enquirer*. "Nothing like this had ever happened in American political history," White notes.[46] Even Eugene Pulliam, owner of the *Phoenix Gazette* and *Arizona Republic*, the man who had done more than any other to midwife the political career of the young Barry Goldwater, cut him loose in 1964.

Otis Chandler came out for Rockefeller in a *Los Angeles Times* editorial on the eve of the Republican primary in California, but his father insisted that the paper include its traditional pledge to back whoever emerged as the Republican nominee. The ensuing conversation reflects the transition taking place in the world of the media from a parochial to an objective depiction of reality:

"We have to put it in," [Norman Chandler] said. "We're Republicans and we always have been.

"No, we aren't," said Otis Chandler.

"Yes we are, and we always have been," said Norman.

"Well, then, let's change," said Otis. "We can't support Goldwater, we can't go that way."

"If you don't put that in, what can I tell my friends at the California Club?" Norman pleaded. "Everyone knows we're a Republican paper, that's our history. What can I tell them?"[47]

Ultimately, reluctantly, Otis did as his father bid him, a victory Norman no doubt found bittersweet. On September 16, Palmer Hoyt had written the Chandlers to warn them what an endorsement of the "radical reactionary" Republican candidate would mean for the family newspaper. "If the Times finds it necessary, for reasons not known to me, to support the Goldwater ticket, I sincerely believe it will do the Los Angeles Times enduring harm and damage the image that Otis Chandler is creating in the newspaper business and in the country generally." Hoyt concluded by pleading, "Please, please, please don't do this to Otis, the newspaper business, the nation, and the world."[48] Norman Chandler replied immediately after the election, conceding that Hoyt's missive was "a masterpiece and I agreed basically with all you had to say. The results of Tuesday's election proved you to be one hundred per cent in your evaluation of Mr. Goldwater. None of us were enthusiastic about the candidate, and it was a difficult and disturbing decision to make. I realize that I made Otis and others—including Buff [Mrs. Chandler]—quite unhappy with the decision. My only alibi is that I could not convince myself that the Times should endorse a Democratic candidate for President. It was probably stupid on my part, so please forgive me."[49]

Many of the publications that chose to reject Goldwater in 1964 used rhetoric in doing so that ironically echoed the Republican nominee's dictum that extremism in the defense of liberty is no vice. In its editorial, the *Christian Century* compared the Goldwater campaign with the Nazi rise to power in 1933: "We hear again the appeal to national pride and self-justification; we hear the brandishing of weapons— any kind of weapons— to fulfill our purposes; we hear the gods invoked in alliance with our claims; we even notice subtle and implicit appeals to those among us who are racist. We have cause to be uneasy."[50]

Goldwater took such criticism personally. "I have never in my life seen such inflammatory language as has been used by some men who should know better, who should write better, who should have enough decency, common ordinary manners about them," he lamented. "I think these people should, frankly, hang their heads in shame because I think they have made the fourth estate a rather sad, sorry mess."[51]

The most scurrilous piece during the campaign was "The Unconsciousness of a Conservative: A Special Issue on the Mind of Barry Goldwater," an article published in the September-October issue of *Fact* magazine. Ralph Ginzburg, the publisher of *Fact*, had rented the mailing list of the American Psychoanalytical Association and sent out a single-question poll: "Do you believe Barry Goldwater is psychologically fit to serve as President of the United States?" By way of reply, *Fact* received the opinions of more than one thousand psychiatrists, a response rate of 20 percent. America's mental health professionals seized this opportunity to depict Goldwater as "a dangerous lunatic" and "paranoid schizophrenic" given to "unconscious sadism" and "suicidal tendencies."

"I believe Goldwater," wrote an Atlanta psychiatrist,

fact:

VOLUME ONE, ISSUE FIVE $1.25

1,189 Psychiatrists Say Goldwater Is Psychologically Unfit To Be President!

Fact magazine never amounted to more than a vehicle for election-year character assassination of 1964 GOP candidate Barry Goldwater— a throwback to the partisan election special editions once produced by the likes of Amos Kendall and Horace Greeley. What really hurt Goldwater was the defection to Lyndon Johnson of a host of legitimate publications that had been loyally Republican for generations. Most of these returned to the fold four years later but the GOP never forgave or forgot their apostasy and the Republican Party has been at loggerheads with the media ever since (author's collection).

"has a mask of sanity covering an inner political madness.... I find myself increasingly thinking of the early 1930s and the rise of another intemperate, impulsive, counterfeit figure of a masculine man, namely, Adolf Hitler."[52]

"I do not think his having had two nervous breakdowns in the past should be held against him," wrote another doctor. "The sickness of his character structure *now present* is his real psychological deficit. Basically, I feel he has a narcissistic character disorder with not too latent paranoid elements." Another doctor called Goldwater a "compensated schizophrenic" like Hitler, Castro and Stalin. A colleague demurred: "Though compensated at present," the Republican candidate would "become more irrational and paranoid when under political attack during the campaign."

One psychiatric professional singled out Goldwater's "frustrated and malcontented" followers, who "reflect his own paranoid and omnipotent tendencies ... as was characteristic of dictators in the '30s and '40s," because the senator from Arizona "appeals to the unconscious sadism and hostility in the average human being." This necessitated subtlety in formulating a response because, as another doctor advised, "Strategy against the paranoid fringe must be *very* carefully worked out. A frontal attack on paranoids causes them to band together and become more efficient." There was no doubt as to the geographic locus of this paranoia. A doctor from New York decried Goldwater's "tremendous following from among ... destructive elements of the South and West."[53]

Was this, then, the tipping point? The Northeastern elite media had on a previous occasion tried and found wanting the mental qualifications of another presidential candidate who represented the same constituency of southern and western "destructive elements." In 1896, William Jennings Bryan had been subjected to exactly the same treatment as Goldwater, described in exactly the same terms, abandoned by the traditional press vehicles of his party. The Republican and Democratic parties were now in the process of turning full circle, each inhabiting the other's electoral heartland. Was the press completing the paradigm by barricading itself as an institution within the Democratic camp? The answer is a qualified no.

All the President's Men

If 1964 truly represented a definitive turning point in the balance of media opinion, the trend away from the Republican Party would have continued into 1968 and beyond. In fact, as soon as Goldwater was out of the picture, the press largely reverted to its establishment, status-quo, conservative stance. But this was no longer enough to satisfy those cadres of New-Right conservatives energized by Goldwater who were engaged in seizing control of the Republican Party at the grassroots. A gulf had opened between the GOP and the "elite" newsmakers. This relatively intimate circle has expanded to include the *New York Times*, *Los Angeles Times*, and *Washington Post*; *Time* and *Newsweek*; ABC, NBC, and especially CBS; CNN and MSNBC; and NPR/PBS. These outlets are essentially what conservatives mean today when they talk of "the media."

Ironically, in the New-Right interpretation of history, the first President to fall victim to the elite opinion makers was not a Republican but rather a Democrat, Lyndon Johnson, who in retirement would himself grumble about being subjected to "tireless assaults on me and my administration" by the media, particularly over policy in Vietnam.[54] Picking up on Johnson's grievances, conservatives have long maintained that the media was responsible for the loss of Southeast Asia to communism, by hewing to an editorial line dedicated to representing the U.S. military commitment in the region as a failure.[55]

This interpretation raises more questions than it answers. Why, if the media was so liberal, it would want to deliberately bring down the most liberal president in history? Why, if liberal bias is so easy to spot, and tends to aggravate rather than manipulate the great, silent majority in America, didn't the media line on Vietnam inflate rather than deflate enthusiasm for the war? In fact, studies do not substantiate the argument that the media, overtly or covertly, was responsible for the outcome of the U.S. intervention in Southeast Asia. Wyatt concludes, "It is difficult to maintain that the press was the profound, even decisive, influence over public opinion and the course of the war that it has been portrayed to be. The press was more a paper soldier than an antiwar, antigovernment crusader."[56] Hammond concurs that the media largely followed rather than led the shift in public opinion against the war.[57]

Analysis by Mueller points out an obvious counter-parallel. American involvement in the Korean War was more "legitimate" than its role in Vietnam. No Gulf of Tonkin incident ambiguity marked the beginning of active U.S. involvement in Korea; it was simply a clear-cut response to an outright, Stalin-endorsed invasion of the South by the North. And U.S. intervention in Korea was sanctioned by the UN Security Council, which brought America's allies on board. Yet the public turned against the Korean War much *sooner* than it did the conflict in Vietnam, despite the fact that television in the early 1950s was in its infancy, censorship was tight, and the World War II ethic of the journalist serving the war effort remained strong.[58] It appears that the public does not require any prodding from the media to draw its own conclusions about the strategic and moral imperatives of a military commitment. After all, blanket propagandizing by the Soviet press did not prevent that nation from undergoing its own Vietnam in Afghanistan.[59] The myth of the *Dolchstoßlegende*, of the Vietnam War effort being deliberately stabbed in the back by the media persists, however; the exact same charge is being leveled today against the media in Iraq.[60]

The ultimate domestic political beneficiary of the stalemate in Vietnam was none other than Richard Nixon. Not that this inclined him more favorably towards the press. "I've earned their hatred," was one of his proudest boasts.[61] About one in ten persons on Nixon's 182-member "enemies list" was a journalist or news executive. The President, who referred to reporters as "that fucking bunch of crew-cut boy scouts," and on one occasion refused to grant an interview to a media outlet on the grounds that "I wouldn't give them the sweat off my balls," even allowed his underlying malice to creep into his already morose sense of humor; he once told the prime minister of England that if astronauts returning from the moon brought back with them rock samples that turned out to be laden with lethal space germs, he would dole them out as presents to journalists.[62] Sometimes Nixon's brooding obsession spilled over into outright paranoia. "*Newsweek* is ... all run by Jews and dominated by them in their editorial pages," he once groused. "The *New York Times*, the *Washington Post*, totally Jewish too."[63]

From day one, the Nixon administration put in place a two-step strategy to deal with the media; bypass it, and subvert it. In pursuit of the former, overt objective, Nixon proceeded to take Roosevelt's "Fireside Chat" technique one step further by projecting himself into American living rooms via television. He gave more televised addresses while in office (32) than Kennedy (9), Johnson (15), and Ford (6) combined.

It was the second, covert aspect of its approach to the media that would mark the administration's legacy. "Nixon spent hours, every day, studying the press, manipulating the press, warning his associates about the press, threatening the press—and then declaring himself indifferent to the press," Liebovich notes.[64] The president directed his staff to treat the media with "the courteous, cool contempt which has been my policy over the last few years." He instructed Chief of Staff H. R. Haldeman that "under absolutely no circumstances" was anyone in the White House to give an interview or respond to any queries from the *New York Times*, "unless I give express permission (and I do not expect to give such permission in the foreseeable future"). Nixon also ordered *Time* and *New Republic* reporters Hugh Sidey and John Osborne excluded from receiving White House news summaries and cut off from interviews. Their sin? The president claimed to have unimpeachable evidence that both reporters had said derogatory things in circles "where you really find out what the people think — the Georgetown cocktail parties." Nixon was adamant: "There is no appeal whatever — I do not want it discussed with me any further."[65]

This attitude flowed faithfully down through the chain of command. "I can't remember all of the reporters and newspeople he [Nixon] asked me to 'go after' in one way or the other," Haldeman wrote in his memoirs, and he did his best to comply.[66] "The Democrats have the press, the network commentators, the Congress and all the media of communications basically on their side," Haldeman advised his subordinates. "The point is we make points by fighting the press, and we've got to do it."[67] In another staff memo, Haldeman wrote in early 1970, "[You are to get out] and run [the story] somewhere about how the President has overcome the great handicaps under which he came into office — specifically the hostile press epitomized by the NEW YORK TIMES, WASHINGTON POST, TIME, NEWSWEEK, the hostile network commentators.... This story has not gotten through."[68]

Led by deputy director Jeb Magruder, the White House Office of Communications maintained an extensive monitoring operation to track trends in press thinking, orchestrated letter-writing campaigns, generated telephone complaints to media outlets about biased coverage, and rigged local polls.[69] According to White House aide Alexander Butterfield, at times the staff had orders to convince Nixon partisans to get "100 vicious dirty calls to the New York Times and Washington Post about their editorials (even though they had no idea what they would be)." Haldeman noted in an addendum to his diary, "The plea for 'vicious dirty calls' to the papers was to keep pressure on them from the public in the hope that they would consider the other viewpoint occasionally."[70] By mid–1970, White House staffers had compiled an extensive list of more than 200 journalists from television, radio, and print, and placed each one into one of six categories: Friendly to Administration; Balanced to Favorable; Balanced; Unpredictable; Usually Negative; and Always Hostile. Each assessment included an executive summary: there was John Chancellor, who generally sides with "the liberals" and is "tricky"; David Brinkley, a "Kennedy Democrat and his cynicism shows through frequently with sarcasm"; Chet Huntley, who "at one time at least was an independent Republican, although not all of his comments would indicate this"; and Walter Cronkite, who at least "doesn't have the tendency to be snide, which is noted in some of the others."[71]

Nixon's utter lack of humor shines through in his obsession with micro-managing this anti-media campaign. In a March 11, 1969, memorandum to John Erlichman, the president noted that he wanted an effort made to "monitor television programs — not only the political programs but the entertainment programs in which there are often deliberately negative comments which deserve some reaction on the part of our friends." Nixon had a specific example in mind — the Smothers Brothers: "In looking at it Sunday night ... one said to the other that he found it difficult to find anything to laugh about — Vietnam, the cities, etc., but 'Richard Nixon is solving these problems' and 'that's really funny.'" Nixon added, "The line didn't get a particularly good reaction," but it was "the kind of line that should ... receive some calls and letters strenuously objecting to that kind of attack."[72]

Nixon was furious with his staff for arranging him to be present when the awards were presented at the White House correspondents' annual dinner in the spring of 1970. All the trophies were handed out, the president raged, "to way out left-wingers ... while the drunken audience laughed in derision." Nixon went on to lay down the law:

What I want everyone to realize is that as we approach the election we are in a fight to the death for the big prize. Ninety-five percent of the members of the Washington press corps are unalterably opposed to us because of their intellectual and philosophical background. Some of them will smirk and pander to us for the purpose of getting a story but we must remember that they are just waiting for the chance to stick the knife in deep and to twist it.

"We simply have to start growing up and being just as tough, ruthless and unfeeling as they are," the president concluded, "otherwise, they will sink us without trace."[73]

Control was Nixon's obsession, not merely self-control but control over the words and deeds of everyone within his inner circle. Hostile media were to be blackballed entirely. When the *St. Louis Post-Dispatch* reported on a dispute among "high Administration officials," Nixon wrote to Haldeman, "I have told [press secretary Ron Ziegler] not to have our people talk to the *Post-Dispatch*— or *N.Y. Times* or *Washington Post. Knock It Off!!!*" On another occasion, the president told Haldeman and Erlichman, "*Newsweek* is loaded against us. Cut them like we cut the *Times*."[74] Speaking of himself in the third person, Nixon summed up his efforts in September 1970 in a memo to Herb Klein: "Instead of trying to win the press, to cater to them, to have backgrounders with them, RN has ignored them and talked directly to the country by TV whenever possible. He has used the press and not let the press use him. He has particularly not allowed the press, whenever he could avoid it, to filter his ideas to the public. This is a remarkable achievement."[75]

Conservatives were only too happy to indulge the administration in this agenda because, by and large, they shared Nixon's perspective on the Fourth Estate: it was the enemy. It was true, as the figures show, editorial support for Nixon did actually *increase* every time he ran for president: from 57.7 percent of the newspapers in 1960 to 60.8 percent in 1968 to 71.4 percent in 1972. In Nixon's last race, his opponent, George McGovern, was endorsed by only 5.3 percent of the papers. And it was true that in addition to Nixon loyalists in the big media markets, like the *Detroit News*, the *Dallas Morning News*, the *Chicago Tribune*, the *Wall Street Journal*, and the *New York Daily News*, the President could rely on favorable coverage from the *St. Louis Globe-Democrat*, the Houston papers, the *Fort Worth Star-Telegram*, the *Los Angeles Herald-Examiner*, and the *San Francisco Chronicle*. And it was true, as Teddy White pointed out, that "once below the top fifty newspapers of the country, support for the President grew overwhelmingly."[76] But discerning bias in the media was no longer simply a matter of totaling up editorial endorsements in the newspapers. The real enemy was on television.

By the time Nixon took office, television had already cemented its place in the media pantheon as the primary source for political information. Its rise had been astonishingly swift. Whereas only 940,000 American households had television sets in 1949, 34,900,000 homes had at least one television by 1956. Although one-third of all Americans had claimed radio was their most important source of campaign information in 1952, by 1960 only 6 percent chose radio, while 65 percent named television as their most important source. A 1959 Roper poll found 32 percent claiming newspapers as their most credible news source while 29 percent claimed television. By 1968 only 21 percent still claimed newspapers while 44 percent placed the most trust in television.[77] The media was now dominated by television, and "between this newest and most potent form of news delivery, on the one hand, and the President, on the other, was growing up an institutional hatred," White noted.[78] And conservatives were taking note, too. According to a groundbreaking study by Nora Efron, "all three networks clearly tried to defeat Mr. Nixon in his campaign for the Presidency of the United States" in 1968. "If Mr. Nixon is President of the United States today, it is in spite of ABC-TV, CBS-TV and NBC-TV."[79]

The new ground rules established by the Republican Party in its relationship with the press were expressed in a speech by Vice President Spiro Agnew in Des Moines on November 13, 1969. Agnew had been warned against a frontal assault on the media by none other than Lyndon Johnson, who, as he left the White House, had told the incoming vice president:

"We have in this country two big television networks, NBC and CBS. We have two news magazines, *Newsweek* and *Time*. We have two wire services, AP and UPI. We have two pollsters, Gallup and Harris. We have two big newspapers, the *Washington Post* and the *New York Times*. They're all so damn big they think they own the country. But, young man, don't get any ideas about fighting."[80] But after less than a year in office, a fight was just what Agnew was in the mood for. In a speech penned by Pat Buchanan, he identified the elite against which the Nixon White House, and all subsequent Republican administrations, have defined themselves: "A small group of men, numbering perhaps no more than a dozen anchormen, commentators and executive producers."[81]

> No medium has a more profound influence over public opinion. Nowhere in our system are there fewer checks on vast power. So, nowhere should there be more conscientious responsibility exercised than by the news media. The question is, are we demanding enough of our television news presentations? And are the men of this medium demanding enough of themselves?[82]
>
> We do know that to a man these commentators and producers live and work in the geographical and intellectual confines of Washington, D.C., or New York City.... Both communities bask in their own provincialism, their own parochialism. We can deduce that these men read the same newspapers. They draw their political and social views from the same sources. Worse, they talk constantly to one another, thereby providing artificial reinforcement to their shared viewpoints.[83]
>
> Is it not fair and relevant to question its concentration in the hands of a tiny, enclosed fraternity of privileged men elected by no one and enjoying a monopoly sanctioned and licensed by Government? The views of the majority of this fraternity do not ... represent the views of America.[84]

"The day when the network commentators and even the gentlemen of the *New York Times* enjoyed a form of diplomatic immunity from comment and criticism of what they said is over," Agnew said in Des Moines. "Yes, gentlemen, that day is passed."

> Just as a politician's words — wise and foolish — are dutifully recorded by press and television to be thrown up at him at the appropriate time, so their words should be likewise recorded and likewise recalled.
>
> When they go beyond fair comment and criticism they will be called upon to defend their statesmen and their positions just as we must defend ours. And when their criticism becomes excessive or unjust, we shall invite them down from their ivory towers to enjoy the rough and tumble of public debate.
>
> I don't seek to intimidate the press, or the networks or anyone else from speaking out. But the time for blind acceptance of their opinions is past. And the time for naïve belief in their neutrality is gone.[85]

The challenge had been thrown down. In February 1970 Agnew extended his assault on the "liberal news media," telling an Atlanta audience that he was meeting the "need for a strong voice to penetrate the cacophony of seditious drivel emanating from the best-publicized clowns of our society and from their fans in the fourth estate."[86]

Behind the scenes, the administration's high-profile assault on the press was complemented by an ongoing shadow campaign being directed out of the White House to neutralize those opinion makers deemed hostile by a panoply of legal and quasi-illegal means. The Nixon administration's methods of influencing the media included initiating legal action against publishing companies; publicly signaling that it was looking at options to strike back at its enemies via anti-trust legislation and withholding of broadcasting licenses; and harassment and intimidation of individual reporters, including the use of wiretaps.[87] Less than four months after Nixon took office, the White House hired two New York City detectives, Jack Caulfield and Tony Ulasewicz, to spy on political opponents and reporters. Columnist Joseph

Kraft was one of their first targets; listening devices were planted in his home and in a hotel where he stayed in Paris in the spring of 1971. From 1969 to 1971, the Nixon White House, with the help of FBI director J. Edgar Hoover, placed wiretaps in the homes of eighteen individuals, including five in the media, along with thirteen White House, State Department and Defense Department aides.

No one was immune from this prevailing paranoia. Nixon speechwriter William Safire later recognized that the President "was saying exactly what he meant: 'the press is the enemy,' to be hated and beaten, and in that vein of vengeance that ran through his relationship with another power center, in his indulgence of his most combative and abrasive instincts against what he saw to be an unelected and unrepresentative elite, lay Nixon's greatest personal and political weakness."[88] Safire himself paid the price for his defiance of presidential directives against speaking with the press. "Not until mid–1973 did I realize that these contacts with the press had caused my phone to be tapped in 1969 by the FBI at the direction of a suspicious President and national security adviser [Henry Kissinger]."[89] Others wiretapped included Hedrick Smith and William Beecher of the *New York Times* and Marvin Kalb of CBS News.

In a memorandum written in October 1969, Jeb Magruder suggested using the Antitrust Division of the Justice Department in order to tame media organs considered hostile: "Even the possible threat of anti-trust action I think would be effective in changing their views." In addition, Magruder suggested the Internal Revenue Service be used to tame recalcitrant news organizations because "just a threat of an IRS investigation will probably turn their approach."[90]

This line of reasoning jibed with Nixon, who had never forgotten nor forgiven the *Los Angeles Times* for its supposed treachery during his ill-fated California gubernatorial campaign in 1962. During his presidency he ordered the IRS and the INS to investigate the entire Chandler family. "We're going after the Chandlers," he told Attorney General John Mitchell, "every one, individually, collectively, their income tax ... [e]very one of those sons of bitches.... I want you to direct the most trusted person you have in the Immigration Service that they are to look over all of the activities of the *Los Angeles Times*.... Otis Chandler — I want him checked with regard to his gardener. I understand he's a wetback."[91]

In November 1970, Haldeman, at Nixon's direction, called J. Edgar Hoover and asked for "a rundown on the homosexuals known and suspected" to be lurking in the Washington press corps. The director confirmed that the material in question was already available — he would not need to conduct any specific investigation. The files were sent to the White House.[92]

Trying another angle, allegedly on the grounds that CBS correspondent Daniel Schorr was being considered as assistant to the chairman of the Council on Environmental Quality, Haldeman requested an FBI check on his background in August 1971. Of course, the prospect of Schorr being fast-tracked into a career in public service was simply a ruse. The White House just wanted to see if there was any dirt it could dig out. ("We just ran a name check on the son-of-a-bitch," Nixon snapped.")[93]

Meanwhile, the administration continued to muse about the possibility of using legal action to break up the entrenched position of the major networks. In a speech a week after his Des Moines address, in Montgomery, Alabama, Agnew upped the ante, publicly airing the administration's flirtation with using antitrust action to bring the media to heel. Patrick Buchanan later cut out the middle man and himself scored the bias of the three channels, warning that if they continued to "freeze out opposing points of view you're going to find something done in the area of antitrust type action."[94] The administration did file an action against the networks in the spring of 1972, but struggled to overcome the recalcitrance of the Antitrust Division of the Department of Justice, and particularly its chief, Robert McLaren. ("I never liked that son-of-a-bitch," Nixon growled).[95]

Arm twisting the networks was nothing new. After CBS had broadcast the results of a survey relating to Jack Kennedy's Catholicism during the 1960 campaign, first Bobby Kennedy and then the candidate himself called CBS President Frank Stanton to register their ire at attention being drawn to an issue they felt would be better left alone. "What are you doing to me?" Jack demanded. When Stanton pointed out that CBS had done nothing more than many newspapers, Kennedy replied, not very cryptically, "Yes, but they're not licensed by the Federal Government."[96] But the Nixon administration's constant probing for opportunities that fell within its purview was unprecedented. Everything from the FCC to public broadcasting was subjected to immense pressure directly from the White House. The administration displayed its displeasure with the fledgling Corporation for Public Broadcasting by vetoing the 1972 Public Broadcasting Bill and killing its funding for a two-year period.[97]

According to Halberstam, in addition to its frontal assault on the media, "the Nixon administration had also found and sliced at the soft underbelly of the networks, their affiliate stations.... [T]here was no doubt as the Nixon administration orchestrated its assault against the network news teams that it found a receptive response among affiliate owners, most of whom were Republicans."[98] According to Grossman and Kumar, the "all-out attack on the media" conducted by the Nixon administration "was well planned and was successful in intimidating large segments of broadcasting and publishing enterprises."[99]

Nixon's cold war against the press even emerged as a campaign issue: "We are determined that never again shall government seek to censor the newspapers and television," the 1972 Democratic platform declared. "The Nixon policy of intimidation of the media ... must end, if free speech is to be preserved." [100]

Did the media play along with its role as defined by the administration? Was the liberal ideological homogeneity that Nixon so obsessed over reflected in media coverage of the campaign in 1972? Did the media create the dark-horse candidacy of Democratic nominee George McGovern in order to hitch a ride on his star? In fact, McGovern broke through in the New Hampshire primary not because of the media but despite it. His surprisingly strong second place "moral victory" attracted media attention only because of the horse-race potentialities it suddenly opened up. Prior to that, McGovern had been largely ignored. As Perry notes, "we weren't interested in George McGovern, who was obviously the candidate of the 'liberal establishment' we were supposed to be welded to."[101]

Once McGovern had secured the nomination, the only homogeneity exhibited by the media was its almost universal contempt for his candidacy. Leader of the pack, as always, was William Loeb's *Manchester Union Leader*, which tagged McGovern from the start as "dangerous to the safety and security of this nation.... Furthermore, we consider Senator McGovern to be personally responsible for the deaths of thousands of American boys." The main target of the *Union Leader's* guns in New Hampshire, however, was Democratic frontrunner Ed Muskie, whom Loeb literally reduced to tears.

With Muskie safely disposed of in the primaries, Loeb could unleash anti–McGovern missives at his leisure through the summer and fall. "The McGovern push is the main drive for power in the United States by the Communist Party," was a typical effort.[102] The *New York Daily News* warned in a June 8 editorial after the South Dakotan effectively clinched the Democratic nomination by winning the California primary, "All real Republicans, we believe, and all patriotic Democrats, should begin working now to defeat McGovern." "If McGovern becomes President, he can be counted on to do his utmost to wreck the Vietnam war effort and betray Southeast Asia to the Communists," the paper added. "Also, you can look for him to strive to weaken the U.S.A. militarily throughout the world ... to bankrupt the government via outlandish handouts and giveaways ... to cripple initiative and destroy work incentives with idiotic tax 'reforms' ... and in other ways to make America over into a ruinous hulk of a great nation."

For the *St. Louis Globe-Democrat*, in an editorial on September 28, "Senator George McGovern has been an utter disappointment from the day he was nominated. He has been a weak, vacillating, confused, opportunistic blunderer." On October 8, the *Richmond Times-Dispatch* described McGovern as "one of the most unattractive presidential candidates any major party ever presented to the nation," whose program "features proposals that are irresponsible, dangerous and philosophically repugnant," and who "has shown no capacity for leadership." The election of McGovern "is simply unacceptable," the *Boston Herald* wrote on October 12, characterizing the Democrat as "an indecisive, impractical and impulsive challenger whose radical views, wild accusations and ever-changing positions inspire no confidence that he would be capable of leading the nation."

Even those papers prepared to take a stand against Nixon did so almost apologetically. "It is undeniable that since his nomination Senator McGovern has been on the defensive, partly because of the Eagleton episode, partly because of ill-considered comments on specific points that he has subsequently modified or corrected, and partly because of the confused management of his own campaign," the *New York Times* acknowledged on September 28. But, the paper hoped, "Senator McGovern may yet touch a chord in the American voter that will respond to his own practical vision of an American society that cares and an American democracy that works." In a similar vein, on October 30 the *New York Post*, at the time one of the last bastions of liberal sentiment, sought to downplay McGovern's manifest incompetence ("He has at least had the courage to acknowledge mistakes"), and concluded, "We cannot offer any certainty that he provides the promise of greatness. We are confident, however, that his voice will be steadfastly addressed to the best instincts of the American people."[103]

In the final analysis, projected by circulation figures, ten times as many Americans were exposed to a pro–Nixon as a pro–McGovern newspaper during the 1972 campaign. Some conservatives were forced to admit this represented something like objectivity. According to Shogan, in the aftermath of the campaign "Victor Gold, veteran of countless battles with the media as press secretary to Spiro Agnew in 1972 and before that as press aide to Barry Goldwater in 1964, told me: 'I used to think you guys were out for our blood. But I can see now that you're out for anybody's blood.'"[104] But not even this triumph could heal the breech between the president and the Fourth Estate. And there was a cancer in the Nixon White House that would widen that divide to a chasm of unprecedented proportions.

Two post–1972 election tracts written by reporters, *The Boys on the Bus*, by Timothy Crouse, and *The Politics of Lying*, by David Wise, reflected the media's increasing frustration and sense of unease in its relationship with the Nixon administration. Crouse wrote that Nixon "was different" from his predecessors; that he "felt a deep, abiding, and vindictive hatred for the press that no president, with the possible exception of Lyndon Johnson, had ever shared.... No other president had ever worked so lovingly or painstakingly to emasculate reporters." "Under the Nixon Administration, there has been an unprecedented effort," Wise agreed, "to downgrade and discredit the American press."[105] This campaign would only intensify once Nixon was reelected. "What lay at issue in 1972 between Richard Nixon, on the one hand, and the adversary press and media of America, on the other, was simple," Teddy White notes, "it was power."[106] Flush with victory, Nixon's underlings laid at his feet various proposals by which to settle scores with the hated press. In mid–December, Buchanan outlined an "Attack Operation" against the national press corps:

> [It is] vitally important for the credibility of this Administration that neither the Post nor CBS get away scot-free with what they did in the campaign. Should they do so, then any hostile media institution can consider us a paper tiger, and the word will go forth for networks to carve up the more conservative candidate — two weeks before an election — and nothing will

happen. We need a strategy of how to deal with CBS, and that should go into the final product. We need a strategy for dealing with the problems raised by the PBS situation, and public broadcasting in general....

We need a listing — not extended — of perhaps the 10–20 most serious media problems we face — in terms of hostile TV reporters, commentators, columnists, and their counterparts in the writing press. And this memorandum should name them — and include specific measures which the White House can and will take to deny those individuals materials to use against us. A black-out is one tactic, and could be enforced in the present environment, for example, by firing the first guy in the bureaucracy found talking to Daniel Schorr. But, unless there is a campaign to specifically deny privileged access to our adversaries, then any strategy is something of a joke.[107]

Others within the administration immediately began to apply pressure. Clay Whitehead, the director of the White House Office of Telecommunications Policy, called on local television stations to refuse to carry "biased" news accounts from the networks, warning them that failure "to correct imbalance or consistent bias from the networks" would make local broadcasters "fully accountable" at license-renewal time.[108] Chuck Colson took a direct approach, calling CBS President Frank Stanton and warning him, according to an affidavit of Stanton's, "that unless CBS substantially changed its news treatment of the Nixon administration 'things will get much worse for CBS.'" Specifically, since the network "'didn't play ball during the campaign ... [w]e'll bring you to your knees in Wall Street and on Madison Avenue.'"[109]

The administration would expire from the self-inflicted wounds suffered during the Watergate scandal before this agenda could be consummated, but it would be a mistake to represent this as the president being hounded from office by a collaborative phalanx of activist liberals in the media collectively conspiring on a pre-determined agenda to bring him down. Quite the opposite, in fact. Liebovich decries what he calls "a shameful lack of aggressiveness in the early months of the Watergate investigation.... Nixon was not hounded from office by a malevolent press corps; he was allowed to stay in office too long by a reluctant press brigade."[110]

The investigative reporting on the part of Bob Woodward and Carl Bernstein, two young reporters for the *Washington Post*, whose sleuthing uncovered the link between the Watergate burglary and the White House, has passed into legend.[111] The *Post* came under immense pressure from the highest authorities during this period. Publicly, the administration fought back with scathing denunciations of the paper's coverage, charging that by "using innuendo, third-person hearsay, unsubstantiated charges, anonymous sources, and scare headlines, the *Post* has maliciously sought to give the appearance of a direct connection between the White House and the Watergate." Inevitably, the charge of conspiracy was leveled: to Nixon, the Woodward and Bernstein investigation was evidence of "a political effort by the *Washington Post*, well conceived and coordinated, to discredit this administration."[112] Privately, the intimidation was even worse, and more personal. "All that crap, you're putting it in the paper? It's all been denied," Attorney General John Mitchell snapped to Carl Bernstein. "Katie Graham's going to get her tit caught in a big fat wringer if that's published."

Nixon told Haldeman that he was willing to use all of the $5 million left in his campaign treasury "to take the *Washington Post* down a notch." The Oval Office tapes record Nixon, clearly agitated, concluding, "We're going to stop it. I don't care how much it costs."[113] Three months after the *Post* began its investigation into Watergate, Nixon instructed his aides to have political allies in Jacksonville and Miami challenge the license renewals of the two TV stations in Florida owned by the Washington Post Company on the grounds that they were not providing the community service programming requisite under state law. "The *Post* is going to have damnable — damnable — problems out of this one," Nixon assured Halde-man. "Its going to be goddamn active here. The game has to be played awfully rough." Three and a half months after that conversation, Nixon's supporters formally challenged the license renewal applications made by the two stations — the first time either had ever been contested. George Champion, Jr., Florida finance chairman for Nixon's 1972 campaign, filed the chal-lenge against WJXT-TV in Jacksonville; partners of Senator George A. Smathers, a close friend of Nixon's closest confidant, Bebe Rebozo, filed the challenge against WPLG-TV in Miami. Both stations overcame the challenges only after documenting that they had, in fact, fulfilled the community service requirement.[114]

Nixon spun the *Post's* reporting into the web of the pan-media conspiracy against him that had formed a staple of his worldview since the inception of his career. In late 1973, the President accused the media of "outrageous, vicious, distorted reporting" on a scale that sur-passed anything he had ever before seen "in 27 years of public life."[115] "Don't get the impres-sion that you arouse my anger," Nixon told CBS's Robert Pierpont on October 26, 1973. "I'm afraid, sir, that I have that impression," Pierpont replied, to which the president responded, "You see, one can only be angry with those he respects."[116]

But one of the more remarkable aspects of the entire Watergate saga was just how slow the vast majority of the media was in appreciating its true extent. Woodward and Bernstein effectively had the story to themselves during the summer and fall of 1972. Outside of Wash-ington the scandal made little impression on the loyalties of the voters. According to Liebovich, "A major scandal was largely ignored and an election was held under false pretences."[117] Long after the election, the *Post* was left isolated, subjected to the full brunt of White House retal-iation. "For months we were out there alone on this story," said *Post* managing editor Howard Simons. "We used to ask ourselves: 'Where are the AP, the UPI, the *New York Times*, *Newsweek*?' It was months of loneliness."[118] "If this is such a hell of a story," wondered the *Post's* belea-guered publisher, Katherine Graham, "then where is everybody else?"[119]

Bar a few exceptions — Sandy Smith of *Time*, Jack Nelson and Ron Ostrow of the *Los Angeles Times*, and, sporadically, the *New York Times*, *Newsday*, and *Newsweek* — the big guns of the American press failed to support their embattled colleagues with any solid investiga-tive reporting of their own. According to Lukas, "The press shied away from it in large part because the administration's three-year campaign of intimidation had succeeded — beyond its wildest expectations. The television networks in particular ... feared a head-on confrontation with the President. Newspapers and magazines were beset by irresolution and self-doubt, half believing that they really were part of some coterie of effete Eastern intellectuals out to get the President."

Joseph Kraft, for example, one of those on Nixon's enemies list, managed to convince himself that Nixon and Mitchell couldn't have been involved in Watergate because "they are too honorable and high-minded, too sensitive to the requirements of decency, fair play, and law."[120]

Yet the legend of the press mobilized against malfeasance in high office endures, partic-ularly among observers who like to point out the oedipal symmetry of a president brought down by that which he feared and hated most. "Instead of accepting the changed role of media as one of the quirks of destiny, Nixon brooded about it and plotted against an amorphous monster that he could never defeat," Liebovich concludes.[121] As a character sketch that holds true, and Nixon would continue to manifest those traits until the day he died. In noting that the TV networks "have the same bias for the Communist rebels in El Salvador that they now have for the Communist government in Nicaragua" during the 1980s, he would sneer ,"Their pink slip is showing."[122] But in the final analysis no other institution or individual was respon-sible for destroying Richard Nixon; only Richard Nixon could do that.[123]

Epilogue: The Past as Prologue

By the mid–1970s, the question of bias in the media was being subjected to an ever increasing array of studies employing more or less scientific models usually tailored to suit the particular bias of whomever conducted or commissioned them, in order to produce results vindicating one or other points of view. This crisscross of data notwithstanding, many people persisted in tracing the rise and fall of presidential hopefuls to an active agenda on the part of the media. Writing in the *New York Times Book Review*, Lester Bernstein, a former editor of *Newsweek*, noted, "Jimmy Carter as a national figure was almost invented by the media. He owed more to the engines of publicity for his emergence from obscurity to a Presidential nomination than any other politician since Wendell Willkie in 1940."[124] But if so, isn't that just another way of saying Carter was better at playing the media to his advantage than his rivals? Aren't media relations skills exactly the quality primary voters are looking for in candidate in this, the age of "electability?" In other words, were primary voters being manipulated by the media into endorsing Carter, or were they factoring in his ability to get good press when determining who would make the best candidate for the fall campaign?

In any case, if the Carter presidency was spawned by the media, the media turned against its creation with remarkable alacrity. The ambivalence with which it greeted Carter's inauguration tipped into antipathy early in his term and culminated in outright disgust.[125] Consider the following election year 1980 missive from the erstwhile liberal *Washington Post*:

> Mr. Carter, as a candidate, tends to convey a mean and frantic nature [and has a] miserable record of personally savaging political opponents (Hubert Humphrey, Edward Kennedy) when the going gets rough....
>
>   So the President calls names, and he badly recreates his record (for the better) and that of everyone else (for the worse) and he displays an alarming absence of magnanimity, generosity and size when he is campaigning.... Jimmy Carter, as before, seems to have few limits beyond which he will not go in the abuse of opponents and reconstruction of history.[126]

According to Heineman, the president "loathed the *Washington Post*" and "despised the *New York Times*." *Plus ça change, plus c'est la même chose.* "Remarkably, the television networks and newspapers that Carter hated the most were the very ones Richard Nixon had believed were out to get him."[127] By the end of his term Carter had virtually abandoned holding press conferences. "We just thought they weren't helping us," press secretary Jody Powell shrugged.[128] On the other hand, the media certainly wasn't helping Ted Kennedy either when he challenged Carter for the Democratic presidential nomination in the 1980 primaries. The star-gazing hero worship of the liberal media for the liberal senator vanished from the moment he announced his candidacy, not to reappear until after his big speech at the convention conceding his defeat. In between these milestones, his floundering campaign was subject to relentless and merciless criticism, as Kennedy failed to live up to the expectations the media had created for him. Kennedy had failed to understand the first law of the relationship between press and politician: the media only really wants you when it can't have you.

Ronald Reagan took office with a predetermined agenda in dealing with the media. Following the template set by Franklin Roosevelt, wherever possible he would go over the heads of the print and network filters directly to the people. Whenever forced to go through intermediaries, he consistently sought to marginalize their input by implying a gap between their elite perception of reality and that of real Americans. In 1982, for example, he told reporters, "I know that what we've been doing here doesn't read well in the *Washington Post* or the *New York Times*, but, believe me, it reads well in Peoria."[129] It was an approach for which Reagan had the ideological dedication, the charisma, and the oratorical skills honed through years of exposure to the cameras, to make work. There was little the media could do about it. "Upon

Reagan's ascendancy to power in 1981, the press quickly settled into a posture of accommodating passivity from which it never completely arose," Hertsgaard says.[130] This was particularly evident during the major crisis of Reagan's second term. Just as with Watergate, the media was slow out of the starting blocks and never really caught up with events during the Iran-Contra scandal. Although Watergate veteran Pat Buchanan would blast the media as representing the "polemical and publicity arm of American liberalism" while the scandal bubbled, there was no real push to seize the initiative by driving the agenda in a liberal direction, least of all toward impeachment. [131]

Nevertheless, by the 1990s conservatives had fully assimilated the mindset that anything that didn't go their way (e.g., the election of Bill Clinton) could not be an expression of the actual values of the American people but rather could only be the outcome of an orchestrated media conspiracy. In 1996, GOP candidate Bob Dole implored his audiences today to "rise up" against the media: "We've got to stop the liberal bias in this country," he declared to more than 9,000 people packed into the coliseum bleachers at Southern Methodist University. "Don't read that stuff! Don't watch television! You make up your mind! Don't let them make up your mind for you!" Singling out the *New York Times* for the second straight day, Dole continued: "We are not going to let the media steal this election. We're going to win this election. The country belongs to the people, not the *New York Times*."[132] Dole's defeat, of course, only confirmed conservative assumptions. "Eddie, I grit my teeth and I hold my tongue because of my friendship with you, but the networks get under my skin sometimes," Senate Majority Leader Trent Lott told National Association of Broadcasters President Eddie Fritts, a friend since college days at the University of Mississippi, at the NAB's State Leadership Conference in February 1997. The networks, according to Lott, were "prejudiced" and "biased toward the liberal side. Sometimes the networks get into a frenzy that is pretty staggering."[133] The outcome of the Clinton impeachment saga, of course, served merely to reiterate to conservatives yet again the extent of the media monolith standing in their way.[134] So conservatives knew what to expect by the time of the Bush ascendancy at the end of the millennium. But by then the mainstream media no longer held any terror for them. They had constructed their own media universe and were only too happy to subsist within it.

By the 1980s, the Republican Party had fully internalized a worldview in which the media was a collective entity hostile to its interests and, by definition, those of America. In good times the media was a favorite Republican whipping boy; in bad times it was the scapegoat for every problem. President George H. W. Bush took the latter approach while running for reelection in 1992; in this photograph from the campaign trail, he is urging the public to return him to office not based on his record or his merits but in order to defy the nation's media (courtesy Reuters).

Conclusion: Toward a New Understanding of Bias

Objectivity Sells

Rupert Murdoch isn't conservative. It is true that he had this to say to a symposium two decades ago: "The press itself is in danger, if it is allowed to go to extremes without being checked. It does not really matter if there are biases; the people are much smarter than to be misled by simple bias.... [However] the First Amendment was not written for a monopoly press, or a monolithic media, and I maintain it will be in danger one day if this elite does not straighten out its double values, if it does not quit attempting to change the political agenda, and does not at least accommodate the more traditional values of this country."[1]

It is true that Murdoch has personally dedicated the resources of his multinational, multimedia business empire to correcting that imbalance by promulgating a consistent line on policy targeted at a global audience — all 175 Murdoch publications worldwide editorialized in favor of the 2003 war in Iraq, for example.[2] It is true that he launched FOX News specifically in order to meet the needs of the disenfranchised Red State constituency, coloring its "fair and balanced" slant with such a ruby hue the chairman of the Democratic Party was moved to declare, "My view is [that] FOX News is a propaganda outlet for the Republican Party and I don't comment on FOX News."[3] It is even true that Murdoch is prepared to run the *New York Post* at a loss running into the tens of millions of dollars every year just to maintain an outpost behind enemy lines in the heart of Blue State country.

But politics isn't an end to Rupert Murdoch. It's merely a means to an end. Murdoch, in the words of John Lancaster, almost without exception "puts his political interests to work to serve his business interests, and not the reverse." Nowhere is this more apparent than in his strictly enforced policy of appeasement towards China.

In 1993, in an uncharacteristic slip, Murdoch publicly enthused over the manner in which the telecommunications revolution has "proved an unambiguous threat to totalitarian regimes everywhere." One month later the Chinese government banned all satellite dishes in China — inconvenient for the man who had just spent $825 million in Hong Kong to buy the satellite channel Star TV. In order to get back into the good graces of the Beijing regime, Murdoch banned the BBC from Star TV and instituted a policy of purging any critical commentary about China from his multinational media empire. He paid Deng Xiaoping's daughter a substantial advance for her biography of her father, backed out of publishing Chris Patten's book *East and West* (he was later compelled to apologize "unreservedly" to Patten and pay him an undisclosed out-of-court settlement), and derided the Dalai Lama as "a very political old monk shuffling around in Gucci shoes."[4] Demonstrating that appeasement does sometimes run in families, Murdoch progeny James Murdoch, a college dropout who at twenty-eight years old was evidently the ideal man to appoint as CEO of Star TV, described the Falun Gong religious resistance movement in China as "dangerous" and an "apocalyptic cult" which "clearly does not have the success of China at heart." For good measure, young Murdoch counseled Hong Kong's democracy advocates to resign themselves to the reality of life under an "absolutist" regime.[5]

For evidence that the priority of remaining on good terms with China will always override nationalistic chest-thumping for the Murdoch dynasty, you need look no further than the uncharacteristically muted response of the *New York Post* to the spy plane imbroglio of April 2001. Under any other circumstances, the *Post* would have come out with all guns blazing at the spectacle of a U.S. aircraft being forced down and its crew interned by a foreign power. But the foreign power in this instance being China, the *Post* kept the story tucked carefully away inside for the ten-day duration, reserving the front page for such headline news as the narcotics-induced travails of Darryl Strawberry, a Ricky Martin look-alike rape spree, and a Manhattan maître'd being awarded a $16,000 tip.

The *Post*'s commentary on the spy plane standoff was as sparse as it was somber. "It is in neither side's interests for this incident to escalate to the point where more substantive matters are overshadowed," the paper editorialized on April 4. "The U.S. and China ... must move forward with their critical relationship. Hopefully, this incident will lead to an understanding on how vital surveillance and reconnaissance can be carried out, and tolerated, by each side." Only after the crew was released did the *Post* act true to form, splashing a manly portrait of the president on its April 12 front page, headlined "HOMECOMING KING: BUSH BRINGS CREW BACK TO U.S.," with four pages of coverage inside along the same lines ("Prez Passes His First Big Test With Flying Colors") and an editorial pooh-poohing the significance of the crisis for U.S. relations with China. "Crisis, in fact, probably is too strong a word to describe the 10-day standoff.... Think 'situation.'" The *Post* rounded out the saga the following day with a front page featuring the smiling, flag-waving crew on their return to U.S. soil and four more pages of warmhearted coverage inside.[6]

Should the *Post* be congratulated for its statesmanship? Perhaps. But one could easily be excused for being cynical in not anticipating such a cautious, measured response from Murdoch's mouthpiece should a similar "situation" arise involving Mahmoud Ahmadinejad's Iran or Hugo Chavez's Venezuela.

American conservatives would be making a mistake if they assumed Murdoch was their ally. His decision to launch FOX News was a reflection of his business savvy, not his devotion to charitable causes.[7] He has consistently demonstrated that he won't hesitate to flip his support to those politicians of the center-left who meet his standards — just ask Tony Blair or, possibly, Hillary Clinton.[8] Given Murdoch's ultimate allegiance to the bottom line it is his consolidation of the media they embrace, not the persistence of liberal bias in the media they spurn, that should be the primary concern of conservatives.

Murdoch's dedication to making money by any means necessary extends to his entertainment division, which chooses to pay its homage to traditional Christian values by broadcasting such wholesome family entertainment as *The Simple Life, Temptation Island, Skin, The Swan, The Girl Next Door: The Search for a Playboy Centerfold, Who's Your Daddy?* and *Married by America*, which was slapped with a record $1.2 million FCC fine in 2004 after complaints about scenes in which "partygoers lick whipped cream from strippers' bodies" and two female strippers "playfully spank" a man on all fours in his underwear.[9]

"Fox has a schizophrenic personality," Robert Knight, director of the conservative Culture and Family Institute, admits. "Conservatives appreciate Fox news channel for bringing balance, but the Fox entertainment network, on the other hand, has clearly been the leader in driving TV into the sewer with its non-stop sexual emphasis."[10] L. Brent Bozell III faces a similar conundrum with Murdoch's agenda; "Wearing my Media Research Center hat, I'm thrilled with what he's doing with Fox News. Wearing my [Parents Television Council] hat, I'm stunned by what he's done with Fox entertainment."[11]

It amounts to a classic bait and switch approach; attracting a mass audience with populist rhetoric and lascivious innuendo while simultaneously promulgating a neoconservative ideological slant. This strategy isn't anything new. Fifty years ago the *New York Post* under liberal editor James Weschler was described as being "equally concerned with racial integration, disarmament, and Hollywood bust measurements."[12] Under Rupert Murdoch, today's *New York Post* is equally concerned with the War on Terror, opposing gay marriage, and Hollywood bust measurements. Ultimately, the bottom line for Murdoch isn't what's good for America, conservatism, or the Republican Party; the bottom line for Rupert Murdoch is what's good for Rupert Murdoch.

Hollywood isn't liberal. Just because Hollywood has produced some of the most venerated figures in the conservative canon (John Wayne, Ronald Reagan, Charlton Heston), been a source of major star power (Clint Eastwood, Bruce Willis, Kevin Costner) and provided a seemingly inexhaustible pool of GOP candidates for public office (Arnold Schwarzenegger, Fred Thompson, Sonny Bono), doesn't mean that the leading lights of show business typically tilt conservative. They don't. The rank and file of Tinsel Town contributes funds and lends star power to a plethora of liberal causes and charities. But the crucial distinction to make here is that while the bulk of the *people* working in Hollywood are liberal, the *product* is not.

Consider the top money-making movies in U.S. domestic box-office history. Do you notice the overt liberal themes running through these productions? Do you recall having a radical, nonconformist political agenda forced on you when you took your kids to see *Finding Nemo*, *The Lion King*, or *The Chronicles of Narnia*? Bereft of any ideological constructs other than the most elemental good vs. evil, utterly chaste (other than a brief moment of non-explicit premarital sex in *Titanic*), what is there for even the most devout conservative to complain about in any of these films? Certainly not their (sometimes literally) cartoonish violence; the only movie on this list that truly embraces the raw horror of real violence is that paean to the triumph of conservative sensibilities, *The Passion of the Christ*.

TABLE 13. ALL-TIME TOP-RANKED MOVIES BY U.S. DOMESTIC GROSS,
AS OF OCTOBER 1, 2007[13]

Rank	Title	Rank	Title	Rank	Title
1	Titanic	11	Passion of the Christ	21	Lord of the Rings I
2	Star Wars IV	12	Jurassic Park	22	Star Wars II
3	Shrek II	13	Lord of the Rings II	23	Pirates of the Carib. III
4	E.T.	14	Finding Nemo	24	Star Wars VI
5	Star Wars I	15	Spider-Man III	25	Independence Day
6	Pirates of the Carib. II	16	Forrest Gump	26	Pirates of the Carib. I
7	Spider-Man	17	The Lion King	27	The Sixth Sense
8	Star Wars III	18	Shrek III	28	Chronicles of Narnia
9	Lord of the Rings III	19	Harry Potter I	29	Star Wars V
10	Spider-Man II	20	Transformers	30	Harry Potter V

One simple fact pertains here. Hollywood isn't a charity, it's a business, and G-rated, middle-of-the-road popular entertainment is how Hollywood makes its money. Only by raking in the big dollars from movies people actually want to see can the studios afford to indulge auteur directors in R-rated art-film projects (e.g., *Brokeback Mountain*) and major stars in character-driven Oscar vehicles (e.g., George Clooney's *Syriana* and *Good Night, and Good Luck*).[14] Ultimately, the bottom line for Hollywood isn't what's good for America, liberalism, or the Democratic Party; the bottom line for Hollywood is what's good for Hollywood.

The point of drawing these two illustrations is to highlight the dominant economic imperative of the contemporary media. In order to maximize profits it is necessary to secure as wide an advertising revenue base as possible, and accordingly, since "most media organizations are owned by conglomerates or shareholders more interested in balance sheets than in either journalism or politics," as Hackett and Zhao note, "market structures and commercial logic, rather than partisanship as such, have become the primary context of journalism."[15] But if this is true, and it is the struggle for the median that continues to define the business model of the increasingly indiscernible news and entertainment industries, why would the dominant ideological paradigm of the elite media be so skewed to the left?

Survey data leaves no doubt that a gap has opened between the press and the American people. A groundbreaking 1981 study of 240 journalists at national news outlets, conducted by S. Robert Lichter and Stanley Rothman, found that 81 percent said they voted for Democratic candidates for president in every election between 1964 and 1976. Even below the elite level, the division persisted. A 1985 *Los Angeles Times* study of 2,700 journalists at 621 newspapers found this sample to the left of the public on issues relating to abortion, gun control, prayer in schools and defense spending. In 1999, the American Society of Newspaper Editors surveyed 1,037 reporters at 61 newspapers of all sizes. It found that 53 percent said they were liberal or Democrat or leaned that way, compared to only 15 percent who called themselves Republican or conservative or tilted that way. The trend was not as evident at smaller papers, but still existed. An Indiana University School of Journalism survey in 2002 found that although the number of Democrats (37 percent) was at its lowest ebb since 1971, Democrats still topped Republicans by about a 2–1 margin in news rooms.[16] The public in turn is entirely cognizant of the political correctness that suffuses most news sources.[17]

Alan Murray concludes that mainstream newspapers and networks suffered over the years, if not from intentional bias, then at least from a process of self-selection that leads liberal-leaning Americans to choose journalism school over, for example, business school. While conservatives are more likely to choose public relations, advertising or broadcasting there always seems to be a steady stream of advocacy-oriented journalism school graduates ready to re-stock newspaper newsrooms. One analyst theorizes that profit-hungry news corporations tolerate leftward bias because it helps them attract liberal journalists who tend to accept working for a lower wage. Liberal bias therefore "is shown to be consistent with profit maximization."[18]

In rebuttal, one argument runs that even if most reporters are socially liberal, "the countervailing bias of our bosses is generally conservative," as Richard Cohen notes. "Corporate news managers do not rock the boat, and they are in charge. News executives care more about holding on to customers and increasing profits than challenging the establishment. The status quo seems safe."[19]

Moreover, the nature of contemporary political coverage minimizes discussion of process and policy in favor of highlighting the horse-race aspects of partisan competition. According to David Niven, a number of studies point to the ubiquity of horse-race coverage — in which the amount, tone, and subject matter of coverage is largely based on the candidate's positions in the polls — as a major factor that produces political coverage that may be unequal but is in no way based on the media's partisan or ideological preferences.[20] The media accent on a candidate's electoral viability minimizes discussion of what it is she will actually do when in office, thereby minimizing the opportunity for editorializing.

Competition, above all else, feeds this process. The primary objective of the media is to generate competition because competition generates interest and boosts sales. "They are adversarial," was how George Stephanopoulos described the political slant of the media, "in an obsession with conflict, controversy and scandal."[21] This perspective is echoed from the other side of the aisle. "My conclusion is that the press is biased — biased in favor of conflict," former White House press secretary Ari Fleischer says. "There is an ideological element — a subtle bias on policy issues, particularly on social policy issues, that favors Democrats more than Republicans. But that bias is secondary. Conflict comes first, regardless of whether the press is covering a Democrat or a Republican."[22]

And yet the orthodox interpretation of media coverage remains that it reflects a pervasive liberal bias. At an essential level this is an inescapable reality; the fact remains that most people working in the news industry are more liberal than the national median. This liberalism does not apply to the entire spectrum of issues, being much more social than economic; America's trade unions, for example, must be wondering where this legendary media bias is given the consistent pattern of the media to marginalize advocates for tariff protection in favor of those promoting free trade. However, taken as a whole, journalists can be labeled reflexively liberal. Their first response to any issue is interpreted through an essentially liberal ideological framework, and this spills over into the totality of their work. But at the same time they are inhibited by the tenets of impartiality in which aspiring journalists are schooled and the standards of objectivity that the business model of the contemporary mainstream media demands. Although capable of raising questions, the mainstream media is prohibited from delivering answers. It thereby secures the worst of both worlds— endlessly needling conservatives while doing nothing to rally or inspire liberals.

While the media has succeeded in raising the profile of a number of liberal social trends since World War II, such as feminism, environmentalism, gay rights, and the sexual revolution, in each instance this increased prominence provoked a conservative backlash in the polling booth, endowing the Republican Party with the rich vein of votes it has successfully mined in election after election since the end of the 1960s. The only issue on which the media can honestly be said to have shaped a broad public consensus and directly influenced a policy agenda is civil rights. Otherwise, for all the blame and/or credit assigned by either side of the partisan divide, the cupboard is bare. The self-satisfied self-congratulation of *Good Night, and Good Luck* notwithstanding, the media did not bring down Joe McCarthy. It was a co-conspirator, however unwittingly, in his rise and little more than mute witness to his self-immolation. There was no media conspiracy to end the war in Vietnam; the media did not turn the nation against the war; the media did not lose the war. There was no media conspiracy to bring down Richard Nixon; the Rube Goldberg superstructure of the Watergate cover-up held together just long enough for the president to be reelected, and then collapsed under the weight of its own accumulated mendacity.[23] Just as with the last days of McCarthy, the media only piled on to the Watergate story after it was clear that the momentum had already broken against the administration.

And where was the coordinated mainstream media assault on the president's rationale for initiating military action against Iraq in 2003? Where was the investigative journalism that scrutinized his evidence and exposed the fallacy of launching a preemptive and unilateral war to neutralize weapons of mass destruction that didn't exist?[24] If the media was so biased during this period, why did those two doyens of elite media liberalism, the *New York Times* and the *Washington Post*, both feel constrained to issue apologies to their readers about the quality of their coverage of the issues leading up to the war?[25]

Most of all, there is not, there never has been, and there never could be any grand pan-media liberal conspiracy to deliberately "fix" elections in this country by skewing coverage and reporting. Dave D'Alessio and Mike Allen, who conducted the most extensive meta-analysis of media bias in the 20th century by incorporating 59 studies employing 132 measurements of the extent of media bias across thirteen presidential elections, concluded that "there is no evidence whatsoever of a monolithic liberal bias in the newspaper industry, at least as manifest in presidential campaign coverage." The study did find that "analyses of coverage bias and statement bias in TV network news coverage of presidential campaigns reveal a very small, and not completely consistent, liberal (or at least pro–Democratic) bias," but at the same time, "a slight pro–Republican coverage bias and an even slighter pro–Republican statement bias."[26] Far from sharpening the political divide, newspaper editorials have consistently been on the retreat from the definitive partisan advocacy of yesteryear. In 1940, over 85 percent of all U.S. newspapers endorsed a candidate in the presidential election. By 1996 this figure had decreased to less than one in three newspapers (see Appendix 1). If anything, the only pattern of favoritism to have emerged in the editorials of those still willing to make a call is a pronounced bias in favor of incumbency.[27]

The Conservative Agenda

These facts notwithstanding, the conservative Greek Chorus condemning the media for its bias against Bush in 2004 was echoing exactly the same lines from four years earlier, even though no evidence exists to support the assertion that there was a coordinated media campaign to elect Al Gore.[28] Quite the opposite, in fact. "It's George W. Bush — big time," Greg Mitchell reported at the end of campaign 2000, citing a TIPP poll of 193 newspaper executives across the country. By a 55 to 14 percent margin they anticipated a Bush victory. Bush won 48 percent of the endorsements, to 23 percent for Gore. Smaller papers went for Bush almost 3–1, midsize papers 5–3, and larger papers 5–4. The papers that backed Bush represented 58 percent of total national circulation, to 42 percent for Gore. "The nation's newspaper editors and publishers strongly believe the Texas governor will beat Al Gore in Tuesday's election for president," Mitchell summed up. "By a wide margin, they plan to vote for him themselves. And, to complete this Republican trifecta, newspapers endorsed Bush by about 2-to-1 nationally. One has to wonder: whatever happened to the so-called 'liberal press'?"[29]

The media is a fickle goddess, choosing to destroy without scruple that which she has created, a case in point being the viability of the erstwhile frontrunner for the 1988 Democratic presidential nomination, Gary Hart, whose extramarital hi-jinks were relentlessly sniffed-out and gleefully exposed by investigative reporters for whom policy was the last thing on their minds. Does the saturation coverage of Barack Obama indicate a liberal bias in the media? If so, why were the other presidential contenders, real or imagined, it has overtly boosted for the White House over the past quarter century both Republicans? Why, for example, did it proselytize so fervently for Republican Colin Powell to enter the 1996 presidential campaign? Was it because Powell was more liberal than GOP heir apparent Bob Dole? No. It was simply because journalists liked and respected Powell personally, they were enchanted by his all–American personal history which, coupled with his political virginity, represented the foundation on which to construct the all–American candidate, and they sensed that Dole would be easy meat for Clinton, while Powell could shake up the race, thereby generating interest, hence news, hence business. The media craves a story; for this reason, as Shogan says, newsmakers fixated on Powell, creating a presidential boom that had little connection with political reality.[30]

The same phenomenon repeated itself with a vengeance during the next electoral cycle where the unprecedented pan-media enthusiasm for John McCain effectively rendered it as a collective entity, for all intents and purposes an unofficial adjunct to his campaign.[31] Rather than serving to further his cause, however, this adulation may in fact have worked against him. Any suggestion the media may actually be playing favorites with a Republican only serves as further evidence of the extent of the liberal conspiracy. Unable to take on the conservative juggernaut frontally, liberals seek to deceive the faithful by whispering in their ear about false idols. "When the media talks about how much they like Jack Kemp," L. Brent Bozell IIII told Oliver North at the 1996 GOP convention, "it's opposed to the other Republicans who they hate."[32] McCain might have enjoyed taking his turn to bathe in the indulgent glow of the media spotlight during primary season in 2000, but by doing so he only inherited the inevitable back-lash from the right. "It's only natural that leftists would take the media lovefest over Arizona Republican Sen. John McCain's 'trash-talk express' to mean only one thing," Bozell snapped, meaning the suggestion that maybe the whole liberal media conspiracy thing might be just a tad exaggerated. But like the rest of the true believers, Bozell wasn't buying it, and if he was angry at liberals for this new effrontery, he was even angrier at those "network TV pundits trotted out as representative of 'conservative' thinking"—including *Weekly Standard* editor Bill Kristol (who told the *New Yorker*, "The whole idea of the 'liberal media' was often used as an excuse by conservatives for conservative failures"), David Brooks, and Tucker Carl-son—who were prepared to play along. On behalf of the faithful everywhere, Bozell uncere-moniously read these apostates out of the ranks of the elect: "They have lost touch with the conservative movement and now echo elite media opinion.... We might say each of these polit-ical analysts has forsaken loyalty to conservative principles and partisans on so many different issues in the interests of getting his own face, byline and paycheck in the plush environs of the liberal media corporations."[33]

Conservatives have yet to forgive McCain for this cardinal sin of courting, and earning, the respect of non-conservatives. In their estimation, the friend of my enemy is my enemy. The same formula applies to any other Republican presidential hopeful who makes the mis-take of getting too chummy with the mainstream media. "The best way to win the Republi-can caucuses in Iowa is to get the *New York Times* to attack you," says GOP lobbyist and author Craig Shirley. "It's almost formulaic."[34] Ipso facto, the guaranteed way to lose the Republican nomination is to be highly esteemed by the paper of record, a burden none of the contempo-rary contenders aspires to shoulder.[35]

A key point to always bear in mind in the debate over bias is that the more obsessed with bias someone is, the more biased they are. Those driving the war against liberal bias are them-selves far from being disinterested and altruistic third parties prepared to recuse themselves from the partisan fray in order to uphold the sacred torch of objectivity. They are highly moti-vated and tightly organized conservative activists dedicated to securing an overtly partisan outcome in the interests of the Republican Party.

The leading light in this regard is the Media Research Center, founded in 1987 by L. Brent Bozell III, the nephew of conservative icon William F. Buckley, Jr. A finance chairman for Pat Buchanan's 1992 presidential bid, and finance director and later president of the for-mer National Conservative Political Action Committee (NCPAC), Bozell also launched the Parents Television Council in 1995.[36] Bozell first caught the public eye at the GOP convention in 1996, where he published a daily convention newsletter, "Media Reality Check '96," and rented a booth in the convention's merchandise mart to give away T-shirts featuring carica-tures of ABC's Peter Jennings, CBS's Dan Rather and NBC's Bryant Gumbel under the words "Team Clinton." Bozell's then chief lieutenant, Brent Baker, argued that the work of dedi-cated activists outside party circles represented a boon to the Republican Party: "The more

For conservatives, the media now constitutes an explicit threat, not just to the social values of Americans but to national security itself. This placard was just one of nearly a dozen on display during a protest against the *New York Times* for its 2006 decision to publish a feature on the SWIFT monitoring of international financial transactions. By conservative reasoning this decision undermined the "War on Terror" and constituted treason, the penalty for which is death. In reality such empty threats and feeble demonstrations were but a pale shadow of the media divide during previous conflicts, for example the Civil War, when mobs sacked presses and editors disappeared in the middle of the night into federal prisons. This forgotten history needs to be considered in order to bring context to the debate about the role of the media (courtesy Matt Stoller).

that people distrust the media the better it is for conservatives because the media is the largest force in tearing down conservatives."[37]

By its own account, the Media Research Center has grown to be the largest and most sophisticated television-monitoring operation in the United States, now employing sixty professional staff with a $6 million annual budget. For the 2004 campaign alone, the MRC raised $2.8 million for newspaper ads in fifteen markets, billboards in forty cities and a talk-radio blitz aimed at countering the "liberal jihad" against George W. Bush.[38] Bozell, who founded the Cybercast News Network ("The Right News: Right Now"), also sits on the Board of Directors of the American Conservative Union, and is executive director of the Conservative Victory Committee, a political-action committee that contributed $53,500 to Republican Senate and House candidates in the 2004 election cycle alone, none to Democrats.[39]

Bozell's agenda is a component of a multi-faceted strategy on the part of conservatives, one that has been gathering momentum for at least the past four decades, to marginalize and ultimately entirely ostracize alternate modes of thought from American political discourse. The conservative program does not end merely with liberalism purged from the corporate structures of the media empires. In order to be fully consummated it requires their conversion to a norm that exclusively reflects conservative values.

The irony at the heart of the debate over media bias is the fact that no one in the media is more biased than those conservatives who have built their careers on a foundation of incessantly criticizing the bias of others. This trait is most explicit in the new media of talk radio and the Internet. It's certainly no secret that when you listen to Rush Limbaugh and his ilk you have tapped into a direct conduit to the Republican Party.[40] But conservatives tend to hew more closely to an ideological line even within the mainstream media itself.[41]

Response time and message discipline among conservatives in the media have been honed to a fine art. For example, within twenty-four hours of the news breaking that W. Mark Felt was the legendary "Deep Throat" of Watergate fame, the official conservative line, promulgated across the entire spectrum of the new and old media, was that by bringing down Nixon, Felt was directly responsible for the fall of South Vietnam and the killing fields of Cambodia. Another classic manifestation of this phenomenon was the conservative rejoinder to the publication by the *New York Times* on June 23, 2006, of a feature article on the Bush administration's tapping into the database of international financial transactions maintained by the banking consortium Society for Worldwide Interbank Financial Telecommunication (SWIFT), in order to monitor the flow of funds to terrorist organizations. The instantaneously mobilized and universally outraged reaction across the entire spectrum of the conservative media was to brand the *Times* a threat to national security and demand stringent legal sanctions against those responsible, on a charge of treason.[42] Even the *Wall Street Journal* joined in the fracas, condemning the publication of the article and accusing *Times* executive editor Bill Keller of being committed to "not winning the war on terror but obstructing it," despite having itself featured an article on exactly the same subject on exactly the same day the story broke.[43] Such chutzpah, endorsed as a matter of course by the *Journal's* ideological soul mates on the radio waves and online, leads to the conclusion, as Michael Tomasky puts it, that "conservatives don't want *The New York Times* to be 'fairer.' They want it to cease to exist."[44]

When conservatives complain that the media has a liberal bias, therefore, they don't mean that it should be neutral but that it should have a conservative bias; they aspire to a world where every TV channel is some variant on FOX News, where every newspaper is some variant on the *New York Post* and the *Washington Times*, and where the magazine racks only offer your choice on such alternatives as the *National Review*, the *Weekly Standard*, and the *American Spectator*.[45] Until arriving at this promised land conservatives, feeling more and more isolated from what they consider the mainstream media, will adhere ever more tightly to the alternatives. This is a reflection of a broad social trend that is reshaping the political map in the United States.

Bias Sells

The deepening social cleavages in this country are not the invention of the media. Simply put, the media is following, not leading, this balkanization. Thanks to the revolutions in transportation and communications technology, Americans today have greater choice than ever before in where to live. Increasingly, they are choosing to express this unprecedented social mobility by living with like-minded individuals in communities of interest, linked more closely to similar communities in other locations via the Internet than they are to their neighbors in physical proximity.[46] This phenomenon is especially obvious in the college towns scattered like oases throughout the "flyover country" in heartland America. These liberal enclaves are like self-contained worlds whose inhabitants share infinitely more in common with their counterparts in Boston, New York or San Francisco than with their fellow citizens in Oklahoma, Kansas or Idaho. Thanks to the Internet, Red State liberals are able to retreat into isolation from the hostile environment surrounding them, participating in everything from consciousness-raising forums to fundraising with kindred spirits online. A similar process of cocooning goes on in those conservative redoubts trapped behind enemy lines in the Blue States.

These demographic shifts are being expressed politically, a pattern that is most obvious at the county level. For thirty years after the end of World War II, the trend was towards social homogenization. In the down-to-the-wire election between Jimmy Carter and Gerald Ford in 1976, only 26.8 percent of American voters lived in counties with landslide election results, where one party secured 60 percent or more of the vote. Analysts spoke of an era of dealignment, of the decline of party and the rise of the independent voter. But that paradigm has reversed itself to the point where six elections later, in the even tighter contest between George W. Bush and Al Gore in 2000, the share of the electorate living in counties with landslide election results had increased to 45.3 percent. Three of every five voters now live in counties where children have been born, graduated from high school and gone off to college without ever experiencing a local change in presidential party preference. "Today, most Americans live in communities that are becoming more politically homogenous," the *Austin American-Statesman* noted before the last presidential election. "And that grouping of like-minded people is feeding the nation's increasingly rancorous and partisan politics."[47]

This cocktail of geographic socialization, partisan attachment, and advocacy media is collectively responsible for the one unambiguously positive trend in contemporary American political culture, the rise in voter turnout. Throughout past eras when the express purpose of the press was to mobilize the electorate on behalf of the respective parties, it acted as a powerful force impelling citizens to show up at the ballot-box and strike a blow for their particular brand of freedom. The real triumph of the party papers was their success in making partisan loyalty among its readers synonymous with their personal identity. Turnout spiraled downward across the board once the mutually reinforcing principles of media objectivity and partisan dealignment became the established norms. In an era where candidate-focused campaigns targeted swing voters by blurring policy distinctions, disillusioned blocs of the electorate detached from the political system and drifted out of involvement. By the dawn of the last decade of the 20th century, commentators such as Entman were concerned enough at the long-term implications of this hollowing-out of American democracy to argue that "the decline of participation in the U.S. has historically paralleled the dwindling of the partisan press and the rise of objectivity; perhaps an injection of party media would reverse the trend."[48] This prescription has been realized. With the ideological divisions between the two parties becoming more strictly defined, and the respective party cadres being effectively rallied by the new wave of partisan advocates in the media, turnout has jumped sharply, 2006 being the first midterm election in over a decade in which turnout was over 40 percent, and 2004 being the first presidential election in over three decades in which turnout was over 60 percent.

As community identities solidify around partisan interests, they naturally gravitate towards sources of information that reflect those interests. The surge in explicit media bias, therefore, may be following, not leading, this trend. A key component of a successful marketing strategy is identification of a viable market; given that George W. Bush could not convince one in five citizens in New York City or Washington D.C. to vote for him in 2004, it would be unrealistic to expect the *New York Times* or the *Washington Post* to be anything other than biased against him.[49] By these standards, the publications defying economic rationality are the conservative *New York Post* and *Washington Times*. The owners of both papers are only able to sustain these ideological indulgences by siphoning off capital from those facets of their multinational multimedia empires which actually generate profits.[50]

The new reality is that bias, properly targeted, sells. This fact explains the transition from objectivity to opinion across the entire spectrum of both the "new" and "old" media.[51] Decades ago the hippie counterculture was born when New Age guru Timothy Leary advised Baby Boomers everywhere to "Turn On, Tune In, Drop Out," in order to achieve spiritual satisfaction. The new, conservative counterculture is following the same agenda — turning on FOX News and tuning in to talk radio in order to drop out of a world corrupted by secularism, pacifism, humanism, socialism, and a host of additional un–American "isms" propagated by what is in their minds a monolithically liberal mainstream media.[52]

An instructive exemplar of this new mood took place during the final moments of the 2004 Republican National Convention. After the balloons had fallen and the cameras had turned away, an unusual commotion broke out in the seats surrounding CNN's convention-floor set. Dozens of delegates turned to where Judy Woodruff and Wolf Blitzer were conducting interviews, and started loudly chanting, "WATCH FOX NEWS! WATCH FOX NEWS!" This was not mere tomfoolery. "For all intents and purposes, we now have a Republican TV news network — Fox News — and a Democratic one, CNN," Tim Rutten notes. According to Pew Research Center for the People and the Press data, 70 percent of voters who said they got most of their election news from Fox planned to vote for Bush, while just 21 percent intended to support Kerry. Among voters who relied on CNN for their news, 67 percent support Kerry and 26 percent said they'd back Bush.[53] The issue that Fox News now has to finesse is maintaining the delicate balance between serving as a platform for Republican advocacy and maintaining its credibility as an objective news agency. The signs are that this may no longer be possible. The decision in 2007 by the Democratic contenders for the 2008 presidential nomination, after coming under immense pressure from the Internet grass roots of the party ("netroots"), to boycott a debate being hosted by Fox News, may represent a critical turning point in the ongoing "balkanization" of American politics and the American media into rival, mutually incompatible, insular communities. The netroots represent the belated arrival of a liberal counterpart to the conservative New Right that emerged in the 1960s and ultimately seized control of the Republican Party from its establishment elite. The netroots are following the same template, starting with the isolation of — and, where necessary, purging of — status quo figures, most notably Joseph Lieberman, within the Democratic Party.[54]

Conservatives have succeeded in constructing their own multimedia channels for the dissemination of information, and they are much more effective in partisan terms than the timid, conflicted liberalism of the mainstream media, because, entirely free of the constraints of objectivity, they can deliver the unadulterated, red-blooded Americanism their target audience craves.[55] Conservatives now have the capacity for total immersion in a conservative multimedia environment. Frustrated with the liberal bias of the Daily Show, they can turn to the Half-Hour News Hour. Frustrated with the liberal bias of YouTube, they can log on to Qubetv; frustrated with the liberal bias of Wikipedia, they now have Conservapedia as an alternative.

"Twenty-five years ago, most people got their news from ABC, CBS or NBC," Ralph Reed, a regional coordinator for the Bush-Cheney campaign and a former head of the Christian Coalition, reminded his fellow Republicans during campaign '04. "Fortunately, that is no longer the case. The gatekeepers of dominant media have lost their monopoly on information." "I have not watched a newscast of a major network in years," Reed boasted. "I get in the car in the morning and listen to Rush Limbaugh. On the way home, I listen to Sean Hannity. At night I watch Fox News."[56]

"Let me talk to you about five good things of late," the late Jerry Falwell told his flock after the election of 2004, "for which this week I hope you and your family around your Thanksgiving table will praise the Lord." And the No. 5 blessing for which to give praise unto the one true God? That "America has alternative news media and is no longer held hostage by the major print and broadcast media." Falwell continued, "I remember a day when ABC, CBS, NBC, and CNN and the major print media controlled all the news flow to the American people and we found ourselves getting warped and distorted news. I thank God now in the 21st century for talk radio, that three hours a day people like Sean Hannity, Rush Limbaugh and hundreds of others are telling the truth of what really is going on. I thank God for FOX News Channel [applause]. I thank God for the Internet bloggers and the news producers like NewsMax.com, WorldNetDaily.com, even The Drudge Report."[57]

Alan Murray believes that the rise of Fox News, which has deliberately sought out right-leaning anchors to push a conservative line, hasn't just been an antidote to the leftward tilt of the mainstream press, but a catalyst for a new era of partisan journalism. The actors involved, notwithstanding their "fair and balanced" moniker, are comfortable serving as the locus of this partisan attachment. "If Fox News is a conservative channel — and I'm going to use the word 'if' — so what?" Bill O'Reilly shrugged while covering the 2004 GOP convention. "You've got 50 other media that are blatantly left. Now, I don't think Fox is a conservative channel. I think it's a traditional channel. There's a difference. We are willing to hear points of view that you'll never hear on ABC, CBS or NBC."[58]

This ideologically-driven consumerism is reshaping marketing in such commercial fields as publishing.[59] It's those same consumers who are choosing news sources that support their own biases.[60] And increasingly media outlets are, consciously or unconsciously, enthusiastically or reluctantly, shaping their perspective on the news to satisfy this expectation of bias.[61]

The quarantine they maintain against the virus of media bias enables conservatives to dismiss negative commentary on reconstruction in Iraq as liberal "brainwashing" equivalent to "gang rape."[62] Ideology will always triumph over reality, a case in point being the July 2006 Harris Poll that showed 50 percent of Americans believed Saddam Hussein was in possession of weapons of mass destruction when the U.S. began military operations in 2003, up from 36 percent the previous year.[63] This epitomizes the mindset of the conservative counterculture for whom any information received via the mainstream media by definition is suspect, whereas the tightly interwoven campaign of innuendo and conspiracy theory saturating conservative talk radio, blogs, and cable television automatically has credence.[64]

This process begins at the very apex of the conservative pyramid and is disseminated all the way down the chain of command.[65] Bush-Cheney 2004 campaign manager and former GOP chair Ken Mehlman recently remarked that while in previous years political campaigns were driven by the content of evening newscasts of CBS, NBC and ABC, in 2004 there was a shift toward focusing on cable news, Internet and talk radio: "Without the Web or talk radio, [a campaign] has no word of mouth."[66] True to this vision, during the 2004 campaign, GOP opposition research nuggets on John Kerry were almost always leaked first to the Drudge Report because, according to Mehlman, it inevitably drove wider coverage, including to old media organizations: "He puts something up and they have to follow it." At the Republican National Committee, leaking items to the Drudge Report is now an official part of communications strategy. In a bid to make this relationship more intimate, a delegation of RNC officials flew to Miami Beach in 2005 for a dinner at the Forge Steakhouse to introduce Drudge to Matt Rhoades, the party's new opposition research director.[67]

The Bush White House has consistently undertaken to stonewall ideologically unreliable publications while feeding information to sympathetic ones through such ongoing political operations as "Friends & Allies."[68] Other tactics employed by this administration and its party to neutralize the mainstream media include proffering payola to sympathetic talking heads, setting up dummy news organizations to provide accreditation for conservative reporters both domestically and abroad, and restructuring the public broadcasting that falls within its purview on more favorable terms.[69]

As the political climate deteriorated in 2006, Bush adopted a strategy of meeting informally with radio talk-show hosts in order to more effectively coordinate their message, inviting Rush Limbaugh to the Oval Office in June and playing host to Mike Gallagher, Neal Boortz, Laura Ingraham, Sean Hannity and Michael Medved for a 90-minute private conference in September.[70] This approach reached its apotheosis on October 24 when the White House set up a tent on the North Lawn and allowed forty-two radio hosts to broadcast live throughout the day. As an illustration of the faith it placed in the power of the alternative media, the administration ensured that all its key players, from key presidential adviser Karl Rove to Secretary of State Condoleezza Rice and Defense Secretary Donald Rumsfeld, were available for interviews.[71]

In many respects, the emerging partisan media environment today has picked up right where the partisan media model left off during the New Deal era. The same causes are being advocated in the same terms and by strikingly interchangeable personalities. In employing the multimedia empire at his disposal to promulgate his standardized free-market/manifest-destiny agenda across multiple markets, Rupert Murdoch has adopted the business model established by William Randolph Hearst. Rush Limbaugh and Bill O'Reilly are the lineal descendants of Charles Coughlin, who pioneered the use of talk radio as a mechanism by which to circumvent the elite-dominated mainstream media and appeal directly to the American heartland.[72] Matt Drudge is the modern incarnation of Walter Winchell, the man who tore down the wall between the personal and the political, exposing the intimate details of celebrity to the public domain. In Ann Coulter's casual advocacy of the liquidation of her enemies, one can discern the ghost of Westbrook Pegler, in whose columns, which were carried in 186 papers during the 1940s, he once mused over "what sort of a world we might have had now had [Giuseppe] Zangara been a better shot that day in Bayfront Park, Miami, when Tony Cermak was called to his reward" instead of the intended target, that "feeble-minded fuehrer" Franklin Roosevelt.[73]

But if America is returning full circle to the halcyon days of the partisan press of the early republic, then the process is being driven furthest and fastest online. The bloggers of today are the contemporary counterparts to the editors of yesteryear. The most striking similarity is the youth common to the pioneers of both eras. Bloggers live by the old rules; driven by their ideology, they make whatever revenue they can by advertising, typically events, campaigns and publications exclusively targeted at those who share their ideology. Through a miasma of news largely poached from established sources, rumor, and outright conjecture, they present a completely one-sided perspective on reality, relentlessly liberal or conservative, probing for weaknesses in the words and deeds of the opposition while boosting (and where necessary exonerating) those of their own side. At election time they serve as rallying points for the respective parties, helping link the hierarchies with the grass roots.

Many of these sites allow for interactive responses to the host's commentary or open-mike participation by the online communities that congregate there. The ensuing debates can be quite heated but are always refracted through the prism of partisan interest: namely, how can this issue best be resolved in the interest of our party? And the debates are held strictly in-house. On Red State sites the enemies are referred to as "rats" and "dimocrats," while their online equivalents are referred to as "moonbats." On Blue State sites the foes are known as "rethugs" or "repugs," who in their online incarnation are dubbed "wingnuts." Neither are welcome at the haunts of the other; strangers, provocateurs, effectively anyone with a difference of opinion, are labeled "trolls" and flamed out of the conversation, even if they make it past the gatekeepers, who on some sites police and enforce rigid ideological conformity.[74] In a significant manifestation of the maturation of the new media, blogs, once seen as spontaneous expressions of anti-establishment dissent on the part of concerned citizens, are becoming mainstream, as leading bloggers enter into formal or informal relationships with particular candidates for office.[75]

It doesn't take long while bouncing from Red to Blue sites online to appreciate the key characteristic of the partisan divide in the new media: the sites don't offer differing perspectives on the same news, they offer an entirely distinct, self-contained universe of news compatible with the personal ideological perspective of their readers. And this represents not a departure from the established pattern, but a return to the mode of news dissemination that was an everyday reality for most Americans for most of the history of the republic. The evidence is right there in black and white. On election day, November 5, 1844, the editorial page of Horace Greeley's *New York Tribune* included the ubiquitous, flag-draped Whig ballot at its masthead; a brief declaration of Whig principles, accompanied by a statement from presidential candidate Henry Clay himself; encouraging reports of early returns from other states; an account of electoral chicanery involving forged ballots on the part of the Democrats, complete with the offer of a $100 reward for information regarding the perpetrators; and a barrage of exhortations reminding Whigs that it was their patriotic obligation to turn out and vote. Under the heading "DON'T MIND THE RAIN," Greeley conceded, "It may be bad weather today," but reminded his readers that autumnal showers were "nothing to what the election of Polk would bring upon us. Let no Whig be deterred by rain from doing his whole duty," the editor insisted. After all, "who values his coat more than his country?" In plain language, Horace Greeley and the editors of yesteryear have been reincarnated as the bloggers of today, and as they will increasingly come to dominate the news making agenda on their explicitly partisan terms, they will render the debate over bias irrelevant.

Déjà Vu All Over Again

We arrive at last at the contradiction at the heart of the conservative animus toward the mainstream media. Conservatives continue to pour so much of their time, effort and money into proving the existence and exposing the extent of liberal bias. But it is an open question whether all of this endeavor, and the hostility that underlies it, is warranted. Throughout American history, the press has helped build parties, shape policy, and launch political careers. In 1876, one enterprising editor was able to seize an opportunity to shape the aftermath of the Hayes-Tilden contest and may have set in motion a process that culminated in the elevation of his preferred candidate to the White House. But there is nothing whatsoever to substantiate the claim that the media has the capacity to shape public opinion to the extent that it can decide the outcome of an election. There is no evidence to contradict the conclusion reached over six decades ago by Frank Mott that "there seems to be no correlation, positive or negative, between the support of a majority of newspapers during a campaign and success at the polls" (see Table 14).[76] Even if there is a grand pan-media liberal conspiracy to prevent the election of Republican candidates for the presidency, it isn't doing a particularly good job, bearing in mind that Republican candidates have won seven out of the past ten presidential elections, and have been endorsed by at least a plurality of newspapers in all but three presidential elections over the past one hundred years.

TABLE 14. ESTIMATED PERCENTAGES OF PRESS SUPPORT FOR SUCCESSFUL PRESIDENTIAL CANDIDATES, 1789–2004[77]

Year	Candidate Elected	% Press	Year	Candidate Elected	% Press
1789	Washington	—	1900	McKinley	62
1793	Washington	—	1904	Theodore Roosevelt	52
1796	John Adams	80	1908	Taft	55
1800	Jefferson	33	1912	Wilson	41
1804	Jefferson	—	1916	Wilson	49
1808	Madison	47	1920	Harding	60
1812	Madison	55	1924	Coolidge	57
1816	Monroe	67	1928	Hoover	59
1820	Monroe	—	1932	Franklin D. Roosevelt	41
1824	John Q. Adams	40	1936	Franklin D. Roosevelt	37
1828	Jackson	40	1940	Franklin D. Roosevelt	26
1832	Jackson	40	1944	Franklin D. Roosevelt	27
1836	Van Buren	35	1948	Truman	18
1840	William H. Harrison	67	1952	Eisenhower	82
1844	Polk	40	1956	Eisenhower	80
1848	Taylor	51	1960	Kennedy	22
1852	Pierce	48	1964	Lyndon B. Johnson	55
1856	Buchanan	52	1968	Nixon	80
1860	Lincoln	30	1972	Nixon	93
1864	Lincoln	65	1976	Carter	16
1868	Grant	62	1980	Reagan	73
1872	Grant	55	1984	Reagan	86
1876	Hayes	49	1988	George H.W. Bush	79
1880	Garfield	49	1992	Clinton	54
1884	Cleveland	53	1996	Clinton	38
1888	Benjamin Harrison	47	2000	Bush	54
1892	Cleveland	53	2004	Bush	46
1896	McKinley	67			

But if the media doesn't present any real threat, why are conservatives so obsessed with it? This is the schizophrenia lying at the heart of modern conservatism. Consider Hanson's argument:

> The East and West Coasts and the big cities may reflect the sway of the universities, the media, Hollywood, and the arts, but the folks in between somehow ignore what the professors preach to their children, what they read in the major newspapers, and what they are told on TV. The Internet, right-wing radio, and cable news do not so much move Middle America as reflect its preexisting deep skepticism of our aristocracy and its engineered morality imposed from on high.... *60 Minutes, Nightline,* ABC News — these are now seen by millions as mere highbrow versions of *Fahrenheit 9/11.*[78]

The question remains: if this is such a truism, why continue to highlight it? If the public has proved so consistently able to pierce the veil of partisan advocacy in the press, why keep reminding them of it? If the mainstream media has been rendered so utterly impotent, why keep flogging a dead horse? To find the answer all you had to do was be one of the more than 950 people who packed into the Grand Ballroom of the J. W. Marriott in Washington, D.C. on April 21, 2005, to attend that year's Dishonor Awards. This annual event, hosted by the Media Research Center, is dedicated to "Roasting the Most Outrageously Biased Liberal Reporters" of the preceding year. In 2005 the event also took a moment to honor the Swift Boat Veterans and POWs for Truth; co-founder of the group, John O'Neill, was awarded the MRC's Conservative of the Year Award. The event always attracts a who's who of American conservatism; the panel of judges, who were asked to decide on such categories as the "Barbra Streisand Political IQ Award (For Celebrity Vapidity)," "Good Morning Morons," and "The Madness of King George (For Bush Bashing)," included conservative luminaries Ann Coulter, Lucianne Goldberg, Sean Hannity, Laura Ingraham, Michelle Malkin, and Rush Limbaugh.

This ceremony amounts to nothing less than a total inversion of social and political reality. The entire premise assumed that those attending represented a marginalized and persecuted minority struggling to find expression beneath the yoke of absolutist tyranny. But in fact the audience — which, at the 2004 awards, "through its cheering, clapping and Dean-like screams" picked from among all the outrages perpetrated by the liberal media the "Quote of the Year" — was the physical manifestation of the white, wealthy, conservative, heterosexual, Christian constituency which held an absolute monopoly on power in this country.

The Republican Party at the end of 2004 controlled the White House, both houses of Congress, and had appointed thirteen of the last fifteen justices to the Supreme Court; a majority of the states had Republican governors and legislatures; and — far more important than these transient partisan realities — business and the military, the twin pillars of the global pax–Americana, are institutionally Republican. And yet Republicans, congressional majorities or no, are fixated on their self-perception as helpless victims of an arbitrary and unrepresentative power, subjected every day to indignities perpetrated at the whim of the liberal axis of evil between academia, Hollywood, and the media. This mindset, this self identification with the oppressed majority, is the binding force that makes conservatism so powerful.[79] It has the best of both worlds; all the advantages that come with incumbency, coupled with a backs-to-the-wall mindset that informs them that *they* are the outsiders, heroic underdogs fighting back against entrenched elites. The Dishonor Awards therefore are perfectly representative of the conservative worldview precisely because the participants see nothing incongruous in the spectacle of millionaires at black-tie gala events, that could not be more ideologically pure, expressing outrage at the lack of objectivity on the part of others.

This psychology is far from being unique in American history. In 1800, in 1828, and in 1932, Thomas Jefferson, Andrew Jackson and Franklin Roosevelt won elections that cemented the Democratic Party's dominance of the presidency and Congress. Their triumphant electoral coalitions were based on aligning the frontier states of the South and West against those of the Northeast. Unifying these coalitions, binding them together and driving them on, was their all-consuming contempt for, fear of and resentment toward the establishment in its heartland of New England. What does this establishment represent? Why, nothing less than the Wizard of Oz, Dorothy — the elite that not only controlled the financial destiny of the nation but dictated its cultural values and social mores through its monopoly of the modes of entertainment, education, and information.[80] The fact that the organs of the news were solidly against Jefferson, Jackson and Roosevelt served only to further galvanize their supporters against the establishment behind the news. Having secured a monopoly of political power, the Democrats, in the name of the people, were determined to emasculate the one institution still in establishment hands that could counteract their agenda — the judiciary.[81]

Today, the Republican Party of Nixon, Reagan and George W. Bush represents those same frontier states, mobilizing a coalition of voters from South and West against their ancestral enemy, the establishment of the Northeast. Having secured a monopoly of political power they too, in the name of the people, are determined to bring the judiciary to heel. The fact that long ago the curtain was pulled back on the establishment — dissipating whatever capacity it ever actually possessed to guide the destiny of the nation — is irrelevant. No one has a greater interest in sustaining the illusion that an unrepresentative, media controlling, all-pervasive elite represents a threat to this country, than its ostensible enemy. The longer this charade is played out, the more united and focused the Republican Party becomes.

This agenda harbors one final irony. No context has ever been considered as to what standards of objectivity the perceived liberal bias of the contemporary mainstream media should be measured against. With the uncompromisingly partisan fulmination of the press in bygone eras having receded beyond the threshold of memory, it registered with no one that the media is in fact less partisan than at any time in the past. The conservative assault on the credibility of the media, as orchestrated as it is relentless, has succeeded in sponsoring the emergence of alternative anti-media to satisfy the needs of a distinct, self-contained, conservative cultural milieu. But the inevitable corollary of this ideological isolationism has been a parallel emigration by liberals from dependence on the media toward their own unabashedly liberal alternatives. Having been set in motion, this process will culminate in the demise of the mainstream media concept, proving it to be an aberration in American history, and leading to the reemergence of a business model wherein news is contested between rival, mutually exclusive, partisan worldviews, each convinced of their own uncompromising objectivity. This process both feeds from and contributes to the polarization on either side of the cultural and socioeconomic fault line dividing America, which, after a period of transition through decades of dealignment, divides two ideologically homogenous camps. A partisan press complements the other key trends — election strategies based on motivating core constituencies as opposed to targeting swing voters; higher turnout; and enhanced caucus discipline among legislators — that will dominate the future of American politics just as they once dominated in the past.[82]

Appendix:
Newspaper Endorsements
for President, 1940–1996 *

*"Newspaper Endorsements for President Since 1940," *Editor and Publisher*, October 26, 1996, p. 28.

EDITORIAL ENDORSEMENTS: 1940

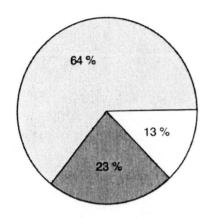

Candidate	Endorsements
☐ Willkie (R)	813
◼ Roosevelt (D)	289
☐ None	171
TOTAL	1,273

EDITORIAL ENDORSEMENTS: 1944

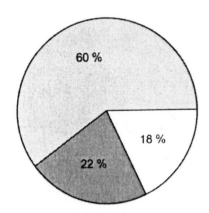

Candidate	Endorsements
☐ Dewey (R)	796
◼ Roosevelt (D)	291
☐ None	237
TOTAL	1,324

EDITORIAL ENDORSEMENTS: 1948

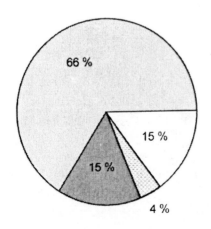

Candidate	Endorsements
☐ Dewey (R)	771
◼ Truman (D)	182
☐ Other	48
☐ None	182
TOTAL	1,183

EDITORIAL ENDORSEMENTS: 1952

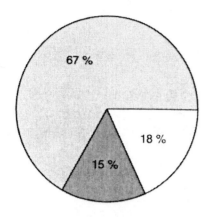

Candidate		Endorsements
☐	Eisenhower (R)	933
◼	Stevenson (D)	202
☐	None	250
	TOTAL	1,385

EDITORIAL ENDORSEMENTS: 1956

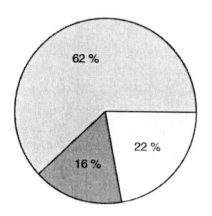

Candidate		Endorsements
☐	Eisenhower (R)	740
◼	Stevenson (D)	189
☐	None	270
	TOTAL	1,199

EDITORIAL ENDORSEMENTS: 1960

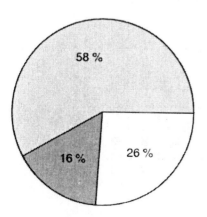

Candidate		Endorsements
☐	Nixon (R)	731
◼	Kennedy (D)	208
☐	None	328
	TOTAL	1,267

EDITORIAL ENDORSEMENTS: 1964

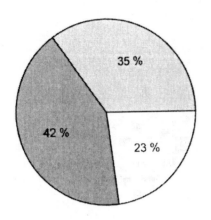

Candidate		Endorsements
□	Goldwater (R)	259
■	Johnson (D)	440
□	None	237
	TOTAL	1,036

EDITORIAL ENDORSEMENTS: 1968

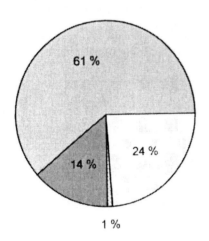

Candidate		Endorsements
▨	Nixon (R)	634
▦	Humphrey (D)	146
▨	Other	12
□	None	250
	TOTAL	1,042

EDITORIAL ENDORSEMENTS: 1972

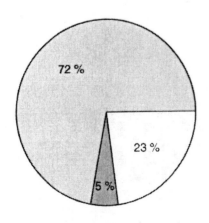

Candidate		Endorsements
□	Nixon (R)	753
■	McGovern (D)	56
□	None	245
	TOTAL	1,054

EDITORIAL ENDORSEMENTS: 1976

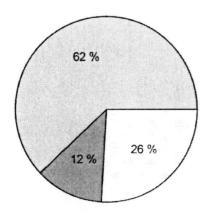

Candidate		Endorsements
☐	Ford (R)	411
▨	Carter (D)	80
☐	None	168
	TOTAL	659

EDITORIAL ENDORSEMENTS: 1980

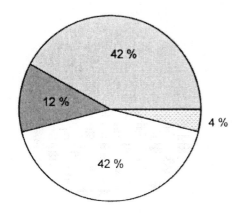

Candidate		Endorsements
☐	Reagan (R)	443
▨	Carter (D)	126
☐	Other	40
☐	None	439
	TOTAL	1,048

EDITORIAL ENDORSEMENTS: 1984

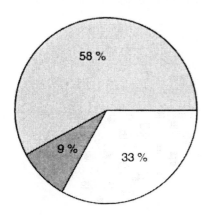

Candidate		Endorsements
☐	Reagan (R)	381
▨	Mondale (D)	62
☐	None	216
	TOTAL	659

EDITORIAL ENDORSEMENTS: 1988

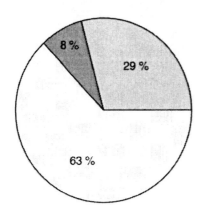

	Candidate	Endorsements
▨	Bush (R)	195
▧	Dukakis (D)	51
☐	None	416
	TOTAL	662

EDITORIAL ENDORSEMENTS: 1992

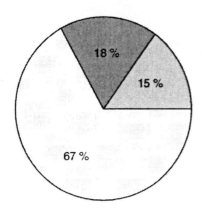

	Candidate	Endorsements
▨	Bush (R)	125
▧	Clinton (D)	149
☐	None	542
	TOTAL	816

EDITORIAL ENDORSEMENTS: 1996

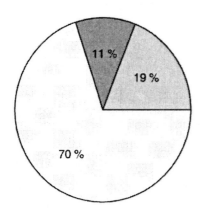

	Candidate	Endorsements
▨	Dole (R)	111
▧	Clinton (D)	65
☐	None	415
	TOTAL	591

Chapter Notes

Preface

1. Though oft repeated, the aphorism that the pen is mightier than the sword retains a surprising amount of heft. Throughout history the high and the mighty have trembled at the power of the press. "I fear three newspapers more than a hundred thousand bayonets," Napoleon Bonaparte is supposed to have said. David L. Paletz and Robert M. Entman, *Media, Power, Politics* (New York: The Free Press, 1981), 54.

2. Bias, whether deliberate or subliminal, has suffused the American press at all levels in its coverage of politics, both domestic and international. In order to participate in the electoral process directly or indirectly, a key priority for emerging interest groups has been the creation of advocacy media to promulgate a common agenda among the membership and advance the cause to the general public. Examples include publications launched by third parties (Anti-Masons in the 1820s and 30s, Know Nothings in the 1850s, Populists in the 1890s, etc.) and such reformist coalitions as the abolitionists, trade unions, and suffragists. These concerns were picked up and debated in the mainstream media, in terms defined by subjective criteria, alongside the defining questions of foreign and economic policy. In order to explore the issue of bias in sufficient depth, this study will focus on the media and its relationship with the two-party system at the presidential level.

3. Richard Hofstadter, *The Paranoid Style in American Politics* (New York: Knopf, 1965).

4. Michael O'Neill, former editor of the *New York Daily News*, raised this issue in an address to the American Society of Newspaper Editors when he warned his peers, "We are deeply embedded in the democratic process itself, as principal actors rather than bit players or mere audience." Jay Rosen, *What Are Journalists For?* (New Haven: Yale University Press, 1999), 35.

5. Lynda Lee Kaid and Clifford A. Jones, "United States of America," in *The Media and Elections: A Handbook and Comparative Study*, ed. Bernd-Peter Lange and David Ward (Mahwah, NJ: Lawrence Erlbaum, 2004), 26.

6. Lance Bennett, *News: The Politics of Illusion* (New York: Longman, 1996), xii. According to Blumler and Gurevitch, communications processes are involved in the legitimatization of authority, and serve functions of political articulation, mobilization and conflict-management.

All political systems generate principles derived from the tenets of their political cultures for regulating the political role of the mass media. Jay G. Blumler and Michael Gurevitch, *The Crisis of Public Communication* (New York: Routledge, 1995), 19.

7. Asa Briggs and Peter Burke, *A Social History of the Media: From Gutenberg to the Internet* (Cambridge: Polity, 2002), 202.

8. Stephen J. A. Ward, *The Invention of Journalism Ethics: The Path to Objectivity and Beyond* (Montreal: McGill-Queen's University Press, 2004), 147.

9. For studies of the challenge faced by the established media outlets, especially the newspapers, see David T. Z. Mindich, *Tuned Out: Why Americans Under 40 Don't Follow the News* (New York: Oxford University Press, 2005) and Philip Meyer, *The Vanishing Newspaper: Saving Journalism in the Information Age* (Columbia: University of Missouri Press, 2004). The viability of the newspaper itself is now being openly called into question — Philip Meyer, for one, foresees a future in which the last newspaper is discarded in 2043. For commentary signaling the alarm over what the slow death of the newspaper means at the community level, see John Nichols, "Newspapers.... And After?" *The Nation* 284, no. 4, (January 29, 2007), 11–18.

Introduction

1. James Poniewozik and Andrea Sachs, "Bush vs. Kerry vs. the Media," *Time* 164, no. 20 (November 15, 2004), 87. Also worth reading for a useful overview of the media bias issue in the run-up to the election are Jack Shafer, "The Varieties of Media Bias, Part 1: Who Threw the First Punch in the Press Bias Brawl?" *Slate.com*, February 5, 2003, www.slate.com/id/2078200, and Jack Shafer, "The Varieties of Media Bias, Part 2: The Old Litmus Tests that Sort Journalists into Left and Right Don't Work Anymore," *Slate.com*, February 12, 2003, www.slate.com/id/2078494.

2. The call to arms was being sounded months prior to Labor Day via posts to conservative forums online: "The lying socialist treasonous liberal media will do everything in its power to defeat the president and turn our country into a province of France. They will lie, cheat and propagandize shamelessly to advance an

anti–American agenda and get a lying socialist treasonous Democratic candidate elected president. Even a $200 million war chest may *not be enough* to counter them." Polipundit.com, 06/18/2003. Associating the media with the French is a compulsion with a long history among conservatives. Maureen Dowd recalls being told by one delegate to the 1988 Republican convention, "You can write this down. The media are a bunch of left wing, liberal communists. No, take out communists. Put down French Socialists." Maureen Dowd, "For the Republicans, a final day of boos and hisses and hugs and kisses," *New York Times*, August 19, 1988, A15.

3. Greg Hitt, "Media-Bias Charges Rally Republican Base; Party Energizes Loyalists with Complaints about Coverage of Presidential Race," *Wall Street Journal*, October 28, 2004, A4.

4. Stephen F. Hayes, "The Other Losers Tuesday Night," *Weekly Standard* 10, no. 9, (November 15, 2004), www.weeklystandard.com/Content/Public/Articles/000/000/004/885haqnt.asp. BoycottCBS.com, a project of the Framers Institute whose first target was the network's made-for-TV Reagan biopic, rejoined the fray after the National Guard imbroglio: "They smeared the President with fake documents just weeks before Election Day," the organization declared. "They coordinated their attack with the John Kerry campaign before they aired their smear. They covered up theft coordination for 13 days until other media outlets forced them to admit it. Want your election hijacked by a media conglomerate? If not, join us." Joseph A. D'Agostino, "BoycottCBS.com," *Human Events* 60, no. 33 (September 27, 2004), 16.

5. Peggy Noonan, "So Much to Savor: A Big Win for America, and a Loss for the Mainstream Media," *Wall Street Journal*, November 4, 2004, www.opinionjournal.com/columnists/pnoonan/?id=110005844. Noonan singled out Rush Limbaugh, Sean Hannity and Laura Ingraham for their dedication to preserving the traditional, Christian family values they represented: "She is one tough girl and they are two tough men. Savor them too." Of course, there were other fallen foes over whom to gloat: "The elites of Old Europe are depressed. Savor.... George Soros cannot buy a presidential election. Savor."

6. James Q. Wilson, "Why Did Kerry Lose? (Answer: It Wasn't 'Values')," *Wall Street Journal*, November 8, 2004, A14.

7. Greg Mitchell, "Daily Endorsement Tally: Kerry Wins, Without Re-count," *Editor & Publisher*, November 5, 2004. The President himself professed his lack of concern at the trend: "If I worried about editorials, I'd be a nervous wreck. My job is not to try to win the kudos of those who write the editorials." "Bush on Editorials: 'What, Me Worry?'" *Editor & Publisher*, November 1, 2004.

8. John O'Sullivan, "The Limits of Media Bias," *National Review* 56, no. 22 (November 29, 2004), 46.

9. David Limbaugh, "A Media Cover-Up of Watergate Proportions," *WorldNetDaily*, November 2, 2004, www.wnd.com/news/article.asp?ARTICLE_ID=41234.

10. Victor Davis Hanson, "The Ironies Ahead," *National Review Online*, November 12, 2004, www.nationalreview.com/hanson/hanson200411120830.asp.

11. Patrick Buchanan, "Big Media drop the mask," *WorldNetDaily*, November 1, 2004, www.wnd.com/news/article.asp?ARTICLE_ID=41216.

12. Jed Babbin, "Post-Election SGO," *American Spectator*, November 8, 2004, www.spectator.org/dsp_article.asp?art_id=7359.

13. See Davis Merritt, *Knightfall: Knight Ridder and How the Erosion of Newspaper Journalism is Putting Democracy at Risk* (New York: American Management

Association, 2005); Stephen J. Farnsworth and S. Robert Lichter, *The Nightly News Nightmare: Network Television's Coverage of U.S. Presidential Elections, 1988–2000* (New York: Rowman & Littlefield, 2003); Matthew Robinson, *Mobocracy: How the Media's Obsession with Polling Twists the News, Alters Elections, and Undermines Democracy* (Roseville, CA: Forum, 2002); Robert Shogan, *Bad News: Where the Press Goes Wrong in the Making of the President* (Chicago: Ivan R. Dee, 2001); Patricia Moy, *With Malice Toward All? The Media and Public Confidence in Democratic Institutions* (Westport, CT: Praeger, 2000); Kenneth Dautrich and Thomas H. Hartley, *How the News Media Fail American Voters: Causes, Consequences and Remedies* (New York: Columbia University Press, 1999); James M. Fallows, *Breaking the News: How the Media Undermine American Democracy* (New York: Pantheon, 1996); Benjamin I. Page, *Who Deliberates? Mass Media in Modern Democracy* (Chicago: University of Chicago Press, 1996); Larry Sabato, *Feeding Frenzy: How Attack Journalism has Transformed American Politics* (Toronto: Free Press, 1991). A useful background to the role of agenda setting in the media is Karen S. Johnson-Cartee, *News Narratives and News Framing: Constructing Political Reality* (Lanham, MD: Rowman & Littlefield), 2005. See also Doris A. Graber, *Media Power in Politics* (Washington, DC: CQ Press, 2000); Doris A. Graber, *Mass Media and American Politics* (Washington, DC: CQ Press, 1997); and Richard Davis, *The Press and American Politics: The New Mediator* (New York: Longman, 1992). For recent perspectives on the relations between the press and the political process, see Kenneth T. Walsh, *Feeding the Beast: The White House Versus the Press* (New York: Random House, 2001) and Michael Janeway, *Republic of Denial: Press, Politics, and Public Life* (New Haven: Yale University Press, 1999). Relatively objective analysis of media trends is available from such institutions as Media Tenor International (www.mediatenor.com).

14. See Eric Boehlert, *Lap Dogs: How the Press Rolled Over for Bush* (New York: The Free Press, 2006); Tom Fenton, *Bad News: The Decline of Reporting, the Business of News, and the Danger to Us All* (Regan Books, 2005); John Nichols and Robert W. McChesney, *Tragedy and Farce: How the American Media Sell Wars, Spin Elections, and Destroy Democracy* (New York: New Press, 2005); Elliot D. Cohen (ed.), *News Incorporated: Corporate Media Ownership and its Threat to Democracy* (Amherst, NY: Prometheus Books, 2005); Seth Mnookin, *Hard News: The Scandals at the New York Times and their meaning for American Media* (New York: Random House, 2004); Eric Alterman, *What Liberal Media? The Truth about Bias and the News* (New York: Basic Books, 2003); Joe Conason, *Big Lies: The Right-Wing Propaganda Machine and How it Distorts the Truth* (New York: Thomas Dunne Books, 2003); Robert W. McChesney, *Rich Media, Poor Democracy: Communication Politics in Dubious Times* (Urbana: University of Illinois Press, 2000); Dennis Mazzocco, *Networks of Power: Corporate TV's Threat to Democracy* (Boston: South End Press, 1994); Lee Martin, *Unreliable Sources: A Guide to Detecting Bias in News Media* (New York: Carol Publishing Group, 1990).

15. Laurie Kelliher, "Fox Watch," *Columbia Journalism Review* 42, no. 6 (March/April 2004), 8. The business can get ugly; when MoveOn lobbied the *New York Post* to drop syndicated columnist Robert Novak in response to the Plame affair, the paper's editorial page editor, Bob McManus, responded with a leak of his own, running "Fox Watch" coordinator Noah Winer's home telephone number in the headline of an editorial with instructions to "swarm him." An organization fulfilling a similar function can be found at www.newshounds.us. See also Robert

Greenwald's documentary *Outfoxed: Rupert Murdoch's War on Journalism*. For more liberal advocacy, see the Media Reform Information Center at www.corporations.org/media.

16. For a representative sample of conservative tomes targeting liberal media bias this decade alone, see L. Brent Bozell III, *Weapons of Mass Distortion: The Coming Meltdown of the Liberal Media* (New York: Crown Forum, 2004); Bernard Goldberg, *Arrogance: Rescuing America from the Media Elite* (New York: Warner Books, 2003); Jim A. Kuypers, *Press Bias and Politics: How the Media Frame Controversial Issues* (Westport, CT: Praeger, 2002); Bernard Goldberg, *Bias: A CBS Insider Exposes how the Media Distort the News* (Washington, DC: Regnery, 2002); Ann Coulter, *Slander: Liberal Lies About the American Right* (New York: Crown, 2002); William McGowan, *Coloring the News: How Political Correctness Has Corrupted American Journalism* (San Francisco: Encounter Books, 2001). Recent academic studies include "A Measure of Media Bias" by Tim Groseclose of the University of California at Los Angeles and Jeff Milyo of the University of Chicago, available online at http://mason.gmu.edu/~atabarro/MediaBias.doc. The findings are summarized in Robert J. Barro, "The Liberal Media: It's No Myth," *Business Week*, June 14, 2004, 28.

17. Always bear in mind the great double standard: the more overtly partisan a conservative media publication, the more obsessed it is with liberal bias in the media. The *Wall Street Journal*, in referring to the expansion of the child tax credit in June 2003, typically paired responsibility on "a PR offensive by Democrats and their media echo chamber." Editorial, "Delay's Finest Hour — Keep Obstructing, Mr. Majority Leader," *The Wall Street Journal*, June 19, 2003, A14. An entire election-year-2004 issue of the *National Review* was dedicated to attacking those institutions within the media which manifest liberal bias — all three networks, Peter Jennings ("Worse than Tom and Dan?" — note that conservative critiques of the late Peter Jennings were never complete without incorporating the phrase "Canadian-born"), *Time* and *Newsweek*, Reuters, the *Washington Post*, the *New York Times*, Chris Matthews, and editorial cartoonists everywhere, while boosting Lou Dobbs, Brit Hume and Dennis Miller as "things we like." The *National Review* 56, no. 14 (July 26, 2004).

18. The best way to trace the existence of any ideological agenda in these watchdog organizations is to follow the money. The purportedly nonpartisan nature of the Center for Media and Public Affairs, for example, is compromised somewhat by the fact that records from 1986 to 2002 show that the overwhelming majority of its funding has been derived from conservative sources, including the Carthage Foundation, part of the Scaife Foundations ($267,000 from five donations), the John M. Olin Foundation ($730,000 from fifteen donations), the Sarah Scaife Foundation, part of the Scaife Foundations ($760,000 from nine donations), and the Smith Richardson Foundation ($416,916 from three donations).

19. This applies most explicitly to social issues such as abortion, euthanasia, and stem cell research, where, "whether or not its members recognize it, America's journalistic elite is a functional ally of the party of death." Ramesh Ponnuru, *Party of Death* (Washington, DC: Regnery, 2006), 199.

20. Evan Gahr, "Uncovering the politics of women's magazines," *Wall Street Journal*, August 21, 1997, A14.

21. Myrna Blyth, *Spin Sisters: How the Women of the Media Sell Unhappiness — and Liberalism — to the Women of America* (New York: St. Martin's Press, 2004), 8.

22. Kevin Lamb, "Gould Obits Reveal Media Bias," *Human Events* 58, no. 21 (June 3, 2002), 16. According to the same publication, the "Annual Survey of Commencement Speakers" (a survey of commencement addresses conducted by Young America's Foundation of the nation's 100 most prestigious colleges) "provides another insight into how college commencement exercises, instead of providing a new beginning, continue the liberal bias that makes up much of a four year undergraduate education." Ron Robinson, "1995 commencement exercises dominated by liberal speakers," *Human Events* 51, no. 26 (July 7, 1995), 18.

23. Ward, 19.

24. Robert A. Hackett and Yuezhi Zhao, *Sustaining Democracy? Journalism and the Politics of Objectivity* (Toronto: Garamond Press, 1998), 89.

25. The level playing field for the media may be tilted during peacetime too; in France, the incoming Socialist Party administration conducted "a rapid purge of the directors of the three national networks, of news editors and anchormen" under its purview after taking power in 1981. Julius W. Friend, *The Long Presidency: France in the Mitterrand Years, 1981–1995* (Boulder, CO: Westview Press, 1998), 34. See also *ibid.*, 162–167, and Raymond Kuhn, *The Media in France* (New York: Routledge, 1994).

26. Thompson concludes of Northcliffe that "in the war years he developed a degree of power over political and public opinion that was real, not illusory." J. Lee Thompson, *Politicians, the Press, & Propaganda: Lord Northcliffe & the Great War, 1914–1919* (Kent, OH: Kent State University Press, 1999), 238. In his 1956 autobiography, David Low quoted H. G. Wells as saying of Beaverbrook: "If ever Max ... gets to Heaven, he won't last long. He will be chucked out for trying to pull off a merger between Heaven and Hell after having secured a controlling interest in key subsidiary companies in both places, of course."

27. The definitive critique of Berlusconi is Alexander Stille, *The Sack of Rome* (New York: Penguin, 2005). For a specific focus on the legitimacy of Berlusconi's media influence as it related to the democratic process, see Gianpietro Mazzoleni, "With the Media, Without the Media: Reasons and Implications of the Electoral Success of Silvio Berlusconi in 2001," in *European Culture and the Media*, ed. Ib Bondebjerg and Peter Golding (Portland, OR: Intellect, 2004), 257–276; Teresa Perrucci and Marina Villa, "Italy," in *The Media and Elections: A Handbook and Comparative Study*, ed. Bernd-Peter Lange and David Ward (Mahwah, NJ: Lawrence Erlbaum, 2004), 1–24. Even controlling his own media empire couldn't stop Berlusconi from complaining that the "left-wing press declared war when I came back on the political scene" and that "eighty-five percent of the press is left-wing, and the judges are worse. There is a cancer in Italy that we must cure — the politicization of the bench." See "Berlusconi lashes out at Italy's 'left-wing' press, courts," *Agence France Presse*, June 30, 2003. For biographies of Murdoch, see Neil Chenoweth, *Virtual Murdoch: Reality Wars on the Information Highway* (London: Secker & Warburg, 2001); William Shawcross, *Murdoch* (New York: Simon & Schuster, 1993); Jerome Tuccille, *Rupert Murdoch* (New York: D.I. Fine, 1989); Thomas Kiernan, *Citizen Murdoch* (New York: Dodd, Mead, 1986); George Munster, *A Paper Prince* (New York: Viking, 1985); and Michael Leapman, *Arrogant Aussie: The Rupert Murdoch Story* (Secaucus, NJ: L. Stuart, 1985). For criticisms of Murdoch's dominance of the Australian media, see David Flint, *Malice in Media Land* (Australia: Freedom Publishing, 2005); Rodney Tiffen, *News and Power* (Sydney: Allen & Unwin, 1989); and Scott Balson, *Murder by Media: Death of Democracy in Australia* (Mt. Crosby, Queensland: Interactive Presentations, 1999). For criticisms of

Murdoch's multinational influence, see Gaby Hinsliff, "The PM, the Mogul and the Secret Agenda," *Observer*, July 23, 2006, http://observer.guardian.co.uk/politics/story/0,,1827023,00.html.

28. As James Madison put it in a post-presidential digression on the role of the press, dated April 23, 1828, "The effect of their falsehood and slanders must always be controuled in a certain degree by contradictions in rival or hostile papers, where the press is free." Hazel Dicken-Garcia, *Journalistic Standards in Nineteenth Century America* (Madison: University of Wisconsin Press, 1989), 102.

29. Russell J. Dalton, et. al., "Partisan Cues in the Media: Cross-National Comparisons of Election Coverage" (paper presented at the Annual Meeting of the Mid-West Political Science Association, Chicago, April 1997), 28.

30. Colin Seymour-Ure, *The Political Impact of Mass Media* (London: Constable, 1974), 157.

31. David H. Stevens, *Party Politics and English Journalism, 1702–1742* (Ph.D. dissertation, University of Chicago Libraries, 1916), 61.

32. Mark Knights, *Representation and Misrepresentation in Later Stuart Britain: Partisanship and Political Culture* (Oxford: Oxford University Press, 2005), 242–243. See also John A. Downie, *Robert Harley and the Press: Propaganda and Public Opinion in the Age of Swift and Defoe* (Cambridge: Cambridge University Press, 1979) and Hannah Barker, *Newspapers, Politics, and Public Opinion in Late Eighteenth-Century England* (New York: Clarendon Press, 1998).

33. See Stevens, *Party Politics and English Journalism*, 81–103 ("Whig Rewards Under George I").

34. Bob Harris, *Politics and the Rise of the Press: Britain and France, 1620–1800* (New York: Routledge, 1996), 1. Many inhabitants of the only recently united United Kingdom harbored deep misgivings about the influence of the fourth estate, especially one so open to blatant partisan manipulation. In 1722, for example, Walpole's government purchased the *London Journal*; in 1726 Tory politicians financed the *Craftsman*. Some observers, such as Joseph Addison, professed concern about the role played by the press in thus dividing the kingdom into two tribes of "strangers." Stephen J. A. Ward, 140. Others sought to articulate their grievances in verse, such as William Cowper: "Thou God of our idolatry, the Press / By thee, worse plagues than Pharaoh's land befell, / Diffus'd, make earth the vestibule of Hell...." William L. Rivers, Wilbur Schramm, and Clifford G. Christians, *Responsibility in Mass Communication* (New York: Harper & Row, 1980), 2.

35. Hannah Barker, *Newspapers, Politics, and Public Opinion in Late Eighteenth-Century England* (New York: Clarendon Press, 1998), 45.

36. *Ibid.*, 43–72.

37. Harris, 29–52. Aspinall in his authoritative study of the issue states that "during the last decades of the eighteenth century, when newspapers were beginning to play an important part in politics, they were not independent and responsible organs of public opinion.... The great majority of the London newspapers accepted subsidies either from the Government or from the Opposition, and were tied in various ways to the Party organizations." Arthur Aspinall, *Politics and the Press, c. 1780–1850* (New York: Barnes & Noble, 1974), v.

38. Stephen Koss, *The Rise and Fall of the Political Press in Britain, volume 1* (London: Hamish Hamilton, 1984), 36.

39. Stevens, *Party Politics,* 76–77.

40. Wilkes was charged with seditious libel over attacks on the King's speech at the opening of Parliament, attacks made in issue 45 of the *North Britain* published April 23, 1763. General warrants were issued for the arrest of Wilkes and the publishers on the April 30. Almost fifty people were arrested under the warrants. Wilkes was expelled from the House of Commons, and he ultimately fled to Paris where he was found guilty, *in absentia*, of obscene libel and seditious libel, and was declared an outlaw on January 19, 1764. While in exile, Wilkes met Madame Pompadour, mistress of King Louis XV, who expressed amazement that he had been able to abuse the royal family in print. "How far does liberty of the press extend in England?" she asked. "That is exactly what I am trying to find out!" Wilkes replied. After returning to England in 1768 he was elected MP for Middlesex only to be imprisoned again for severely criticizing King George III in the *North Briton* Expelled from Parliament in February 1769 he was reelected by Middlesex in the same month, only to be expelled and reelected in March. In April, Wilkes having been expelled and having won election again, Parliament declared his opponent the winner. In defiance, Wilkes had himself elected an alderman of London before he eventually succeeded in convincing Parliament to expunge the resolution barring him from sitting. See Arthur H. Cash, *John Wilkes: The Scandalous Father of Civil Liberty* (New Haven: Yale University Press, 2006); Audrey Williamson, *Wilkes: A Friend to Liberty* (London: Allen & Unwin, 1974); and George Rudé, *Wilkes and Liberty: A Social Study of 1763 to 1774* (Oxford: Clarendon Press, 1962).

41. Andrew W. Robertson, *The Language of Democracy: Political Rhetoric in the United States and Britain, 1790–1900* (Ithaca: Cornell University Press, 1995), 54–55.

42. Aspinall, 382. See also Barker, 65–94 (chap. four, "Politicians and the Press") and Robertson, 96–115 (chap. five, "Parliamentary Reform and the Repeal of Constraints on Expression, 1832–1855").

43. See Aled Jones, *Powers of the Press: Newspapers, Power and the Public in Nineteenth-Century England* (Brookfield, VT: Ashgate, 1996).

44. Koss, 95–96. See also Alan J. Lee, *The Origins of the Popular Press in England, 1855–1914* (London: Croom Helm, 1980).

45. Koss, 11–12.

46. Disraeli's appreciation of the power of the press is reflected in his 1844 novel *Coningsby*, where one character remarks, "God made man in his own image, but the Public is made by Newspapers." Briggs and Burke, 204.

47. Koss, 198.

48. *Ibid.*, 138. As late as March 17, 1876, Queen Victoria could still lecture Disraeli on "the importance of securing some newspaper as an organ for the Government." *Ibid.*, 207.

49. *Ibid.*, 90.

50. *Ibid.*, 150.

51. *Ibid.*, 149.

52. Robertson, 164.

53. *Ibid.*, 144.

54. *Ibid.*, 143.

55. Robertson draws an earlier parallel: "As Lincoln had used his debates with Douglas, Gladstone used the Midlothian tour: as a dramatic setting to build a national audience." *Ibid.*, 145.

56. Koss, 14.

57. James Thomas, *Popular Newspapers, the Labour Party and British Politics* (New York: Routledge, 2005), 8.

58. Thomas, 8.

59. *Ibid.*, 14.

60. Koss, 16.
61. See Huw Richards, *The Bloody Circus: The Daily Herald and the Left* (Chicago: Pluto Press, 1997).
62. Thomas, 14.
63. *Ibid.*, 34.
64. See *ibid.*, 35–60 (chap. 2, "The Popular Press and the 1964 General Election").
65. David Butler and Denis Kavanagh, *The British General Election of February 1974* (London: Macmillan, 1974), 172.
66. Martin Harrop, "The Press and Post-War Elections," in *Political Communications: The General Election Campaign of 1983*, ed. Ivor Crewe and Martin Harrop (Cambridge: Cambridge University Press, 1986), 141. Thomas also notes, "It was only from the mid-1970s that there was a marked shift to the right in the politics of the popular press." Thomas, 61.
67. Thomas, 76.
68. See Jeremy Tunstall, *Newspaper Power: The New National Press in Britain* (New York: Clarendon Press, 1996), 240–241. Tunstall also makes the point that ideological conviction was not the only imperative for Murdoch in his decision to back the Conservatives in 1979—market competition was a contributing factor. From this perspective, the launch of the pro-Tory *Daily Star* in 1978 required the *Sun* to shift its position because an endorsement of Labour would have left the newcomer as the sole working-class paper backing Thatcher. Tunstall, 251.
69. Thomas, 81.
70. *Ibid.*, 86. Butler and Cavanagh confirm this perspective in their analysis of the election that brought Thatcher to power: "The strongest impression of Fleet Street's role during the campaign was the extent of bias among the popular dailies. The uncommitted voter could not have relied for informed election coverage upon any of the tabloids." Butler and Kavanagh, 253.
71. Ian Gilmour, *Dancing with Dogma* (London: Simon and Schuster, 1993), 2.
72. Doling out honors to loyal acolytes in the media is nothing new in U.K. politics: Four journalists at the *Daily Mirror* (Lords Cudlipp, Beavan, Jacobson, and Castle) received their titles from Harold Wilson.
73. Tunstall, 247. See also Jean Seaton and Ben Pimlott, eds., *The Media in British Politics* (Brookfield, VT: Gower, 1987).
74. Alan Clarke, "Thatcherism and the Media: The Blueprint for the General Election," in *Political Communications: The General Election Campaign of 1983*, ed. Ivor Crewe and Martin Harrop (Cambridge: Cambridge University Press, 1986), 29.
75. Harrop in Crewe and Harrop, 142.
76. Thomas, 88.
77. For an overview see *ibid.*, 87–117 (chap. 4, "A 'Nightmare on Kinnock Street'").
78. David McKie, "'Fact is Free but Comment is Sacred': Or was it The Sun wot won it?" in *Political Communications: The General Election Campaign of 1992*, ed. Ivor Crewe and Brian Gosschalk (Cambridge: Cambridge University Press, 1995), 128.
79. According to Bevins, at the 1991 Conservative Party conference, the government Chief Whip, Richard Ryder, was seen sitting at a *Daily Mail* keyboard reviewing a story for the next day's paper. McKie in Crewe and Gosschalk, 129.
80. To cite just one example, on April 6 the *Daily Mail* published a feature in which it presented a series of questions it had put to the three party leaders, accompanied by their responses. Kinnock refused to participate; the *Daily Mail* printed the questions anyway, leaving the space for answers blank, and criticizing his pusillanimity: "How arrogant of him to turn down this perfectly civil request to clarify his views." Considering the format, one should not be surprised at his reticence. While Conservative prime minister John Major was invited to answer queries like, "Can I ask whether you think Mr. Kinnock was wise to admit to grave errors of judgement?" Kinnock was expected to respond to such loaded questions as, "Socialism has been ditched in Eastern Europe and discredited here in the West. What makes you think Britain needs another dose of it?" and "Your manifesto is stuffed with spending promises which Labour won't cost and the nation cannot afford. Is not this manifesto a fraud?" McKie in Crewe and Gosschalk, 126.
81. Thomas, 1.
82. McKie in Crewe and Gosschalk, 130.
83. John Curtice, "Was it the Sun Wot Won it Again? The Influence of Newspapers in the 1997 Election Campaign," *Crest Working Paper No. 75*, September 1999, available online at www.crest.ox.ac.uk/papers/p75.pdf#search ='It%20Was%20the%20Sun%20Wot%20Won%20It', 2.
84. John Curtice and Holli Semetko, "Does it Matter What the Papers Say?" in *Labour's Last Chance? The 1992 Election and Beyond*, ed. Anthony Heath, Roger Jowell, and John Curtice (Aldershot: Dartmouth, 1994), 55. See also Martin Harrop and Margaret Scammell, "A Tabloid War," in *The British General Election of 1992*, ed. David Butler and Dennis Kavanagh (New York: St. Martin's Press, 1992), chap. 9.
85. For analysis of "New" Labour's "Spin Doctors" in operation, see Colin Seymour-Ure, *Prime Ministers and the Media: Issues of Power and Control* (Malden, MA: Blackwell Publishers, 2003); Nicholas Jones, *The Control Freaks: How New Labour Gets its Own Way* (London: Politico's, 2001); and Nicholas Jones, *Sultans of Spin* (London: Orion, 2000). For material on concern that in exchange for the support of the media barons Blair's Labour has betrayed its agenda see Thomas, 118–146 (chap. 5, "Vote Conservative — Vote Blair").
86. John Curtice, "Is *The Sun* shining on Tony Blair? The Electoral Influence of British Newspapers," *Harvard International Journal of Press/Politics* 2, no. 2 (1997), 23.
87. Baldasty, *The Press and Politics in the Age of Jackson*, The Association for Education in Journalism and Mass Communication, 1984, 21. The July 9, 1828, Louisville *Public Advertiser* used similar terms when it condemned a purportedly neutral Indiana paper: "We do not know how it is in Indiana, but, in this State, people have more respect for an open, independent adversary than for dumb partisans or shuttlecock politicians, who are considered too imbecile to form an opinion, or too servile to express an opinion when formed." Gerald J. Baldasty, *The Commercialization of the News in the Nineteenth Century* (Madison: University of Wisconsin Press, 1992), 25.
88. See also Jeremy Tunstall and David Machin, *The Anglo-American Media Connection* (New York: Oxford University Press, 1999).
89. Dicken-Garcia, 99–100.
90. The new technology also changed the rules of the media game on a very personal level. Leaving even the most partisan papers lying around the house was one thing, but no one in the 1950s would feel comfortable bringing some frothing demagogue into their living room every evening via the flickering medium of the television set. How times have changed.
91. "As the country entered the postwar era, objectivity was universally acknowledged to be the spine of the journalist's moral code," Schudson and Tifft say. "It was asserted in the textbooks used in journalism schools, it was asserted in codes of ethics of professional associations. It was at last a code of professional honor." Michael

Schudson and Susan E. Tifft, "American Journalism in Historical Perspective," in *The Press*, Geneva Overholser and Kathleen Hall Jamieson (Oxford University Press, 2005), 27. Hackett and Zhao confirm that this obeisance to codes of objectivity within the journalistic profession, which reached its zenith in the 1940s and 1950s, was dominant for only a few decades in the twentieth century. Hackett and Zhao, 215.

92. See Robert M. Entman, "Faith and Mystification in Broadcast Deregulation," in *Democracy Without Citizens: Media and the Decay of American Politics* (New York: Oxford University Press, 1989), 102–124.

93. Howard Fineman, "The 'Media Party' is Over," *MSNBC*, January 13, 2005, msnbc.msn.com/id/6813945. According to Gallup, those having a "great deal" or "quite a lot" of confidence in newspapers and television fell to 28 percent in 2005, ranking the media only just ahead of big business and Congress (both at 22 percent) and HMOs (17 percent) in public esteem. "Gallup: Public Confidence in Newspapers, TV News Falls to All-Time Low," *Editor & Publisher*, June 10, 2005. See also Terry Eastland, "Starting Over," *Wilson Quarterly* 29, no. 2 (Spring 2005), 40–47; the Pew Research Center study, "News Audiences Increasingly Polarized," released on June 8, 2004, available online at people-press.org/reports/display.php3?ReportID=215; and Bill Kovach and Tom Rosenstiel, *Warp Speed: America in the Age of Mixed Media* (New York: Century Foundation Press, 1999), 1–9 (chap. 1, "The Journalism of Assertion,") and 77–88 (chap. 8, "The Press and Cultural Civil War").

94. "When I was growing up there were three networks and basically the same information," Hollywood's George Clooney recalls. "Now, because we've fractioned into little pieces, you go look for the things that reinforce what you already believe to be fact and don't get a common truth." "Clooney's Attack on an Age of Dishonesty," *Contactmusic.com*, September 2, 2005, contactmusic.com/new/xmlfeed.nsf/mndwebpages/clooneys%20attack%20on%20an%20age%20of%20dishonesty.

95. Editorial, "Red News, Blue News: A Search for Meaning in a Fog of Facts," *Columbia Journalism Review*, November/December 2004, http://www.cjr.org/issues/2004/6/editorial.asp. See also Dana Milbank, "My Bias for Mainstream News," *Washington Post*, March 20, 2005, B1, *http://www.washingtonpost.com/wp-dyn/articles/A48952-2005Mar19.html*.

96. Cass Sunstein, *Republic.com* (Princeton, NJ: Princeton University Press, 2001), 5.

97. *Ibid.*, 8–9. Rosen arrived at a similar conclusion, warning his peers in journalism that "it's not just readers disappearing, it's the *public disintegrating*, at least from our grasp." Rosen, 84. See also Thomas C. Leonard, *News for All: America's Coming-of-Age with the Press* (London: Oxford University Press, 1995, 177–201. For further discussion of the role of technology in the fragmentation of the media market, see Merrill Morris and Christine Ogan, "The Internet as Mass Medium," in *The Media, Journalism and Democracy*, ed. Margaret Scammell and Holli Semetko (Burlington: Ashgate, 2000), 389–400, and Elihu Katz, "And Deliver Us From Segmentation," in *The Media and Politics*, ed. Kathleen Hall Jamieson (Thousand Oaks, CA: Sage Periodicals Press, 1996), 22–33. For an old media perspective, see Brian Williams, "Enough About You," *Time*, December 25, 2006, 78.

98. Chris Anderson, *The Long Tail: Why the Future of Business is Selling Less of More* (New York: Hyperion, 2006), 190.

99. *Ibid.*, 191. The potential for developments in communications technology acting to restore the intimacy of political debate was recognized by Marshall McLuhan

three decades prior to the rise of the Internet when he noted that, thanks to the electronic media, "we everywhere resume person-to-person relations as if on the smallest village scale." Marshall McLuhan, *Understanding Media: The Extensions of Man* (New York: McGraw-Hill, 1965), 255–256. For more on the interface between modern technology and the media, see the study conduced by Noor Ali-Hasan available online: www.noor.bz/blog study. See also Nicholas Lehman, "Amateur Hour: Journalism without Journalists," *New Yorker* 82, no. 24 (August 7 & 14, 2006), 44–49; Henry Jenkins and David Thorburn, eds., *Democracy and New Media* (Cambridge, MA: MIT Press, 2003); Marshall Van Alstyne and Erik Brynjolfsson, "Electronic Communities: Global Village or Cyberbalkans," available online at web.mit.edu/marshall/www/Abstracts.html; and James R. Beniger, *The Control Revolution: Technological and Economic Origins of the Information Society* (Cambridge, MA: Harvard University Press, 1986).

100. Morton Keller is another observer to recognize the trend towards partisan bias in the media being a cyclical one: "Over most of its long history, political commitment has been a dependable spur to one-sidedness and distortion. A special mix of journalistic beliefs and publisher self-interest made possible a brief age of objectivity. Now, it appears, conditions have changed, and the media are, so to speak, reverting to type." Morton Keller, "The Media: What They Are Today, and How They Got That Way," *The Forum* 3, no. 1 (2005), 7. Available online at www.bepress.com/forum/vol3/iss1/art1.

101. Arriving independently at this conclusion is Richard A. Posner, "Bad News," *New York Times Book Review*, July 31, 2005, 1, 8–11. A study conducted by Shanto Iyengar and Richard Morin for the *Washington Post* confirmed that "Fox News is the dominant news source for Americans whose political leanings are Republican or conservative (the results ... are even stronger if we substitute ideology for party identification)." This preference transcended the boundaries of the overtly political. While "Fox's brand advantage among Republicans is especially strong when the news deals with political subjects.... Republicans prefer Fox News, even when reading about possible vacation destinations." In conclusion: "One thing is certain. The importance of source labels to news consumption will only grow as technology diffuses and consumers increasingly customize their online news menus. As this trend progresses, there is the real possibility that news will no longer serve as a 'social glue' that connects all Americans; instead, the very same lines that divide voters will also divide news audiences." Shanto Iyengar and Richard Morin, "Red Media, Blue Media: Evidence for a Political Litmus Test in Online News Readership, *Washington Post*, May 3, 2006, www.washingtonpost.com/wp-dyn/content/article/2006/05/03/AR2006050300865.html.

Chapter I

1. See Eric Burns, *Infamous Scribblers: The Founding Fathers and the Rowdy Beginnings of American Journalism* (New York: Public Affairs, 2006), Parts I and II; Carol Sue Humphrey, *"This Popular Engine": New England Newspapers during the American Revolution, 1775–1789* (Newark, University of Delaware Press, 1992); Patrick M. Garry, *The American Vision of a Free Press* (New York: Garland, 1990); Jeffrey A. Smith, *Printers and Press Freedom: The Ideology of Early American Journalism* (New York: Oxford University Press, 1988); and Arthur M. Schlesinger, *Prelude to Independence: The Newspaper War on Britain, 1764–1776* (Boston: Northeastern University

Press, 1957). See also George Henry Payne, *History of Journalism in the United States* (Westport, CT: Greenwood Press, 1970), especially chap. 9, and Willard Grosvenor Bleyer, *Main Currents in the History of American Journalism* (Boston: Houghton Mifflin, 1927), chap. 3. For an overview, see Rodger Streitmatter, *Mightier than the Sword: How the News Media have Shaped American History* (Boulder, CO: Westview Press, 1997).

2. John Tebbel and Sarah Miles Watts, *The Press and the Presidency: From George Washington to Ronald Reagan* (Oxford: Oxford University Press, 1985), 5.

3. See Payne, chap. 11–13. Timothy E. Cook describes the continuity of the adversarial nature of the American press from colonial to revolutionary and party eras accordingly: "Newspapers in the colonial and revolutionary eras were supported by political patronage, factional disputes, and the participation of politicians in the assembly of the newspaper. If the first hundred years of American newspapers saw government's punitive authority against newspapers wane somewhat, the press was far from independent: their ability to criticize government depended on powerful factions to provide copy, support, and political cover." Timothy E. Cook, *Governing with the News: The News Media as a Political Institution* (Chicago: University of Chicago Press, 1998), 25.

4. Morton Borden, *Parties and Politics in the Early Republic, 1789–1815* (New York: Thomas Y. Crowell, 1967), 28.

5. For more on the heated nature of political rhetoric during the early years of the republic, see John R. Howe, Jr., "Political Thought and the Political Violence of the 1790s," *American Quarterly* 19, no. 2 (Summer 1967), 147–165, and Marshall Smelser, "The Federalist Period as an Age of Passion," *American Quarterly* 10, no. 4 (Winter 1958), 391–419.

6. William J. Small, *Political Power and the Press* (New York: W. W. Norton, 1972), 55.

7. Leonard D. White, *The Federalists: A Study in Administrative History, 1789–1801* (New York: Free Press, 1948), 111.

8. *Ibid.*

9. Frank L. Mott, *Jefferson and the Press* (Baton Rouge: Louisiana State University Press, 1943), 56–57.

10. Walt Brown, *John Adams and the American Press: Politics and Journalism at the Birth of the Republic* (Jefferson, NC: McFarland, 1995), 39. Nerone, on the other hand, says that "it is not true that common newspapers were as a rule partisan throughout the early national period." He argues that the true party press emerged during the 1820s, and the penny press emerged as a reaction against this trend in the 1830s. John C. Nerone, "The Mythology of the Penny Press," *Critical Studies in Mass Communication* 4, no. 4 (December 1987), 389. Of course, the newspapers were only one aspect of the multimedia campaigns employed to mobilize voters in the early republic, which were much more personal, social, and interactive than today; see David Waldstreicher, *In the Midst of Perpetual Fetes: The Making of American Nationalism, 1776–1820* (Chapel Hill: University of North Carolina Press, 1997). The Internet in some senses may be acting as a means to restore, on a virtual basis at least, some of the spirit of this first political milieu.

11. James Melvin Lee, *History of American Journalism* (Garden City, NY: Garden City Publishing, 1923), 143.

12. William David Sloan, "Scurrility and the Party Press," *American Journalism* 5, no. 2 (1988), 98.

13. Jerry W. Knudson, *Jefferson and the Press: Crucible of Liberty* (Columbia: University of South Carolina Press, 2006), 1. As the number of Republican — or, to a Federalist, Jacobin — publications increased during the 1790s,

the *Gazette* issued a strident call to all like-minded printers everywhere to report any antigovernment newspaper items to its office. However, this experiment did not survive the next twenty-four hours. As the paper's editor explained to his readers: "Upon experiment, we find, that to notice everything which would come under the two heads of *folly* and *falsehood*, would be to copy every *original* article which appears in the Jacobin papers the consequence is, that we must content ourselves with occasional selections fully persuaded that our readers will be satisfied with these, as specimens of the whole." *Ibid.*, 3.

14. Bleyer, 125.

15. Marcus L. Daniel, *"Ribaldry and Billingsgate": Popular Journalism, Political Culture and the Public Sphere in the Early Republic* (Ph.D. dissertation, Princeton University, 1998), 410.

16. Richard N. Rosenfeld, *American Aurora* (New York: St. Martin's Press, 1997), 690.

17. Bleyer, 126.

18. Knudson, 10.

19. Clarence S. Brigham, *Journals and Journeymen* (Philadelphia: University of Pennsylvania Press, 1950), 64.

20. Robertson, 9.

21. Knudson, 5–6.

22. Leonard W. Levy, ed., *Freedom of the Press from Zenger to Jefferson* (New York: Bobbs-Merrill, 1966), 333. Jefferson told another French correspondent, "This formidable censor of the public functionaries, by arraigning them at the tribunal of public opinion, produces reform peaceably, which must otherwise be done by revolution." Mott, 6–7. Jefferson upheld these principles, in the rarefied atmosphere of political theory at least, for the balance of his life. Offering advice on a proposed French constitution in 1823, he recommended that it include "freedom of the press, subject only to liability for personal injuries." "This formidable censor of the public functionaries," he said of the press, "by arraigning them at the tribunal of public opinion, produces reform peaceably, which must otherwise be done by revolution. It is also the best instrument for enlightening the mind of man, and improving him as a rational, moral, and social being." Knudson, 169. That same year Jefferson wrote to the Marquis de Lafayette: "The only security of all, is a free press. The force of public opinion cannot be resisted, when permitted freely to be expressed. The agitation it produces must be submitted to. It is necessary to keep the waters pure." *Ibid.*, 171.

23. Richard L. Rubin, *Press, Party and Presidency* (New York: W. W. Norton, 1981), 11.

24. Tebbel and Watts, 7.

25. To be fair to the representatives of the people, the standard of House reporting was variable at best. Correspondent Thomas Lloyd struggled to identify members of the House and would refer to some speakers as "a baldheaded man" or a "man in blue coat and wig." James Madison believed that Lloyd "sometimes filled up blanks from his notes from memory or imagination" and in later years recalled that Lloyd "became a votary of the bottle and perhaps made too free use of it sometimes at the period of his printed debates." See Marion Tinling, "Thomas Lloyd's Reports of the First Federal Congress," *William and Mary Quarterly* 18, no. 4 (October 1961), 519–545.

26. Donald A. Ritchie, *Press Gallery: Congress and the Washington Correspondents* (Cambridge, MA: Harvard University Press, 1991), 7. House reporters had it easy — the Senate, too, banned journalists from the floor and only opened a gallery in December 1794. Even then the public was only indulged in access to legislative debates — all treaties and nominations continued to be debated in

secret until the twentieth century. After the House voted 47–28 in January 1802 to find room on the floor for reporters, the Senate shortly followed suit. Federalist senator Gouvernor Morris, who found himself among the first to have his speech recorded under the new arrangement, labeled it "the beginning of mischief" in the safety of his diary. *Ibid.*, 12.

27. The first Washington correspondents were hired by two Philadelphia Federalist papers, the *United States Gazette* and the *Freeman's Journal*, as early as 1808. Knudson, 9. See also Frederick B. Marbut, "Early Washington Correspondents: Some Early Pioneers," *Journalism Quarterly* 25, no. 4 (December 1948), 369–374.

28. Carol Sue Humphrey, *The Press of the Young Republic, 1783–1833* (Westport, CT: Greenwood Press, 1996), 44. For more on Fenno, see Daniel, chap. 1 ("'The Formation of a National Character': John Fenno and the Gazette of the United States").

29. Culver H. Smith, *The Press, Politics and Patronage: The American Government's Use of Newspapers, 1989–1875* (Athens: University of Georgia Press, 1977), 14.

30. Jeffrey L. Pasley, *"The Tyranny of Printers" Newspaper Politics in the Early American Republic* (Charlottesville: University of Virginia Press, 2001), 61–62.

31. Michael Lienesch, "Thomas Jefferson and the American Democratic Experience: The Origins of the Partisan Press, Popular Political Parties, and Public Opinion," in *Jeffersonian Legacies*, ed. Peter S. Onuf (Charlottesville: University Press of Virginia, 1993), 321.

32. Jules Witcover, *Party of the People: A History of the Democrats* (New York: Random House, 2003), 26.

33. There was printer's ink in Bache's blood; his illustrious grandfather had been editor of the *Pennsylvania Gazette* from 1729 to 1748.

34. Lienesch in Onuf, 318.

35. Pasley, 63. See also Jacob Axelrad, *Philip Freneau: Champion of Democracy* (Austin: University of Texas Press, 1967), chap. 20–25; Philip M. Marsh, *Philip Freneau: Poet and Journalist* (Minneapolis: Dillon Press, 1967), chap. 11–12; and Lewis Leary, *That Rascal Freneau* (New Brunswick, NJ: Rutgers University Press, 1941), chap. 7–8.

36. Small, 48–49.

37. See Leonard D. White, chap. 19 ("The Hamilton-Jefferson Feud").

38. William David Sloan, "'Purse and Pen': Party-Press Relationships, 1789–1816," *American Journalism* 6, no. 2 (1989), 109. The financial burden of sustaining the *National Gazette* was met by Freneau's partners, Francis Childs and John Swaine, who were in turn receiving lucrative printing contracts from the federal government. Daniel maintains that between 1789 and 1797, "they exercised a virtual monopoly on Congressional printing" and received a "considerable share of Jefferson's departmental printing." See also Claude G. Bowers, *Jefferson and Hamilton: The Struggle for Democracy in America* (Boston: Houghton Mifflin, 1966), 152–160.

39. Lienesch in Onuf, 320.

40. *Ibid.*, 319–320.

41. Pasley, 67. Madison's concern to keep this operation secret is reflected in a letter he wrote to Jefferson: "The possibility of its falling into base [i.e., pro-Hamilton] hands cannot be too carefully guarded against. I beg you to let me know its fate the moment it is in your power." Garry Wills, *James Madison* (New York: Times Books, 2002), 46. Federalist control of the mail was a constant source of apprehension for those Republicans concerned to keep their political ambitions anonymous. "I owe you a political letter," Jefferson wrote John Taylor in 1798, "yet the infidelities of the post office and the cir-

cumstances of the times are against my writing freely and fully." Leonard D. White, 191.

42. Eric Burns, 281.

43. *Ibid.*, 285.

44. Stanley Elkins and Eric McKitrick, *The Age of Federalism: The Early American Republic, 1788–1800* (New York: Oxford University Press, 1993), 284.

45. Daniel, 110. Pasley maintains that it was Freneau, in a sketch called "Sentiments of a Republican," who gave the "real friends" the name they would use in the party battles of the 1790s. Pasley, 68.

46. Bleyer, 125. For more on this cloak-and-dagger feud, see "A Tissue of Machinations," in *Hamilton, Vol. II: 1789–1804*, Robert Hendrickson (New York: Mason/Charter, 1976), 168–188.

47. Elkins and McKitrick, 284.

48. Bleyer, 110.

49. Knudson, 3.

50. John Hohnberg, *Free Press/Free People* (New York: Columbia University Press, 1971), 64. Hamilton would continue to use Fenno's *Gazette* as his mouthpiece against Jefferson even after stepping down from the cabinet. In 1796, under the name "Phocion," Hamilton expressed his alarm at the "pretensions of Thomas Jefferson to the Presidency." Hamilton classified Jefferson as belonging to that class of men who are "most dangerous" and warned his fellow citizens to be constantly "on our guard" against such a "demagogue" who wore the *"garb of patriotism"* only as a disguise and spoke the *"language of liberty"* only to deceive the unwary as to his true intentions. Eric Burns, 266.

51. Lienesch in Onuf, 322–323.

52. *Ibid.*, 323.

53. Washington was singularly unimpressed by the argument put forward by Freneau and other Republican critics that they made a distinction between the administration and the president himself. Washington insisted that if they attacked the government they condemned him, "for if they thought there were measures pursued contrary to his sentiment, they must conceive him too careless to attend to them or too stupid to understand them." Elkins and McKitrick, 290. The president was deeply concerned about the license of the press in general. Even in 1792 he fretted that "if the government and the officers of it are to be the constant theme for newspaper abuse ... it will be impossible, I conceive, for any man living to manage the helm or to keep the machine together." Much worse was to come. Jeffrey Manber and Neil Dahlstrom, *Lincoln's Wrath: Fierce Mobs, Brilliant Scoundrels and a President's Mission to Destroy the Press* (Naperville, IL: Sourcebooks, 2005), 9.

54. Small, 49.

55. Mott, 1943, 20.

56. Bleyer, 111.

57. Small, 50. Then again, Freneau himself was far from forthcoming about the true nature of the relationship with his employer. In a sworn affidavit, the editor insisted "that no negotiation was ever opened with him by Thomas Jefferson, Secretary of State, for the establishment or institution of the National Gazette; that the dependent's coming to the city of Philadelphia as the publisher of a newspaper was at no time urged, advised or influenced by the above officer, but that it was his own voluntary act; that the Gazette or the Editor thereof was never directed, controlled or attempted to be influenced in any manner either by the Secretary or any of his friends; that not a line was ever directly or indirectly written, dictated or composed for it by that officer, but that the Editor has consulted his own judgment alone in conducting it—free, unfettered and uninfluenced." Mott, 1943, 19.

For more on Freneau's relationship with Jefferson and Madison, see Philip Marsh, "Madison's Defense of Freneau," *William and Mary Quarterly* 3, no. 2 (April 1946), 269–274, and Philip Marsh, "The Griswold Story of Freneau and Jefferson," *American Historical Review* 51, no. 1 (October 1945), 68–73.

58. Daniel, 210.

59. Pasley, 72.

60. Leary, 202.

61. Sidney Kobre, *Development of American Journalism* (Dubuque, IA: William C. Brown, 1969), 130. Another Freneau ode to Fenno ran:

> One national paper, you think is enough
> To flatter and lie, to palaver and puff;
> To preach up in favor of monarchs and titles,
> And garters and ribbons, to prey on our vitals;
> Who knows but our Congress will give it in free,
> And make Mr. Fenno the grand patentee!

Donald Avery, "Battle Without a Rule Book," in *The Press in Times of Crisis*, ed. Lloyd Chiasson, Jr. (Westport, CT: Greenwood Press, 1995), 33.

62. Pasley, 59.

63. *Ibid.*

64. Freneau moved on to the New York *Time Piece.* When he began to shift the focus of that publication from a literary journal to a political organ, Noah Webster commented acidly, "The dog returns to his vomit." Walt Brown, 48.

65. Rubin, 9.

66. Sloan, 1989, 126.

67. Daniel, 111.

68. Pasley, 96.

69. John C. Miller, *Crisis in Freedom: The Alien and Sedition Acts* (Boston: Little, Brown, 1951), 60. The *Mercury* further referred to the *Aurora* as "this fountain head and source of calumny that the various political streams have issued which have defiled our towns and cities." Eric Burns, 317.

70. Miller, 61.

71. James Tagg, *Benjamin Franklin Bache and the Philadelphia Aurora* (Philadelphia: University of Pennsylvania Press, 1991), 395.

72. Mott, 1943, 28.

73. Jeffrey A. Smith, *Franklin and Bache: Envisioning the Enlightened Republic* (New York: Oxford University Press, 1990), 152.

74. Avery in Chiasson, 30.

75. Bleyer, 115.

76. In February 1791, Bache had warmly endorsed the festivities planned to mark the occasion upon which "our beloved PRESIDENT entered his 60th year." The following year he helped to organize a ball in Washington's honor under the auspices of the Philadelphia New City Dancing Assembly.

77. Eric Burns, 317.

78. Donald H. Stewart, *The Opposition Press of the Federalist Period* (New York: State University of New York Press, 1969), 520. For the role of the rival presses in shaping debate over foreign policy during the 1790s, see chaps. 5–8.

79. See Susan Dunn, *Sister Revolutions: French Lightning, American Light* (New York: Faber & Faber, 1999).

80. Walt Brown, 53.

81. See "'The Desacralization of George Washington': Benjamin Franklin Bache and the Aurora General Advertiser," in Daniel, 1998 (chap. 3).

82. Walt Brown, 53.

83. Tagg, 278.

84. *Ibid.*, 79.

85. Miller, 27–28.

86. Tagg, 287.

87. Sometimes the *Aurora* got too far ahead of its patrons, for example when it charged that Washington had never truly been a supporter of America's revolutionary ideals, as "twenty years after the establishment of the Republic" he was still "possessed of FIVE HUNDRED of the HUMAN SPECIES IN SLAVERY." Sean Wilentz, *The Rise of American Democracy: Jefferson to Lincoln* (New York: W. W. Norton, 2005), 62. Perhaps embarrassed by the inherent contradiction of criticizing Washington on this score while extolling the virtues of his fellow plantation aristocrats Jefferson and Madison, Duane subsequently subjected himself to a considerable degree of self-censorship on the subject.

88. Donald H. Stewart, 1969, 521.

89. *Ibid.*, 1969, 528. John Adams wrote his wife Abigail that Washington had told him that Paine's missive was "the most insulting letter he ever received." Walt Brown, 58. William Cobbett replied on behalf of the establishment, berating Paine in the pages of *Porcupine's Gazette* as "the Apostle of the Devil, and the nuisance of the world." Eric Burns, 343.

90. Leonard D. White, 111.

91. Mott, 1943, 21.

92. Rosenfeld, 31.

93. "It is even said," Washington's friend Benjamin Rush remarked, "that [Bache's] paper induced [Washington] to retire from the president's chair of the United States." Eric Burns, 326.

94. Walt Brown, 57.

95. Donald H. Stewart, 1969, 533.

96. Allan Nevins, *American Press Opinion: Washington to Coolidge* (Boston: D. C. Heath, 1928), 21.

97. Tebbel and Watts, 19.

98. Tagg, 286.

99. Jeffrey A. Smith, 1990, 160–161.

100. Tagg, 284.

101. Pasley, 97.

102. Jeffrey A. Smith, 1990, 150.

103. Michael Durey, *"With the Hammer of Truth": James Thomson Callender and America's Early National Heroes* (Charlottesville: University Press of Virginia, 1990), 96. Fenno took the same tone, grousing that "the only credit that any man can derive from that paper (which has been not inaptly styled the 'Infernal Gazette') is to receive its abuse." Arthur Scherr, "'Vox Populi' versus the Patriot President: Benjamin Franklin Bache's Philadelphia Aurora and John Adams (1797)," *Pennsylvania History* 62, no. 4 (Fall 1995), 518.

104. Bernard A. Weisberger, *America Afire: Jefferson, Adams, and the Revolutionary Election of 1800* (New York: HarperCollins, 2000), 205. Certainly, the president's son bridled under the lash of Bache's pen. After John Adams was criticized by the *Aurora* for appointing his boy John Quincy as ambassador to the Court of Sweden, the younger Adams, who had shared classes with Bache in Paris during the Revolutionary War while their father and grandfather, respectively, were utilizing their diplomatic skills in the patriot cause, remarked in a letter to his mother, "As for Mr. Bache, he was once my schoolmate; one of the companions of those infant years when the Heart should be open to strong and deep impressions of attachment.... Mr. Bache must have lost those feelings." Rosenfeld, 43–44.

105. Federalists were unforgiving of their literary nemesis to the last. "The Jacobins are all whining at the exit of the vile Benjamin Franklin Bache," *Russell's Gazette* observed, "so they would do if one of their gang was hung for stealing. The memory of this scoundrel cannot be too highly execrated." Eric Burns, 365.

106. Tagg, 329.
107. William David Sloan, "The Early Party Press," *Journalism History* 9, no. 1 (Spring 1982), 22.
108. Rosenfeld, 211.
109. *Ibid.*, 212.
110. William Reitzel, "William Cobbett and Philadelphia Journalism, 1794–1800," in *Highlights in the History of the American Press*, ed. Edwin H. Ford and Edwin Emery (Minneapolis: University of Minnesota Press, 1954), 114.
111. Cobbett had a matchless capacity for scrutinizing the targets of his barbs in order to best get under their skins. He certainly had the measure of Jefferson, skewering the intellectual hypocrisy of his pseudoscientific pursuits in the burlesque *Last Will and Testament*, in which Cobbett bequeathed to the then vice president "a curious Norway spider, with a hundred legs and nine pairs of eyes; likewise the first black cut-throat general he can catch hold of, to be flayed alive, in order to determine with more certainty the real cause of the dark colour of his skin." In addition, in the event that Jefferson survived African American intellectual Benjamin Banneker, Cobbett mockingly specified that "he will get the brains of said Philomath carefully dissected, to satisfy the world in what respect they differ from those of a white man." Hamilton enjoyed similar sport at Jefferson's expense, on one occasion offering his readers "a few comments on T. Jefferson's very ridiculous and elaborate attempt to prove that the *negroes are an inferior race of animals.*" Hamilton hoped that his comments "will place in just light the *philosophical* merits of the author." Eric Burns, 266. David A. Wilson, *William Cobbett: Peter Porcupine in America* (Ithaca: Cornell University Press, 1994), 233–234. For more on Cobbett, see Scott M. Howell, *William Cobbett and American Society in the Age of the French Revolution* (Ph.D. dissertation, University of California at Riverside, 2001) and Daniel, chap. 5 ("'Ribaldry and Billingsgate': William Cobbett and Porcupine's Gazette"). See also Keith Arbour, "Benjamin Franklin as Weird Sister: William Cobbett and Federalist Philadelphia's Fears of Democracy," in *Federalists Reconsidered*, ed. Doron Ben-Atar and Barbara B. Oberg (Charlottesville: University Press of Virginia, 1998), chap 9.
112. Sloan, 1982, 19. A New Jersey newspaper marked Cobbett's arrival on the literary scene with the warning: "Ye Democrats now beware, and hasten to gird on your armour and shield, that you may render yourselves invulnerable to the piercing quills of that groveling animal, the Porcupine." Walt Brown, 47.
113. Weisberger, 208.
114. Humphrey, 1996, 59.
115. Pasley, 100. Anti-Semitism was a recurring theme in Cobbett's writing. On one occasion *Porcupine's Gazette* derided then House minority leader Albert Gallatin with the following story: "When Mr. Gallatin rose from his seat ... there was an old farmer sitting beside me.... 'Ah, ah!' says he, 'what's little Moses in Congress?' I sharply reprimand him for taking one of our representatives for a Jew: but to confess a truth, the Gentleman from Geneva has an accent not unlike that of a wandering Israelite." Geoffrey R. Stone, *Perilous Times: Free Speech in Wartime* (New York: W. W. Norton, 2004), 27.
116. Tagg, 345. To be fair to Cobbett, in the first issue of *Porcupine's Gazette* he did offer Bache a political truce; he promised to avoid "all personality whatsoever" in his discussion of politics, provided Bache agreed to do the same. "I do not wish to fill my paper with personal satire and abuse," he wrote. "Our readers, especially those of this city, know already everything about you and I. Nothing that we say will alter their opinions of us; and as for

us altering our opinions of one another, that is a thing not to be thought of.... It is therefore useless, my dear Bache, to say any more about the matter. Let us disappoint them; let us walk arm in arm: many a couple, even of different sex, do this, and at the same time like one another no better than we do." Daniel, 432.
117. Jeffrey A. Smith, 1990, 158. See also Bernard Fay, *The Two Franklins: Fathers of American Democracy* (Boston: Little, Brown, 1933).
118. Rosenfeld, 70. Fenno was referring to Callender when he archly noted that "the chance of truth in the *Aurora* was always bad, but its editor has recently taken into employ some assistants which afford it no chance at all." Eric Burns, 330.
119. Durey, 103. Fenno is no less vivid in his characterization of the Scottish hired gun as "the *vagrant Callender* ... a miserable, ragged vagabond, who has been whipped and kicked out of one of our capital cities, and applied for relief as a pauper in another, whose very appearance gives a disgustful idea of the collected dregs of corruptible meanness and filthy beggary, who would not be picked out of a ditch by even a *good* Samaritan." Eric Burns, 331. Yet another critic depicted Callender as "a dirty, little toper with shaved head and greasy jacket, nantucket pantaloons, and woolen stockings." Miller, 214.
120. Bleyer, 119.
121. Sloan, 1988, 104.
122. Kobre, 1969, 120. Similarly, Abigail Adams remarked that Cobbett "frequently injures the cause he means to advocate for want of prudence and direction." She found a "strange mixture" in him. "He can write very handsomely, and he can descend and be as low and vulgar as a fish woman." David A. Wilson, *William Cobbett: Peter Porcupine in America* (Ithaca, NY: Cornell University Press, 1994), 36–37. Cobbett was not without his advocates, however; the first issue of the monthly *Anti-Jacobin Review and Magazine* in July 1798 depicted him as the victim of "vindictive, malignant, oppressive and intolerant" Jacobins, and saluted *Porcupine's Gazette* for "having contributed to give a proper tone to the public spirit in America." Editorial, *Anti-Jacobin Review and Magazine* 1, no. 1 (July 1798), 10.
123. Miller, 96.
124. John Lofton, *The Press as Guardian of the First Amendment* (Columbia: University of South Carolina Press, 1980), 37.
125. Rosenfeld, 235.
126. Miller, 40.
127. Donald H. Stewart, 1969, 625. "The style of *Porcupine's Gazette* is unquestionably the most base and wretched of any newspaper in Christendom," Carey continued. Outside of revolutionary France, he asserted, "I believe there never was a Gazette so infamous for scurrility, abuse, cursing, swearing, [and] blasphemy." Daniel, 514. Carey was later challenged to a duel by Federalist Eleazer Oswald and received a wound that required more than a year to fully recover from. Brigham, 68. Another Carey, James, under the pseudonym "Henry Hedgehog," expressed his disapprobation of Cobbett in the pamphlet *Anticipation! Peter Porcupine's Descent into Hell: Or an Elegy on his Death.*
128. Humphrey, 1996, 46. For more on Cobbett's checkered but always lively career, see Arthur Scherr, "'Sambos' and 'Black Cut-Throats': Peter Porcupine on Slavery and Race in the 1790s," *American Periodicals* 13 (2003), 3–30.
129. Rosenfeld, 734.
130. Reitzel in Ford and Emery, 125.
131. Michael Farquhar, *A Treasury of Great American Scandals* (New York: Penguin, 2003), 276.

132. Robertson, 33.

133. Rosenfeld, 632. For more on Duane, see Kim Tousley Phillips, *William Duane, Radical Journalist in the Age of Jefferson* (New York: Garland), 1989.

134. Pasley, 187.

135. Rosenfeld, 601.

136. *Ibid.*, 639–640.

137. *Ibid.*, 722.

138. *Ibid.*, 725.

139. *Ibid.*, 802. The now Fenno-less *Gazette* struggled on until 1818.

140. Pasley, 188.

141. Sloan, 1989, 114.

142. Rosenfeld, 81–82.

143. Miller, 21.

144. Brigham, 61.

145. Sloan, 108.

146. Tagg, 370. Bache, who in a lighter mood described Adams as "his rotundity," "has the malice & falsehood of Satan," Abigail Adams snarled. "The wrath of an insulted people will by & by break upon him." Jeffrey A. Smith, 1990, 154. Adams himself was not entirely without humor in dealing with the abuses of the press. One campaign rumor that circulated in 1800 had the President sending his running mate Charles Cotesworth Pinckney to England to procure four mistresses, two for Adams and two for himself. "I do declare upon my honor," Adams wryly commented, "if this be true, General Pinckney has kept them all for himself and cheated me out of my two." Farquhar, 156.

147. Geoffrey R. Stone, 34.

148. Miller, 57.

149. Lofton, 22.

150. Walt Brown, 143.

151. Geoffrey R. Stone, 35.

152. Rosenfeld, 188.

153. See Weisberger, chap. 11 ("Gagging the Press"); Humphrey, 1996, chap. 4 ("The Challenge of the Sedition Act, 1798–1800"); Elkins and McKitrick, 694–713; Leonard W. Levy, "The Gestation of an American Libertarian Theory," in *Emergence of a Free Press*, (Oxford University Press, Oxford, 1985), chap. 9; and James M. Smith, "The Sedition Law, Free Speech, and the American Political Process," *William and Mary Quarterly* 9, no. 4 (October 1952), 497–511.

154. For a useful overview of Congressional debate on the Sedition Bill, see Lofton, chap. 2 ("Sedition and the Press"). One of the few Federalists to oppose the bill was Alexander Hamilton, who labeled it politically inexpedient on the grounds that it would tend to make martyrs of Republicans. See Robert Martin, "Reforming Republicanism: Alexander Hamilton's Theory of Republican Citizenship and Press Liberty," *Journal of the Early Republic* 25, no. 1 (Spring 2005), 21–46. Ironically, Hamilton himself came close to being made an example of during the Sedition Act witch hunt. See Dumas Malone, "The Threatened Prosecution of Alexander Hamilton under the Sedition Act by Thomas Cooper," *American Historical Review* 29, no. 1 (October 1923), 76–81.

155. Lofton, 25.

156. Rosenfeld, 190.

157. Miller, 1951, 91–92.

158. *Ibid.*, 1951, 91.

159. Rosenfeld, 195.

160. *Ibid.*, 153.

161. Walt Brown, 31. See also Tagg, chap. 12 ("Sedition").

162. Miller, 57.

163. *Ibid.*, 73.

164. Lofton, 34.

165. Geoffrey R. Stone, 46.

166. Miller, 92.

167. Aleine Austin, *Matthew Lyon: "New Man" of the Democratic Revolution, 1749–1822* (University Park: Pennsylvania State University Press, 1981), 76.

168. Austin, 78.

169. Major General Arthur St. Clair, who convened the court martial that cashiered Lyon and the other officers associated with the incident, later recommended that he be reinstated to the Continental Army. Lyon was promoted to captain and served at Saratoga.

170. Austin, 105–106. Elsewhere Lyon warned that under the Sedition Act people "had better hold their tongues and make toothpicks of their pens."

171. *Ibid.*, 108. Lyon declared that the "great object" *The Scourge* "shall be to oppose truth to falsehood, and to lay before the public such facts as may tend to elucidate the real situation of this country … at this agitated and awful crisis, when everything is industriously circulated, which can corrupt or mislead the public sentiment, and prepare the American mind for a state of abject slavery, and degrading subjection to a set of assuming High Mightinesses in our own country, and a close connection with a corrupt, tottering monarchy in Europe." Austin, 121.

172. *Ibid.*, 119.

173. Sloan, 1988, 102. For more on Lyon's travails, see Miller, 102–111.

174. "A meaner, more artful or a more malicious libel has not appeared," the thin-skinned president complained after one of Cooper's many diatribes was brought to his attention. "As far as it alludes to me, I despise it; but I have no doubt it is a libel against the whole government, and as such ought to be prosecuted." Eric Burns, 361.

175. Brigham, 66. See also James M. Smith, "President John Adams, Thomas Cooper, and Sedition: A Case Study in Suppression," *Mississippi Valley Historical Review* 42, no. 3 (December 1955), 438–465.

176. Lofton, 40.

177. Knudson, 16.

178. Knudson, 15.

179. *Ibid.*, 16.

180. Miller, 197.

181. Geoffrey R. Stone, 65–66.

182. Knudson, 17–18.

183. *Ibid.*, 18.

184. Durey, 29.

185. Daniel, 472.

186. In fact, Callender had an evil reputation throughout the print trade, irrespective of party affiliation. Joseph Gales, Sr., who was working as a printer in Philadelphia, made the transition into reporting at the exhortation of his employer: "You seem able to do everything that is wanted: pray, could you not do these Congressional Reports for us better than this drunken Callender, who gives us so much trouble?" Donald A. Ritchie, *Press Gallery: Congress and the Washington Correspondents* (Cambridge, MA: Harvard University Press, 1991), 14.

187. Miller, 214. Callender refused to let Hamilton off the hook so easily, asserting that the confession of sexual infidelity was a cover story concocted by Hamilton and James Reynolds to mask more dastardly crimes. "So much correspondence could not refer exclusively to wenching," Callender maintained. "Hence it must have implicated some connection still more dishonourable, in Mr. Hamilton's eyes, than that of incontinency." Eric Burns, 310.

188. Durey, 107–108.

189. Knudson, 38–39.

190. Sloan, 1989, 108.

191. Thomas Fleming, *Duel: Alexander Hamilton,*

Aaron Burr and the Future of America (New York: Basic Books, 1999), 167.

192. Geoffrey R. Stone, 61.

193. Knudson, 39.

194. Sloan, 1989, 121.

195. Geoffrey R. Stone, 62.

196. *Ibid.*

197. Walt Brown, 126.

198. Geoffrey R. Stone, 62–63.

199. *Ibid.*, 69.

200. *Ibid.*, 73. Federalists never did appreciate the damage they had inflicted upon themselves by their conduct. The *Wasp*, on January 6, 1803, wondered, "Why did the Democrats call the Federal sedition-law the 'gag law?' It only punished them for lying, while it left them free liberty to publish truth. 'Aye, there's the rub!' Nothing can so completely gag a Democrat as to restrain him from lying. If you forbid his lying, you forbid his speaking." For a summary of the brief life of the Sedition Act, see Donald Avery, "The Legislation of Prior Restraint," in *The Press in Times of Crisis*, ed. Lloyd Chiasson, Jr. (Westport, CT: Greenwood Press, 1995). See also Daniel, 541–555.

201. Pasley, 126.

202. Rosenfeld, 216.

203. *Ibid.*, 720.

204. Miller, 221.

205. David Hackett Fischer, *The Revolution of Conservatism: The Federalist Party in the Era of Jeffersonian Democracy* (New York: Harper & Row, 1965), 135.

206. Walt Brown, 125.

207. Miller, 223.

208. Sloan, 1989, 112.

209. Culver H. Smith, 39–40.

210. Miller, 31. See also Leonard D. White, chap. 15–16.

211. Miller, 30.

212. Pasley, 117.

213. Sloan, 1982, 23.

214. Mott, 1943, 36.

215. Pasley, 154.

216. *Ibid.*, 153–154.

217. Noble E. Cunningham, *The Jeffersonian Republicans: The Formation of a Party Organization, 1789–1801* (Chapel Hill: University of North Carolina Press, 1957), 168.

218. Rosenfeld, 765–766.

219. Pasley, 162.

220. Cunningham, 1957, 168–169.

221. Pasley, 163.

222. Cunningham, 1957, 173.

223. Fischer, 129.

224. Sloan, 1989, 107–108.

225. *Ibid.*, 112.

226. *Ibid.*, 108.

227. Cunningham, 1957, 173.

228. See Donald H. Stewart, "The Press and Political Corruption during the Federalist Administrations," *Political Science Quarterly* 67, no. 3 (September 1952), 426–446.

229. Fischer, 131. For further state-by-state analysis of patterns in partisan journalism during the term of office of John Adams. see Walt Brown, 43.

230. Pasley, 169. See also Carl E. Prince, "The Federalist Party and Creation of a Court Press, 1789–1801," *Journalism Quarterly* 53, no. 2 (Summer 1976), 238–241.

231. Donald H. Stewart, 1969, 622.

232. Sloan, 1989, 117.

233. Walt Brown, 128–129.

234. *Ibid.*, 135. Adams certainly enjoyed no favors from Cobbett, who referred to the president as "a precipitate old ass."

235. *Ibid.*, 137.

236. Pasley, 233.

237. Nancy McPhee, *The Book of Insults — Ancient and Modern* (Toronto: Jonathan-James, 1978), 112.

238. Fischer, 169.

239. Noble E. Cunningham, Jr., "Election of 1800," in *Running for President: The Candidates and their Images, Vol. 1: 1789–1896*, ed. Arthur M. Schlesinger, Jr., (New York: Simon & Schuster, 1994), 32.

240. *Ibid.*

241. Mott, 38–39.

242. Eric Burns, 369–370.

243. Jefferson once said that he was always determined "to keep my name out of newspapers, because I find the pain of a little censure, even when it is unfounded, is more acute than the pleasure of much praise." If so, this particular personal quality was the first to be sacrificed on the altar of his political ambition. Knudson, 170.

244. Walt Brown, 47.

245. Sloan, 1988, 111. Duane concluded in the *Aurora* on December 24, 1800: "Our former contest with England was merely a matter of strength. The contest which has just been closed was a war of interest, vice and corruption against principle, virtue and patriotism. Our country became filled with foreign spies and domestic traitors who were on the eve of subverting our constitution and liberty — but the irresistible voice of a free people have banished them forever." Rosenfeld, 894.

246. Some historians have suggested that the assault on Jefferson by the Federalist press was actually counterproductive, in that it created a backlash in favor of the Republican nominee. Knudson disputes this, arguing that for all their limitations Jefferson's critics in the Federalist press were the most serious threat to the Virginian's presidential aspirations: "The Federalist press did not lose the election; on the contrary, it came remarkably close to winning it." Knudson, 66.

247. Pasley, 238. For more on the role of the Republican Press during the campaign of 1800, see Donald H. Stewart, 1969, chap. 8–9. To further explore this, one of the most well-chronicled of America's election, see Susan Dunn, *Jefferson's Second Revolution* (New York: Houghton Mifflin, 2004); John Ferling, *Adams vs. Jefferson: The Tumultuous Election of 1800* (New York: Oxford University Press, 2004); James Horn, Jan Ellis Lewis and Peter S. Onuf, *The Revolution of 1800: Democracy, Race, and the New Republic* (Charlottesville: University of Virginia Press, 2002); Bernard Weisberger, *America Afire: Jefferson, Adams, and the Revolutionary Election of 1800* (New York: William Morrow, 2000); Frank van der Linden, *The Turning Point: Jefferson's Battle for the Presidency* (Golden, CO: Fulcrum Publishing, 2000); and Daniel Sisson, *The American Revolution of 1800* (New York: Knopf, 1974). See also Matthew Q. Dawson, *Partisanship and the Birth of America's Second Party, 1796–1800* (Westport, CT: Greenwood Press, 2000).

248. Rosenfeld, 901.

249. Bleyer, 125. Adams later expanded the list of his tormentors, sparing neither Republican nor Federalist in asserting, "The causes of my retirement are to be found in the writings of Freneau, Markoe, Ned Church, Andrew Brown, Paine, Callender, Hamilton, Cobbett, and John Ward Fenno." Joanne B. Freeman, *Affairs of Honor: National Politics in the New Republic* (New Haven, CT: Yale University Press, 2001), 131. His xenophobia was a recurring trait among Federalists, who typically were themselves manifestations of the established families, classes and churches. On August 10, 1801, the *Gazette of the United States* noted the expiry of the Alien and Sedition Laws by commenting, "It is well known to all men of common discernment, Jacobins as well as others, that the

present unhappy and perilous state of public affairs, in this country, is owing in a great measure, to the unrestricted licentiousness of presses imprudently suffered to remain in the hands of wicked and seditious foreigners.... Every avenue and every byway passage... will be seen thronged with motley gangs, whose faces we know not and whose languages we cannot understand, strangers, Jews, and proselytes ... and Arabians." Knudson, 6

250. Walt Brown, 144.

251. Some Republican editors couldn't resist taking a parting shot at Adams as his administration wound down. Duane opened the pages of the *Aurora* to Congressman Matthew Lyon, who spat at the outgoing president, "I hope and pray that your fate may be a warning to all usurpers and tyrants, and that you may before you leave this world, become a true and sincere penitent and be forgiven all your manifold sins in the next." Knudson, 62–63

252. *Ibid.*, 55.

253. *Ibid.*, 61–62.

254. Durey, 117.

255. Charles H. Ambler, *Thomas Ritchie: A Study in Virginia Politics* (Richmond, VA: Bell, 1913), 17.

256. For coverage of the process of Republican encroachment on Federalist turf, see Pasley, 203–215. Republicans were also underrepresented at the other extreme of the expanding nation, on the western frontier. Partisans in Ohio grumbled that "the printers there do not give the republicans a fair chance; print every thing for aristocrats, and only now & then a piece for Democrats." Donald J. Ratcliffe, *Party Spirit in a Frontier Republic: Democratic Politics in Ohio 1793–1821* (Columbus: Ohio State University Press, 1998), 65.

257. Sloan, 1989, 106.

258. Timothy E. Cook, 28.

259. Culver H. Smith, 43–44.

260. Knudson, 13–14.

261. *Ibid.*, 14.

262. Mott, 1943, 50. As late as May 31, 1824, Jefferson could still write to Duane, "I am long since withdrawn from the political world. I think little, read less, and know all but nothing of what is going on; but I have not forgotten the past, nor those who were fellow-laborers in the gloomy hours of federal ascendancy, when the spirit of republicanism was beaten down, its votaries arraigned as criminals, and such threats denounced as posterity will never believe." Knudson, 25.

263. Mott, 1943, 50.

264. Knudson, 19.

265. For further analysis of Duane's losing out to Samuel Harrison Smith and the *National Intelligencer* for Jeffersonian patronage, see Phillips, 130–143. For more on Duane's political influence in Pennsylvania, see Sanford W. Higginbotham, *The Keystone in the Democratic Arch: Pennsylvania Politics 1800–1816* (Harrisburg: Pennsylvania Historical and Museum Commission, 1952). As the Republican Party strayed from its founding principles after the War of 1812, the *Aurora* turned increasingly critical. In January 1817, the paper published a series of scathing criticisms of the Monroe Administration which it accused of misleading the nation in its schemes to acquire Florida from Spain. Apparently with a straight face Duane accused the administration of "bad faith and public deception" for its policy of causing "articles to be written in public offices" for publication in proadministration newspapers such as the Washington *National Intelligencer*, the *Boston Patriot*, and the *Richmond Enquirer*. "By means of these *machines* the people are *managed*—an impulse is then given to the class of sycophants ... who in every populous place, return the service of slaves for the emoluments or promises of petty

offices." William Earl Weeks, *John Quincy Adams & American Global Empire* (Lexington: University Press of Kentucky, 1992), 68.

266. In addition, the *Centinel of Liberty*, a Federalist paper that had been published for two years in Georgetown, established the *Museum and Washington and George-Town Advertiser* on November 18. Thus, by the time Congress assembled, Washington already had two Republican and two Federalist newspapers. Knudson, 12.

267. *Ibid.*

268. William E. Ames, *A History of the National Intelligencer* (Chapel Hill: University of North Carolina Press, 1972), 67. Jefferson's vice president Aaron Burr confirmed the exalted status of the *National Intelligencer* when he commented, "The Washington paper edited by Smith has the countenance and support of the administration. His explanations of the Measures of the Government and of the Motives which produce them are, I believe, the result of information and advice from high authority." Timothy E. Cook, 28.

269. Culver H. Smith, 27.

270. Bleyer, 131.

271. Knudson, 3.

272. Sloan, 1982, 22.

273. Knudson, 13.

274. Ritchie, 1991, 12–13.

275. Ames, 98.

276. Ritchie, 1991, 16. Occasionally, Republicans might cross party lines to raise trial balloons too risky to flirt with in the pages of their own press. One Republican representative, John Bacon, allowed the *Washington Federalist* to print a speech he withheld from the *Intelligencer* on the grounds that while its publication might have caused divisions within his own party's ranks, its appearance in the organ of the opposition could cause no harm, since "all the readers of that paper were of the same opinion before." *Ibid.*

277. Knudson, 27–28. Bronson tempted fate along the way by flirting with objectivity, entirely contrary to the rules of the game. Criticism of John Adams in the *Gazette* attracted the rebuke of Timothy Dwight, who wrote the editor on January 21, 1802: "I have, since my arrival in this town [Philadelphia], been informed, that some disadvantageous observations have been made concerning Mr. Adams in your paper. I cannot but think any such thing would better be wholly omitted. Were I present, I would, I think, persuade you of this truth. I know it to be the opinion of the most respectable men, of my acquaintance, from Boston to New York. I think the most exact delicacy should be observed on this subject. I know you will believe this hint kindly given, & will therefore receive it kindly." *Ibid.*, 28–29.

278. See Jerry W. Knudson, "The Jeffersonian Assault on the Federalist Judiciary, 1802–1805: Political Forces and Press Reaction," *American Journal of Legal History* 14, no. 1 (January 1970), 55–75.

279. Knudson, 27.

280. *Ibid.*, 29.

281. *Ibid.*, 169.

282. *Ibid.*, 30.

283. After Jefferson's election, Coleman sent the new president a bombastic epistle, accusing him of pulling down the old temple of morality and religion, and erecting in its place "a foul and filthy temple consecrated to atheism and lewdness." Coleman was content to recognize his place as the mouthpiece of Hamilton. "Whenever anything occurs on which I feel the want of information," he once confessed, "I state matters to [Hamilton,] sometimes in a note. He appears at a time when I may see him, usually a late hour in the evening. He always keeps

himself minutely informed on all political matters. As soon as I see him, he begins in a deliberate manner to dictate and I to note down in shorthand. When he stops, my article is completed." Eric Burns, 397.

284. Knudson, 33. James Cheetham of the Republican New York *American Citizen* was less flattering: "He may, in fact, be called a mere hireling." *Ibid.*, p. 33.

285. The third issue of the *New York Evening Post* was in fact dedicated to partisan unity: "It has been long since observed, that the cause of FEDERALISM has received as much injury from the indiscreet contentions and bickerings among those who profess to be its friends, as from the open assaults of its enemies." *Ibid.*, 31.

286. *Ibid.*, 34.

287. Bleyer, 134. The *Aurora* in turn referred to William Coleman as an "impious, disorganized wretch!" Avery in Chiasson, 30.

288. Knudson, 35.

289. Fischer, 133.

290. Robertson, 38.

291. Knudson asserts that "once Jefferson was in office he neglected to exert leadership over his partisan press." Knudson, 172. While Jefferson may no longer have been actively involved in the operational management of the Republican papers, he effectively delegated this responsibility to the party hierarchy.

292. Noble E. Cunningham, *The Jeffersonian Republicans in Power: Party Operations, 1801–1809* (Chapel Hill: University of North Carolina Press, 1963), 239.

293. Bleyer, 133. On another occasion Cheetham labeled the editor of the Boston *Repertory* "an impertinent meddling ignoramus." Fleming, 256.

294. Allan Nevins, *The Evening Post: A Century of Journalism* (New York: Russell & Russell, 1968), 48–49. Coleman's successor, William Cullen Bryant, noted of his employer that "he was of full make, with a broad chest, muscular arms, which he wielded lightly and easily, and a deep-toned voice; but his legs dangled like strings." Ibid, 134. Brigham, 67. At this stage of his career Duane felt that he would be more vulnerable outside of the editorial business than actively engaged in it. As he explained in a letter to Jefferson dated May 10, 1801, "I had determined before the election, that upon the success of the people's choice, I should dispose of the paper and pursue another profession, but I find the hatred so violent against me that it would follow me for ever, and in any other situation I should not possess such formidable means of defence." Knudson, 24.

296. Levy, 1966, 354. It is clear that "Porcupine" (William Cobbett) and Fenno were doing their job in getting under Jefferson's skin. In a letter to Abigail Adams dated July 22, 1804, the president wrote, "With respect to the calumnies and falsehoods which writers and printers at large published against Mr. Adams, I was as far from stooping to any concern or approbation of them, as Mr. Adams was respecting those of Porcupine, Fenno, or Russell, who published volumes against me for every sentence vended by their opponents against Mr. Adams.... I am not afraid to appeal to the nation at large, to posterity, and still less to that Being who sees himself our motives, who will judge us from his own knowledge of them, and not on the testimony of Porcupine or Fenno." Levy, 1966, 365–366.

297. Durey, 142.

298. Knudson, 41.

299. *Ibid.*

300. Knudson, 42.

301. *Ibid.*

302. Witcover, 71.

303. Durey, 156–157.

304. *Ibid.*, 158.

305. Eric Burns, 384–385. Like Hamilton and Cobbett before him, Callender explicitly twitted Jefferson's hypocrisy on the question of race: "'Tis supposed that, at the time, when Mr. Jefferson wrote so smartly concerning Negroes, when he had endeavored so much to *belittle* the African race, he had no idea that the chief magistrate of the United States was to be the ringleader in shewing that his opinion was erroneous; or, that he should chuse an African stock whereupon he was to engraft his own descendants."

306. Knudson, 43.

307. Avery in Chiasson, 23.

308. Humphrey, 1996, 76. Abigail Adams, on the other hand, found the entire episode hilarious, and relished the opportunity to rub it in. "The serpent you cherished and warmed, bit the hand that nourished him," she wrote Jefferson. Richard Brookhiser, *America's First Dynasty: The Adamses, 1735–1918* (New York: Free Press, 2002), 55.

309. "What would this unfortunate figure give to recall the moment, when he refused to pay Callender his fine?" Callender asked of Jefferson on May 28, 1803, less than two months prior to his death. "Chastisement was promised; and the promise has been kept with the most rigid punctuality.... Such, O democrats! is the faithful portrait of your favorite hero!" This reaction against a personal betrayal suffuses all of Callender's attacks on his erstwhile patron. He described the president's decision to receive Thomas Paine upon his return to America as evidence that "divine providence has predestined the disgrace and dismission on Thomas Jefferson." Callender called Paine the "*chosen vessel* of our beloved president! He sends twelve hundred leagues for an auxiliary writer." Projecting his own bitter experience in a third-person *Recorder* editorial, Callender predicted that the association between Jefferson and Paine would soon end in bitter recrimination: "It is quite as probable as otherwise that Jefferson will treat Paine as he did Callender—He'll scarcely rent him a part of his house—I tender you the homage of my high respects for the services you rendered me in vilifying Washington, Adams and the constitution, but you see how 'tis, Mr. Paine; I-I-did not think you would come 'in event'—I-I-should be happy to see your services rewarded—by 'the gratitude of nations,' the only reward a true philosopher wishes." But Callender could not resist adding, "On second consideration, I think it more probable than otherwise, that Paine and Jefferson will not break friends: *the executive bought his wit dear enough in quarrelling with Callender.*" Knudson, 79–80.

310. Durey, 159. For more on the Hemings affair, see Joshua D. Rothman, "James Callender and Social Knowledge of Interracial Sex in Antebellum America," in *Sally Hemings and Thomas Jefferson: History, Memory and Civic Culture*, Jan Ellen Lewis and Peter S. Onuf (Charlottesville: University Press of Virginia, 1999), chap. 4; Annette Gordon-Read, *Thomas Jefferson and Sally Hemings: An American Controversy* (Charlottesville: University Press of Virginia, 1997), especially chap. 2, "James Callender."

311. Knudson, 45.

312. Fleming, 166. Callender's legacy was to be remembered by history as "a hardened and habitual liar, a traitorous and truculent scoundrel," and "the most outrageous and wretched scandalmonger of a scurrilous age ... drunken, vicious and depraved, albeit talented." Charles A. Jellison, "That Scoundrel Callender," *Virginia Magazine of History and Biography* 64 (1959), 306; and Virginius Dabney, *The Jefferson Scandals: A Rebuttal* (New York: Dodd, Mead, 1981), 65. Jefferson himself characterized his one-time hireling as "a poor creature ... drunken, penniless & unprincipled." Eric Burns, 393.

313. Fleming, 167.

314. Dumas Malone, *Jefferson the President: First Term, 1801–1805* (Boston: Little, Brown, 1970), 225.

315. Guido H. Stempel III, "Media Coverage of Presidential Campaigns as a Political Issue," in *The Media in the 1984 and 1988 Presidential Campaigns*, ed. Guido H. Stempel III and John W. Windhauser (New York: Greenwood Press, 1991), 1.

316. Malone, 1970, 229.

317. Levy, 1966, 350–352. For comments on the degree to which the Virginia and Kentucky Resolves actually hurt the Republican cause, see Miller, 177–179.

318. Mott, 1943, 6.

319. Levy, 1966, 364.

320. *Ibid.*

321. Mott, 1943, 39.

322. Malone, 1970, 231. When Callender's allegations first surfaced, Dennie had gone to print with a less inspired piece of doggerel: "Dear Thomas, deem it no disgrace / With slaves to mend thy breed, / Nor let the wench's smutty face / Deter thee from the deed." Mott, 1943, 40.

323. Donna L. Dickerson, *The Course of Tolerance: Freedom of the Press in Nineteenth-Century America* (New York: Greenwood Press, 1990), 26. McKean wasn't finished yet in his crusade against the license of the press. After instituting criminal proceedings against renegade Republican William Duane (who had called for the governor's impeachment, remarking, "The United Kingdom belongs to George the Third, so does Pennsylvania belong to Thomas the First"), McKean returned to the legislature in December 1806, asking for the libel laws to given more teeth. "Libeling has become the crying sin of the nation and the times," he argued. It was, he said, "the general prostitution of the liberty of the press, the overwhelming torrent of political dissension; the indiscriminate demolition of public characters; and the barbarous inroads upon the peace and happiness of private individuals." The legislature rejected this plea in March 1809, passing a law which stated that no person could be charged with a criminal libel for publications which examined the legislature, any branch of government, or any official conduct of public officeholders. McKean's case against Duane promptly collapsed. Ibid, 28–29.

324. Malone, 1970, 215.

325. Malone, 1970, 232.

326. See Hendrickson, chap. 29 ("The Freedom of the Press"). See also Fleming, 169–176, 273–275.

327. Lofton, 45–47. As the countdown to Jefferson's inauguration in 1801 had begun, the *Connecticut Courant* had greeted the forthcoming event with two and a half columns of invective in verse, typified by the following stanza: "While to the Union's utmost bounds, / The Jacobinic Tocsin sounds, / Thieves, traitors, Irish renegades, / Scape-gallowless, and desperadoes, / All sorts of rogues stripped off the mask / And entered on the glorious task."

328. Mott, 1943, 41.

329. Levy, 1966, 367–368.

330. Bleyer, 139.

331. Sloan, 1989, 107.

332. Pasley, 235–236.

333. *Ibid.*, 238.

334. Fischer, 142.

335. Dickerson, 43.

336. Fischer, 168–169.

337. Dickerson, 44.

338. Richard Buel, Jr., *America on the Brink: How the Political Struggle over the War of 1812 Almost Destroyed the Young Republic* (New York: Palgrave, 2005), 178. For more on press freedom during the War of 1812, see Lofton, chap. 3 ("First Wartime Test of the First Amendment").

339. Some Federalist editors simply found they could not lower themselves to the level at which their Republican rivals operated. "READER, it has given me much pain to write such lies as I have presented you in this number," Harry Croswell apologized to the subscribers of the Hudson *Wasp* in January 1803. "If it has been such a task for me to fill this one little paper with them, how the devil does [Charles Holt of the New London, Connecticut, *Bee*] get along with such a piece of work from year to year? Perhaps by being accustomed to it. However, I despair of acquiring the habit; and therefore must give up the idea of becoming a democrat." Dicken-Garcia, 97.

340. Pasley, 239.

341. *Ibid.*, 254.

342. *Ibid.*, 253. Some Federalists actively promoted secession as the best means to defend their interest, and Federalist newspapers toyed with this concept in public. Theodore Dwight, who founded the Hartford *Connecticut Mirror* in 1809, was a leading critic of the War of 1812 and a motivating force behind the Hartford Convention, where he served as secretary.

343. William C. Dowling, *Literary Federalism in the Age of Jefferson: Joseph Dennie and The Port Folio, 1801–1812* (Columbia: University of South Carolina Press, 1999), 69.

344. Knudson, 8.

345. Dowling, ix.

346. Norman K. Risjord, "Election of 1812," in Schlesinger, 1994, 71.

347. Frank Luther Mott, "Newspapers in Presidential Campaigns," *Public Opinion Quarterly* 8, no. 3 (Autumn 1944), 363.

348. Mott, 1943, 54–55. Jefferson expressed similar sentiment towards the press on another occasion: "When I read the newspapers and see what a mass of falsehood and what an atom of truth they contain, I am mortified with the consideration that 90/100th of mankind pass through life imagining they have known what was going forward when they would have been nearer the truth had they heard nothing." Knudson, 167. Jefferson was not alone among presidents in adopting this antithetical approach to the press. "I am not surprised that your faith is shaken as to the reliability of all you see in the papers," Ulysses Grant once wrote to a friend. "For some time I have believed everything except what I see in print."

Chapter II

1. Harry J. Maihafer, *War of Words: Abraham Lincoln and the Civil War Press* (Washington, D.C.: Brassey's, 2001), 48.

2. Maihafer, 2001, 37. Russell noted that the American public regarded the "chiefs of the most notorious journals very much as people in Italian cities of past time might have talked of the most infamous band of assassins." Russell's sojourn in the former colonies was destined to be brief. The correspondent had been greeted upon his arrival with Lincoln's usual flattery for the press. "The London *Times* is one of the greatest powers in the world," the president remarked. "In fact, I don't know anything which has much more power — except perhaps the Mississippi." But after issuing caustic remarks about the Union performance at the First Battle of Bull Run,

Russell felt his welcome turn abruptly cooler. The following year the secretary of war denied him a military pass to travel with the Union army. After Lincoln refused to intervene, Russell left the United States in disgust, in April 1862. Manber and Dahlstrom, 69.

3. Page Smith, *The Nation Comes of Age: A People's History of the Ante-Bellum Years* (New York: McGraw-Hill, 1981), 257. Other choice epithets that Dickens directed at the American press included "foul," "licentious," "vicious," "a disgrace," "moral poison," and "rampant ignorance and base dishonesty." He concluded that "while the newspaper press of America is in, or near, its present abject state, high moral improvement in that country is hopeless." Mitchell Stephens and David T.Z. Mindich, "The Press and the Politics of Representation," *The Press*, Geneva Overholser and Kathleen Hall Jamieson (Oxford: Oxford University Press, 2005), 373–374.

4. Robertson, 68. In his *American Notes* from 1842, Dickens warned his hosts that "any man who attains a high place among you ... may date his downfall from that moment; for any printed lie that any notorious villain pens ... appeals at once to your distrust, and is believed." When read between the lines, another acerbic trans-Atlantic observation, this one by Frances Trollope in her 1832 tome *Domestic Manners of the Americans*, may at least be considered a back-handed compliment to the extent of newspaper consumption in the erstwhile colonies: "In truth, there are many reasons which render a very general diffusion of literature impossible in America. I can scarcely class the universal reading of newspapers as an exception to this remark; if I could, my statement would be exactly the reverse, and I should say that Americans beat the world in letters."

5. Cooper's animus towards the press of his day spilled over into the pages of his *The American Democrat*, 1838: "If newspapers are useful in overthrowing tyrants, it is only to establish a tyranny of their own ... it is gradually establishing a despotism as ruthless, as grasping, and one that is quite as vulgar as that of any christian state ever known. With loud professions of freedom of opinion, there is no tolerance; with a parade of patriotism, no sacrifice of interests; and with fulsome panegyrics on propriety, too frequently, no decency." Michael Schudson, *Discovering the News: A Social History of American Newspapers* (New York: Basic Books, 1978), 13.

6. Carl R. Osthaus, *Partisans of the Southern Press: Editorial Spokesmen of the Nineteenth Century* (Lexington: University Press of Kentucky, 1994), 5–6.

7. Knudson, 26.

8. Douglas Fermer, *James Gordon Bennett and the New York Herald: A Study of Editorial Opinion in the Civil War Era 1854–1867* (New York: St. Martin's Press, 1986), 5.

9. William E. Gienapp, "'Politics Seems to Enter into Everything': Political Culture in the North, 1840–1860, in *Essays on American Antebellum Politics, 1840–1860*, William E. Gienapp et al. (Arlington: Texas A&M University Press, 1982), 42. For a contemporary perspective on the cut-throat world of the antebellum editors, see Lambert A. Wilmer, *Our Press Gang* (Philadelphia: J.T. Lloyd, 1859), especially chap. 4, "The Foreign and Anti-American Character of our Newspaper Press."

10. Alexis de Tocqueville, *Democracy in America* (New York: Knopf, 1945), 120. A prestigious American authority on the subject of the indigenous media also remarked on its role in stimulating debate: "It is certain that, could the journals agree, they might, by their united efforts, give a powerful inclination to the common will. But, in point of fact, they do not agree on any one subject or set of subjects, except, perhaps, on those which directly affect their own interests. They, consequently, counteract, instead of

aiding each other, on all points of disputed policy; and it is in the bold and sturdy discussions that follows that men arrive at truth." James Fenimore Cooper, *The American Democrat and Other Political Writings* (Washington, D.C.: Regnery, 2000), 152.

11. Richard B. Kielbowicz, *News in the Mail: The Press, Post Office, and Public Information, 1700–1860s* (New York: Greenwood Press, 1989), 179.

12. John Gerald, *Tippecanoe and the Party Press too: Mass Communication, Politics, Culture, and the Fabled Presidential Election of 1840* (Ph.D. dissertation, University of Illinois at Urbana-Champaign, 1999), 205.

13. Kielbowicz, 63, 71.

14. In addition to noting its vital role in the dissemination of news, Baltimore editor Hezekiah Niles sourly commented in 1813 on the network's potential for plagiarism: "The rounds that these things take are curious—for instance, I have an article before me that *I* myself *made*, that was published at *Boston* as original, copied into a *Baltimore* paper without credit, and inserted in an *Albany* paper as belonging to the newspaper last noted." Gerald, 206.

15. Baldasty, 1984, 6.

16. Baldasty, 1992, 5.

17. Carl Russell Fish, *The Civil Service and Patronage* (New York: Russell & Russell, 1967), 123.

18. Baldasty, 1984, 7.

19. Robertson, 71.

20. Baldasty, 1992, 25.

21. Gienapp in Gienapp et al., 42.

22. Dickerson, 63.

23. Jeffrey Rutenbeck, "The Stagnation and Decline of Partisan Journalism in Late Nineteenth-Century America: Changes in the New York World, 1860–76," *American Journalism* 10, no. 1–2 (Winter-Spring 1993), 46.

24. Dicken-Garcia, 114–115. "The deeply rooted political role had far-reaching implications that sustained it, despite the claims of the new journalism," Dicken-Garcia notes. "Even as they debunked partisanism in the 1830s and 1840s, journalists sought political roles and used newspapers to advance political views and parties." *Ibid.*, 47.

25. Gerald, 210. On November 1, 1842, the editor of the Hannibal, Missouri, *Courier* went so far as to argue that newspapers should not support politicians who were not subscribers: "No newspaper ought to support any man for office ... unless he is a regular subscriber to it. The press has long enough been drudge for the elevation of illiberal and selfish men." Dicken-Garcia, 114. A similar scenario was playing out north of the border. One reason for the rapid expansion of the newspaper industry in mid-nineteenth-century Canada was the "perceived need for both a Tory publication and a Reform one in every important population centre so that each could block the outrages of the others." Douglas Fethering, *The Rise of the Canadian Newspaper* (Toronto: Oxford University Press, 1990), 78. By the 1860s, the federal Conservative Party was spending $100,000 per year to buy favorable newspaper treatment. *Ibid.*, 79.

26. Baldasty, 1984, 16. The ideological component of such transactions has persisted through the centuries. In 1964 the DuPont family, which effectively monopolized the news in Delaware, was musing about the sale of its papers through its holding company, Christiana Securities. In an internal memo, the managing editor advocated "outright sale to an outside newspaper organization whose political and economic views closely parallel those of the present ownership. There are a number of such organizations. To avoid having the papers fall into unfriendly hands through a second sale, the sales agreement should

give Christiana or its successors the first opportunity to purchase the papers if they should be again put up for sale." Ben H. Bagdikian, *The Effete Conspiracy, and other Crimes by the Press* (New York: Harper & Row, 1974), 12. More recently, when Lee Enterprises Inc. agreed to purchase Pulitzer Inc. for $1.46 billion in May 2005, it also agreed that the flagship *St. Louis Post-Dispatch* would keep its longstanding liberal editorial slant for at least the next five years, according to the purchase agreement mailed to Pulitzer shareholders. "For a period of at least five years following the Effective Time, Parent (Lee Enterprises) will cause the St. Louis *Post-Dispatch* to maintain its current name and editorial page platform statement and to maintain its news and editorial headquarters in the City of St. Louis, Missouri," the agreement states. Mark Fitzgerald, "In Unusual Agreement, 'Post-Dispatch' Will Remain Liberal Under Lee," *Editor & Publisher*, May 13, 2005.

27. Mark W. Summers, *The Plundering Generation: Corruption and the Crisis of the Union, 1849–1861* (Oxford: Oxford University Press, 1987), 40.

28. Mott, 1943, 355. Military allusions saturate the partisan press of the era. "The editors of both parties," *Niles' National Register* noted in 1844, "appear to think there is much to be gained from the game of brag.... Arguing from the maxim that most people are desirous of being upon the strong side, they calculate upon making something out of a show of confidence. No general should allow his men to doubt of a victory, if he expects to obtain one." Richard Jensen, "Armies, Admen and Crusaders: Types of Presidential Crusaders," *History Teacher* 2, no. 2 (January 1969), 38.

29. Gerald, 228. Politicians were not shy about retaliating to such obloquy in kind, often with interest. When an editor accused one congressional candidate of adultery, the candidate shot back in print that his accuser was "some spindle-shanked, toad-eating, man-granny ... some *puling* sentimental, *he*-old maid whose cold liver and pulseless heart never felt a desire which could be tempted!" On another occasion an Illinois senator expressed his conviction that the editor of an opposition paper had the features of one who had "been vomited from the depths of the infernal regions." Of course, it was a confrontational environment in which the purveyors of the print trade interacted with each other. One Tennessee editor, alluding to his "ugly, blear-eyed, monkey faced" rival at the *Nashville Union*, could not be satisfied without making the world aware that "there is not a more contemptible being roaming the face of the earth." *Ibid.*, 228.

30. Schudson, 1978, 16.

31. Pasley, 354.

32. Joel H. Silbey, *The Partisan Imperative: the Dynamics of American Politics before the Civil War* (New York: Oxford University Press, 1985), 54.

33. See Chilton Williamson, *American Suffrage: From Property to Democracy, 1760–1860* (Princeton, NJ: Princeton University Press, 1960).

34. Ward, 190.

35. Sales were the key to the survival of the penny paper. Deliberately turning his back on the networks of patronage that received wisdom deemed vital to the survival of any publication, Day gambled that he could break out of the subscription-based business model. The gamble paid off, thanks both to pricing the *Sun* to meet the needs of the lowest common denominator and to the decisive marketing innovation of hiring newsboys to hawk his paper in the streets. The *Sun* had a daily circulation of 5,000, the largest in New York, by January of 1834. By June 1835, the combined circulation of the *Sun* and the two penny papers to emerge in its wake, the *Evening Transcript* and the *Herald*, was 44,000. On the day that the *Sun*

debuted, the combined circulation of the city's eleven dailies had been 26,500. The concept spread like wildfire. The *Boston Daily Times*, Philadelphia *Public Ledger*, and Baltimore-based *The Sun* were all market leaders within months or even weeks of their debuts. Schudson, 1978, 18. Advertising, as well as sales, took on a more democratic cast in the penny papers, being pitched to households rather than mercantile interests. On this basis Schudson concludes that "the penny papers expressed and built the culture of a democratic market society." *Ibid.*, 60. Innis also notes the increasing salience of commercial advertising to the viability of the popular press, asserting that under the new business model, news increasingly became "a device for advertising the paper as an advertising medium." Harold A. Innis, *The Bias of Communications* (Toronto: University of Toronto Press, 1951), 162.

36. David T.Z. Mindich, *Just the Facts: How "Objectivity" Came to Define American Journalism* (New York: New York University Press, 1998), 53. On November 21, 1837, Bennett opined that only the penny press could be a free press, "simply because it is subservient to none of its readers — known to none of its readers — and entirely ignorant of who are its readers and who are not." Bennett's peers in the penny press issued similar manifestos of partisan independence. The New York *Evening Transcript*, in its inaugural issue, declared that so far as politics goes, "we have none." The *Boston Daily Times* claimed to be "neutral in politics" while the Baltimore *Sun* proclaimed, "Our object will be the common good, without regard for that of sects, factions, or parties." Schudson, 1978, 21–22.

37. Briggs and Burke, 202. In a series of articles on the history of the American newspaper for *Collier's* magazine in 1911, William Irwin credited Bennett with the invention of news as distinct from editorial journalism: "And before the Civil War we find our press transformed." William H. Irwin, *The American Newspaper* (Ames: Iowa State University Press, 1969), 12. See also Andie Tucher, *Froth & Scum: Truth, Beauty, Goodness, and the Ax Murder in America's First Mass Medium* (Chapel Hill: University of North Carolina Press, 1994).

38. Schudson, 1978, 17.

39. Ritchie, 1991, 31.

40. Crouthamel, 1989, 45.

41. Ritchie, 1991, 32. Challenges to the incestuous relationship between the political hierarchy and the Washington press had emerged at an earlier date, however. In 1835 the Senate passed a rule restricting access to the floor exclusively to reporters from Washington-based publications. When reporters for the *New York Herald* arrived at the Senate in 1841, the president pro tempore, Samuel Southard, notified them they would not be admitted to the floor. After Bennett lobbied Southard's fellow Whig, Henry Clay, suggesting that the *Herald's* reporters could transcribe debate as efficiently as the publicly supported stenographers, the Senate repealed the previous language and bade the secretary to "cause suitable accommodation to be prepared in the eastern gallery for such reporters as may be admitted by the rules of the Senate." The established monopoly of the Washington papers as conduits to news outlets throughout the nation was thus broken, even prior to the invention of the telegraph and the emergence of the Associated Press later in the decade. Timothy E. Cook, 35. Congress continued to maintain that journalistic access to its august chambers was a privilege, not a right, and when that privilege was abused, retribution could be swift. In February 1848, a Washington correspondent for the *New York Tribune*, writing under the pseudonym "Persimmon," sketched the luncheon habits of Representative William Sawyer of Ohio, detailing how each day at two o'clock Sawyer moved from his seat in the

House to a place behind and to the left of the Speaker's chair, near the window, unfolded a greasy paper and ate the bread and sausage it contained, and wiped his hands on the paper before throwing it out the window, climaxing his repast by using his jackknife for a toothpick and his pantaloons and coat sleeves for a napkin. An aggrieved Sawyer prevailed upon the House to pass a resolution (by a vote of 119–46) ousting all *Tribune* reporters from their seats or desks on the House floor. Schudson, 1978, 29.

42. Robert H. Wiebe, *The Search for Order* (New York: Hill and Wang, 1967), xiii.

43. Innis, 170.

44. Mindich, 64.

45. James Keogh, *President Nixon and the Press* (New York: Funk & Wagnalls, 1972), 21.

46. The collapse of national identity subsequent to the introduction of the telegraph as a mass medium of information exchange may reflect an instance of what Lewis Mumford labeled "the paradox of communication," whereby greater and more intensive interaction between individuals, sections, and nations can serve at least initially to "increase the areas of friction," to "hasten mass-reactions," and perhaps, more generally, to highlight disagreements and differences that previously were only latent. Lewis Mumford, *Technics and Civilization* (New York: Harcourt, Brace and World, 1963), 239–241.

47. Not all politics in 1824 revolved around personalities—sectional interests played a key role in determining editorial allegiance. See Paul C. Nagel, The Election of 1824: A Reconsideration Based on Newspaper Opinion," *The Journal of Southern History* 26, no. 3 (Fall 1960), 315–329. See also James W. Tankard, Jr., "Public Opinion Polling by Newspapers in the Presidential Election Campaign of 1824," *Journalism Quarterly* 49, no. 2 (Summer 1972), 361–365, and Robert P. Hay, "'The Presidential Question': Letters to Southern Editors, *Tennessee Historical Quarterly* 31, no. 2 (1972), 170–186. For an editorial perspective from what was then the frontier, see Thomas H. Howard, "Indiana Newspapers and the Presidential Election of 1824," *Indiana Magazine of History* 63, no. 3 (Fall 1967), 177–206. For an overview, see Payne, chap. 17. See also Ernest R. May, "Domestic Politics," in *The Making of the Monroe Doctrine*, (Harvard University Press, Cambridge, 1975), chap. 4.

48. Tebbel and Watts, 64–65.

49. See Ames, chap. 8 ("The Loss of Executive Patronage").

50. Dickerson, 65.

51. William E. Ames and S. Dean Olson, "Washington's Political Press and the Election of 1824," *Journalism Quarterly* 40, no. 3 (Summer 1963), 348.

52. Dickerson, 66.

53. Ames and Olson, 345.

54. *Ibid.*, 350.

55. Culver H. Smith, 57–58.

56. Robert K. Stewart, *The Jackson Press and the Elections of 1824 and 1828* (MA thesis, University of Washington, 1984), 100.

57. Robert V. Remini, *Henry Clay: Statesman for the Union* (New York: W. W. Norton, 1991, 241.

58. Pasley, 389–390.

59. Marquis James, *The Life of Andrew Jackson* (Indianapolis: Bobbs-Merrill, 1938), 93.

60. Humphrey, 1996, 115.

61. George Dangerfield, *The Era of Good Feelings* (Chicago: Elephant Paperbacks, 1989), 345.

62. Culver S. Smith, 110.

63. Robert K. Stewart, 100.

64. Dickerson, 69–70.

65. William S. Belko, *Duff Green: A Public Life, 1791–1840* (Ph.D. dissertation, Mississippi State University, Starkville, 2002), 229.

66. Gretchen G. Ewing, "Duff Green, John C. Calhoun, and the Election of 1828," *South Carolina Historical Magazine* 79, no. 2 (April 1978), 127.

67. For more on Green, see Marshall T. Phelps, *Duff Green: American Warwick or Man of Principle?* (Ph.D. dissertation, University of Memphis, 1995); David W. Moore, *Duff Green and the South, 1824–45* (Ph.D. dissertation, Miami University, 1983); and Kenneth L. Smith, *Duff Green and the United States Telegraph, 1826–1837* (Ph.D. dissertation, College of William and Mary, 1981).

68. Belko, 87–88.

69. *Ibid.*, 64.

70. See Gretchen G. Ewing, "Duff Green: Independent Editor of a Party Press," *Journalism Quarterly* 54, no. 1 (Winter 1977), 733–739.

71. Ames, 157. The charge had a greater significance than perhaps Adams realized. Although Green perforce advocated the cause of Jackson, his abiding interest, as would later become clear, was always to advance the career of Calhoun. After Green took control of the *Telegraph*, the *National Journal* wryly commented that although ostensibly a vehicle for the promotion of Jackson, the paper "almost exclusively devotes its columns to the Vice President." Ewing, 1978, 129.

72. Dicken-Garcia, 101.

73. Fletcher M. Green, "Duff Green, Militant Journalist of the Old School," *The American Historical Review* 52 (October 1946), 251.

74. After the Jacksonians took control of the House in the elections in 1828, Green secured the printing rights for that chamber also, for the Twentieth Congress. During the Twenty-Second Congress (1831–33) Green received $34,152.51 for the Senate printing and $108,566.14 for the House printing, in addition to $6,000 for the Supreme Court printing. Baldasty, 1984, 14.

75. Culver S. Smith, 80.

76. Robert V. Remini, *The Election of Andrew Jackson* (Philadelphia: J.B. Lippincott, 1963), 124.

77. Claude G. Bowers, *The Party Battles of the Jackson Period* (Boston: Houghton Mifflin, 1922), 35.

78. Mary W. M. Hargreaves, *The Presidency of John Quincy Adams* (Lawrence: University Press of Kansas, 1985), 285.

79. Mott, 1944, 351–352.

80. Remini, 1963, 118–119.

81. Bowers, 1922, 32.

82. Culver S. Smith, 60.

83. Tebbel and Watts, 75.

84. Lee Benson, "Who Led the Democrats and the Whigs?" in *New Perspectives on Jacksonian Parties and Politics*, Edward Pessen (Boston: Allyn and Bacon, 1969), 74. Croswell's father had founded and edited the *Catskill Recorder*, and had made him an apprentice by 1811 and a partner by 1819. Croswell averaged over $15,000 per annum in state printing contracts for the *Albany Argus* between 1827 and 1832. "I would go through grape-shot to turn Croswell out of his office," an envious Horace Greeley remarked in a letter dated May 30, 1839. Gerald, 213.

85. Donald B. Cole, *Martin Van Buren and the American Political System* (Princeton, NJ: Princeton University Press, 1984), 87.

86. Baldasty, 1984, 11.

87. Elbert B. Smith, *Francis Preston Blair* (New York: Free Press, 1980), 31.

88. See Harry Ammon, "The Richmond Junto, 1800–1824," *The Virginia Magazine of History and Biography* 51 (1953), 395–418.

89. Ted Widmer, *Martin Van Buren* (New York: Times Books, 2005), 60.

90. Richard H. Brown, "The Jacksonian Pro-Slavery Party," in Pessen, 285–286.

91. Richard P. McCormick, *The Second American Party System: Party Formation in the Jacksonian Era* (Chapel Hill: University of North Carolina Press, 1966), 61.

92. Baldasty, 1984, 12. For more on the emerging Democratic press in Massachusetts, see Gerald J. Baldasty, *The Political Press in the Second American Party System: The 1832 Election*, (Ph.D. dissertation, University of Washington, 1978), chap. 3–4.

93. Remini, 1963, 49.

94. Widmer, 2005, 60.

95. Baldasty, 1992, 18.

96. Culver S. Smith, 69.

97. Ames, 166.

98. Wilentz, 306. Webster agreed, telling Clay that Hammond's publication was "certainly ably & vigorously conducted." See also Norma Basch, "Marriage, Morals, and Politics in the Election of 1828," *Journal of American History*, Vol. 80, No. 3, December 1993, pp. 890–918.

99. Remini, 1963, 128.

100. Bowers, 1922, 32.

101. Robert K. Stewart, 117.

102. See Culver H. Smith, "Propaganda Technique in the Jackson Campaign of 1828," *East Tennessee Historical Society Publication*, no. 6 (1934).

103. M.J. Heale, *The Presidential Quest: Candidates and Images in American Political Culture, 1787–1852* (New York: Longman, 1982), 74.

104. For more on Green's role during the election of 1828 see Belko, especially chap. 8–13.

105. Rubin, 36.

106. John Hampden Pleasants, editor of the *Richmond Whig*, had first published the circular ten days earlier. Samuel Flagg Bemis, *John Quincy Adams and the Union* (New York: Alfred A. Knopf, 1965), 141. The attack on Jackson's marital status concluded by asserting that "anyone approving of Andrew Jackson must therefore declare in favor of the philosophy that any man wanting anyone else's pretty wife has nothing to do but take his pistol in one hand a horsewhip in another and possess her." Kerwin C. Swint, *Mudslingers: The Top 25 Negative Political Campaigns of All Time* (Westport, CT: Praeger, 2006), 215–216.

107. Belko, 153–154.

108. Robert V. Remini, "Election of 1828," in Schlesinger, 1994, 110.

109. Remini in Schlesinger, 1994, 111. The Jackson men enjoyed the last laugh. Following the election, the citizens of Philadelphia resolved to punish Binns by carrying him through the streets of the City of Brotherly Love in an open coffin. As they assembled before his house, Binns bolted his doors and fled to the roof with his wife. After failing to force the entrance, the mob settled down to throw stones at the editor's windows and hoot invitations for him to join them on a moonlight ride. The scene was repeated for three nights before the Jackson men gave up their fun. Stefan Lorant, *The Glorious Burden* (New York: Harper & Row, 1968), 123.

110. Belko, 141.

111. James E. Pollard, *The Presidents and the Press* (New York: Macmillan, 1947), 152.

112. Robert V. Remini, *Andrew Jackson, Vol. II: The Course of American Freedom, 1822–1832* (Baltimore: Johns Hopkins University Press, 1981), 145.

113. Remini, 1963, 185.

114. Culver S. Smith, 82.

115. Green, 249.

116. *Ibid.*, 250.

117. Tebbel and Watts, 88.

118. Remini, 1981, 154.

119. Bowers, 1922, 66.

120. James, 190.

121. Meg Jacobs, William J. Novak and Julian E. Zelizer, *The Democratic Experiment: New Directions in American Political History* (Princeton, NJ: Princeton University Press, 2003), 61.

122. Bowers, 1922, 51.

123. Tebbel and Watts, 81.

124. Edward Pessen, *Jacksonian America: Society, Personality, and Politics* (Homewood, IL: Dorsey Press, 1969), 338.

125. See Donald B. Cole, *A Jackson Man: Amos Kendall and the Rise of American Democracy* (Baton Rouge: Louisiana State University Press, 2004), chap. 9 ("Reform").

126. Culver S. Smith, 91–92.

127. Ames, 181.

128. "Invade the freedom of the Press, and the freedom of Election, by showering patronage too much on Editors of newspapers and on members of Congress, and the rights of the people themselves are exposed to imminent danger," Ritchie concluded. "I know this was not the *motive* of such appointments; but I argue about *effects*." Dicken-Garcia, 105.

129. Culver S. Smith, 93. "I have, I assure you, none of those fears, and forebodings, which appears to disturb the repose of mr Ritchie," Jackson concluded. "Say to him, before he condemns the Tree, he ought to wait and see it fruit." Jackson called on Van Buren to give Ritchie a good "dressing down" in "the most delicate manner," but on this point of principle the editor refused to toe the party line. In an editorial for the *National Journal* dated August 18, Ritchie expressed his earnest wish that "the Executive would let the Press alone. We cannot any more approve of the appointments of so many of its conductors to office, although they be required to give up their papers, than we approved of the great pains which were taken by Mr. Clay to turn obnoxious editors out ... and to put in his devoted Partizans." This attitude cut little ice with the president. In a reply to another correspondent, dated May 13, 1829, while conceding the truth that "the press being an important essential in the maintenance of our republican institutions, its freedom and purity can not be too carefully guarded," Jackson reiterated the point that editors "were actuated by the same generous and patriotic impulse that the people were," and asked, "why should this class of citizens be excluded from offices to which others, not more patriotic, nor presenting stronger claims as to qualification may aspire?" Proscribing newspaper editors from public office would only mean "men of uncompromising and sterling integrity will no longer be found in the ranks of those who edit our public journals." Jackson emphasized this association of patronage with editorial talent in a letter to John Randolph on November 11, 1831:

> I was never sensible of the justness of the exceptions stated to the employment of Printers in the public service. The press is the Palladium of our liberties. Disenfranchise those who conduct it: or what is the same thing make the calling of an editor a disqualification for the possession of those rewards which are calculated to enlarge the sphere of talent and merit, and which are accessible to other callings in life, and you necessarily degrade it ... it is the object of all who really take an interest in the honor and welfare of our country to elevate the character of the press and make it the vehicle of truth and useful knowledge. What scheme

can be more subversive of this object than one which virtually withdraws from the service of the press those who aspire to some higher character in life than that of mere agents for the advancement and distinction of others?

In his last word on the subject, Jackson informed Randolph, "I refuse to consider the editorial calling as unfit to offer a candidate to office." Dicken-Garcia, 103–106.

130. See Bowers, 1922, 80–87.

131. Rubin, 39.

132. Culver S. Smith, 100.

133. Green, 253.

134. Belko, 242.

135. *Ibid.*, 244.

136. See Belko, chap. 15 ("Appointments and Patronage"), and Robert P. Patrick, Jr., *In the Interest of the South: The Life and Career of Duff Green* (Ph.D. dissertation, University of South Carolina, 2000), 66–76.

137. Terry L. Shoptaugh, *Amos Kendall: A Political Biography* (Ph.D. dissertation, University of New Hampshire, 1984), 166.

138. Cole, 2004, 96–97.

139. Elbert B. Smith, 37.

140. See John F. Marszalek, *The Petticoat Affair* (New York: Free Press, 1997), especially 149–156. See also Belko, chap. 18 ("The Eaton Affairs").

141. Belko, 259.

142. Remini, 1981, 236.

143. Culver S. Smith, 122. See also William E. Smith, "Francis P. Blair, Pen-Executive of Andrew Jackson," *Mississippi Valley Historical Review* 17, no. 1 (March 1931), 545–547.

144. Baldasty, 1978, 32.

145. Remini, 1981, 294.

146. For more on the origins of the *Globe*, see Michael W. Singletary, "The New Editorial Voice for Andrew Jackson: Happenstance, or Plan?" *Journalism Quarterly* 54, no. 4 (Winter 1976), 672–678, and William Ernest Smith, *The Francis Preston Blair Family in Politics, Vol. 1* (New York: Macmillan, 1933), chap. 6–7.

147. Wilentz, 289–290.

148. William Ernest Smith, 68.

149. Baldasty, 1978, 40.

150. Elbert B. Smith, 54.

151. *Ibid.*, 55.

152. Belko, 261–262.

153. *Ibid.*, 263–264.

154. Donald B. Cole, *The Presidency of Andrew Jackson* (Lawrence: University Press of Kansas, 1993), 90.

155. Kielbowicz, 69.

156. Baldasty, 1984, 14. See also Tebbel and Watts, 81–82.

157. A Senate investigation conducted by the Whigs in 1834 revealed that between December 1, 1831 and October 26, 1833, Blair received $21,634.90 for Post Office printing, far in excess of the $14,371.57 reported by Postmaster General Barry. The rates paid to Blair "are enormous, and, in our opinion, are not to be justified by reference to anything which has occurred in the past history of this department," the Whigs complained. Baldasty, 1978, 41.

158. *Ibid.*, 41–42.

159. Frederic Hudson, quoted in Tebbel and Watts, 90. This perspective was endorsed by the powerful Jacksonian senator Thomas Hart Benton: "The *Globe* was a powerful assistant, both as an ally working in its own columns, and as a vehicle of communication for our daily debates." Ritchie, 1991, 24–25.

160. See Bowers, 1922, chap. 6 ("Kitchen Cabinet Portraits"). See also Richard B. Latner, "The Kitchen Cabi-

net and Andrew Jackson's Advisory System," *The Journal of American History* 65, no. 2 (September, 1978), 367–388, and Cole, 2004, chap. 11 ("The Kitchen Cabinet").

161. According to Congressman Henry Wise, Kendall's function was to give an everyday elegance to the languid intellect of the President, insofar as Jackson "could think, but could not write; he knew what nerve to touch, but he was no surgeon skilled in the instrument of dissection." Wise found Kendall personally "unscrupulous" but "indefatigable" and "able." Andrew Burstein, *The Passions of Andrew Jackson* (New York: Alfred A. Knopf, 2003), 196.

162. Noble E. Cunningham, Jr., *Popular Images of the Presidency: From Washington to Lincoln* (Columbia: University of Missouri Press, 1991), 149.

163. Schlesinger, 1946, 67.

164. Cole, 2004, 163.

165. William E. Smith, "Francis P. Blair, Pen-Executive of Andrew Jackson," in Ford and Emery (Minneapolis: University of Minnesota Press, 1954), 144. Even after succeeding Jackson to the presidency, Van Buren lacked the authority to impose his will on Blair, whose overriding priority was to prevent the emergence of an upstart editor with the potential to impose on him the same fate he had inflicted on Green. When John L. O'Sullivan, the twenty-three-year-old co-owner of the Georgetown *Metropolitan*, launched the *Democratic Review* in 1837, a publication with aspirations to national influence, he sincerely believed that he was doing so on the basis of an understanding with Van Buren whereby the new venture would receive a share of the executive branch's printing contracts, "of which," as he pointed out to the President, "a single word of General Jackson has controlled the dispersal." The hostility of Blair, who would not tolerate the emergence of a rival to the *Globe*, led to Van Buren's reneging on this commitment. Robert D. Sampson, *John L. O'Sullivan and His Times* (Kent, OH: Kent State University Press, 2003), 25.

166. Belko, 280–281.

167. *Ibid.*, 307.

168. Marszalek, 1997, 153–154.

169. Belko, 276.

170. Culver S. Smith, 120.

171. Marszalek, 1997, 161.

172. *Ibid.*, 165.

173. Remini, 1981, 309.

174. Baldasty, 1978, 34.

175. Belko, 314.

176. Baldasty, 1984, 8–9.

177. Culver S. Smith, 134.

178. Remini, 1981, 309.

179. Green, 252. Even the *National Gazette* was moved to comment that Blair's attack represented "one of the most brutal, cowardly, and disgraceful outrages, it has ever been our duty to record." Green later sued Blair for damages, being awarded $350. The volatile Blair committed suicide less than two years later, after reading part of a love letter from his wife to Governor John Murphy of Alabama.

180. Shoptaugh, 294–295.

181. Cole, 2004, 176. In Jackson's second term, Green tried to keep the old fires stoked. The president's adamantine stance against nullification, he asserted, represented "in all its naïve deformity, the despotic principles of the Executive." Belko, 367–368. But his heart was not in the struggle; he ultimately sold out of the *Telegraph* (which folded on February 21, 1837) to pursue other interests.

182. For more on Kendall, see Baxter F. Melton, Jr., *Amos Kendall in Kentucky, 1814–1829: The Journalistic Beginnings of the "Master Mind" of Andrew Jackson's "Kitchen Cabinet"* (Ph.D. dissertation, Southern Illinois

University at Carbondale, 1978); James D. Daniels, *Amos Kendall: Cabinet-Politician, 1829–1841* (Ph.D. dissertation, University of North Carolina at Chapel Hill, 1968); Lynne L. Marshall, *The Early Career of Amos Kendall: The Making of a Jacksonian* (Ph.D. dissertation, University of California, Berkeley, 1962); and Powrie V. Doctor, *Amos Kendall, Propagandist of Jacksonian Democracy* (Ph.D. dissertation, Georgetown University, 1940).

183. Schlesinger, 1946, 72–73. Although *in* the highest circles of the land Kendall was always subject to reminders that he was not *of* them, even by those he served. Jackson's Tennessee confidant, Alfred Balch, encountering Kendall at a presidential dinner, sniffed that his "watchfulness and awkwardness" contrasted poorly with "the polished conversation the graceful manner & high tone" of the real elite. "To me he does not look like a Gentleman and therefore I could not talk to him. The truth is if a man is not raised as a gentleman he can never be one." Cole, 2004, 195; Lynn L. Marshall, "Opposing Democratic and Whig Concepts of Party Organization," in *New Perspectives on Jacksonian Parties and Politics*, Edward Pessen (Boston: Allyn and Bacon, 1969), 47.

184. Marshall in Pessen, 1969, 44. For more on Kendall's role in shaping this message, see Lynn L. Marshall, "The Authorship of Jackson's Bank Veto Message," *Mississippi Valley Historical Review* 50, no. 3 (December, 1963), 466–477. See also the conclusion reached in Cole, 2004, 165.

185. Pessen, 1969, 332.

186. *Ibid.*, 334. See also Frank Otto Gatell, "Spoils of the Bank War: Political Bias in the Selection of Pet Banks," *American Historical Review* 70, no. 1 (October 1964), 35–58.

187. See Dickerson, chap. 4 ("'Their Mad and Wicked Schemes': Abolitionists and the Post Office").

188. Belko, 339–340.

189. Baldasty, 1984, 12.

190. Ames, 191.

191. Tebbel and Watts, 88.

192. Robert V. Remini, "Election of 1832," in Schlesinger, 1994, 124.

193. Baldasty, 1984, 10.

194. Bowers, 1922, 221.

195. Robertson, 76–77.

196. Remini, 1981, 377.

197. Pessen, 1969, 176.

198. Remini in Schlesinger, 1994, 125.

199. Humphrey, 1996, 126.

200. Baldasty, 1978, 50–52.

201. Oliver Carlson, *The Man Who Made News: James Gordon Bennett* (New York: Duell, Sloan & Pearce, 1942), 100.

202. Belko, 341.

203. Carlson, 101.

204. James L. Crouthamel, *James Watson Webb: A Biography* (Middletown, CT: Wesleyan University Press, 1969), 25.

205. Crouthamel, 1969, chap. 4.

206. Remini, 1981, 375.

207. Bowers, 1922, 228. See also Thomas Payne Govan, *Nicholas Biddle: Nationalist and Public Banker, 1786–1844* (Chicago: University of Chicago Press, 1959).

208. This is the standard account, but Belko, 429–430, suggests it was Duff Green who first popularized the term "Whig."

209. Robert Gray Gunderson, *The Log-Cabin Campaign* (Lexington: University of Kentucky Press, 1957), 9.

210. Page Smith, 1981, 906.

211. George H. Douglas, *The Golden Age of the Newspaper* (Westport, CT: Greenwood Press, 1999), 19–20.

Webb was a staunch anti-abolitionist during the infancy of the movement. "Are we to tamely look on and see this most dangerous species of fanaticism extending itself through society?" he asked in 1833. Was it not the duty of every citizen to crush "this many-headed hydra in the bud?" Dickerson, 117.

212. Crouthamel, 1969, 72.

213. See Donald E. Emerson, *Richard Hildreth* (Baltimore: Johns Hopkins University Press, 1946), especially chap. 3 ("A Whig Journalist").

214. William Preston Vaughn, *The Antimasonic Party in the United States, 1826–1843* (Lexington: University Press of Kentucky, 1983), 26. For more on the Anti-Masons, see Baldasty, 1978, chap. 5 ("Antimasons and the Press").

215. Milton W. Hamilton, *The Country Printer: New York State, 1785–1830* (New York: Columbia University Press, 1936), 130.

216. Benson in Pessen, 1969, 77.

217. Sidney David Brummer, "Political History of New York State During the Period of the Civil War," *Studies in History, Economics and Public Law* 39, no. 2 (1911), 19. See also Glyndon G. Van Deusen, *Thurlow Weed: Wizard of the Lobby* (Boston: Little, Brown, 1947).

218. Gunderson, 31.

219. Manber and Dahlstrom, 25.

220. Edwin Emery, 182.

221. Witcover, 154. Weed's contempt for Van Buren was as palpable as it was consistent. In 1844 the editor labeled the ex-president, then angling for a comeback, "a little, old, red-faced, fat man." Thurlow Weed to Francis Granger, March 11, 1844, *Thurlow Weed Papers*, University of Rochester, New York.

222. Gunderson, 13.

223. Nevins, 1928, 139.

224. Elbert B. Smith, 129.

225. William Ernest Smith, 140.

226. For background, see Gerald, 104–106.

227. See William Groneman III, *David Crockett: Hero of the Common Man* (New York: Tom Doherty Associates, 2005), especially chap. 6–8, and Buddy Levy, *American Legend: The Real-Life Adventures of David Crockett* (New York: Putnam's, 2005), especially chap. 12–13.

228. Gunderson, 110.

229. Gerald, 246–247.

230. Gregory Borchard, *The Firm of Greeley, Weed, and Seward: New York Partisanship and the Press, 1840–1860* (Ph.D. dissertation, University of Florida, 2003), 46.

231. Elbert B. Smith, 130.

232. Todd smoothly integrated this responsibility into the role of the President's private secretary once Harrison took office. Nevins, 1928, 141.

233. Elbert B. Smith, 134.

234. Gerald, 290. The campaign witnessed the emergence of a new angle of attack in the Democratic press, linking the Whigs with the campaign for the abolition of slavery, which had increased in salience during the 1830s. As early as December 23, 1839, the *Globe* was asking its readers, "Will any tell us there is no sympathy between Whigs and these fanatics of the North?" The assault continued on New Year's Day, 1840: "Whiggery at the North," the *Globe* declared, "is naturally allied to Abolitionism and accordingly in whatever State, district or town the Whigs have the ascendancy there we find the Abolitionists strongest and most numerous." In the West, the *Ohio Statesman* picked up on this cue and chimed in with a prediction that upon the election of Harrison, "the TWENTY-SIX MILLIONS of the surplus revenue now deposited with the States will be appropriated to the purchase of refugee negroes, to be set free and overrun our country." Gerald, 241–242.

235. William Ernest Smith, 135.
236. Gunderson, 127.
237. See L. D. Ingersoll, "Chiefly of the 'Log Cabin' Campaign," in *The Life of Horace Greeley* (Chicago: Union Publishing, 1873), chap. 6.
238. William Miles, *The People's Voice: An Annotated Bibliography of American Presidential Campaign Newspapers, 1828–1984* (Westport, CT: Greenwood Press, 1987), 9–53.
239. Robert C. Williams, *Horace Greeley: Champion of American Freedom* (New York: New York University Press, 2006), 45.
240. Robertson, 70.
241. Gunderson, 132. Greeley made the same point in launching the *Tribune* the following year, when he promised that the new publication would be "anti-slavery, anti-war, anti-rum, anti-tobacco, anti-seduction and anti-grogshops, brothels, and gambling houses." Louis Heren, *The Power of the Press?* (London: Orbis, 1985), 41–42.
242. Gunderson, 157.
243. Tebbel and Watts, 101.
244. For more on Greeley's role in Whig politics, see Glyndon G. Van Deusen, *Horace Greeley: Nineteenth-Century Crusader* (Philadelphia: University of Pennsylvania Press, 1953), chap. 8–11.
245. Gunderson, 105.
246. *Ibid.*, 107.
247. *Ibid.*, 127.
248. Pessen, 1969, 177. Having recognized this fact, editor John L. O'Sullivan was not prepared to accept its inevitability. Comparing the campaign to a "holy war," he asserted that it was vital that Van Buren not only win but crush the Whigs, administering a "rebuke, a punishment not soon to be forgotten," not only for their policy objectives but for the "great national insult," the "deep disgrace" that constituted their campaign, which had succeeded only in bringing democracy "into contempt in the eyes of the rest of the world." Sampson, 82–84.
249. Despite this subterfuge, the Whig won. Storey did publish a retraction saying that his report of the victor's demise had been without foundation—but he published this four days *after* the election. William E. Huntzicker, *The Popular Press, 1833–1865* (Westport, CT: Greenwood Press, 1999), 38.
250. Gunderson, 86.
251. Kielbowicz, 70.
252. Gunderson, 233.
253. *Ibid.*, 194.
254. *Ibid.*, 200.
255. Pollard, 208.
256. Democratic papers, of course, had a different spin on the outcome of the election. "The people of the country have been wronged, their intelligence insulted; their understanding trifled with; they have been cheated out of their rights," the *Globe* wailed. For the first time in U.S. history—or at least since 1824—"profligacy, villainy and fraud" had "overthrown the popular will." O'Sullivan chimed in by adding that "never was astonishment more sincere or more profound" than at the necessity of admitting the American people "capable of this foolish thing.... Nations, too, it would seem, like individuals, have their occasional fits of delirium ... when reason yields her throne to a brief insanity." Sampson, 85, 86. Interestingly, Greeley refused to claim his legitimate place at the patronage teat for services rendered during the campaign. "I s'pose I might have got some wretched claw at 'the spoils' by hard elbowing," he wrote a friend, "but I have told all the magnates that I won't have the smell of anything." Robert C. Williams, 54.
257. Cole, 2004, 224.

258. Elbert B. Smith, 145.
259. Horace Greeley, *Recollections of a Busy Life* (New York: J.B. Ford, 1868), 138.
260. Elbert B. Smith, 146.
261. Ames, 263.
262. See William W. Freehling, *The Road to Disunion, Vol. I: Secessionists at Bay, 1776–1854* (New York: Oxford University Press, 1990), chap. 21 ("An Extremist's Zany Pilgrimage"). For more on Green's pro-slavery machinations, see Patrick, chap. 5 ("The Pilot, Foreign Activities, and a Last Attempt to Make Calhoun President"). Upon returning to the United States, Green established the *New York Republic* on January 22, 1844, as a vehicle for Calhoun's phantasmagorical presidential ambitions and later as a booster of Polk. Subsequent forays into print included the *Daily American Telegraph* in 1852 and the *American Statesman* in 1857, short-lived efforts to defend slavery and Southern rights. During the Civil War, Green offered more active support to slavery, manufacturing material for the front lines at his Jonesboro, Tennessee, iron works on contract with the Confederate government.
263. John M. Belohlaver, "The Democracy in a Dilemma: George M. Dallas, Pennsylvania, and the Election of 1844," *Pennsylvania History* 41, no. 4 (Fall 1974), 399.
264. Remini, 1991, 647.
265. Elbert B. Smith, 159. For further manifestations of rivalry between the partisan presses, see Steven W. Short, *Texas Annexation and the Presidential Election of 1844 in the Richmond, Virginia and New Orleans, Louisiana, Newspapers* (MA Thesis, University of North Texas, 2001).
266. Silbey, 55.
267. Sheldon H. Harris, "John Louis O'Sullivan and the Election of 1844 in New York," *New York History* 41, no. 3 (Summer 1960), 288.
268. Sampson, 175. When a Whig writer contemptuously dismissed Polk as "Young Hickory," it was O'Sullivan who seized on the charge, emphasizing it honored rather than denigrated the Democratic nominee. The nickname stuck. *Ibid.*, 169.
269. Harris, 293, 295. For an excellent depiction of the influence of O'Sullivan at the nexus of politics and literature during this period, see Edward L. Widmer, *Young America: The Flowering of Democracy in New York City* (New York: Oxford University Press, 1999).
270. Frederick Merk, *The Monroe Doctrine and American Expansion, 1843–1849,* (New York: Alfred A. Knopf, 1966), 75. For an interesting etymological digression, see Julius W. Pratt, "The Origin of 'Manifest Destiny,'" *American Historical Review* 32, no. 4 (July 1927), 795–798. After selling out of his literary interests, O'Sullivan was arrested and tried for violation of the Neutrality Act after playing a role in a filibustering exhibition against Cuba. He subsequently served two Democratic administrations as consul to Portugal during the 1850s before selling out his country by advancing the cause of, and accepting citizenship in, the Confederacy during the Civil War.
271. Ames, 273.
272. Ingersoll, 162–163. Greeley's devotion was at least reciprocated by its recipient. Clay considered the *Tribune* a "very great" newspaper (while regretting its "eccentricities") and considered Greeley "surpassed by no other editor in the Union." Robert C. Williams, 54.
273. Vernon L. Volpe, "The Liberty Party and Polk's Election," *Historian* 53, no. 4 (Summer 1991). Greeley's commenced his lamentations the moment the result of the election became undeniable: "It will take some time to shake wholly off the nightmare which weighed us to the earth from the announcement of the extraordinary, unexpected, and most foully won majority in this city," he editorialized on November 7. Weed held out hope that the

election result, "however disastrous in other respects," would "open the eyes of the people to the reckless designs and fatal tendencies of ultra Abolitionists." But the defeat of Clay weighed heavily on him. "The country owes much of its misrule and misery," he wrote bitterly, "to the action of minorities—well-meaning, patriotic, but misguided minorities." He actively considered quitting the newspaper trade and, for a period, politics altogether. Word reached Lieutenant Governor George Washington Patterson, who wrote the editor "I hear some talk about your leaving the 'Evening Journal,' and I protest against it most earnestly and solemnly." Borchard, 83.

274. The press would be intimately associated with Cameron's own political aspirations. By the time he was twenty-two, he was already editor of two Pennsylvania papers, the *Bucks County Messenger* and the *Doylestown Democrat*. Within a year he moved to Washington where he worked as a journeyman printer for the *National Intelligencer*, returning to the Keystone State to enter into a partnership with the *Pennsylvania Intelligencer*, the Jacksonian organ in the state capital, Harrisburg. After two years as the state printer in Pennsylvania, Cameron became associated with a number of business interests, including the operation of several railroad companies and the founding of a bank, which in 1845 led to the first of two non-consecutive terms in the U.S. Senate (the second being an appointment to a vacated seat in 1857). By the time the 1860 Republican convention opened at the Wigwam in Chicago, Cameron was Pennsylvania's favorite son and had the state's most influential newspaper, the *Evening Bulletin*, in his pocket. It wasn't enough to win him the nomination, but it did secure him a place in Lincoln's Cabinet.

275. See Elbert B. Smith, chap. 11, and William Ernest Smith, chap. 15. Bitterness at the Southern cabal that had ousted him drove Blair to support the Free Soil crusade in 1848 and ultimately into the Republican Party. During the campaign of 1856, Blair announced that "*the Democracy has been 'sold out'* to Mr. Calhoun's nullifying party." This "spurious Democracy," dancing to the tune of the "perfect Southern phalanx" that threatened disunion, had "perfected its system in the Kansas[-Nebraska] act, and made it their test." In defiance of this sectional agenda, "I, as a Democrat of the Jefferson, Jackson, and Van Buren school, enter my protest." Wilentz, 704.

276. Wilentz, 578. Vindicating Jackson's concern over the sectional implications of evicting Blair, O'Sullivan commented that Polk's agenda left the remaining Democratic newspapers in Washington "Southern — Southern and rotten." Sampson, 186.

277. Witcover, 176. Even Polk had mixed feelings about the capacities of his new editorial advocate. "Mr. Ritchie meant well," the president admitted on one occasion; indeed, he "might occasionally make mistakes, but he was always ready to correct them when informed of them." Polk's misgivings would only grow over time.

278. See Osthaus, chap. 2 ("Between Nationalism and Nullification").

279. *Ibid.*, 12–13.

280. *Ibid.*, 30. For more on Ritchie, see Wade L. Shaffer, *The Richmond Junto and Politics in Jacksonian Virginia* (Ph.D. dissertation, College of William and Mary, 1993) and Bert M. Mutersbaugh, *Jeffersonian Journalist: Thomas Ritchie and the Richmond Enquirer, 1804–1820,* (Ph.D. dissertation, University of Missouri at Columbia, 1973).

281. Osthaus, 29–30.

282. *Ibid.*, 31.

283. Barbara Holland, *Gentlemen's Blood: A History of Dueling, from Swords at Dawn to Pistols at Dusk* (New York: Bloomsbury, 2003), 178. William & Mary educated,

a onetime attaché with the U.S. legations in Berlin and Paris, Wise fought no fewer than eight duels in less than two years. Incredibly, he never succeeded in hitting an opponent, and was never even scratched in return. His luck finally ran out during the Civil War when he was killed in Confederate service.

284. Holland, 180–181.

285. See John H. Franklin, *The Militant South* (Cambridge, MA: Harvard University Press, 1956), 33–61.

286. Jack K. Williams, *Dueling in the Old South: Vignettes of Social History* (College Station: Texas A&M University Press, 1980), 11. Georgians were touchy too; Governor James Jackson was compelled to kill the state's lieutenant governor because the latter had accused him of having an overbearing personality.

287. *Ibid.*, 32–33.

288. Holland, 176–177.

289. *Ibid.*, 177.

290. Holland, 176.

291. David Dary, *Red Blood and Black Ink: Journalism in the Old West* (New York: Alfred A. Knopf, 1998), 119.

292. Holland, 175–176.

293. Holland, 176.

294. Frederick B. Marbut, "Decline of the Official Press in Washington," *Journalism Quarterly* 33, no. 2 (Summer 1956), 336–337.

295. Ritchie, 1991, 28.

296. Osthaus, 17.

297. Ames, 282. Allen's good fortune extended to his being able to sell out of the *Madisonian* after Tyler's departure from the White House rendered it no longer viable. The new proprietor, Jesse Dow, had purchased the paper, only for the incoming Polk to pass it over in favor of Ritchie's *Washington Union*, which subsequently secured a clean sweep of the patronage by being elected official printer to both houses of Congress. Dow led the *Madisonian* into an editorial stance of plague-on-both-your-houses objectivity, only for it to inevitably fold shortly thereafter.

298. Culver S. Smith, 191.

299. Nevins, 174.

300. John Gerring, *Party Ideologies in America, 1828–1996* (Cambridge, MA: Cambridge University Press, 1998), 175.

301. The first hint of the factionalization within the Democratic Party over slavery, that would culminate in the Free Soil bolt, was the battle between the Barnburners and Hunkers for the state printing privileges for their respective newspapers, the *Albany Atlas* and *Albany Argus*, in 1843. See John Niven, *Martin Van Buren: The Romantic Age of American Politics* (New York: Oxford University Press, 1983), 513–514. A notable advocate for the Free Soil campaign of 1848 was the Brooklyn *Daily Freeman*, founded and edited by Walt Whitman.

302. Culver S. Smith, 181.

303. See Ames, 294–296.

304. Dickerson, 73.

305. Culver S. Smith, 185. Speaking for the administration "by authority," the *Register* dubbed Weed "Generalissimo-in-chief of the Abolition forces." In his zeal to effect sectional reconciliation, Fillmore concentrated the power of the patronage at his disposal in a bid to purge the Whig Party of abolition sympathizers. All federal office holders suspected of fidelity to Weed were requested to resign their posts. Borchard, 119.

306. Culver S. Smith, 219.

307. See Mark W. Summers, 1987, chap. 2 ("The Hireling Press").

308. Culver S. Smith, 219–220

309. *Ibid.*, 224.

310. Mark W. Summers, 1987, 50.

311. Pollard, 299.

312. Culver S. Smith, 230.

313. Howard C. Perkins, "The Defense of Slavery in the Northern Press on the Eve of the Civil War," *Journal of Southern History* 9, no. 4 (November 1943), 517.

314. Neither did many publications survive that had grown up inside this system and evolved in a symbiotic fashion to the point that they could no longer survive without it. In its twilight, the *National Intelligencer*, once the clearinghouse of official Washington opinion, had become, in the words of Mark Twain, the kind of journal "that regularly comes out in the most sensational and aggressive manner, every morning, with news it ought to have printed the day before." Gales died in August 1860, after forty-eight years at the helm. Seaton retired in December 1864. The paper itself folded four years later. Ritchie, 1991, 33.

315. See Streitmatter, chap. 2 ("Abolition: Turning America's Conscience Against the Sins of Slavery") and Bernell Tripp, "Journalism for God and Man," in *The Press in Times of Crisis*, ed. Lloyd Chiasson, Jr. (Westport, CT: Greenwood Press, 1995), chap. 4.

316. See Hohnberg, 114–118. For more on mob violence against abolitionists, see Dickerson, chap. 5 ("'The Savage Populace': Violence Against Abolitionists").

317. H. Edward Richardson, *Cassius Marcellus Clay: Firebrand of Freedom* (Lexington: University Press of Kentucky, 1976), 45–46.

318. Osthaus, 42–43.

319. John L. Brooke, "To be 'Read by the Whole People': Press, Party, and Public Sphere in the United States, 1789–1840," *Proceedings of the American Antiquarian Society* 110, Part 1 (2002), 61.

320. Osthaus, 10.

321. Typical of editorial reaction in the South to the Charles Sumner/Preston Brooks imbroglio on the floor of the Senate, the *Richmond Enquirer* declared, "We consider the act good in conception, better in execution, and best of all in consequences. The vulgar Abolitionists in the Senate are getting above themselves.... They must be lashed into submission." Wilentz, 691.

322. See Kenneth S. Greenberg, *Masters and Statesmen: The Political Culture of American Slavery* (Baltimore: Johns Hopkins University Press, 1985). For the role of the media in promulgating this insularity, see Donald B. Kelley, "Intellectual Isolation: Gateway to Secession in Mississippi," *Journal of Mississippi History* 36, no. 1 (February 1974), 17–37. It should be noted that although all Southerners were united in their defiance of Yankee interference in Southern institutions, only a minority advocated secession at the beginning of the 1850s. As late as 1857 the *Richmond Enquirer* could still attack the "idle twaddle" of the fire eaters, who considered themselves the "anointed defenders" of the South and slavery, singling out the *Charleston Mercury* for its "editorial ravings" and "hopeless insanity." By the end of the decade, however, a consensus had emerged that a Republican victory in 1860 justified the dissolution of the Union. The outbreak of war removed any lingering doubts.

323. Mark W. Summers, 1987, 37.

324. Rubin, 52.

325. Jensen, 37.

326. Stephen Ponder, *Managing the Press: Origins of the Media Presidency, 1897–1933* (New York: St. Martin's Press, 1998), xiii.

327. Osthaus, 3.

328. Greeley, 280.

329. Thurlow Weed, *Life of Thurlow Weed, Vol. II* (New York: Houghton Mifflin, 1883–1884), 125.

330. See Tyler Anbinder, *Nativism and Slavery: The Northern Know Nothings and the Politics of the 1850s* (New York: Oxford University Press, 1992).

331. The standard texts on this subject are Eric Foner, *Free Soil, Free Labor, Free Men: The Ideology of the Republican Party before the Civil War* (New York: Oxford University Press, 1995) and Richard H. Sewell, *Ballots for Freedom: Antislavery Politics in the United States, 1827–1860* (New York: W. W. Norton, 1976). For a case study, see Michael F. Holt, *Forging a Majority: The Formation of the Republican Party in Pittsburgh, 1848–1860* (New Haven, CT: Yale University Press, 1969).

332. Joseph S. Myers, "The Genius of Horace Greeley," *Journalism Series No. 6* (Columbus: Ohio State University Press, 1929), 22.

333. Henry L. Stoddard, *Horace Greeley: Printer, Editor, Crusader* (New York: Putnam's, 1946), 166.

334. Stoddard, 167. Greeley's passionate advocacy of the new party swiftly landed him in yet another physical confrontation. When Democratic representative Albert Rust of Arkansas proposed that all leading contenders withdraw in favor of a compromise candidate after the badly fragmented House elected in 1854 cast its 118th unsuccessful ballot in a bid to elect a Speaker, Greeley, who saw the proposal as a ruse by which to thwart the election of the Republican nominee, reacted indignantly. "I have had some acquaintance with human degradation," he fulminated, but nothing apparently on a par with Rust's gambit, "a more discreditable proposition than I had ever known gravely submitted to a legislative body." Rust subsequently added his name to the ever-lengthening list of people to have responded to Greeley in a violent fashion, by giving the editor a sound beating at their next encounter. Ritchie, 1991, 50.

335. Thorton K. Lothrop, *William Henry Seward* (New York: Houghton Mifflin, 1896), 150.

336. Weed, 280. The lack of concern exhibited by Weed and Seward over Greeley's ultimatum was probably conditioned by their years of experience in soothing the excitable editor's ruffled feathers on the numerous occasions that his political ambition was disappointed. As far back as September 10, 1842, Greeley wrote Weed, "You have pleased on several occasions to take me to task for differing from you, as though such conditions were an evidence, not merely of weakness on my part, but of some black ingratitude, or heartless treachery." Greeley asserted that he had "never desired offices of distinction, avenues to fortune," at Weed's expense. He acknowledged his subordinate role in their relationship, that of client to patron, but denied that this gave Weed the right to override his autonomy or overlook his legitimate claims to political advancement. "I have ever been ready to give you any service within my power," he said, "but my understanding, my judgment, my consciousness of convictions, of duty and public good, these I can surrender to no man. You wrong yourself in asking them, and taking me to task, like a school-boy, for expressing my sentiments respectfully when they differ from yours." Greeley concluded his letter by apparently dissolving the partnership between the two men: "Henceforth, I pray you," he wrote, "differ from me when you see occasion, favor me in nothing, treat me as you do others." Borchard, 70–71.

337. Tebbel and Watts, 75.

338. *Ibid.*, 98–99.

339. Fermer, 15.

340. James L. Crouthamel, *Bennett's New York Herald and the Rise of the Popular Press* (Syracuse, NY: Syracuse University Press, 1989), 18.

341. Paul Peebles, "James Gordon Bennett's Brilliant Scintillations," in Ford and Edwin Emery, 153.

342. Even William Duane, combative editor of the *Aurora*, recognized the moral obligations of a newspaper editor of his day. He reflected with pride even in the twilight of his career that "I never admit into my paper accounts of murders, robberies, crimes and desperations, because habits make good or bad news, and familiarity with tales of crimes will blunt the faculties and form habits of indifference to crime." Knudson, 23.

343. Fermer, 28.

344. Francis Brown, *Raymond of the Times* (New York: W. W. Norton, 1951), 104–105. Bennett's ego did little to sooth the ruffled feathers of his editorial counterparts. In his own words, "Shakespeare is the genius of the drama, Scott of the novel, Milton and Byron of the poem — and I mean to be the genius of the newspaper press." Heren, 35.

345. Leading the charge against Bennett in the 1840 "Moral War" were the three avatars of New York's business elite, the *Journal of Commerce*, the *Commercial Advertiser*, and the *Courier and Enquirer*. In addition to ad hominem attacks, these papers kept up pressure on Bennett's advertisers and subscribers. It would take years for his circulation figures to recover.

346. Peebles in Ford and Emery, 151.

347. Borchard, 69.

348. Crouthamel, 1989, 33.

349. *Ibid.*, 1989, 36.

350. Mindich, 21–22.

351. Peebles in Ford and Emery, 156.

352. Crouthamel, 1969, 72.

353. Nevins, 1928, 118. Newspaper editors were still swinging at each other as late as 1906, when Joseph Pulitzer II threw a punch at William Randolph Hearst for maligning his father during his bid for the New York governorship. That the punch hadn't landed, the young Pulitzer later said, was "always ... one of my regrets." Daniel W. Pfaff, *Joseph Pulitzer II and the Post-Dispatch: A Newspaperman's Life* (University Park, PA: Penn State University Press, 1991), 71.

354. Peebles in Ford and Emery, 156.

355. Huntzicker, 44.

356. Page Smith, 1981, 904.

357. Crouthamel, 1989, 57.

358. *Ibid.*, 1989, 33.

359. Fermer, 62.

360. Carlson, 266. In the wake of John Brown's raid on Harpers Ferry, Bennett listed Greeley among other abolitionist conspirators who should be arraigned in court as "accomplices in treason and murder." The racist venom of the *New York Herald* was by no means restricted to African Americans. During the 1888 campaign, the paper referred to alleged Chinese supporters of Republican candidate Benjamin Harrison as "Hallison's Flends." Mark Wahlgren Summers, *Party Games: Getting, Keeping and Using Power in Gilded Age Politics* (Chapel Hill: University of North Carolina Press, 2004), 7.

361. Fermer, 83, 85.

362. Carlson, 267–268.

363. See Fermer, 91105.

364. For the standard texts on the era, see William W. Freehling, *The Road to Disunion, Vol. II: Bleeding Kansas to Fort Sumter* (New York: Oxford University Press, 2007); Michael F. Holt, *The Political Crisis of the 1850s* (New York: John Wiley & Sons, 1978); David M. Potter, *The Impending Crisis, 1848–1861* (New York: Harper & Row, 1976); Roy F. Nichols, *The Disruption of American Democracy* (New York: Macmillan, 1948); and the first two volumes of Allan Nevins' *Ordeal of the Union* series, reprinted by Collier Books, New York, 1992.

365. Tebbel and Watts, 168.

366. Small, 53.

367. *Ibid.*, 53–54.

368. Robert S. Harper, *Lincoln and the Press* (New York: McGraw-Hill, 1951), 19–20.

369. See Don C. Seitz, *Horace Greeley: Founder of the New York Tribune* (New York: AMS Press, 1970), chap. 8 ("The Republican Party"); Van Deusen, 1953, chap. 15 ("A Republican Operator"); and Ralph Ray Fahrney, *Horace Greeley and the Tribune in the Civil War* (Cedar Rapids, IA: Torch Press, 1936), chap. 1 ("Seward, Weed and Greeley").

370. See Isley, chap. 8 ("The Democratic Party is Split"). In private, Greeley was less enamored of Douglas, labeling him "a low and dangerous demagogue," a "great political sinner," and a "walking magazine of mischief" responsible for "hateful scheming and reckless legislation." Robert C. Williams, 201.

371. Stoddard, 184.

372. Robert C. Williams, 199.

373. *Ibid.*, 200.

374. Harper, 40.

375. Kobre, 1969, 288.

376. Pollard, 335.

377. Tebbel and Watts, 173.

378. Charles Adams, *When in the Course of Human Events: Arguing the Case for Southern Secession* (Lanham, MD: Rowman & Littlefield, 2000), 204. Medill served one term as mayor of Chicago, 1871–73.

379. Harper, 53. For more on the roll of Medill in "booming" Lincoln, see Tracy Elmer Strevey, *Joseph Medill and the Chicago Tribune during the Civil War Period* (PhD. dissertation, University of Chicago, 1930), chap. 3.

380. Greeley maintained he had "discharged a public duty" at Chicago. For Greeley's role at the convention, see Isely, chap. 9 ("Greeley's Contender Fails at Chicago") and Marvin R. Cain, *Lincoln's Attorney General: Edward Bates of Missouri* (Columbia: University of Missouri Press, 1965), chap. 4. See also Borchard, especially chap. 8 ("The 1860 Campaign: Splitting Rails").

381. For more on the role of New York's editors in Lincoln's tilt at the Republican nomination, see Harold Holzer, *Lincoln at Cooper Union: The Speech that Made Abraham Lincoln President* (New York: Simon & Schuster, 2005).

382. Brummer, 65–66. Weed secured a modicum of revenge by blocking Greeley's bid to fill the vacant seat in the Senate when Lincoln appointed Seward as his secretary of state.

383. Melvin L. Hayes, *Mr. Lincoln Runs for President* (New York: Citadel Press, 1960), 180.

384. Mark E. Neely, Jr., *The Boundaries of American Political Culture in the Civil War Era* (Chapel Hill: University of North Carolina Press, 2005), 5.

385. Silbey, 102. Responding in kind, the Muscogee, Alabama, *Herald* defined the Republican Party as "conglomeration of greasy mechanics, filthy operatives, small-fisted farmers, and moonstruck theorists." Wilentz, 705.

386. Howard Cecil Perkins, ed., *Northern Editorials on Secession* (Gloucester, MA: Peter Smith, 1964), 14–15.

387. Harper, 56.

388. Crouthamel, 1989, 111.

389. Albert Shaw, *Abraham Lincoln: The Year of his Election* (New York: Review of Reviews, 1929), 46.

390. Hayes, 119, 120–121.

391. *Ibid.*, 116.

392. Donald F. Reynolds, *Editors Make War: Southern Newspapers in the Secession Crisis* (Nashville: Vanderbilt University Press, 1970), 216.

393. For examples by state, see Lenette S. Taylor, "Polemics and Partisanship: The Arkansas Press in the

1860 Election," *Arkansas Historical Quarterly* 44, no. 4 (Winter 1985), 314–335; David L. Porter, "Attitudes of the Georgia Press in the Presidential Election of 1860," *Georgia Historical Quarterly* 59 (Supplement 1975), 127–133; David L. Porter, "The Kentucky Press and the Election of 1860," *Filson Club Historical Quarterly* 46, no. 1 (January 1972), 49–52; and Thomas S. Graham, "Florida Politics and the Tallahassee Press, 1845–1861," *Florida Historical Quarterly* 46, no. 3 (January 1968), 234–242.

394. Reynolds, 10.
395. Hayes, 86–87.
396. Reynolds, 36.
397. *Ibid.*, 72–75.
398. *Ibid.*, 35, 51.
399. *Ibid.*, 63.
400. *Ibid.*, 76–77.
401. David L. Porter, "The Southern Press and the Presidential Election of 1860," *West Virginia History* 33, no. 1 (October 1971), 5.
402. David L. Porter, "Attitude of the Tennessee Press Toward the Presidential Election of 1860," *Tennessee Historical Quarterly* 29, no. 4 (Winter 1970–71), 392.
403. Tebbel and Watts, 177.
404. Reynolds, 187.
405. Hayes, 106.
406. Meade Minnigerode, *Presidential Years: 1787–1860* (New York: Putnam's, 1928), 378.
407. Tebbel and Watts, 177.
408. Reynolds, 58.
409. Jay Monaghan, *The Man who Elected Lincoln* (Indianapolis: Bobbs-Merrill, 1956), 217.

Chapter III

1. See Mark E. Neely, Jr., "'Odious to Honorable Men': The Press and its Freedom in the Civil War," in *The Union Divided: Party Conflict in the Civil War North*, (Cambridge, MA: Harvard University Press, 2002), chap. 4; Robertson, 116–128 ("The Rhetorical Civil War in the Northern Press: New York, 1860–1868"); Ritchie, 1991, 57–72 ("Horace White Speculates on the War"); and Lofton, chap. 6 ("War and the First Amendment: New Tests"). For an overview, see Brayton Harris, *Blue and Gray in Black and White: Newspapers in the Civil War* (Washington, DC: Batsford Brassey, 1999), and Huntzicker, Chapters 7–8. A useful depiction of military-press relations is John F. Marszalek, *Sherman's Other War: The General and the Civil War Press* (Kent, OH: Kent State University Press, 1999). To get the perspective from both sides of the Mason-Dixon Line, see J. Cutler Andrews, *The South Reports the Civil War* (Princeton, NJ: Princeton University Press, 1970), and, conversely, J. Cutler Andrews, *The North Reports the Civil War* (Pittsburgh: University of Pittsburgh Press, 1955). For a summary, see Lorman A. Ratner and Dwight L. Teeter, Jr., *Fanatics and Fire-eaters: Newspapers and the Coming of the Civil War* (Urbana: University of Illinois Press, 2003).
2. Dicken-Garcia, 53.
3. Page Smith, 1981, 815.
4. Alfred McClung Lee, *The Daily Newspaper in America: The Evolution of a Social Instrument* (New York: Macmillan, 1937), 64–65.
5. Michael E. McGerr, *The Decline of Popular Politics: The American North, 1865–1928* (Oxford: Oxford University Press, 1986), 108.
6. Linda Lawson, *Truth in Publishing: Federal Regulation of the Press's Business Practices, 1880–1920* (Carbondale, IL: Southern Illinois University Press, 1993), 9.
7. Ponder, xiii.

8. Richard L. Kaplan, *Politics and the American Press: The Rise of Objectivity, 1865–1920* (Cambridge: Cambridge University Press, Cambridge, 2002), 129.
9. Kaplan, 129. A somewhat similar conclusion, that the rising objectivity of the media "was the result of the rising scale and competitiveness in the newspaper industry," was reached by Gentzkow, Glaeser, and Goldin. They write that by the end of the nineteenth century, "declining costs and increased city populations caused a huge increase in scale. In 1870, a newspaperman might make more money pleasing a local politician than in selling papers and advertisements. By 1920 newspapers had become big business, and they increased readership and revenue by presenting factual and informative news. Following these financial incentives, newspapers changed from being political tools to at least trying to present a façade of impartial reporting." Gentzkow, Glaeser, and Goldin. For a class-based analysis of the rise of media objectivity, see Dan Schiller, "A New Press for a New Public," *Objectivity and the News: The Public and the Rise of Commercial Journalism* (Philadelphia: University of Pennsylvania Press, 1981), 12–46.
10. Donald L. Shaw, "News Bias and the Telegraph: A Study of Historical Change," *Journalism Quarterly*, Spring 1967, 6.
11. Ritchie, 1991, 142–143.
12. Ted Curtis Smythe, *The Gilded Age Press, 1865–1900* (Westport, CT: Praeger, 2003), 18.
13. Rutenbeck, 1993, 41.
14. Ward, 200.
15. McGerr, 116.
16. For a reference to the stance of the Mugwumps, see John M. Dobson, "George William Curtis and the Election of 1884: The Dilemma of the New York Mugwumps," *New York Historical Society Quarterly* 52, no. 3 (Fall 1968), 215–234. See also Nevins, 1968, 458–475.
17. See Ritchie, 1991, 131–144 ("James G. Blaine, Journalist and Politician").
18. *Ibid.*, 67.
19. Frederic Hudson, *Journalism in the United States from 1690–1872* (New York: Haskell House, 1873), 410, 414. See also Robertson, 146–163 ("Loss of Public Principles and Public Interest: Gilded Age Rhetoric, 1872–1896").
20. Jean H. Baker, *Affairs of Party: The Political Culture of Northern Democrats in the Mid-Nineteenth Century* (Ithaca, NY: Cornell University Press, 1983), 48–49.
21. Dicken-Garcia, 176.
22. Kaplan, 189.
23. Rutenbeck, 1993, 42.
24. From Jeffrey B. Rutenbeck, "Newspaper Trends in the 1870s: Proliferation, Polarization, and Political Independence," *Journalism and Mass Communication Quarterly* 72, no. 2 (Summer 1995), 364–365.
25. *Ibid.*
26. Kaplan, 27.
27. McGerr, 120. See also Michael Schudson, *The Power of News* (Cambridge, MA: Harvard University Press, 1995), 189–203 ("Was There Ever a Public Sphere?").
28. Kaplan, 22.
29. According to Dicken-Garcia, "At most, independent seemed to mean that a paper had no formal party alliance; in practice, it did not mean that it would not in other ways play the same role or one similar to that of the party papers." Dicken-Garcia, 49.
30. Mark Wahlgren Summers, *The Press Gang: Newspapers and Politics, 1865–1878* (Chapel Hill: University of North Carolina Press, 1994), 48.
31. *Ibid.*, 5, 26.
32. Rubin, 59.
33. Witcover, 215. Some involved in the print business

couldn't keep their cynicism about "reform" to themselves, at least in their more maudlin moments. In a response to a toast to "the independent press" at a meeting of the New York Press Association, John Swinton replied: "There is no such thing in America as an independent press.... You know it, and I know it. There is not one of you who dare express an honest opinion. If you express it you know beforehand that it would never appear in print. I am paid $150 per week for keeping my honest opinions out of the paper I am connected with. Others of you are paid similar salaries for doing similar things.... The business of the New York journalist is to distort the truth, to lie outright, to pervert, to vilify, to fawn at the feet of Mammon, and sell his country and race for his daily bread.... You know this, and I know it; and what foolery to be toasting to an 'independent press.' We are tools, and the vassals of rich men behind the scenes.... They pull the strings and we dance.... We are intellectual prostitutes." Page Smith, *The Rise of Industrial America, Vol. VI* (New York: McGraw-Hill, 1984), 378–379.

34. Mark Wahlgren Summers, 1994, 294.

35. *Ibid.*, 303.

36. Thomas B. Littlewood, *Calling Elections: The History of Horse-Race Journalism* (Notre Dame, IN: University of Notre Dame Press, 1998), 48. For further evidence of pro-Hayes bias in the Associated Press throughout the 1876 campaign, see Menahem Blondheim, *News Over the Wires: The Telegraph and the Flow of Public Information in America, 1844–1897* (Cambridge, MA: Harvard University Press, 1994), 175–182.

37. Mark Wahlgren Summers, *The Era of Good Stealings* (Oxford: Oxford University Press, 1993), 75. The mid-nineteenth-century newspaper, industry veteran Beman Brockway insisted in 1891, "was not a newspaper at all. It contained little news of a general character, and almost no local intelligence. It was simply the organ of a party." 18. Another old hand remarked the same year that "devotion to party was the test of the value of the journal. All else was subordinated to this feature." McGerr, 19.

38. Simon N. D. North, *History and Present Condition of the Newspaper and Periodical Press of the United States* (Washington, D.C.: U.S. Census Bureau, 1881), 37.

39. Mark Wahlgren Summers, 1994, 45.

40. Richard Watson Gilder, looking back at the end of the century on his career as a journalist in Newark, New Jersey, during the 1860s, recalled that "men and women were common who swore by one paper, and they'd no more think of taking some other paper of a different stripe of politics than they would of drinking milk on lobster." McGerr, 22.

41. McGerr, 17.

42. Justin E. Walsh, *To Print the News and Raise Hell! A Biography of Wilbur F. Storey* (Chapel Hill: University of North Carolina Press, 1968), 194.

43. Mark Wahlgren Summers, 1994, 156. During Reconstruction, Pomeroy demanded "the equality of the states or another war." Charles H. Coleman, *The Election of 1868* (New York: Octagon Books, 1971), 297.

44. Ted C. Hinckley, "The Politics of Sinophobia: Garfield, the Morey Letter, and the Presidential Election of 1880," *Ohio History* 89, no. 4 (1980), 395.

45. McGerr, 20. Samuel Bowles in the Springfield, Massachusetts, *Republican* on September 30, 1858, confirmed that a partisan press dependent on patronage could be "no more expected to give a true account of political affairs" than an attorney was "expected to give the jury a truthful and just exposition of the facts." Dicken-Garcia, 176

46. Smythe, 113.

47. Farquhar, 162–163.

48. Harper, 67.

49. Reynolds, 217.

50. For an investigation of the Southern state of mind during this period, see Dwight Lowell Dumond, ed., *Southern Editorials on Secession* (New York: Century, 1931). See also Osthaus, chap. 4 ("The Triumph of Sectional Journalism"); Nancy McKenzie Dupont, "Mississippi's Fire-Eating Editor Ethelbert Barksdale and the Election of 1860," Sachsman et al., eds., *The Civil War and the Press* (New Brunswick, NJ: Transaction Publishers, 2000), chap. 10.

51. Reynolds, 155.

52. Harper, 92.

53. Reynolds, 171.

54. *Ibid.*, 169.

55. Reynolds, 206. For further analysis of the pressure on Unionist papers in the South see *ibid.*, 132–135, 171–173.

56. Harper, 69.

57. See Harper, chap. 19 ("'Until Hell Freezes Over'").

58. Richard H. Abbott, *For Free Press and Equal Rights: Republican Newspapers in the Reconstruction South* (Athens, GA: University of Georgia Press), 98. See also Steve Humphrey, *"That D----d Brownlow": Being a Saucy and Malicious Description of William Gannaway Brownlow* (Boone, NC: Appalachian Consortium Press, 1978). Although pro-Union voices had been suppressed throughout the Confederacy at the outbreak of the Civil War, the government in Richmond was hardly immune from criticism in the newspapers of the South. While the Confederate fighting man was lionized, and General Robert E. Lee idolized, President Jefferson Davis, in particular, found himself under incessant editorial assault. But this dissatisfaction was motivated not by a desire for peace but rather for more effective direction of the war effort. See Bell Irvin Wiley, *Embattled Confederates: An Illustrated History of Southerners at War* (New York: Bonanza Books, 1964), chap. 11 ("Journalism and Literature").

59. Perkins, 1943, 516. For a case study of the everyday travails faced by a typical Northern paper openly sympathetic with the Southern cause during the war, see Ford Risley, "The Albany Patriot, 1861–1865: Struggling to Publish and Struggling to Remain Optimistic," in Sachsman et al., chap. 16.

60. Keogh, 22.

61. Marbut, 339–340.

62. Harry James Carman, *Lincoln and the Patronage* (Gloucester, MA: P. Smith, 1964), 125.

63. Carman, 126–128.

64. *Ibid.*, p. 119–121. For more on Lincoln's relationship with Forney, see Manber and Dahlstrom, 243–246.

65. Carman, 122.

66. *Ibid.*

67. *Ibid.*, 128. This cornucopia of federal largesse was described as "a disgrace to journalism" by Murat Halstead of the *Cincinnati Gazette*, who printed all of the names and the sinecures enjoyed by each. Manber and Dahlstrom, 61.

68. Perkins, 1943, 520.

69. Manber and Dahlstrom, 83.

70. Frank L. Klement, *Lincoln's Critics: The Copperheads of the North* (Shippensburg, PA: White Mane Books, 1999), 114.

71. Klement, 10.

72. Tebbel and Watts, 189.

73. Justin E. Walsh, 5.

74. Mark Wahlgren Summers, 1993, 78.

75. Justin E. Walsh, 165.

76. *Ibid.*, 168.

77. *Ibid.*, 167.

78. *Ibid.*, 147.

79. *Ibid.*, 184.

80. *Ibid.*, 6.

81. McPhee, 121.

82. Kobre, 1969, 289.

83. Justin E. Walsh, 192.

84. *Ibid.*, 159–160.

85. *Ibid.*, 198–199. See also Donald Bridgman Sanger, "The Chicago Times and the Civil War," *Mississippi Valley Historical Review* 17, no. 4 (March 1931), 557–580.

86. Klement, 136.

87. *Ibid.*, 137.

88. *Ibid.*, 36.

89. *Ibid.*, 141–142.

90. *Ibid.*, 36.

91. *Ibid.*, 143.

92. *Ibid.*, 37.

93. Charles Seymour, "The Press," in *History of La-Crosse County, Wisconsin* (Chicago: Western Historical Co., 1881), 545.

94. Reed W. Smith, "The Paradox of Samuel Medary, Copperhead Newspaper Publisher," in Sachsman et al., 297, 298.

95. Reed W. Smith, *Samuel Medary & the Crisis: Testing the Limits of Press Freedom* (Columbus: Ohio State University Press, 1995), 88.

96. *Ibid.*, 130.

97. Smith in Sachsman et al., 291.

98. Donald Reynolds, "Words for War," in Lloyd Chiasson, Jr., ed., *The Press in Times of Crisis* (Westport, CT: Greenwood Press), 1995, 92.

99. Reynolds in Chiasson, 92.

100. Swinton certainly fared better than Augustus Cazaran of the *Boston Traveller*, who was sentenced to dig trenches on the front line for sixty days by Major General Benjamin F. Butler. Cazaran was at least able to solicit the sympathy of Confederate sharpshooters on the far side of no-man's-land; when he held up his ball and chain they would cease firing in his direction.

101. Emmet Crozier, *Yankee Reporters 1861–65* (New York: Oxford University Press, 1956), 394.

102. Reynolds in Chiasson, 94.

103. Hohnberg, 123–124.

104. John Glen, "Journalistic Impedimenta: William Tecumseh Sherman and Free Expression," in Sachsman et al., 411.

105. Reynolds in Chiasson, 91.

106. Marszalek, 1981, 79, 81.

107. *Ibid.*, 104. Grant also ordered Associated Press correspondent L. W. Meyers arrested and jailed in Memphis.

108. Tebbel and Watts, 197.

109. See Crozier, chap. 18 ("Spy and Infamous Dog").

110. Dickerson, 161.

111. *Ibid.*, 162.

112. Maihafer, 2001, 98–99.

113. Manber and Dahlstrom, 112–113.

114. *Ibid.*, 132–133.

115. Robert C. Williams, 25.

116. Manber and Dahlstrom, 124–125.

117. *Ibid.*, 129.

118. Klement, 29.

119. Dickerson, 165.

120. Klement, 29. Manber and Dahlstrom is the definitive resource on Hodgson's travails.

121. Geoffrey R. Stone, 128–129.

122. Klement, 11, 28, 101.

123. *Ibid.*, 97.

124. *Ibid.*, 101–102.

125. *Ibid.*, 10–11.

126. Geoffrey R. Stone, 129.

127. Reed W. Smith, 95.

128. Klement, 30.

129. Maihafer, 2001, 101.

130. *Ibid.*, 2001, 103.

131. Reed W. Smith, 120.

132. Geoffrey R. Stone, 131.

133. Klement, 29.

134. Klement, 31.

135. *Ibid.*

136. Harper, 135.

137. Reed W. Smith, 136.

138. Geoffrey R. Stone, 131–132.

139. Harper, 189.

140. Klement, 30.

141. Harper, 197.

142. "Abler and stronger men I may have met," Greeley wrote of Raymond, "a cleverer, readier, more generally efficient journalist, I never saw." After Raymond launched his own paper, the *New York Times*, which debuted on September 18, 1851, his erstwhile employer dubbed him "The Little Villain." Borchard, 107–108.

143. See Thurlow Weed Banks, *Memoir of Thurlow Weed* (Boston: Houghton, Mifflin, 1884), chap. 21, and Harper, 58–61.

144. Francis Brown, 255.

145. Harper, 101.

146. Robert C. Williams, 225–227.

147. See Maihafer, 2001, chap. 14 ("Get Down you Damn Fool!").

148. John G. Nicolay, *Abraham Lincoln: A History, Vol. IX* (New York: Century, 1917), 184–200.

149. Maihafer, 2001, 204.

150. Fermer, 209.

151. Fermer, 134–135.

152. Carlson, 308.

153. Carlson, 313.

154. See Crozier, chap. 3 ("The Ball is Opened!").

155. Fermer, 187.

156. Carman, 123. Although seizing on the opportunity to curry favor with the administration, Bennett remained unreconciled with Weed and continued to refer to him as the "superannuated imbecile." Fermer, 198. This mission was in fact Weed's last major contribution to national politics in a career that spanned over four decades. He stepped down as editor of the *Albany Evening Journal* in 1863. He tried to make a comeback as a journalist by taking the helm of the *New York Commercial Advertiser* in 1867 but had to give up the position because of failing health. He died in retirement in 1882.

157. Don C. Seitz, *The James Gordon Bennetts*, Bobbs-Merrill, Indianapolis, 1928, p. 180–182.

158. Fermer, 218–219.

159. Farquhar, 163–164.

160. Crouthamel, 1989, 146. See also Fermer, chap. 11 ("The Campaign Against the Politicians, 1863–4").

161. Harper, 309.

162. *Ibid.*, 308.

163. Maihafer, 2001, 183.

164. Harper, 304.

165. Nevins, 1928, 292.

166. Strevey, 161–163.

167. Maihafer, 2001, 216–217. Bennett ultimately made his peace with Lincoln, allegedly because the president dangled the mission to France under his nose; see Crouthamel, 1989, 148–149.

168. See Harper, chap. 36 ("The Belling of the Cats").

169. William Frank Zornow, *Lincoln and the Party Divided* (Norman: University of Oklahoma Press, 1954), 187.

170. Swint, 200–201. Alongside Democratic newspapers, Democratic politicians, ever eager to seize on any evidence of the threat that the Republican Party posed to white racial purity, kept the story alive throughout 1864. Ohio congressman Samuel Cox declared that the pamphlet proved that the Republican agenda was to propel the nation into "perfect social equality of black and white." See Sidney Kaplan, "The Miscegenation Issue in the Election of 1864," *The Journal of Negro History* 34, no. 3 (July 1949), 274–343.

171. Crouthamel, 1989, 150.

172. Harper, 349.

173. Abbott, 41. Porter's estimates for pre-war Southern publications are higher: 91 dailies, 807 weeklies, 34 tri-weeklies, and 24 semiweeklies, meaning that one-fourth of the national dailies and one-third of the national weeklies in 1860 originated below the Mason-Dixon Line. In either case, the extent of the impact of the war is clear. Porter, 1971, 1.

174. Abbott, 48.

175. Thomas D. Clark, *The Southern Country Editor* (New York: Bobbs-Merrill, 1948, 202. For more on efforts to secure a combined line of attack in the Democratic Press, North and South, see Osthaus, 135–136.

176. The Southern state of mind is reflected in an anecdote related by "L. A. G." of the Murray, Georgia, *News Letter* in 1899. The author remarked that while much had been written about the corrupt nature of "Negroes," he had found a sixteen-year-old African American boy who had "never taken a drink of whiskey, never smoked a cigar or cigarette, never engaged in a game of baseball, never tried to dance a step, never cussed an oath, and doesn't know one card from another." "I remarked to him," the author concluded, "that I thought now was a good time to kill him, that maybe we could get one Negro in Heaven." Clark, 200. See also Dickerson, chap. 7 ("'The Rule of Reticence': War and Reconstruction in the South") and Charles F. Ritter, *The Press in Florida, Louisiana, and South Carolina and the End of Reconstruction, 1865–1877: Southern Men with Northern Interests* (PhD dissertation, Catholic University of America, 1976).

177. Lawrence J. Friedman, *The White Savage: Racial Fantasies in the Postbellum South* (Englewood Cliffs, NJ: Prentice-Hall, 1970), 35.

178. Friedman, 28–29.

179. Clark, 285.

180. Osthaus, 1994, 131.

181. Abbott, 49.

182. *Ibid.*, 51.

183. Osthaus, 6.

184. Page Smith, 1981, 906.

185. Abbott, 53.

186. Clark, 36.

187. Abbott, 182. The two Republican papers in Georgia, both in Atlanta, were matched against eight independent papers and the seventy-eight organs of the Democratic Party. Rutenbeck, 1995, 373. See also Richard H. Abbott, "The Republican Party Press in Reconstruction Georgia, 1867–1874," *The Journal of Southern History* 61, no. 4 (November 1995), 725–760.

188. Clark, 203.

189. *Ibid.*, 205.

190. *Ibid.*, 206.

191. Smythe, 4.

192. Mark Wahlgren Summers, 2004, 59.

193. See Lawrence J. Friedman, "Wattersonia: The Road to Autonomy" in *The White Savage: Racial Fantasies in the Postbellum South* (Englewood Cliffs, NJ: Prentice-Hall, 1970), chap. 3.

194. Rutenbeck, 1995, 362.

195. Abbott, 41.

196. George McJimsey, *Genteel Partisan: Manton Marble, 1834–1917* (Ames: Iowa State University Press, 1971), 39.

197. McJimsey, 42.

198. Kaplan, 61.

199. Mark Wahlgren Summers, 1994, 49.

200. Irving Stone, *They Also Ran: The Story of the Men Who Were Defeated for the Presidency*, (New York: Signet, 1966), 311.

201. Coleman, 297.

202. McJimsey, 131.

203. *Ibid.*, 132. The apostasy of the *World* was attributed to a $40,000 bribe distributed by a patent medicine advertiser, but it is more likely to have merely reflected the editor's independent frame of mind.

204. William Best Hesseltine, *Ulysses S. Grant, Politician*, (New York: F. Ungar, 1957), 130. See also Coleman, 344–359.

205. Rutenbeck, 1993, 48.

206. *Ibid.*, 49.

207. Mark Wahlgren Summers, 2004, 78.

208. Kaplan, 61.

209. *Ibid.*, 89.

210. *Ibid.*, 65.

211. Tebbel and Watts, 223.

212. McGerr, 113.

213. Harry J. Maihafer, *The General and the Journalists*, (Washington, D.C.: Brassey's, 1998), 230–231.

214. James G. Smart, "Whitelaw Reid and the Nomination of Horace Greeley," *Mid America* 49, no. 4 (October 1967), 227–243. See also Matthew T. Downey, "Horace Greeley and the Politicians: The Liberal Republican Convention in 1872," *Journal of American History* 53, no. 1 (March 1967), 727–750.

215. Sidney Kobre, *The Yellow Press and Gilded Age Journalism* (Tallahassee: Florida State University, 1964), 32.

216. Irving Stone, 17.

217. Janet E. Steele, *The Sun Shines for All: Journalism and Ideology in the Life of Charles A. Dana* (Syracuse, NY: Syracuse University Press, 1993), 112. For more on Dana's mixed motives in his advocacy of Greeley, see Candace Stone, *Dana and the Sun* (New York: Dodd, Mead, 1938), 115–123.

218. Tebbel and Watts, 224. See also Jeffrey B. Rutenbeck, "Editorial Perception of Newspaper Independence and the Presidential Campaign of 1872: An Ideological Turning Point for American Journalism," *Journalism History* 17, no. 1–2 (Spring–Summer 1990), 13–22.

219. Nevins, 1968, 396–398. Bryant, who considered Greeley a "blackguard," had long nursed a personal grievance toward the man who had commenced a reply to a *Post* editorial in 1849 by blurting out, "You lie, villain! willfully, wickedly, basely lie!" Bryant didn't appreciate the company Greeley kept, either. "With such a head," the *New York Post* intoned, "as is on Greeley's shoulders, the affairs of the nation would not, under his direction, be wisely administered; with such manners as his, they could not be administered with common decorum; with such associates as he has taken to his bosom, they could not be administered with common integrity." Lorant, 315. President Grant was relatively mild when he described his opponent as "a genius without common sense." Robert C. Williams, 296.

220. Lorant, 312.

221. Mark Wahlgren Summers, 1993, 221.

222. Maihafer, 1998, 240.

223. Greeley largely devoted his brief stint in Congress to uncovering exposés for his paper, most notoriously by

obtaining access to other members' travel vouchers and then comparing the routes for which they claimed reimbursement to the most direct mail routes and then calculating the differences. Published in the *Tribune*, the results embarrassed members of both parties, including Illinois representative Abraham Lincoln, whom Greeley accused of over-billing the government by $676.80. In a remarkably brief span of time Greeley had made himself, in his own words, "the most thoroughly detested man who ever sat in Congress" and his erstwhile colleagues were only too glad to see the back of him. Greeley found the experience rewarding, however. "I thought it would be a nuisance and a sacrifice for me to go to Congress," he later mused to Schuyler Colfax, "but I was mistaken; it did me lasting good. I never was brought so palpably and tryingly into collision with the embodied scoundrelism of the nation as while in Congress." Ritchie, 1991, 42–43.

224. Van Deusen, 1953, 414.
225. Lorant, 321.
226. Kaplan, 59.
227. *Ibid.*, 60.
228. *Ibid.*, 23–24.
229. For studies of the Greeley campaign, see Robert C. Williams, 279–307 ("Liberal-Republican"); Mark Wahlgren Summers, 1994, chap. 15 ("The Worst Thing Yet! 1872"); Seitz, 1970, chap. 14 ("Inconsistent Independence"); Van Deusen, 1953, chap. 25 ("End of the Rainbow"); Stoddard, chap. 28–29; and Royal Cortissoz, *The Life of Whitelaw Reid*, Vol. I (London: Thornton Butterworth, 1921), chap. 14 ("Greeley and the Presidency").
230. Maihafer, 1998, 245.
231. See Bingham Duncan, *Whitelaw Reid: Journalist, Politician, Diplomat* (Athens: University of Georgia Press, 1975), chap. 6 ("Editor in Politics"). Having usurped Greeley, Reid was determined to keep the *Tribune* in the family thereafter. His son, Ogden Mills Reid, was the next editor of the *Tribune*, assisted and succeeded by his wife, Helen Rogers Reid, who retained control until the paper folded in 1966.
232. See Kobre, 1964, 207.
233. Rutenbeck, 1993, 51.
234. *Ibid.*, 51–52.
235. *Ibid.*, 52.
236. *Ibid.*, 53.
237. *Ibid.*, 54.
238. See McJimsey, chap. 9.
239. Marble wrote a letter to Belmont just before he sold his failing paper, explaining that he could not compete with the independent sheets that were offering more news at a cheaper price and making more money off a greater volume of advertising. Rutenbeck, 1995, 370–371.
240. Rutenbeck, 1993, 58.
241. "New York: Why the State Went Democratic," *Chicago Tribune*, November 13, 1876, 3. The Chicago man also mentioned that the *Evening Post*, which inclined towards Tilden but was manhandled back into the Republican camp by veteran editor William Cullen Bryant, "pulled through the campaign, without giving any unusual signs of life, in its heavy, dull, logy manner."
242. Hamilton J. Eckenrode, *Rutherford B. Hayes: Statesman of Reunion* (Port Washington, NY: Kennikat Press, 1930, 142.
243. Robert L. Bishop and Stephen Friedman, "Campaign Coverage—1876 Style by the Chicago Tribune," *Journalism Quarterly* 45, no. 3 (Autumn 1968), 481.
244. John Bigelow, ed., *Letters and Literary Memorials of Samuel J. Tilden, Vol. I*, (New York: Harper & Brothers, 1908), 273.
245. "Vote for Samuel J. Tilden," *New York Times*, November 6, 1871, 4. Even in July 1874, the *Times*, in

considering that year's crop of Democratic hopefuls for the gubernatorial election, was moved to declare "Mr. TILDEN would make a very good candidate, for he is a gentleman, an able man, and a man of very high character ... a man of unsullied honor, public and private; a good, public-spirited man, who would be no discredit, but much the reverse, to our State." The *Times* warned Tilden against entering the race, however, on the grounds he would surely lose; it was when he chose to disregard this warning that the gloves came off. "State Politics," *New York Times*, July 24, 1874, 4.
246. Eckenrode, 178.
247. Alexander Clarence Flick, *Samuel Jones Tilden: A Study in Political Sagacity* (Port Washington, NY: Kennikat Press, 1939), 324.
248. "The Democratic Ticket," *New York Times*, August 23, 1876, 9.
249. See "Gov. Tilden's Perjury," *New York Times*, August 28, 1876, 5; "Tilden's Perjury; His Explanation Evasive and Unsatisfactory," *New York Times*, September 23, 1876, 5; "Tilden's Perjury; His Explanation only a Confession of Guilt—Additional Expressions from the Press of the Country," *New York Times*, September 25, 1876, 5; "Tilden's Perjury; Further Extracts Showing How Widely He is Condemned by the Press," *New York Times*, October 22, 1876, 2; and "Tilden's Perjury; The Guilty Man Not Fit to be a Candidate for President of the United States," *New York Times*, November 3, 1876, 3.
250. "'Managing' the Country Press," *New York Times*, August 25, 1876, 4.
251. "The Close of the Canvass," *New York Times*, November 6, 1876, 1.
252. Lloyd Robinson, *The Stolen Election: Hayes versus Tilden, 1876* (New York: Forge, 2001), 120.
253. *New York Tribune*, November 8, 1876, 4.
254. Mark Wahlgren Summers, 1993, 287.
255. McGerr, 20–21.
256. Lloyd Robinson, 119.
257. Mark Wahlgren Summers, 1993, 288.
258. *New York Tribune*, November 8, 1876, 4.
259. Another account described Reid as a "red-faced, bloated, hot-tempered tyrant whose greatest joy in life was to tyrannize over the unfortunate reporters under his charge." Leon Burr Richardson, *William E. Chandler: Republican* (New York: Dodd, Mead, 1940), 184.
260. "Just What Chandler Did," *New York Times*, June 15, 1887, 4. See also Mark D. Harmon, "The New York Times and the Theft of the 1876 Presidential Election," *Journal of American Culture* 10, no. 2 (Summer 1987), 35–41. For a different take on the events of election night 1876, see Jerome L. Sternstein, "The Sickles Memorandum: Another Look at the Hayes-Tilden Election-Night Conspiracy," *Journal of Southern History* 32, no. 6 (1966), 342–357.
261. Henry F. Pringle, "Kentucky Bourbon: Marse Henry Watterson," in Ford and Emery, 222.
262. See William H. Rehnquist, *Centennial Crisis: The Disputed Election of 1876* (New York: Knopf, 2004); Roy Morris, *Fraud of the Century: Rutherford B. Hayes, Samuel Tilden and the Stolen Election of 1876* (New York: Simon & Schuster, 2003); Keith Ian Polakoff, *The Politics of Inertia: The Election of 1876 and the End of Reconstruction* (Baton Rouge: Louisiana State University Press, 1973); Paul Leland Haworth, *The Hayes-Tilden Disputed Presidential Election of 1876* (New York: Russell & Russell, 1966).
263. Lloyd Robinson, 191.
264. Candace Stone, 309.
265. Clark, 289.
266. Tebbel and Watts, 240.

267. *Ibid.*, 243.

268. Denis Tilden Lynch, *Grover Cleveland: A Man Four-Square* (New York: Horace Liveright, 1932), 221.

269. Mark Wahlgren Summers, *Rum, Romanism & Rebellion: The Making of a President, 1884* (Chapel Hill: University of North Carolina Press, 2000), 180.

270. Richard E. Welch, Jr., *The Presidencies of Grover Cleveland* (Lawrence: University Press of Kansas, 1988), 37–38.

271. Lynch, 1932, 221.

272. "Infamous Campaign Methods," *Washington Post*, Oct. 24, 1884, 2.

273. Cleveland's chief confidant, Daniel Manning, began his journalistic career during the Civil War as legislative correspondent for the *Brooklyn Eagle*. He later moved to the *Albany Argus*, which he ultimately controlled. Manning was a close friend of Samuel Tilden, who he succeeded as effective head of the Democratic Party in New York after the debacle of 1876, serving as actual chairman from 1881 to 1885, when he entered Cleveland's Cabinet as secretary of the treasury.

274. H. Wayne Morgan, *From Hayes to McKinley: National Party Politics, 1877–1896* (Syracuse, NY: Syracuse University Press, 1969), 210.

275. Welch, 34.

276. Duncan, 103. See also Cortissoz, chap. 5 ("Blaine and Cleveland").

277. McGerr, 119.

278. Littlewood, 50. Cleveland's girth was a perpetual source of fodder for Republican editorialists. During the 1888 campaign, the Philadelphia *Press* described the Democratic ticket of Cleveland and Thurman as "some adipose tissue and a red bandanna." John Edgar McDaniel, Jr., *The Presidential Election of 1888* (PhD dissertation, University of Texas, Austin, 1970), 170.

279. Mark Wahlgren Summers, 2004, 62.

280. "The Candidates Phrenologically Considered," *Cleveland Leader*, October 31, 1884, 1.

281. Farquhar, 167.

282. Pearl Louise Robertson, *Grover Cleveland as Political Leader* (PhD dissertation, University of Chicago, 1937), 235. Cleveland never forgave the press either. In a speech at the 250th Anniversary of Harvard in 1886 he deplored "the silly, mean and cowardly lies that every day are found in the columns of certain newspapers, which violate every instinct of American manliness, and in ghoulish glee desecrate every sacred relation of public life." Keogh, 24.

283. The best source on the events of October 29, 1884, is Mark Wahlgren Summers, 2000, chap. 17 ("Clerical Errors").

284. James Harrison Wilson, *The Life of Charles A. Dana* (New York: Harper & Brothers, 1907), 450. Hancock was derided by other Republican editors for allegedly wearing a corset; he was a "self-maid man" with "pretty-man ideas in dress." Mark Wahlgren Summers, 2004, 49. For more on the role of the press in the campaign of 1880, see Herbert J. Clancy, *The Presidential Election of 1880* (Chicago: Loyola University Press, 1958).

285. See Candace Stone, 155–158. For more on Dana's relationship with Cleveland, see *ibid.*, chapter 9, and Steele, chap. 8.

286. Kobre, 1964, 45, 47.

287. Smythe, 112.

288. Tebbel and Watts, 263.

289. McGerr, 124. See also James Wyman Barrett, *Joseph Pulitzer and his World* (New York: Vanguard Press, 1941), especially chap. 4 ("For Progress and Reform"). Pulitzer learned a useful lesson in the relative merits of his two professions once he entered Congress. Getting drunk one night, he got into trouble with a policeman. His protestations that he was a representative were cutting no ice. Walt McDougall, who was with him, told the policeman, "Say, old man, you don't want to jug this gent. He is Joseph Pulitzer, the owner of the *New York World*." "Holy Chessus!" exclaimed the cop. "Why didn't you say so at first? I'll get you a carriage and you can take him home without anyone seeing him." Smythe, 113.

290. Denis Brian, *Pulitzer: A Life* (New York: John Wiley & Sons, 2001), 88.

291. *Ibid.*, 89–90. Pulitzer and Dana continued their feud into Cleveland's term of office, scrapping over an internecine spat within the Democratic Party during the 1887 race for New York district attorney. Pulitzer labeled Dana "a mendacious blackguard ... an assaulter of women and a mortgaged, broken-down calumniator in the last agonies of humiliation." Dana retaliated with a screed of anti-Semitic personal abuse, describing "Judas" Pulitzer's face as "repulsive" because "[c]unning, malice, falsehood, treachery, dishonesty, greed, and venal self-abasement have stamped their unmistakable traits." After Dana's candidate emerged victorious, the *Sun* headlined "THE PEOPLE REBUKE THE LIARS," and offered its editorial opinion that Pulitzer be given "no more rope than is necessary for the final act of his career." The editorial concluded: "Perhaps your lot will be like that of the mythical unfortunate of the same race you belong to and deny, that weird creation of medieval legend, a creation, by the way, far more prepossessing than you are—we mean, The Wandering Jew! In that case it may shortly please the inscrutable Providence, which has chastened us with your presence, to give you that stern and dreadful signal—'Move on, Pulitzer, move on!'" *Ibid.*, 128–131.

292. Nevins, 378.

293. Brian, 96.

294. Klement, 6.

295. James S. Olson, *Catholic Immigrants in America* (Chicago: Nelson-Hall, 1987), 235. A. James Reichley concludes that with the slavery issue now resolved, the "most important key" to the success of the GOP in the post-Civil War era, even more than the tariff, "was that the Republicans were identified in the North as the party of Protestantism." A. James Reichley, *Faith in Politics* (Washington, D.C.: Brookings Institution Press, 2002), 188. See also George E. Reedy, *From the Ward to the White House: The Irish in American Politics* (New York: Scribner's, 1991).

296. Vincent P. de Santis, "Catholicism and Presidential Elections, 1865–1900," *Mid-America* 42, no. 2 (April 1960), 68.

297. De Santis, 70.

298. Mark Wahlgren Summers, 2000, 216.

299. Marvin and Dorothy Rosenberg, "The Dirtiest Election," *American Heritage* 13, no. 5 (May 1962), 99.

300. See Mark Wahlgren Summers, 2000, chap. 18 ("Lord! But We Skirted the Edge!").

301. Lynch, 282.

302. See Littlewood, 50–52. For a contemporary views of the post-election brouhaha, see "Stock Jobbers at Work," *New York Times*, November 7, 1884, 5, and "Accepting the Verdict," *New York Times*, November 8, 1884, 5. The slant of AP coverage during the campaign, and in particular its refusal to concede Blaine's defeat, led association president David M. Stone to comment in his *Journal of Commerce* regarding the election returns having been collected "under the entire supervision" of Reid: "The partisan character of the service is most painfully apparent and we do not believe that the other members of the association will quietly submit to lose the good name of the body in any such fashion" in future. See Blonheim, 184–187.

303. Marshall Berges, *The Life and Times of Los Angeles* (New York: Atheneum, 1984), 16.

304. Arthur M. Schlesinger, Jr., ed., *History of American Political Parties, Vol. II: 1860–1910, The Gilded Age of Politics* (New York: Chelsea House, 1973), 1479.

305. McDaniel, 5–6.

306. Mark Wahlgren Summers, 2000, 189, 195.

307. According to Larry Sabato, this gentlemen's agreement reached its apogee during the period from 1941 to 1966, when journalists were engaged in what he calls "'lapdog' journalism — reporting that served and reinforced the political establishment. In this period, mainstream journalists rarely challenged prevailing orthodoxy, accepted at face value much of what those in power told them, and protected politicians by revealing little about their nonofficial lives, even when private vices affected their public performance." See Sabato, chap. 2 ("The Press of Yesteryear"). In Sabato's model, the media, energized by Vietnam and Watergate, entered a "watchdog" period from the mid-sixties, and has been in "junkyard dog" mode ever since Nixon resigned.

308. Pollard, 542.

309. Mark Wahlgren Summers, 1994, 306.

310. Duncan, 151. See also Cortissoz, chap. 10 ("The Campaign of 1892").

Chapter IV

1. Theodore H. White, *The Making of the President 1972* (New York: Atheneum, 1973), 246.

2. Jensen, 37.

3. Hackett and Zhao, 191–192.

4. Schudson, 93.

5. Hackett and Zhao, 210.

6. In 1935 the American Newspaper Guild's code of ethics officially endorsed the ethos of objectivity by stating, "The newspapermen's first duty is to give the public accurate and unbiased news reports." Accounts by journalists who experienced the transition from subjective to objective imperatives in the newsroom reflect the rigidity by which the new regime was imposed: "Facts, facts, nothing but facts.... The index of forbidden words was very lengthy, and misuse of them, when they escaped the keen eye of a copyreader and got into print, was punishable by suspension without pay for a week, or immediate discharge. It was a rigid system, rigidly enforced." Julius Chambers, *News Hunting on Three Continents*, New York: Mitchell Kennerly, 1921; 7; "Reporters were to report the news as it happened, like machines, without prejudice, color, and without style; all alike. Humor or any sign of personality in our reports was caught, rebuked, and in time, suppressed." Lincoln Steffens, *The Autobiography of Lincoln Steffens* (New York: Harcourt, Brace, 1931), 179. See also Schudson, 1978, 77–87 ("Occupational Ideals of Journalists"); Joseph A. Milando, "Embracing Objectivity Early On: Journalism Textbooks in the 1880s," *Journal of Mass Media Ethics* 16, no. 1 (2001), 23–32; Stephen A. Banning, "Truth is Our Ultimate Goal: A Mid-Nineteenth Century Concern for Journalism Ethics," *American Journalism* 16, no. 1 (Winter 1999), 17–39; and Harlan S. Stensaas, "Development of the Objectivity Ethic in U.S. Daily Newspapers," *Journal of Mass Media Ethics* 2, no. 1 (Fall–Winter 1986–87), 50–60.

7. For background on the evolution of this agenda, see Fred W. Friendly, *The Good Guys, The Bad Guys and The First Amendment: Free Speech vs. Fairness in Broadcasting* (New York: Random House, 1976). For analysis of the ensuing debate between social responsibility and First Amendment rights, see Edwin Diamond, Norman Sand-

ler, and Milton Mueller, *Telecommunications in Crisis: The First Amendment, Technology, and Deregulation* (Washington, DC: Cato Institute, 1983); and Erwin G. Krasnow, Lawrence D. Longley, and Herbert A. Terry, *The Politics of Broadcast Regulation* (New York: St. Martin's Press, 1982).

8. Graham Knight, "News and Ideology," *Canadian Journal of Communications* 8, no. 4 (September 1982), 23.

9. According to Ward, the type of objectivity to which journalists aspire is not the theoretical, philosophical conception of objectivity as absolute standards or absolute knowledge — what he labels the "ways of truth"— but rather is closer to the form of objectivity that characterizes "ways of practice" such as law and other professions. Ward, 35–36.

10. Hackett and Zhao, 67–68.

11. Michael Barone, "The Return of Partisan Journalism," *American Enterprise* 7, no. 2 (March/April 1996), 30.

12. Mott, 354. For further analysis of this trend see Gentzkow, Glaeser, and Goldin. Some urban papers housed a species of activists determined to use the printed word to prick the nation's conscience about the festering social problems that the political system refused to acknowledge. The sensationalist reporting of this handful of journalistic reformers, dubbed "muckrakers," was a major spur in the rise of the progressive movement during this period. For more on this enterprise, which was not strictly partisan, see Robert Miraldi, ed., *The Muckrakers: Evangelical Crusaders* (Westport, CT: Praeger, 2000); Robert Miraldi, *Muckraking and Objectivity: Journalism's Colliding Traditions* (New York: Greenwood Press, 1990); Fred J. Cook, *The Muckrakers: Crusading Journalists Who Changed America* (Garden City, NY: Doubleday, 1972); Herbert Shapiro, ed., *The Muckrakers and American Society* (Boston: D. C. Heath, 1968); Arthur and Lila Weinberg, eds., *The Muckrakers: The Era in Journalism that Moved America to Reform* (New York: Simon and Schuster, 1961).

13. Dary, 61.

14. *Ibid.*, 49.

15. McGerr, 130.

16. *Ibid.*, 131.

17. It wasn't until the postwar era that the patronage-based partisan press fell into disfavor. In a letter to the president dated December 18, 1946, a month after the Democrats had lost their majorities in both chambers of Congress, State Senator Frank P. Briggs of Truman's home state, Missouri, discussed the potential advantages and pitfalls in setting up a partisan newspaper in the Show Me State "in which the Republican mistakes would be given to the public in no uncertain terms." Truman hedged in his reply on December 28, remarking "I don't want to say whether the project should be started or not," but adding "in my opinion, it would be a fine thing for the Democrats to have a paper which would tell the truth about their plans and aspirations. There is no such paper in Missouri at the present time with a statewide circulation." Nothing came of the proposal. Herbert Lee Williams, *The Newspaperman's President: Harry S. Truman* (Chicago: Nelson-Hall, Chicago, 1984), 18.

18. McGerr, 130.

19. Thomas C. Leonard, *The Power of the Press: The Birth of American Political Reporting* (New York: Oxford University Press, 1986), 133. Despite this pledge of resolute party orthodoxy, White did in fact bolt the GOP to back Teddy Roosevelt's Bull Moose campaign in 1912.

20. Schlesinger, 1973, 1531.

21. *Ibid.*, 1541.

22. Rubin, 91. See also Seymour Lutzky, *The Reform*

Editors and their Press (Ph.D. dissertation, University of Iowa, 1951). For an extensive historiography of the niche political publications of the era, see Joseph R. Conlin, ed., *The American Radical Press, 1880–1960*. Two vols. (Westport, CT: Greenwood Press, 1974).

23. Mark Wahlgren Summers, 2004, 264.

24. Henry F. Graff, *Grover Cleveland* (New York: Times Books, 2002), 129.

25. J. Rogers Hollingsworth, *The Whirligig of Politics: The Democracy of Cleveland and Bryan* (Chicago: University of Chicago Press, 1963), 69–70.

26. "Why Bryan is a Demagogue," *Chicago Tribune*, November 2, 1896, 6.

27. Matthew Josephson, *The Politicos, 1865–1896* (New York: Harcourt, Brace, 1938), 684.

28. Littlewood, 62.

29. Smythe, 179.

30. Paul W. Glad, *McKinley, Bryan and the People* (New York: J.B. Lippincott, 1964), 172.

31. Nevins, 1928, 418.

32. Hollingsworth, 86.

33. "Bolting the Nominee: Opinions of the Democratic Press on Mr. Bryan," *Washington Post*, July 11, 1896, 3.

34. Kobre, 1964, 167.

35. Littlewood, 67.

36. *Literary Digest*, July 18, 1896, 356.

37. Louis W. Koenig, *Bryan: A Political Biography of William Jennings Bryan* (New York: Putnam's, 1971), 243.

38. Kobre, 1964, 176.

39. *Literary Digest*, July 25, 1896, 385.

40. Kaplan, 67.

41. "Loss of Press Allies," *Los Angeles Times*, July 18, 1896, 6.

42. Nevins, 1928, 417.

43. *Ibid.*, 1928, 422.

44. Lawson, 1993, 9.

45. "Mr. Bryan Distrusts the Press," *New York Times*, August 23, 1896, 4. Having exhausted the pejoratives available in the standard political lexicon long before the end of the campaign, the *Times* was forced to resort to neologisms in attacking Bryan, accusing him of suffering from such afflictions as "paranoia querulenta" and "graphomania." Brian, 210.

46. "Mattoid Statesmanship," *New York Times*, October 23, 1896, 6.

47. "Is Mr. Bryan a Mattoid? Leading Alienists Analyze the Democratic Candidate," *New York Times*, September 29, 1896, 3.

48. "The Mattoidism of Bryan," *New York Times*, October 25, 1896, 12.

49. Mark Wahlgren Summers, 2004, ix.

50. *Literary Digest*, November 7, 1896, 4.

51. "The New York Newspapers and the Election," *Washington Post*, November 11, 1896, 6.

52. *Literary Digest*, July 18, 1896, 356–357.

53. Michael Kazin, *A Godly Hero: The Life of William Jennings Bryan* (New York: Knopf, 2006), 72.

54. *Literary Digest*, November 14, 1896, 36.

55. "The Victory: How it is Viewed by the Coast Press," *Los Angeles Times*, November 11, 1896, 10.

56. "The Nation Declares for Honesty," *Chicago Tribune*, November 4, 1896, 12.

57. *Literary Digest*, November 14, 1896, 35.

58. An indifferent student, more devoted to drinking, playing with his pet alligator and selling ads for the *Harvard Lampoon* than to his books, Hearst was finally expelled after sending personalized chamber pots with each man's likeness drawn on the bottom to his professors.

59. Kenneth Stewart and John Tebbel, *Makers of Modern Journalism* (New York: Prentice-Hall, 1952), 107.

60. Koenig, 204.

61. Bleyer, 360.

62. Leon Wolff, *Little Brown Brother: How the United States Purchased and Pacified the Philippine Islands at the Century's Turn* (Garden City, NY: Doubleday, 1961), 79. For more on Hearst and his methods, see Ian Mugridge, *The View from Xanadu: William Randolph Hearst and United States Foreign Policy* (Montreal and Kingston: McGill–Queen's University Press, 1995).

63. Page Smith, 1984, 872. The only paper to deprecate the war fever emanating from the Hearst and Pulitzer presses was that bastion of fine culture and the liberal arts, *New York Evening Post*, which expressed Olympian disapprobation of the bloodlust emanating from its rivals: "A yellow journal office is probably the nearest approach in atmosphere to hell existing in any Christian state." Kobre, 1964, 119. For an in-depth focus on the Pulitzer vs. Hearst imbroglio, see W. Joseph Campbell, *1897: The Year that Defined American Journalism* (New York: Routledge, 2006). See also Streitmatter, chap. 5 ("Journalism as Warmonger: The Spanish-American War"); Sylvia L. Hilton, "The Spanish-American War of 1898: Queries into the Relationship between the Press, Public Opinion and Politics," *Revista Espanola de Esiodios Norte-americanos* 5, no. 7 (1994); Gene Wiggins, "Journey to Cuba: The Yellow Crisis," in *The Press in Times of Crisis*, ed. Lloyd Chiasson, Jr. (Westport, CT: Greenwood Press, 1995), chap. 7; and Richard F. Hamilton, *President McKinley, War and Empire* (New Brunswick, NJ: Transaction Publishers, 2006), chap. 5 ("Cuba and the American Press"). The editorial parallels between the U.S. war against Spain and the U.S. war against Iraq 105 years later are quite eerie, as the following table indicates:

FACTOR	1898	2003
Ultimate justification for war	Spanish brutality in Cuba	Saddam's brutality in Iraq
True?	Yes	Yes
Proximate justification for war	Spanish sink the USS *Maine*	Saddam possesses WMDs
True?	No	No
Media baron fuels war fever	William Randolph Hearst	Keith Rupert Murdoch
Established New York tabloid publisher responds to media baron intrusion on his turf by trying to out-muscle him in spurring war fever?	Joseph Pulitzer (New York *World*)	Mort Zuckerman (*New York Daily News*)
"Splendid Little War?"	Yes	Yes
Bitter and protracted insurgency in aftermath marked by massive loss of civilian life and allegations of abuse by U.S. forces costs more U.S. lives and treasure than the formal hostilities?	Yes (Philippines)	Yes (Iraq)

64. Joseph E. Wisan, *The Cuban Crisis as Reflected in the New York Press, 1895–1898* (New York: Octagon Books, 1965), 458–459. See also Joyce Milton, *Yellow Kids: Foreign Correspondents in the Heyday of Yellow Journalism* (New York: Harper & Row, 1989). For a contrary view, see W. Joseph Campbell, *Yellow Journalism: Puncturing the Myths, Defining the Legacies* (New York: Praeger, 2003).

65. Steve Neal, *Happy Days are Here Again: The 1932 Democratic Convention* (New York: HarperCollins, 2004), 51

66. Neal, 2004, 51–52.

67. *Literary Digest*, October 3, 1936, 5.

68. Neal, 2004, 55.

69. George Juergens, *News from the White House: The Presidential-Press Relationship in the Progressive Era* (Chicago: University of Chicago Press, 1981), 11.

70. Juergens, 61–62.

71. William H. Allen, "The Election of 1900," *Annals of the American Academy of Political and Social Science* 17 (January 1901), 69–70. Typically, one such newspaper asserted that Bryan's electoral coalition represented a "conglomeration of wild theorists, of discontented ignorance, of dishonest debtors, of selfish silver owners, of self-seeking politicians, of objectors to law, order, and the sanctity of the supreme judiciary, following the Jack o'Lantern light of a man void of understanding." In fact, in many quarters Bryan's defeat was celebrated more than McKinley's victory. Bryanism "stands condemned before the world with none so low as to do it reverence," one editorial exulted."All that the Democratic Party, under the leadership of Mr. Bryan, has contended for, has been repudiated." Expanding on this theme, another publication declaimed that the election marked the "deliverance from the combination of all the political lunacies of the past." Not only was "free silver confined to the limbo reserved for the children of a diseased imagination" but America had left behind "the whole congeries of fads and follies and hatreds that greedy and unscrupulous men have gathered together in a modern Cave of Adullam for menace to ordered government." Ibid, 56–57.

72. The universal support for the Democratic nominee in the Southern press, always assured, was particularly energized in 1904 because of the Booker T. Washington affair of 1901. See Clark, chap. 18 ("That Man Teddy Roosevelt").

73. Koenig, 456. Symbolizing the prevailing mood in the nation's editorial offices, the *Brooklyn Eagle* argued after Bryan's nomination that his defeat "is called for by considerations of duty to the Republic." *Literary Digest* 37, no. 3 (July 18, 1908), 69.

74. The three-fourths interest Fairbanks had in the *Indianapolis News*, along with his four-fifths interest in the *Indianapolis Journal*, only came to light at the reading of his will.

75. Juergens, 80–85.

76. *Ibid.*, 87.

77. *Ibid.*, 90. See also Lofton, chap. 8 ("A Presidential Big Stick Against Press Freedom").

78. Ponder, 56.

79. David Halberstam, *The Powers that Be* (New York: Alfred A. Knopf, 1979), 117.

80. Bob Gottlieb and Irene Wolt, *Thinking Big: The Story of the Los Angeles Times, its Publishers, and their Influence on Southern California* (New York: Putnam, 1977), 52.

81. *Ibid.*, 52.

82. Halberstam, 1979, 103.

83. Berges, 26–27. After his election, Governor Johnson would find himself regularly denounced as "bombastic" and "conceited" in the pages of the *Times*.

84. Gottlieb and Wolt, 112–114.

85. "Why Wilson Won," *Literary Digest*, November 18, 1916, 1313. There was no Hiram Johnson in Ohio, the only major state Wilson carried in the East and Midwest, but apparently the president was the beneficiary of a positive spin from the Buckeye press; according to Charles P. Taft of the *Cincinnati Times-Star*, "A large majority of city newspapers in Ohio were with the Democrats in this campaign. That was one of the principle reasons for Democratic success." Then again, Charles was the former

president's half brother, so that response could just be a case of sour grapes. "Why Wilson Won," 1315.

86. Ray Stannard Baker, *Woodrow Wilson: Life and Letters, Vol. 3: Governor, 1910–1913* (Garden City, NY: Doubleday, 1931), chap. 1–2; James Kerney, *The Political Education of Woodrow Wilson* (New York: Century, 1926), chap. 1–3.

87. James B. Startt, *Woodrow Wilson and the Press: Prelude to the Presidency* (New York: Palgrave Macmillan, 2004), 59.

88. Startt, 61.

89. Edmund Ions, *Woodrow Wilson: The Politics of Peace and War* (London: Macdonald, 1972), 24.

90. Startt, 87.

91. *Ibid.*, 106–107.

92. *Ibid.*, 109.

93. See *ibid.*, 143–148; Stannard, 246–254.

94. Pringle in Ford and Emery, 226.

95. Arthur S. Link, *Wilson: The Road to the White House* (Princeton, NJ: Princeton University Press, 1968), 382.

96. Startt, 157.

97. *Ibid.*, 164–165.

98. Link, 382–383.

99. Startt, 160.

100. Link, 412.

101. Startt, 152.

102. Startt, 160.

103. Link, 392.

104. Startt, 177.

105. *Ibid.*, 180. Wilson's campaign manager also wrote to Grasty, expressing his gratitude for the *Sun's* support: "Its work cannot be overestimated."

106. *Ibid.*, 180. For more on Wilson's nomination, see James Chace, *1912: Wilson, Roosevelt, Taft & Debs — The Election that Changed the Country* (New York: Simon & Schuster, 2004), chap. 9 ("Baltimore"); Link, chap. 13 ("The Baltimore Convention"); and Frank K. Kelly, "June: The Battle of Baltimore," in *The Fight for the White House: The Story of 1912* (New York: Thomas Y. Crowell, 1961), chap. 7.

107. Link, 508.

108. Startt, 194.

109. *Ibid.*, 210.

110. *Ibid.*, 193.

111. See George Britt, *Forty Years — Forty Millions: The Career of Frank A. Munsey* (New York: Farrar & Rinehart, 1935), especially chap. 11.

112. Startt, 212.

113. John W. Dean, *Warren G. Harding* (New York: Henry Holt, 2004), 29.

114. Startt, 184.

115. Pringle in Ford and Emery, 224–225.

116. Startt, 211.

117. *Ibid.*, 212.

118. *Ibid.*, 200.

119. *Ibid.*, 228. Josephus Daniels later remarked that these small-town editors had done more "than any other people" to assure Wilson's success.

120. Rubin, 87. Not that Wilson personally approved of those in the press corps he had committed himself to interacting with. "Do not believe anything you read in the newspapers," the President once wrote a friend. "If you read the papers I see, they are utterly untrustworthy.... Their lying is shameless and colossal!" Small, 56.

121. For more on the Wilson administration's assault on press freedom, see Lofton, chap. 9 ("World War I: Pressure for Patriotism Versus Freedom to Dissent"). See also Jeffrey A. Smith, *War & Press Freedom: The Problem of Prerogative Power* (New York: Oxford University Press, 1999), 128–142.

122. Geoffrey R. Stone, 180. See also Juergens, chap. 7 ("The Drums of War"); and Stephen Vaughn, *Holding Fast the Inner Lines: Democracy, Nationalism and the Committee on Public Information* (Chapel Hill: University of North Carolina Press, 1980).

123. For the role of press in the struggle over America's membership in the League of Nations, see Juergens, chap. 9 ("The Final Defeat").

124. Wesley M. Bagby, *The Road to Normalcy: The Presidential Campaign and Election of 1920* (Baltimore: Johns Hopkins Press, 1962), 99–100.

125. Keogh, 27.

126. Interestingly, in light of future developments, whatever they thought of the nominee, nearly every paper in the country congratulated the party on its choice for the vice presidency, Assistant Secretary of the Navy Franklin Delano Roosevelt. The *New York Globe* went so far as to conclude, "If the Democratic ticket is elected, even Republicans will be glad to have Roosevelt in Washington." Irving Stone, 43.

127. *Literary Digest*, November 13, 1920, 12.

128. Ponder, 147.

129. *Ibid.*, 425.

130. Tebbel and Watts, 416–419.

131. *Ibid.*, 428.

132. *Ibid.*, 428–429.

133. Neal, 2004, 57.

134. John K. Winkler, *William Randolph Hearst: A New Appraisal* (New York: Hastings House, 1955), 249–250.

135. Ralph G. Martin, *Ballots and Bandwagons* (Chicago: Rand McNally, 1964), 286.

136. Neal, 2004, 62–63.

137. Quoted in Rodney P. Carlisle, *Hearst and the New Deal: The Progressive as Reactionary* (New York: Garland, 1979), 58.

138. Neal, 2004, 59–60.

139. *Ibid.*, 2004, 89.

140. Martin, 1964, 288.

141. Winkler, 253.

142. The best and most comprehensive analysis is Martin, 1964, chap. 4 ("Democratic National Convention of 1932").

143. Neal, 2004, 5–6.

144. In one of his more personal swipes at Roosevelt, Hearst effectively vetoed his offer to historian Claude Bowers to give his nominating speech. Bowers, a member of the New York delegation, was also covering the convention for the Hearst papers. Neal, 2004, 183–186.

145. Oliver Carlson and Ernest Sutherland Bates, *Hearst: Lord of San Simeon* (New York: Viking Press, 1936), 245–246.

146. Michael R. Beschloss, *Kennedy and Roosevelt: The Uneasy Alliance* (New York: Norton, 1980), 72; David Koskoff, *Joseph P. Kennedy: A Life and Times* (Englewood Cliffs, NJ: Prentice Hall, 1974), 44–45; Arthur Krock, *The Consent of the Governed and Other Deceits* (Boston: Little, Brown, 1971), 90–91; Arthur Krock, *Memoirs: Sixty Years on the Firing Line* (New York: Funk & Wagnalls, 1968), 330; Richard J. Whalen, *The Founding Father: The Story of Joseph P. Kennedy* (New York: New American Library, 1964), 124.

147. Winkler, 254–255.

148. *Ibid.*, 255. For further analysis of the backroom machinations that shaped the ascendancy of Franklin Roosevelt, see Richard Oulahan, *The Man Who... The Story of the 1932 Democratic National Convention* (New York: Dial Press, 1971), 114–130.

149. Winkler, 256.

150. Tebbel and Watts, 438.

151. Rubin, 125. See also Samuel Kernell, *Going Public: New Strategies of Presidential Leadership* (Washington, DC: CQ Press, 1997), chap. 3 ("The President and the Press").

152. Rubin, 128.

153. Donald A. Ritchie, *Reporting from Washington: The History of the Washington Press Corps* (New York: Oxford University Press, 2005), 17.

154. *Ibid.*

155. George Seldes, *Lords of the Press* (New York: Julian Messner, 1938), 351.

156. Leo C. Rostow, *The Washington Correspondents* (New York: Harcourt, Brace, 1937, 222–227.

157. *Ibid.*, 272.

158. Pollard, 806. This distinction between reporters and owners was a recurring theme throughout the New Deal–Fair Deal era; Roosevelt's successor Harry Truman raised it during the run-up to the 1952 election when he noted, "This campaign has brought out another fact about the press. The publishers may be mostly Republicans, but the working newspaper men — like most working people throughout the country — are for Stevenson.... I want to say a word to these newspaper men, especially the ones who have been going around the country with me. Boys, when I take out after the one party press, that doesn't include you. It only includes your publishers — and you and I can agree they are not too bright, anyway. You fellows are all right in my book, and I mean it." Herbert Lee Williams, 32.

159. Ritchie, 2005, 10.

160. Rubin, 132.

161. See Douglas B. Craig, *Fireside Politics: Radio and Political Culture in the United States, 1920–1940* (Baltimore: Johns Hopkins University Press, 2000), and Edward W. Chester, *Radio, Television, and American Politics* (New York: Sheed & Ward, 1969).

162. Gary Dean Best, *The Critical Press and the New Deal: The Press versus Presidential Power, 1933–1938* (Westport, CT: Praeger, 1993), 96.

163. Pollard, 800.

164. George Wolfskill and John A. Hudson, *All but the People: Franklin D. Roosevelt and his Critics, 1933–39* (Toronto: Collier-Macmillan, 1969), 175.

165. Best, 57. See also Richard W. Steele, *Propaganda in an Open Society: The Roosevelt Administration and the Media, 1933–1941* (Westport, CT: Greenwood Press, 1985).

166. Best, 37.

167. See Greg Mitchell, *The Campaign of the Century: Upton Sinclair's Race for Governor of California and the Birth of Media Politics* (New York: Random House, 1992).

168. Swint, 19.

169. *Ibid.*, 20.

170. Gottlieb and Wolt, 211.

171. Rubin, 81.

172. Edwin Emery, 629.

173. Carlisle, 12.

174. *Ibid.*, 11.

175. *Ibid.*, 72.

176. *Ibid.*, 78.

177. Wolfskill and Hudson, 175.

178. Carlisle, 84.

179. Winkler, 262. Best uses this quote as the basis for his assertion that by the end of 1934, "the conviction was near universal among newspapermen that the New Deal was retarding recovery." Best, 79.

180. James MacGregor Burns, *Roosevelt: The Lion and the Fox* (New York: Harcourt, 1956), 241.

181. Winkler, 262.

182. Carlson and Bates, 268.

183. Winkler, 265.

184. Carlisle, 105.

185. Rostow, 298.
186. Winkler, 267.
187. Carlisle, 106. It should be noted that Hearst frequently got as fiercely as he gave. In November 1930, ten years before the release of *Citizen Kane*, George P. West wrote a portrait of the Lord of San Simeon for the *American Mercury*: "A towering vanity, fed for thirty years on dreams of the White House and the power of a Caesar, rests at last on a veritable movie-set of Moorish palaces, rising above the sea to command his four hundred square miles, and on the flattery of that Hollywood circle which is both the creature and the wish-fulfillment of the mob on which Hearst has played all his life. And while he putters about among his shiploads of transplanted marbles, or presides, pale and silent, amid the revelry of these puppets, his newspapers that once harried the captains of finance and industry until they trembled in their beds now lead the chorus in hymns to Mammon and genuflections before his high priests." George P. West, "Hearst: A Psychological Note," in Ford and Emery, 300. Nearly ten years later, in March 1949, an irritated Henry Luce took aim at Hearst in *Time* magazine: "No other press lord ever wielded his power with less sense of responsibility; no other press ever matched the Hearst press for flamboyance, perversity and incitement of mass hysteria. Hearst never believed in anything much, not even Hearst, and his appeal was not to men's minds but to those infantile emotions which he never conquered in himself: arrogance, hatred, frustration, fear." Edwin Emery, "William Randolph Hearst: A Tentative Appraisal," in Ford and Emery, 326.
188. Farquhar, 87. The old school tie at least won Roosevelt some breathing space after he took office during the Depression. *Tribune* editorial writer Clifford Raymond recalled that toward the windup of the 1932 campaign, McCormick called him into his office. "Now Cliff, I want you to treat Roosevelt nicely in your editorials," the Colonel said. "I want that boy that I went to school with at Groton to know I wish him well on his career." Obituary, "Life Story of Col. Robert M. McCormick," *Chicago Tribune*, April 2, 1955, 3.
189. Lloyd Wendt, *Chicago Tribune: Rise of a Great American Newspaper* (Chicago: Rand McNally, 1979), 562.
190. *Ibid.*, 563.
191. Richard Norton Smith, *The Colonel: The Life and Legend of Robert R. McCormick* (New York: Houghton Mifflin, 1997), 342. Ironically, more than one modern commentator has ascribed George W. Bush's policies— which diametrically oppose Roosevelt's— to the same root causes. For more on McCormick, see Joseph Gies, *The Colonel of Chicago* (New York: E. P. Dutton, 1979).
192. Wendt, 587–588.
193. Wolfskill and Hudson, 183. Tugwell was also fair game for Colonel McCormick of the *Chicago Tribune*, who accused him of "preaching the identical doctrines of Karl Marx and Lenin."
194. *Ibid.*, 194. Mencken once remarked of the New Deal, "There is, in fact, only one intelligible idea in the whole More Abundant Life rumble-bumble, and that is the idea that whatever A earns really belongs to B. A is any honest and industrious man or woman; B is any drone or jackass."
195. Best, 93.
196. *Ibid.*, 94.
197. Smith, 344345.
198. Carlisle, 168.
199. Wolfskill and Hudson, 191.
200. Money was the least of Landon's problems; in 1936 the GOP outspent the Democrats by $8,892,972 to $5,194,741. Michael J. Webber and G. William Domhoff,

"Myth and Reality in Business Support for Democrats and Republicans in the 1936 Presidential Election," *American Political Science Review* 90, no. 4 (December 1996), 825.
201. Smith, 346.
202. *Time*, November 2, 1936, 13.
203. Smith, 350.
204. Wolfskill and Hudson, 188.
205. Arthur M. Schlesinger, Jr., *The Politics of Upheaval: The Age of Roosevelt, Vol. III* (Boston: Houghton Mifflin, 1960), 636.
206. W. A. Swanberg, *Citizen Hearst* (New York: Macmillan, 1986), 567.
207. *Literary Digest*, October 3, 1936, 5.
208. Wendt, 593. For more on the communist bogey, see W. Cameron Meyers, "The Chicago Newspaper Hoax in the '36 Election Campaign," *Journalism Quarterly* 37, no. 3 (Summer 1960), 356–364.
209. Wendt, 593.
210. Wolfskill and Hudson, 190.
211. Rostow, 277.
212. *Ibid.*, 298.
213. Carlisle, 174–175.
214. Wolfskill and Hudson, 193.
215. Rubin, 138.
216. Wolfskill and Hudson, 194.
217. Wendt, 595.
218. *Ibid.*, 594.
219. Best, 110.
220. "Roosevelt on the Run," *Chicago Tribune*, November 1, 1936, 16.
221. "Nationwide Air Travelers Tell Landon Swing," *Chicago Tribune*, November 2, 1936, 7.
222. "New Deal Girds for 4 Years of Sweet Revenge," *Chicago Tribune*, November 2, 1936, 1.
223. "Paul Revere Must Ride Again," *Chicago Tribune*, November 2, 1936, 1.
224. Graham J. White, *FDR and the Press* (Chicago: University of Chicago Press, 1979), 57.
225. Such missives would seem entirely at home in today's Rupert Murdoch-era *Post*— if "Osama" was substituted for "Hitler" and "Democrats" for "Republicans."
226. Best, 106.
227. *Ibid.*, 107.
228. Wolfskill and Hudson, 184.
229. Graham J. White, 73.
230. *Time*, November 2, 1936, 14.
231. Wolfskill and Hudson, 184.
232. Seldes, 352–353.
233. James Farley, *Behind the Ballots: The Personal History of a Politician* (New York: Harcourt, Brace, 1938), 287.
234. *Literary Digest*, October 31, 1936, 5.
235. Winkler, 268.
236. Carlisle, 177.
237. "Editorial Comment of Representative Papers on Vote Outcome," *New York Times*, Nov. 5, 1936, 4.
238. Smith, 352. The crowd gathered along Michigan Avenue outside the Tribune Tower to watch the election results come in did little to incline McCormick toward magnanimity. As the night wore on and the Republicans melted away, the increasingly boisterous Democrats lingered to jeer and catcall the editor; copies of the *Tribune* were burned in the Loop by citizens congregating along State Street. Presumably not improving the irascible editor's mood, the letters page of the *Tribune* for weeks after the election was inundated with barbs at his expense, such as, "How many more days to save our country? Or is it too late?" "The publishers of the *Tribune* should now take the editorials off the front page and get down to business and print the news. They are fairly good at that, but know

nothing about politics," and "I think you had better hurry, pack your belongings, and catch the first airplane to either Germany or Italy.... You surely don't want to be here when Stalin arrives." *Chicago Tribune*, November 6, 1936, 16.

239. *Literary Digest*, November 14, 1936, 12.

240. Seldes, 352.

241. James L. Baughman, *Henry R. Luce and the Rise of the American News Media* (Boston: Twayne Publishers, 1987), 57.

242. *Literary Digest*, October 3, 1936, 6.

243. Carlisle, 13.

244. *Ibid.*, 166.

245. Wolfskill and Hudson, 300.

246. The fatal error of the Republican press may have been in not appreciating that after weathering the worst of the Depression, Americans were in no mood to be talked down to by the mouthpieces of the old era. Did H .L. Mencken really detract from Roosevelt's appeal when in the July issue of the *American Mercury* he observed that "we may be treated, next November, to a singular spectacle — the reelection of a President who has been repudiated, either openly or covertly, by almost every literate American not on the dole or employed by the Post Office"? Did Mencken assist Landon's cause when in another article for the *American Mercury* in October he noted that "the waning" of Roosevelt's "popularity has been significantly selective. That is to say, it has been fastest in proportion as one mounts the scale of general intelligence"? Best, 110.

247. Rubin, 125. See also Harold F. Gosnell, *Machine Politics: Chicago Model* (Chicago: University of Chicago Press, 1937), 156–176.

248. Betty Houchin Winfield, *FDR and the News Media* (Urbana: University of Illinois Press, 1990), 132.

249. Pollard, 783–784.

250. Winfield, 145–146. So poisonous was the atmosphere by the late 1930s that an expression of support for Roosevelt could terminate careers, in addition to crippling one's social standing. Columnist Dorothy Thompson was eased off the pages of the *New York Herald-Tribune* after she released a column endorsing the president. James David Barber, *The Pulse of Politics: Electing Presidents in the Media Age* (New York: W. W. Norton, 1980), 140.

251. Tebbel and Watts, 445.

252. Winfield, 130.

253. Rostow, 274. McCormick's struggle with the administration turned even more nasty in 1941 when the Colonel blocked the Associated Press from extending its service to his new rival, department store heir Marshall Field, who sought an AP franchise for his pro–New Deal *Chicago Sun*. That action led the Justice Department to file an antitrust suit against the AP.

254. Best, 123.

255. Graham J. White, 49.

256. Keogh, 29.

257. Graham J. White, 50.

258. Winfield, 144.

259. This by definition excluded Hearst, who on the eve of the midterm elections in 1946, more than a year after Roosevelt went to his maker, was still publishing banner headlines declaring "VOTE AGAINST NEW DEAL COMMUNISM — VOTE REPUBLICAN — VOTE AMERICAN." Ethan Rarick, *California Rising: The Life and Times of Pat Brown* (Berkeley: University of California Press, 2005), 51. It also excluded Colonel McCormick. Even after Willkie's loss in 1940, McCormick still refused to compromise, and almost immediately trained his guns on the putative Republican frontrunner for 1944, Tom Dewey. The *Chicago Tribune*, as early as February 15, 1941,

snapped, "If the Republican Party remains an American party it will not make Mr. Dewey a candidate for President." The editorial of September 7, 1943, labeled Dewey a "deserter" who had "compromised his Americanism" and gone "the anti-American way," who had "finished the pilgrimage to Downing Street by way of Wall Street." Elmer Gertz, "Chicago's Adult Delinquent: 'The Tribune,'" *Public Opinion Quarterly* 8, no. 3 (Autumn 1944), 422–423.

260. Schudson, 1978, 149.

261. Halberstam, 1979, 63.

262. Ralph G. Martin, *Henry and Clare: An Intimate Portrait of the Luces* (New York: Putnam's, 1991), 193–194.

263. Wolfskill and Hudson, 299.

264. Martin, 1991, 121. For more on Luce's politics, see W.A. Swanberg, *Luce and his Empire* (New York: Scribner, 1972).

265. Robert E. Herzstein, *Henry R. Luce: A Political Portrait of the Man who Created the American Century* (New York: Macmillan, 1994), 80.

266. Martin, 1991, 193.

267. Barber, 144.

268. Robert E. Burke, "Election of 1940," in Schlesinger, 1985, 2927.

269. Charles Peters, *Five Days in Philadelphia* (New York: Public Affairs, 2005), 39.

270. Barber, 155.

271. Steve Neal, *Dark Horse: A Biography of Wendell Willkie* (Garden City, NY: Doubleday, 1984), 76.

272. Herzstein, 140–145.

273. Burke in Schlesinger, 1985, 2928.

274. Neal, 1984, 85.

275. *Ibid.*, 86.

276. Peters, p. 98.

277. Obituary, "Life Story of Col. Robert M. McCormick," *Chicago Tribune*, April 2, 1955, 6.

278. Convention coverage in the Luce publications saluted the result as the triumph of a grassroots insurgency over the old guard, "the same old jostling crowds, the same stunts and signs and gadgets, the same well-whiskeyed bedroom conniving.... In petitions, letters, telegrams by the hundreds of thousands the people were demanding that the Republican Party meet the challenge of new times by nominating Willkie. But the Party elders, to a man, still held back, still strove to nominate a safe-and-sound Party Regular.... By Wednesday night when the Willkie opposition broke into boos and physical fighting on the convention floor, progressive observers were about ready to write the G.O.P. off as hopeless.... Thursday night, with the galleries cheering every Willkie vote and the delegates breaking away from their leaders, a tidal wave of popular demand crumbled the opposition, swept the old bosses out and Wendell Willkie and his young followers in to the leadership of the Republican Party." Barber, 157.

279. Baughman, 124. The beginning of the split pitting the Eastern against the Southern and Western wings of the Republican Party can be traced to this convention. The Easterners continued to dominate the party for the next twenty years, having to whisk Dwight Eisenhower back from Europe to hold off Taft in 1952 in the process. The rebellion against this Eastern hegemony propelled Barry Goldwater to the nomination over Nelson Rockefeller in 1964. The last Eastern victory came in 1976 when Gerald Ford inched past the challenge of Ronald Reagan. Since then the South and West have been absolutely dominant.

280. Herzstein, 162.

281. Barber, 157. According to Herzstein, Willkie "listened carefully to Harry's monologues and accepted most of his advice." Herzstein, 140–145.

282. Barber, 158.

283. Winfield, 144.

284. Graham J. White, 1.

285. Winkler, 283.

286. Mott, 1944, 357.

287. *Ibid.*, 348.

288. Barber, 159. However cruel, Luce's instincts as to Willkie's viability were even more correct than he could have known: Willkie died of a heart attack on October 8, 1940.

289. Herzstein, 301–306; 310–323; 335–345.

290. Small, 56–57, 61.

291. Truman's ambivalent assessment of the media barons was on full display during his address to the National Conference of Editorial Writers in 1947. "I have been told that when a fellow fails at everything else, he either starts a hotel or a newspaper," the president told his audience. In a more serious vein he added, "You have a tremendous influence on the welfare of this country. You can either make it or break it. I say that advisedly." Herbert Lee Williams, 19–20. Truman perceived this influence most clearly in foreign policy: "No group of men in this country is of greater importance to our foreign policy than the group your society represents." *Ibid.*, 21.

292. Small, 57.

293. Tebbel and Watts, 460. "The sabotage sheet, the *Washington Times Herald* is Bertie McCormick's outlet in the capital city," Truman opined on another occasion. "His *Chicago Tribune* and the *New York Daily News* are his lie outlets in those two great cities. Roy Howard's chain and the Knight layout are Hearst imitators, but not quite up to the dirtiest Hearst technique. But they are coming along." Kenneth W. Thompson, ed., *Ten Presidents and the Press* (Wasington, DC: University Press of America, 1983), 38.

294. Small, 62.

295. Tebbel and Watts, 460.

296. *Ibid.*, 459.

297. Kenneth W. Thompson, 1983, 31. Truman grumbled in a letter dated December 15, 1951, that he "wouldn't expect the Hearst papers to tell the truth about anything." Herbert Lee Williams, 97.

298. "How We Earned His Hate," *Chicago Tribune*, June 11, 1948, 1. "If McCormick ever said anything good about me," Truman retorted in a letter to an Illinois friend, "I'd know it was wrong." Kenneth W. Thompson, 1983, 30.

299. Barber, 52.

300. Herbert Lee Williams, 156.

301. Jules Abels, *Out of the Jaws of Victory* (New York: Henry Holt, 1959), 251.

302. "Scripps-Howard Papers Announce for Dewey," *Washington Post*, October 15, 1948, 12.

303. Littlewood, 122.

304. Herbert Lee Williams, 91. The salience of "facts" was key to Truman's belief system. See *ibid.*, 89–102 ("A Fight for Facts"). The "truth" as Truman saw it enabled him to maintain his identity distinct from the "fact murderers" of the press. *Ibid.*, 193.

305. Franklin Mitchell, *Harry S. Truman and the News Media: Contentious Relations, Belated Respect* (Columbia: University of Missouri Press, 1998), 51.

306. "Papers Back Dewey," *New York Times*, October 30, 1948, 9.

307. Mitchell, 51.

308. Barber, 62.

309. Editorial, "Today's Election," *Washington Post*, November 2, 1948, 14.

310. Littlewood, 122.

311. Ritchie, 2005, 26.

312. Mitchell, 54. For a sprightly report on how the nation's media coped on election night 1948 — including the delicious reference to pollster George Gallup "looking like an animal eating its young" when he conceded Truman's victory at 3 A.M.— see Lew Wallace, "The Truman-Dewey Upset," *American History Illustrated* 11, no. 6 (June 1976), 20–29.

313. Herbert Lee Williams, 73–74.

314. Kenneth W. Thompson, 1983, 32–33.

315. *Ibid.*, 33.

316. Mitchell, 121. When once asked why newspaper editors had such a poor record in picking the winners of presidential elections, Truman replied, "I will tell you exactly what is the matter with them. They don't know anything about politics." Herbert Lee Williams, 157.

317. Herbert Lee Williams, 137–138.

318. Kenneth W. Thompson, 1983, 31.

319. *Ibid.*, 1983, 35. Truman could also let bygones be bygones. In 1956, the ex-president not only accepted an invitation to dinner from Henry Luce, he played a Paderewski minuet for him afterward.

320. Halberstam, 1979, 89. See also Robert E. Herzstein, *Henry R. Luce, Time, and the American Crusade in Asia* (Cambridge: Cambridge University Press, 2005).

321. Kenneth W. Thompson, 1983, 35.

322. Herbert Lee Williams, 174.

323. Kenneth W. Thompson, 1983, 38.

324. Martin, 1991, 291.

325. Halberstam, 1979, 90–93.

326. Baughman, 163.

327. Halberstam, 1979, 59.

328. "Given all their back room dealings, both Luces had a right to consider Eisenhower's nomination a personal victory, and so they did," Martin says. Martin, 1991, 296.

329. Porter McKeever, *Adlai Stevenson: His Life and Times* (New York: Morrow, 1989), 251.

330. Nathan B. Blumberg, *One-Party Press? Coverage of the 1952 Presidential Campaign in 35 Daily Newspapers* (Lincoln: University of Nebraska Press, 1954, 15–16. Data derived from a poll published in *Editor & Publisher*, November 1, 1952. The poll included 1,385 of 1,773 daily newspapers published in the United States. Total daily circulation of newspapers in the poll was 50,013,420, 92.59 percent of the total daily U.S. circulation.

331. Blumberg, 46. See also Malcolm W. Klein and Nathan Macoby, "Newspaper Objectivity in the 1952 Campaign," *Journalism Quarterly* 31, no. 2 (Summer 1954), 285–286. While confirming the pervasive Republican favoritism during the 1952 campaign, the key point made by Rowse in his conclusion was that "all papers— both Republican and Democratic — showed evidence of favoritism in their news columns in violation of their own accepted rules of conduct." Arthur Edward Rowse, *Slanted News: A Case Study of the Nixon and Stevenson Fund Stories* (Westport, CT: Greenwood Press, 1973), 127.

332. A point noted by Harry Truman when he grumbled that "very few of the slick magazines are friends of mine, or the Democratic party, either." Herbert Lee Williams, 22.

333. John B. Martin, *Adlai Stevenson of Illinois* (New York: Doubleday, 1976), 668; and Kenneth S. Davis, *The Politics of Honor: A Biography of Adlai Stevenson* (New York: Putnam, 1967), 288.

334. "One-Party Press," *Washington Post*, September 9, 1952, 10.

335. Herbert Lee Williams, 158.

336. *Ibid.*, 159.

337. *Ibid.* In one of the more typical incidents of the

campaign, on August 5, the *Los Angeles Times* published a photo of an Eisenhower speech before the Veterans of Foreign Wars at the 100,000-seat Los Angeles Coliseum. Though only 16,000 people showed up, the *Times* angled the photograph to make it appear that Ike was addressing a full house. Gottlieb and Wolt, 279.

339. William E. Porter, *Assault on the Media: The Nixon Years* (Ann Arbor: University of Michigan Press, 1976), 11.

340. Baughman, 163.

341. Herbert Lee Williams, 164.

342. Kenneth W. Thompson, 1983, 38.

343. Baughman, 164.

344. Eisenhower tried to have Clare named ambassador to Brazil in 1959. The Senate overwhelmingly approved her nomination, despite the protracted opposition of Senator Wayne Morse (D-OR). But Clare, fatally, always had to have the last word. Flushed with success in the immediate aftermath of the vote, she remarked, "My difficulties, of course, go some years back when Senator Wayne Morse was kicked in the head by a horse." When she refused to retract her statement, Luce, furious at his wife's invective, dictated her letter of resignation. Baughman, 178–179. Clare would go on to second the nomination of Barry Goldwater at the Republican National Convention in 1964.

345. *Ibid.*, 72.

346. *Ibid.*, 173.

347. Malcolm Moos, "Election of 1956," in Schlesinger, 1985, 3352.

348. For an in-depth analysis of the structuring of media relations by the Eisenhower White House, identifying it as the first television presidency, see Craig Allen, *Eisenhower and the Mass Media* (Chapel Hill: University of North Carolina Press, 1993).

349. David M. Oshinsky, *A Conspiracy so Immense: The World of Joe McCarthy*, (New York: Free Press, 1983), 183–184.

350. *Ibid.*, 180–181.

351. *Ibid.*, 182.

352. See Jim Tuck, *McCarthyism and New York's Hearst Press: A Study of Roles in the Witch Hunt* (Lanham, MD: University Press of America, 1995).

353. Truman fumed over McCarthy's skill in stringing the media along, especially when juxtaposed with his own comparative impotence. He wrote to Senator William Benton on August 15, 1951, "There is a concerted effort on the part of the wire services ... to discredit whatever the administration forces try to do. If you will analyze the manner in which they handled McCarthy and the manner in which they handle people who are members of the Administration you will see what I mean." Ironically, given the political climate of the day, the president concluded, "You will find if you study the lines followed by these press people, that they are just as guilty of sabotaging the news as *Pravda* and *Izvestia* in Russia." Kenneth W. Thompson, 1983, 37–38.

354. James Chace, *Dean Acheson* (New York: Simon & Schuster, 1998), 240. The situation had changed little two years later when Alan Barth, an editorial writer at the *Washington Post*, told the Association for Education in Journalism, "There can be little doubt that the way [McCarthy's charges] have been reported in most papers serves Senator McCarthy's partisan political purposes much more than it serves the purposes of the press, the interest of truth." Brent Cunningham, "Re-Thinking Objectivity," *Columbia Journalism Review* 42, no. 2 (July/August 2003), 27.

355. Oshinsky, 187.

356. Oshinsky, 189–190. Halberstam draws a similar conclusion when he accuses the press of being a "willing accessory" to McCarthy's agenda because even those journalists who appreciated that they were dancing to McCarthy's tune were constrained from critical analysis by the prevailing orthodoxy that mandated that "a story was a story. If Joe said something, you reported it; that was all it took." Reporters were "wedded to a notion of objectivity that made very little distinction between fact and truth." Halberstam, 1979, 194–195. Even a more sympathetic biographer like Arthur Herman recognizes that the relationship between McCarthy and the press was more symbiotic than antagonistic. While he states that "the American media used McCarthy for its own purposes," the fact that the reverse was also true clearly comes through in his narrative. See Arthur Herman, *Joseph McCarthy: Reexamining the Life of America's Most Hated Senator* (New York: Free Press, 2000), especially chap. 12 ("McCarthy Against the Press"). For more on the media's love-hate relationship with McCarthy see Ritchie, 2005, chap. 4 ("The Friends of Joe McCarthy"), and James Aronson, *The Press and the Cold War* (New York: Bobbs-Merrill, 1970), chap. 5 ("The Making of Joe McCarthy"). Perhaps the last word should go to the arch-traitor in McCarthy's pan-global red conspiracy: "The anti-administration press made a glamour boy out of McCarthy," Harry Truman concluded, "then they found they'd made a Frankenstein out of him." Herbert Lee Williams, 11.

357. Edwin R. Bayley, *Joe McCarthy and the Press* (Madison: University of Wisconsin Press, 1981), 173–174.

358. *Ibid.*, 219.

359. Liebovich concludes that after a moment of disorientation at the end of the Second World War, "the news organizations came to accept the inevitability of the Cold War because right-wing elements in the United States had a stronger case to make and made their case better." Louis Liebovich, *The Press and the Origins of the Cold War, 1944–1947* (Westport, CT: Praeger, 1988), 152. See also Daniel Chomsky, *Constructing the Cold War: The New York Times and the Truman Doctrine* (Ph.D. dissertation, Northwestern University, Evanston, 1999).

360. See Stephen Schlesinger and Stephen Kinzer, *Bitter Fruit: The Story of the American Coup in Guatemala* (Cambridge, MA: Harvard University Press, 2005); and David Halberstam, *The Fifties* (New York: Villard Books, 1993), 382–388.

361. See Aronson, chap. 11 ("The Bay of Pigs").

362. See Montague Kern, Patricia W. Levering, and Ralph B. Levering, *The Kennedy Crises: The Press, the Presidency, and Foreign Policy* (Chapel Hill: University of North Carolina Press, 1983), chap. 11 ("The Cuban Missile Crisis: The Administration Dominates the Press") and Aronson, chap. 12 ("The Missile Crisis").

363. Edwin R. Bayley, *Joe McCarthy and the Press* (Madison: University of Wisconsin Press, 1981), 152–156.

364. Robert J. Bresler, "Media Bias and the Culture Wars," *USA Today Magazine* 133, no. 2710 (July 2004), 13–14.

365. When Stanley Kramer's nuclear Armageddon film *On the Beach* was released in 1959, the *New York Daily News* labeled it a "would-be shocker which plays right up the alley of a) the Kremlin, and b) the Western defeatists and/or traitors who yelp for the scrapping of the H-bomb.... [I]t points the way toward eventual communist enslavement of the entire human race." Kim Newman, *Apocalypse Movies: End of the World Cinema* (New York: St. Martin's Griffin, 1999), 150.

366. Stephen E. Ambrose, *Nixon: The Education of a Politician, 1913–1962* (New York: Simon and Schuster, 1987), 359. In an unguarded moment captured years later by the White House tapes, Nixon expanded on the key

role that manipulation of the media had played in his own political ascendancy, describing methods he wanted carried forward into his presidency: "We won the Hiss case in the papers. We did. I had to leak stuff all over the place. Because the Justice Department would not prosecute it. [FBI Director J. Edgar] Hoover didn't even cooperate. It was won in the papers. We have to develop a program, a program for leaking out information. We're destroying these people in the papers."

367. Richard A. Viguerie and David Franke, *America's Right Turn: How Conservatives Used New and Alternative Media to Take Power* (Chicago: Bonus Books, 2004), 52.

Chapter V

1. Joanne Freeman captures the enduring nature of this key distinction between the parties: "Republicans perceive themselves as insiders even when they are out of power, and Democrats perceive themselves as outsiders even when they are in power." Jo Freeman, "The Political Culture of the Democratic and Republican Parties," *Political Science Quarterly* 101, no. 3 (1986), 328.

2. For the antecedents of this sense of noblesse oblige on the part of the party of the establishment towards non-white minorities, especially African Americans and Native Americans, see Harry L. Watson, "The Second American Party System," in *Liberty and Power: The Politics of Jacksonian America* (New York: Hill & Wang, 1990), chap. 8.

3. Gary Donaldson, *Liberalism's Last Hurrah: The Presidential Campaign of 1964* (Armonk, NY: M. E. Sharpe, Armonk, 2003), 174. The assembled journalists half jokingly agreed that if the delegates rushed them, they would throw themselves on the mercy of the *Chicago Tribune*. Barber, 179. One reporter, John Chancellor of NBC, was later hustled off the convention floor by the police. "I'm in custody," Chancellor, still broadcasting, informed his audience. "I want to assure you that NBC is fully staffed with other reporters who are not in the custody of the Daly City Police and the San Mateo Sheriff's office. I formally say this is a disgrace. The press, radio, and television should be allowed to do their work at a convention. I'm being taken down off the arena now.... I'll check in later." He signed off: "This is John Chancellor, somewhere in custody." Rick Perlstein, *Before the Storm: Barry Goldwater and the Unmaking of the American Consensus* (New York: Hill and Wang, 2001), 382.

4. There were some longer-term shifts across the ideological divide. John Cowles continued to endorse Democrats in subsequent elections, and emerged as a liberal voice in the business community during the later 1960s when he served on the Business Council.

5. Daniel Patrick Moynihan, writing in *Commentary* in 1971, noted that the increase in the number of middle-class, college-educated Baby Boomers seeking careers in the media meant that "the press grows more and more influenced by attitudes genuinely hostile to American society and American government." Schudson, 1978, 179

6. From 1910 to 1968, the number of cities with commercially competing dailies declined from 689 to 45. Patrick M. Garry, *Scrambling for Protection: The New Media and the First Amendment* (Pittsburgh: University of Pittsburgh Press, 1994), 81. This process is ongoing; when the first edition of Ben Bagdikian's *The Media Monopoly* was published in 1983, it identified some fifty corporations who controlled the majority of America's major media outlets. Twenty years later, that list was down to ten international news conglomerates.

7. Louis W. Liebovich, *The Press and the Modern Presidency: Myths and Mindsets from Kennedy to Election 2000* (Westport, CT: Praeger, 2001), 5.

8. V. O. Key, Jr., *Public Opinion and American Democracy* (New York: Alfred A. Knopf, 1964), 393.

9. Richard Nixon, *The Memoirs of Richard Nixon* (New York: Simon & Schuster, 1990), 260.

10. Keogh, 6.

11. David Halberstam offers the following perspective on this debate: "I was twenty-six years old and working for the Nashville *Tennessean* that fall and, like every other reporter who covered that campaign, no matter how briefly, I will never forget the difference between the two camps: the ease and camaraderie of the Kennedy plane and camp, the capacity of the Kennedy people to imply that this was one big happy family and to suggest that the Kennedys were for the good, civilized things that mankind wanted; the Nixon camp, by contrast, filled with the shadows of mutual suspicion and distrust and barely concealed anger, a coldness and distance which somehow implied darker things covered up and hidden. Nixon held the press at bay, even the pool press; Kennedy, as Theodore H. White wrote, would as soon have flown off without his copilot as leave his pool reporters behind." David Halberstam, "Press and Prejudice," *Esquire*, April 1974, 228.

12. Halberstam, 1979, 355.

13. For more on Luce's flirtation with Kennedy in 1960, see Martin, 1991, 358–363. Most of the other weeklies also endorsed Nixon, explicitly (such as the *Christian Science Monitor*) or implicitly; one report notes that, "taken together, the news magazines tend to put Republican candidates in a more favorable light than Democratic candidates." Bruce H. Westley, et al., "The News Magazines and the 1960 Conventions," *Journalism Quarterly* 40, no. 4 (Autumn 1963), 525–531, 647.

14. As a representative manifestation of his editorial line, Loeb heralded the news of the first Soviet nuclear-weapons test by advocating an immediate preemptive nuclear strike against the reds: "We cannot sit idle and wait for Armageddon and destruction. We must forestall such a catastrophe and the only way is to strike a proposed aggressor before he is ready to strike. A preventive war ... will be the greatest agency for peace in the world today, as well as our only salvation from impending destruction. We cannot delay longer." Oshinsky, 106.

15. Eric P. Veblen, *The Manchester Union Leader in New Hampshire Elections* (Hanover: University Press of New England, 1975), 160–161.

16. Nixon remains a subject of endless fascination for qualified political psychologists, but in my amateur opinion the ultimate motivation for this hate was Nixon's own profound sense of inadequacy. While he craved recognition from this elite more than anything, his own paranoia denied him the satisfaction of ever truly believing he had secured it.

17. See Gottlieb and Wolt, 277–280. For further analysis of the overwhelming Republican bias in the California media, see James E. Gregg, "Newspaper Editorial Endorsements and California Elections, 1948–62," *Journalism Quarterly* 42 (1965), 532–538. Gregg estimated that 80 percent of the newspapers in California during the period studied were Republican in orientation, 10 percent independent, and 10 percent Democratic.

18. Rarick, 2005, 249.

19. Halberstam, 1979, 256–266. For more on the *Los Angeles Times* incubation of the young Richard Nixon, see Dennis McDougal, *Privileged Son: Otis Chandler and the Rise and Fall of the L.A. Times Dynasty* (Cambridge, MA: Perseus, 2001), 176–179.

20. Editorial, "Nixon for Governor," *Los Angeles Times*, October 21, 1962, K6.

21. Rarick, 2005, 248–249. See also Ambrose, 668–673.

22. "Publisher of Times tells Endorsement," *Los Angeles Times*, November 8, 1962, 1.

23. One aspect of the campaign that did meet with Nixon's approval was the coverage on television, which he praised as particularly fair. In fact, Los Angeles station KTTV had aired so many commentaries favorable to Nixon and critical of Brown that it was ordered by the Federal Communications Commission (comprised of four Republicans and two Democrats) to provide the Democrats with more time.

24. Rarick, 2005, 249–250.

25. Halberstam, 1979, 349. For an interesting perspective on Nixon's changing relationship with the press in California, see Ethan Rarick, "Kicking Nixon around some more: Tricky Dick's career marked a stark change in press-politician relations," *San Francisco Chronicle*, December 1, 2002, sfgate.com/cgi-bin/article.cgi?f=/c/a/2002/12/01/IN234985.DTL.

26. For an example of the mounting conservative grievance against the media, see Morrie Ryskind, "They Toe the Liberal Line on TV," *Los Angeles Times*, October 31, 1962, A5.

27. Ambrose, 13.

28. Veblen, 161.

29. *Time*, Oct. 2, 1964, 74.

30. Theodore H. White, *The Making of the President 1964* (New York: Atheneum, 1965), 334. Goldberg also notes, "In an unprecedented reversal of the pattern, most daily newspapers tilted against the Republican candidate." Robert Alan Goldberg, *Barry Goldwater* (New Haven, CT: Yale University Press, 1995), 223. See also Robert S. Erikson, "The Influence of Newspaper Endorsements in Presidential Elections: The Case of 1964," *American Journal of Political Science* 20, no. 2 (May 1976), 207–233.

31. Erik A. Devereux, "Newspaper, Organized Interests and Party Competition in the 1964 Election," *Media History* 5, no. 1 (June 1999), 44.

32. Perlstein, 457.

33. Liebovich, 2001, 38.

34. John Micklethwait and Adrian Wooldridge, *The Right Nation: Conservative Power in America* (New York: Penguin, 2004), 56.

35. The dozen holdouts for Goldwater included the *Chicago Tribune* and *American* in Illinois, *Los Angeles Times* and *Oakland Tribune* in California, *Cincinnati Enquirer* and *Columbus Dispatch* in Ohio, *Milwaukee Sentinel* in Wisconsin, *Richmond Times-Dispatch* and *News Leader* in Virginia, *Nashville Banner* in Tennessee, *Tulsa World* in Oklahoma, and *Birmingham News* in Alabama (the only state on this list he carried). Other loyalists included the *Arizona Republic, Charleston News and Courier,* Idaho *Daily Statesman,* and *Manchester Union Leader.* Johnson was endorsed by all twenty-two of the major dailies that had supported Kennedy in 1960: the *New York Times, Post, Newsday,* and *Long Island Press, St. Louis Post-Dispatch, Milwaukee Journal,* Louisville *Courier-Journal* and *Times,* Pittsburgh *Post-Gazette,* Toledo *Blade,* Denver *Post,* Hartford *Times, Sacramento Bee, Atlanta Constitution* and *Journal, Miami News, Raleigh News and Observer, Nashville Tennessean, Norfolk Virginian-Pilot, Dayton News, Fresno Bee,* and *Long Beach Press-Telegram.* Johnson also made deep inroads into Nixon's allies in the press, swinging 52 of them including the *San Francisco Chronicle, Chicago Daily News* and *Sun-Times, Miami Herald, Des Moines Register* and *Tribune, New Orleans States-Item,* Baltimore *Sun, Boston Herald, Detroit Free Press, Minneapolis Star* and *Tribune, St. Paul Dispatch* and *Pioneer Press, Kansas City Star* and *Times, Newark News* and *Star-Ledger, New York Herald-Tribune, Rochester Democrat and Chronicle* and *Times Union, Syracuse Post-Standard* and *Herald-Journal, Cleveland Plain Dealer,* Portland *Oregon Journal, Philadelphia Bulletin, Inquirer* and *News, Fargo Forum, Albuquerque Journal, Hartford Courant, Seattle Times, Dallas Times Herald, Fort Worth Star-Telegram, Houston Chronicle* and *Post,* and *Norfolk Ledger-Dispatch,* in addition to eight of the Hearst papers and eleven of the Scripps-Howard papers. Nixon papers declining to make an endorsement in 1964 included the *St. Louis Globe-Democrat, Omaha World-Herald, Dallas News, South Bend Tribune, Honolulu Star-Bulletin,* and *New York Daily News.* Edwin Emery, "Press Support for Johnson and Goldwater," *Journalism Quarterly* 41, no. 4, (Autumn 1964), 485–488.

36. Devereux, 46.

37. *Ibid.,* 52–53.

38. *Ibid.,* 48.

39. *Ibid.,* 49. Hoyt wrote to LBJ on October 5 to assure him "you have the greatest press in history."

40. *Ibid.,* 42.

41. Richard H. Meeker, *Newspaperman: S. I. Newhouse and the Business of News* (New Haven, CT: Ticknor & Fields, 1983), 222.

42. Devereux, 53. The editor of the latter paper wrote Johnson to point out that "we believe this is the first time in 135 years that this newspaper has endorsed a Democrat for the Presidency," adding disingenuously, "As you know, this is a Newhouse newspaper. As usual, Mr. S. I. Newhouse played absolutely no part in our decision. His papers are completely autonomous."

43. *Ibid.,* 47.

44. Perlstein, 432.

45. Emannuel Perlmutter, "Many Papers Shifting Allegiance on Presidency," The *New York Times,* Sep. 8, 1964, A19.

46. Theodore H. White, 1965, 334–335.

47. Halberstam, 1979, 394.

48. Devereux, 51.

49. *Ibid.,* 52.

50. Editorial, "The 1964 Religious Issue," *The Christian Century,* Vol. LXXXI, No. 41, October 7, 1964, p. 1228. This was far from the first occasion this publication drew an analogy between Goldwater and the Third Reich (or at least, the Weimar Republic). One contributor asserted that during the GOP convention "The Cow Palace at times rang with echoes from the Munich beer hall," and concluded, "Goldwater may be the precursor of an American totalitarianism." William Stringfellow, "God, Guilt and Goldwater," *The Christian Century,* Vol. LXXXI, No. 36, September 2, 1964, p. 1082, 1083. If such hostility toward Goldwater was manifested in the ecclesiastical press, the animus of the secular papers can well be imagined.

51. Barber, 182. Goldwater's campaign treasurer, shades of FDR, feels that the blame for the distorted coverage his candidate was subjected to rests not with the beat reporters but with their overseers in the boardrooms: "It may seem hard to believe, but most of the traveling press—especially those who had been with Barry throughout the campaign—liked the man, if not his policies. I think, of the fifty-three reporters on board for the last big swing, only three were really belligerent. Barry's big problem was not with the reporters, but with editors." J. William Middendorf II, *Glorious Disaster: Barry Goldwater's Presidential Campaign and the Origins of the Conservative Movement* (New York: Basic Books, 2006), 220.

52. Robert Alan Goldberg, 223.

53. Perlstein, 438–439. Another coalition of mental health professionals weighing in during the campaign was Psychiatrists for Johnson. Although its members had

never met Goldwater, they deemed him unstable anyway. Goldwater later sued for libel and won.

54. Lyndon B. Johnson, *The Vantage Point* (New York: Holt, Rinehart & Winston, 1971), 96. For more on Johnson's travails in his relationship with the media, see Kathleen J. Turner, *Lyndon Johnson's Dual War: Vietnam and the Press* (Chicago: University of Chicago Press, 1985), and Vaughn D. Bornet, *The Presidency of Lyndon B. Johnson* (Lawrence: University Press of Kansas, 1983), chap. 7 ("In This Corner: The Media").

55. Streitmatter, chap. 12 ("Vietnam War: Bringing the Battlefield into the American Living Room") endorses this perspective, and quotes a number of other authors to the same effect.

56. Clarence R. Wyatt, *Paper Soldiers: The American Press and the Vietnam War* (New York: W. W. Norton, 1993), 218. See also Ted Carpenter, *The Captive Press: Foreign Policy Crises and the First Amendment* (Washington, D.C.: Cato Institute, 1995), chap. 7 ("Losing Control: The Vietnam War"). Galen concludes, "The belief that television ... undermined Washington's war effort is one of the most tenacious but inaccurate aspects of the stab-in-the-back myth," 155. See also Peter Braestrup, *Big Story: How the American Press and Television Reported and Interpreted the Crisis of Tet 1968 in Vietnam and Washington* (Novato, CA: Presidio, 1994), 705, 707. For more detailed analysis, see *ibid.*, 619–673 ("The Debate at Home: How did it Affect Johnson War Policy?").

57. William M. Hammond, *Reporting Vietnam: Media and Military at War* (Lawrence: University Press of Kansas, 1998), 291–296. See also William M. Hammond, "The Press in Vietnam as Agent of Defeat: A Critical Examination," *Reviews in American History* 17, no. 2 (June 1989), 312–323. This is the dominant assessment on the role of the media during the Vietnam conflict — that coverage reflected a fractured reality, not a political agenda. See the conclusions drawn by Daniel C. Hallin, *The "Uncensored War:" The Media and Vietnam* (Berkeley: University of California Press, 1989), 211–215; Wyatt, 216–219; and Braestrup, who concludes in his analysis of how the media reported the Tet Offensive that "rarely has contemporary crisis-journalism turned out, in retrospect, to have veered so widely from reality," does not ascribe this poor performance to agenda setting: "Ideology, per se, played a relatively minor role in the media treatment of the Tet crisis." See also William Prochnow, "The Military and the Media," in *The Press*, by Geneva Overholser and Kathleen Hall Jamieson (Oxford: Oxford University Press, 2005), chap. 19; and Daniel C. Hallin, "The Media, the War in Vietnam, and Political Support: A Critique of the Thesis of an Oppositional Media," *Journal of Politics* 46, no. 1 (February 1984), 2–24.

58. See John E. Mueller, *War, Presidents, and Public Opinion* (New York: Wiley, 1973), 42–65 ("Trends in Popular Support for the Wars in Korea and Vietnam"), 155–167 ("The Similarity of Support for the Wars: Some Explanations and Commentary"). See also Aronson, chap. 7 ("The News from Korea").

59. But the legendary power of the media to break the back of a war effort is invoked time and again, most recently by *1776* author David McCullough who in an interview with Tim Russert on CNBC said, "If [the Revolution] had been covered by the media, and the country had seen how horrible the conditions were, how badly things were being run by the officers, and what a very serious soup we were in, I think that would have been it." "For This W, It's 1776 All Over Again," *US News & World Report*, July 18, 2005.

60. This accusation is leveled notwithstanding the conclusion of the Iraq Study Group that "there is significant underreporting of the violence in Iraq." James A. Baker and Lee H. Hamilton, Co-Chairs, *Iraq Study Group Report* (New York: Vintage, 2006), 94. See also Kevin Baker, "Stabbed in the Back! The Past and Future of a Right-Wing Myth," *Harper's* 312, no. 1873 (May 2006), 31–42.

61. Ironically, Nixon enjoyed a honeymoon upon taking office that was almost unprecedented in length among his twentieth century counterparts. "Overall, Nixon enjoyed better press in his first year than any other twentieth-century president except Theodore Roosevelt," Greenberg says, quoting a study that asserts Theodore Roosevelt's coverage in his first year was 88.8 percent positive, compared to 81.2 percent for Nixon. David Greenberg, *Nixon's Shadow: The History of an Image* (New York: W. W. Norton, 2003), 140.

62. Summers, 330–331.

63. Farquhar, 223.

64. Ambrose, 251. "Nixon hated us," one correspondent at the time recalled. "It was reciprocated in some ways, but not as much as he thought." Lou Cannon, "The Press and the Nixon Presidency," in *The Nixon Presidency: Twenty-Two Intimate Perspectives of Richard M. Nixon*, Kenneth W. Thompson, ed. (Lanham, MD: University Press of America, 1987), 196.

65. Stanley I. Kutler, *The Wars of Watergate: The Last Crisis of Richard Nixon* (New York: Alfred A. Knopf, 1990), 163–164.

66. Michael A. Genovese, *The Nixon Presidency: Power and Politics in Turbulent Times* (New York: Greenwood Press, 1990), 49.

67. Ambrose, 370.

68. Louis W. Liebovich, *Richard Nixon, Watergate, and the Press* (Westport, CT: Praeger, 2003), 4. Nixon even had some advice for Haldeman on how to deal with the press personally. Reporters, the president told his chief of staff in 1970, "have a fetish about fairness, and once they are caught being unfair, they are very sensitive about it and try to compensate it from time to time." (At other times, the president added, "they have no intention whatever to be fair.") David Greenberg, 159.

69. See Julius Duscha, "The White House Watch Over TV and the Press," *New York Times*, August 20, 1972, M9, 92–93, 95–97, 100; see also John Anthony Maltese, *Spin Control: The White House Office of Communications and the Management of Presidential News* (Chapel Hill: University of North Carolina Press, 1994), 71–72.

70. Liebovich, 2003, 7.

71. Lori C. Han, *Governing from Center Stage: White House Communication Strategies During the Television Age of Politics* (Cresskill, New Jersey: Hampton Press, 2001), 80–81. Some with access to the president were uneasy at the direction media policy was taking. Speechwriter Jim Keogh (formerly a journalist with *Time*) expressed his concern to Haldeman in June 1970 that the administration was relying too much on "gimmicks" to promote the president's agenda: "Too many people are spending too much time drawing up too many game plans.... Let's face a few facts. Most of the working media people are 1) against us, and 2) suspicious of us. In the main, they are hard to fool.... It is very difficult for us to put anything over on them; it is practically impossible for us to subvert them. If they were for us we could do these things; since they are not, we can't. When we try a gimmick they usually are waiting at the entrance to the alley and they wind up making us look even more devious than we are. This gives us a credibility problem. The results often turn out to be counter productive. And the media wind up being more suspicious of us than ever." Han, 85. Rebuffed, Keogh quit the administration at the end of 1970. "I left because I didn't like it. I was somewhat frustrated, some-

what uncomfortable, and not pleased with what I was able to do there." James Keogh, "Nixon, the Press, and the White House," in *The Nixon Presidency: Twenty-Two Intimate Perspectives of Richard M. Nixon*, Kenneth W. Thompson, ed. (Lanham, MD: University Press of America, 1987), 206.

72. Genovese, 51.

73. Fred Emery, *Watergate: The Corruption and Fall of Richard Nixon* (London: Jonathan Cape, 1994), 38.

74. Ambrose, 250. On another occasion, Nixon ordered his subordinates to play favorites: "Get *Time* in on Friday and *US News* give them the whole story.... [D]on't tell *Newsweek* anything."

75. Maltese, 46.

76. Theodore H. White, 1973, 262.

77. Herbert B. Asher, *Presidential Elections and American Politics* (Homewood, IL: Dorsey Press, 1976), 222–227.

78. Theodore H. White, 1973, 251.

79. Edith Efron, *The News Twisters* (Los Angeles: Nash Publishing, 1971), 50, 55.

80. Halberstam, 1979, 596.

81. Theodore H. White, 1973, 251–252.

82. Porter, 256–257.

83. *Ibid.*, 258.

84. *Ibid.*, 259.

85. Porter, 265. The public response, in the form of a flood of letters and telegrams to the White House and the networks, was overwhelmingly in favor of Agnew (although, given the administration's vigorous policy of biasing "spontaneous" displays of popular sentiment, this should be somewhat qualified). According to one account, anti-Semitic letters constituted eleven percent of one network's mail, while tirades against blacks made up another ten percent. Kutler, 178.

86. Small, 138. Conservative commentator Robert Novak picked up on this theme, arguing, "[T]he journalist working for the television networks, the big news magazines and the important metropolitan press had now [in 1972] become part of the liberal establishment, both in his manner of living and his ideological commitment.... The national media is a melting pot where the journalists, regardless of background, are welded into a homogenous ideological mold joined to the liberal establishment and alienated from the masses of the country." James Perry, *Us & Them: How the Press Covered the 1972 Election* (New York: Crown Publishers, 1973), 264.

87. See Marilyn A. Lashner, *The Chilling Effect in TV News: Intimidation by the Nixon White House* (New York: Praeger, New York, 1984); Joseph C. Spear, *Presidents and the Press: The Nixon Legacy* (Cambridge, MA: MIT Press, 1984).

88. William Safire, *Before the Fall* (New York: Doubleday, New York), 343.

89. *Ibid.*, 345.

90. Michael Baruch Grossman and Martha Joynt Kumar, *Portraying the President: The White House and the News Media* (Baltimore: Johns Hopkins University Press, 1981), 290–291.

91. Anthony Summers, *The Arrogance of Power: The Secret World of Richard Nixon* (New York: Viking, 2000), 48–49.

92. Kutler, 176.

93. *Ibid.*, 180.

94. "Nixon Aide Scores TV News Practice," *New York Times*, May 6, 1972, 1.

95. Porter, 262.

96. Alexander Kendrick, *Prime Time: The Life of Edward R. Murrow* (Boston: Little, Brown, 1969), 452.

97. See David M. Stone, *Nixon and the Politics of Public Television* (New York: Garland, 1985). See also Steve Knoll, "The Government vs. Television News," *Washington Post*, June 4, 1972, B2; and Les Brown, "Files of Nixon White House Show Bid to Control Public Broadcasting," *New York Times*, February 24, 1979, A1.

98. Halberstam, 1979, 600.

99. Grossman and Kumar, 290.

100. From this perspective, the hammering that the Democratic Party was subjected to in the election of 1972 amounts to little more than collateral damage. Theodore H. White notes that for Nixon his chief adversary during the campaign was not the hapless McGovern, but "the news media of America — and the culture they spoke for, which so contradicted the culture for which he spoke, and on which he was to found his victory." Theodore H. White, 1973, 244.

101. Perry, 265. According to Perry, the media focus on the game, not the agenda. "We are mechanistic, interested chiefly in personalities, power plays, squabbles, the degree of 'professionalism' of the various candidates. Above all else, we are fascinated by one question: Who's ahead?" Note also the media's failure to pursue the Watergate scandal, which broke during the campaign — surely a priority for a partisan media determined to destroy Nixon (234–238). On the other hand, see Richard C. Hofstetter, *Bias in the News: Network Television Coverage of the 1972 Election Campaign* (Columbus: Ohio State University Press, 1976). The 1972 campaign was the first in which the media took to chronicling its own role in presidential politics. See also Timothy Crouse, *Boys on the Bus* (New York: Ballantine, 1973 (including the reference to Candice Bergen of "Murphy Brown" fame telling the press corps "You all suck," 384), and, for a Gonzo perspective, Hunter S. Thompson, *Fear and Loathing: On the Campaign Trail '72* (London: Flamingo, 1973).

102. Veblen, 165–166.

103. Bear in mind that in its pre-Rupert Murdoch days, the *New York Post* was considered by contemporaries to be "probably the most extreme of [the] Nixon-hating newspapers." Keogh, 152.

104. Shogan, 62.

105. David Greenberg, 157. Sabato quotes one Nixon confidant as saying that the President "uses the term 'media asshole' so frequently it sounds like one word." Sabato, 255.

106. Theodore H. White, 1973, 245.

107. Han, 87.

108. Kutler, 183.

109. Genovese, 54.

110. Liebovich, 2001, 91.

111. The inside source is, of course, Carl Bernstein and Bob Woodward, *All the President's Men* (New York: Simon and Schuster, 1974).

112. J. Anthony Lukas, *Nightmare: The Underside of the Nixon Years* (New York: Viking Press, 1976), 274. Other official epithets directed at the *Post*'s coverage included "a collection of absurdities," "a senseless pack of lies," "shabby journalism," "unfounded and unsubstantiated allegations," "mud-slinging," and "guilt by association."

113. Streitmatter, 214.

114. *Ibid.* Nixon also directed his aides to take action against the *Post*'s legal representative. As he told Haldeman, "I would not want to be in Edward Bennett Williams's position after this one. We are going to fix that son of a bitch."

115. Grossman and Kumar, 292.

116. Liebovich, 2001, 78–79.

117. Liebovich, 2003, 71. See also Gladys E. Lane and Kurt Lang, *The Battle for Public Opinion: The President,*

the Press, and the Polls During Watergate (New York: Columbia University Press, 1983).

118. Streitmatter, 210.

119. Ritchie, 2005, 219.

120. Lukas, 275. See also Schudson, 1995, 142–165 ("Watergate and the Press"); Edward J. Epstein, *Between Fact and Fiction: The Problem of the Press* (New York: Vintage Books, 1975), 19–33; and Charles Peters, "Why the White House Press Didn't Get the Watergate Story," *Washington Monthly*, July/August 1973, 7–15.

121. Liebovich, 2003, 115.

122. Gil Troy, *Morning in America: How Ronald Reagan Invented the 1980s* (Princeton, NJ: Princeton University Press, 2005), 243–244.

123. The Nixon debate continues long after his death. See Thomas J. Johnson, *The Rehabilitation of Richard Nixon: The Media's Effect on Collective Memory* (New York: Garland, 1995). See also David Greenberg.

124. Lester Bernstein, "Review of *The Other Side of the Story*," *New York Times Book Review*, April 1, 1984, 7.

125. See Mark Rozell, *The Press and the Carter Presidency* (Boulder, CO: Westview Press, 1988).

126. Editorial, *Washington Post*, September 18, 1980, A18.

127. Kenneth J. Heineman, *God is a Conservative: Religion, Politics and Morality in Contemporary America* (New York: New York University Press, 1998), 103. See also Jody Powell, *The Other Side of the Story* (New York: Morrow, 1984), 74–75, 109–117, 150, 206, 290.

128. Kenneth W. Thompson, 1983, 88. For more on the Carter administration's testy relationship with the press, see Mark J. Rozell, *The Press and the Carter Presidency* (Boulder: Westview Press, 1988).

129. Maltese, 194.

130. Mark Hertsgaard, *On Bended Knee: The Press and the Reagan Presidency* (New York: Farrar Straus Giroux, 1988), 343. See also Schudson, 1995, 124–141 ("The Illusion of Ronald Reagan's Popularity"); Robert E. Denton, Jr., *The Primetime Presidency of Ronald Reagan: The Era of the Television Presidency* (New York: Praeger, 1988), 63–79 ("The Primetime Presidency of Ronald Reagan"); Herbert J. Gans, "Are U.S. Journalists Dangerously Liberal?" *Columbia Journalism Review*, November/December 1985; Michael J. Robinson, "Jesse Helms Takes Stock," *Washington Journalism Review*, April 1985; Michael J. Robinson and Margaret A. Sheehan, *Over the Wire and on TV* (New York: Russell Sage Foundation, 1983); Peter Stoler, *The War Against the Press: Politics, Pressure and Intimidation in the 1980s* (New York: Dodd, Mead, 1986). For the unhappy story of Reagan's successor, George H. W. Bush, and his unhappy experience with the media, see Mark J. Rozell, *The Press and the Bush Presidency* (Westport, CT: Praeger, 1996).

131. Troy, 247.

132. Katharine Q. Seelye, "Dole is imploring voters to 'rise up' against the press," *New York Times*, October 26, 1996, 1. "Taking on the liberal media," Dole's campaign manager Scott Reed later said, "is a huge motivator." See also John E. Yang, "Gingrich tells activists to outgun 'elite media,'" *Washington Post*, April 23, 1996, A6; Allan Levite, "Bias basics," *National Review* 48, no. 20 (October 28, 1996), 63–67. Despite Dole's fervor there is no evidence of a media conspiracy to deliberately hamstring him. Both *Time* and the *Washington Post* had the option during the campaign to break the story of the GOP candidate's engaging in an affair with a woman from 1968 through 1970 while still married to his first wife, but both sat on the story. Shogan, 194–195.

133. Heather Fleming, "Lott complains of 'liberal' bias by networks," *Broadcasting & Cable* 127, no. 9 (March 3, 1997), 16. Ironically, it was no media frenzy that was responsible for costing Lott his position as Senate Majority Leader; his remarks at Strom Thurmond's testimonial dinner went right over the heads of the media and never would have surfaced had they not been picked up and rebroadcast by liberal bloggers, forcing the media to pay attention.

134. The assumption that Bill Clinton got a free ride from the media during his administration won't stand up to any objective analysis. According to studies conducted by the Center for Media and Public Affairs of evaluations by sources and reporters on the network evening news shows, Bill Clinton's coverage was 72 percent negative during his first year in office in 1993; 62 percent negative after the Republicans took control of Congress in 1995; 56 percent negative after the Monica Lewinsky scandal broke and 67 percent negative during his impeachment hearings in 1998; and 65 percent negative after he left office in 2001, amid controversies over last-minute pardons. Analysis available online at www.cmpa.com/press-Releases/MediaThrowtheBookatClinton.htm. For more on Clinton's relations with the media, see Howard Kurtz, *Spin Cycle: Inside the Clinton Propaganda Machine* (New York: Free Press, 1998).

Conclusion

1. Nick Thimmesch, ed., *A Liberal Media Elite?* (Washington, DC: American Enterprise Institute for Public Policy Research, 1985), 10. The idea that the monolithic liberal bias of the media represents a threat to the balance of the American body politic, to the principle of free speech, even to democracy itself, has been a recurring theme in conservative thought. In the mid-seventies, Kevin Phillips argued in *Human Events* that the First Amendment was "obsolescent" since it "cannot ... cope with Big Media power," a situation that "invites—even obliges—the government to move in and in the name, of course, of the free press, correct the situation." Before this can happen, he concluded, "we need a new socioprudential approach that can solve the problem before the government throws the baby of a free press out with the bathwater of Liberal Establishment bunk." Alan Crawford, *Thunder on the Right* (New York: Pantheon, 1980), 207. "The general reportorial practices of the press today are abhorrent," Jim Kuypers alleged more recently. "The level of speculation, hearsay, arrogant assertion, and outright political advocacy makes a mockery of the press's professed role of objective disseminator of the news." He concludes that "in its role as provider of objective, balanced information for the American polity, the press fails miserably. As it now exists, the mainstream press is clearly an anti-Democratic institution." Kuypers, 246. In September 2004, Rep. Dan Barton (R-TX), who chairs the Commerce Committee, told a trade group that newscasts "need to have safeguards to prevent reporters from infusing their opinions into news reports." Editorial, "Big Brother Barton," *Wall Street Journal*, September 30, 2004, A16.

2. Roy Greenslade, "Their Master's Voice," *Guardian*, February 17, 2003, 2.

3. Dean was still maintaining this stonewall position during the midterm campaign of 2006. "I happen to despise Fox News because I think they're nothing but the propaganda arm of the Republican Party." Paul Bedard, "Washington Whispers," *US News & World Report*, October 15, 2006, www.usnews.com/usnews/politics/whispers/articles/061015/23whisplead.htm. One wonders if the good doctor has yet purchased the ultimate accessory for

the conscientious liberal determined to absolutely isolate himself from the world of conservative opinion: the FOXBlocker. See Mark Jurkowitz, "Hunting for Fox: Device Blacks Out Network's News." *Boston Globe*, April 14, 2005, D1. For a "gotcha" scoop on the proud conservatism of FOX, see Timothy Noah, "Fox News Admits Bias," *Slate.com*, May 31, 2005, slate.com/id/2119864. For analysis on the dangerous game of Fox-baiting, see Lorne Manly, "In Taking on Fox, Democrats See Reward in the Risk," *New York Times*, October 1, 2006.

4. John Lancaster, "Bravo L'Artiste," *London Review of Books* 26, no. 3 (February 5, 2005), 6.

5. Tunku Varadarajan, "Bowing Low to China," *Wall Street Journal*, March 27, 2001, A22. Murdoch's figurative kowtowing has certainly paid off. At the end of 1998, Chinese president Jiang Zemin "expressed appreciation for the efforts made by world media mogul Rupert Murdoch in presenting China objectively and cooperating with the Chinese press over the past two years," according to the state-run Xinhua news agency

6. The *Post's* coverage for the duration of the incident was as follows: 2/3 of page 5 on Monday, April 2, as the story broke; pages 6–7 on April 3; pages 4–5 and the first cautious editorial on April 4. On April 5 there was coverage on pages 4–5 and two op-ed pieces: an aggressive shot across China's bow by syndicated columnist George Will ("Why Is Beijing Blowing It? Time to Grow Up") balanced by a measured response from Dale Brown ("If Tables Were Turned, We'd Hold *Their* Plane"). On April 6, the only coverage was on page 7; on April 7, the *Post* dedicated page 5 and half of page 4; on April 8, half of page 7; on April 9, page 5 and a neutral Robert Novak op-ed; on April 10, half of page 2 and a neutral E. J. Dionne op-ed; on April 11, page 5 and a second cautious editorial. On April 12 came the big front page, with news of the resolution to the "situation," coverage on pages 2–5, and a breezy editorial. The following day there was another happy front-page splash and coverage on pages 2–5.

7. See Marshall Sella, "The Red State Network," *New York Times Magazine*, June 24, 2001, 26–34, 62–63.

8. It would be more accurate to say that Murdoch is carefully attuned to which way the wind is blowing and knows when to jump ship from a doomed vessel (e.g., the U.K. Conservative Party in the mid-1990s). To this end, there is increasing chatter regarding his flirtation with Hillary Clinton; see Ben Smith, "The Odd Couple '08," *New York Observer*, June 15, 2005; David Carr, "Murdoch and Clinton: An Unlikely Alliance," *New York Times*, August 15, 2005; Tina Brown, "Rupert Murdoch: Bending with the Wind," *Washington Post*, September 15, 2005, C1; Caroline Daniel, "Murdoch to Host Fundraiser for Hillary Clinton," *Financial Times*, May 8, 2006, news.ft.com/cms/s/61faabde-deb8-11da-acee-0000779e2340.html; Robert B. Bluey, "Murdoch Defends Plan to Host Hillary Fundraiser: Calls Her 'Effective, Good Senator,'" *Human Events Online*, May 10, 2006, www.humaneventsonline.com/blog-detail.php?id=14727; John Cassidy, "Murdoch's Game," *New Yorker*, October 16, 2006, 68–85. Murdoch himself appears to have dampened this speculation; see Nicholas Wapshott, "The World according to Rupert," *Independent*, July 23, 2005, news.independent.co.uk/media/article1191891.ece. But the *New York Post* did endorse Hillary Clinton's reelection to the Senate in 2006, so his bets may still be hedged.

9. Frank Rich, "On 'Moral Values' It's Blue In a Landslide," *New York Times*, November 14, 2004. See also Cynthia Tucker, "Red States Tuning to Trash TV," *Sun* [Baltimore], January 4, 2005, 11. For evidence that Murdoch's motivation is making money, one need look no further than the movie *The Day After Tomorrow* which

despite amounting to little more than environmental, catastrophist, hippie propaganda was not only distributed by 20th Century Fox, everyone on screen watches Fox News (or its U.K. equivalent, Sky.)

10. Alan Cooperman, "Conservative Christians Protest Movie on Kinsey," *Washington Post*, November 22, 2004, A3.

11. Bob Thompson, "Fighting Indecency, One Bleep at a Time: Only Popular Culture and Big Media Stand in the Parents Television Council's Way," *Washington Post*, December 9, 2004, C1. Thompson maintains that this contradiction lies at the heart of a ratings-inducing circular strategy: "My theory has always been that Fox News and Fox Broadcasting are the perfect synergy. One produces this outrageous programming that pundits on the other channel can complain about." George Rush and Corky Siemaszko, "Rupe is in Soup with Troops," *New York Daily News*, November 18, 2006. This schizophrenia on the part of FOX is the source of an ongoing headache for conservatives. "Murdoch happily rakes the cash in from both sides of the cultural divide," Timothy A. Chichester, president of the Catholic Family Association of America, argues. "In one hand he holds FOX-Sleaze and the other FOX-News. The first caters to the social liberals based on the proposition that the deeper the TV dumpster the bigger the bottom-feeder bucks to be hauled up. FOX-News caters to those who seek refuge from the nauseating reek of the pit. Wow, what a market straddle! What a two-headed money machine." Timothy A. Chichester, "The Music Man." Cliff Kincaid, "Fox News Versus Fox Sleaze," *Accuracy in Media*, November 3, 2003, *http://www.aim. org/media_monitor/A234_0_2_0_C/*. See also Shmuley Boteach, "A Plea to Conservative Networks: Practice What You Preach," Beliefnet; www.beliefnet.com/story/156/story_15614_1.html. What conservatives make of Murdoch personally, particularly his Woody Allen-esque marriage, heaven only knows.

12. Kevin Matson, *When America was Great: The Fighting Faith of Postwar Liberalism* (New York: Routledge, 2004), 31.

13. Figures as of October 1, 2007; available online at www.boxofficemojo.com/alltime/domestic.htm. Note that adjusting the figures for inflation generates some shuffling of the rankings, but only succeeds in making the overall picture even more conservative (for example, by restoring *Gone with the Wind* to the No. 1 slot and placing *The Sound of Music* at 3, *The Ten Commandments* at 5, and *Dr. Zhivago* at 8). Figures available online at www.boxofficemojo.com/alltime/adjusted.htm.

14. See Steve Sailer, "Left Coast's Right Turn," *American Conservative* 4, no. 12 (June 20, 2005), 7–10.

15. Hackett and Zhao, 64–65.

16. For more recent data, see Joe Strupp, "New Survey Finds Huge Gap Between Press and Public on Many Issues," *Editor & Publisher*, May 15, 2005. It should be noted that regardless of what's happening in the newsroom, conservatives more than hold their own on the editorial pages. A 2002 *Editor & Publisher* study found 35 conservative, 30 liberal, and dozens of harder-to-categorize columnists distributed by the eight biggest syndicates; more recent numbers are similar. In addition, the two op-ed columnists with the most newspapers—a combined 1,000 or so—were conservatives Cal Thomas (syndicated by Tribune Media Services) and George Will (Washington Post Writers Group). Dave Astor, "Where the Right has the Write Stuff," *Editor & Publisher* 137, no. 8 (August 2004), 32.

17. A Zogby poll of 1,757 likely voters, released in March 2007 in conjunction with the George Washington University Institute for Politics, Democracy and the Inter-

net, found that 83 percent thought bias was "alive and well." Of that number, 64 percent (including 97 of Republican respondents) said the press had a liberal bias while 28 percent said there was a conservative bias. Jennifer Harper, "Poll: Bias 'Alive and Well' in Press," *Washington Times*, March 16, 2007. A Gallup poll of 1,025 Americans conducted in September 2003 found 45 percent considered the media too liberal, compared to 14 percent who said the media is too conservative (39 percent said it's just about right, 2 percent had no opinion). A Princeton Survey Research Associates July 2002 survey of 1,201 Americans found 51 percent of respondents said that news organizations are liberal, while 26 percent said that news organizations are conservative (14 percent said neither phrase applied, 9 percent didn't know). See Joe Strupp, "The Bias Wars," *Editor & Publisher* 137, no. 8 (August 2004), 22–32; David A. Jones, "Why Americans Don't Trust the Media," *Harvard International Journal of Press/Politics* 9, no. 2 (Spring 2004), 60–75; Daniel Sutter, "Can the Media be so Liberal? The Economics of Media Bias," *CATO Journal* 20, no. 3 (Winter 2001), 431–452; David Domke and Mark D. Watts, "The Politics of Conservative Elites and the 'Liberal Media' Argument," *Journal of Communication* 49, no. 4 (Autumn 1999), 35–58; Mark D. Watts, et al., "Elite Cues and Media Bias in Presidential Campaigns: Explaining Public Perceptions of a Liberal Press," *Communication Research* 26, no. 2 (April 1999), 144–175.

18. David P. Baron, "Persistent Media Bias," *Research Paper No. 1845*, Stanford University, February 2004, www.nyu.edu/gsas/dept/politics/seminars/baron.pdf.

19. Richard M. Cohen, "Extra! The press is liberal (so what?)," *Nation* 264, no. 20 (May 26, 1997), 10. Reacting to a story that had just run, about a Texas bill requiring abortion doctors to counsel patients that an abortion might increase their risk of breast cancer, *Los Angeles Times* editor John Carroll sent out a staff memo in May 2003 warning his reporters, "I want everyone to know about how serious I am about purging all political *bias* from our coverage. We may happen to live in a political atmosphere that is suffused with liberal values (and is unreflective of the nation as a whole), but we are not going to push a liberal agenda in the news pages of the Times." Many commentators have remarked on the unlikelihood of the Watergate scandal breaking in the contemporary media environment. See Frank Rich, "Don't Follow the Money," *New York Times*, June 12, 2005; Jonathan Alter, "If Watergate Happened Now," *Newsweek*, June 13, 2005, 33.

20. David Niven, *Tilt? The Search for Media Bias* (Westport, CT: Praeger, 2002), 68.

21. Richard M. Cohen, 10.

22. Mike Allen, "Gingrich finds God in Washington," *Washington Post*, January 10, 2005, A7.

23. John Dean, closer to the truth than anyone, scornfully rejects the assertion that the press in general, and the *Washington Post* in particular, was responsible for forcing the resignation of Richard Nixon. "They couldn't have been further from the story as to what was going on. They didn't have anything really on the cover-up at all.... They had no idea of the width and breadth of the abuse of power that was going on inside the White House." Liebovich, 2003, 119. Epstein, another to ridicule the notion that Woodward and Bernstein had "solved" the Watergate puzzle, argues all they had done was serve as conduits for leaks from government insiders to investigators. Edward J. Epstein, "Did the Press Uncover Watergate?" *Commentary*, July 1974, 21–24. Hunter S. Thompson, in the October 10, 1974 issue of *Rolling Stone*, best captured true diffidence of the press during the Nixon era when he noted

that "the climate of those years was so grim that half the Washington press corps spent more time worrying about having their telephones tapped than they did about risking the wrath of Haldeman, Ehrlichman, and Colson by poking at the weak seams of a Mafia-style administration that began cannibalizing the whole government just as soon as it came into power. Nixon's *capos* were never subtle; they swaggered into Washington like a conquering army, and the climate of fear they engendered apparently neutralized *The New York Times* along with all the other pockets of potential resistance. Nixon had to do everything but fall on his own sword before anybody in the Washington socio-political establishment was willing to take him on."

24. For criticism of the role of the media in the debate leading up to the start of Operation Iraqi Freedom, see Justin Lewis et al., *Shoot First and Ask Questions Later: Media Coverage of the 2003 Iraq War* (New York: Peter Lang, 2006); Danny Schechter, *When News Lies: Media Complicity and the Iraq War* (New York: SelectBooks, 2006); Alexander G. Nikolaev and Ernest A. Hakanen, eds., *Leading to the 2003 Iraq War: The Global Media Debate* (New York: Palgrave Macmillan, 2006); Lee Artz and Yahya R. Kamalipour, eds., *Bring 'em On: Media and Politics in the Iraq War* (Lanham, MD: Rowman & Littlefield, 2005); Douglas Kellner, *Media Spectacle and the Crisis of Democracy: Terrorism, War, and Election Battles* (Boulder, CO: Paradigm Publishers, 2005); Steven Kull, Ramsay Clay, and Evan Lewis, "Misperceptions, the Media, and the Iraq War," *Political Science Quarterly* 118, no. 4 (Winter 2003–2004), 569–598.

25. In an editorial, "The Times and Iraq," *New York Times*, May 26, 2004, A10, the paper of record admitted, "We have found a number of instances of coverage that was not as rigorous as it should have been," specifically listing instances where "information that was controversial then, and seems questionable now, was insufficiently qualified or allowed to stand unchallenged. Looking back, we wish we had been more aggressive in re-examining the claims as new evidence emerged — or failed to emerge." Even some others at the paper felt this mea culpa was incomplete; see Daniel Okrent, "Weapons of Mass Destruction? Or Mass Distraction?" *New York Times*, May 30, 2004. Howard Kurtz admitted on behalf of his paper, the *Washington Post*, that it too was guilty of reporting that "in hindsight looks strikingly one-sided at times." Howard Kurtz, "The Post on WMDs," *Washington Post*, August 12, 2004, A1. Similarly, Chris Hedges of the *Philadelphia Inquirer* concludes, "The failure of the coverage leading up to the invasion of Iraq was the failure to be wary of the powerful, the failure to listen to those who are not our own." Chris Hedges, "Journalists' objectivity needs balance of truth," *Philadelphia Inquirer*, January 23, 2005. For additional commentary, see Chris Mooney, "The Editorial Pages and the Case for War," *Columbia Journalism Review* 42, no. 6 (March/April 2004), 28–34. Mooney ascribes the failure of the major media outlets to effectively critique the administration's case for preemptive military action to prevailing conventions of objectivity. "By faithfully refracting his message, major U.S. editorial pages conditioned themselves to treat Bush's national security argument with deference during the days leading up to war," he writes. See also Howard Friel and Richard Falk, *The Record of the Paper: How the New York Times Misreports US Foreign Policy* (New York: Verso, 2004); Steven Kull, "The Press and Public Misperceptions About the Iraq War," *Nieman Reports* 58, no. 2 (Summer 2004), 64–66; Susan Moeller, "The President, Press and Weapons of Mass Destruction," *Nieman Reports* 58, no. 2 (Summer 2004), 66–68. For an overview, see the Bill Moyers PBS

documentary *Buying the War*, www.pbs.org/moyers/journal/btw/watch.html.

26. Dave D'Alessio and Mike Allen, "Media Bias in Presidential Elections: A Meta-Analysis," *Journal of Communications* 50, no. 4 (Autumn 2000), 148–149.

27. See Stephen Ansolabehere, Rebecca Lessem and James M. Snyder Jr., "The Political Orientation of Newspaper Endorsements in U.S. Elections, 1940–2002," March, 2004, econ-www.mit.edu/faculty/download_pdf.php?id=1148.

28. Jamieson and Waldman conclude that "ultimately, the dominant press frame in the 2000 election hurt Gore more than Bush." Kathleen Hall Jamieson and Paul Waldman, *The Press Effect: Politicians, Journalists and the Stories that Shape the Political World* (Oxford: Oxford University Press, 2003), 41. See also Shogan, chap. 11–12, and Eric Boehlhart, "The Media vs. Al Gore," *Rolling Stone*, November 26, 2001.

29. Greg Mitchell, "Bird in the hand for Bush?" *Editor & Publisher*, November 6, 2000, 25. As a corollary, perhaps, according to a TIPP poll of 2,200 potential voters, newspaper voters favored Bush over Gore by a margin of 47.5 percent to 42.8 percent. Greg Mitchell, "Readers support Bush, say coverage was good," *Editor & Publisher*, November 6, 2000, 7–8.

30. Shogan, 178. In the space of two years, Powell appeared twice on the cover of *Time*, *Newsweek* and *US News & World Report*.

31. See *ibid.*, 209–216. Tucker Carlson recollects that in 2000, "McCain ran an entire presidential campaign aimed primarily at journalists. He understood that the first contest in a presidential race is always the media primary. He campaigned hard to win it. To a greater degree than any candidate in thirty years, McCain offered reporters the three things they want most: total access all the time, an endless stream of amusing quotes, and vast quantities of free booze.... I saw reporters call McCain 'John,' sometimes even to his face and in public. I heard others, usually at night in the hotel bar, slip into the habit of referring to the McCain campaign as 'we'—as in, 'I hope we kill Bush.'" Tucker Carlson, *Politicians, Partisans, and Parasites: My Adventures in Cable News* (New York: Warner Books, 2003).

32. Bob Davis, "Self-styled media critic dissects TV coverage to expose perceived liberal bias at networks," *Wall Street Journal*, August 15, 1996, A12.

33. Brent L. Bozell, "McCain's Media Lapdogs Rip Conservative Critics," *Insight on the News* 16, no. 13 (April 3, 2000), 44–45. Of course, the question then arises as to why the media would rush to anoint a man who had voted to impeach Clinton, for tax cuts, for a missile defense system, against abortion, or, in Bozell's words, the "other conservative stance he's (sometimes) [actually 85 percent of the time] taken" in the first place. As David Limbaugh explained, it all occurred within the context of the great liberal media conspiracy: "Forget McCain's prior voting record. During the primary season, which is the only relevant time period here, he was running decidedly to the left of Gov. Bush. That is when the media began glorifying McCain. Why wouldn't they, when McCain's signature issue (campaign finance reform) would effectively emasculate conservatives?" David Limbaugh, "Liberal Bias Shapes Media Coverage," *Human Events* 56, no. 37 (October 13, 2000), 10.

34. Howard Fineman, "Torn Between Faith and Science," MSNBC.com, April 17, 2005, www.msnbc.msn.com/id/7529448/site/newsweek/page/2.

35. Another potential GOP presidential aspirant with the positive media problem is Nebraska Senator Chuck Hagel, like McCain a westerner with a distinguished military career and a solidly conservative voting record but handicapped by a propensity to publicly buck the party line that has earned him plaudits from the press and thus rendered him unacceptable to key conservative movers and shakers; see George Neumayr, "Chuck McHagel," *American Spectator* 38, no. 1 (February 2005), 28–33. The Greek chorus of conservative lamentation over media bias against them in the 2008 campaign is already well underway; Fred Barnes has preemptively targeted "the media, more aptly called the Republican-hating media. We've already seen what they are willing to do to protect Hillary Clinton. They trashed a perfectly respectable, though highly critical, biography of Hillary by veteran newsman Ed Klein. It got so bad that conservatives, too, began attacking his book. If this is happening in 2005, imagine what lengths the press will be willing to go to in 2008 on Hillary's, or another Democrat's, behalf." Fred Barnes, "Rough Road," *Weekly Standard*, September 28, 2005, www.weeklystandard.com/Content/Public/Articles/000/000/006/133mmdsn.asp?pg=2.

36. The latter organization itself made news when it was disclosed that nearly all (99.8 percent) of the more than 240,000 indecency complaints to the Federal Communications Commission in 2003 (up from roughly 14,000 in 2002, and from fewer than 350 in each of the two previous years) were filed by the Parents Television Council. This organization set out to make an impact in 2003, including what it called "a massive, coordinated and determined campaign" for more action against broadcast indecency. "We delivered on that promise," Bozell said in the group's annual report. Todd Shields, "Activists Dominate Content Complaints," *Mediaweek*, December 6, 2004.

37. Bob Davis, "Self-styled media critic dissects TV coverage to expose perceived liberal bias at networks," *Wall Street Journal*, August 15, 1996, A12. See also Brent H. Baker, *How to Identify, Expose and Correct Liberal Media Bias* (Alexandria, VA: Media Research Center, 1994). Financial contributors to Bozell's efforts have included textile magnate Roger Milliken, Valhi, Inc. Chairman Harold Simmons and the John M. Olin Foundation.

38. Howard Kurtz, "Hear No Lichtblau, See No Lichtblau," *Washington Post*, June 28, 2004, C1.

39. Figures available at www.campaignmoney.com/committee.asp?committeeID=C00218172&cycle=04.

40. Joe Scarborough, a former Republican congressman from Florida who now hosts MSNBC's nightly *Scarborough Country*, may be an exception to this rule. He says the challenge for conservative hosts during the second Bush term will be to prove "that we're more than just the *Pravda* of the right." He adds, "I think that's going to be difficult for some people. I honestly don't know what Sean Hannity is going to be able to talk about. If you've been reading off the Republican National Committee's talking points like he has for the past four years, it's going to be hard to be critical of the status quo." Paul Farhi, "Right-Wing Wins Take Wind Out of Talk-Show Hosts," *Washington Post*, November 17, 2004, C1.

41. One study concluded that conservative editorial pages, represented by the *Wall Street Journal* and the *Washington Times*, are much less willing to take on a Republican administration than liberal pages like the *New York Times* and the *Washington Post* are willing to criticize a Democratic one. The study compared ten similar episodes in the Clinton and Bush administrations (disregarding the Monica Lewinsky affair, in which case everyone took the president to the woodshed). In these incidents, the liberal papers criticized the Clinton administration 30 percent of the time, lauded Clinton 36

percent of the time and criticized Bush 67 percent of the time. Conversely, the conservative papers criticized Bush only 7 percent of the time, lauded Bush 77 percent of the time and criticized Clinton 89 percent of the time. "Bias in the Media," *Christian Century* 120, no. 18 (September 6, 2003), 7.

42. A not uncharacteristic response was to declaim, "The legal remedy for what the *New York Times* has done is the death penalty and confiscation of the newspaper." Mithridate Ombud, "Time to Confiscate the *New York Times*," Newsbusters.org, June 28, 2006, newsbusters. org/node/6150. For representative examples of the conservative media response, see Andrew C. McCarthy, "The Media's War against the War Continues," *National Review Online*, June 23, 2006; Michael Barone, "Why do 'they' hate us? *Townhall.com*, Jun 26, 2006; and Heather Mac Donald, "National Security Be Damned: The guiding philosophy on West 43rd Street," *Weekly Standard* 11, no. 40 (July 3, 2006), www.weeklystandard.com/Content/Public/Articles/000/000/012/386syqsr.asp. The latter asserts, "By now it's undeniable: The *New York Times* is a national security threat." For an executive summary, see Howard Kurtz, "Piling on the New York Times with a Scoop: Story on Secret Program Further Rouses Critics," *Washington Post*, June 28, 2006, C01, and "'[T]reason, plain and simple': Right-Wing Media Figures Attack *NY Times* Over Bank-Tracking Story," *Media Matters For America*, June 27, 2006, mediamatters.org/items/200606270010. Representative Peter King (R-NY) did in fact fulminate that "the New York Times is putting its own arrogant elitest left wing agenda before the interests of the American people" and called on the Attorney General to begin a criminal investigation and prosecution of the paper's reporters, the editors who worked on story, and the publisher, on charges violating the Espionage Act. King's colleagues declined to endorse his course of action, but on June 29 the House of Representatives did approve—on a largely party-line 227–183 vote—a resolution asserting that the House "expects the cooperation of all news media organizations in protecting the lives of Americans and the capability of the government to identify, disrupt and capture terrorists by not disclosing classified intelligence programs."

43. Editorial, "Fit and Unfit to Print," *Wall Street Journal*, June 30, 2006, www.opinionjournal.com/editorial/feature.html?id=110008585. Two recent examples of conservative new media "swarming" on an issue—in both instances under false pretenses—include attacking the credibility of Associated Press reports out of Iraq by questioning the existence of source police chief Jamil Hussein, and disseminating allegations that Democratic senator Barack Obama was raised as a Muslim and educated in a madrasa.

44. Michael Tomasky, "Keller Must Stay," *American Prospect*, June 30, 2006, www.prospect.org/web/page.ww?section=root&name=ViewWeb&articleId=11689.

45. There is an interesting subtext to bear in mind about all these titles, one that relates to the terms of the political debate in the United States from 2003–2007. The election of 2004 was heralded as a triumph for conservatism over liberalism, but it could equally be interpreted as a triumph for one form of conservatism—neoconservatism—over any other form. FOX News and the publications listed above all exclusively expound the virtues of this dominant strain of big government, deregulatory, free-trade, morally interventionist and internationally proactive conservatism, which is fully subscribed to by the administration and therefore, though not without some misgivings, the Republican Party.

46. See David Brooks, "For Democrats, Time to Meet the Exurban Voter," *New York Times*, November 10, 2003. This article is an examination of the political ramifications outlined in David Brooks, *Bobos in Paradise: The New Upper Class and How They Got There* (New York: Simon & Schuster, 2000), and was expanded in David Brooks, *On Paradise Drive: How We Live Now (And Always Have) in the Future Tense* (New York: Simon & Schuster, 2004). See also Lawrence C. Levy, "Keystone Suburbs," *Newsday*, November 10, 2004, A43; Ronald Brownstein and Richard Rainey, "GOP Plants Flag on New Voting Frontier," *Los Angeles Times*, November 22, 2004, A1.

47. Bill Bishop, "The Great Divide: Where We Live, What We Think, How We Vote," *Austin American-Statesman*, April 4, 2004, A1. See also David Von Drehle, "Political Split is Pervasive: Clash of Cultures is Driven by Targeted Appeals and Reinforced by Geography," *Washington Post*, April 25, 2004, A1; Phillip A. Klinkner and Ann Hapanowicz, "Red and Blue in Déjà vu: Measuring Political Polarization in the 2004 Election," *Forum* 3, no. 2 (July 2005). The trend toward polarization is even more marked at the congressional district level; only 59 of the 435 Congressional districts in the United States split their vote for president and House in 2004. Dan Balz, "Partisan Polarization Intensified in 2004 Election," *Washington Post*, March 29, 2005, A4.

48. Entman, 137.

49. See Daniel Okrent, "Is the New York Times a Liberal Newspaper?" *New York Times*, July 25, 2004. In answering his own question in the affirmative, Okrent is refreshingly up-front about the reality of his own media environment.

50. By 2002, the Unification Church had spent approximately $1.7 billion in subsidies for the *Washington Times*; the paper has lost money every year of publication since 1982. Frank Ahrens, "Moon Speech raises Old Ghosts as the Times turns 20," *Washington Post*, May 23, 2002, p. E1.

51. Michael Kinsley, "The Twilight of Objectivity: How Opinion Journalism Could Change the Face of the News," *Slate.com*, March 31, 2006, www.slate.com/id/2139042.

52. This process is achieving its apotheosis among America's religious communities. See Mariah Blake, "Stations of the Cross: How evangelical Christians are creating an alternative universe of faith-based news," *Columbia Journalism Review*, May/June 2005, www.cjr.org/issues/2005/3/blake-evangelist.asp.

53. Tim Rutten, "Campaign's lasting effect for media," *Christian Science Monitor* 96 no. 238 (November 3, 2004), 9. See also the Pew Research Center study, "News Audiences Increasingly Polarized," released on June 8, 2004, people-press.org/reports/display.php3?ReportID=215.

54. For a balanced introduction to this phenomenon, see Jonathan Chait, "The Left's New Machine," *New Republic* 236, no. 4,812 (May 7, 2007), 18–28.

55. The best source on this process is Viguerie and Franke. For a specific case study, see William G. Mayer, "Why Talk Radio is Conservative," *Public Interest*, no. 156 (Summer 2004), 86–103. See also Don Feder, "Why Liberals Find Talk Radio so Threatening," *American Enterprise* 7, no. 2 (March/April 1996), 24–28.

56. Scott Sonner, "Ex-Christian Coalition leader Reed says he watches only Fox News," *San Francisco Chronicle*, April 30, 2004.

57. "If it hadn't been for Fox, I don't know what I would have done for the news," Senate Majority Leader Trent Lott confessed during the 2000 imbroglio in Florida. Micklethwait and Wooldridge, 163.

58. Mark Memmott, "Fox Newspeople say Allegations of Bias Unfounded," *USA Today*, September 2, 2004, A8.

Fox is touchy about allegations that it serves as a communications arm of the Republican Party. After ABC News correspondent Terry Moran called Fox "a friendly channel" to the Bush administration and asked White House press secretary Scott McClellan if "Fox News and other Republican surrogates" were being handed information directly from Karl Rove, a Fox News spokesperson retorted, "[Moran's] the last person who should be casting aspersions on anyone's else 'bias' or credibility. He has plenty of the first and almost none of the latter." "Follow-Up: Terry Moran & Fox News," *Media Bistro*, July 12, 2005, www.mediabistro.com/tvnewser/abc/follow up_terry_moran_fox_news_23536.asp.

59. For further analysis of partisan trends in publishing, see this study of patterns in Internet book purchasing via Amazon.com: Valdis Krebs, "Divided we Stand," available online at: www.orgnet.com/divided.html.

60. Alan Murray, "As in Olden Days, U.S. Media Reflect the Partisan Divide," *Wall Street Journal*, September 14, 2004, A4. See also Howard Kurtz, "Political Perspectives with Tunnel Vision," *Washington Post*, February 7, 2005, C1. For evidence of this process of fragmentation, see the Pew Research Center study available online at people-press.org/reports/display.php3?ReportID=200. William Powers, for one, supports this perspective that a genuinely adversarial press would represent a positive development: "Now that one ideological faction controls all three branches of the government, I find myself longing for some authentic liberal bias. Not the weasely, between-the-lines bias that we've grown used to, but open, crusading, unembarrassed bias. And not just in the opinion columns, but on the front page. Call me a hopeless independent, but I think both political parties have dangerous tendencies and need somebody to keep them honest. Who's going to keep the Republicans honest now? Not the donkey party — they're a laughingstock. Who does that leave but the media? When the president is a Democrat, liberal media bias is a genuine hazard. But when the Republicans are in power, a dose of the very same bias can be healthy. America's most powerful newsrooms are packed with people who oppose much of what the Republican Party stands for. Let's unleash a few of those Lefties from the shackles of journalistic convention and see what happens." William Powers, "Bias, Anyone?" *National Journal* 34, no. 46 (November 16, 2002), 3419. Matthew Yglesias, too, endorses this scenario: "After all, England, France, and — as far as I know — pretty much all European countries seem to get on just fine without a broadsheet that aspires to American-style neutrality... After all, ideology need not be the enemy of quality." Matthew Yglesias, "Against Objectivity," *American Prospect*, June 30, 2006.

61. See James T. Hamilton, *All the News that's Fit to Sell: How the Market Transforms Information into News* (Princeton, NJ: Princeton University Press, 2006). For a fresh perspective on this phenomenon, see Matthew Gentzkow and Jesse M. Shapiro, "Media Bias and Reputation," *Journal of Political Economy* 114, no. 2 (April 2006), 280–316. For an executive summary, see Jack Shafer, "I Agree With You, Completely. Honest. Just Read My Piece," *Slate.com*, April 3, 2006, www.slate.com/id/2139172.

62. Daniel Henninger argues that the media coverage in Iraq "amounts to a kind of contemporary brainwashing of both the American public and Washington elites." Daniel Henninger, "Pour It On," *Wall Street Journal*, March 24, 2006. According to Rush Limbaugh, "It is going to be a gang rape. There is going to be a gang rape by the Democratic Party, the American left and the Drive-By Media, to finally take us out in the war against Iraq. Make no bones about it." Thinkprogress.org, June 6,

2006, thinkprogress.org/2006/06/06/limbaugh-haditha. Predictably, in addition to its costing them the war in Iraq, conservatives interpreted the Republican defeat in the midterm elections of 2006 as being masterminded by the mainstream media. "I will say this unequivocally," L. Brent Bozell III concluded, "In 25 years of looking at the national media, I have never in my life seen a more one-sided, distorted, vicious presentation of news and non-news by the national press." These sentiments were universally seconded in election-night posts to leading conservative message board Free Republic: "I will never believe that we lost by such large numbers due just to the GOP missteps. The media orchestrated this mess. Their unbalanced reporting was the major culprit." "[R]elentless media bashing is why we lost — the old media were a cornered rat — they bashed 24 hours a day and lied — whether it was on the radio or tv — their tactics worked." "Even with Rush, Hannity and all the other conservative talk radio hosts and the internet out there, America takes the lazy way out and allows 'news' to be spoon-fed to them by the likes of CNN, MSNBC, ABC, CBS, NBC, NPR, NY Times, USA Today, Time, Newsweak, etc." "We have no choice now, the commie vampire media must be destroyed." http://www.freerepublic.com/focus/f-news/1734539/posts?q=1&&page=1.

63. See Charles J. Hanley, "Half of U.S. Still Believes Iraq Had WMD," *Newsday*, August 6, 2006.

64. A classic instance of this process was the conservative anti-media campaign to discredit the existence of an Associated Press source in Iraq, Jamil Hussein. See Joe Strupp, "AP's Editor Criticizes Those Who Questioned Iraq Source," *Editor & Publisher*, January 5, 2007; "Shocking Twist: Disputed AP Source in Iraq Does Exist — And Now Faces Arrest for Talking to Media," *Editor & Publisher*, January 4, 2007.

65. A revealing glimpse into the prevailing attitude toward the mainstream media was accorded at the George Washington University Graduate School of Political Management in July 2006. "Some decry the professional role of politics, they would like to see it disappear," presidential alter-ego Karl Rove told graduating students. "Some argue political professionals are ruining American politics trapping candidates in daily competition for the news cycle instead of long-term strategic thinking in the best interest of the country." But Rove turned that criticism on journalists. "It's odd to me that most of these critics are journalists and columnists," he said. "Perhaps they don't like sharing the field of play. Perhaps they want to draw attention away from the corrosive role their coverage has played focusing attention on process and not substance." Will Lester, "Rove Blasts Journalists' Role in Politics," *ABC News*, July 29, 2006, abcnews.go.com/Politics/wireStory?id=2251920&CMP=OTC-RSSFeeds0312.

66. Sara Foley, "Campaign managers share tales of the trade," *The Battalion*, January 27, 2005, www.thebatt.com/news/2005/01/27/News/Campaign.Managers.Share.Tales.Of.The.Trade-842895.shtml.

67. John F. Harris, "New Media a Weapon in New World of Politics," *Washington Post*, October 6, 2006, A1. In January 2005, in one of his first acts as RNC Chair, Mehlman solicited the party faithful for funds by reminding them that "we need your help to get the president's message past the liberal media filter and directly to the American people." Dana Milbank, "Read his Lips," *Washington Post*, January 30, 2005, A5. For more on the Republican mastery of the new media, see Mark Halperin and John F. Harris, *The Way to Win: Taking the White House in 2008* (New York: Random House, 2006), 3–64.

68. See "Another Win for 'Friends & Allies,'" *US News & World Report*, September 26, 2005, www.usnews.com/

usnews/politics/whispers/articles/050926/26whisplead.ht m. As Howard Fineman notes, "By dividing the press corps into Red versus Blue—and talking only to the Red—administration strategists are inviting attacks from one side. But that might be precisely what they want. After all, they won two national elections that way." Howard Fineman, "The Physics of Unaccountable Power," *MSNBC*, July 13, 2005, www.msnbc.msn.com/id/8562223.

69. Paul Farhi, "Public Broadcasting Targeted by House," *Washington Post*, June 10, 2005, A1. For a partisan investigation into the payola issue see blog.dccc.org/mt/archives/003443.html.

70. Jim Rutenberg, "As Talk Radio Wavers, Bush Moves to Firm Up Support," *New York Times*, October 17, 2006, A16.

71. Other administration bigwigs on hand included Attorney General Alberto Gonzales, Treasury Secretary Henry M. Paulson Jr., Homeland Security Secretary Michael Chertoff, Energy Secretary Samuel Bodman, Agriculture Secretary Mike Johanns, Health and Human Services Secretary Mike Leavitt, national security adviser Stephen J. Hadley, presidential counselor Dan Bartlett, White House homeland security adviser Frances Fragos Townsend, and budget director Rob Portman. Peter Baker, "The GOP Leans on a Proven Strategy," *Washington Post*, October 25, 2006, A1.

72. See especially Donald Warren, *Radio Priest: Charles Coughlin, the Father of Hate Radio* (New York: Free Press, 1996). See also Marcus Sheldon, *Father Coughlin: The Tumultuous Life of the Priest of the Little Flower* (Boston: Little, Brown, 1973), and Alan Brinkley, *Voices of Protest: Huey Long, Father Coughlin, and the Great Depression* (New York: Knopf, 1982).

73. Oliver R. Pilat, *Pegler, Angry Man of the Press* (Boston: Beacon Press, 1963), 12. See also Finis Farr, *Fair Enough: The Life of Westbrook Pegler* (New Rochelle, NY: Arlington House Publishers, 1975). Pegler started as he meant to go on—his first nationally syndicated column in 1933 was dedicated to a defense of lynching. "As one member of the rabble," it began, "I will admit that I said, 'Fine, that is swell,' when the papers came up that day telling of the lynching of two men who killed the young fellow in California, and that I haven't changed my mind yet for all the storm of right-mindedness which has blown up since." Allan Fotheringham, *Birds of a Feather: The Press and the Politicians* (Toronto: Key Porter Books, 1989), 121. His course of action regarding striking copper miners in Butte, Montana was characteristic: "The thing to do is blow their heads off." Seizing on a remark by Eleanor Roosevelt that she and Franklin "had a lot of queer friends" during their early married life, Pegler suggested, "It is not cynicism to wonder whether the Empress Eleanor was being naïve or imposing on the naïveté of the public when she said on the air that she always had lots of queer friends. She certainly is a woman of the world, and some of her associates considered, can hardly be expected to be regarded as an ignoramus in such matters. Queer was right!" Pilat, 12. The parallel between this observation and Coulter's assertion that Bill Clinton's "rampant promiscuity does show some level of latent homosexuality," her reference to Al Gore as a "total fag," her conviction that there is "about even money" on Hillary Clinton "coming out of the closet," and her allusion to John Edwards as being a "faggot," is self-evidently manifest. "Coulter comes out against Gay Clinton marriage," *Wonkette.com*, www.wonkette.com/politics/movies/coulter-comes-out-against-gay-clinton-marriage-189845.php.

74. Even one of the more intelligent political forums, Redstate.org, states in its posting rules that "this site is explicitly meant to serve as a *conservative and Republican community*. Postings, comments, etc., contrary to this purpose fall under the rubric of 'disruptive behavior' and *will result in banning*." For a fascinating study on the partisan dynamics of blogging, see the study by Lada Adamic and Natalie Glance, "The Political Blogosphere and the 2004 U.S. Election: Divided they Blog," available online at: www.blogpulse.com/papers/2005/AdamicGlanceBlogWWW.pdf.

75. In an early but increasingly representative manifestation of this trend, Jerome Armstrong, the founder of MyDD, teamed with Markos Moulitsas, the founder of DailyKos, to launch a political consulting partnership called Armstrong Zuniga in January 2003. They were briefly retained that year by Howard Dean as technical consultants before formally dissolving their partnership in December 2004. Armstrong went on to offer Internet and campaign-strategy consulting services through the firm Political Technologies LLC. Beneficiaries of these services include former Virginia Governor Mark Warner ($65,000 over twelve months) and 2006 Ohio senate candidate Sherrod Brown ($115,000-plus over fifteen months). K. Daniel Glover, "New on the Web: Politics as Usual," *New York Times*, December 3, 2006. See also Armstrong's Wikipedia entry at: en.wikipedia.org/wiki/Jerome_Armstrong.

76. Mott, 1944, 358. For recent election-specific studies into this question, see Tim Counts, "Editorial Influence on GOP Vote in 1948 Presidential Election," *Journalism Quarterly* 66, no. 1 (Spring 1989), 177–181; Robert E. Hurd and Michael W. Singletary, "Newspaper Endorsement Influence on the 1980 Presidential Vote," *Journalism Quarterly* 61, no. 2 (Summer 1984), 332–338; John P. Robinson, "The Press as King-Maker: What Surveys From Last Five Campaigns Show," *Journalism Quarterly* 51, no. 4 (Winter 1974), 587–594, 606. See also William M. Mason, "The Impact of Endorsements on Voting," *Sociological Methods and Research* 1, no. 4 (May 1973), 463–495. Mott's conclusion is challenged by a study titled "The Fox News Effect: Media Bias and Voting," by Stefano DellaVigna of the University of California, Berkeley, and Ethan Kaplan of the Institute for International Economic Studies at Stockholm University, available online at elsa.berkeley.edu/~sdellavi/wp/foxvote06–03–30.pdf. (For an executive summary, see Richard Morin, "The Fox News Effect," *Washington Post*, May 4, 2006, A2). The authors conclude that between 1996 and 2000, "Fox News convinced between 3 and 8 percent of its non-Republican listeners to vote Republican.... Exposure to the conservative coverage of Fox News, therefore, had a sizable persuasive effect." (3). The authors estimate this effect to be worth 0.15 to 0.20 points in the popular vote, or 200,000 votes nationwide, enough to swing Florida, and therefore the election, to George W. Bush. However, an earlier study by the same authors found that while the Republican vote in those towns exposed to Fox News increased by 6 percent between 1996 and 2000, the Republican vote increased by 7 percent over the same period in towns which did not offer Fox News (see Alan B. Krueger, "Fair? Balanced? A Study Finds It Does Not Matter," *New York Times*, August 18, 2005). In any event, there is a difference between the ideological bias of a particular media outlet and its actively conspiring with a political party or candidate to secure a partisan outcome; Fox News may be guilty of the former but cannot be accused of the latter.

77. Mott, 1944, 362; "Newspaper Endorsements for President since 1940," *Editor & Publisher*, October 26, 1996, 28; "Endorsements by Newspapers and Magazines," www.gwu.edu/~action/natendorse5.html; Howard Kurtz, "36 Papers Abandon Bush for Kerry," *Washington Post*,

October 27, 2004, A13. The table only incorporates those papers making an endorsement.

78. Victor Davis Hanson, "American Exceptionalism," *National Review Online*, November 5, 2004, www.nationalreview.com/hanson/hanson200411050826.asp. Hanson, who received a Ph.D. from Stanford University, was until recently a professor at California State University, Fresno, and is currently a Senior Fellow at the Hoover Institute. The fact that the American people are capable of drawing their own conclusions on the issues and candidacies of the day independently of the elite media is hardly a revelation. Andrew D. White, the first president of Cornell, wrote in 1905 of Grant's landslide reelection in 1872: "Years afterward I was asked in London by one of the most eminent of English journalists how such a thing could have taken place. Said he, 'The leading papers of the United States, almost without exception, were in favor of Mr. Greeley; how, then, did it happen that he was in such a hopeless minority?' I explained the matter as best I could, whereupon he said, 'Whatever the explanation may be, it proves that the American press, by its wild statements in political campaigns, and especially by its reckless attacks upon individuals, has lost that hold upon American opinion which it ought to have; and depend upon it, this is a great misfortune for your country.'" Andrew D. White, *Autobiography of Andrew Dickson White* (New York: Century, 1905), 172–173.

79. Thomas Frank coined this term. He observes that to the conservative, "Liberalism is beyond politics, a tyrant that dominates our lives in countless ways great and small, and which is virtually incapable of being overthrown. Conservatism, on the other hand, is the doctrine of the oppressed majority.... [T]he Republicans are the party of the disrespected, the downtrodden, the forgotten. They are always the underdog, always in rebellion against a haughty establishment, always rising up from below." Thomas Frank, *What's the Matter with Kansas? How Conservatives Won the Heart of America* (New York: Metropolitan Books, 2004), 119. Former House Speaker Newt Gingrich, for example, in his latest nonfiction book *Winning the Future: A 21st Century Contract With America*, is still arguing that "since the 1960s, the conservative majority has been intimidated, manipulated and bullied by the liberal minority. The liberal elites who dominate academia, the courts, the press and much of the government bureaucracy share an essentially European secular-socialist value system. Yet they have set the terms of the debate." Michiko Kakutani, "Does Tomorrow Belong to Gingrich's 'Popular Majority?'" *New York Times*, February 1, 2005, E8. See also Ruben Navarrette, Jr., "Republican Majority as Victims," *San Diego Union-Tribune*, April 22, 2005, B7. For a conservative perspective on conservative anti-establishmentarianism, see Brian C. Anderson, *South Park Conservatives: The Revolt Against Liberal Media*

Bias (Washington, DC: Regnery, 2005). For a hyperextension of this conservative ethos in graphic novel form, *Liberality for All*, see accstudios.com/f/july20b_05.htm. The worldview expressed in the pages of *Liberality For All* ("Can Sean Hannity, G. Gordon Liddy and Oliver North save America from an Orwellian Nightmare of Ultra-Leftist Oppression?") is beyond even the satire of *The Daily Show*: "Why can't the Republicans just admit it — you're in charge," host Jon Stewart laments. "You're not a bunch of ragtag rebels fighting the Empire—*you are the Empire.*" *The Daily Show*, February 16, 2006.

80. This analogy has been drawn before; see David B. Parker, "The Rise and Fall of the Wonderful Wizard of Oz as a 'Parable on Populism,'" *Journal of the Georgia Association of Historians* 15 (1994), 49–63.

81. Jackson, of course, chose simply to ignore it. On March 3, 1832, the old Federalist Chief Justice of the Supreme Court John Marshall, speaking for the majority, ruled in *Worcester v. Georgia* that state law dealing with the Cherokee nation was unconstitutional, null, void, and of no effect, thereby throwing a major spanner into the works of the administration's cherished policy of Indian removal. Years later, Jackson was reported by Horace Greeley to have responded by remarking, "Well, John Marshall has made his decision: now let him enforce it." In fact, the president said no such thing. But there is no doubt that the apocryphal phrase captures his mood; in his State of the Union Address of 1830, he declared that the states were "not responsible" to the central government for the "justice" of their laws. See Robert V. Remini, *Andrew Jackson and his Indian Wars* (New York: Viking, 2001), and Cole, 1993, chap. 5 ("The Bank Veto and Indian Removal").

82. For a brief introduction to the rise of ideological polarization and partisan identification in the American electorate, see David C. Kimball and Cassie A. Gross, "The Growing Polarization of American Voters," in *The State of the Parties: The Changing Role of Contemporary American Politics*, 5th edition, John C. Green and Daniel J. Coffey eds. (Lanham, MD: Rowman & Littlefield, 2007), 265–278; John Petrocik, "Party Coalitions in the American Public: Morality Politics, Issue Agendas, and the 2004 Election," in *ibid.*, 279–298; and Kyle L. Saunders and Alan I. Abramowitz, "The Rise of the Ideological Voter: The Changing Bases of Partisanship in the American Electorate," in *ibid.*, 299–316; David G. Lawrence, "On the Resurgence of Party Identification in the 1990s," in *American Political Parties: Decline or Resurgence?* Jeffrey A. Cohen et al., eds. (Washington, DC: CQ Press, 2001), 30–54; Richard Fleisher and Jon R. Bond, "Evidence of Increasing Polarization Among Ordinary Citizens," in *ibid.*, 55–77; and Arthur Paulson, "Ideological Homogenization and Party Revival," in *Realignment and Party Revival* (Westport, CT: Praeger, 2000), 148–171.

Bibliography

This bibliography is divided into sections: Books, Dissertations and Theses, Articles, Online Resources, Web Sites, and Comparative Resources

Books

Abbott, Richard H. *For Free Press and Equal Rights: Republican Newspapers in the Reconstruction South.* Athens: University of Georgia Press, 2004.

Abels, Jules. *Out of the Jaws of Victory.* New York: Henry Holt, New York, 1959.

Adams, Charles. *When in the Course of Human Events: Arguing the Case for Southern Secession.* Lanham, MD: Rowman & Littlefield, 2000.

Allen, Craig. *Eisenhower and the Mass Media.* Chapel Hill: University of North Carolina Press, 1993.

Alterman, Eric. *What Liberal Media? The Truth about Bias and the News.* New York: Basic Books, 2003.

Altschuler, Glenn C., and Stuart M. Blumin. *Rude Republic: Americans and their Politics in the Nineteenth Century.* Princeton, NJ: Princeton University Press, 2000.

Ambler, Charles H. *Thomas Ritchie: A Study in Virginia Politics.* Richmond, VA: Bell, 1913.

Ambrose, Stephen E. *Nixon: The Education of a Politician, 1913–1962.* New York: Simon and Schuster, 1987.

Ames, William E. *A History of the National Intelligencer.* Chapel Hill: University of North Carolina Press.

Anbinder, Tyler. *Nativism and Slavery: The Northern Know Nothings and the Politics of the 1850s.* New York: Oxford University Press, 1992.

Anderson, Brian C. *South Park Conservatives: The Revolt Against Liberal Media Bias.* Washington, DC: Regnery, 2005.

Anderson, Chris. *The Long Tail: Why the Future of Business is Selling Less of More.* New York: Hyperion, 2006.

Andrews, J. Cutler. *The North Reports the Civil War.* Pittsburgh: University of Pittsburgh Press, 1955.

_____. *The South Reports the Civil War.* Princeton, NJ: Princeton University Press, 1970.

Aronson, James. *The Press and the Cold War.* New York: Bobbs-Merrill, 1970.

Artz, Lee, and Yahya R. Kamalipour, eds. *Bring 'em On: Media and Politics in the Iraq War.* Lanham, MD: Rowman & Littlefield, 2005.

Asher, Herbert B. *Presidential Elections and American Politics.* Homewood, IL: Dorsey Press, 1976.

Auletta, Ken. *Backstory: Inside the Business of News.* New York: Penguin, 2003.

Austin, Aleine. *Matthew Lyon: "New Man" of the Democratic Revolution, 1749–1822.* University Park: Pennsylvania State University Press, 1981.

Axelrad, Jacob. *Philip Freneau: Champion of Democracy.* Austin: University of Texas Press, 1967.

Bagby, Wesley M. *The Road to Normalcy: The Presidential Campaign and Election of 1920.* Baltimore: Johns Hopkins Press, 1962.

Bagdikian, Ben H. *The Effete Conspiracy, and other Crimes by the Press.* New York: Harper & Row, 1974.

Baker, Jean H. *Affairs of Party: The Political Culture of Northern Democrats in the Mid-Nineteenth Century.* Ithaca, NY: Cornell University Press, 1983.

Baker, Ray Stannard. *Woodrow Wilson: Life and Letters, Vol. 3: Governor, 1910–1913.* Garden City, NY: Doubleday, 1931.

Baldasty, Gerald J. *The Commercialization of the News in the Nineteenth Century.* Madison: University of Wisconsin Press, 1992.

Baldasty, Gerald J. *The Press and Politics in the Age of Jackson.* Association for Education in Journalism and Mass Communication, 1984.

Barber, James David. *The Pulse of Politics: Electing Presidents in the Media Age.* New York: W. W. Norton, 1980.

Barlow, Aaron. *Rise of the Blogosphere.* New York: Praeger, 2006.

Barrett, James Wyman. *Joseph Pulitzer and his World.* New York: Vanguard Press, 1941.

Baughman, James L. *Henry R. Luce and the Rise of the American News Media.* Boston: Twayne Publishers, 1987.

Bayley, Edwin R. *Joe McCarthy and the Press.* New York: Pantheon Books, 1981.

Belko, W. Stephen. *The Invincible Duff Green: Whig of*

the West. Columbia: University of Missouri Press, 2006.

Bemis, Samuel Flagg. *John Quincy Adams and the Union*. New York: Alfred A. Knopf, 1965.

Ben-Atar, Doron, and Barbara B. Oberg, eds. *Federalists Reconsidered*. Charlottesville: University Press of Virginia, 1998.

Bennett, Lance. *News: The Politics of Illusion*. New York: Longman, 1996.

Berges, Marshall. *The Life and Times of Los Angeles*. New York: Atheneum, 1984.

Bernstein, Carl, and Bob Woodward. *All the President's Men*. New York: Simon and Schuster, 1974.

Beschloss, Michael R. *Kennedy and Roosevelt: The Uneasy Alliance*. New York: Norton, 1980.

Best, Gary Dean. *The Critical Press and the New Deal: The Press versus Presidential Power, 1933–1938*. Westport, CT: Praeger, 1993.

Bigelow, John, ed. *Letters and Literary Memorials of Samuel J. Tilden*, Vol. I. New York: Harper & Brothers, 1908.

Bleyer, Willard Grosvenor. *Main Currents in the History of American Journalism*. Boston: Houghton Mifflin, 1927.

Blondheim, Menahem. *News Over the Wires: The Telegraph and the Flow of Public Information in America, 1844–1897*. Cambridge, MA: Harvard University Press, 1994.

Blumberg, Nathan B. *One-Party Press? Coverage of the 1952 Presidential Campaign in 35 Daily Newspapers*. Lincoln: University of Nebraska Press, 1954.

Blumler, Jay G., and Michael Gurevitch. *The Crisis of Public Communication*. New York: Routledge, 1995.

Blyth, Myrna. *Spin Sisters: How the Women of the Media Sell Unhappiness — and Liberalism — to the Women of America*. New York: St. Martin's Press, 2004.

Boehlert, Eric. *Lap Dogs: How the Press Rolled Over for Bush*. New York: Free Press, 2006.

Borden, Morton. *Parties and Politics in the Early Republic, 1789–1815*. New York: Thomas Y. Crowell, 1967.

Bornet, Vaughn D. *The Presidency of Lyndon B. Johnson*. Lawrence: University Press of Kansas, 1983.

Bowers, Claude G. *Jefferson and Hamilton: The Struggle for Democracy in America*. Boston: Houghton Mifflin, 1966.

Bowers, Claude G. *The Party Battles of the Jackson Period*. Boston: Houghton Mifflin, 1922.

Bozell, L. Brent III. *Weapons of Mass Distortion: The Coming Meltdown of the Liberal Media*. New York: Crown Forum, 2004.

Braestrup, Peter. *Big Story: How the American Press and Television Reported and Interpreted the Crisis of Tet 1968 in Vietnam and Washington*. Presidio, CA: Presidio, 1994.

Brian, Denis. *Pulitzer: A Life*. New York: John Wiley & Sons, 2001.

Briggs, Asa, and Peter Burke. *A Social History of the Media: From Gutenberg to the Internet*. Cambridge, MA: Polity, 2002.

Brigham, Clarence S. *Journals and Journeymen*. Philadelphia: University of Pennsylvania Press, 1950.

Brinkley, Alan. *Voices of Protest: Huey Long, Father Coughlin, and the Great Depression*. New York: Knopf, 1982.

Britt, George. *Forty Years — Forty Millions: The Career of Frank A. Munsey*. New York: Farrar & Rinehart, 1935.

Brooks, David. *Bobos in Paradise: The New Upper Class and How They Got There*. New York: Simon & Schuster, 2000.

_____. *On Paradise Drive: How We Live Now (And Always Have) in the Future Tense*. Simon & Schuster, New York, 2004.

Brown, Francis. *Raymond of the Times*. New York: W. W. Norton, 1951.

Brown, Walt. *John Adams and the American Press: Politics and Journalism at the Birth of the Republic*. Jefferson, NC: McFarland, 1995.

Buel, Richard, Jr. *America on the Brink: How the Political Struggle over the War of 1812 Almost Destroyed the Young Republic*. New York: Palgrave, 2005.

Burlingame, Michael, ed. *Lincoln's Journalist: John Hay's Anonymous Writings for the Press, 1860–1864*. Carbondale: Southern Illinois University Press, 1998.

Burns, Eric. *Infamous Scribblers: The Founding Fathers and the Rowdy Beginnings of American Journalism*. New York: Public Affairs, 2006.

Burns, James MacGregor. *Roosevelt: The Lion and the Fox*. New York: Harcourt, 1956.

Burstein, Andrew. *The Passions of Andrew Jackson*. New York: Alfred A. Knopf, 2003.

Cain, Marvin R. *Lincoln's Attorney General: Edward Bates of Missouri*. Columbia: University of Missouri Press, 1965.

Campbell, W. Joseph. *1897: The Year that Defined American Journalism*. New York: Routledge, 2006.

Campbell, W. Joseph. *Yellow Journalism: Puncturing the Myths, Defining the Legacies*. New York: Praeger, 2003.

Carlisle, Rodney P. *Hearst and the New Deal: The Progressive as Reactionary*. New York: Garland, 1979.

Carlson, Oliver. *The Man Who Made News: James Gordon Bennett*. New York: Duell, Sloan & Pearce, 1942.

Carlson, Oliver, and Ernest Sutherland Bates. *Hearst: Lord of San Simeon*. New York: Viking Press, 1936.

Carman, Harry James. *Lincoln and the Patronage*. Gloucester, Massachusetts: P. Smith, 1964.

Carpenter, Ted. *The Captive Press: Foreign Policy Crises and the First Amendment*. Washington, DC: Cato Institute, 1995.

Caute, David. *News from Nowhere*. New York: Random House, 1973.

Chace, James. *Dean Acheson*. New York: Simon & Schuster, 1998.

_____. *1912: Wilson, Roosevelt, Taft & Debs — The Election that Changed the Country*. New York: Simon & Schuster, 2004.

Chernow, Ron. *Alexander Hamilton*. New York: Penguin, 2004.

Chester, Edward W. *Radio, Television, and American Politics*. New York: Sheed & Ward, New York, 1969.

Chiasson, Lloyd, Jr., ed. *The Press in Times of Crisis*. Westport, CT: Greenwood Press, 1995.

Clancy, Herbert J. *The Presidential Election of 1880*. Chicago: Loyola University Press, 1958.

Clark, Thomas D. *The Southern Country Editor*. New York: Bobbs-Merrill, 1948.

Cohen, Elliot D., ed. *News Incorporated: Corporate Media Ownership and its Threat to Democracy*. Amherst, NY: Prometheus Books, 2005.

Cole, Donald B. *A Jackson Man: Amos Kendall and the Rise of American Democracy*. Baton Rouge: Louisiana State University Press, 2004.

_____. *Martin Van Buren and the American Political System*. Princeton, NJ: Princeton University Press, 1984.

_____. *The Presidency of Andrew Jackson*. Lawrence: University Press of Kansas, 1993.

Coleman, Charles H. *The Election of 1868*. New York: Octagon Books, 1971.

Conason, Joe. *Big Lies: The Right-Wing Propaganda Machine and how it Distorts the Truth*. New York: Thomas Dunne Books, 2003.

Conlin, Joseph R., ed. *The American Radical Press, 1880–1960*. Two volumes. Westport, CT: Greenwood Press, 1974.

Cook, Fred J. *The Muckrakers: Crusading Journalists Who Changed America*. Garden City, NY: Doubleday, 1972.

Cook, Timothy E. *Governing with the News: The News Media as a Political Institution*. Chicago: University of Chicago Press, 1998.

Cortissoz, Royal. *The Life of Whitelaw Reid*, volume 1. London: Thornton Butterworth, 1921.

Coulter, Ann. *Slander: Liberal Lies About the American Right*. New York: Crown, 2002.

Craig, Douglas B. *Fireside Politics: Radio and Political Culture in the United States, 1920–1940*. Baltimore: Johns Hopkins University Press, 2000.

Crouthamel, James L. *Bennett's New York Herald and the Rise of the Popular Press*. Syracuse, NY: Syracuse University Press, 1989.

_____. *James Watson Webb: A Biography*. Middletown, CT: Wesleyan University Press, 1969.

Crozier, Emmet. *Yankee Reporters 1861–65*. New York: Oxford University Press, 1956.

Cunningham, Noble E. *The Jeffersonian Republicans in Power: Party Operations, 1801–1809*. Chapel Hill: University of North Carolina Press, 1963.

Cunningham, Noble E. *The Jeffersonian Republicans: The Formation of a Party Organization, 1789–1801*. Chapel Hill: University of North Carolina Press, 1957.

Cunningham, Noble E., Jr. *Popular Images of the Presidency: From Washington to Lincoln*. Columbia: University of Missouri Press, 1991.

Dabney, Virginius. *The Jefferson Scandals: A Rebuttal*. New York: Dodd, Mead, 1981.

Dangerfield, George. *The Era of Good Feelings*. Chicago: Elephant Paperbacks, 1989.

Dary, David. *Red Blood and Black Ink: Journalism in the Old West*. New York: Alfred A. Knopf, 1998.

Dautrich, Kenneth and Thomas H. Hartley. *How the News Media Fail American Voters: Causes, Consequences and Remedies*. New York: Columbia University Press, 1999.

Davis, Kenneth S. *The Politics of Honor: A Biography of Adlai Stevenson*. New York: Putnam, 1967.

Davis, Richard. *The Press and American Politics: The New Mediator*. New York: Longman, 1992.

Dawson, Matthew Q. *Partisanship and the Birth of America's Second Party, 1796–1800*. Westport, CT: Greenwood Press, 2000.

Dean, John W. *Warren G. Harding*. New York: Henry Holt, 2004.

Denton, Jr., Robert E. *The Primetime Presidency of Ronald Reagan: The Era of the Television Presidency*. New York: Praeger, 1988.

Dicken-Garcia, Hazel. *Journalistic Standards in Nineteenth Century America*. Madison: University of Wisconsin Press, 1989.

Dickerson, Donna L. *The Course of Tolerance: Freedom of the Press in Nineteenth-Century America*. New York: Greenwood Press, 1990.

Donaldson, Gary. *Liberalism's Last Hurrah: The Presidential Campaign of 1964*. Armonk, NY: M. E. Sharpe, 2003.

Dowling, William C. *Literary Federalism in the Age of Jefferson: Joseph Dennie and The Port Folio, 1801–1812*. Columbia: University of South Carolina Press, 1999.

Dumond, Dwight Lowell, ed. *Southern Editorials on Secession*. New York: Century, 1931.

Duncan, Bingham. *Whitelaw Reid: Journalist, Politician, Diplomat*. Athens: University of Georgia Press, 1975.

Dunn, Susan. *Jefferson's Second Revolution*. New York: Houghton Mifflin, 2004.

_____. *Sister Revolutions: French Lightning, American Light*. New York: Faber & Faber, 1999.

Durey, Michael. *"With the Hammer of Truth": James Thomson Callender and America's Early National Heroes*. Charlottesville: University Press of Virginia, 1990.

Eckenrode, Hamilton J. *Rutherford B. Hayes: Statesman of Reunion*. Port Washington, NY: Kennikat Press, 1930.

Efron, Edith. *The News Twisters*. Los Angeles: Nash Publishing, 1971.

Eisenstein, Elizabeth L. *The Printing Press as an Agent of Change: Communications and Cultural Transformations in Early Modern Europe*. Cambridge: Cambridge University Press, Cambridge, 1979.

Elkins, Stanley, and Eric McKitrick. *The Age of Federalism: The Early American Republic, 1788–1800*. New York: Oxford University Press, 1993.

Emerson, Donald E. *Richard Hildreth*. Baltimore: Johns Hopkins University Press, 1946.

Emery, Edwin. *The Press and America: An Interpretive History of the Mass Media*. Englewood Cliffs, New Jersey: Prentice-Hall, 1972.

Emery, Fred. *Watergate: The Corruption and Fall of Richard Nixon*. London: Jonathan Cape, 1994.

Entman, Robert M. *Democracy without Citizens*. New York: Oxford University Press, 1989.

Fahrney, Ralph Ray. *Horace Greeley and the Tribune in the Civil War*. Cedar Rapids, IA: Torch Press, 1936.

Fallows, James M. *Breaking the News: How the Media Undermine American Democracy*. New York: Pantheon, 1996.

Farley, James. *Behind the Ballots: The Personal History of a Politician*. New York: Harcourt, Brace, 1938.

Farnsworth, Stephen J. and S. Robert Lichter. *The Nightly News Nightmare: Network Television's Coverage of U.S. Presidential Elections, 1988–2000*. New York: Rowman & Littlefield, 2003.

Farquhar, Michael. *A Treasury of Great American Scandals*. New York: Penguin, 2003.

Farr, Finis. *Fair Enough: The Life of Westbrook Pegler*. New Rochelle, NY: Arlington House Publishers, 1975.

Fay, Bernard. *The Two Franklins: Fathers of American Democracy*. Boston: Little, Brown, 1933.

Fenton, Tom. *Bad News: The Decline of Reporting, the Business of News, and the Danger to Us All*. New York: Regan Books, 2005.

Ferling, John. *Adams vs. Jefferson: The Tumultuous Election of 1800*. New York: Oxford University Press, 2004.

Fermer, Douglas. *James Gordon Bennett and the New York Herald: A Study of Editorial Opinion in the Civil War Era 1854–1867*. New York: St. Martin's Press, 1986.

Fidler, Roger. *Mediamorphosis: Understanding New Media*. Thousand Oaks, CA: Pine Forge Press, 1997.

Fischer, David Hackett. *The Revolution of Conservatism: The Federalist Party in the Era of Jeffersonian Democracy*. New York: Harper & Row, 1965.

Fish, Carl Russell. *The Civil Service and Patronage*. New York: Russell & Russell, 1967.

Fleming, Thomas. *Duel: Alexander Hamilton, Aaron Burr and the Future of America*. New York: Basic Books, 1999.

Flick, Alexander Clarence. *Samuel Jones Tilden: A Study in Political Sagacity*. Port Washington: Kennikat Press, 1939.

Foner, Eric. *Free Soil, Free Labor, Free Men: The Ideology of the Republican Party before the Civil War*. New York: Oxford University Press, 1995.

Ford, Edwin H., and Edwin Emery, eds. *Highlights in the History of the American Press*. Minneapolis: University of Minnesota Press, 1954.

Fotheringham, Allan. *Birds of a Feather: The Press and the Politicians*. Toronto: Key Porter Books, 1989.

Frank, Thomas. *What's the Matter with Kansas? How Conservatives Won the Heart of America*. New York: Metropolitan Books, 2004.

Franklin, John H. *The Militant South*. Cambridge, MA: Harvard University Press, Cambridge, 1956.

Freehling, William W. *The Road to Disunion, Vol. I: Secessionists at Bay, 1776–1854*. New York: Oxford University Press, 1990.

Freeman, Joanne B. *Affairs of Honor: National Politics in the New Republic*. New Haven, CT: Yale University Press, 2001.

Friedman, Lawrence J. *The White Savage: Racial Fantasies in the Postbellum South*. Englewood Cliffs, NJ: Prentice-Hall, 1970.

Friel, Howard, and Richard Falk. *The Record of the Paper: How the New York Times Misreports US Foreign Policy*. New York: Verso, 2004.

Garry, Patrick M. *The American Vision of a Free Press*. New York: Garland, 1990.

_____. *Scrambling for Protection: The New Media and the First Amendment*. Pittsburgh: University of Pittsburgh Press, 1994.

Genovese, Michael A. *The Nixon Presidency: Power and Politics in Turbulent Times*. New York: Greenwood Press, 1990.

Gerring, John. *Party Ideologies in America, 1828–1996*. Cambridge: Cambridge University Press, 1998.

Gienapp, William E., Stephen E. Maizlish, and John J. Kushma. *Essays on American Antebellum Politics, 1840–1860*. Arlington: Texas A&M University Press, 1982.

Gies, Joseph. *The Colonel of Chicago*. New York: E. P. Dutton, 1979.

Glad, Paul W. *McKinley, Bryan and the People*. New York: J. B. Lippincott, 1964.

Goldberg, Bernard. *Arrogance: Rescuing America from the Media Elite*. New York: Warner Books, 2003.

_____. *Bias: A CBS Insider Exposes how the Media Distort the News*. Washington, DC: Regnery, 2002.

Goldberg, Robert Alan. *Barry Goldwater*. New Haven, CT: Yale University Press, 1995.

Gordon-Read, Annette. *Thomas Jefferson and Sally Hemings: An American Controversy*. Charlotteville: University Press of Virginia, 1997.

Gosnell, Harold F. *Machine Politics: Chicago Model*. Chicago: University of Chicago Press, 1937.

Gottlieb, Bob, and Irene Wolt. *Thinking Big: The Story of the Los Angeles Times, Its Publishers, and Their Influence on Southern California*. New York: Putnam, 1977.

Govan, Thomas Payne. *Nicholas Biddle: Nationalist and Public Banker, 1786–1844*. Chicago: University of Chicago Press, 1959.

Graber, Doris A. *Mass Media and American Politics*. Washington, DC: CQ Press, 1997.

_____. *Media Power in Politics*, Washington, DC: CQ Press, 2000.

Graff, Henry F. *Grover Cleveland*. New York: Times Books, 2002.

Greeley, Horace. *Recollections of a Busy Life*. New York: J.B. Ford, 1868.

Greenberg, David. *Nixon's Shadow: The History of an Image*. New York: W. W. Norton, 2003.

Greenberg, Kenneth S. *Masters and Statesmen: The Political Culture of American Slavery*. Baltimore: Johns Hopkins University Press, 1985.

Groneman, William III. *David Crockett: Hero of the Common Man*. New York: Tom Doherty Associates, 2005.

Grossman, Michael Baruch, and Martha Joynt Kumar. *Portraying the President: The White House and the News Media*. Baltimore: Johns Hopkins University Press, 1981.

Gunderson, Robert Gray. *The Log-Cabin Campaign*. Lexington: University of Kentucky Press, 1957.

Hackett, Robert A., and Yuezhi Zhao: *Sustaining Democracy? Journalism and the Politics of Objectivity*. Toronto: Garamond Press, 1998.

Halbertsam, David. *The Fifties*. New York: Villard Books, 1993.

_____. The Powers That Be. New York: Alfred A. Knopf, 1979.

Hallin, Daniel C. *The "Uncensored War:" The Media and Vietnam*. Berkeley: University of California Press, 1989.

Hallock, Steven M. *Editorial & Opinion: The Dwindling Marketplace of Ideas in Today's News*. New York: Praeger, 2006.

Hamilton, James T. *All the News that's Fit to Sell: How the Market Transforms Information into News*. Princeton, NJ: Princeton University Press, 2006.

Hamilton, Milton W. *The Country Printer: New York State, 1785–1830*. New York: Columbia University Press, 1936.

Hammond, William M. *Reporting Vietnam: Media and Military at War*. Lawrence: University Press of Kansas, 1998.

Han, Lori C. *Governing from Center Stage: White House Communication Strategies During the Television Age of Politics*. Cresskill, NJ: Hampton Press, 2001.

Hargreaves, Mary W. M. *The Presidency of John Quincy Adams*. Lawrence: University Press of Kansas, 1985.

Harper, Robert S. *Lincoln and the Press*. New York: McGraw-Hill, 1951.

Harris, Brayton. *Blue and Gray in Black and White: Newspapers in the Civil War*. Washington, DC: Batsford Brassey, 1999.

Haworth, Paul Leland. *The Hayes-Tilden Disputed Presidential Election of 1876*. New York: Russell & Russell, 1966.

Hayes, Melvin L. *Mr. Lincoln Runs for President*. New York: Citadel Press, 1960.

Heale, M. J. *The Presidential Quest: Candidates and Images in American Political Culture, 1787–1852*. New York: Longman, 1982.

Heineman, Kenneth J. *God is a Conservative: Religion, Politics and Morality in Contemporary America*. New York: New York University Press, 1998.

Hendrickson, Robert. *Hamilton, Vol. II: 1789–1804*. New York: Mason/Charter, 1976.

Heren, Louis. *The Power of the Press?* London: Orbis, 1985.

Herman, Arthur. *Joseph McCarthy: Reexamining the Life*

of America's Most Hated Senator. New York: Free Press, 2000.

Hertsgaard, Mark. *On Bended Knee: The Press and the Reagan Presidency*. New York: Farrar Straus Giroux, 1988.

Herzstein, Robert E. *Henry R. Luce: A Political Portrait of the Man Who Created the American Century*. New York: Macmillan, 1994.

_____. *Henry R. Luce, Time, and the American Crusade in Asia*. Cambridge: Cambridge University Press, 2005.

Hesseltine, William Best. *Ulysses S. Grant, Politician*. New York: F. Ungar, 1957.

Higginbotham, Sanford W. *The Keystone in the Democratic Arch: Pennsylvania Politics 1800–1816*. Harrisburg: Pennsylvania Historical and Museum Commission, 1952.

Hofstetter, Richard C. *Bias in the News: Network Television Coverage of the 1972 Election Campaign*. Columbus: Ohio State University Press, 1976.

Hohnberg, John. *Free Press/Free People*. New York: Columbia University Press, 1971.

Hollingsworth, J. Rogers. *The Whirligig of Politics: The Democracy of Cleveland and Bryan*. Chicago: University of Chicago Press, 1963.

Holland, Barbara. *Gentlemen's Blood: A History of Dueling from Swords at Dawn to Pistols at Dusk*. New York: Bloomsbury, 2003.

Holt, Michael F. *Forging a Majority: The Formation of the Republican Party in Pittsburgh, 1848–1860*. New Haven, CT: Yale University Press, 1969.

_____. *The Political Crisis of the 1850s*. New York: John Wiley & Sons, 1978.

Holzer, Harold. *Lincoln at Cooper Union: The Speech that Made Abraham Lincoln President*. New York: Simon & Schuster, 2005.

Horn, James, Jan Ellis Lewis, and Peter S. Onuf. *The Revolution of 1800: Democracy, Race, and the New Republic*. Charlottesville: University of Virginia Press, 2002.

Hudson, Frederic. *Journalism in the United States from 1690–1872*. New York: Haskell House, 1873.

Humphrey, Carol Sue. *The Press of the Young Republic, 1783–1833*. Westport, CT: Greenwood Press, 1996.

_____. *"This Popular Engine": New England Newspapers during the American Revolution, 1775–1789*. Newark: University of Delaware Press, 1992.

Humphrey, Steve. *"That D----d Brownlow": Being a Saucy and Malicious Description of William Gannaway Brownlow*. Boone, NC: Appalachian Consortium Press, 1978.

Huntzicker, William E. *The Popular Press, 1833–1865*. Westport, CT: Greenwood Press, 1999.

Ingersoll, L.D. *The Life of Horace Greeley*. Chicago: Union Publishing, 1873.

Innis, Harold A. *The Bias of Communications*. Toronto: University of Toronto Press, 1951.

Ions, Edmund. *Woodrow Wilson: The Politics of Peace and War*. London: Macdonald, 1972.

Irwin, William H. *The American Newspaper*. Ames: Iowa State University Press, 1969.

Isley, Jeter Allen. *Horace Greeley and the Republican Party, 1853–1861*. Princeton, NJ: Princeton University Press, 1947.

Iyengar, Shanto, and Donald R. Kinder. *News that Matters: Television and American Opinion*. Chicago: University of Chicago Press, 1987.

Jacobs, Meg, William J. Novak, and Julian E. Zelizer.

The Democratic Experiment: New Directions in American Political History. Princeton, NJ: Princeton University Press, 2003.

James, Marquis. *The Life of Andrew Jackson*. Indianapolis: Bobbs-Merrill, 1938.

Jamieson, Kathleen Hall, ed. *The Media and Politics*. Thousand Oaks, CA: Sage Periodicals Press, 1996.

Jamieson, Kathleen Hall, and Paul Waldman. *The Press Effect: Politicians, Journalists and the Stories that Shape the Political World*. Oxford: Oxford University Press, 2003.

Janeway, Michael. *Republic of Denial: Press, Politics, and Public Life*. New Haven, CT: Yale University Press, 1999.

Jenkins, Henry, and David Thorburn, eds. *Democracy and New Media*. Cambridge, MA: MIT Press, 2003.

Johnson, Lyndon B. *The Vantage Point*. New York: Holt, Rinehart & Winston, 1971.

Johnson, Thomas J. *The Rehabilitation of Richard Nixon: The Media's Effect on Collective Memory*. New York: Garland, 1995.

Johnson-Cartee, Karen S. *News Narratives and News Framing: Constructing Political Reality*. Lanham, MD: Rowman & Littlefield, 2005.

Josephson, Matthew. *The Politicos, 1865–1896*. New York: Harcourt, Brace, 1938.

Juergens, George. *News from the White House: The Presidential-Press Relationship in the Progressive Era*. Chicago: University of Chicago Press, 1981.

Kaplan, Richard L. *Politics and the American Press: The Rise of Objectivity, 1865–1920*. Cambridge: Cambridge University Press, 2002.

Kazin, Michael. *A Godly Hero: The Life of William Jennings Bryan*. New York: Knopf, 2006.

Kellner, Douglas. *Media Spectacle and the Crisis of Democracy: Terrorism, War, and Election Battles*. Boulder, CO: Paradigm Publishers, 2005.

Kelly, Frank K. *The Fight for the White House: The Story of 1912*. New York: Thomas Y. Crowell, 1961.

Kendrick, Alexander. *Prime Time: The Life of Edward R. Murrow*. Boston: Little, Brown, 1969.

Keogh, James. *President Nixon and the Press*. New York: Funk & Wagnalls, 1972.

Kern, Montague, Patricia W. Levering, and Ralph B. Levering. *The Kennedy Crises: The Press, the Presidency, and Foreign Policy*. Chapel Hill: University of North Carolina Press, 1983.

Kernell, Samuel. *Going Public: New Strategies of Presidential Leadership*. Washington, DC: CQ Press, 1997.

Kerney, James. *The Political Education of Woodrow Wilson*. New York: Century, 1926.

Key, V. O., Jr. *Public Opinion and American Democracy*. New York: Alfred A. Knopf, 1964.

Kielbowicz, Richard B. *News in the Mail: The Press, Post Office, and Public Information, 1700–1860s*. New York: Greenwood Press, 1989.

Klement, Frank L. *Lincoln's Critics: The Copperheads of the North*. Shippensburg, Pennsylvania: White Mane Books, 1999.

Knudson, Jerry W. *Jefferson and the Press: Crucible of Liberty*. Columbia: University of South Carolina Press, 2006.

Kobre, Sidney. *Development of American Journalism*. Dubuque, IA: Wm. C. Brown, 1969.

_____. *The Yellow Press and Gilded Age Journalism*. Tallahassee: Florida State University, 1964.

Koenig, Louis W. *Bryan: A Political Biography of William Jennings Bryan*. New York: Putnam's, 1971.

Koskoff, David. *Joseph P. Kennedy: A Life and Times.* Englewood Cliffs, NJ: Prentice Hall, 1974.

Kovach, Bill, and Tom Rosenstiel. *Warp Speed: America in the Age of Mixed Media.* New York: Century Foundation Press, 1999.

Krock, Arthur. *The Consent of the Governed and Other Deceits.* Boston: Little, Brown, 1971.

_____. *Memoirs: Sixty Years on the Firing Line.* New York: Funk & Wagnalls, 1968.

Kurtz, Howard. *Spin Cycle: Inside the Clinton Propaganda Machine.* New York: Free Press, 1998.

Kutler, Stanley I. *The Wars of Watergate: The Last Crisis of Richard Nixon.* New York: Alfred A. Knopf, 1990.

Kuypers, Jim A. *Press Bias and Politics: How the Media Frame Controversial Issues.* Westport , CT: Praeger, 2002.

Lane, Gladys E., and Kurt Lang. *The Battle for Public Opinion: The President, the Press, and the Polls During Watergate.* New York: Columbia University Press, 1983.

Lange, Bernd-Peter, and David Ward, eds. *The Media and Elections: A Handbook and Comparative Study.* Mahwah, NJ: Lawrence Erlbaum, 2004.

Lashner, Marilyn A. *The Chilling Effect in TV News: Intimidation by the Nixon White House.* New York: Praeger, 1984.

Lawson, Linda. *Truth in Publishing: Federal Regulation of the Press's Business Practices, 1880–1920.* Carbondale: Southern Illinois University Press, 1993.

Leary, Lewis. *That Rascal Freneau.* New Brunswick, NJ: Rutgers University Press, 1941.

Lee, Alfred McClung. *The Daily Newspaper in America: The Evolution of a Social Instrument.* New York: Macmillan, 1937.

Lee, James Melvin. *History of American Journalism.* Garden City, NY: Garden City Publishing, 1923.

Leonard, Thomas C. *News for All: America's Coming-of-Age with the Press.* London: Oxford University Press, 1995.

_____. *The Power of the Press: The Birth of American Political Reporting.* New York: Oxford University Press, 1986.

Levy, Buddy. *American Legend: The Real-Life Adventures of David Crockett.* New York: Putnam's, 2005.

Levy, Leonard W. *Emergence of a Free Press.* Oxford: Oxford University Press, 1985.

Levy, Leonard W., ed. *Freedom of the Press from Zenger to Jefferson.* New York: Bobbs-Merrill, 1966.

Lewis, Jan Ellen, and Peter S Onuf. *Sally Hemings and Thomas Jefferson: History, Memory and Civic Culture.* Charlottesville: University Press of Virginia, 1999.

Lewis, Justin, et al. *Shoot First and Ask Questions Later: Media Coverage of the 2003 Iraq War.* New York: Peter Lang, 2006.

Lichter, S. Robert, Stanley Rothman, and Linda S. Lichter. *The Media Elite.* Bethesda, MD: Adler & Adler, 1986.

Liebovich, Louis W. *The Press and the Modern Presidency: Myths and Mindsets from Kennedy to Election 2000.* Westport, CT: Praeger, 2001.

_____. *Richard Nixon, Watergate, and the Press.* Westport, CT: Praeger, 2003.

Linden, Frank van der. *The Turning Point: Jefferson's Battle for the Presidency.* Golden, CO: Fulcrum Publishing, 2000.

Link, Arthur S. *Wilson: The Road to the White House.* Princeton, NJ: Princeton University Press, 1968.

Littlewood, Thomas B. *Calling Elections: The History of Horse-Race Journalism.* Notre Dame, IN: University of Notre Dame Press, 1998.

Lofton, John. *The Press as Guardian of the First Amendment.* Columbia: University of South Carolina Press, 1980.

Lorant, Stefan. *The Glorious Burden.* New York: Harper & Row, 1968.

Lothrop, Thorton K. *William Henry Seward.* New York: Houghton Mifflin, 1896.

Lukas, J. Anthony. *Nightmare. The Underside of the Nixon Years.* New York: Viking Press, 1976.

Lynch, Denis Tilden. *Grover Cleveland: A Man Four-Square.* New York: Horace Liveright, 1932.

MacKuen, Michael Bruce, and Steven Lane Coombs. *More than News: Media Power in Public Affairs.* Beverly Hills, CA: Sage Publications, 1981.

Maihafer, Harry J. *The General and the Journalists.* Washington, DC: Brassey's, 1998.

Malone, Dumas. *Jefferson the President: First Term, 1801–1805.* Boston: Little, Brown, 1970.

Maihafer, Harry J. *War of Words: Abraham Lincoln and the Civil War Press.* Washington, DC: Brassey's, 2001.

Maltese, John Anthony. *Spin Control: The White House Office of Communications and the Management of Presidential News.* Chapel Hill: University of North Carolina Press, 1994.

Manber, Jeffrey, and Neil Dahlstrom. *Lincoln's Wrath: Fierce Mobs, Brilliant Scoundrels, and a President's Mission to Destroy the Press.* Naperville, IL: Sourcebooks, 2005.

Marsh, Philip M. *Philip Freneau: Poet and Journalist.* Minneapolis: Dillon Press, 1967.

Martin, Lee. *Unreliable Sources: A Guide to Detecting Bias in News Media.* New York: Carol Publishing Group, 1990.

Martin, Ralph G. *Ballots and Bandwagons.* Chicago: Rand McNally, 1964.

_____. *Henry and Clare: An Intimate Portrait of the Luces.* New York: Putnam's, 1991.

Marszalek, John F. *The Petticoat Affair.* New York: Free Press, 1997.

_____. *Sherman's Other War: The General and the Civil War Press.* Kent, OH: Kent State University Press, 1999.

Martin, John B. *Adlai Stevenson of Illinois.* New York: Doubleday, 1976.

Matson, Kevin. *When America was Great: The Fighting Faith of Postwar Liberalism.* New York: Routledge, 2004.

Mazzocco, Dennis. *Networks of Power: Corporate TV's Threat to Democracy.* Boston: South End Press, 1994.

McChesney, Robert W. *Rich Media, Poor Democracy: Communication Politics in Dubious Times.* Urbana: University of Illinois Press, 1999.

McCormick, Richard P. *The Second American Party System: Party Formation in the Jacksonian Era.* Chapel Hill: University of North Carolina Press, 1966.

McDougal, Dennis. *Privileged Son: Otis Chandler and the Rise and Fall of the L.A. Times Dynasty.* Cambridge, MA: Perseus, 2001.

McGerr, Michael E. *The Decline of Popular Politics: The American North, 1865–1928.* Oxford: Oxford University Press, 1986.

McGowan, William. *Coloring the News: How Political Correctness Has Corrupted American Journalism.* San Francisco: Encounter Books, 2001.

McJimsey, George. *Genteel Partisan: Manton Marble, 1834–1917.* Ames: Iowa State University Press, 1971.

McKeever, Porter. *Adlai Stevenson: His Life and Times.* New York: Morrow, 1989.

McLuhan, Marshall. *Understanding Media: The Extensions of Man.* New York: McGraw-Hill, 1965.

McPhee, Nancy. *The Book of Insults — Ancient and Modern.* Toronto: Jonathan-James, 1978.

Meeker, Richard H. *Newspaperman: S. I. Newhouse and the Business of News.* New Haven: Ticknor & Fields, 1983.

Merk, Frederick. *The Monroe Doctrine and American Expansion, 1843–1849.* New York: Alfred A. Knopf, 1966.

Merritt, Davis. *Knightfall: Knight Ridder and How the Erosion of Newspaper Journalism is Putting Democracy at Risk.* New York: American Management Association, 2005.

Meyer, Philip. *The Vanishing Newspaper: Saving Journalism in the Information Age.* Columbia: University of Missouri Press, 2004.

Micklethwait John, and Adrian Wooldridge. *The Right Nation: Conservative Power in America.* New York: Penguin, 2004.

Middendorf, J. William, II. *Glorious Disaster: Barry Goldwater's Presidential Campaign and the Origins of the Conservative Movement.* New York: Basic Books, 2006.

Miles, William. *The People's Voice: An Annotated Bibliography of American Presidential Campaign Newspapers, 1828–1984.* Westport, CT: Greenwood Press, 1987.

Miller, John C. *Crisis in Freedom: The Alien and Sedition Acts.* Boston: Little, Brown, 1951.

Milton, Joyce. *Yellow Kids: Foreign Correspondents in the Heyday of Yellow Journalism.* New York: Harper & Row, 1989.

Mindich, David T. Z. *Just the Facts: How "Objectivity" Came to Define American Journalism.* New York: New York University Press, 1998.

Minnigerode, Meade. *Presidential Years: 1787–1860,* New York: Putnam's, 1928.

Miraldi, Robert, ed. *The Muckrakers: Evangelical Crusaders.* Westport, CT: Praeger, 2000.

Miraldi, Robert. *Muckraking and Objectivity: Journalism's Colliding Traditions.* New York,: Greenwood Press, 1990.

Mitchell, Franklin. *Harry S. Truman and the News Media: Contentious Relations, Belated Respect.* Columbia: University of Missouri Press, 1998.

Mitchell, Greg. *The Campaign of the Century: Upton Sinclair's Race for Governor of California and the Birth of Media Politics.* New York: Random House, 1992.

Monaghan, Jay. *The Man Who Elected Lincoln.* Indianapolis: Bobbs-Merrill, 1956.

Mondak, Jeffrey J. *Nothing to Read: Newspapers and Elections in a Social Experiment.* Ann Arbor: University of Michigan Press, 1995.

Morgan, H. Wayne. *From Hayes to McKinley: National Party Politics, 1877–1896.* Syracuse, NY: Syracuse University Press, 1969.

Mott, Frank L. *Jefferson and the Press.* Baton Rouge: Louisiana State University Press, 1943.

Moy, Patricia. *With Malice Toward All? The Media and Public Confidence in Democratic Institutions.* Westport, CT: Praeger, 2000.

Mnookin, Seth. *Hard News: The Scandals at the New York Times and Their Meaning for American Media.* New York: Random House, 2004.

Morris, Roy. *Fraud of the Century: Rutherford B. Hayes, Samuel Tilden and the Stolen Election of 1876.* New York: Simon & Schuster, 2003.

Mueller, John E. *War, Presidents, and Public Opinion.* New York: Wiley, 1973.

Mugridge, Ian. *The View from Xanadu: William Randolph Hearst and United States Foreign Policy.* Montreal & Kingston: McGill-Queen's University Press, 1995.

Myers, Joseph S. *The Genius of Horace Greeley.* Columbus: Ohio State University Press, 1929.

Neal, Steve. *Dark Horse: A Biography of Wendell Willkie.* Garden City, NY: Doubleday, 1984.

_____. *Happy Days Are Here Again: The 1932 Democratic Convention.* New York: HarperCollins, 2004.

Neely, Jr., Mark E. *The Boundaries of American Political Culture in the Civil War Era.* Chapel Hill: University of North Carolina Press, 2005.

_____. *The Union Divided: Party Conflict in the Civil War North.* Cambridge, MA: Harvard University Press, 2002.

Nevins, Allan. *American Press Opinion: Washington to Coolidge.* Boston: D. C. Heath, 1928.

_____. *The Evening Post: A Century of Journalism.* New York: Russell & Russell, 1968.

_____. *Ordeal of the Union.* Volumes 1–7. New York: Collier Books, 1992.

Nichols, John, and Robert W. McChesney. *Tragedy and Farce: How the American Media Sell Wars, Spin Elections, and Destroy Democracy.* New York: New Press, 2005.

Nichols, Roy F. *The Disruption of American Democracy.* New York: Macmillan, 1948.

Nikolaev, Alexander G., and Ernest A. Hakanen, eds. *Leading to the 2003 Iraq War: The Global Media Debate.* New York: Palgrave Macmillan, 2006.

Niven, David. *Tilt? The Search for Media Bias.* Westport, CT: Praeger, 2002.

Niven, John. *Martin Van Buren: The Romantic Age of American Politics.* New York: Oxford University Press, 1983.

Nixon, Richard. *The Memoirs of Richard Nixon.* New York: Simon & Schuster, 1990.

Norris, Pippa. *Politics and the Press: The News Media and their Influences.* Boulder, CO: L. Rienner Publishers, 1997.

Olson, James S. *Catholic Immigrants in America.* Chicago: Nelson-Hall, 1987.

Onuf, Peter S., ed. *Jeffersonian Legacies.* Charlottesville,: University Press of Virginia, 1993.

Oshinsky, David M. *A Conspiracy so Immense: The World of Joe McCarthy.* New York: Free Press, 1983.

Ostertag, Bob. *People's Movements, People's Press: The Journalism of Social Justice Movements.* Boston,: Beacon Press, 2006.

Osthaus, Carl R. *Partisans of the Southern Press: Editorial Spokesmen of the Nineteenth Century.* Lexington: University Press of Kentucky, 1994.

Overholser, Geneva, and Kathleen Hall Jamieson. *The Press.* Oxford: Oxford University Press, 2005.

Page, Benjamin I. *Who Deliberates? Mass Media in Modern Democracy.* Chicago: University of Chicago Press, 1996.

Paletz, David L., and Robert M. Entman. *Media, Power, Politics.* New York: Free Press, 1981.

Pasley, Jeffrey L. *"The Tyranny of Printers": Newspaper Politics in the Early American Republic.* Charlottesville: University of Virginia Press, 2001.

Pavlik, John V. *Journalism and the New Media.* New York: Columbia University Press, 2001.

Payne, George Henry. *History of Journalism in the United States.* Westport, CT: Greenwood Press, 1970.

Perkins, Howard Cecil, ed. *Northern Editorials on Secession*. Gloucester, MA: Peter Smith, 1964.

Perlstein, Rick. *Before the Storm: Barry Goldwater and the Unmaking of the American Consensus*. New York: Hill and Wang, 2001.

Perry, James. *Us & Them: How the Press Covered the 1972 Election*. New York: Crown Publishers, 1973.

Pessen, Edward. *Jacksonian America: Society, Personality, and Politics*. Homewood, IL: Dorsey Press, 1969.

_____. *New Perspectives on Jacksonian Parties and Politics*. Boston: Allyn and Bacon, 1969.

Peters, Charles. *Five Days in Philadelphia*. New York: Public Affairs, 2005.

Pfaff, Daniel W. *Joseph Pulitzer II and the Post-Dispatch: A Newspaperman's Life*. University Park: Penn State University Press, 1991.

Phillips, Kim Tousley. *William Duane, Radical Journalist in the Age of Jefferson*. New York: Garland, 1989.

Pilat, Oliver R. *Pegler, Angry Man of the Press*. Boston: Beacon Press, 1963.

Polakoff, Keith Ian. *The Politics of Inertia: The Election of 1876 and the End of Reconstruction*. Baton Rouge: Louisiana State University Press, 1973.

Pollard, James E. *The Presidents and the Press*. New York: Macmillan, 1947.

Ponder, Stephen. *Managing the Press: Origins of the Media Presidency, 1897–1933*. New York: St. Martin's Press, 1998.

Porter, William E. *Assault on the Media: The Nixon Years*. Ann Arbor: University of Michigan Press, 1976.

Potter, David M. *The Impending Crisis, 1848–1861*. New York: Harper & Row, 1976.

Rarick, Ethan. *California Rising: The Life and Times of Pat Brown*. Berkeley, CA: University of California Press, 2005.

Ratcliffe, Donald J. *Party Spirit in a Frontier Republic: Democratic Politics in Ohio 1793–1821*. Columbus: Ohio State University Press, 1998.

Ratner, Lorman A., and Dwight L. Teeter, Jr. *Fanatics and Fire-eaters: Newspapers and the Coming of the Civil War*. Urbana: University of Illinois Press, 2003.

Reedy, George E. *From the Ward to the White House: The Irish in American Politics*. New York: Scribner's, 1991.

Rehnquist, William H. *Centennial Crisis: The Disputed Election of 1876*. New York: Knopf, 2004.

Reichley, A. James. *Faith in Politics*. Washington, DC: Brookings Institution Press, 2002.

Remini, Robert V. *Andrew Jackson, Vol. II: The Course of American Freedom, 1822–1832*. Baltimore: Johns Hopkins University Press, 1981.

_____. *The Election of Andrew Jackson*. Philadelphia: J. B. Lippincott, 1963.

_____. *Henry Clay: Statesman for the Union*. New York: W. W. Norton, 1991.

Reynolds, Donald F. *Editors Make War: Southern Newspapers in the Secession Crisis*. Nashville: Vanderbilt University Press, 1970.

Richardson, H. Edward. *Cassius Marcellus Clay: Firebrand of Freedom*. Lexington: University Press of Kentucky, 1976.

Richardson, Leon Burr. *William E. Chandler: Republican*. New York: Dodd, Mead, 1940.

Ritchie, Donald A. *Reporting from Washington: The History of the Washington Press Corps*. New York: Oxford University Press, 2005.

Rivers, William L., Wilbur Schramm, and Clifford G. Christians. *Responsibility in Mass Communication*. New York: Harper & Row, 1980.

Robertson, Andrew W. *The Language of Democracy: Political Rhetoric in the United States and Britain, 1790–1900*. Ithaca, NY: Cornell University Press, 1995.

Robinson, Lloyd. *The Stolen Election: Hayes versus Tilden, 1876*. New York: Forge, 2001.

Robinson, Matthew. *Mobocracy: How the Media's Obsession with Polling Twists the News, Alters Elections, and Undermines Democracy*. Roseville, CA: Forum, 2002.

Robinson, Michael J., and Margaret A. Sheehan. *Over the Wire and on TV*, New York: Russell Sage Foundation, 1983.

Rosen, Jay. *What are Journalists For?* New Haven, CT: Yale University Press, 1999.

Rosenfeld, Richard N. *American Aurora*. New York: St. Martin's Press, 1997.

Rostow, Leo C. *The Washington Correspondents*. New York: Harcourt, Brace, 1937.

Rowse, Arthur E. *Slanted News: A Case Study of the Nixon and Stevenson Fund Stories*. Westport, CT: Greenwood Press, 1973.

Rozell, Mark J. *The Press and the Bush Presidency*. Westport, CT: Praeger, 1996.

_____. *The Press and the Carter Presidency*. Boulder, CO: Westview Press, 1988.

Rubin, Richard L. *Press, Party and Presidency*. New York: W. W. Norton, 1981.

Rudenstine, David. *The Day the Presses Stopped: A History of the Pentagon Papers Case*. Berkeley: University of California Press, 1996.

Sabato, Larry. *Feeding Frenzy: How Attack Journalism has Transformed American Politics*. Toronto: Free Press, 1991.

Sachsman, David B., S. Kittrell Rushing, and Debra Reddin Van Tuyll, eds. *The Civil War and the Press*. New Brunswick, NJ: Transaction Publishers, 2000.

Safire, William. *Before the Fall*. New York: Doubleday, 1975.

Sampson, Robert D. *John L. O'Sullivan and His Times*. Kent, OH: Kent State University Press, 2003.

Scammell, Margaret, and Holli Semetko, eds. *The Media, Journalism and Democracy*. Burlington: Ashgate, 2000.

Schechter, Danny. *When News Lies: Media Complicity and the Iraq War*. New York: SelectBooks, 2006.

Schiller, Dan. *Objectivity and the News: The Public and the Rise of Commercial Journalism*. Philadelphia: University of Pennsylvania Press, 1981.

Schlesinger, Arthur M., Jr. *The Age of Jackson*. Boston: Little, Brown, 1946.

_____, ed. *History of American Political Parties, Vol. II: 1860–1910, The Gilded Age of Politics*. New York: Chelsea House, 1973.

_____. *The Politics of Upheaval: The Age of Roosevelt, Vol. III*. Boston: Houghton Mifflin, 1960.

_____. *Prelude to Independence: The Newspaper War on Britain, 1764–1776*. Boston: Northeastern University Press, 1957.

_____, ed. *Running for President: The Candidates and their Images, Vol. 1: 1789–1896*. New York: Simon & Schuster, 1994.

Schudson, Michael. *Discovering the News: A Social History of American Newspapers*. New York,: Basic Books, 1978.

Schudson, Michael. *The Power of News*. Cambridge, MA: Harvard University Press, 1995.

Seitz, Don C. *Horace Greeley: Founder of the New York Tribune,*. New York: AMS Press, 1970.

_____. *The James Gordon Bennetts*. Indianapolis: Bobbs-Merrill, 1928.

Seldes, George. *Lords of the Press.* New York: Julian Messner, 1938.

Sewell, Richard H. *Ballots for Freedom: Antislavery Politics in the United States, 1827–1860.* New York: W. W. Norton, 1976.

Shapiro, Herbert, ed. *The Muckrakers and American Society.* Boston: D. C. Heath, 1968.

Shaw, Albert. *Abraham Lincoln: The Year of his Election.* New York: Review of Reviews, 1929.

Sheldon, Marcus. *Father Coughlin: The Tumultuous Life of the Priest of the Little Flower.* Boston: Little, Brown, 1973.

Shogan, Robert. *Bad News: Where the Press Goes Wrong in the Making of the President.* Chicago: Ivan R. Dee, 2001.

Silbey, Joel H. *The Partisan Imperative: the Dynamics of American Politics before the Civil War.* New York: Oxford University Press, 1985.

Sisson, Daniel. *The American Revolution of 1800.* New York: Knopf, 1974.

Small, William J. *Political Power and the Press.* New York: W. W. Norton, 1972.

Smith, Culver H. *The Press, Politics and Patronage: The American Government's Use of Newspapers, 1789–1875.* Athens: University of Georgia Press, 1977.

Smith, Elbert B. *Francis Preston Blair.* New York: Free Press, 1980.

Smith, Jeffrey A. *Franklin and Bache: Envisioning the Enlightened Republic.* New York: Oxford University Press, 1990.

Smith, Jeffrey A. *Printers and Press Freedom: The Ideology of Early American Journalism.* New York: Oxford University Press, 1988.

Smith, Jeffrey A. *War & Press Freedom: The Problem of Prerogative Power.* New York: Oxford University Press, 1999.

Smith, Page. *The Nation Comes of Age: A People's History of the Ante-Bellum Years.* New York: McGraw-Hill, 1981.

Smith, Page. *The Rise of Industrial America, Vol. VI.* New York: McGraw-Hill, 1984.

Smith, Reed W. *Samuel Medary & the Crisis: Testing the Limits of Press Freedom.* Columbus: Ohio State University Press, 1995.

Smith, Richard Norton. *The Colonel: The Life and Legend of Robert R. McCormick.* New York: Houghton Mifflin, 1997.

Smith, Ron F. *Groping for Ethics in Journalism.* Ames: Iowa State University Press, 2003.

Smith, William Ernest. *The Francis Preston Blair Family in Politics, Vol. 1.* New York: Macmillan, 1933.

Smythe, Ted Curtis. *The Gilded Age Press, 1865–1900.* Westport, CT: Praeger, 2003.

Spear, Joseph C. *Presidents and the Press: The Nixon Legacy.* Cambridge, MA: MIT Press, 1984.

Startt, James B. *Woodrow Wilson and the Press: Prelude to the Presidency.* New York: Palgrave Macmillan, 2004.

Steele, Janet E. *The Sun Shines for All: Journalism and Ideology in the Life of Charles A. Dana.* Syracuse, NY: Syracuse University Press, 1993.

Steele, Richard W. *Propaganda in an Open Society: The Roosevelt Administration and the Media, 1933–1941.* Westport, CT: Greenwood Press, 1985.

Stempel, Guido H. III, and John W. Windhauser, eds. *The Media in the 1984 and 1988 Presidential Campaigns.* New York: Greenwood Press, 1991.

Stewart, Donald H. *The Opposition Press of the Federalist Period.* Albany: State University of New York Press, 1969.

Stewart, Kenneth, and John Tebbel. *Makers of Modern Journalism.* New York: Prentice-Hall, 1952.

Stoddard, Henry L. *Horace Greeley: Printer, Editor, Crusader.* New York: Putnam's, 1946.

Stoler, Peter. *The War Against the Press: Politics, Pressure and Intimidation in the 1980s.* New York: Dodd, Mead, 1986.

Stone, Candace. *Dana and the Sun.* New York,: Dodd, Mead, 1938.

Stone, David M. *Nixon and the Politics of Public Television.* New York: Garland, 1985.

Stone, Geoffrey R. *Perilous Times: Free Speech in Wartime.* New York: W. W. Norton, 2004.

Stone, Irving. *They Also Ran: The Story of the Men who Were Defeated for the Presidency.* New York: Signet, 1966.

Streitmatter, Rodger. *Mightier than the Sword: How the News Media Have Shaped American History.* Boulder, CO: Westview Press, 1997.

Summers, Anthony. *The Arrogance of Power: The Secret World of Richard Nixon.* New York: Viking, 2000.

Summers, Mark Wahlgren. *The Era of Good Stealings.* Oxford: Oxford University Press, 1993.

_____. *Party Games: Getting, Keeping and Using Power in Gilded Age Politics.* Chapel Hill: University of North Carolina Press, 2004.

_____. *The Plundering Generation: Corruption and the Crisis of the Union, 1849–1861.* Oxford: Oxford University Press, 1987.

_____. *The Press Gang: Newspapers and Politics, 1865–1878.* Chapel Hill: University of North Carolina Press, 1994.

_____. *Rum, Romanism & Rebellion: The Making of a President, 1884.* Chapel Hill: University of North Carolina Press, 2000.

Sunstein, Cass. *Republic.com.* Princeton, NJ: Princeton University Press, 2001.

Swanberg, W. A. *Citizen Hearst.* New York: Macmillan, 1986.

_____. *Luce and his Empire.* New York: Scribner, 1972.

Swint, Kerwin C. *Mudslingers: The Top 25 Negative Political Campaigns of All Time.* Westport, CT: Praeger, 2006.

Tagg, James. *Benjamin Franklin Bache and the Philadelphia Aurora.* Philadelphia: University of Pennsylvania Press, 1991.

Tebbel, John, and Sarah Miles Watts. *The Press and the Presidency: From George Washington to Ronald Reagan.* Oxford: Oxford University Press, 1985.

Thimmesch, Nick, ed. *A Liberal Media Elite?* Washington, DC: American Enterprise Institute for Public Policy Research, 1985.

Thompson, Hunter S. *Fear and Loathing on the Campaign Trail '72.* London: Flamingo, 1973.

Thompson, Kenneth W., ed. *The Nixon Presidency: Twenty-Two Intimate Perspectives of Richard M. Nixon.* Lanham, MD: University Press of America, 1987.

_____, ed. *Ten Presidents and the Press.* Washington, DC: University Press of America, 1983.

Tocqueville, Alexis de. *Democracy in America.* New York: Knopf, 1945.

Troy, Gil. *Morning in America: How Ronald Reagan Invented the 1980s.* Princeton, NJ: Princeton University Press, 2005.

Tucher, Andie. *Froth & Scum: Truth, Beauty, Goodness, and the Ax Murder in America's First Mass Medium.* Chapel Hill: University of North Carolina Press, 1994.

Tuck, Jim. *McCarthyism and New York's Hearst Press: A Study of Roles in the Witch Hunt,*. Lanham, MD: University Press of America, 1995.

Turner, Kathleen J. *Lyndon Johnson's Dual War: Vietnam and the Press.* Chicago: University of Chicago Press, 1985.

Van Deusen, Glyndon G. *Horace Greeley: Nineteenth-Century Crusader.* Philadelphia: University of Pennsylvania Press, 1953.

_____. *Thurlow Weed: Wizard of the Lobby.* Boston: Little, Brown, 1947.

Vaughn, Stephen. *Holding Fast the Inner Lines: Democracy, Nationalism and the Committee on Public Information.* Chapel Hill: University of North Carolina Press, 1980.

Vaughn, William Preston. *The Antimasonic party in the United States, 1826–1843.* Lexington: University Press of Kentucky, 1983.

Veblen, Eric P. *The Manchester Union Leader in New Hampshire Elections.* Hanover: University Press of New England, 1975.

Viguerie, Richard A., and David Franke. *America's Right Turn: How Conservatives Used New and Alternative Media to Take Power.* Chicago: Bonus Books, 2004.

Waldstreicher, David. *In the Midst of Perpetual Fetes: The Making of American Nationalism, 1776–1820.* Chapel Hill: University of North Carolina Press, 1997.

Walsh, Justin E. *To Print the News and Raise Hell! A Biography of Wilbur F. Storey.* Chapel Hill: University of North Carolina Press, 1968.

Walsh, Kenneth T. *Feeding the Beast: The White House Versus the Press.* New York: Random House, 2001.

Ward, Stephen J. A. *The Invention of Journalism Ethics: The Path to Objectivity and Beyond.* Montreal: McGill-Queen's University Press, 2004.

Warren, Donald. *Radio Priest: Charles Coughlin, the Father of Hate Radio.* New York: Free Press, 1996.

Watson, Harry L. *Liberty and Power: The Politics of Jacksonian America.* New York: Hill & Wang, 1990.

Weed, Thurlow. *Life of Thurlow Weed, Vol. II.* New York: Houghton Mifflin, 1883–1884.

Weeks, William Earl. *John Quincy Adams & American Global Empire.* Lexington: University Press of Kentucky, 1992.

Weinberg, Arthur, and Lila Weinberg, eds. *The Muckrakers: The Era in Journalism that Moved America to Reform.* New York: Simon and Schuster, 1961.

Weisberger, Bernard A. *America Afire: Jefferson, Adams, and the Revolutionary Election of 1800.* New York: HarperCollins, 2000.

Welch, Richard E., Jr. *The Presidencies of Grover Cleveland.* Lawrence: University Press of Kansas, 1988.

Wendt, Lloyd. *Chicago Tribune: Rise of a Great American Newspaper.* Chicago: Rand McNally, 1979.

Whalen, Richard J. *The Founding Father: The Story of Joseph P. Kennedy.* New York: New American Library, 1964.

White, Graham J. *FDR and the Press.* Chicago: University of Chicago Press, 1979.

White, Leonard D. *The Federalists: A Study in Administrative History, 1789–1801.* New York: Free Press, 1948.

White, Theodore. *The Making of the President 1972.* New York: Atheneum, 1973.

_____. *The Making of the President 1964.* New York: Atheneum, 1965.

Widmer, Edward L. *Young America: The Flowering of Democracy in New York City.* Oxford: Oxford University Press, 1999.

Widmer, Ted [Edward L.] *Martin Van Buren.* New York: Times Books, 2005.

Wiebe, Robert H. *The Search for Order.* New York: Hill and Wang, 1967.

Wilentz, Sean. *The Rise of American Democracy: Jefferson to Lincoln.* New York: W. W. Norton, 2005.

Williams, Herbert Lee. *The Newspaperman's President: Harry S. Truman.* Chicago: Nelson-Hall, 1984.

Williams, Jack K. *Dueling in the Old South: Vignettes of Social History.* College Station: Texas A&M University Press, 1980.

Williams, Robert C. *Horace Greeley: Champion of American Freedom.* New York: New York University Press, 2006.

Wills, Garry. *James Madison.* New York: Times Books, 2002.

Wilmer, Lambert A. *Our Press Gang.* Philadelphia: J. T. Lloyd, 1859.

Wilson, James Harrison. *The Life of Charles A. Dana.* New York: Harper & Brothers, 1907.

Winfield, Betty Houchin. *FDR and the News Media.* Urbana: University of Illinois Press, 1990.

Winkler, John K. *William Randolph Hearst: A New Appraisal.* New York: Hastings House, 1955.

Wisan, Joseph E. *The Cuban Crisis as Reflected in the New York Press, 1895–1898.* New York: Octagon Books, 1965.

Witcover, Jules. *Party of the People: A History of the Democrats.* New York: Random House, 2003.

Wolfskill, George, and John A. Hudson. *All but the People: Franklin D. Roosevelt and his Critics, 1933–39.* Toronto: Collier-Macmillan, 1969.

Wyatt, Clarence R. *Paper Soldiers: The American Press and the Vietnam War.* New York: W. W. Norton, 1993.

Zornow, William Frank. *Lincoln and the Party Divided.* Norman: University of Oklahoma Press, 1954.

Dissertations and Theses

Avery, Donald R. *The Newspaper on the Eve of the War of 1812: Changes in Content Patterns, 1808–1812.* Ph.D. dissertation, Southern Illinois University, 1982.

Baldasty, Gerald J. *The Political Press in the Second American Party System: The 1832 Election.* Ph.D. dissertation, University of Washington, 1978.

Belko, William S. *Duff Green: A Public Life, 1791–1840.* Ph.D. dissertation, Mississippi State University, 2002.

Borchard, Gregory A. *The Firm of Greeley, Weed and Seward: New York Partisanship and the Press, 1840–1860.* Ph.D. dissertation, University of Florida, 2003.

Chomsky, Daniel. *Constructing the Cold War: The New York Times and the Truman Doctrine.* Ph.D. dissertation, Northwestern University, 1999.

Daniel, Marcus L. *"Ribaldry and Billingsgate": Popular Journalism, Political Culture and the Public Sphere in the Early Republic.* Ph.D. dissertation, Princeton University, 1998.

Daniels, James D. *Amos Kendall: Cabinet-Politician, 1829–1841.* Ph.D. dissertation, University of North Carolina at Chapel Hill, 1968.

Doctor, Powrie V. *Amos Kendall, Propagandist of Jacksonian Democracy.* Ph.D. dissertation, Georgetown University, 1940.

Gerald, John. *Tippecanoe and the Party Press too: Mass Communication, Politics, Culture, and the Fabled Presidential Election of 1840.* Ph.D. dissertation, University of Illinois at Urbana-Champaign, 1999.

Howell, Scott M. *William Cobbett and American Society in the Age of the French Revolution.* Ph.D. dissertation, University of California at Riverside, 2001.

Lutzky, Seymour. *The Reform Editors and their Press.* Ph.D. dissertation, University of Iowa, 1951.

Marshall, Lynne L. *The Early Career of Amos Kendall: The Making of a Jacksonian.* Ph.D. dissertation, University of California at Berkeley, 1962.

McDaniel, John Edgar, Jr. *The Presidential Election of 1888.* Ph.D. dissertation, University of Texas, 1970.

Melton, Baxter F., Jr. *Amos Kendall in Kentucky, 1814–1829: The Journalistic Beginnings of the "Master Mind" of Andrew Jackson's "Kitchen Cabinet."* Ph.D. dissertation, Southern Illinois University at Carbondale, 1978.

Moore, David W. *Duff Green and the South, 1824–45,* Ph.D. dissertation, Miami University, 1983.

Mutersbaugh, Bert M. *Jeffersonian Journalist: Thomas Ritchie and the Richmond Enquirer, 1804–1820.* Ph.D. dissertation, University of Missouri at Columbia, 1973.

Patrick, Robert P., Jr. *In the Interest of the South: The Life and Career of Duff Green.* Ph.D. dissertation, University of South Carolina, 2000.

Phelps, Marshall T. *Duff Green: American Warwick or Man of Principle?* Ph.D. dissertation, University of Memphis, 1995.

Ritter, Charles F. *The Press in Florida, Louisiana, and South Carolina and the End of Reconstruction, 1865–1877: Southern Men with Northern Interests.* Ph.D. dissertation, Catholic University of America, 1976.

Robertson, Pearl Louise. *Grover Cleveland as Political Leader.* Ph.D. dissertation, University of Chicago, 1937.

Shaffer, Wade L. *The Richmond Junto and Politics in Jacksonian Virginia.* Ph.D. dissertation, College of William and Mary, 1993.

Shaw, Donald L. *Bias in the News: A Study of National Presidential Campaign Coverage in the Wisconsin English Daily Press, 1852–1916.* Ph.D. dissertation, University of Wisconsin, 1966.

Shoptaugh, Terry L. *Amos Kendall: A Political Biography.* Ph.D. dissertation, University of New Hampshire, 1984.

Short, Steven W. *Texas Annexation and the Presidential Election of 1844 in the Richmond, Virginia and New Orleans, Louisiana, Newspapers.* MA Thesis, University of North Texas, 2001.

Smith, Kenneth L. *Duff Green and the United States Telegraph, 1826^–1837.* Ph.D. dissertation, College of William and Mary, 1981.

Stewart, Robert K. *The Jackson Press and the Elections of 1824 and 1828.* MA Thesis, University of Washington, 1984.

Strevey, Elmer. *Joseph Medill and the Chicago Tribune during the Civil War Period.* PhD. dissertation, University of Chicago, 1930.

Articles

Abbott, Richard H. "The Republican Party Press in Reconstruction Georgia, 1867–1874," *The Journal of Southern History* 61, no. 4 (November 1995), 725–760.

Allen, William H. "The Election of 1900," *Annals of the American Academy of Political and Social Science* Vol. 17 (January 1901), 53–73.

Ames, William E., and S. Dean Olson. "Washington's Political Press and the Election of 1824," *Journalism Quarterly* 40, no. 3 (Summer 1963), 343–350.

Ammon, Harry. "The Richmond Junto, 1800–1824," *Virginia Magazine of History and Biography* 61 (1953), 395–418.

Banning, Stephen A. "Truth is Our Ultimate Goal: A Mid-Nineteenth Century Concern for Journalism Ethics," *American Journalism* 16, no. 1 (Winter 1999), 17–39.

Barone, Michael. "The Return of Partisan Journalism," *American Enterprise* 7, no. 2 (March/April 1996), 29–31.

Basch, Norma. "Marriage, Morals, and Politics in the Election of 1828," *Journal of American History* 80, no. 3 (December 1993), 890–918.

Belohlaver, John M. "The Democracy in a Dilemma: George M. Dallas, Pennsylvania, and the Election of 1844," *Pennsylvania History,* Vol. 41, No. 4, Fall 1974, pp. 391–411

Bishop, Robert L., and Stephen Friedman. "Campaign Coverage—1876 Style by the Chicago Tribune," *Journalism Quarterly* 45, no. 3 (Autumn 1968), 481–486, 495.

Brooke, John L. "To be 'Read by the Whole People': Press, Party, and Public Sphere in the United States, 1789–1840," *Proceedings of the American Antiquarian Society* 110, (Part 1, 2002), 41–118.

Brummer, Sidney David. "Political History of New York State During the Period of the Civil War," *Studies in History, Economics and Public Law* 39, no. 2 (1911), 17–98.

Counts, Tim. "Editorial Influence on GOP Vote in 1948 Presidential Election," *Journalism Quarterly* 66, no. 1 (Spring 1989), 177–181.

Covert, Tawnya, J. Adkins, and Philo C. Wasburn. "Measuring Media Bias: A Content Analysis of Time and Newsweek Coverage of Domestic Social Issues, 1975–2000," *Social Science Quarterly* 88, no. 3 (September 2007), 690–706.

Cunningham, Brent. "Re-Thinking Objectivity," *Columbia Journalism Review* 42, no. 2 (July/August 2003), 24–32.

D'Alessio, Dave, and Mike Allen. "Media Bias in Presidential Elections: A Meta-Analysis," *Journal of Communications* 50, no. 4 (Autumn 2000), 133–156.

De Santis, Vincent P. "Catholicism and Presidential Elections, 1865–1900," *Mid-America* 42, no. 2 (April 1960), 67–79.

Devereux, Erik A. "Newspaper, Organized Interests and Party Competition in the 1964 Election," *Media History* 5, no. 1 (June 1999), 33–64.

Dobson, John M. "George William Curtis and the Election of 1884: The Dilemma of the New York Mugwumps," *New York Historical Society Quarterly* 52, no. 3 (Fall 1968), 215–234.

Domke, David, and Mark D. Watts. "The Politics of Conservative Elites and the 'Liberal Media' Argument," *Journal of Communication* 49, no. 4 (Autumn 1999), 35–58.

Downey, Matthew T. "Horace Greeley and the Politicians: The Liberal Republican Convention in 1872," *Journal of American History* 53, no. 1 (March 1967), 727–750.

Eastland, Terry. "Starting Over," *Wilson Quarterly* 29, no. 2 (Spring 2005), 40–47.

Epstein, Edward J. "Did the Press Uncover Watergate?" *Commentary,* July 1974, 21–24.

Erikson, Robert S. "The Influence of Newspaper

Endorsements in Presidential Elections: The Case of 1964," *American Journal of Political Science* 20, no. 2 (May 1976), 207–233.

Ewing, Gretchen G. "Duff Green: Independent Editor of a Party Press," *Journalism Quarterly* 54, no. 1 (Winter 1977), 733–739.

Ewing, Gretchen G. "Duff Green, John C. Calhoun, and the Election of 1828," *South Carolina Historical Magazine* 79, no. 2 (April 1978), 126–137.

Feder, Don. "Why Liberals Find Talk Radio so Threatening," *American Enterprise* 7, no. 2 (March/April 1996), 24–28.

Freeman, Joanne. "The Political Culture of the Democratic and Republican Parties," *Political Science Quarterly* 101, no. 3 (1986), 327–356.

Gans, Herbert J. "Are U.S. Journalists Dangerously Liberal?" *Columbia Journalism Review*, November/December 1985, 29–33

Gatell, Frank Otto. "Spoils of the Bank War: Political Bias in the Selection of Pet Banks," *American Historical Review* 70, no. 1 (October 1964), 35–58.

Gentzkow, Matthew, and Jesse M. Shapiro. "Media Bias and Reputation," *The Journal of Political Economy*, Vol. 114, No. 2, April 2006, pp. 280–316.

Gertz, Elmer. "Chicago's Adult Delinquent: 'The Tribune,'" *Public Opinion Quarterly* 8, no. 3 (Autumn 1944), 416–424.

Graham, Thomas S. "Florida Politics and the Tallahassee Press, 1845–1861," *Florida Historical Quarterly* 46, no. 3 (January 1968), 234–242.

Gregg, James E. "Newspaper Editorial Endorsements and California Elections, 1948–62," *Journalism Quarterly* 42 (1965), 532–538.

Green, Fletcher M. "Duff Green, Militant Journalist of the Old School," *American Historical Review* 52 (October 1946), 247–264.

Groseclose, Tim, and Jeffrey Milyo. "A Measure of Media Bias," *Quarterly Journal of Economics* 120, no. 4 (November 2005), 1191–1237.

Hallin, Daniel C. "The Media, the War in Vietnam, and Political Support: A Critique of the Thesis of an Oppositional Media," *Journal of Politics* 46, no. 1. (February 1984), 2–24.

Hammond, William M. "The Press in Vietnam as Agent of Defeat: A Critical Examination," *Reviews in American History* 17, no. 2 (June 1989), 312–323.

Harmon, Mark D. "The New York *Times* and the Theft of the 1876 Presidential Election," *Journal of American Culture* 10, no. 2 (Summer 1987), 35–41.

Harris, Sheldon H. "John Louis O'Sullivan and the Election of 1844 in New York," *New York History* 41, no. 3 (Summer 1960), 278–298.

Hay, Robert P. "'The Presidential Question': Letters to Southern Editors, *Tennessee Historical Quarterly* 31, no. 2 (1972), 170–186.

Hernandez, Debra Gersh. "Nixon and the Press," *Editor & Publisher* 127, no. 26 (June 25, 1994), 82–91.

Hinckley, Ted C. "The Politics of Sinophobia: Garfield, the Morey Letter, and the Presidential Election of 1880," *Ohio History* 89, no. 4 (1980), 381–399.

Howard, Thomas H. "Indiana Newspapers and the Presidential Election of 1824," *Indiana Magazine of History* 63, no. 3 (Fall 1967), 177–206.

Howe, John R., Jr. "Political Thought and the Political Violence of the 1790s," *American Quarterly* 19, no. 2 (Summer 1967), 147–165.

Hurd, Robert E., and Michael W. Singletary. "Newspaper Endorsement Influence on the 1980 Presidential

Vote," *Journalism Quarterly* 61, no. 2 (Summer 1984), 332–338.

Iyengar, Shanto, and Richard Morin. "Red Media, Blue Media: Evidence for a Political Litmus Test in Online News Readership," *Washington Post*, May 3, 2006.

Jellison, Charles A. "That Scoundrel Callender," *Virginia Magazine of History and Biography* 64 (1959), 295–306.

Jensen, Richard. "Armies, Admen and Crusaders: Types of Presidential Crusaders," *History Teacher* 2, no. 2 (January 1969), 33–50.

Jones, David A. "Why Americans Don't Trust the Media," *Harvard International Journal of Press/Politics* 9, no. 2 (Spring 2004), 60–75.

Kaplan, Sidney. "The Miscegenation Issue in the Election of 1864," *Journal of Negro History* 34, no. 3 (July 1949), 274–343.

Keller, Morton. "The Media: What They Are Today, and How They Got That Way," *The Forum* 3, no. 1 (2005).

Kelley, Donald B. "Intellectual Isolation: Gateway to Secession in Mississippi," *Journal of Mississippi History* 36, no. 1 (February 1974), 17–37.

Kim, Kyun Soo, and Pasadeos Yorgo. "Study of Partisan News Readers Reveals Hostile Media Perceptions of Balanced Stories," *Newspaper Research Journal* 28, no. 2 (Spring 2007), 99–106.

Klein, Malcolm W., and Nathan Macoby. "Newspaper Objectivity in the 1952 Campaign," *Journalism Quarterly* 31, no. 2 (Summer 1954), 285–286.

Knudson, Jerry W. "The Jeffersonian Assault on the Federalist Judiciary, 1802–1805: Political Forces and Press Reaction," *American Journal of Legal History* 14, no. 1 (January 1970), 55–75.

Kull, Steven, Ramsay Clay, and Evan Lewis. "Misperceptions, the Media, and the Iraq War," *Political Science Quarterly* 118, no. 4 (Winter 2003–2004), 569–598.

Latner, Richard B. "The Kitchen Cabinet and Andrew Jackson's Advisory System," *Journal of American History* 65, no. 2 (September 1978), 367–388.

Malone, Dumas. "The Threatened Prosecution of Alexander Hamilton under the Sedition Act by Thomas Cooper," *American Historical Review* 29, no. 1 (October 1923), 76–81.

Marbut, Frederick B. "Decline of the Official Press in Washington," *Journalism Quarterly* 33, no. 2 (Summer 1956), 335–341.

_____. "Early Washington Correspondents: Some Early Pioneers," *Journalism Quarterly* 25, no. 4 (December 1948), 369–374.

Marsh, Philip. "The Griswold Story of Freneau and Jefferson," *American Historical Review* 51, no. 1 (October 1945), 68–73.

_____. "Madison's Defense of Freneau," *William and Mary Quarterly* 3, no. 2 (April 1946), 269–274.

Marshall, Lynn L. "The Authorship of Jackson's Bank Veto Message," *The Mississippi Valley Historical Review*, Vol. 50, No. 3, December, 1963, pp. 466–477.

Martin, Robert. "Reforming Republicanism: Alexander Hamilton's Theory of Republican Citizenship and Press Liberty," *Journal of the Early Republic* 25, no. 1 (Spring 2005), 21–46.

Mason, William M. "The Impact of Endorsements on Voting," *Sociological Methods and Research* 1, no. 4 (May 1973), 463–495.

Mayer, William G. "Why Talk Radio is Conservative," *Public Interest*, no. 156 (Summer 2004), 86–103.

McCombs, Maxwell. "Editorial Endorsements: A Study

of Influence," *Journalism Quarterly* 44, no. 3 (Autumn 1967), 545–548.

Meyers, W. Cameron. "The Chicago Newspaper Hoax in the '36 Election Campaign," *Journalism Quarterly* 37, no. 3 (Summer 1960), 356–364.

Milando, Joseph A. "Embracing Objectivity Early On: Journalism Textbooks in the 1880s," *Journal of Mass Media Ethics* 16, no. 1 (2001), 23–32.

Moeller, Susan. "The President, Press and Weapons of Mass Destruction," *Nieman Reports* 58, no. 2 (Summer 2004), 66–68.

Mott, Frank Luther. "Newspapers in Presidential Campaigns," *Public Opinion Quarterly* 8, no. 3 (Autumn 1944), 348–367.

Nagel, Paul C. "The Election of 1824: A Reconsideration Based on Newspaper Opinion," *The Journal of Southern History* 26, no. 3 (Fall 1960), 315–329.

Nerone, John C. "The Mythology of the Penny Press," *Critical Studies in Mass Communication* 4, no. 4 (December 1987), 376–404.

Nichols, John. "Newspapers... And After?" *Nation* 284, no. 4 (January 29, 2007), 11–18.

Parker, David B. "The Rise and Fall of the Wonderful Wizard of Oz as a 'Parable on Populism,'" *Journal of the Georgia Association of Historians* 15 (1994), 49–63.

Perkins, Howard C. "The Defense of Slavery in the Northern Press on the Eve of the Civil War," *Journal of Southern History* 9, no. 4 (November 1943), 501–531.

Peters, Charles. "Why the White House Press Didn't Get the Watergate Story," *Washington Monthly*, July/August 1973, 7–15.

Porter, David L. "Attitude of the Tennessee Press Toward the Presidential Election of 1860," *Tennessee Historical Quarterly* 29, no. 4 (Winter 1970–71), 390–395.

_____. "Attitudes of the Georgia Press in the Presidential Election of 1860," *Georgia Historical Quarterly* 59 (Supplement 1975), 127–133.

_____. "The Kentucky Press and the Election of 1860," *Filson Club Historical Quarterly* 46, no. 1 (January 1972), 49–52.

_____. "The Southern Press and the Presidential Election of 1860," *West Virginia History* 33, no. 1 (October 1971), 1–13.

Posner, Richard A. "Bad News," *New York Times Book Review*, July 31, 2005, 1, 8–11.

Pratt, Julius W. "The Origin of 'Manifest Destiny,'" *American Historical Review* 32, no. 4 (July 1927), 795–798.

Prince, Carl E. "The Federalist Party and Creation of a Court Press, 1789–1801," *Journalism Quarterly* 53, no. 2 (Summer 1976), 238–241.

Robinson, John P. "The Press as King-Maker: What Surveys From Last Five Campaigns Show," *Journalism Quarterly* 51, no. 4 (Winter 1974), 587–594, 606.

Rosenberg, Marvin, and Dorothy Rosenberg. "The Dirtiest Election," *American Heritage* 13, no. 5 (May 1962), 4–9, 97–100.

Rutenbeck, Jeffrey B. "Editorial Perception of Newspaper Independence and the Presidential Campaign of 1872: An Ideological Turning Point for American Journalism," *Journalism History* 17, no. 1–2 (Spring-Summer 1990), 13–22.

_____. "Newspaper Trends in the 1870s: Proliferation, Polarization, and Political Independence," *Journalism and Mass Communication Quarterly* 72, no. 2 (Summer 1995), 361–375.

_____. "The Stagnation and Decline of Partisan Journal-ism in Late Nineteenth-Century America: Changes in the New York World, 1860–76," *American Journalism* 10, no. 1–2 (Winter–Spring 1993), 38–60.

Sanger, Donald Bridgman. "The Chicago Times and the Civil War," *Mississippi Valley Historical Review* 17, no. 4 (March 1931), 557–580.

Scherr, Arthur. "'Sambos' and 'Black Cut-Throats': Peter Porcupine on Slavery and Race in the 1790s," *American Periodicals* 13 (2003), 3–30.

_____. "'Vox Populi' versus the Patriot President: Benjamin Franklin Bache's Philadelphia Aurora and John Adams (1797)," *Pennsylvania History* 62, no. 4 (Fall 1995), 503–531.

Sella, Marshall. "The Red State Network," *New York Times Magazine*, June 24, 2001, 26–34, 62–63.

Shaw, Donald L. "News Bias and the Telegraph: A Study of Historical Change," *Journalism Quarterly* 44, no. 1 (Spring 1967), 3–12.

Singletary, Michael W. "The New Editorial Voice for Andrew Jackson: Happenstance or Plan?" *Journalism Quarterly* 54, no. 4 (Winter 1976), 672–678.

Sloan, William David. "The Early Party Press," *Journalism History* 9, no. 1 (Spring 1982), 18–24.

Sloan, William David. "'Purse and Pen': Party-Press Relationships, 1789–1816," *American Journalism* 6, no. 2 (1989), 103–127.

_____. "Scurrility and the Party Press," *American Journalism* 5, no. 2 (1988), 97–112.

_____, and Jenn Burleson Mackay. *Media Bias: Finding It, Fixing It*, McFarland & Co., Jefferson, N.C., 2007.

Smart, James G. "Whitelaw Reid and the Nomination of Horace Greeley," *Mid America* 49, no. 4 (October 1967), 227–243.

Smelser, Marshall. "The Federalist Period as an Age of Passion," *American Quarterly* 10, no. 4 (Winter 1958), 391–419.

Smith, James M. "President John Adams, Thomas Cooper, and Sedition: A Case Study in Suppression," *Mississippi Valley Historical Review* 42, no. 3 (December 1955), 438–465.

_____. "The Sedition Law, Free Speech, and the American Political Process," *William and Mary Quarterly* 9, no. 4 (October 1952), 497–511.

Smith, William E. "Francis P. Blair, Pen-Executive of Andrew Jackson," *Mississippi Valley Historical Review* 17, no. 1 (March 1931), 545–547.

Stensaas, Harlan S. "Development of the Objectivity Ethic in U.S. Daily Newspapers," *Journal of Mass Media Ethics* 2, no. 1 (Fall–Winter 1986–87), 50–60.

Sternstein, Jerome L. "The Sickles Memorandum: Another Look at the Hayes-Tilden Election-Night Conspiracy," *Journal of Southern History* 32, no. 6 (1966), 342–357.

Stewart, Donald H. "The Press and Political Corruption during the Federalist Administrations," *Political Science Quarterly* 67, no. 3 (September 1952), 426–446.

Strupp, Joe, Hawn Moynihan, and Charles Geraci. "The Bias Wars," *Editor & Publisher* 137, no. 8 (August 2004), 22–32.

Sutter, Daniel. "Can the Media be so Liberal? The Economics of Media Bias," *CATO Journal* 20, no. 3 (Winter 2001), 431–452.

Tankard, James W., Jr. "Public Opinion Polling by Newspapers in the Presidential Election Campaign of 1824," *Journalism Quarterly* 49, no. 2 (Summer 1972), 361–365.

Taylor, Lenette S. "Polemics and Partisanship: The Arkansas Press in the 1860 Election," *Arkansas Historical Quarterly* 44, no. 4 (Winter 1985), 314–335.

Tinling, Marion. "Thomas Lloyd's Reports of the First Federal Congress," *William and Mary Quarterly* 18, no. 4 (October 1961), 519–545.

Towne, Stephen E. "Killing the Serpent Speedily: Governor Morton, General Hascall, and the Suppression of the Democratic Press in Indiana, 1863," *Civil War History* 52, no. 1 (March 2006), 41–65.

Wallace, Lew. "The Truman-Dewey Upset," *American History Illustrated* 11, no. 6 (June 1976), 20–29.

Watts, Mark D., et al. "Elite Cues and Media Bias in Presidential Campaigns: Explaining Public Perceptions of a Liberal Press," *Communication Research* 26, no. 2 (April 1999), 144–175

Webber, Michael J., and G. William Domhoff. "Myth and Reality in Business Support for Democrats and Republicans in the 1936 Presidential Election," *American Political Science Review* 90, no. 4 (December 1996), 824–833.

Westley, Bruce H. "The News Magazines and the 1960 Conventions," *Journalism Quarterly* 40, no. 4 (Autumn 1963), 525–531, 647.

Online Resources

Adamic, Lada, and Natalie Glance. "The Political Blogosphere and the 2004 U.S. Election: Divided they Blog," www.blogpulse.com/papers/2005/Adamic GlanceBlogWWW.pdf.

Ansolabehere, Stephen, Rebecaa Lessem, and James M. Snyder, Jr. "The Political Orientation of Newspaper Endorsements in U.S. Elections, 1940–2002," March 2004, econ-www.mit.edu/faculty/download_pdf.php ?id=1148.

Baron, David P. "Persistent Media Bias," *Research Paper No. 1845*, Stanford University, February 2004, www. nyu.edu/gsas/dept/politics/seminars/baron.pdf.

Besley, Timothy J., and Andrea Prat. "Handcuffs for the Grabbing Hand? Media Capture and Government Accountability," *CEPR Discussion Paper*, No. 3132, January 2002, papers.ssrn.com/sol3/papers.cfm?ab stract_id=298049.

DellaVigna, Stefano, and Ethan Kaplan. "The Fox News Effect," March 30, 2006, elsa.berkeley.edu/~sdellavi/ wp/foxvote06–03–30.pdf.

Gentzkow, Matthew, Edward L. Glaeser, and Claudia Goldin. "The Rise of the Fourth Estate: How Newspapers Became Informative and Why it Mattered," *NBER Working Paper 10791* (September 2004), www. nber.org/papers/w10791.

Groseclose, Tim, and Jeff Milyo. "A Measure of Media Bias," mason.gmu.edu/~atabarro/MediaBias.doc.

Krebs, Valdis. "Top Political Books," www.orgnet.com/ divided.html.

Lott, John R., and Kevin A. Hassett. "Is Newspaper Coverage of Economic Events Politically Biased?" October 19, 2004, ssrn.com/abstract=588453.

Pew Research Center. "Cable and Internet Loom Large in Fragmented Political News Universe," released on January 11, 2004, people-press.org/reports/display. php3?ReportID=200.

Pew Research Center. "News Audiences Increasingly Polarized," released on June 8, 2004, people-press.org /reports/display.php3?ReportID=215.

Project for Excellence in Journalism. "The State of the News Media 2007," released March 12, 2007, www. stateofthenewsmedia.org/2007/index.asp.

Puglisi, Riccardo. "Being the New York Times: The Political Behaviour of a Newspaper," March 10, 2006, ssrn.com/abstract=573801.

Van Alstyne, Marshall, and Erik Brynjolfsson. "Electronic Communities: Global Village or Cyberbalkans," web.mit.edu/marshall/www/Abstracts.html.

Web Sites

Accuracy in Media: www.aim.org

Center for Media and Public Affairs, The: www.cmpa. com

Daily Kos: www.dailykos.com

Fair Press: www.fairpress.org

Fairness and Accuracy in Reporting: www.fair.org

Fight the Bias: www.fightthebias.com

Free Republic: www.freerepublic.com

Media Bias Page, The: www.akdart.com/media.html

Media Matters for America: mediamatters.org

Media Research Center, The: www.mrc.org

Media Tenor International: www.mediatenor.com

Media Transparency: mediatransparency.org

National Review Online, The Corner: corner.national review.com

Newsbusters: newsbusters.org/blog/43

That Liberal Media: www.thatliberalmedia.com

Times Watch: www.timeswatch.org

Comparative Resources

Aspinall, Arthur. *Politics and the Press, c. 1780–1850*. New York: Barnes & Noble, 1974.

Balson, Scott. *Murder by Media: Death of Democracy in Australia*. Mt. Crosby, Queensland: Interactive Presentations, 1999.

Barker, Hannah. *Newspapers, Politics and English Society, 1695–1855*. New York: Longman, 2000.

_____. *Newspapers, Politics, and Public Opinion in Late Eighteenth-Century England*, New York: Clarendon Press, 1998.

Black, Jeremy. *The English Press in the Eighteenth Century*, London: Croom Helm, 1987.

Bondebjerg, Ib, and Peter Golding, eds. *European Culture and the Media*. Portland, OR: Intellect, 2004.

Butler, David, and Dennis Kavanagh, eds. *The British General Election of 1992*. New York: St. Martin's Press, 1992.

Chenoweth, Neil. *Virtual Murdoch: Reality Wars on the Information Highway*. London: Secker & Warburg, 2001.

Crewe, Ivor, and Brian Gosschalk, eds. *Political Communications: The General Election Campaign of 1992*. Cambridge: Cambridge University Press, 1995.

Crewe, Ivor, and Martin Harrop, eds. *Political Communications: The General Election Campaign of 1983*. Cambridge: Cambridge University Press, 1986.

Curtice, John. "Is *The Sun* shining on Tony Blair? The Electoral Influence of British Newspapers," *Harvard International Journal of Press/Politics* 2, no. 2, (1997): 9–26.

Curtice, John. "Was it the Sun Wot Won it Again? The Influence of Newspapers in the 1997 Election Campaign." *Crest Working Paper No. 75*, September 1999. *http://www.crest.ox.ac.uk/papers/p75.pdf.*

Downie, John A. *Robert Harley and the Press: Propaganda and Public Opinion in the Age of Swift and Defoe.* Cambridge: Cambridge University Press, 1979.

Flint, David. *Malice in Media Land.* Australia: Freedom Publishing, 2005.

Frank, Joseph. *The Beginnings of the English Newspaper, 1620–1660.* Cambridge, MA: Harvard University Press, 1961.

Harris, Bob. *Politics and the Rise of the Press: Britain and France, 1620–1800.* New York: Routledge, 1996.

Heath, Anthony, Roger Jowell, and John Curtice, eds. *Labour's Last Chance? The 1992 Election and Beyond.* Aldershot: Dartmouth, 1994.

Jones, Aled. *Powers of the Press: Newspapers, Power and the Public in Nineteenth-Century England*, Ashgate Pub. Co., Brookfield, Vt., 1996.

Jones, Nicholas. *The Control Freaks: How New Labour Gets its Own Way*, Politico's, London, 2001.

Jones, Nicolas. *Sultans of Spin*, Orion, London, 2000.

Kelly, Mary, Gianpietro Mazzoleni, and Denis McQuail (eds.). *The Media in Europe*, SAGE, Thousand Oaks, Calif., 2004.

Kiernan, Thomas. *Citizen Murdoch*, Dodd, Mead, New York, 1986.

Koss, Stephen. *The Rise and Fall of the Political Press in Britain*: volume 2: twentieth century. London: Hamish Hamilton, 1984.

Koss, Stephen. *The Rise and Fall of the Political Press in Britain*: volume 1: nineteenth century. London: Hamish Hamilton, 1981.

Knights, Mark. *Representation and Misrepresentation in Later Stuart Britain: Partisanship and Political Culture.* Oxford: Oxford University Press, 2005.

Kuhn, Raymond. *The Media in France.* New York: Routledge, 1994.

Leapman, Michael. *Arrogant Aussie: The Rupert Murdoch Story.* Seacaucus, NJ: L. Stuart, 1985.

Lee, Alan J. *The Origins of the Popular Press in England, 1855–1914.* London: Croom Helm, 1980.

Munster, George. *A Paper Prince.* New York: Viking, 1985.

Rea, Robert. *The English Press in Politics, 1760–1774.* Lincoln: University of Nebraska Press, 1963.

Richards, Huw. *The Bloody Circus: The Daily Herald and the Left.* Chicago: Pluto Press,.

Seaton, Jean, and Ben Pimlott, eds. *The Media in British Politics.* Brookfield, VT: Gower, 1987.

Seymour-Ure, Colin. *Prime Ministers and the Media: Issues of Power and Control.* Malden, MA: Blackwell Publishers, 2003.

Seymour-Ure, Colin. *The Political Impact of Mass Media.* London: Constable, 1974.

Shawcross, William. *Murdoch.* New York: Simon & Schuster, 1993.

Siebert, Fredrick S. *Freedom of the Press in England, 1476–1776.* Urbana: University of Illinois Press, 1965.

Stevens, David H. *Party Politics and English Journalism 1702–1742.* Ph.D. Dissertation, University of Chicago, Urbana, 1916.

Thomas, James. *Popular Newspapers, the Labour Party and British Politics.* New York: Routledge, 2005.

Thompson, J. Lee. *Politicians, the Press, & Propaganda: Lord Northcliffe & the Great War, 1914–1919.* Kent, OH: Kent State University Press, 1999.

Tiffen, Rodney. *News and Power.* Sydney: Allen & Unwin, 1989.

Tuccille, Jerome. *Rupert Murdoch.* New York: D.I. Fine, 1989.

Tunstall, Jeremy. *Newspaper Power: The New National Press in Britain.* New York: Clarendon Press, 1996.

Tunstall, Jeremy, and David Machin. *The Anglo-American Media Connection.* New York: Oxford University Press, 1999.

Index